MUNDO)real

Teacher's Edition

CAMBRIDGE
UNIVERSITY PRESS

Edi
numen

© Editorial Edinumen, 2014

Authors:
Julia Caballero, María Carmen Cabeza, Francisca Fernández, Patricia Fontanals,
Luisa Galán, Amelia Guerrero, Peter Hearn, Debra L. King, Emilio José Marín, Celia Meana, Liliana Pereyra
and Francisco Fidel Riva.
Coordination Team: Celia Meana.

ISBN - Teacher's Edition: 978-1-107-65477-8

Printed in the United States of America

Editorial Coordination:
Mar Menéndez

Cover Design:
Juanjo López

Design and Layout:
Juanjo López

Cambridge University Press
32 Avenue of the Americas
New York, NY 10013

Editorial Edinumen
José Celestino Mutis, 4. 28028 Madrid. España
Telephone: (34) 91 308 51 42
Fax: (34) 91 319 93 09
e-mail: edinumen@edinumen.es
www.edinumen.es

MUNDO)real

TABLE OF CONTENTS

INTRODUCTION TO THE PROGRAM

PROGRAM AT A GLANCE	TE4
COMPONENTS AT A GLANCE: PRINT + TECHNOLOGY	TE5
PRINT AND DIGITAL COMPONENTS FOR THE TEACHER	TE6
ONLINE RESOURCES FOR TEACHERS AND STUDENTS	TE7
TEACHER'S WEBSITE AND TECHNOLOGICAL RESOURCES	TE8
FEATURES OF THE TEACHER'S EDITION	TE9
UNIT STRUCTURE	TE12
ASSESSMENT	TE13
PROFESSIONAL ORGANIZATIONS AND RESOURCES	TE14
BIBLIOGRAPHICAL REFERENCES	TE15

STUDENT BOOK

APPENDIX

PROGRAM AT A GLANCE

Mundo Real is a three-level Spanish language program designed for high school students that uses lively and compelling content, images, and video to teach the language that learners need to succeed in and outside the classroom.

Each level of *Mundo Real* provides a complete curriculum of instruction for one year of high school Spanish.

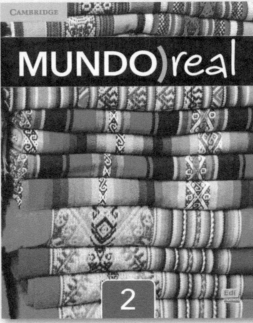

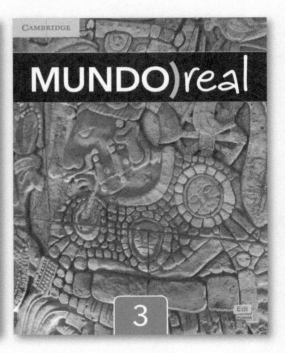

COMPONENTS AT A GLANCE: PRINT + TECHNOLOGY

Mundo Real offers a communicative approach that focuses on functional, real-life language. The program's guided and manageable content encourages students to begin speaking the language immediately. With real-life themes, high-interest content, and natural speech, *Mundo Real* teaches the language relevant to students' lives.

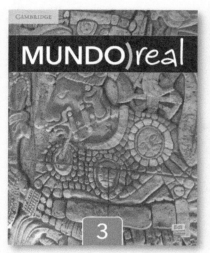

Student Book

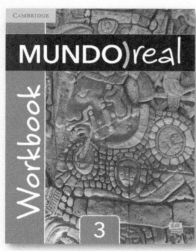

Workbook

Teacher's Edition

DVD

eBooks

Digital Master Guide

ELEteca, Cambridge / Edinumen's educational platform (**www.edinumen.es/cambridge-eleteca**), offers **additional material** for teachers and students which expands and complements all three levels of the program.

FOR THE TEACHER

The easy-to-use **Teacher's Edition** includes teacher's notes, expansion activities, and answer keys for activities in the Student's Book.

Mundo Real **ELEteca**, a Learning Management System designed for both students and teachers, includes interactive and collaborative activities, audiovisual resources and materials for self-assessment and independent study. For the teacher, *Mundo Real* **ELEteca** provides access to the **Digital Master Guide**, which provides added support through Student and Teacher eBooks, suggestions for exploration, answer keys, cultural and grammatical notes, audio recordings, transcripts, projectable material, and much more!

The **DVD** contains all the video material corresponding to the *¡Acción!* section of the Student Book, as well as *Casa de Español*, a series of street interview-style videos that focus on high-impact grammar and common Spanish phrases.

ONLINE RESOURCES FOR TEACHERS AND STUDENTS

Your online extension of *Mundo Real*

ELEteca, Cambridge / Edinumen's educational platform (**www.edinumen.es/cambridge-eleteca**), offers **supplementary material** which expands and complements this course.

WHAT IS ELETECA?

ELEteca is an **online learning management platform** that adds value to the Spanish learning / teaching process for teachers and students that use *Mundo Real*.

WHAT CAN STUDENTS FIND IN ELETECA?

For each level of *Mundo Real*, students can find the following **resources**:

- **Supplementary interactive activities** focusing on the grammar, vocabulary, communication, etc., covered in each unit.
- **Recordings** from the listening exercises in the Student Book and in the Workbook.
- **Extra interactive review tests** for each unit.
- An **assessment test** for each unit.
- **Collaborative activities** with wikis and forums.

> In addition, this platform gives teachers the opportunity to track the results online of the activities that their students perform in ELEteca.

HOW TO ACCESS ELETECA

To access ELEteca, just follow a process of three simple steps:

1. Go to ELEteca (www.edinumen.es/cambridge-eleteca) and sign up by filling out the short form.
2. Select ***Mundo Real*** and the appropriate level. At each level, teachers will find: ***Teacher Resources*** and ***Student Resources***. These are easily accessible with Web codes. We highly recommend that teachers log on to both the ***Teacher Resources*** and ***Student Resources*** for complete access to all the technology available in the program.
3. Enter the different access codes provided for the online ***Teacher Resources*** and ***Student Resources***.

> Mundo Real 3 Student Access code:
> 07670921

> Mundo Real 3 Teacher Access code:
> Find your code printed on the inside front cover.

ELETECA FOR TEACHERS

The **ELEteca** online learning management platform provides additional teaching options with the following technology resources:

DIGITAL MASTER GUIDE

The Digital Master Guide is a Digital Teacher's Edition including related resources that allows teachers to access and use the materials dynamically anywhere, using any kind of device (iPad and Android tablets, PC and Apple computers), or in the classroom with a computer and an interactive whiteboard to engage students.

IMPORTANT: To download and install the Digital Master Guide, the teacher should first enter and register in ELEteca and follow the instructions to complete the process.

Assessments

A comprehensive bank of downloadable, editable assessments.

Appendix and extra resources

Downloadable documents with all the material needed to get the best experience from the course: audioscripts, videoscripts for *¡Acción!* Section, Workbook answer keys and audioscripts, User's Guide for the cooperative activities suggested for students on ELEteca.

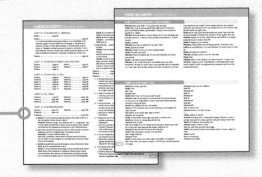

Interactive Whiteboard Lessons

The Interactive Whiteboard Lessons are additional resources which are downloadable from ELEteca and inter-referenced throughout the Teacher's Guide, that provide additional opportunities for teachers to present new material and for students to practice in a dynamic way.

Extension Activities (Photocopiable)

The Extension Activities are downloadable from ELEteca and can be printed and distributed to students for classroom group activities that enhance learning.

USING THE SPECIAL FEATURES OF TEACHER'S EDITION

UNIT OPENER

Objectives for the Unit Opener
This section provides a quick summary of objectives for the unit opener and how it connects the unit's learning outcomes.

Objectives for the Unit
The unit's learning objectives are an organizational tool for both the teacher and the students. Teachers can use them to preview what students will learn, and they serve as a way to assess whether students have mastered the main ideas and skills.

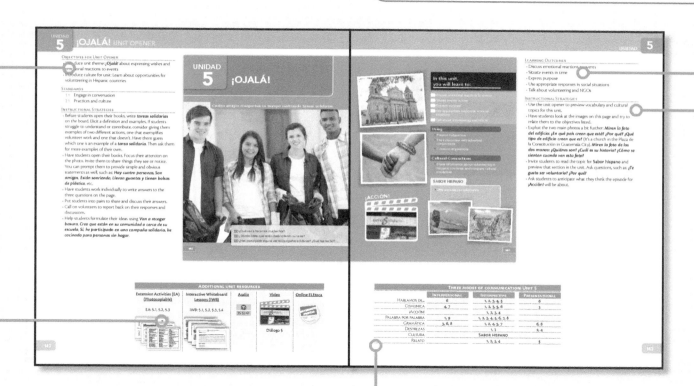

Unit Resources at a Glance
All of the teacher's resources available for the unit are listed here for quick reference.

Instructional Strategies
These provide specific recommendations to the teacher for presenting and teaching the material to students.

Common Core Standards
A correlation to the four strands of the Common Core Standards is provided in the Unit Opener, listing which activities in each section of the unit correspond to each of these strands.

Core Resources

This lists the specific instructional resources *Mundo Real* provides for each section of the unit.

Objectives for the Lessons

Each section starts with a list of learning objectives that teachers can use as an organizational tool. Teachers can use them to preview what students will learn in this section, and they serve as a way to assess whether students have mastered the main ideas and skills.

Activity-Specific Instructional Strategies

These instructional strategies provide specific recommendations to the teacher for teaching the unit content and for guiding students on how to carry out specific activities.

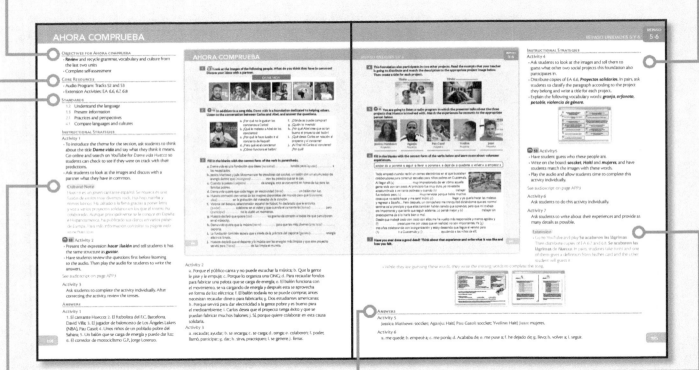

Cultural Notes

These notes provide support for the teacher, with additional cultural information to share with students, bringing Hispanic culture alive for students and motivating them to learn.

Extensions and Alternative Activities

These supplementary activities allow teachers to give students more practice, if needed.

Standards for Learning Languages

This lists the Standards for Learning Languages covered in this section.

Answers

An answer key is provided immediately below the activities for quick reference and to facilitate feedback to students.

UNIT STRUCTURE

Each unit of *Mundo Real* follows a consistent, clear sequence of instruction.

UNIT SECTION	PEDAGOGICAL PURPOSE
UNIDAD	**UNIT OPENER** • This is a visual introduction to the unit theme. Each unit focuses on a different real-world content area. • Discussion questions act as a springboard for students to begin using the language immediately, creatively adapting language they have learned previously to respond to new situations.
HABLAMOS DE...	**PREVIEWING LANGUAGE AND STRUCTURES** • A sample dialogue, featuring engaging images related to the unit theme, previews important structures and vocabulary from the unit. • These dialogues immediately engage students in the language, improving their listening and reading comprehension skills.
COMUNICA	**COMMUNICATIVE FUNCTIONS** • Develops speaking skills and oral interaction using communicative structures and activities.
¡ACCIÓN!	**INTEGRATED LANGUAGE VIDEO** • Built around a video segment following the lives of students in Spain. This authentic language input not only strengthens comprehension and listening skills, but also acts as a model for speaking. • Before, during, and after viewing activities provide a structured approach to viewing the video. The video contextualizes the content of the unit in a familiar scenario.
PALABRA POR PALABRA	**LANGUAGE AND VOCABULARY** • Introduces high-frequency vocabulary, which is practiced and expanded throughout the unit.
GRAMÁTICA	**GRAMMAR IN CONTEXT** • Presents three to four grammar points in each unit. • *Gramática* allows students to examine and practice specific grammar points and language functions from the unit while enabling them to sharpen their listening and speaking skills. • Accessible and contextualized grammar charts and presentations provide students with added clarity.
DESTREZAS	**COMMUNICATIVE SKILLS** • Integrates key language skills (listening and reading comprehension, oral and written expression) • Provides guided strategies and activities related to the unit theme to further student comprehension and learning.
PRONUNCIACIÓN	**PRONUNCIATION** • Activities focus on the high-priority features of phonetics, stress, and intonation, to help students improve overall speech.
SABOR HISPANO	**CULTURE IN CONTEXT** • Presents different aspects of Hispanic cultures using images, maps, and other cultural realia to provide students with a window into the Hispanic world.

RELATO	**COMPREHENSION PRACTICE** • Brings the unit's content together through a fictional text and encourages students to build their reading and listening comprehension skills.
EVALUACIÓN	**SELF-ASSESSMENT** • An integrated self-assessment section for students to assess their knowledge of the content covered in each unit.
EN RESUMEN: VOCABULARIO/ GRAMÁTICA	**UNIT REVIEW** • A one-page glossary of the unit vocabulary and a one-page summary of grammar structures covered in each unit for easy reference and review. • Teacher's Edition models for students how to review vocabulary and grammar and provides instructional strategies to help students develop learning and study skills.
AHORA COMPRUEBA	**CUMULATIVE REVIEW** • An integrated cumulative self-assessment every two units for students to assess their knowledge of the content covered in the previous units. • Teachers can assign point values to each activity as a way for students to self-assess. If students achieve less than 80% on each activity, teachers can direct them to *En resumen* in the previous units for unit sections to review.

ADDITIONAL RESOURCES AT THE END OF THE BOOK

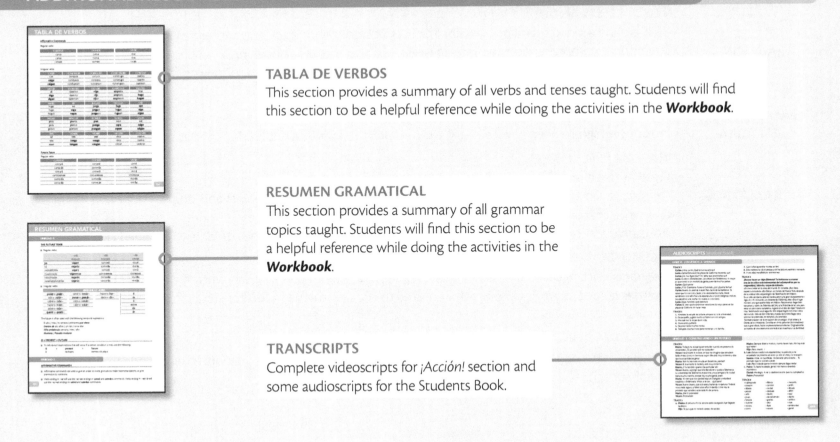

TABLA DE VERBOS
This section provides a summary of all verbs and tenses taught. Students will find this section to be a helpful reference while doing the activities in the ***Workbook***.

RESUMEN GRAMATICAL
This section provides a summary of all grammar topics taught. Students will find this section to be a helpful reference while doing the activities in the ***Workbook***.

TRANSCRIPTS
Complete videoscripts for *¡Acción!* section and some audioscripts for the Students Book.

• Additional resources for the teacher can be found in the ***ELEteca*** Platform and the ***Digital Master Guide*** (see page TE8).

ASSESSMENT

Mundo Real offers a range of print and digital assessment opportunities.

Informal Assessment

- Student Book
  - **Activities** These are provided throughout with opportunities for peer-supported learning in pair, group, and whole-class activities.
  - **Self-Assessment** Each unit provides an end-of-unit *Evaluación* that students can use for self-assessment and teachers can use to monitor students' progress.
  - **Cumulative Assessment** In *Ahora comprueba* the Student Book provides a cumulative self-assessment every two units that students and teachers can use to monitor progress.
- **Technology: ELEteca** Interactive review tests for each unit provide immediate feedback to students, helping them monitor their own progress.

FORMAL ASSESSMENTS

Mundo Real provides three types of assessments to measure both achievement and proficiency in Spanish. The printable, photocopiable version of the tests is provided as editable Word files, allowing teachers to customize them to meet specific classroom needs. The Word files and the answer key are available as downloadable teacher resources on ELEteca.

UNIT QUIZ

Unit quizzes help monitor progress and identify what students need to review and practice before taking the unit test.

UNIT TEST

Teachers can use the unit tests to give additional practice to students who have done well on the unit quiz, or as an alternate test, before giving the Comprehensive Unit Test.

COMPREHENSIVE UNIT TEST

These comprehensive unit tests assess students in listening, speaking, reading, and writing. It includes open-ended, performance-based assessment, as well as targeted assessment of discrete grammar and vocabulary items based on unit objectives.

ELETECA DATA MANAGEMENT SYSTEM

ELEteca collects data for the teachers to help adapt their pedagogical approach, gathering information on student use of the online activities and tests and how well students have performed on these. Teachers can use ELEteca to generate reports on individual students and for the class as a whole.

Class Reports

These reports summarize data for the whole class collected by ELEteca, based on individual student responses, allowing teachers to make decisions about student grouping and inform further review, revision, practice, and instruction.

Individual Student Reports

- These reports provide information on what activities and tests an individual student has completed and their scores, including dates completed.
- Teachers can retrieve the tests completed by students to gain further insight into a student's level of command of the language and provide personalized, individual feedback.

PROFESSIONAL ORGANIZATIONS AND RESOURCES

These organizations provide a wealth of teaching resources with online materials, conferences, and workshops.

American Association of Teachers of Spanish and Portuguese (AATSP)
AATSP's mission is to promote the study and teaching of the Spanish and Portuguese languages and their corresponding literatures and cultures at all levels of education.
http://www.aatsp.org/

The American Council on the Teaching of Foreign Languages (ACTFL)
ACTFL is an individual membership organization of more than 12,000 language educators and administrators, dedicated to the improvement and expansion of the teaching and learning of all languages at all levels of instruction.
www.actfl.org
In addition, ACTFL provides an "Alignment of the National Standards for Learning Languages with the Common Core Standards" at the following URL:
http://www.actfl.org/news/reports/alignment-the-national-standards-learning-languages-the-common-core-state-standards

Center for Applied Linguistics (CAL)
Language acquisition experts at the Center for Applied Linguistics focus on language education at all levels of instruction. They conduct language research, professional development for language teachers, information collection and dissemination, and program evaluation.
www.cal.org

National Capital Language Resource Center
NCLRC is a joint project of Georgetown University, The George Washington University, and the Center for Applied Linguistics. NCLRC is located in Washington, DC, and is one of fifteen nonprofit Language Resource Centers funded by the U.S. Department of Education.
http://www.nclrc.org

Partnership for 21st Century Skills (P21)
P21's mission is "To serve as a catalyst to position 21st century readiness at the center of US K12 education by building collaborative partnerships among education, business, community and government leaders." P21's focus includes the learning of foreign languages in K–12.
http://www.p21.org

Regional Foreign Language Conferences and Teacher Organizations
- The Central States Conference on the Teaching of Foreign Languages (CSCTFL)
  http://www.csctfl.org/
- The Greater Washington Association of Teachers of Foreign Languages http://www.gwatfl.org/
- Southern Conference on Language Teaching
  http://scolt.webnode.com/
- Southwest Conference on Language Teaching
  http://www.swcolt.org/
- Northeast Conference on the Teaching of Foreign Languages
  http://alpha.dickinson.edu/prorg/nectfl/index.html
- Pacific Northwest Council for Languages (PNCFL)
  http://www.pncfl.org

BIBLIOGRAPHICAL REFERENCES

Teaching Methods

Gattegno, C. (1976). *The Common Sense of Teaching Foreign Languages.* New York: Educational Solutions.

Holt, D. (1993). *Cooperative Learning: A Response to Linguistic and Cultural Diversity.* McHenry, IL, and Washington, DC: Delta Systems and Center for Applied Linguistics.

Johnson, K. (1982). *Communicative Syllabus Design and Methodology.* Oxford: Pergamon.

Krashen, S.D. (1981). *Second Language Acquisition and Second Language Learning.* Oxford: Pergamon.

Krashen, S.D., & Terrell, T.D. (1983). *The Natural Approach: Language Acquisition in the Classroom.* Englewood Cliffs, NJ: Prentice Hall.

Larsen-Freeman, D. (2000). *Techniques and Principles in Language Teaching* (2nd ed.). Oxford: Oxford University Press.

Littlewood, W. (1982). *Communicative Language Teaching: An Introduction.* Cambridge: Cambridge University Press.

Littlewood, W. (1992). *Teaching Oral Communication: A Methodological Framework.* Oxford: Blackwell.

Lozanov, G. (1978). *Suggestology and Outlines of Suggestopedy.* New York: Gordon and Breach.

Lozanov, G., & Gateva, E. (1988). *The Foreign Language Teacher's Suggestopedic Manual.* New York: Gordon and Breach.

National Standards in Foreign Language Education Project (1999, 2006). *Standards for Foreign Language Learning in the 21st Century (SFFLL)* (2nd & 3rd edns.). Lawrence, KS: Allen Press.

Nunan, D. (1999). Second Language Teaching and Learning. Boston: Heinle & Heinle.

Richards, J. C., & Rodgers, T.S. (2001). *Approaches and Methods in Language Teaching.* (2nd ed.). Cambridge: Cambridge University Press.

Stern, H.H. (1983). *Fundamental Concepts of Language Teaching.* Oxford: Oxford University Press.

Access for All Students / Differentiated Instruction

Downey, D.M. (1992, April). *Accommodating the foreign language learning disabled student.* Paper presented at the Foreign Language and Learning Disabilities Conference, The American University, Washington, DC.

Ganschow, L., Myer, B.J., & Roeger, K. (1989). Foreign language policies and procedures for students with specific learning disabilities. *Learning Disabilities Focus,* 5(1), 50-58.

Ganschow, L. and Schneider, E. (2006). *Assisting Students With Foreign Language Learning Difficulties in School. From Perspectives on Language and Literacy, Special Edition 2006.* Baltimore, MD:International Dyslexia Association.

Gardner, Howard E. (1993). *Multiple Intelligences: The Theory in Practice.* New York: Basic Books.

Teaching Spanish to Spanish Heritage Speakers

American Association of Teachers of Spanish and Portuguese. (2000). Volume I. *Spanish for native speakers: AATSP Professional Development Series Handbook for Teachers K-16. A handbook for teachers.* Fort Worth, TX: Harcourt College Publishers.

Jim Cummins "Beyond Curricular Scripts and Instructional Techniques: Implementing Classroom Interactions that Foster Power, Identity, Imagination, and Intellect Among Bilingual Students." NABE conference. Philadelphia, PA. March 2002.

Poey, Delia and Virgil Suárez. (1992) *Iguana Dreams.* New York, Harper Collins. Samaniego et al. (2002).

Webb, J.B., & Miller, B.L. (Eds.) (2000). *Teaching Heritage Language Learners: Voices from the Classroom.* Yonkers, NY: American Council on the Teaching of Foreign Languages.

Additional Bibliographical References

For additional reading suggestions and teaching materials, visit the following sites.

- **CAL Resource Guides Online**
  http://www.cal.org/resources/archive/rgos/methods.html
- **NCLRC Teaching Materials for Spanish**
  http://nclrc.org/teaching_materials/materials_by_language/spanish.html
- **Resource Publications from AATSP**
  http://www.aatsp.org/?page=RESOURCPUB

MUNDO)real

Student Book

Cover Photograph:

Relieve azteca. *"América es un grandioso escenario donde se mezclan múltiples culturas y lenguas, muchas de ellas de considerable antigüedad, como la azteca, maya e inca. Estas grandes civilizaciones han constituido la base de una diversidad cultural americana de valor universal".* David Isa.

© Editorial Edinumen, 2014

Authors:
Eduardo Aparicio, Cecilia Bembibre, María Carmen Cabeza, Noemí Cámara, Francisca Fernández, Patricia Fontanals, Luisa Galán, Amelia Guerrero, Emilio José Marín, Celia Meana, Liliana Pereyra and Francisco Fidel Riva.
Coordination Team: David Isa, Celia Meana and Nazaret Puente.

ISBN - Student Book: 978-1-107-67092-1

Printed in the United States of America

Editorial Coordination:
Mar Menéndez

Cover Design:
Juanjo López

Design and Layout:
Juanjo López, Carlos Casado,
Analia García and Lucila Bembibre

Illustrations:
Carlos Casado

Photos:
See page 270

Cambridge University Press
32 Avenue of the Americas
New York, NY 10013

Editorial Edinumen
José Celestino Mutis, 4. 28028 Madrid. España
Telephone: (34) 91 308 51 42
Fax: (34) 91 319 93 09
Email: edinumen@edinumen.es
www.edinumen.es

EXTENSIÓN DIGITAL

Access code
07670921
www.edinumen.es/cambridge-eleteca

The **Student Book** contains eight units of high-interest content that help students learn and practice Spanish in and outside the classroom.

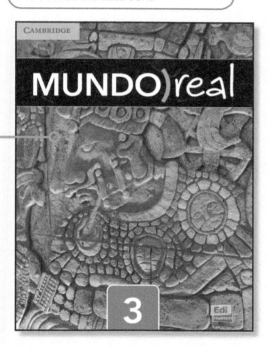

The **Workbook** provides additional practice for the skills covered in the Student Book. Workbook activities focus on reading and listening comprehension and written expression, perfect for independent study in the classroom or at home.

eBooks are available for each level and allow learners to access Student Book content online. eBooks include highlighting and note-taking features, as well as integrated audio and video.

Mundo Real **ELEteca**, a Learning Management System designed for both students and teachers, includes both interactive and collaborative activities and audiovisual resources and materials for self-assessment and independent study.

FOR THE TEACHER

The easy-to-use **Teacher's Edition** includes teacher's notes, expansion activities, and answer keys for activities in the Student Book.

***Mundo Real* ELEteca**, a Learning Management System designed for both students and teachers, includes interactive and collaborative activities, audiovisual resources and materials for self-assessment and independent study. For the teacher, ***Mundo Real* ELEteca** provides access to the **Digital Master Guide**, which provides added support through Student and Teacher eBooks, suggestions for exploration, answer keys, cultural and grammatical notes, audio recordings, transcripts, projectable material, and much more!

The **DVD** contains all the video material corresponding to the *¡Acción!* section of the Student Book, as well as *Casa de Español*, a series of street interview-style videos that focus on high-impact grammar and common Spanish phrases.

ELETECA *MUNDO REAL*

Your online extension of *Mundo Real*

ELEteca, Cambridge / Edinumen's educational platform (www.edinumen.es/cambridge-eleteca), offers **supplementary material** which expands and complements this course.

WHAT IS ELETECA?

ELEteca is an **online learning management platform** that adds value to the Spanish learning / teaching process for teachers and students that use *Mundo Real*.

WHAT CAN STUDENTS FIND IN ELETECA?

For each level of *Mundo Real*, students can find the following **resources**:

- **Supplementary interactive activities** focusing on the grammar, vocabulary, communication, etc., covered in each unit.
- **Recordings** from the listening exercises in the Student Book.
- **Extra interactive review tests** for each unit.
- An **assessment test** for each unit.
- **Collaborative activities** with wikis and forums.

In addition, this platform gives teachers the opportunity to track the results online of the activities that their students perform in ELEteca.

HOW TO ACCESS ELETECA

To access ELEteca, just follow a process of three simple steps:

1. Go to ELEteca (www.edinumen.es/cambridge-eleteca) and sign up by filling out the short form.
2. Select the *Mundo Real* course to access the corresponding resources.
3. Enter the book's access code

ACCESS CODE:
○ 07670921

El flamenco es la música y baile típicos del sur de España.

La hamburguesa se considera un ejemplo de comida rápida en España.

Thalía, cantante y actriz mexicana, conocida como «la reina de las telenovelas».

Turistas visitan una pirámide en Teotihuacán, México.

Una banda de mariachi de Puebla, México.

Parque Nacional de Los Picos de Europa, Asturias.

Lionel Messi.

La Danza de los Voladores en Teotihuacán.

Guillermo del Toro, en la presentación de la película *Don't be Afraid of the Dark*.

Parque Nacional del Teide, Tenerife, Islas Canarias.

Shakira.

La paella, un plato típico de la dieta mediterránea.

MUNDO)real

A dynamic image provides a visual introduction to the unit theme. Each unit theme focuses on a different real-world content area.

A discussion question acts as a springboard for students to begin using the language immediately, creatively adapting language they have learned previously to respond to new situations.

Each unit of *Mundo Real* contains eleven focused sections:

Hablamos de…	Destrezas / Pronunciación
Comunica	Sabor hispano
¡Acción!	Relato
Palabra por palabra	Evaluación
Gramática	En resumen

HABLAMOS DE..., a sample dialogue featuring engaging images related to the unit theme, previews important structures and vocabulary from the unit. These dialogues immediately engage students in the language, improving their listening and reading comprehension skills.

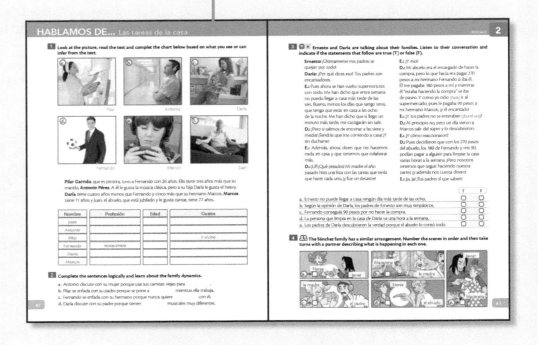

COMUNICA develops speaking skills and oral interaction using communicative structures and activities.

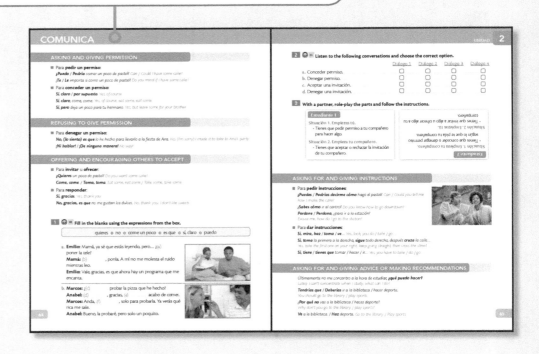

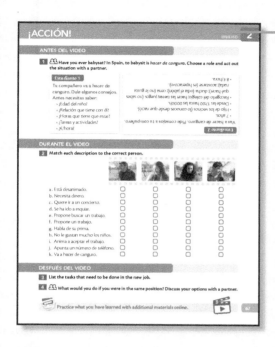

¡ACCIÓN! is built around a video segment following the lives of students in Spain. This authentic language input not only strengthens comprehension and listening skills, but also acts as a model for speaking. Before, during, and after viewing activities provide a structured approach to viewing the video. The video contextualizes the content of the unit in a familiar scenario.

PALABRA POR PALABRA introduces high-frequency vocabulary, which is practiced and expanded throughout the unit.

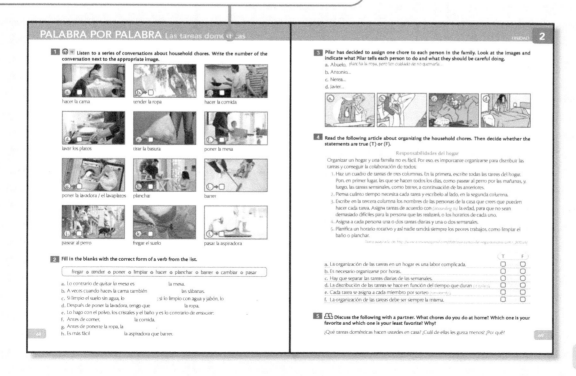

EXPLORE A UNIT

GRAMÁTICA presents three to four grammar points in each unit. **Gramática** allows students to examine and practice specific grammar points and language functions from the unit while enabling them to sharpen their listening and speaking skills.

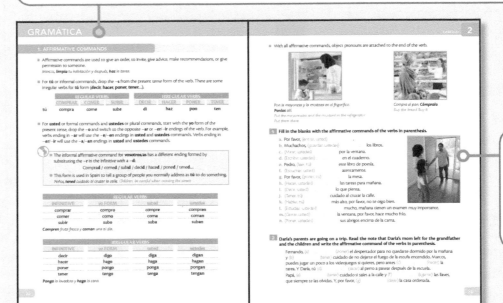

Accessible and contextualized grammar charts and presentations provide students with added clarity.

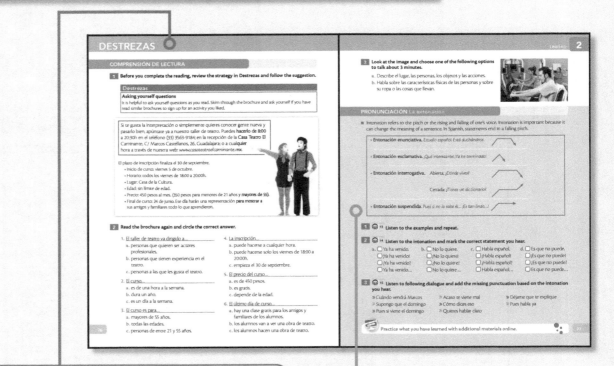

DESTREZAS integrates key language skills –listening and reading comprehension, oral and written expression– and provides guided strategies and activities related to the unit theme to further student comprehension and learning.

PRONUNCIACIÓN activities focus on the high-priority features of stress and intonation, to help students improve overall speech.

SABOR HISPANO presents different aspects of Hispanic cultures using images, maps, and other cultural realia to provide students with a window into the Hispanic world.

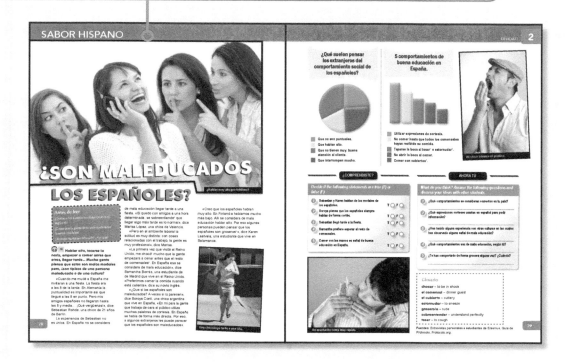

RELATO brings the unit's content together through a fictional text and encourages students to build their reading and listening comprehension skills.

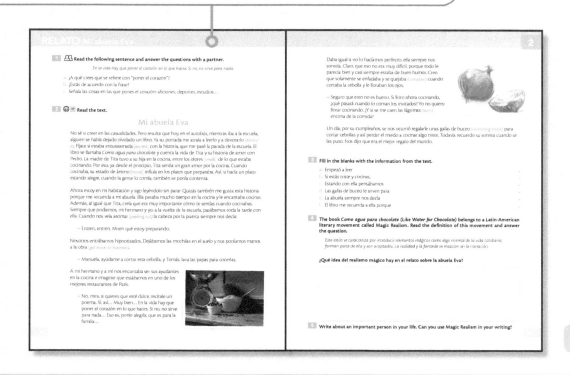

EVALUACIÓN is an integrated review for students to assess their knowledge of the content covered in each unit.

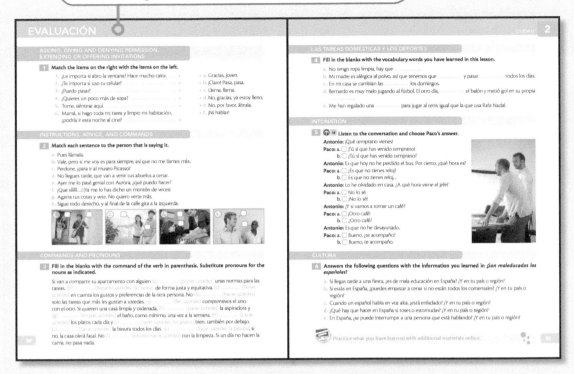

EN RESUMEN contains a glossary of the vocabulary and grammar structures covered in each unit for easy reference and review.

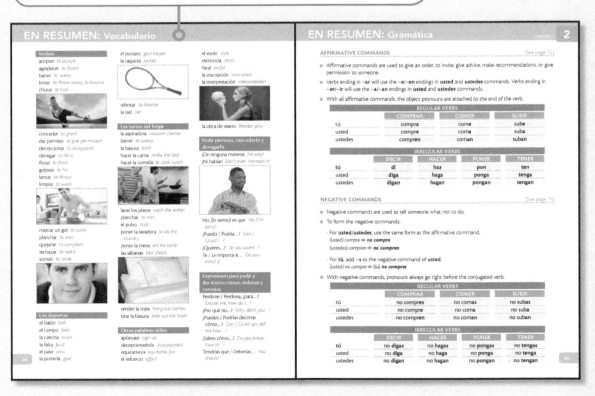

SCOPE AND SEQUENCE

Hablamos de... / Comunica
COMMUNICATION

- Talking about everyday activities in the past
- Relating a story or anecdote
- Giving orders
- Expressing opinions
- Talking about trips and vacations

Palabra por palabra
VOCABULARY

- Ocio y tiempo libre
- Los viajes y las vacaciones

Gramática
GRAMMAR

- The Present progressive
- The verbs *ser* / *estar*
- Informal affirmative commands
- Contrast of the preterit, the imperfect and the present perfect

Destrezas
SKILLS

- N/A

Pronunciación
PRONUNCIATION

- N/A

Sabor hispano
CULTURE

- Tesoros latinoamericanos

En resumen
SUMMARY

Pair icon: indicates that the activity is designed to be done by students working in pairs.

Group icon: indicates that the activity is designed to be done by students working in small groups or as a whole class.

Audio icon: XX indicates recorded material either as part of an activity or a reading text.

Language icon: provides additional language and grammar support in presentations and for activities.

Regional variation icon: provides examples of regional variations in the language.

Recycling icon: provides a reminder of previously taught material that students will need to use in an activity.

OBJECTIVES FOR UNIT OPENER

- Introduce unit theme: **Volvemos a vernos**, about activities in the past and vacation time
- Introduce culture for the unit: Learn about vacation time in Hispanic countries

STANDARDS

- 1.1 Interpersonal communication
- 1.2 Understand the language
- 2.1 Practices and perspectives

INSTRUCTIONAL STRATEGIES

- Introduce unit theme and objectives and explain to students that this unit is a review of vocabulary and grammatical functions from previous levels.
- Talk about the photo and have students state who these people are, where they are, what they are doing, how they feel, etc.
- Have the students discuss the questions and call on several students to respond. Help students recall verb forms and expressions from **Mundo real**, Levels 1 & 2 by modeling answers as necessary.
- Use the photographs to review vocabulary: **¿Dónde vas de vacaciones? ¿Con quién vas? ¿Cuál es tu lugar favorito? ¿Por qué? ¿Cuándo fue la última vez que fuiste? ¿Qué tiempo hizo? ¿Qué actividades hiciste?**
- Ask related questions: **¿Qué te gusta hacer cuando vas a la playa / a la montaña / al extranjero? ¿Por qué? ¿Cuál es tu actividad favorita? ¿Por qué?**
- Help students formulate their ideas using: **A mí me gusta hacer surf… porque me encanta el mar y el buen tiempo, no hay clases y me divierto mucho**, etc.

ANSWERS

Answers will vary. Possible answers are:
- Hola, ¿qué tal te fue?
- ¿Dónde fuiste de vacaciones? ¿Qué hiciste? ¿Cuánto tiempo estuviste? ¿Con quién fuiste? ¿Te gustó?, etc.
- Answers will vary.

UNIDAD
0
VOLVEMOS A VERNOS

Unos amigos saludan.

- ¿Cómo saludas a tus amigos cuando los vuelves a ver después de las vacaciones?
- ¿Qué les preguntas?
- ¿Y tú? ¿Qué hiciste durante tus vacaciones? ¿Lo pasaste bien?

18

ADDITIONAL UNIT RESOURCES

Extension Activities (EA) (Photocopiable)	Interactive Whiteboard Lessons (IWB)	Audio
EA: 0.1	IWB: 0.1, 0.2	🎧 1 to 3

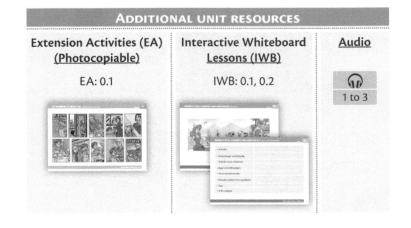

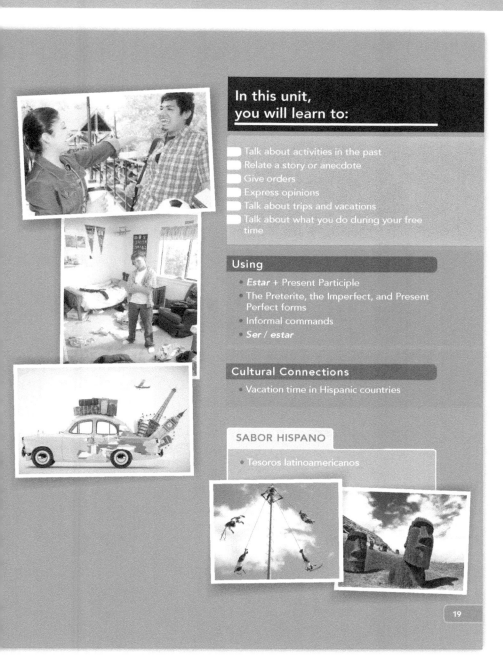

**In this unit,
you will learn to:**

- Talk about activities in the past
- Relate a story or anecdote
- Give orders
- Express opinions
- Talk about trips and vacations
- Talk about what you do during your free time

Using

- *Estar* + Present Participle
- The Preterite, the Imperfect, and Present Perfect forms
- Informal commands
- *Ser / estar*

Cultural Connections

- Vacation time in Hispanic countries

SABOR HISPANO

- Tesoros latinoamericanos

19

LEARNING OUTCOMES

- Talk about activities in the past
- Relate a story or anecdote
- Give orders
- Express opinions
- Talk about trips and vacations
- Talk about what you do during your free time

INSTRUCTIONAL STRATEGIES

- Explain to students that the purpose of this unit is to help them determine what they already know, and also help them focus on what they personally need to improve upon. Review the learning outcomes with students and then change them to questions. For example: *Are you able to talk about activities in the past?* and so on.
- Have students look at the images on this page and try to relate them to the objectives listed. Ask questions using the grammatical structures listed as prompts. Ask: **¿Cómo están los muchachos? ¿Por qué? ¿Qué tiene la muchacha en la mano? ¿Y el muchacho? ¿Por qué? ¿Qué crees que va a hacer? ¿Qué quieres decirle al muchacho de la segunda imagen? Describe su habitación. ¿Qué no ha hecho últimamente? ¿Por qué crees que no lo ha hecho? ¿Estaba de mal humor? ¿Tenía mucha tarea?** and so on.
- Invite students to read the topic for **Sabor hispano** and preview that section in the unit. Ask questions such as: **¿Cuáles son algunos tesoros de tu país? ¿Dónde están? ¿A cuántos has ido? ¿Cuál te gustó más?**

Note Common Core State Standards (CCSS)
The four strands of the *Common Core State Standards for English Language Arts (ELA) and Literacy in History/Social Studies, Science, and Technical Subjects* (Reading, Writing, Speaking and Listening, and Language) are represented in the National Standards for Learning Languages by the Communication standards: Interpersonal, Interpretive, and Presentational. The three modes of communication align with the goals in Reading, Writing, Speaking, and Listening by emphasizing the purpose behind the communication.

THREE MODES OF COMMUNICATION: UNIT 0			
	INTERPERSONAL	**INTERPRETIVE**	**PRESENTATIONAL**
LAS VACACIONES	3, 4, 7	1, 2, 5, 6, 7, 8, 9, 10, 11	
RECUERDOS DE LA ESCUELA	8	1, 2, 3, 4, 5, 6, 7	1, 4, 7, 9
UN POCO MÁS		1, 2, 3, 4, 5, 6	
CULTURA		SABOR HISPANO	

OBJECTIVES FOR LAS VACACIONES

- Review vocabulary related to travel and free-time activities
- Review grammatical structures: Present progressive tense; preterit, and present perfect
- Talk about past vacations and what you did

CORE RESOURCES

- Audio Program: Track 1
- Interactive Whiteboard Lessons: IWB 0.1, 0.2

STANDARDS

1.1 Engage in conversation
1.2 Understand the language
1.3 Present information
4.2 Compare cultures

INSTRUCTIONAL STRATEGIES

- Explain to students that **Unidad 0** is a brief review of vocabulary and grammatical structures. Content is grouped thematically by sections. The purpose is to guide students to begin at a similar point while providing practice before new material is presented. Remind students that none of the material should be new to them.

Activity 1

- Ask students to look at the image and ask: **¿Dónde están los muchachos que aparecen en la imagen? ¿Qué relación hay entre ellos? ¿De qué están hablando?**
- Have students write then say the sentences for each one.
- Tell students to expand upon the information and create a short conversation between Carlos and Lucía. Call on student volunteers to present their conversation for the class.

🎧 1 Activity 2

- Play the audio and have students listen to the conversation between Carlos and Lucía and fill in the missing words.
- Play the audio a second time and have students check their answers.

ANSWERS

Activity 1

Carlos: Fui a Colorado y estuve haciendo senderismo.
Lucía: Fui a las playas de California y estuve haciendo surf.

Activity 2

a. ¡No me digas!; **b.** bastante bien; **c.** montón; **d.** Cuéntame;
e. de miedo; **f.** cansadísimo; **g.** peligrosa; **h.** No vuelvo a ir;
i. ¡Vaya, hombre!; **j.** nada.

LAS VACACIONES

1 Carlos and Lucía are seeing each other for the first time after their summer break. What have they done during their vacation? Arrange the words to create sentences about their summer.

Carlos
estuve ○ haciendo ○ a ○ Fui ○ y ○ Colorado ○ senderismo

Lucía
surf ○ playas ○ haciendo ○ Fui ○ y ○ California ○ las ○ estuve ○ a ○ de

Carlos: Fui ....

Lucía: Fui ....

2 🎧 1 Listen to the conversation between Carlos and Lucía and fill in the missing words from the list below.

> bastante bien ○ cansadísimo ○ cuéntame ○ de miedo ○ montón ○ nada
> no me digas ○ peligrosa ○ vaya, hombre ○ no vuelvo a ir

Carlos: ¡Hola, Lucía! ¿Qué tal tus vacaciones?
Lucía: ¡Genial! Estuve en las playas de California haciendo surf.
Carlos: ¡(a) ....! ¿Surf? No sabía que practicabas surf.
Lucía: Sí, estuvo (b) .... Las playas son fantásticas y lo mejor es que conocí a un (c) .... de gente joven de muchos países.
Carlos: ¡Qué suerte!
Lucía: ¿Y tú? (d) .... Fuiste a Colorado, ¿no? ¿Qué tal te fue?
Carlos: Bueno, ¡lo pasé (e) ....! Pero terminé (f) .... Ya sabes que fui con Luis y Javier y no descansamos nada. Hacer senderismo con ellos fue una experiencia un poco (g) .... Incluso, nos perdimos una noche. (h) .... con ellos.
Lucía: ¡(i) ....!, ¡qué aventura!
Carlos: Sí, creo que las próximas vacaciones las voy a pasar en las playas de California sin hacer (j) ....

3 🗨 **What is the best way to spend your vacation? Read the sentences below and choose a response that best expresses your opinion about the comment. Then, share your opinions with a partner. Do you agree on many of the same things?**

a. Ir a un hotel es mejor que ir de camping.
b. Pasar las vacaciones en la playa es la mejor manera de descansar.
c. Viajar en avión es la forma más fácil de viajar.
d. Visitar una ciudad y descubrir una cultura nueva es lo mejor de las vacaciones.
e. La montaña es mejor que la playa.
f. Los campamentos de verano son aburridos.

🔄
• A mí me parece que sí.
• A mí me parece que no.
• Yo creo que sí.
• Yo pienso que no.
• No sé qué decir.
• ¡Yo qué sé!
• No te puedo decir.

4 🗨 **What about you? Where did you go on your last vacation? What did you do? Where did you stay? Talk about it with your partner.**

5 **These people are enjoying their vacation time. Follow the model to write complete sentences for each one and match them with the corresponding image.**

🔟 a. (leer) Está leyendo un libro.
☐ b. (dormir) .... la siesta.
☐ c. (entrar) .... a los servicios.
☐ d. (vestirse) ....
☐ e. (construir) .... un castillo.
☐ f. (bañarse) ....
☐ g. (comer) .... un helado.
☐ h. (tomar) .... una foto.
☐ i. (tomar) .... el sol.
☐ j. (salir) .... del agua.

21

INSTRUCTIONAL STRATEGIES

Activity 3
• Have students first read through the sentences and ask questions about vocabulary. Then review the recycling box to practice expressions. Have students repeat after you. Use gestures and appropriate emphasis to help students access meaning. For example, shrug your shoulders as you review the last three expressions to indicate that you don't feel strongly either way.
• Put students in pairs so they can practice orally, taking turns reading the statements and reacting.
• Have students build conversations by giving a reason or explanation for their opinions. Encourage students to use appropriate intonation in their responses.

Activity 4
• Review typical vacation activities such as **bañarse, descansar, divertirse, hacer surf / senderismo, pasear, tomar el sol, ir en avión, alojarse en un hotel, hacer la maleta, llevar el pasaporte**, etc.
• Remind them how to talk about the past and review some of the most common verbs (**fui, estuve**, etc.).
• Ask students to share their experiences and offer details.
• Go around the class and help students to clarify questions they might have.
• Ask students to write about their vacations and collect them so you can assess their writing skills as well.

Activity 5
• Before doing the activity, call a student to the front of the room and ask him/her to mime something: reading a book, writing on the board, eating a banana, drinking a cup of coffee, etc.
• Ask the class what the student is doing. When they guess the sentence, write it on the board and remind them about the structure (**estar** + present participle) and its use: for actions that are happening at the moment.

• Have students complete the sentences with the progressive form and them match the sentences with the people in the picture.
• Project IWB 0.1, **En la playa** to review the answers. Encourage students to include additional comments about the scene.

ANSWERS

Activity 5
a. 10, Está leyendo; b. 4, Está durmiendo; c. 9, Está entrando; d. 8, Está vistiéndose; e. 7, Está construyendo; f. 2, Está bañándose; g. 5, Está comiendo; h. 6, Está tomando; i. 1, Está tomando; j. 3, Está saliendo.

LAS VACACIONES

Activity 6

- Ask students to do this activity individually first.
- Working in pairs, students compare their answers.
- Call on students to share their answers and explain in Spanish what each of the boldface words mean. Get students started by providing cues such as: *lo/la usas para..., es una persona que..., es lo que haces...*
- Ask students to be creative and write two more sentences related to the topic.
- With another pair, students ask for the correct answers to the sentences they have created.

Activity 7

- Project IWB 0.2, *Actividades de tiempo libre* and review the situations with students with books closed. Brainstorm vocabulary students need to talk about these topics. Use the printed questions as a guide to prompt students, but without reading them aloud. Write the words and expressions in the spaces next to each situation.

- In pairs, ask students to choose one of the pastimes and talk about it with their partners. Each student should choose a different topic.
- As a follow-up, have students practice either the same topic or a new one with a different partner. In this round, students are encouraged to build a conversation by asking as many questions as possible of each other and giving as many details as possible.
- Have students volunteer to present to the class. Allow students to choose their topic to present, but ensure that all are represented. You may have student pairs compete to see which one conducted the most exchanges. You and the rest of the students can ask questions as well.

Alternative Activity

- After practicing with their partner, allow students to ask you questions on a topic, again to see how many exchanges they can conduct.
- Another option is to call on a student and ask him/her to respond to your questions.
- All or any variety of these options promote student oral interaction and encourage students to participate.

ANSWERS

Activity 6

a. pasaporte; **b.** los boletos; **c.** te alojas, reservación; **d.** propina; **e.** El guía del hotel; **f.** tarjeta de crédito.

LAS VACACIONES

6 Pedro is going on a trip and his parents are giving him some advice. Circle the right word in each sentence.

a. Si vas a un país extranjero, necesitas tu **pasaporte** / **cuaderno**.
b. No te olvides de **los boletos** / **las maletas** de avión.
c. Si **duermes** / **te alojas** en un hotel, necesitas hacer una **maleta** / **reservación**.
d. Si tomas un taxi, no te olvides de darle una **propina** / **llave** al conductor.
e. **El recepcionista** / **El guía del hotel** te puede dar información útil.
f. Puedes pagar el hotel con **tarjeta de crédito** / **llave**.

7 Choose one of the pastimes from the table below and talk to your partner about it. Use the questions as a guide.

• Ir al cine	¿Qué tipo de películas te gusta ver? Comedias, dramas, horror, suspense, documentales…
• Pasar tiempo con la familia	¿Qué te gusta hacer con tu familia? ¿Ir de vacaciones con ellos? ¿Por qué?
• Trabajar como voluntario	¿Dónde haces de voluntario?
• Jugar a los videojuegos	¿Cuál es tu videojuego favorito? ¿Con quién te gusta jugar? ¿Cuánto rato pasas jugando a los videojuegos?
• Tocar un instrumento	¿Tocas algún instrumento? ¿Solo o en grupo?
• Escuchar música e ir a conciertos	¿Qué tipo de música te gusta escuchar? ¿Por qué vas a conciertos?
• Leer	¿Qué te gusta leer? Novelas, noticias, poesía, revistas…
• Ir de compras	¿Dónde te gusta ir de compras? ¿Prefieres ir solo o acompañado?

22

8 Complete the crossword puzzle with the correct forms of the preterit to uncover the secret word.

1. venir (yo)
2. traer (ustedes)
3. hacer (yo)
4. traducir (ella)
5. conducir (tú)
6. decir (tú)
7. dormir (él)
8. andar (nosotros)
9. leer (ellos)
10. ir (nosotros)

9 Complete the following sentences with the correct form of the verb in the present perfect.

a. Este verano (hacer, nosotros) .... muchas excursiones al campo.
b. Hace un rato (ver, yo) .... a Luis en la cafetería.
c. ¿(Estar, tú) .... alguna vez en Barcelona?
d. Este fin de semana (ponerse, yo) .... morena porque (ir, yo) .... a la playa.
e. Siempre (querer, ellos) .... viajar en barco pero nunca lo (hacer) ....
f. El viento (abrir) .... la ventana y (romperse) .... el cristal.
g. Este año (volver, ustedes) .... de vacaciones antes que el año pasado.

23

INSTRUCTIONAL STRATEGIES

Activity 8

- Ask students to do this activity individually first.
- Working in pairs, students compare their answers. Ask students to identify the secret word (**vacaciones**).
- In pairs, ask students to classify the verbs into regular and irregular. They should recognize all as being irregular. Then ask students to explain how they are irregular. For example: **–ir** stem-changing verbs (**dormir**), **i ➡ y** stem-changing verbs (**leer**), verbs with new stems (**venir, traer, hacer, traducir, decir, conducir, andar**), and completely irregular verbs (**ir**).
- Ask students to be creative and write a sentence with each of the verbs.
- Ask a couple of students to read two or three sentences they have created.

Activity 9

- Ask for volunteers to provide examples of the present perfect form in Spanish and write them on the board, making corrections as needed. Review the parts of the present perfect (**haber** + past participle).
- Ask if there are any irregulars and have students identify which verbs in the activity are irregular (**hacer, ver, ponerse, abrir, romperse, volver**).
- Give students five minutes to do the activity individually and then correct with the entire class.
- With a partner, ask students to discuss what they have done **este verano**, **hace un rato**, **alguna vez**, etc.

ANSWERS

Activity 8

1. VINE; 2. TRAJERON; 3. HICE; 4. TRADUJO; 5. CONDUJISTE; 6. DIJISTE; 7. DURMIÓ; 8. ANDUVIMOS; 9. LEYERON; 10. FUIMOS.
Palabra secreta: vacaciones.

Activity 9

a. hemos hecho; b. he visto; c. Has estado; d. me he puesto, he ido; e. han querido, han hecho; f. ha abierto, se ha roto; g. han vuelto.

INSTRUCTIONAL STRATEGIES

Activity 10

- Read the text with students and address any questions about vocabulary.
- Ask students if they remember the names of the two tenses highlighted in the reading: present perfect and preterit.
- Call on volunteers to explain their use.

Extension

Tell students to write back to Elena as if they were Sara and tell her what they have done during their vacation. Students should also include questions for Elena to demonstrate interest in her vacation.

Cultural Note

Las ferias son fiestas que tienen lugar en ciudades y pueblos de toda Hispanoamérica. Pueden ser un mercado que se celebra ciertos días del año para la venta de determinados productos, o también pueden ser las instalaciones recreativas que ponen para celebrar fiestas (circos, puestos de ventas, atracciones, lugares con música…).

Activity 11

- Have students read the text again carefully to themselves.
- Give students some minutes to do the activity individually and then correct with the entire class.
- Without looking at the book, challenge students to retell Elena's story using the verbs from their lists and in third person. Have them recreate as much as they can remember.
- In pairs, ask students to compare their texts to see who had the most details and correct information.

ANSWERS

Activity 10

The preterit is used to talk about actions that were completed at a fixed point in the past and have no relation with the present. The present perfect is used to say what a person has done.

Activity 11

Present perfect: lo he pasado (pasar); ha dicho (decir); he estado (estar); he vuelto (volver); he escrito (escribir); he hecho (hacer).

Preterit: decidieron (decidir); llegué (llegar); me gustó (gustar); me aburrí (aburrir); tuve (tener); conocí (conocer); nos hicimos (hacer); fuimos (ir); nos encontramos (encontrar); estuvimos (estar); nos divertimos (divertirse); pidió (pedir).

a. preterit; **b.** present perfect.

LAS VACACIONES

10 Read the post card Elena wrote to her friend Sara on her last day of the vacation. Look at the verbs that are highlighted. Do you remember what they express and when they are used?

¡Hola, Sara!

¿Qué tal tus vacaciones? ¡Este verano me lo he pasado genial! Ya sabes que mis padres decidieron ir a visitar a mis abuelos en Montana.

El viaje en auto fue muy largo y aburrido, pero cuando llegué, me gustó mucho el sitio. Los primeros días me aburrí un poco y, además, tuve que ir con mis padres a visitar a toda la familia. Por suerte, hace dos semanas conocí a Fani, la nieta de los vecinos de mis abuelos, y desde ese día nos hicimos muy amigas. El viernes pasado fuimos a la feria del pueblo y nos encontramos a sus primos, estuvimos todo el rato con ellos y nos divertimos mucho. El mayor, Jorge, ¡es guapísimo! Creo que me gusta. Esta mañana Fani me ha dicho que yo también le gusto y que ayer le pidió mi correo electrónico. Hoy es mi último día aquí, así que he estado toda la mañana en la piscina con Fani y después he vuelto a casa y les he escrito a todos. Ahora te dejo porque quiero despedirme de todo el mundo y ¡todavía no he hecho la maleta! Me da lástima irme, pero también tengo ganas de empezar el curso para verles de nuevo a todos. ¡¡Muchos besos!!

¡Hasta pronto! Elena

SARA MARTÍNEZ

3333 Rock Avenue

Albuquerque,

New Mexico 33333

11 Look at the verbs in Elena's card. Sort them in two columns according to their tense and write the infinitive for each. Then, fill in the blanks to describe the use of each tense.

PRESENT PERFECT	PRETERIT
lo he pasado ➡ pasar(lo)	decidieron ➡ decidir

a. Usamos el .... para hablar de acciones pasadas en un **tiempo terminado.**
b. Usamos el .... para hablar de acciones pasadas en un **tiempo no terminado o en relación con el presente.**

24

RECUERDOS DE LA ESCUELA

UNIDAD **0**

1 🔗 Elena's grandfather, Gregorio Fernández, is thinking back on his life. Look at the images and use them to complete the sentences with a partner.

- Cuando era niño ....
- A los 18 años ....
- Cuando cumplí los 30 ....
- Hoy ....

2 🎧 ² Listen as Gregorio talks about his life and write the number of the statement that corresponds to the appropriate time frame.

a. Cuando era niño ....   c. Cuando cumplí los 30 ....
b. A los 18 años ....   d. Hoy ....

3 🎧 ² Listen again to the audio and write the forms of the verbs you hear and the correct tense.

a. empezar ....   d. estar ....   g. aprender ....
b. jugar ....   e. tener ....   h. ir ....
c. casarme ....   f. trabajar ....   i. afeitarse ....

25

OBJECTIVES FOR RECUERDOS DE LA ESCUELA

- Talk about activities in the past
- Relate a story or anecdote
- Describe physical characteristics and personality traits in the past

CORE RESOURCES

- Audio Program: Track 2
- Extension Activities: EA 0.1

STANDARDS

1.1   Engage in conversation
1.2   Understand the language
1.3   Present information
4.1   Compare cultures

INSTRUCTIONAL STRATEGIES

Activity 1

- Review the vocabulary and grammatical structures corresponding to activities in the past using the images as a guide. Ask students to look at the thought bubbles and brainstorm related words and expressions. For example, **ser estudiante**, **ir a la Universidad**, **casarse**, **tener un hijo**, **jubilarse**, etc.
- Then tell students to work with a partner to complete the sentences about Gregorio's life. Remind them to think about what past tenses they should use with each.

🎧 2 Activity 2

- Play the audio and tell students to write the number of the statement that corresponds to when the action takes place. Point out that there will be more than one sentence per timeframe.
- Play the audio again and ask students to check their answers.
- Ask students to compare what they wrote in Activity 1 with what they heard in the audio. Did they use the correct tenses?

See audioscript on page APP1

🎧 2 Activity 3

- Play the audio one more time so students write the forms of each verb.
- Write all the forms on the board for students to check their answers.

Extension

Play the audio again and have students write the sentences they hear as a dictation. Pause the audio after each statement and remind students to use the verbs already listed on the board as a reference. This will help students review the use of the different tenses in context.

ANSWERS

Activity 2

a. 2, 7; b. 1, 5, 9; c. 3, 6; d. 4, 8.

Activity 3

a. empecé; b. jugaba; c. me casé; d. estoy; e. tenía; f. trabajaba; g. aprendí; h. he ido; i. me afeité.

Activity 4

- To introduce the activity, write the following sentence on the board: *Cuando pienso en mi infancia me vienen a la memoria muy buenos recuerdos*. Ask students: *¿Recuerdan algún momento especial de su infancia que quieran compartir con el resto de la clase?*
- With books closed, distribute copies of EA 0.1, *Mi primer día de la escuela* to student pairs. Tell students to put the images in order to recreate Gregorio's first day at school and to practice retelling what happened.
- Ask students to present their stories in class. You may also have students tape the images to the board as they present their version to the class. Ask the class if they agree with the order presented: *¿Están de acuerdo?*
- Correct vocabulary and grammar and review tenses if necessary.
- Have students open their books to confirm the correct order.

Activity 5

- Ask students to do the activity individually and correct with the entire class.
- Take opportunities to review tenses.

Extension

- For additional oral practice, string together the retelling of the story by having each student add the next line. Start with: *Cuando el señor Gregorio piensa en su época de estudiante le vienen a la memoria muy buenos recuerdos, bueno, menos el primer día de la escuela, porque...* To ensure that all students have a chance to participate, encourage them to go beyond the events presented in the images and provide additional details.
- Another option is to have students write out the story, this time describing the opposite experience. In this case, tell students to use the opposite meaning of the adjectives in the original story and verbs to turn the story around. Have students begin the story as follows: *Cuando pienso en mi época de estudiante vienen a mi memoria muy malos (en vez de buenos) recuerdos...*

RECUERDOS DE LA ESCUELA

4 Gregorio has never forgotten his first day of school. Look at the images and take turns with a partner describing what happened that day.

5 Check your descriptions. Fill in the blanks with the verbs in the preterit, the imperfect, or the present perfect form.

Cuando pienso en mi época de estudiante siempre vienen a mi memoria muy buenos recuerdos, bueno, menos el de mi primer día de escuela... Se puede decir que para mí (1) .... (ser) toda una experiencia y, aunque ya (2) .... (pasar) muchos años desde entonces, me acuerdo perfectamente de lo que (3) .... (sentir).

Recuerdo que ese día mi mamá me (4) .... (despertar) muy temprano. (5) .... (Levantarse), (6) .... (vestirse) yo solo y (7) .... (desayunar) muy bien, porque mi mamá siempre (8) .... (decir) que "antes de estudiar, tu barriga debes llenar". Después mi mamá me (9) .... (ayudar) a peinarme, yo (10) .... (agarrar) mi mochila nueva y (11) .... (salir) hacia la escuela. Yo (12) .... (estar) muy emocionado porque (13) .... (ser) mi primer día de cole y ya (14) .... (ser) un niño mayor. Además, como toda mi vida (15) .... (ser) una persona muy curiosa e inquieta, (16) .... (sentir) mucha curiosidad por saber qué (17) .... (ser) eso del cole. (18) .... (Ir) todo el camino contento, iba a conocer la escuela, a mis compañeros, a mi maestra... Sin embargo, cuando mi mamá me (19) .... (dejar) en la puerta de la escuela junto a los demás niños, (20) .... (ponerse) tan nervioso que (21) .... (empezar) a llorar y, para mi desconsuelo, ¡los demás niños también (22) .... (llorar)!

Enseguida (23) .... (venir) mi maestra e (24) .... (intentar) consolarme, pero (25) .... (estar) todo el día triste y de mal humor, tanto, que al final la maestra (26) .... (llamar) a mi mamá por teléfono y ella (27) .... (venir) a buscarme a la escuela. Cuando (28) .... (acostumbrarse), la escuela me (29) .... (encantar) y la maestra Margarita (30) .... (ser) la mejor maestra que (31) .... (tener) nunca.

Activity 5

1. fue; **2.** han pasado; **3.** sentí; **4.** despertó; **5.** me levanté; **6.** me vestí; **7.** desayuné; **8.** decía; **9.** ayudó; **10.** agarré; **11.** salí; **12.** estaba; **13.** era; **14.** era; **15.** he sido; **16.** sentía; **17.** era; **18.** Fui; **19.** dejó; **20.** me puse; **21.** empecé; **22.** lloraban; **23.** vino; **24.** intentó; **25.** estuve; **26.** llamó; **27.** vino; **28.** me acostumbré; **29.** encantaba; **30.** fue; **31.** he tenido.

6 Read the following sentences from the text above. Then write the letter of the sentence in the box corresponding to the use of the past tense.

a. Se puede decir que para mí fue toda una experiencia.

b. Ya han pasado muchos años desde entonces.

c. Recuerdo que ese día mi mamá me despertó muy temprano.

d. Mi mamá siempre decía que "antes de estudiar, tu barriga debes llenar".

e. Yo estaba muy emocionado porque era mi primer día de escuela y ya era un niño mayor.

f. Toda mi vida he sido una persona muy curiosa e inquieta.

g. Sentía mucha curiosidad por saber qué era eso del cole.

h. Enseguida vino mi maestra e intentó consolarme, pero estuve todo el día triste y de mal humor.

i. Margarita fue la mejor maestra que he tenido nunca.

Acción sin relación con el presente	Descripción de una situación	Acción en un pasado reciente o en relación con el presente	Acción habitual	Valoración
				a

7 Write four sentences about one of your classmate's first day of school and how you think it went.

a. ....

b. ....

c. ....

d. ....

8 📖 Do you remember your first day of school? Talk about it with your partner. Are his/her sentences close to your experience?

Modelo: Yo tenía 6 años cuando empecé la escuela.

9 Now write what your partner's first day of school was really like.

INSTRUCTIONAL STRATEGIES

Activity 6

• Introduce the activity by asking students how many past tenses they know in Spanish (preterit, present perfect, imperfect). Call on volunteers to explain what they remember about the uses of these forms.

• Have students do this activity individually first.

• Ask them to compare their answers with a partner.

• Correct the activity with the entire class.

• While correcting, take the opportunity to review all the past tenses.

Activity 7

• Give the students a few minutes to think about what their partner's first day of school was like. Tell students to write four sentences about their classmate's experience. Encourage them to be creative yet realistic in their descriptions.

• Explain to students that they will have an opportunity to share their version in the next activity.

Activity 8

• In pairs, ask students to retell their first day of school to their partner. Circulate around the room to check that students are on task and actively participating. Note down any errors to correct later as a class.

• Then have students share with their partners the sentences they prepared in Activity 7. How close were they?

Activity 9

• For this activity, students are asked to recall their partner's story and write about it.

• Collect all the texts and correct them to check vocabulary and grammar of this unit. You can also have students exchange papers with their partner for peer correction.

ANSWERS

Activity 6

Acción sin relación con el presente: c, h.

Descripción de una situación: e, g.

Acción en un pasado reciente o en relación con el presente: b.

Acción habitual: d, f.

Valoración: a, i.

UN POCO MÁS

OBJECTIVES FOR UN POCO MÁS

- Review verbs **ser** / **estar**
- Review informal commands

STANDARDS

1.2 Understand the language
1.4 Present information

INSTRUCTIONAL STRATEGIES

Activity 1

- Ask students to describe the images to provide context for the activity.
- Then have students work individually and match the statements with the images.
- After you review answers, ask students what these expressions all have in common (they are giving instructions, advice, orders, and permission to do something).
- Ask students to tell you who they think is making the statements to the people in the images.

Activity 2

- Ask students to classify the commands according to their use.
- In pairs, have students compare their answers.

Activity 3

- Practice first with commands by telling students to do the following: **Carla, cierra el libro**; **Albert, sal a la pizarra**; **Emma, dame tu libro**. Call on volunteers to explain the formation of **tú** commands (**tú** form, drop the **s**). Ask others what happens to the pronoun (it's attached to the end of the command).
- Have students complete this activity individually and time it to see who finishes first.
- After completing the activity, ask a student to come to the front of the class and act out what his/her classmates tell him/her to do. Remind the student to do the action only if the command was properly stated.

Extension

Have students write two linked commands on a piece of paper (it must be possible to do them in the classroom). For example: **Quítate un zapato y métolo en tu mochila**. Then divide the class into small groups and distribute commands. The first student reads the instructions, carries out the action, and the rest of the group writes what he/she did. The group who performs all the actions first and gets the forms correct is the winner.

ANSWERS

Activity 1

1. e; **2.** a; **3.** d; **4.** c; **5.** b.

Activity 2

Dar órdenes: e; Dar permiso: b; Invitar: d; Dar consejos: c; Dar instrucciones: a.

Activity 3

a. Sal a la pizarra; **b.** Abre la ventana; **c.** Recoge el libro; **d.** Siéntate bien; **e.** Cierra la puerta; **f.** Quítate la gorra.

---

1 Match the following statements with their corresponding image.

1. ☐ ¡Ordena tu cuarto!
2. ☐ Respire, por favor.
3. ☐ Coman ensalada.
4. ☐ Haz tu tarea.
5. ☐ Entra.

2 List the commands from the preceding activity according to their use.

Dar órdenes	Dar permiso	Invitar	Dar consejos	Dar instrucciones

3 Look at the images. Pretend you are the teacher of these students. Tell each one what to do using the following verbs.

- cerrar
- abrir
- ~~salir~~
- recoger
- quitarse
- sentarse

a. Sal a la pizarra
b. _____
c. _____
d. _____
e. _____
f. _____

4 **Complete the sentences with the correct form of *ser* or *estar*. Then match each sentence to its use.**

1. Mariela .... argentina.
2. Barcelona .... en España.
3. Lola .... una muchacha muy antipática.
4. Roberto .... un muchacho muy guapo.
5. Pedro .... informático.
6. La puerta .... de cristal.
7. Carlos .... el primo de Lucía.
8. .... las diez de la mañana.
9. Laura .... enferma.

- **a.** Decir el material de una cosa.
- **b.** Describir características físicas.
- **c.** Decir la nacionalidad.
- **d.** Describir situaciones temporales.
- **e.** Describir personalidad o rasgos de carácter.
- **f.** Decir la hora.
- **g.** Decir la profesión.
- **h.** Identificar a personas.
- **i.** Expresar localización.

5 **Choose the appropriate verb according to the context.**

a. Madrid **es** / **está** la capital de España.
b. El avión **es** / **está** más rápido que el tren.
c. **Soy** / **Estoy** muy contento porque este año voy a ir de vacaciones a la playa.
d. En esta época del año siempre **es** / **está** nublado.
e. ¿**Eres** / **Estás** cansado?
f. Mi hermano **es** / **está** más alto que yo.
g. Los libros **son** / **están** encima de la mesa.

6 **Fill in the blanks with *ser* or *estar* and an appropriate adjective from the list.**

| aburrido/a ○ abierto/a ○ listo/a ○ malo/a ○ rico/os |

a. Pedro .... un muchacho muy ...., por eso habla con todo el mundo.
b. Hoy yo .... en casa, sin saber qué hacer, y he dedicido preparar un pastel, por cierto, ... muy ....
c. Hoy, cuando he llegado a casa, he visto que la puerta ....
d. Ayer Laura no fue a clase porque ...., tenía un poco de fiebre y ganas de vomitar.
e. Los vecinos de mi padre ...., tienen mucho dinero, pero tienen un hijo que .... muy ...., y es que no se puede tener todo en esta vida.
f. ¡Muchachos! ¡A comer! La comida ....
g. Esta película .... muy ...., mejor la quitamos y hacemos otra cosa.
h. .... un muchacho muy ...., siempre tiene muy buenas notas en la escuela.

Activity 4

- With books closed, read aloud the uses of ***ser*** and ***estar*** from the activity. Tell students to show one finger for ***ser*** and two fingers for ***estar***. Explain that they should hold their hands in front of their chests to keep their answers private. In this way, the teacher can see individual responses to better assess how much students recall. You can correct answers now or after students complete the activity.
- Then have students work individually and match the sentences with the uses of verbs ***ser*** and ***estar***.
- Ask students to compare their answers with another partner.

Activity 5

- Ask students to choose the appropriate verbs and add two more sentences.
- Have students compare their answers in pairs.

Activity 6

- Review the use of adjectives with ***ser*** and ***estar***. Ask students to recall which adjectives change in meaning when used with both ***ser*** and ***estar***. Use the adjectives in the word bank to prompt students.
- Have students complete this activity individually paying attention to the context.
- Project activity and review the answers together as a class. Be sure students used the correct forms of the adjectives to show agreement.

ANSWERS

Activity 4

1. es, c; **2.** está, i; **3.** es, e; **4.** es, b; **5.** es, g; **6.** es, a; **7.** es, h; **8.** Son, f; **9.** está, d.

Activity 5

a. es; **b.** es; **c.** Estoy; **d.** está; **e.** Estás; **f.** es; **g.** están.

Activity 6

a. es, abierto; **b.** estoy, aburrido; está, rico; **c.** estaba, abierta; **d.** estaba, mala; **e.** son, ricos; es, malo; **f.** está, lista; **g.** es, mala; **h.** Es, listo.

OBJECTIVES FOR SABOR HISPANO

- Learn about Hispanic treasures
- Compare similarities

CORE RESOURCES

- Audio Program: Track 3

STANDARDS

2.1	Practices and perspectives
2.2	Products and perspectives
3.2	Acquire information
5.2	Using language for personal enjoyment and enrichment

INSTRUCTIONAL STRATEGIES

🎧 3

- Introduce the topic by asking what the students know about Hispanic treasures.
- Put students in pairs to discuss the questions in the **Antes de leer** box.
- Monitor their conversations and assist as needed.
- Call on volunteers to report back on their discussions.
- Focus students' attention on the images and their captions. Ask what they see, where the images are from, why they are famous. Tell students to talk about the images and elicit what they already know and can share.
- Before playing the audio, tell students to listen for the question posed at the beginning of the audio and be prepared to answer it. Either have students close their books while they listen or follow along with the text in the book.
- Elicit responses to the target question. For more detail, ask: **¿Qué tipo de lugares van a presentar?**
- To help build vocabulary, have students locate and underline any words from the glossary on the next page in the text. Then have them make and share new sentences with the words. You may choose to have them work individually or in pairs.

SABOR HISPANO

TESOROS

Turistas visitan una pirámide en Teotihuacán, México.

LATINOAMERICANOS

Antes de leer

¿Qué aspectos te atraen de los lugares que visitas, o que quieres visitar? (la historia, las actividades, las compras, etc.).

¿Qué sabes de las culturas prehispánicas en México?

🎧 3 **¿Buscas hacer un viaje diferente? Te invitamos a conocer tres de los sitios más interesantes de Latinoamérica por su originalidad, historia y toque de misterio.**

«Es como estar en la cima° del mundo. Es increíble. ¡Pero lleva zapatos cómodos!», dice Devyn, un turista de Nueva York, después de su visita al sitio arqueológico de Teotihuacán en México. Es un sitio donde los aztecas construyeron una gran ciudad entre los siglos II y VII. Armando, un visitante° de California, dice: «Era el lugar número uno que quería visitar en México. Recomiendo llegar bien temprano y subir a la Pirámide del Sol y a la Pirámide de la Luna para tener un panorama completo», sugiere en el sitio de viajes Tripadvisor.

Hoy, Teotihuacán es el segundo sitio arqueológico con más visitas del mundo. Más de dos millones y medio de turistas llegan para admirar las pirámides, los templos y las avenidas.

También pueden ver la recreación de un antiguo ritual azteca, la Danza de los Voladores. Consiste en cinco personas (los voladores) que, a gran altura, hacen impresionantes acrobacias. Originalmente, se trataba de una ceremonia asociada a las cosechas° y a la fertilidad.

La Danza de los Voladores en Teotihuacán.

30

Las líneas de Nazca

Estas líneas son dibujos en el suelo' hechos por la civilización prehispánica nazca. Se conservaron muy bien porque están en una zona donde casi nunca llueve. No se sabe exactamente cuál es la función de las líneas, aunque hay varias teorías. Este es un resumen numérico del lugar:

Están a **200** millas de Lima, capital de Perú.

Son Patrimonio de la Humanidad desde **1994**.

Hay cerca de **800** dibujos de animales y humanos.

Las líneas tienen **30** cm de profundidad'.

Se investigaron por primera vez en **1932**.

Rapa Nui

Rapa Nui, o Isla de Pascua, es parte del territorio de Chile en el Pacífico Sur. El atractivo turístico de la isla son las esculturas gigantes con forma de cabezas, creadas entre los siglos XII y XVII. No se conoce con certeza' por qué se construyeron.

1. En la isla hay más de 800 estatuas. Se llaman **«moái»**.

2. Las esculturas tienen entre **3,5** y **12** metros de alto.

3. Están **talladas' en piedra** de un volcán extinguido.

4. Se cree que representan a los **antepasados'**.

5. Hoy viven en la isla **5.000** personas.

Los moáis de la isla de Pascua.

¿COMPRENDISTE?

Decide if the following statements are true (T) or false (F).

1. Teotihuacán es el sitio arqueológico más visitado del mundo. T ◯ F ◯

2. Los turistas recomiendan ir a primera hora. T ◯ F ◯

3. Los moáis están hechos de piedra volcánica. T ◯ F ◯

4. La función de los moáis fue descubierta en 1932. T ◯ F ◯

5. Las líneas de Nazca tienen poca profundidad. T ◯ F ◯

Un colibrí' dibujado en Nazca, Perú.

AHORA TÚ

What do you think? Answer the following questions and discuss your ideas with other students.

1. ¿Cuál fue el viaje más interesante que hiciste? ¿Por qué?

2. ¿Qué consejo le puedes dar a alguien que quiere hacer ese mismo viaje?

3. ¿Cuál de estos tres sitios recomiendas a alguien interesado en la escultura? ¿Por qué?

4. ¿Cuál de estos tres sitios es ideal para alguien que quiere hacer ejercicio? ¿Por qué?

5. ¿Cuál de estos tres sitios te gustaría visitar a ti? ¿Por qué?

Glosario:

el antepasado – ancestor
la certeza – certainty
la cima – top
el colibrí – hummingbird
la cosecha – harvest
la profundidad – depth
el suelo – ground
tallado/a – carved
el visitante – visitor

Fuentes: *El Cronista*, Tripadvisor, INAH.

31

INSTRUCTIONAL STRATEGIES

Las líneas de Nazca

- Call on a volunteer to read the text and another student to read the data aloud.
- Point out the image of Nazca at the bottom and ask students if they can recognize the figure.
- Go online and project other images from Nazca and ask students to describe what they see.
- Tell students that they were designated as a UNESCO World Heritage Site in 1994 and encourage them to do additional research.

Rapa Nui

- Call on a volunteer to read the title and information that follows.
- Check students' understanding of the information by asking questions, such as: **¿Dónde se encuentran estas esculturas? ¿A qué país pertenecen? ¿Qué no se sabe de ellas?**
- Call on volunteers to read the facts about Rapa Nui. Ask them to demonstrate their height. Encourage students to share other information they know about this site.

¿Comprendiste?

- Have students work individually to answer true or false.
- Monitor their progress and assist as needed.
- Go over the answers as a class. Have them explain the false answers.

Ahora tú

- Have students work individually to answer the questions.
- Monitor their progress and assist as needed.
- Put students into pairs or small groups to share their ideas. Have them take turns asking and answering the questions. Encourage them to ask each other follow-up questions for more information.
- Ask each pair or group to report back to the class on something interesting from their conversation.

ANSWERS

¿Comprendiste?

1. F; 2. T; 3. T; 4. F; 5. F.

OBJECTIVES FOR EN RESUMEN: VOCABULARIO

- Review unit vocabulary and expressions
- Practice communicative skills

STANDARDS

1.2 Understand the language

1.3 Present information

4.1 Evaluate similarities and differences in language

INSTRUCTIONAL STRATEGIES

- Encourage students to use index cards used as flashcards with the Spanish term on one side and the English term on the other, or a picture or drawing.
- Students work in pairs or groups, using vocabulary flashcards as they would the cards of a board game to help each other practice unit vocabulary.
- Encourage students to write labels or captions for the photos on this page. Remind them to use the vocabulary and expressions they have learned in this unit.

EN RESUMEN: Vocabulario

Verbos

aburrirse *to be bored*
acostumbrarse *to get used to*
agarrar *to take*
bañarse *to swim*
conocer *to know*
construir *to build*

decidir *to decide*
desayunar *to have breakfast*
descansar *to rest*
descubrir *to discover*
despertarse *to wake up*
divertirse *to have fun*
dormir *to sleep*
encontrar *to find*
entrar *to come in*
hacer senderismo *to hike*

hacer surf *to surf*
intentar *to try*
leer *to read*
levantarse *to get up*
ordenar *to clean up*
pasear *to walk*
pedir *to ask for*
relajarse *to relax*

respirar *to breathe*
sentir *to feel*
tener *to have*
tomar el sol *to sunbathe*
vestirse *to get dressed*
volver *to go back*

Los viajes y las vacaciones

el aeropuerto *airport*
el avión *plane*

el boleto / billete *ticket*

el campamento de verano *summer camp*

el extranjero *foreigner*
el hotel *hotel*
la llave *key*
la maleta *suitcase*

la montaña *mountain*
el paisaje *landscape*

el pasaporte *passport*
la propina *tip*
la tarjeta de crédito *credit card*

Ocio y tiempo libre

escuchar música *to listen to music*

hacer deporte *to do sports*
ir a museos o a eventos culturales *to go to museums or cultural events*

ir al cine *to go to the movies*
ir de compras *to go shopping*

jugar a los videojuegos *to play videogames*
leer *to read*
pasar tiempo con la familia *to spend time with family*
salir con amigos *to go out with friends*

tocar un instrumento *to play an instrument*

trabajar como voluntario *to work as a volunteer*
ver la televisión *to watch TV*

EN RESUMEN: Gramática

PRESENT PROGRESSIVE TENSE

(See page 21)

■ Use **estar** + present participle to express an action in progress or the continuity of an action.

*Esta semana **estoy estudiando** mucho.*
This week, I'm studying a lot.

*Ahora mismo **estoy comiendo**, te llamo luego.*
Right now I'm eating, I will call you later.

■ The present participle in Spanish is formed by removing the **–ar** ending and replacing it with **–ando** or by removing the **–er** or **–ir** ending and replacing it with **–iendo**.

PRESENT PARTICIPLE
traba**jar** = traba**jando** *to work = working*
co**rrer** = co**rriendo** *to run = running*
escri**bir** = escri**biendo** *to write = writing*

USING THE PRETERIT, IMPERFECT AND PRESENT PERFECT

(See page 23)

Preterit	Imperfect	Present Perfect
■ The preterit tense is used to talk about actions that were **completed** at a fixed point in the past and have **no relation** with the **present**. · *Ayer **fui** en bici a clase.* · *El año pasado **fui** de vacaciones a Ecuador.*	■ Use the imperfect to describe **ongoing** or **habitual actions** in the past. · *Aquel día **llovía** mucho.* · *Antes yo siempre **iba** a Florida de vacaciones.*	■ We use the present perfect to say what a person **has done**. You generally use it in the same way you use its English equivalent. · *Ya **he hablado** con mi profesor de Matemáticas.* · *Luis y Rob **han comido** aquí.*

INFORMAL COMMANDS

(See page 28)

■ Use an imperative **tú** command when you want to order or tell someone to do something. Also it can be used to give advice or suggestions.

■ The affirmative **tú** commands are formed the same way as the present-tense forms that you use for **usted**, **él**, *or* **ella**.

Infinitive	Tú ➡ drop s	Affirmative *tú* commands
hab**lar**	habla	*Habla más lentamente. Speak more slowly.*
co**mer**	come	*Come la cena. Eat dinner.*
escri**bir**	escribe	*Escribe la carta. Write the letter.*

The following verbs have irregular **tú** commands in the affirmative:

Infinitive	oír	tener	venir	salir	ser	poner	hacer	decir	ir
Imperative	oye	ten	ven	sal	sé	pon	haz	di	ve

33

OBJECTIVES FOR EN RESUMEN: GRAMÁTICA

· Review unit grammar
· Practice communication skills

STANDARDS

1.2   Understand the language
1.3   Present information

INSTRUCTIONAL STRATEGIES

· Model how to review grammar.
· Have the students review the Learning Outcomes in the unit opener to assess whether they feel they have mastered the main ideas and skills.
· Ask them if they can remember additional examples for each grammar topic.
· Model how to find and go back to the appropriate page in the unit to review any grammar topic they may need help with.
· Invite students to review the grammar activities they completed in this unit.
· Ask them what grammar activities they found easy and which they found challenging. Encourage them to rework any activities they found particularly challenging.

OBJECTIVES FOR UNIT OPENER

- Introduce unit theme: *Construyendo un futuro*, about making plans for the future
- Introduce culture for unit: Learn about politics and the environment in Hispanic countries and compare cultural similarities

STANDARDS

1.1 Interpersonal communication
1.2 Understand the language
2.1 Practices and perspectives
4.2 Compare cultures

INSTRUCTIONAL STRATEGIES

- Introduce unit theme and objectives. Talk about the photo and have students make guesses about who the two people are: *Son compañeros de clase*, *El muchacho parece mayor*, *Tienen las mismas clases*, etc.
- Have the students discuss the questions and talk about themselves in the same context.
- Use the photograph to preview unit vocabulary: *¿Cuántos años crees que tienen? ¿Qué tipo de carrera crees que van a elegir? Y a ti ¿qué carrera te gustaría hacer?*, etc.
- Ask related questions: *¿Tienes hermanos en la universidad? ¿Qué carrera estudian? ¿Te gustaría estudiar la misma carrera? ¿Te gustaría estudiar en otra ciudad/otro país?*, etc.
- Help students formulate their ideas using *Tengo un hermano que estudia arquitectura en Boston*, *Me gustaría estudiar contabilidad*, *No tengo ni idea*, etc.

UNIDAD 1

CONSTRUYENDO UN FUTURO

Descansando entre clase y clase.

>> ¿Cuántos años crees que tienen estos muchachos?
>> ¿Qué crees que van a hacer después de graduarse?
>> ¿Y tú? ¿Qué planes tienes para el futuro?
>> ¿Qué crees que es lo más importante a la hora de elegir una carrera?

34

ADDITIONAL UNIT RESOURCES

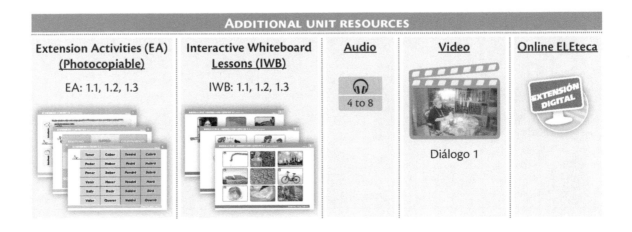

Extension Activities (EA) (Photocopiable)	Interactive Whiteboard Lessons (IWB)	Audio	Video	Online ELEteca
EA: 1.1, 1.2, 1.3	IWB: 1.1, 1.2, 1.3	4 to 8	Diálogo 1	EXTENSIÓN DIGITAL

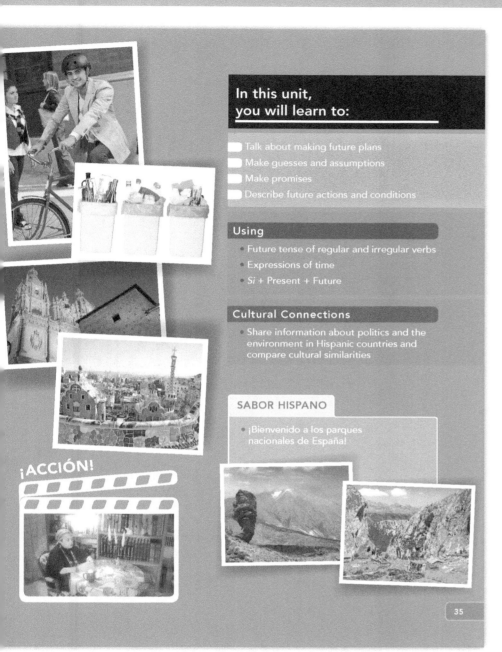

In this unit, you will learn to:

- Talk about making future plans
- Make guesses and assumptions
- Make promises
- Describe future actions and conditions

Using

- Future tense of regular and irregular verbs
- Expressions of time
- *Si* + Present + Future

Cultural Connections

- Share information about politics and the environment in Hispanic countries and compare cultural similarities

SABOR HISPANO

- ¡Bienvenido a los parques nacionales de España!

¡ACCIÓN!

INTRODUCTION TO LEARNING OUTCOMES

- The unit's learning objectives are an organizational tool for you and your students. Use them to preview what students will learn, and they serve as a way for you to assess whether your students have mastered the main ideas and skills. Encourage students to read the learning outcomes both before starting the unit and when they prepare for a test.

LEARNING OUTCOMES

- Talk about making future plans
- Make guesses and assumptions
- Make promises
- Describe future actions and conditions

INSTRUCTIONAL STRATEGIES

- Use unit opener to preview vocabulary and cultural topics for this unit.
- Have students look at the images on this page and relate them to the objectives listed. Ask questions such as: *¿Qué hace el hombre? ¿Por qué lleva casco? ¿Por qué va en bicicleta? ¿Cómo vienes a clase? ¿Tus padres usan la bici? ¿Qué hay en los contenedores? ¿En tu casa reciclan la basura? ¿En qué ciudades se encuentran estos sitios?*, etc.
- Invite students to read the topic for **Sabor hispano** and preview that section in the unit. Ask questions such as: *¿Hay parques nacionales cerca de aquí? ¿Qué se puede ver / hacer allí? ¿Conoces algún parque nacional en otro país?*
- Ask students to anticipate what they think the episode for **¡Acción!** will be about. Ask: *¿Qué hace esta mujer? ¿Dónde está?*
- Have students work in pairs to talk about the images using the questions you have modeled. Then ask for volunteers to present to the class what they understand this unit to be about.

35

Note Common Core State Standards (CCSS) The four strands of the *Common Core State Standards for English Language Arts (ELA) and Literacy in History/Social Studies, Science, and Technical Subjects* (Reading, Writing, Speaking and Listening, and Language) are represented in the National Standards for Learning Languages by the Communication standards: Interpersonal, Interpretive, and Presentational. The three modes of communication align with the goals in Reading, Writing, Speaking, and Listening by emphasizing the purpose behind the communication.

THREE MODES OF COMMUNICATION: UNIT 1			
	INTERPERSONAL	**INTERPRETIVE**	**PRESENTATIONAL**
HABLAMOS DE...	6	1, 2, 3, 4, 5	
COMUNICA	5, 6, 9	1, 2, 4, 7	3, 8, 9
¡ACCIÓN!	4	1, 2, 3	
PALABRA POR PALABRA	5, 6	1, 3, 4, 7, 8	2, 6, 9
GRAMÁTICA	2	1, 3, 4	5, 6
DESTREZAS		1, 2, 3	4
CULTURA		SABOR HISPANO	
RELATO	3, 5	1, 2, 3	4, 6

OBJECTIVES FOR HABLAMOS DE...

- Understand language in context
- Preview vocabulary: Talking about what people plan to do in the future
- Preview grammatical structures: Future of regular and irregular verbs; Time expressions; **Si** + present + future
- Read and listen to a conversation between two young people talking about their plans

CORE RESOURCES

- Audio Program: Track 4

STANDARDS

- 1.1   Engage in conversation
- 1.2   Understand the language
- 4.2   Compare cultures

INSTRUCTIONAL STRATEGIES

Activity 1

- Ask students to talk about the people in the photo and say what they are wearing, where they are or what they are holding. Ask if they are friends or a family and who they think each person is. Ask them what kind of job they think each one would like to have.
- Have the students cover the images of Víctor and Marta and do the activity without looking at the images.
- Have them decide which person each sentence refers to (some are for both and some for neither) and check the boxes, then have them compare their ideas with a partner and look at the images.
- Ask random students to read a sentence and other students to give the corresponding answer.
- Ask students when they think they are going to do all these things and remind them that the **ir a** + infinitive structure is used to talk about plans and intentions, usually in the near future.

Activity 2

- Have the students match the two parts of the sentences using what they already know about the two young people.
- Have them share their answers with a partner.
- Invite individual students to read one of the completed sentences and the rest of the class say who it refers to.

ANSWERS

Activity 1

a. Marta; **b.** Ninguno; **c.** Víctor; **d.** Los dos; **e.** Víctor; **f.** Víctor; **g.** Marta.

Activity 2

1. b; **2.** c; **3.** d; **4.** e; **5.** a.

HABLAMOS DE... El futuro

1 Look at the images of Víctor and Marta and match the sentences to the correct person.

 VÍCTOR

 MARTA

	Víctor	Marta	Los dos	Ninguno
a. Va a hacer deporte.	☐	☐	☐	☐
b. Va a pintar.	☐	☐	☐	☐
c. Va a tocar un instrumento.	☐	☐	☐	☐
d. Lleva una camiseta.	☐	☐	☐	☐
e. No va a jugar al tenis.	☐	☐	☐	☐
f. Va a practicar con su banda.	☐	☐	☐	☐
g. Va a ganar el partido.	☐	☐	☐	☐

2 Match the items to complete the activities Víctor and Marta are going to do this afternoon.

1. Va a ponerse   •   • **a.** el día.
2. Va a practicar su   •   • **b.** protección solar.
3. Va a ir a clase   •   • **c.** deporte favorito.
4. Va a tocar   •   • **d.** de música.
5. Van a disfrutar   •   • **e.** la guitarra.

36

3 🎧 4 **Listen to Marta and Víctor talk about the future and fill in the blanks with the missing words.**

Marta: Todavía no sé qué quiero estudiar cuando empecemos (a) .... ¿Tú ya sabes qué vas a estudiar?
Víctor: Me encanta la música, así que me imagino que estudiaré (b) ...., como mi hermana mayor. Ella está muy contenta y dice que la universidad es genial.
Marta: Pero tu hermana estudia en (c) ...., ¿verdad?
Víctor: Sí, le encanta la ciudad y está muy contenta.
Marta: ¿Y tú también quieres irte a estudiar allí?
Víctor: Bueno, supongo que iré a Barcelona o quizás a (d) .... La universidad de Salamanca es preciosa y muy antigua y la ciudad tiene mucha marcha *(lively)*, porque hay mucha gente joven.
Marta: Yo creo que me quedaré aquí en Zaragoza y estudiaré (e) .... o Enfermería. Víctor, si te vas... ¡qué pena!
Víctor: Bueno, bueno, que solo estoy haciendo (f) .... Todavía no es nada seguro, ¡y faltan unos años! Además, si me voy, te prometo que vendré a verte cada fin de semana.
Marta: ¿Me lo prometes?
Víctor: ¡Prometido!

Casa de las Conchas, Salamanca.

Parque Güell, Barcelona.

Basílica del Pilar, Zaragoza.

4 🎧 4 **Listen again to the conversation. Indicate whether the following sentences are true (T) or false (F).**

	T	F
a. Marta no tiene claro qué va a estudiar.	☐	☐
b. La hermana de Víctor estudia Bellas Artes.	☐	☐
c. Víctor ya sabe que va a estudiar en Salamanca.	☐	☐
d. Víctor y Marta viven en Zaragoza.	☐	☐
e. Víctor dice que en Barcelona hay mucha marcha.	☐	☐
f. A Marta le da igual si Víctor se va a estudiar a otra ciudad.	☐	☐
g. Víctor le hace una promesa a Marta.	☐	☐

37

🎧 4 **Activity 3**

• Write the word **universidad** on the board and ask students to talk about college and what it means to them. Ask: **¿Si vas a la Universidad, qué quieres estudiar? ¿Quieres ir a una universidad cerca de casa o en otro estado? ¿Qué universidades hay cerca de aquí? ¿Cómo son? ¿Quieres estudiar en el extranjero?**
• Inform the students that they are going to listen to a conversation between Marta and Víctor in which they talk about their plans for college.
• Have students close their books and listen to the audio.
• Ask how much they understood and have those who understood more explain what they understood.
• Play the audio again while the students follow in their books and fill in the missing words.
• Ask for volunteers to say the missing words and write them on the board.
• Have the students look at the photos and discuss them. Then find the cities on the map of Spain.

Cultural Note

Salamanca es una ciudad en la región de Castilla y León, muy famosa en España por sus monumentos y por su vida universitaria. Zaragoza es la capital de la Comunidad de Aragón, cerca de Cataluña. En ella, entre otros monumentos, se encuentra la Basílica de El Pilar, uno de los centros de peregrinación más importantes para los católicos.

🎧 4 **Activity 4**

• Have the students read the sentences and decide whether they are true or false as they listen one more time to the audio.
• Encourage students to cover the text and focus only on the audio.
• Invite volunteers to say the answers for the rest of the class.
• As a follow-up, ask students what they know of **la Universidad de Salamanca** based on their previous knowledge of the topic.
• You might ask students go online and visit the websites for these universities and report back on the types of degrees and programs offered at the university and what types of courses they offer foreign students. Or if time permits, visit these websites in class to find the equivalent in Spanish for common programs of studies.

Activity 3

a. la universidad; **b.** Bellas Artes; **c.** Barcelona; **d.** Salamanca; **e.** Medicina; **f.** conjeturas.

Activity 4

a. T; **b.** T; **c.** F; **d.** T; **e.** F; **f.** F; **g.** T.

Activity 5

- This activity previews the forms of the future and its use to make predictions.
- Have the students read the sentences and ask them if these statements refer to something that has already happened, is happening now, or hasn't happened yet. Ask students to identify the expressions that confirm their choice.
- Now ask them to match each sentence to an image.
- Have them compare answers with a partner.
- Ask one student to read a sentence and another to say which image it refers to.
- Point out that some of the expressions are followed by the future tense, which they will study later in the unit. For now, explain to students that they should just focus on becoming familiar with the form.
- If you like, you can ask students to describe what patterns they are beginning to see in this structure (infinitive form).

Activity 6

- Have the students read the questions and ask what other structure also refers to a future action (**ir a** + infinitive).
- Divide the students into pairs to and ask answer the questions in turns. Encourage students to make this activity as similar as possible to a real conversation.
- Circulate around the class as they work, providing assistance where required.
- Invite volunteers to say their answers aloud.

Extension

- Have student pairs present this activity to the class as a television or person-on-the-street type of interview. Tell students to create a "persona" for the interviewer and set up a context for the situation. For example, taking a survey, doing a show for Spanish language television about American students, as part of a comedy skit for a late-night talk show.
- Have the interviewer simulate a microphone and allow him/her to use note cards for the questions. The interviewer should react to the responses in a comical or serious way and ask follow-up questions as necessary.
- Have the class vote on the best interview, interviewer, or person on the street.
- The interviewer might also interview random students in the class without prior practice to see how well students think on their feet.

ANSWERS

Activity 5

1. e; **2.** b; **3.** h; **4.** g; **5.** c; **6.** a; **7.** f; **8.** d.

HABLAMOS DE... El futuro

5 **Match each sentence to the appropriate image.**

a. Me imagino que tendré que lavar los platos.
b. Voy a subir a poner la lavadora.
c. Te prometo que todo saldrá bien.
d. Espero tener tiempo de verlo todo.
e. Creo que este año sí aprobaré.
f. Este verano tengo la intención de ponerme en forma.
g. Te juro que te compraré otras.
h. Para mi fiesta de cumpleaños, este año pienso ir a un karaoke.

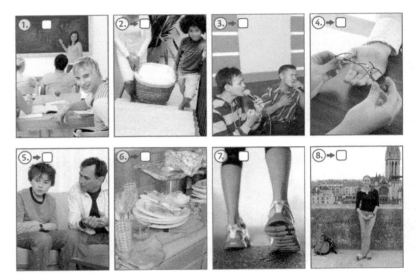

6 **Take turns asking and answering the following questions about your own future plans.**

a. ¿Ya sabes qué vas a hacer después de la escuela secundaria? ¿Qué?
b. ¿Tienes claro qué vas a estudiar en la universidad o escuela técnica? ¿Qué?
c. ¿Quieres ir a otra ciudad para estudiar o trabajar? ¿Por qué?
d. ¿Has ido alguna vez a un karaoke? ¿Cómo fue?
e. ¿Practicas algún deporte? ¿Cuál? ¿Con qué frecuencia?
f. ¿Cuál fue la última ciudad que visitaste? ¿Y la próxima que quieres visitar?

38

COMUNICA

MAKING ASSUMPTIONS

■ Para **hacer suposiciones o conjeturas**:

Creo que mañana lloverá. I believe that it will rain tomorrow.

Me imagino que no podremos ir a la playa. I imagine that we won't be able to go the beach.

Supongo que nos quedaremos en casa. I guess that we will stay at home.

1 Write what the following people have already done.

Alicia	el abuelo Paco	Iván	el tío Pepe	Patricia
(estudiar)	(pescar)	(hacer excursiones)	(tener un accidente)	(escalar montañas)

Alicia ha estudiado mucho.

2 👥 With a partner, match the people in Activity 1 to the image of what they are probably going to do next.

3 👥 Using the people from Activity 1, choose an activity from the list to describe what each one is going to do next according to the image you selected. Did you match them correctly?

> Irá al mecánico ○ Irá de expedición a la selva ○ Subirá al Everest ○
> Irá a la universidad ○ Cocinará pescado a la plancha

a. ....
b. ....
c. ....
d. ....
e. ....

OBJECTIVES FOR COMUNICA

- Present communicative functions of the unit:
  - Make assumptions or conjectures
  - Make promises

CORE RESOURCES

- Audio Program: Track 5
- Extension Activities: EA 1.1
- Interactive Whiteboard Lesson: IWB 1.1, 1.2
- Interactive Online Materials – ELEteca

STANDARDS

1.1 Engage in conversation
1.2 Understand the language
4.2 Compare cultures

INSTRUCTIONAL STRATEGIES FOR MAKING ASSUMPTIONS

- Project the conversation in Activity 3 (page 37) and ask students to identify the sentences that express assumptions or conjecture: **Me imagino que estudiaré Bellas Artes**, **Supongo que iré a Barcelona o quizás a Salamanca**, **Yo creo que me quedaré aquí en Zaragoza**. Ask students: **Cuando Víctor y Marta dicen estas cosas, ¿están seguros de lo que dicen o están haciendo una suposición?**
- Project IWB 1.1, **Conjeturas**. With books closed, tell students to guess what they think the people in the images are going to do using the expressions **Imagino / Supongo / Creo que**. Prompt students by asking, **¿Quién es? ¿Dónde va?** to elicit responses such as **Me imagino que va a ir a la biblioteca porque lleva libros**.

- Then walk students through the sample sentences in the book, pointing out the forms of the future.

Activities 1 and 2

- In addition to recycling the present perfect tense, the purpose of this activity is to establish a context for students to see the relationship between actions and tenses, between what already happened and what might happen next.
- Have the students express what the people have already done using the verbs and the model provided.
- Have students look at the images and decide which one most likely correspond to the people in Activity 1.

Activity 3

Have students work with a partner to choose an activity from the list to describe what the people in Activity 1 are going to do next.

ANSWERS

Activity 1

a. Alicia ha estudiado mucho; **b.** El abuelo Paco ha pescado un pez grande; **c.** Iván ha hecho excursiones a las pirámides centroamericanas; **d.** El tío Pepe ha tenido un accidente; **e.** Patricia ha escalado una montaña.

Activity 2

1. c; **2.** e; **3.** d; **4.** a; **5.** b.

← Previous Page

Activity 3

a. Alicia irá a la Universidad; b. El abuelo Paco cocinará el pescado a la plancha; c. Iván irá de expedición a la selva. d. El tío Pepe irá al mecánico; e. Patricia subirá al Everest.

INSTRUCTIONAL STRATEGIES

Activity 4

- Call on students to read the statements aloud after you to ensure correct pronunciation. Help students put the stress on the last syllable of each verb.
- Have them use the first column to check the activities they think they will do in the future and mark an X in those they don't think they will do. Ask them to provide their own ideas for the last three statements.
- Circulate around the room as they work, providing assistance where required.
- Continue to circulate around the room, listening in and correcting pronunciation and grammar when necessary.

Activity 5

- Have the students sit in a different place in the room and first talk to the student on their right.
- Read the model and remind them of some of the other possibilities for conjectures: **Me imagino que**, **Creo que**, etc.
- Students talk to their new partner about what they think they may do in the future and ask about his/her plans. They should take note of each other's responses.
- Circulate around the room while they talk and provide corrections and assistance where required.

Activity 6

- Have students do the same as in the previous activity, but with the student on their left.
- When they finish, have them think about which one they have more in common with.

Extension

- If you feel your group is ready, expand the activity by introducing the **usted**/**él**/**ella** form of the future.
- Begin by asking students to reflect on the forms of the future they have seen so far. Ask what form of the verb (**yo**) and the ending (add –**é** to infinitive). Explain that to express the **usted**/**él**/**ella** form, students need to add –**á** instead of –**é**. For example: **Pedro cree que hablará español perfectamente**.
- Then call on students to report back on the information they gathered from their classmates.

INSTRUCTIONAL STRATEGIES FOR MAKING PROMISES

- Review the expressions for making promises. Then have students turn back to the conversation in Activity 3 and pick out instances when these are used.
- Ask students to explain what the person is promising to do: **¿Qué promete hacer?** (**Te prometo que vendré a verte cada fin de semana**).
- For additional practice, have students take the last three lines of the conversation and substitute with a different expression.

COMUNICA

4 Put a check (√) next to the activities you think you will do in the future and an X next to those you don't think you will do. Complete the last three with your own information.

	Yo	Compañero 1	Compañero 2
a. Hablaré español perfectamente.			
b. Hablaré muchos idiomas.			
c. Seré un deportista profesional.			
d. Viviré en muchos países.			
e. Tocaré un instrumento.			
f. Escribiré un libro.			
g. Correré maratones.			
h. Iré			
i. Estudiaré			
j. Conoceré			

5 Talk to your classmate on the right about what you think you will or won't do in the future and ask about his/her plans. Take note of your classmate's responses.

Modelo: E1: Supongo que viajaré a España.
E2: Yo también.

6 Now, have the same discussion with your classmate on the left and take note of his/her answers. With which of the two do you have more in common?

MAKING PROMISES

- Para **hacer promesas**:
  - **Te prometo que...** I promise you that...
  - **Te lo prometo / juro.** I promise / swear it...
  - **Te doy mi palabra.** I give you my word.
  - **Te juro que...** I swear that...
  - **¡Prometido!** Promise!
  - **Lo haré sin falta.** I will be sure to do it.

¡Prometido!

40

7  **5** Listen to the following conversations and fill in the blanks with the missing words. Then match each conversation to the appropriate image.

1. ➡ ☐

a. **Madre:** ¡El próximo fin de semana estás castigado (*punished*)! Ayer llegaste tardísimo.
   Hijo: .... que no volverá a pasar, de verdad.
   Madre: Siempre dices lo mismo y nunca haces caso. ¡No hay más que hablar!
   Hijo: ¡Pero, mamá…!

2. ➡ ☐

b. **Luis:** ¡Estuve media hora esperándote y la película ya ha empezado! La próxima vez entro yo solo al cine y no te espero.
   Sandra: Anda, no te enfades. He llamado para avisarte… .... que no volverá a pasar.
   Luis: ¡Pero si desde que te conozco siempre llegas tarde!

3. ➡ ☐

c. **Pedro:** Tu fiesta ha estado genial. Nos hemos divertido muchísimo.
   Daniel: Me alegro. A ver si celebramos otra para tu cumpleaños.
   Pedro: ....

8 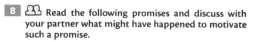 Read the following promises and discuss with your partner what might have happened to motivate such a promise.

a. Te prometo que no me meteré en tu correo electrónico.
b. Te juro que tendré mucho cuidado con él.
c. De verdad que lo haré sin falta. ¡Prometido!

9 Choose one of the promises from the activity above and prepare a conversation with your partner. Use the conversations in Activity 7 as a guide. Be prepared to present to the class.

Practice what you have learned with additional materials online.

INSTRUCTIONAL STRATEGIES

🎧 **5** **Activity 7**

Project IWB 1.2, **¿Qué está pasando?** and ask students to predict what expression the person in the illustration will use according to the scene depicted. Prompt students by signalling which of the characters is making the promise. For more accelerated groups, ask them to complete the promise.

• Then play the audio with books closed and ask students to match each conversation to the correct illustration.
• Have the students open their books and listen to the audio again as they fill in the blanks with the missing expressions from the explanation above.
• Invite pairs of students to perform each exchange for the class.

Activity 8

• In pairs, students imagine what must have happened for the promises to have been made. Help students think of some possibilities by suggesting they identify who made the promise to whom and what the person has done.
• Have volunteers share their ideas with the class.

Extension

• To continue practice, distribute copies of EA 1.1, *Hacer promesas* to student pairs. Each student selects a role and writes a promise for each of the situations presented on his/her card.
• Then each student shares the promise with his/her partner. He/She will try to guess the situation.

Activity 9

• Read through the situations in Activity 8 again and have students in pairs choose one.
• Each pair prepares a conversation for the chosen situation, using Activity 7 as a model. Have the students practice their conversations in pairs.
• Circulate around the class as they talk, listening in and providing assistance and corrections where required.
• Invite volunteers to present to the class.

ANSWERS

Activity 7

1. c: ¡Prometido!; **2.** a: Te juro; **3.** b: Te prometo.

OBJECTIVES FOR ¡ACCIÓN!

- Provide students with a structured approach to viewing the video
- Contextualize the content of the unit in a familiar scenario

CORE RESOURCES

- Unit Video 1
- Interactive Online Materials – ELEteca

STANDARDS

1.3 Understand the language
2.1 Practices and perspectives
3.2 Acquire information
4.2 Compare cultures

INSTRUCTIONAL STRATEGIES

Previewing: Antes del video

Activity 1

- Have students look at the frames and say what they think the video segment will be about.
- Ask the questions for each frame and have volunteers suggest answers.
- Ask for any alternative answers.
- List some of the possibilities on the board.
- Before playing the video, point out that students may notice that the fortune teller or **adivina** has a different accent or way of speaking. The woman uses the pronoun **vos** in place of **tú**.
- You may also ask students to observe the cards the **adivina** uses, which are not Tarot cards. Ask them if they have ever seen this type before.

Cultural Notes

- Also known as **el voseo**, **vos** is used in Latin America in such countries as Argentina, Costa Rica, El Salvador, Nicaragua, Paraguay, Uruguay and Venezuela when addressing a person in informal situations. In the video segment, the fortune teller is from Argentina and says **Cerrá los ojos** for **Cierra los ojos**, **Ya podés abrir los ojos** for **Ya puedes abrir los ojos**, etc.
- A Spanish deck of cards is made up of four suits and has the same type of number and picture cards as a poker deck. The suits are **copas** (cups), **oros** (coins), **bastos** (clubs), and **espadas** (swords) and are highly illustrated with a medieval look and feel to them.

ANSWERS

Activity 1

Answers will vary. Possible answers include: **a.** De una consulta en el que una adivina predice el futuro; **b.** Cartas o naipes; **c.** Normalmente para hacer juegos de mesa, pero también se usan para adivinar el futuro (tarot) o para hacer trucos de magia; **d.** En este caso, los adivinos; **e.** Una adivina; **f.** Predecir el futuro de las personas; **g.** Las personas que quieren conocer su futuro en diversos ámbitos: trabajo, amor, dinero...; **h.** Para conocer su futuro; **i.** Cosas sobre su futuro.

¡ACCIÓN!

ANTES DEL VIDEO

1 Answer the following questions.

a. ¿De qué crees que es ese rótulo?

b. ¿Qué ves entre las manos de la imagen?
c. ¿Para qué se usan?
d. ¿Quién crees que las está usando?

e. ¿Quién es esa señora?
f. ¿Qué crees que hará?
g. ¿Quién crees que irá a verla?

h. ¿Para qué crees que va la muchacha a la adivina?
i. ¿Qué crees que le preguntará?

42

DURANTE EL VIDEO

2 Watch the video and check your answers.

DESPUÉS DEL VIDEO

3 Answer the questions according to the sequence of images.

a. ¿Qué quiere saber la chica?

d. ¿Qué le vuelve a preguntar?
e. ¿Por qué está nerviosa la muchacha?

b. ¿Qué le responde la adivina?

f. ¿Qué le responde en esta ocasión?
g. ¿Qué tendrá que hacer para saber la respuesta?

c. ¿Por qué está tan contenta?

4 👥 **Answer the following questions. Work with a partner.**

a. ¿Crees en los adivinos? ¿Por qué?
b. ¿Alguna vez te han adivinado el futuro? ¿Acertaron?

Practice what you have learned with additional materials online.

43

INSTRUCTIONAL STRATEGIES

Viewing: Durante el video

Activity 2

- Play the video and have the students verify their answers for Activity 1. How accurate were their assumptions?
- Answer any questions they may have about the vocabulary.
- Play the entire video without pauses.
- Ask students what they understood.
- Play the video again and allow students to ask you to pause, as needed.
- Replay sections students found hard to understand.
- Have volunteers who understand help those students who understood less.
- Show the entire video again without pauses. Ask students to share how their understanding has improved.

After viewing: Después del video

Activity 3

- Have the students look at the frames from the video and answer the questions in pairs.
- Circulate while they work, providing assistance as required.
- Ask for volunteers to report their answers to the class.
- If students feel comfortable sharing, ask students to talk about any experiences they have had with a prediction or a fortune teller. How were their experiences similar or different from the ones in the video segment?

Activity 4

Have students discuss the questions and report their ideas back to the class.

Extension

- Have the students work in pairs to write a dialogue between the fortune-teller and a client.
- Provide assistance as required.
- When they are ready, invite pairs to act out their scene for the class.

ANSWERS

Activity 3

Answers will vary. Possible answers include: **a.** Quiere saber algo sobre su futuro, en qué universidad estudiará y qué estudiará; **b.** Que corte la baraja con la mano izquierda, que cierre los ojos y que se concentre; **c.** Porque, según las visiones de la adivina, cree que va a estudiar con su amiga Celia; **d.** Que qué va a estudiar; **e.** Porque no sabe si va a estudiar medicina o arquitectura; **f.** Que no ve nada más; **g.** Tendrá que volver al día siguiente.

OBJECTIVES FOR EL MEDIOAMBIENTE

- Present vocabulary needed to practice communicative and grammatical functions for the unit: The environment and the future
- Talk about ways to preserve natural resources

CORE RESOURCES

- Extension Activities: EA 1.2
- Interactive Whiteboard Lesson: IWB 1.3
- Interactive Online Materials – ELEteca

STANDARDS

1.1   Engage in conversation
1.2   Understand the language
1.3   Present information
3.2   Acquire information
4.1   Compare languages and cultures

INSTRUCTIONAL STRATEGIES

- Introduce the topic by projecting IWB 1.3, **El medioambiente**. With books closed, ask students to look at the images and draw conclusions about what they think the images represent. Ask students to describe some of the images. For example, **La muchacha lleva las botellas de plástico a reciclar**, **El hombre corta un árbol**...
- Then ask students to get into groups of four and distribute an equal number of cards from EA 1.2, **El medioambiente** to each group. Call on a student from each group to match their word to the correct image on the board. Ask the class, **¿Están de acuerdo? ¿Por qué?** Encourage students to justify their choices.
- Have students open their books and check their answers.

Activity 1

- Have the students decide which images show something with a negative impact on the environment and which show something positive, and write them in the correct column.
- Ask students to share their answers with a partner. Then call on volunteers to read from their lists and give examples or more information about the topics.
- Ask students to add other words connected with the topic.

PALABRA POR PALABRA El medioambiente

1 Look at the images and sort them according to their positive or negative impact on the environment. Add other environmental issues to the lists.

consumo responsable   reciclaje   contaminación

energía renovable   sequía   transporte ecológico

calentamiento global   deshielo   deforestación

Positivos	Negativos

2 What's your perspective on the future of the environment? With a partner take turns role-playing a positive and a negative outlook.

Modelo: Pesimista: En el futuro habrá sequía y no habrá suficiente agua para todos.
Optimista: Pero si consumimos el agua de forma responsable, eso no pasará.

- To talk about future actions or events:
  - Use the future tense to express an action that is less likely to occur.
    Esta tarde **visitaremos** la exposición.
  - Use **ir a** + infinitive to express an action that is more likely to occur.
    Vamos a visitar la exposición.
- To make predictions, use the future tense:
  Dentro de cien años **desaparecerán** algunos animales.

44

Activity 2

- Read the model with the class and pre-teach the future form of **hay** ➡ **habrá**.
- Ask them to read the box with the explanation for **ir a** + infinitive and the future tense.
- Call on student volunteers to role-play the model. Then allow students time to prepare a positive and a negative outlook to share with a partner.
- Ask for volunteers to present to the class. Encourage students to show appropriate emotion.

ANSWERS

Activity 1

Positivo: a; b; d; f. **Negativo:** c; e; g; h; i.

3 Read the following article with tips on how to preserve our natural resources and conserve energy. Then list four things the article suggests doing and compare your answers with a partner.

Ideas sencillas para salvar el planeta

El día a día nos ofrece muchas posibilidades para poner nuestro granito de arena en la protección y salvación del planeta. Si no sabes por dónde empezar, nosotros te damos algunas sugerencias *(suggestions)*.

Además de modificar los hábitos, se trata de que estos cambios sean sencillos de realizar *(easy to do)* para conseguir una repetición constante y resultados a largo plazo *(long term)*, los verdaderamente productivos.

Pero, ¿por dónde empezar? Podemos cambiar el chip sin esfuerzo en cuestiones cotidianas como la compra diaria, el uso de la computadora, nuestra basura, la publicidad comercial en papel que llena nuestro buzón *(mailbox)* o, entre muchos aspectos, la climatización de nuestro hogar.

Al ir a hacer la compra, infórmate del origen de los productos y las condiciones en que se elaboran, eso te ayudará a comprar con responsabilidad. Además, intenta consumir frutas y verduras orgánicas, mejorarás tu alimentación y ayudarás a mejorar el medioambiente.

Si utilizamos el portátil en lugar de una computadora ya estamos haciéndole un favor al medioambiente, y también a nuestro bolsillo *(pocket)* pues, por lo general, con él gastaremos aproximadamente la mitad de energía.

Otra idea es evitar *(avoid)* en nuestro buzón la publicidad en papel contactando con las empresas para que nos borren de sus listados. Si necesitamos ver algún catálogo, siempre podemos acudir a la versión *online* para consultarlo en un momento determinado. Piensa, además, que los recursos naturales no son infinitos y compara cuánto se tarda en cortar un árbol y cuánto tardará en crecer. Por eso, no malgastes el papel.

No gastar demasiado en climatización es otra cosa que podemos hacer teniendo un termostato programable y siguiendo consejos básicos para el aire acondicionado y la calefacción *(heating)*, así como evitar el transporte privado y preferir la bicicleta o el tren al coche o al avión.

También conviene revisar la temperatura a la que tenemos regulado el refrigerador, un par de puntos por encima de lo necesario supone un ahorro *(saving)* económico y eléctrico. Además, cambia tus electrodomésticos viejos por otros más modernos que causan un menor impacto medioambiental al consumir menos energía.

Un truco que nos ayudará a pensar qué hacer ante situaciones nuevas es recordar las famosas "tres erres" como propuesta de hábitos de consumo: Reducir, Reutilizar y Reciclar. Recicla los desechos domésticos de forma adecuada, separando los materiales; el reciclaje es básico para ayudar al planeta y son muchas las cosas y los materiales que pueden ser reutilizados.

Lógicamente, una sola persona no consigue cambios suficientes pero sí ayuda a hacerlos realidad si sus esfuerzos *(efforts)* se suman a los de otras muchas personas. El trabajo en equipo resulta totalmente imprescindible. Como ves, se pueden hacer más cosas de las que parece sin mucho esfuerzo. ¿Colaboras?

Texto adaptado de: *http://www.ecologiaverde.com/ideas-sencillas-para-ayudar-a-salvar-el-planeta/*

45

INSTRUCTIONAL STRATEGIES

Activity 4

• Have students look at the images and say a word or sentence to describe what they see and how it relates to the environment.

• Then have students read the statements and match each to an image.

• Have them share with a partner, before asking random students to give the correct answers.

Activity 5

• Students sit in pairs to discuss which ideas they already knew and which are new to them.

• Have them mark each idea with C (*conocida*) or N (*nueva*) in the margin.

• Ask for volunteers to report back to the class.

Extension

Have the class draw up a list of ideas, using the previous activities as a basis.

Divide the class into small groups to write a few sentences and illustrate one of the ideas.

Have the students make illustrated posters to show the results.

Activity 6

• Refer students to the questions and have them talk in small groups about what they already do to protect the environment and what new ideas they have gained from the text.

• Ask them to report back to the class.

Extension

As a follow-up, ask students to report on what environmental practices their school and community participate in. If students are unable to come up with many, encourage them to think about what the school and community can do based on some of the ideas discussed and ask students to draw up a list of recommendations. These should be bilingual so as to reach all members of the community and school staff. Tell students to use expressions such as **hay que**, **tener que** and **deber** for their recommendations. Have students work in small groups of three.

ANSWERS

Activity 4

1. a; **2.** f; **3.** c; **4.** b; **5.** h; **6.** e; **7.** d; **8.** g.

PALABRA POR PALABRA

4 **Match the following sentences from the text to the appropriate image.**

a. Infórmate del origen de los productos y las condiciones en que se elaboran.

b. Intenta consumir frutas y verduras orgánicas.

c. Compara cuánto se tarda en cortar un árbol y cuánto tardará en crecer, no malgastes el papel.

d. Usa un termostato programable y sigue los consejos básicos para el aire acondicionado y la calefacción.

e. Prefiere la bicicleta o el tren al coche o al avión.

f. Si utilizamos el portátil en lugar de una computadora, ya estamos haciéndole un favor al medioambiente.

g. Cambia tus electrodomésticos viejos por otros más modernos que causan un impacto medioambiental menor al consumir menos energía.

h. Recicla los desechos domésticos de forma adecuada, separando los materiales.

5 Talk with a partner about some of the things you learned in the article that are new to you. Use the following questions as a guide:

• ¿Qué ideas prácticas de las que aparecen en el artículo ya conocías?

• ¿Qué información es nueva para ti?

6 In small groups, talk about the things you do to protect the environment.

• ¿Qué cosas haces ya para proteger el medioambiente?

• ¿Crees que vas a hacer alguna más después de leer el artículo?

46

Next Page

OBJECTIVES FOR LA POLÍTICA

• Present vocabulary needed to practice communicative and grammatical functions for the unit: Politics and elections

• Talk about candidates and campaign promises

STANDARDS

1.2 Understand the language

1.3 Present information

3.2 Acquire information

PALABRA POR PALABRA La política

7 Read the following newspaper article.

Unas elecciones muy reñidas

Mañana se celebrarán las elecciones a la presidencia del país. Las encuestas de estos días señalan *(indicate)* que los dos principales partidos están muy igualados y que puede pasar cualquier cosa. Pablo Tomeu y Francisco Torres, los dos principales candidatos a presidente, se muestran optimistas ante estas elecciones, aunque habrá que esperar hasta contar todos los votos para conocer el resultado final.

Los dos partidos *(parties)* han prometido hacer grandes cambios en el país si consiguen ganar las elecciones. El candidato Pablo Tomeu ha dicho que si gana, hará una gran reforma en educación. También ha dicho que mejorará *(will improve)* la salud pública y que abrirá varios hospitales nuevos.

El programa del partido de Francisco Torres apuesta por *(supports)* el medioambiente. Como ha dicho a lo largo de toda su campaña, este será un punto fundamental: si el partido de Torres sale elegido, se incentivará el uso del transporte público, se bajará el precio a los autos eléctricos, se trabajará en las energías renovables, etc. Hasta mañana por la tarde no conoceremos quién será el futuro presidente del país y los cambios que viviremos en los próximos cuatro años.

8 Read the statements and decide whether the sentences below are true (T) or false (F).

	T	F
a. El partido de Tomeu es el favorito.	☐	☐
b. Los dos principales candidatos piensan que pueden obtener buenos resultados.	☐	☐
c. Se presentan más de dos partidos a estas elecciones.	☐	☐
d. El partido que quiere mejorar la sanidad, también quiere mejorar el transporte.	☐	☐
e. Las elecciones se celebran cada cinco años.	☐	☐

9 Elections for a new mayor are being held in your town and you are one of the candidates! What is your platform? Write a speech using the vocabulary you have learned and the following issues.

> medioambiente ○ educación ○ trabajo ○ transporte ○ salud

Estimados ciudadanos:
Prometo que construiré más zonas verdes, así los niños podrán jugar en los parques. Además, si votan por mí, el transporte en la ciudad será más barato. Si mi partido gana, les prometo que no habrá tanta contaminación y...

 Practice what you have learned with additional materials online.

47

Instructional Strategies

Activity 7

- With books closed, draw 8 dashes on the board to represent the letters of the word **política**. Play Hangman with the students until they discover the word.
- Ask students what they know about politics in the U.S. Ask questions such as: **¿Qué partido lidera el Presidente? ¿Dónde se reúnen los senadores?**, etc.
- Ask what they know about politics in any of the countries in Latin America, for instance: **¿Quién es el Presidente del Gobierno? ¿Qué tipo de gobierno es? ¿Una democracia, una monarquía, una dictadura, un gobierno militar?**, etc. You might prepare ahead the names of the heads of state in these countries.
- Ask students to open their books and focus on the highlighted words in the text.
- Ask them to spell out the words while you write them on the board under the heading **Política**. Ask for volunteers to explain the meaning of the words.
- Have the students read quickly through the article and then read aloud in sections.

Activity 8

- Have the students read the statements and mark each as either true or false.
- When they have finished, they share their ideas with a partner.
- Ask for volunteers to give the correct answers.

Activity 9

- Ask for three students to volunteer to be candidates of their political party in the next mayoral elections. Select a team for each candidate to form political parties.
- Read the instructions and have the students write the rest of the speech in their groups, mentioning each of the topics in the box and using the expressions they have learned for making promises.
- Circulate around the room as they work offering assistance.

- When they have finished, have each candidate read their speech to the class, pretending to be a politician and exaggerating any gestures to make it more fun.
- Finally, have the students vote for the best speech and candidate.
- The winning speech can be put up on the classroom wall and the winner can become the class representative.

Extension

- Ask for a volunteer to come to the front and sit facing the rest of the class (unable to see the board).
- Write one of the words from the **Política** list in Activity 7 on the board.
- The other students attempt to define the word without saying it, until the first student guesses. He/she can ask questions such as: **¿Se mete en un sobre? ¿Se celebran cada cuatro años?**, etc.

Answers

Activity 8
a. F; b. T; c. T; d. F; e. F.

OBJECTIVES FOR GRAMÁTICA 1

- Present grammatical structures needed to practice communicative functions of the unit:
  The future tense of regular and irregular verbs
- Use the future tense to make predictions and talk about what will happen

CORE RESOURCES

- Interactive Online Materials – ELEteca

STANDARDS

1.1 Engage in conversation
1.2 Understand the language
1.3 Present information
4.1 Compare languages

INSTRUCTIONAL STRATEGIES

1. The Future Tense

- Write the following sentences on the board: **Te prometo que estaré allí a las ocho**, **Imagino que hablaré muy bien español**, **El próximo año estudiaré en la universidad**. Ask students to identify the sentence that expresses a promise, an assumption, and a future prediction. Then ask what they all have in common (use future tense).
- Walk students through the grammatical explanation in the book. Focus first on the regular forms. Point out that all verbs share the same endings and that all forms except **nosotros** have written accents on the last syllable.
- Provide practice by saying one of the verbs and asking students to say the correct future form of the person given. Say **hablar ➡ él** to elicit **hablará**.
- Focus attention next on the irregular verbs and point out that the endings are still the same, and it is the stem that is irregular. Review new verbs **caber** (*to fit*) and **valer** (*to be worth*).
- Again practice by saying an irregular verb and having the students say the correct future form for the person given.

Activity 1

- Have the students focus first on the verbs in parenthesis and say whether they are regular or irregular. If irregular they should give the correct stem for each.
- Have them read through the text and fill in the correct form of the future.
- Ask for volunteers to read the text aloud while you write the answers on the board, paying particular attention to accents.

Activity 2

- Look at the time expressions in the box with the students and have them provide examples using the future, such as: **Mañana vendré a clase pronto**.

GRAMÁTICA

1. THE FUTURE TENSE

■ The future tense expresses what will happen. Regular verbs in the future tense are conjugated by adding the following endings to the infinitive form of the verb:

REGULAR VERBS			
	ESTUDIAR	COMER	VIVIR
yo	estudiaré	comeré	viviré
tú	estudiarás	comerás	vivirás
usted/el/ella	estudiará	comerá	vivirá
nosotros/as	estudiaremos	comeremos	viviremos
vosotros/as	estudiaréis	comeréis	viviréis
ustedes/ellos/ellas	estudiarán	comerán	vivirán

■ Irregular verbs in the future tense have irregular stems, but use the same endings as regular verbs.

IRREGULAR VERBS			
poder ➡ podr-			é
salir ➡ saldr-	tener ➡ tendr-		ás
caber ➡ cabr-	poner ➡ pondr-	hacer ➡ har-	á
haber ➡ habr-	venir ➡ vendr-	decir ➡ dir-	emos
saber ➡ sabr-	valer ➡ valdr-		éis
querer ➡ querr-			án

■ The future tense is often used with the following expressions of time:

- El año / el mes / la semana / la primavera **que viene**.
- **Dentro de** dos años / un rato / unos días.
- El / la **próximo/a** semana / mes / año.
- **Mañana / Pasado mañana**.

- *El año que viene* iré a España.
- *Dentro de* unos días vendrá a casa.
- *El próximo* año tendré 17 años.
- *Pasado mañana* tendré un examen.

1 What event do you think the fortune teller is referring to? Fill in the blanks with the future tense of the verbs in parenthesis to find out.

Veo… que dentro de poco (conocer, tú) .... a una persona que (ser) .... muy importante para ti. (Salir, ustedes) .... juntos. Un día esta persona (querer) .... hacerte un regalo, pero tú le (decir) .... que no puedes aceptarlo. (Venir, tú) .... otra vez aquí porque (tener, tú) .... muchas dudas y me (pedir) .... consejo.

2 Arrange the following expressions of the timeline of the next page starting with the one closest to the present. Then take turns with a partner saying what you will do at each point in the future.

> el mes que viene ○ dentro de dos años ○ dentro de un rato ○ mañana
> pasado mañana ○ el año que viene ○ las próximas Navidades

- Have the students write the time expressions in the correct place on the timeline on the next page. Then ask them to compare answers with a partner.
- Ask for volunteers to say a sentence using an expression from the box and a verb in the future.

ANSWERS

Activity 1

Conocerás, será, Saldrán, querrá, dirás, Vendrás, tendrás, pedirás.

Activity 2

a. dentro de un rato; **b.** mañana; **c.** pasado mañana; **d.** el mes que viene; **e.** las próximas Navidades; **f.** el año que viene; **g.** dentro de dos años.

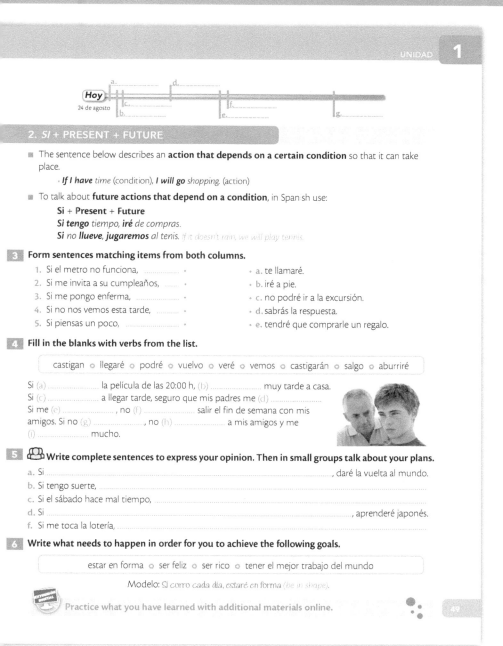

2. SI + PRESENT + FUTURE

■ The sentence below describes an **action that depends on a certain condition** so that it can take place.

· **If I have** time (condition), **I will go** shopping. (action)

■ To talk about **future actions that depend on a condition**, in Spanish use:

Si + Present + Future
Si tengo tiempo, **iré** de compras.
Si no llueve, jugaremos al tenis. If it doesn't rain, we will play tennis.

3 Form sentences matching items from both columns.

1. Si el metro no funciona, ... •
2. Si me invita a su cumpleaños, ... •
3. Si me pongo enferma, ... •
4. Si no nos vemos esta tarde, ... •
5. Si piensas un poco, ... •

· a. te llamaré.
· b. iré a pie.
· c. no podré ir a la excursión.
· d. sabrás la respuesta.
· e. tendré que comprarle un regalo.

4 Fill in the blanks with verbs from the list.

castigan ○ llegaré ○ podré ○ vuelvo ○ veré ○ vemos ○ castigarán ○ salgo ○ aburriré

Si (a) .... la película de las 20:00 h, (b) .... muy tarde a casa.
Si (c) .... a llegar tarde, seguro que mis padres me (d) ....
Si me (e) .... , no (f) .... salir el fin de semana con mis
amigos. Si no (g) .... , no (h) .... a mis amigos y me
(i) .... mucho.

5 Write complete sentences to express your opinion. Then in small groups talk about your plans.
a. Si ...., daré la vuelta al mundo.
b. Si tengo suerte, ...
c. Si el sábado hace mal tiempo, ...
d. Si ...., aprenderé japonés.
f. Si me toca la lotería, ...

6 Write what needs to happen in order for you to achieve the following goals.

estar en forma ○ ser feliz ○ ser rico ○ tener el mejor trabajo del mundo

Modelo: Si corro cada día, estaré en forma (be in shape).

Practice what you have learned with additional materials online.

OBJECTIVES FOR GRAMÁTICA 2

· Present grammatical structures needed to practice communicative functions of the unit:
Si + present + future
· Make predictions about what will happen under certain conditions

STANDARDS

1.1 Engage in conversation
1.5 Understand the language
1.6 Present information
4.1 Compare languages

INSTRUCTIONAL STRATEGIES

2. Si + Present + Future

· Walk the students through the explanation in the book. Point out that **si** is followed by the present tense and refers to the condition that needs to be met. The future tense refers to what will happen, just as in English.

Activity 3

· Have the students look at the sentences and find the correct ending for each.
· Ask them to share their answers with a partner. Then call on students to read out the answers.

Activity 4

· Have the students look at the image and say who they think the two people are and how they feel. Have them read quickly through the sentences to get a general idea.
· Then tell students to choose a verb from the list to fill each blank.
· Ask them to share their answers with a partner to see if they agree. Review correct answers.

Activity 5

· Have the students complete the sentences expressing their opinion.
· Circulate around the room as they work, checking that they are using the correct grammatical structure and providing assistance where required.
· When they have finished, ask them to sit in small groups to share their ideas. Ask some groups to share their ideas with the class.

Activity 6

· Tell students to create at least one sentence for each expression given. Ask for volunteers to read some of their ideas to the class.
· Tell the students they are going to link their sentences, with each person saying the next idea. Say: **Si quiero hablar español...** and invite a student to say: **Si quiero hablar español, tendré que estudiar mucho**. The next student takes the end of the last sentence and begins: **Si tengo que estudiar mucho, no podré salir con**..., etc. Continue round the room so that all the students can practice.

ANSWERS

Activity 3

1. b.; **2.** e; **3.** c; **4.** a; **5.** d.

Activity 4

a. vemos; **b.** llegaré; **c.** vuelvo; **d.** castigarán; **e.** castigan; **f.** podré; **g.** salgo; **h.** veré; **i.** aburriré.

OBJECTIVES FOR DESTREZAS

- Scan for specific information
- Organize information in a logical order

STANDARDS

1.1 Interpersonal communication

1.2 Understand the language

1.3 Present information

Note

The design of the activities in this section is meant to simulate standardized testing formats students may encounter as part of international testing certificates as the DELE (*Diploma de Español como Lengua Extranjera*) or in preparation for other state and / or national assessments. For this reason, it is recommended you do not pre-teach any of the vocabulary. In addition, students should complete the tasks individually.

INSTRUCTIONAL STRATEGIES

Comprensión de lectura

Activity 1

- Have the students look at the images and use them to predict what the email is going to be about.
- Talk the students through the strategy, and have them read through the questions at the end. Have them write key words in the box.

Activity 2

- Ask the students to read the text and choose the best way to complete each statement.
- Ask for volunteers to say the correct answers.

ANSWERS

Activity 2

1. c; 2. c; 3. a; 4. b; 5. a.

DESTREZAS

COMPRENSIÓN DE LECTURA

1 Before you complete the reading, review the strategy in Destrezas and follow the suggestion.

Destrezas

Scanning for specific information

Use the comprehension questions at the end of the activity to help you decide what information to search for as you read.

List some key words or phrases you should focus your attention on.

....

....

Asunto: Mi viaje a Los Ángeles

De: teo@gmail.com   Para: luis@hotmail.com

Hola, Luis:

¿Qué tal va todo? Me imagino que seguirás de exámenes. ¡Con lo estudioso que eres, seguro que sacas unas notas increíbles!

Te escribo para decirte que el mes que viene tendré unos días de vacaciones y quiero ir a Los Ángeles. Supongo que estarás allí y que podremos hacer muchas cosas juntos. Por cierto, pienso llevarme mi tabla de surf. Me han dicho que allí hay unas olas fantásticas, ¿me puedes dar alguna información sobre las playas? También quiero ir un día a la isla Santa Catalina. He leído en Internet que es muy bonita y que se puede ir a ver delfines. ¿Vendrás conmigo? Me imagino que tú sabrás dónde están los botes que te llevan hasta allí. Por cierto, ¿conoces algún lugar para ir de acampada? Como ves, no pienso parar ni un solo día. Y por la noche, supongo que me enseñarás los lugares donde va la gente joven…

¡Espero tu correo! Un abrazo,

Teo

---

2 Read the email again and select the correct answer.

1. Teo escribe un correo sobre...
   a. sus últimas vacaciones.
   b. sus exámenes.
   c. sus próximas vacaciones.

2. Teo tiene información sobre la isla...
   a. por sus amigos.
   b. porque se la ha dado Luis.
   c. porque se lo han contado y por Internet.

3. Teo pide información sobre...
   a. playas y alojamiento.
   b. playas y gastronomía.
   c. playas, gastronomía y alojamiento.

4. En el correo, Teo...
   a. solo pide información a su amigo.
   b. pide información a su amigo y le propone hacer actividades juntos.
   c. solo le propone a su amigo hacer actividades juntos.

5. Teo quiere practicar...

a.   b.   c.

50

[Next Page]

INSTRUCTIONAL STRATEGIES

Expresión e interacción escritas

Activity 3

- Read the information in the **Destrezas** box with the students and have them make their own notes, based on the information provided.
- Tell students to organize their ideas in logical order.

Activity 4

- Students write their email using the notes they made earlier. They should include all the information provided in the **Destrezas** box as well as their own ideas.
- Circulate around the room as they work, answering questions and providing assistance where required.
- Ask for volunteers to read their email to the class.
- The completed emails can be mounted for display on the classroom walls.

EXPRESIÓN E INTERACCIÓN ESCRITAS

3 You want to spend a few days camping in a state park and need some information about the facilities. Before you begin to write, read the strategy in Destrezas and follow the suggestion.

Destrezas

Organizing your information in a logical order

Think about the information you need and prepare your questions. Include the specific vocabulary you will need.

Information: availability for dates you want, access to pools and sports facilities included in price, pets allowed.

Vocabulary: plazas libres, wi-fi, restaurante, luz eléctrica…

4 Write your email to the campsite to ask for information.

PRONUNCIACIÓN La acentuación

As you know, all words in Spanish have a syllable that is pronounced with more stress than the other syllables in the word, and in some cases, a written accent is needed to identify the stressed syllable.

1 🎧 6 **Listen to the following words and underline the syllable in each word that carries the main stress.**

• cuéntamelo	• historia	• ciudad	• lápiz	• aquí
• corazón	• carácter	• después	• verano	• rápido
• sábado	• música	• dáselo	• maravilla	• político
• pensar	• cómic	• devuélvemelo	• jardín	• casa
• salió	• fábrica	• gracias	• dímelo	• envíanoslas
• joven	• canción	• palo	• difícil	• genial

2 **Now classify them according to where the stress falls.**

• Palabras **agudas** ☐☐☐

• Palabras **esdrújulas** ☐☐☐

• Palabras **llanas** difícil ☐☐☐

• Palabras **sobreesdrújulas** ☐☐☐☐

3 **Look at the words that have a written accent mark and fill in the blanks in the basic rules below.**

a. Las palabras agudas se acentúan cuando terminan en ...., ... o ....
b. Las palabras llanas se acentúan cuando terminan en una consonante distinta de .... o ....
c. Las palabras esdrújulas o sobreesdrújulas se acentúan ....
d. Recuerda que las palabras **qué, cómo, dónde, cuándo** y **cuánto** tienen tilde solamente en las frases .... y .... Por ejemplo: ¿De dónde eres? ¡Qué calor!

 Practice what you have learned with additional materials online.

OBJECTIVES FOR PRONUNCIACIÓN

• Practice separating syllables and using stress correctly

CORE RESOURCES

• Audio Program: Track 6
• Interactive Online Materials – ELEteca

STANDARDS

1.2 Understand the language
3.2 Acquire information
4.1 Compare languages

INSTRUCTIONAL STRATEGIES

• Walk the students through the explanation and give them an example, such as **teléfono**. Have them clap or tap out the word on their desks, tapping louder on the stressed syllable.
• Do the same with a few more words to practice, for instance: **reciclaje**, **prometemos**, **escribiré**, etc.
• Point out that words that carry an accent are stressed on that syllable.

🎧 6 **Activity 1**

• Play the audio and have the students listen and repeat, raising their hand as they hear / say the stressed syllable.
• Repeat the audio and have the students underline the syllable in the word that carries the main stress.
• Ask random students to say each word and clap or tap out the syllables, indicating which syllable carries the main stress.

Activity 2

• Have students look at the four types of words in the activity. Tell students to clap or tap out the syllables for each type as indicated by the blanks and accents. Begin with the example: **difícil**.
• Have the students classify the words from Activity 1 according to where the stress falls as indicated by the white boxes that follow
• When they have finished, have them compare their answers with a partner.
• Ask individual students to give the correct answers.

Activity 3

• Have the students focus on the words that carry an accent.
• Students complete the rules for accents, referring back to the previous activities.
• Ask for volunteers to read the rules.

ANSWERS

Activity 1

Cuéntamelo, his**to**ria, ciu**dad**, **lá**piz, a**quí**, cora**zón**, ca**rác**ter, des**pués**, ve**ra**no, **rá**pido, **sá**bado, **mú**sica, **dá**selo, mara**vi**lla, po**lí**tico, pen**sar**, **có**mic, de**vuél**vemelo, jar**dín**, **ca**sa, sa**lió**, **fá**brica, **gra**cias, **dí**melo, en**ví**anoslas, **jo**ven, can**ción**, **pa**lo, di**fí**cil, ge**nial**.

Activity 2

Agudas: corazón, pensar, salió, canción, ciudad, después, jardín, aquí, genial; **Llanas:** joven, historia, carácter, cómic, gracias, palo, lápiz, verano, maravilla, difícil, casa; **Esdrújulas:** sábado, música, fábrica, dáselo, dímelo, rápido, político; **Sobreesdrújulas:** cuéntamelo, devuélvemelo, envíanoslas.

Activity 3

a. *n, s* o vocal; b. *n* o *s*; c. siempre; d. interrogativas y exclamativas.

OBJECTIVES FOR SABOR HISPANO

- Learn about Spanish national parks
- Activate vocabulary connected with the environment

CORE RESOURCES

- Audio Program: Track 7

STANDARDS

2.1 Culture: practices and perspectives

2.2 Products and perspectives

3.2 Acquire information

5.2 Using language for personal enjoyment and enrichment

INSTRUCTIONAL STRATEGIES

- Introduce the topic by asking if the students know what a national park is and to explain what it means.
- Look at the images with them and elicit what they already know and can share.
- Have them look at the questions in **Antes de leer** and discuss them.
- Tell students to skim the reading and find different explanations of what a national park is and is not.
- Tell the students to look at the **Glosario** on the next page to help them with any vocabulary they may not know.
- Read the first section of the text and invite a volunteer to read after you. After each section, ask questions such as: **¿Dónde está el volcán más grande del mundo? ¿Cómo se llama?**, etc.
- Ask what the students have understood and invite those who understood more to help those who understood less.
- You can also play the audio while students follow along with the text.

SABOR HISPANO

¡BIENVENIDOS A LOS PARQUES

Parque Nacional del Teide, Tenerife, Islas Canarias.

NACIONALES DE ESPAÑA!

Antes de leer

¿Hay parques nacionales en tu país?

¿Has visitado alguno?

¿Qué características tienen estos parques?

 7 **Naturaleza espectacular, flora única y fauna salvaje°. Estos son algunos de los elementos de los parques nacionales. ¡Visítalos!**

«Es nuestro mayor tesoro°», dice Humberto Gutiérrez, Jefe de Medioambiente de Tenerife, «el Parque Nacional del Teide es el que recibe más visitas de toda Europa y el segundo del mundo. Además, en él está el volcán más grande del mundo». El Parque Nacional del Teide, en las islas Canarias, España, es uno de los 15 parques nacionales de este país.

Los parques nacionales se caracterizan por su impresionante naturaleza y su fauna. A menudo están formados por cordilleras o montañas, volcanes, lagos, desiertos, cascadas°, bosques, rocas, barrancos°, calderas° o glaciares.

«No es suficiente con tener hectáreas de terreno. Para que una extensión sea declarada Parque Nacional, esta debe tener una belleza, fauna y flora especiales. El gobierno de un país la acota° y protege para que no se construya en ella», dicen desde el Ministerio de Agricultura, Alimentación y Medioambiente de España.

Otros parques nacionales importantes son el Parque Nacional de Doñana, el Parque Nacional de Sierra Nevada, el Parque Nacional Marítimo-Terrestre del Archipiélago de Cabrera y el Parque Nacional de los Picos de Europa.

Muchos de estos parques han sido declarados Patrimonio de la Humanidad por la UNESCO.

Parque Nacional de Ordesa y Monte Perdido, Aragón.

Parques Nacionales

Aquí están los 5 parques nacionales más importantes de España.

- Parque Nacional del Teide
- Parque Nacional de Doñana
- Parque Nacional de Sierra Nevada
- Parque Nacional Marítimo-Terrestre del Archipiélago de Cabrera
- Parque Nacional de los Picos de Europa

Atractivos

Estos son los elementos más atractivos de un Parque Nacional, según sus visitantes.

65%

30%

5%

- La geografía
- La fauna
- La flora

Parque Nacional de Sierra Nevada, Granada, Andalucía.

¿COMPRENDISTE?

Connect the following sentences.

1. Los parques nacionales
2. En el Parque Nacional de Sierra Nevada
3. El Parque Nacional del Teide
4. En los parques nacionales a menudo hay
5. El Parque Nacional de los Picos de Europa

a. está en el norte de España.
b. está en una isla.
c. nieva mucho.
d. son terrenos protegidos por el gobierno.
e. montañas, barrancos y bosques.

Parque Nacional de Los Picos de Europa, Asturias.

AHORA TÚ

What do you think? Answer the following questions and discuss your ideas with other students.

1. ¿Es importante para un país tener parques nacionales? ¿Por qué?

2. ¿Crees que el número de visitantes a un parque nacional es positivo o negativo para el parque? ¿Por qué?

3. ¿Crees que un parque nacional aporta riqueza* a un país? ¿Cómo?

4. ¿Qué elementos famosos hay en algún parque nacional que conozcas?

5. ¿Qué parque te gustaría visitar? ¿Por qué?

Glosario

acotar – enclose
el barranco – ravine
la caldera – crater
la cascada – waterfall
la riqueza – wealth
salvaje – wild
el tesoro – treasure

Fuentes: *El viajero (El País)*, *Viajar (El Periódico)*, Oficina de Turismo de España, *El Mundo*, *La Nación*, Red de Parques Nacionales, Compañía de Parques Nacionales, Parques Nacionales Naturales, Reservas Parques Nacionales, Gobierno de Canarias, Gobierno de España.

53

INSTRUCTIONAL STRATEGIES

Call on students to interpret the information presented in the graphs and make statements about what they see.

Parques Nacionales

Ask questions about their location according to the map.

Atractivos

Have students make comparisons using the information in the pie chart. For example, **A los visitantes les atrae más la geografía de los parques nacionales que la flora** and so on.

¿Comprendiste?

- Have the students read the statements in the box and match the two parts of the sentences. Then have them check through the text to see if they are correct.
- Have them compare their answers with a partner.
- Invite individual students to share their answers with the class.

Ahora tú

- Read the questions with the students and have them think about the answers.
- Have the students answer the questions in pairs or small groups and then ask for volunteers to present to the class.

Extension

- Have the students make a list of the national parks in other Latin American countries (using the Internet).
- Divide the students into groups and have each group research one of the parks.
- Ask them to write a short article about the park and illustrate it with images from the Internet or from travel brochures.
- Invite each group to present their park to the class.
- The completed work can be mounted and displayed on the classroom walls.

ANSWERS

¿Comprendiste?

1. d; **2.** c; **3.** b; **4.** e; **5.** a.

OBJECTIVES FOR RELATO

- Revisit unit themes, grammar, vocabulary and culture in a new context
- Improve reading comprehension skills

CORE RESOURCES

- Audio Program: Track 8

STANDARDS

1.1 Engage in conversation

1.2 Understand the language

1.3 Present information

2.1 Practices and perspectives

5.3 Using language for personal enjoyment and enrichment

INSTRUCTIONAL STRATEGIES

Activity 1

- Have the students look at the image and title and guess what they think the text will be about.
- Ask them what changes they think may occur in the future, in 20 years, 100 years, for example.
- With a partner, have them look at the vocabulary and definitions and match them.
- Ask for volunteers to share their ideas with the class.

🎧 8 Activity 2

- Have the students look through the text to find and underline the words in Activity 1.
- Play the audio while the students follow in their books.
- Ask questions such as: **¿Alberto se sentó a la mesa? ¿Qué premio ha recibido la persona que da la entrevista?**, etc.
- Have those students who understood more help those who understood less.

ANSWERS

Activity 1

1. c; **2.** d; **3.** a; **4.** b.

RELATO Viaje al futuro

1 Match the following expressions with their corresponding definition.

1. efecto invernadero .... •
2. combustibles fósiles .... •
3. vertedero .... •
4. sensores .... •

- **a.** Lugar para depositar los residuos y la basura de una zona o ciudad.
- **b.** Dispositivos que detectan una acción externa como la temperatura o la presión y que transmiten la información.
- **c.** Calentamiento del planeta provocado por diversos gases.
- **d.** Lo son el carbón, el petróleo y el gas natural.

2 🎧 8 **Before you read the story, underline the words above to help you focus on meaning.**

Viaje al futuro

Alberto llegó de la escuela, comió, encendió la tele, agarró el mando a distancia *(remote control)* y se tumbó en el sofá. ¡ZAP!

—Si quiere disfrutar de unas vacaciones de ensueño, Florida es su destino. ¡ZAP!

—Siempre te querré a ti, mi amor. ¡ZAP!

—Quiero hacerle una pregunta; usted, al recibir el Premio Nobel de Energía afirmó que el futuro que nos espera es mucho más negro de lo que pensamos —interesante, pensó Alberto.

—Sí, efectivamente. Las grandes ciudades del futuro provocarán el efecto invernadero y una megapolución si no hacemos algo. Habrá tanta superpoblación que tendremos que cultivar en grandes huertos urbanos para alimentarnos. Para no terminar con los combustibles fósiles, tendremos que reducir el número de carros y los kilómetros recorridos por los aviones. Habrá islas-vertedero para eliminar los residuos *(waste)*. Se tendrá que ahorrar energía utilizando los elementos de la naturaleza como el sol, el viento o la lluvia. ¡ZAP!

—Buenos días, les presento a William Mitchell, del Instituto Tecnológico de Massachusetts. ¿Cómo piensa usted que serán las ciudades del futuro?

—Bueno, yo pienso que estarán diseñadas como organismos vivos, con inteligencia propia. Las calles y edificios tendrán luces inteligentes que cambiarán de color e intensidad dependiendo de la hora del día. Tanto dentro como fuera de la casa, habrá sensores que nos informarán de todo lo que sucede *(takes place)*, como, por ejemplo, tener información de los edificios o monumentos de una ciudad solo con enfocarlos con un celular. ¡ZAP!

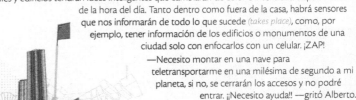

—Necesito montar en una nave para teletransportarme en una milésima de segundo a mi planeta, si no, se cerrarán los accesos y no podré entrar. ¡¡Necesito ayuda!! —gritó Alberto.

—Despierta, hijo. Has tenido una pesadilla.

Alberto miró primero a su madre, luego a su alrededor, y se sintió feliz de encontrarse en el siglo XXI.

54

3 👥 **Answer the following questions. Work with your partner.**

a. ¿Qué cuenta el relato?
   ☐ Un día en la vida de Alberto.
   ☐ Un sueño.
   ☐ Un viaje al futuro.
b. ¿Cuántos canales diferentes de televisión ve Alberto?
c. ¿Cuál de las visiones sobre el futuro te parece más optimista: la del primer científico o la del segundo?
d. ¿Cuál te parece más realista?
e. ¿Con cuál de los dos estás más de acuerdo?
f. ¿Por qué crees que Alberto se alegra cuando su madre lo despierta?

4 **Imagine how life will be in 100 years from now.**

Alimentación: ....

Vivienda: ....

Educación: ....

Transporte: ....

Trabajo: ....

Energías: ....

Familia: ....

Salud / Enfermedades: ....

5 👥 **Compare your view of the future with your partner's. Do you share the same perspective?**

6 **Read the following phrase: "Piensa globalmente, actúa localmente." What do you think it means? Think about what you can do to create a better future.**

> "Piensa globalmente, actúa localmente"
>
> Prometo...
> · que intentaré no malgastar el papel que utilizo en clase y lo reciclaré.
> ·
> ·

INSTRUCTIONAL STRATEGIES

Activity 3

- Ask the students to answer the questions about the text without referring to the text.
- Have them compare their answers with a partner and check in the text.
- Ask different students to say the correct answers aloud.

Activity 4

- Ask students to look at the headings and write one sentence for each.
- Remind them to use the future tense.
- Have them share their sentences with a partner.
- Invite students to read one of their sentences to the class.
- Have the class make a poster for each heading and write their sentences on the posters.

Activity 5

Have the students discuss their ideas about the future with their partner and find out how much they agree or disagree.

Activity 6

- Read the quotation and ask the students what they think it means.
- Ask them to discuss the quotation in small groups and make a list of ideas of what they can do to help create a better future, following the model provided.
- Circulate around the room as they work, providing assistance where necessary.
- Have different groups present their ideas to the class.
- Students may vote for the best proposals.

ANSWERS

Activity 3

a. un sueño; b. 4; c, d, e, f: Answers will vary.

EVALUACIÓN SELF-ASSESSMENT

OBJECTIVES FOR EVALUACIÓN
- Review grammar, vocabulary and culture from the unit
- Complete self-assessment

CORE RESOURCES
- Extension Activities: EA 1.3
- Interactive Online Materials – ELEteca

STANDARDS

1.2 Understand the language
2.1 Practices and perspectives
4.1 Compare cultures

INSTRUCTIONAL STRATEGIES
- Activities can be completed individually and then reviewed with the class. Vary by asking students if they agree with the answer given and then writing it on the board. Provide explanations as needed.
- You may wish to assign point value to each activity as a way for students to monitor their progress.
- Direct students to the indicated pages in **En resumen** if they make more than one or two mistakes in any one section.

Extension
- For additional practice with the forms of the irregular future, use EA 1.3, *Memory del futuro irregular* to play a memory game.
- Have students cut up the cards or have them ready ahead of time. Put students in groups of 4 and give each group a set of cards. Ask them to put all the cards face down but keep infinitive cards separate from conjugated forms. The first student draws an infinitive card and gives the correct *yo* form of the verb. He/she then picks a card from the conjugated side to find the match. The player with the most matched pairs wins.

EVALUACIÓN

MAKING ASSUMPTIONS AND PROMISES

1 Read the sentences and indicate if each sentence is an assumption (A) or a promise (P).

	A	P
a. Me imagino que mañana tendré que ir a hacer la compra.	☐	☐
b. Te prometo que no lo volveré a hacer.	☐	☐
c. Me imagino que no irá a la fiesta.	☐	☐
d. Mañana te traeré el libro sin falta.	☐	☐
e. Te juro que no lo contaré.	☐	☐
f. Supongo que esta tarde cenaremos en casa de Juan.	☐	☐

THE FUTURE TENSE

2 Write the following verbs in the future tense.

a. Tener, yo ....
b. Caber, ella/él ....
c. Poder, Uds. ....
d. Saber, ellos ....
e. Venir, nosotros ....
f. Ir, Uds. ....
g. Salir, usted ....
h. Valer, ellos/ellas ....
i. Ser, yo ....
j. Haber, él/ella ....
k. Poner, tú ....
l. Hacer, Uds. ....
m. Decir, yo ....
n. Querer, tú ....

3 Arrange the following expressions from closest to the present to farthest in time. Then write a sentence with each one.

a. ☐ Pasado mañana ....
b. ☐ El año que viene ....
c. ☐ El próximo verano ....
d. ☐ Dentro de poco ....
e. ☐ Dentro de 10 años ....
f. ☐ Mañana ....

SI + PRESENT + FUTURE

4 Complete the sentences with the verb in parenthesis in the correct tense.

a. Si todo (ir) .... bien, dentro de dos años (ir, yo) .... a la universidad.
b. (Llegar, nosotros) .... tarde si (perder, nosotros) .... el autobús.
c. Si no me (llamar) .... Juan, lo (llamar, yo) ....
d. (Ir, yo) .... a la fiesta si tú (ir) ....

56

ANSWERS

Activity 1
a. A; **b.** P; **c.** A; **d.** P; **e.** P; **f.** A.

Activity 2
a. tendré; **b.** cabrá; **c.** podrán; **d.** sabrán; **e.** vendremos; **f.** irán; **g.** saldrá; **h.** valdrán; **i.** seré; **j.** habrá; **k.** pondrás; **l.** harán; **m.** diré; **n.** querrás.

Activity 3
f, a, d, c, b, e.

Activity 4
a. va, iré; **b.** Llegaremos, perdemos **c.** llama, llamaré; **d.** Iré, vas.

UNIDAD 1

EL MEDIOAMBIENTE Y LA POLÍTICA

5 **Fill in the blanks with the words from the list.**

> sequía ○ deforestación ○ consumo responsable ○ energías renovables ○
> calentamiento global ○ contaminación ○ deshielo

a. Si no llueve, habrá ....
b. El .... del planeta está provocando el .... de los polos.
c. Los países deberían apostar por las .... y el .... para reducir la ....
d. Si no detenemos la ...., nos quedaremos sin selva.

6 **Write complete sentences with the words in parenthesis.**

a. Antes de ...., ... políticos presentan .... para dar a conocer sus proyectos. (los partidos, su programa, las elecciones)
b. Hasta que no se cuentan .... no se puede saber qué .... ha conseguido .... (candidato, la victoria, todos los votos)

WORD STRESS

7 **Circle the word that does not belong and explain what's different about it.**

a. café / amor / mesa / ratón / color ....
b. médico / fábula / manzana / sábado / fábrica ....
c. Jesús / comí / camión / reloj / salón ....
d. árbol / cárcel / mesa / cosa / azul ....
e. quien / que / como / cuesta / donde ....
f. dímelo / cuéntaselo / mecánica / recíbelo ....

CULTURA

8 **Answer the questions according to the information you learned in** *¡Bienvenidos a los parques nacionales de España!*

a. ¿Qué aspectos necesitan tener los parques para clasificarlos como parques nacionales?
b. ¿Cuáles son los parques nacionales más importantes de España y dónde están?
c. Según los visitantes de los parques, ¿cuáles son los elementos más atractivos? ¿Y para ti?
d. ¿Cómo son los parques nacionales de tu estado? ¿Qué puedes hacer allí?

 Practice what you have learned with additional materials online.

Activity 5

a. sequía; **b.** calentamiento global, deshielo; **c.** energías renovables, consumo responsable, contaminación; **d.** deforestación.

Activity 6

a. las elecciones, los partidos, su programa; **b.** todos los votos, candidato, la victoria.

Activity 7

a. mesa – llana entre agudas; **b.** manzana – llana entre esdrújulas; **c.** reloj – aguda sin tilde; **d.** azul – aguda entre llanas; **e.** cuesta – verbo entre pronombres interrogativos; **f.** cuéntaselo – sobreesdrújula entre esdrújulas.

Activity 8

Answers will vary. Possible answers include: **a.** Necesitan poseer una belleza, fauna y flora especiales además de una naturaleza impresionante; **b.** El Parque Nacional de Doñana que está en Huelva y Sevilla (Andalucía); el Parque Nacional de Sierra Nevada que está en Granada (Andalucía); el Parque Nacional Marítimo-Terrestre del Archipiélago de Cabrera que está en las Islas Baleares; el Parque Nacional de los Picos de Europa que está en Asturias; el Parque Nacional del Teide que está en la isla de Tenerife (islas Canarias); **c.** La geografía; **d.** Answers will vary.

OBJECTIVES FOR EN RESUMEN: VOCABULARIO

- Review unit vocabulary and expressions
- Practice communicative skills

STANDARDS

1.2 Understand the language

1.3 Present information

4.1 Evaluate similarities and differences in language

INSTRUCTIONAL STRATEGIES

- Encourage students to use self-adhesive notes to place on correct objects in their house.
- Index cards can be used as flashcards with the Spanish term on one side and the English term on the other, or a picture or drawing.
- Students work in pairs or groups, using vocabulary flashcards as they would the cards of a board game to help each other practice unit vocabulary.
- Encourage students to write labels or captions for the photos on this page. Remind them to use the vocabulary and expressions they have learned in this unit.

EN RESUMEN: Vocabulario

Verbos

aburrirse *to be bored*

aprobar *to pass (a test, a course)*
caber *to fit*
castigar *to punish*

dar igual *to care less*
diseñar *to design*
eliminar *to eliminate*
estar en forma *to be in shape*
prometer *to promise*

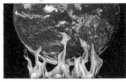

quedarse *to stay*
valer *to be worth*

Expresiones temporales

dentro de.... (periodo de tiempo) *within a (period of time)*
dentro de un rato *in a moment*
el mes que viene *next month*
pasado mañana *day after tomorrow*

Hacer conjeturas y promesas

Creo que... *I believe that...*
Lo haré sin falta. *I'll be sure to do it.*

Me imagino que... *I imagine that...*
¡Prometido! *Promised!*
Supongo que... *I guess that...*
Te juro que... *I promise you that...*
Te prometo que... *I promise you that...*
Te doy mi palabra. *I give you my word.*

El medioambiente

la basura *garbage*

el calentamiento global *global warming*

la climatización *heating and cooling sytems*

los combustibles fósiles *fossil fuels*
consumir *to consume*
la contaminación *pollution*

la deforestación *deforestation*

los desechos *trash, waste*
el deshielo *melting*
el efecto invernadero *greenhouse effect*
la energía renovable *renewable energy*
malgastar *to waste*
reciclar *to recycle*
los recursos naturales *natural resources*
reducir *to reduce*
reutilizar *to reuse*
la sequía *drought*

el transporte ecológico *ecologically friendly transportation*
el vertedero *dumping site*

La política

el alcalde *mayor*
la campaña *campaign*
el candidato *candidate*
las elecciones *elections*
el partido político *political party*
el presidente *president*
el programa *platform*
la reforma *reform*
el voto *vote*

58

EN RESUMEN: Gramática

MAKING PROMISES

(See page 40)

- **Te prometo que…**
- **Te lo prometo / juro.**
- **Te doy mi palabra.**
- **Te juro que…**
- **¡Prometido!**
- **Lo haré sin falta.**

THE FUTURE TENSE

(See page 48)

■ The future tense expresses what will happen. Regular verbs in the future tense are conjugated by adding the following endings to the infinitive form of the verb: **-é, -ás, -á, -emos, -éis, -án**.

	ESTUDIAR	COMER	VIVIR
yo	estudiar**é**	comer**é**	vivir**é**
tú	estudiar**ás**	comer**ás**	vivir**ás**
usted/él/ella	estudiar**á**	comer**á**	vivir**á**
nosotros/as	estudiar**emos**	comer**emos**	vivir**emos**
vosotros/as	estudiar**éis**	comer**éis**	vivir**éis**
ustedes/ellos/ellas	estudiar**án**	comer**án**	vivir**án**

■ There are twelve common verbs that are irregular in the future tense. Their endings are regular, but their stems change.

IRREGULAR VERBS			
poder ➡ podr-			é
salir ➡ saldr-	tener ➡ tendr-		ás
caber ➡ cabr-	poner ➡ pondr-	hacer ➡ har-	á
haber ➡ habr-	venir ➡ vendr-	decir ➡ dir-	emos
saber ➡ sabr-	valer ➡ valdr-		éis
querer ➡ querr-			án

■ The future tense is often used with the following expressions of time:

- El **año / mes / la semana / primavera que viene**
- **Dentro de** dos años / un rato / unos días
- El/la **próximo/a** semana / mes / año
- **Mañana / Pasado mañana**

El año que viene iré a España.
Dentro de unos días vendrá a casa.
El próximo año tendré 17 años.
Pasado mañana tendré un examen.

SI + PRESENT + FUTURE

(See page 49)

To talk about **future actions that depend on a condition**, use the following:
- **Si** + **present** + **future**
- *Si* *no llueve,* *iremos a la playa.*

59

OBJECTIVES FOR EN RESUMEN: GRAMÁTICA

- Review unit grammar
- Practice communication skills

STANDARDS

1.2   Understand the language

1.3   Present information

INSTRUCTIONAL STRATEGIES

- Model how to review grammar.
- Have the students review the Learning Outcomes in the unit opener to assess whether they feel they have mastered the main ideas and skills.
- Ask them if they can remember additional examples for each grammar topic.
- Model how to find and go back to the appropriate page in the unit to review any grammar topic they may need help with.
- Invite students to review the grammar activities they completed in this unit.
- Ask them what grammar activities they found easy and which they found challenging. Encourage them to rework any activities they found particularly challenging.

OBJECTIVES FOR UNIT OPENER

- Introduce unit theme: **Cosas de casa**, about families and household chores
- Introduce culture for the unit: Learn about what is considered polite in Spanish culture and what is not

STANDARDS

1.1 Interpersonal communication
1.2 Understand the language
2.1 Practices and perspectives
4.2 Compare cultures

INSTRUCTIONAL STRATEGIES

- Introduce unit theme and objectives. Talk about the photo and have students state who they think the different people are: **Son hermanos**, **Este es el hermano mayor/menor**, **Tienen la misma cara**, etc.
- Have the students discuss the questions and talk about themselves in the same context.
- Use the photograph to preview unit vocabulary: **¿Cuántos años crees que tienen? ¿Qué tipo de música crees que les gusta? ¿Y a ti?**
- Ask related questions to recycle vocabulary and structures: **¿Tienes hermanos? ¿Son mayores o menores que tú? ¿Te llevas bien con ellos? ¿Eres hijo único? ¿Crees que es importante tener hermanos? ¿Por qué? Si tienes hijos en el futuro, ¿cómo crees que serán? ¿Qué cosas harán igual que tú?**
- Help students formulate their ideas using **Tengo (tres hermanos mayores)**, **Soy (hijo único)**, **No tengo (primos)**, **Me llevo bien/mal con mi hermano/a mayor/menor**, etc.

UNIDAD 2
COSAS DE CASA

Tres hermanos en su casa.

≫≫ ¿Crees que se llevan bien estos hermanos?

≫≫ ¿Y tú? ¿Tienes hermanos? ¿Cuántos? ¿Son mayores o menores que tú?

≫≫ ¿Se llevan bien? ¿Les gusta hacer las mismas cosas?

60

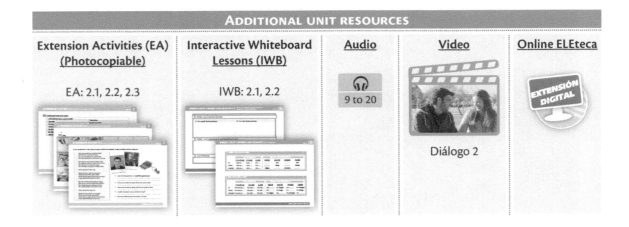

ADDITIONAL UNIT RESOURCES

Extension Activities (EA) (Photocopiable)	Interactive Whiteboard Lessons (IWB)	Audio	Video	Online ELEteca
EA: 2.1, 2.2, 2.3	IWB: 2.1, 2.2	9 to 20	Diálogo 2	EXTENSIÓN DIGITAL

**In this unit,
you will learn to:**

- [ ] Ask, give and refuse permission
- [ ] Give advice, orders and instructions
- [ ] Extend invitations

Using
- Affirmative and negative commands
- Commands and pronouns

Cultural Connections
- Giving commands and being polite

SABOR HISPANO

- ¿Son maleducados los españoles?

¡ACCIÓN!

61

LEARNING OUTCOMES

- Ask, give and refuse permission
- Give advice, orders and instructions
- Extend invitations

INSTRUCTIONAL STRATEGIES

- Use unit opener to preview vocabulary and cultural topics for this unit.
- Have students look at the images on this page and relate them to the objectives listed. Ask questions such as: *¿Qué hace el hombre? ¿Quién plancha en tu casa? ¿Ayudas en casa? ¿Qué haces para ayudar? ¿A qué deporte juegan? ¿Qué deportes haces tú? ¿Te gusta el deporte?*
- Invite students to read the topic for **Sabor hispano** and preview that section in the unit. Ask questions such as: *¿Qué hace la muchacha? ¿Qué hacen las otras muchachas? ¿Por qué abre la boca el hombre? ¿Crees que está bien visto hacer esto en público? ¿Por qué? ¿Crees que estará bien visto en los países hispanos?*
- Ask students to anticipate what they think the episode for **¡Acción!** will be about. Ask: *¿Quiénes hablan?*
- Have students work in pairs to talk about the images using the questions you have modeled. Then have volunteers present to the class what they understand this unit to be about.

THREE MODES OF COMMUNICATION: UNIT 2			
	INTERPERSONAL	**INTERPRETIVE**	**PRESENTATIONAL**
HABLAMOS DE...	4	1, 2, 3	4
COMUNICA	3, 6	1, 2, 4, 5	3, 6
¡ACCIÓN!	1, 4	2, 3	1
PALABRA POR PALABRA	5, 8	1, 2, 4, 6, 7, 9	3, 8, 10
GRAMÁTICA		1, 2, 3, 4, 5, 6, 7	
DESTREZAS		1, 2	3
CULTURA		SABOR HISPANO	
RELATO	1	2, 3, 4	4, 5

OBJECTIVES FOR HABLAMOS DE...

- Understand language in context
- Preview vocabulary: Talking about what people do in the family context
- Preview grammatical structures: Affirmative and negative commands; Commands and pronouns
- Read and listen to a conversation between two young people talking about their families

CORE RESOURCES

- Audio Program: Track 9

STANDARDS

1.1	Engage in conversation
1.2	Understand the language
4.2	Compare cultures

INSTRUCTIONAL STRATEGIES

Activity 1

- Ask students to talk about the people in the photos and say what they are doing and where students think they are. Ask students to predict the relationship between the people. Ask: **¿Son amigos o familia? ¿Quién creen que es Pilar?**, and so on.
- Read the text with the students and explain that not all the information has been provided. Tell students to use the information in the text and images to draw other conclusions in order to complete the chart accurately.
- Have them fill in the blanks in the chart with the profession, age and tastes or preferences of each person in the family.
- Ask individual students to give the class the information for one person. Ask the class if they agree. Then have the student explain how they arrived at the correct answer.

Activity 2

- To introduce the activity, ask students about typical family dynamics: **¿De qué cosas suelen discutir los hermanos? ¿Y los padres e hijos? ¿Con quién sueles discutir más en tu familia? ¿Por qué? ¿Quién se enfada más contigo?**
- Remind students that **discutir** in Spanish means to argue.
- Have the students complete the sentences using what they already know about the family.
- Have them share with a partner.
- To follow up, ask students what aspects in the Garrido family seem to be typical of most families: **¿Piensan que los Pérez-Garrido es una familia típica?**

ANSWERS

Activity 1

Juan: jubilado, 77, cantar; **Antonio:** médico, 43, música clásica; **Pilar:** pintora, 46, ir al cine; **Fernando:** recepcionista, 20, fútbol; **Daría:** estudiante, 16, música heavy; **Marcos:** estudiante, 11, videojuegos.

Activity 2

a. pintar; **b.** cantar; **c.** jugar; **d.** gustos.

HABLAMOS DE... Las tareas de la casa

1 Look at the picture, read the text and complete the chart below based on what you see or can infer from the text.

a.
Pilar

b.
Antonio

c.
Daría

d.
Fernando

e.
Marcos

f.
Juan

Pilar Garrido, que es pintora, tuvo a Fernando con 26 años. Ella tiene tres años más que su marido, **Antonio Pérez**. A él le gusta la música clásica, pero a su hija Daría le gusta el heavy. **Daría** tiene cuatro años menos que Fernando y cinco más que su hermano Marcos. **Marcos** tiene 11 años y Juan, el abuelo, que está jubilado y le gusta cantar, tiene 77 años.

Nombre	Profesión	Edad	Gustos
Juan			
Antonio			
Pilar			ir al cine
Fernando	recepcionista		
Daría			
Marcos			

2 Complete the sentences logically and learn about the family dynamics.

a. Antonio discute con su mujer porque usa sus camisas viejas para ....
b. Pilar se enfada con su padre porque se pone a .... mientras ella trabaja.
c. Fernando se enfada con su hermano porque nunca quiere .... con él.
d. Daría discute con su padre porque tienen .... musicales muy diferentes.

62

3 🎧 **9** **Ernesto and Daría are talking about their families. Listen to their conversation and indicate if the statements that follow are true (T) or false (F).**

Ernesto: ¡Últimamente mis padres se quejan por todo!

Daría: ¿Por qué dices eso? Tus padres son encantadores.

E.: Pues ahora se han vuelto superestrictos con todo. Me han dicho que entre semana no puedo llegar a casa más tarde de las seis. Bueno, menos los días que tengo tenis, que tengo que estar en casa a las ocho de la noche. Me han dicho que si llego un minuto más tarde, me castigarán sin salir.

D.: ¡Pero si salimos de entrenar a las siete y media! ¡Tendrás que irte corriendo a casa! ¡Y sin ducharte!

E.: Además, ahora dicen que no hacemos nada en casa y que tenemos que colaborar más.

D.: ¡Uf! ¡Qué pesados! Mi madre el año pasado hizo una lista con las tareas que tenía que hacer cada uno, ¡y fue un desastre!

E.: ¿Y eso?

D.: Mi abuelo era el encargado de hacer la compra, pero lo que hacía era pagar 270 pesos a mi hermano Fernando si iba él. Él me pagaba 180 pesos a mí y mientras él "estaba haciendo la compra" se iba de paseo. Y como yo odio (hate) ir al supermercado, pues le pagaba 90 pesos a mi hermano Marcos, ¡y él encantado!

E.: ¿Y tus padres no se enteraban (found out)?

D.: Al principio no, pero un día vieron a Marcos salir del súper y lo descubrieron.

E.: ¿Y cómo reaccionaron?

D.: Pues decidieron que con los 270 pesos del abuelo, los 180 de Fernando y mis 90, podían pagar a alguien para limpiar la casa varias horas a la semana. ¡Pero nosotros tenemos que seguir haciendo nuestra parte!, ¡y además nos cuesta dinero!

E.: ¡Ja, ja! ¡Tus padres sí que saben!

	T	F
a. Ernesto no puede llegar a casa ningún día más tarde de las ocho.	☐	☐
b. Según la opinión de Daría, los padres de Ernesto son muy simpáticos.	☐	☐
c. Fernando conseguía 90 pesos por no hacer la compra.	☐	☐
d. La persona que limpia en la casa de Daría va una hora a la semana.	☐	☐
e. Los padres de Daría descubrieron la verdad porque el abuelo lo contó todo.	☐	☐

4 👥 **The Sánchez family has a similar arrangement. Number the scenes in order and then take turns with a partner describing what is happening in each one.**

INSTRUCTIONAL STRATEGIES

🎧 **9** **Activity 3**

- Inform the students that they are going to listen to a conversation between Daría and Ernesto in which they talk about their families.
- Project the True or False questions and review them with students before playing the audio. Have them listen first with books closed and complete the activity.
- Play the audio again while the students follow in their books and confirm their answers.
- Ask for volunteers to say whether each sentence is true or false.
- Ask for volunteers to make each sentence true.

Activity 4

- Have the students look at the images of the Sánchez family and ask students to make a summary statement of what they think is happening. For example: *Nadie quiere hacer la compra*, *La más joven de la familia hace la compra*.
- Have students work in pairs and number the images accordingly.
- Have students retell the story, taking turns with the images.
- Remind them to refer to the conversation in Activity 3 for help.
- Invite volunteers to retell the story to the class while you project the images.

Extension

- In small groups of three, have students talk about their own families. Put the following prompts on the boards as a guide: *¿Cómo son sus familias? ¿Qué tienen en común con la familia Pérez-Garrido? ¿Cuántos son en casa? ¿Qué aficiones tienen? ¿Tienen alguna hora de llegada o tareas domésticas asignadas?*
- You may also assign this as a written activity.

ANSWERS

Activity 3

a. T; **b.** T; **c.** F; **d.** F; **e.** F.

Activity 4

1. d; **2.** a; **3.** e; **4.** b; **5.** c.

OBJECTIVES FOR COMUNICA

- Present communicative functions of the unit:
  - Ask and give permission
  - Refuse permission
  - Offer and encourage others to accept

CORE RESOURCES

- Audio Program: Tracks 10 and 11
- Extension Activities: EA 2.1
- Interactive Whiteboard Lesson: IWB 2.1
- Interactive Online Materials – ELEteca

STANDARDS

1.1 Engage in conversation
1.2 Understand the language
4.2 Compare cultures

INSTRUCTIONAL STRATEGIES

FOR ASKING, GIVING AND REFUSING PERMISSION, OFFERING AND ENCOURAGING OTHERS TO ACCEPT

- Distribute copies of EA 2.1, **Pedir permiso, invitar y ofrecer** to student pairs and tell them to list the expressions in the appropriate categories in the chart according to their function: **pedir permiso, concederlo, denegarlo, invitar u ofrecer** y **responder a una invitación**. The purpose is to have students decipher the meaning of these expressions before reading the chart in the book.

- Once students have completed the chart, have them check their work against the information in the book and ask how many listed the expressions in the correct category.
- Have students repeat chorally to ensure proper pronunciation and intonation. Then call on individual students to answer your prompts giving a thumbs up to indicate whether the student should respond affirmatively or deny permission.

 10 Activity 1

- Focus attention on the photographs of people together. Then have students complete the conversation individually and fill in the blanks with words from the box.
- Play the audio while students listen and follow in the books to confirm their answers.
- Invite pairs of students to read the conversations aloud with their partner. Encourage students to use gestures and appropriate emotion in their presentations.

ANSWERS

Activity 1

a. Puedo; b. Sí, claro; c. Quieres; d. No; e. es que; f. come un poco.

COMUNICA

ASKING AND GIVING PERMISSION

- Para **pedir un permiso**:
  ¿Puedo / Podría comer un poco de pastel? Can / Could I have some cake?
  ¿Te / Le importa si como un poco de pastel? Do you mind if I have some cake?
- Para **conceder un permiso**:
  Sí, claro / por supuesto. Yes, of course.
  Sí, claro, come, come. Yes, of course, eat some, eat some.
  Sí, pero deja un poco para tu hermano. Yes, but leave some for your brother.

REFUSING TO GIVE PERMISSION

- Para **denegar un permiso**:
  No, (lo siento) es que lo he hecho para llevarlo a la fiesta de Ana. No, (I'm sorry) I made it to take to Ana's party.
  ¡Ni hablar! / ¡De ninguna manera! No way!

OFFERING AND ENCOURAGING OTHERS TO ACCEPT

- Para **invitar** u **ofrecer**:
  ¿Quieres un poco de pastel? Do you want some cake?
  Come, come. / Toma, toma. Eat some, eat some./ Take some, take some.
- Para **responder**:
  Sí, gracias. Yes, thank you.
  No, gracias, es que no me gustan los dulces. No, thank you, I don't like sweets.

1 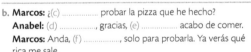 **10 Fill in the blanks using the expressions from the box.**

> quieres ○ no ○ come un poco ○ es que ○ sí, claro ○ puedo

a. **Emilio:** Mamá, ya sé que estás leyendo, pero… ¿(a) .... poner la tele?
Mamá: (b) ...., ponla. A mí no me molesta el ruido mientras leo.
Emilio: Vale, gracias, es que ahora hay un programa que me encanta.

b. **Marcos:** ¿(c) .... probar la pizza que he hecho?
Anabel: (d) ...., gracias, (e) .... acabo de comer.
Marcos: Anda, (f) ...., solo para probarla. Ya verás qué rica me sale.
Anabel: Bueno, la probaré, pero solo un poquito.

64

2 🎧 **11** Listen to the following conversations and choose the correct option.

	Diálogo 1	Diálogo 2	Diálogo 3	Diálogo 4
a. Conceder permiso.	☐	☐	☐	☐
b. Denegar permiso.	☐	☐	☐	☐
c. Aceptar una invitación.	☐	☐	☐	☐
d. Denegar una invitación.	☐	☐	☐	☐

3 With a partner, role-play the parts and follow the instructions.

Estudiante 1

Situación 1. Empiezas tú.
- Tienes que pedir permiso a tu compañero para hacer algo.

Situación 2. Empieza tu compañero.
- Tienes que aceptar o rechazar la invitación de tu compañero.

compañero.
- Tienes que invitar a algo u ofrecer algo a tu

Situación 2. Empiezas tú.
según lo que te pida tu compañero.
- Tienes que conceder o denegar permiso

Situación 1. Empieza tu compañero.

Estudiante 2

ASKING FOR AND GIVING INSTRUCTIONS

■ Para **pedir instrucciones**:
¿Puedes / Podrías decirme cómo hago el pastel? *Can / Could you tell me how I make the cake?*

¿Sabes cómo ir al centro? *Do you know how to go downtown?*

Perdone / Perdona, ¿para ir a la estación? Excuse me, how do I go to the station?

■ Para **dar instrucciones**:
Sí, mira, haz / toma / ve... Yes, look, you do / take / go...

Sí, toma la primera a la derecha, sigue todo derecho, después cruza la calle... Yes, take the first on your right, keep going straight, then cross the street...

Sí, tiene / tienes que tomar / hacer / ir... Yes, you have to take / do / go...

ASKING FOR AND GIVING ADVICE OR MAKING RECOMMENDATIONS

Últimamente no me concentro a la hora de estudiar, ¿qué puedo hacer? Lately I can't concentrate when I study, what can I do?

Tendrías que / Deberías ir a la biblioteca / hacer deporte. You should go to the library / play sports.

¿Por qué no vas a la biblioteca / haces deporte? Why don't you go to the library / play sports?

Ve a la biblioteca. / Haz deporte. Go to the library. / Play sports.

65

INSTRUCTIONAL STRATEGIES

🎧 **11** Activity 2

- Explain that this activity consists of four conversations and students choose the correct option for each.
- Play the audio while students listen and indicate the outcome of each conversation.
- Repeat the audio for students to confirm their answers.
- Ask students to give the answers for the class.

Audioscript

1. **Carlos:** ¡Uf! ¡Qué calor!
   Paco: Pues abre la ventana.
   Carlos: ¿De verdad no te importa?
   Paco: Claro, ábrela, ábrela sin problemas.

2. **Celia:** ¿Te vienes con nosotros a casa de Mercedes? Tiene el último videojuego de…
   Mario: No, gracias, es que tengo mucho que estudiar.
   Celia: Anda, solo un rato, nos lo pasaremos bien.
   Mario: Bueno, iré, pero tengo que estar en casa antes de las 7.

3. **Carmen:** ¿Puedo ponerme tu camiseta?
   Juanjo: No, lo siento, es que luego te echas perfume y se queda el olor y no me gusta.
   Carmen: De acuerdo.

4. **Carolina:** Toma, ¿quieres un poco? Es una tarta que he hecho.
   Pepe: No, muchas gracias.
   Carolina: Venga, pruébala, que está muy buena.
   Pepe: Seguro, pero es que no me gusta mucho el dulce.

Cultural Note

Point out that in the second conversation Marcos at first refuses the offer and gives a reason why. But at the end he does accept the offer with a condition. Explain to students that this is a very common social practice in Hispanic countries in that it's socially accepted to say no the first time and then allow yourself to be convinced or to convince others to do something.

Activity 3

- Have students work with a partner, with each student looking at a different set of instructions (one students holds the book upside down).
- Student 1 begins the conversation according to the instructions, and student 2 responds appropriately.
- Circulate around the room as they talk, checking pronunciation and assisting with vocabulary or expressions as required.
- Ask for volunteers to perform for the class.

ANSWERS

Activity 2

a. diálogo 1; b. diálogo 3; c. diálogo 2; d. diálogo 4.

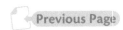
Previous Page

INSTRUCTIONAL STRATEGIES
FOR GIVING ORDERS

- Use IWB 2.1, **Pedir y dar instrucciones, consejos o recomendaciones y órdenes** to introduce the next set of expressions. Project the chart and review the headings with students.
- Tell students to listen to the examples you provide and identify the correct function according to the chart. Ask the class if they agree with the answer. Then write the example in the chart. Use examples from the text such as: **Sí, mira, toma la primera a la derecha, ¿Por qué no vas a la biblioteca?**...
- Finally, ask students to confirm answers with the chart in the book.

Activity 4

- Tell the students to cover the text and look at the images. Ask them to describe who the people are and predict what they are saying.
- Explain to students that the text about the images is a speech bubble and that they have to match the best response for each.
- Ask them to compare with a partner. Have the students read each one as a conversation.
- Invite pairs of students to perform an exchange for the class.

Activity 5

- In this activity, students match the function listed with examples from Activity 4 that exemplify the function. Use the numbers to reference the first part of the conversation and the letters for the second part or response. Classify each according to its function in the conversation.
- Have the students share their answers with a partner.
- Ask individual students to say their answers aloud.

Activity 6

- Read through all the situations in the activity together. Ask students to brainstorm important vocabulary for each one. This will later provide linguistic support while students practice with their partners.
- Then have each student choose one situation and prepare what he/she will say and ask his/her partner. This should

---

COMUNICA

GIVING ORDERS

- **Come / Haz / Ven**... Eat / Do / Go...
  Pedro, haz las tareas antes de ver la tele. Pedro, do your homework before watching TV.

4 Match each picture with the correct response.

Perdona, ¿podrías decirme cómo llegar al Palacio de los Deportes?

No sé si voy a aprobar el examen de Historia. Entran siete temas y solo me sé uno. ¿Qué puedo hacer?

Óscar, haz las tareas, deja de navegar por Internet y baja el volumen de la radio.

- a. ◯ Sí, claro. Sigue todo derecho y después toma la primera calle a la izquierda...
- b. ◯ Que sí, mamá, ¡ya voy...!
- c. ◯ ¿Y por qué no empiezas a estudiar ya? Estudia un tema cada día. Aún falta una semana...

5 Match the image number and response letter in Activity 4 to the appropriate description below.

	a	b	c	1	2	3
a. Pedir y dar consejos.	◯	◯	◯	◯	◯	◯
b. Pedir instrucciones.	◯	◯	◯	◯	◯	◯
c. Dar instrucciones.	◯	◯	◯	◯	◯	◯
d. Dar y aceptar órdenes.	◯	◯	◯	◯	◯	◯

6 Choose one of the situations and ask your partner for advice. He/She will respond with instructions or advice. Then switch roles.

- a. Últimamente duermes poco, solo dos o tres horas. Pide consejo a tu compañero/a.
- b. No sabes cómo mandar un mensaje de texto desde tu celular nuevo. Pregunta a tu compañero/a.
- c. Necesitas ir a la oficina de tu escuela y no sabes dónde está. Tu compañero/a sí lo sabe.
- d. Quieres irte de viaje el fin de semana, pero el lunes tienes un examen y no sabes qué hacer. Pide consejo a tu compañero/a.

Practice what you have learned with additional materials online.

---

not be a scripted activity. Allow students to work only from notes or nothing at all.
- The partner responds appropriately. Then have them switch roles.
- Circulate around the class as they talk, listening in and providing assistance and corrections where required.

ANSWERS

Activity 4
1. a; **2.** c; **3.** b.

Activity 5
a. c, 2; **b.** 1; **c.** a, 1; **d.** b, 3.

¡ACCIÓN!

UNIDAD 2

ANTES DEL VIDEO

1 Have you ever babysat? In Spain, to babysit is *hacer de canguro*. Choose a role and act out the situation with a partner.

Estudiante 1

Tu compañero va a hacer de canguro. Dale algunos consejos. Antes necesitas saber:

- ¿Edad del niño?
- ¿Relación que tiene con él?
- ¿Horas que tiene que estar?
- ¿Tareas y actividades?
- ¿€/hora?

Estudiante 2

Vas a hacer de canguro. Pide consejos a tu compañero.

- 7 años.
- Hijo de los vecinos (lo conoces desde que nació).
- Desde las 17:00 hasta las 00:00h.
- Recogerlo del colegio; hacer las tareas; juegos (no sabes qué hacer); ducha (odia el jabón); cena (no le gusta nada); acostarse (es hiperactivo).
- 8 €/hora.

DURANTE EL VIDEO

2 Match each description to the correct person.

a. Está desanimado. ⬜ ⬜ ⬜ ⬜
b. Necesita dinero. ⬜ ⬜ ⬜ ⬜
c. Quiere ir a un concierto. ⬜ ⬜ ⬜ ⬜
d. Se ha ido a esquiar. ⬜ ⬜ ⬜ ⬜
e. Propone buscar un trabajo. ⬜ ⬜ ⬜ ⬜
f. Propone un trabajo. ⬜ ⬜ ⬜ ⬜
g. Habla de su prima. ⬜ ⬜ ⬜ ⬜
h. No le gustan mucho los niños. ⬜ ⬜ ⬜ ⬜
i. Anima a aceptar el trabajo. ⬜ ⬜ ⬜ ⬜
j. Apunta un número de teléfono. ⬜ ⬜ ⬜ ⬜
k. Va a hacer de canguro. ⬜ ⬜ ⬜ ⬜

DESPUÉS DEL VIDEO

3 List the tasks that need to be done in the new job.

4 What would you do if you were in the same position? Discuss your options with a partner.

Practice what you have learned with additional materials online.

67

OBJECTIVES FOR ¡ACCIÓN!

- Provide students with a structured approach to viewing the video
- Contextualize the content of the unit in a familiar scenario

CORE RESOURCES

- Unit Video 2
- Interactive Online Materials – ELEteca

STANDARDS

1.3 Understand the language
2.1 Practices and perspectives
3.2 Acquire information
4.2 Compare cultures

INSTRUCTIONAL STRATEGIES

Previewing: Antes del video

Activity 1

- Ask students what animal they think a ***canguro*** is and why they think this word is used here. Then they choose one of the roles to act out with a partner. When they finish, invite some pairs of students to perform their conversations for the class.

Cultural Note

In Spain, ***hacer de canguro*** is the expression used for babysitting. The idea is that a babysitter would look after his/her charge much as a mother kangaroo would do.

Viewing: Durante el video

Activity 2

- Have the students look at the images and read through the descriptions. Ask students to identify each of the characters according to their photos.
- Answer any questions they may have about the vocabulary.
- Play the entire video without pauses and ask students what they understood.
- Play again and allow students to ask you to pause, as needed, while they check the boxes.
- Replay sections students found hard to understand.

- Show the entire video again without pauses. Ask students to share how their understanding has improved.
- Have some students give the correct answers.

After viewing: Después del video

Activity 3

Give the students a few minutes to list the tasks, then have them compare answers in pairs.

Activity 4

Have students discuss the question and report their ideas back to the class.

ANSWERS

Activity 2

Marcos: **a, b, c, d, h, j, k;** Eva: **f, g, i;** Paula: **e, i;** Santi: **i.**

Activity 3

Tiene que buscar al niño al colegio y llevarle un rato al parque, solo una hora.

PALABRA POR PALABRA LANGUAGE AND VOCABULARY

OBJECTIVES FOR LAS TAREAS DOMÉSTICAS

- Present vocabulary needed to practice communicative and grammatical functions for the unit: Household chores
- Talk about how to organize family members to do household chores

CORE RESOURCES

- Audio Program: Track 12
- Extension Activities: EA 2.2
- Interactive Online Materials – ELEteca

STANDARDS

- 1.1 Engage in conversation
- 1.2 Understand the language
- 1.3 Present information
- 3.2 Acquire information
- 4.1 Compare languages and cultures

INSTRUCTIONAL STRATEGIES

🎧 12 **Activity 1**

- Invite the students to look at the images and ask: **¿Dónde están las personas que aparecen en las imágenes? ¿Qué tipo de actividades están realizando, de tiempo libre, de trabajo...?**
- Ask students to make a sentence about each picture using the expression provided: **La muchacha hace la cama**, etc.
- Tell the students they are going to listen to a number of conversations about household chores and they will have to number each image.
- Play the audio while the students listen and number the images.
- Play the audio again for the students to confirm their answers.
- Ask different students to give their answers.

Audioscript

1. » A mí, la tarea que menos me gusta hacer es barrer.
   » A mí tampoco me gusta nada, es un rollo.

2. » ¡Jaime! Pon la mesa, por favor.
   » Sí, ya voy. Ahora la pongo.

3. » Luisa, ¿vienes a ver la tele?
   » Sí, un momento que termino de lavar los platos y voy.

4. » Laura, ya que sales, tira también la basura.
   » Vale.

5. » Ya veo que eres muy buen cocinero.
   » Bueno, me gusta mucho la cocina. En casa siempre soy yo el que hace la comida.

6. » ¿Quieres que planche tu blusa?
   » Sí, genial. Muchas gracias.

7. » No entres ahora en la cocina, que estoy fregando el suelo.
   » Pero, mamá, tengo hambre.

8. » No puedo escuchar la tele con el ruido de la aspiradora.
   » Entonces, ¿por qué no la pasas tú y ves tu programa después?

9. » Mi madre no me deja bajar a desayunar si no he hecho la cama.
   » ¿Sí? Pues yo siempre la hago después del desayuno.

10. » ¿Puedes echar esto a lavar cuando pongas la lavadora?
    » Sí, claro.

11. » Qué rollo! Tengo que tender la ropa.
    » ¡Venga!, si es solo un momento. Si quieres, te ayudo.

12. » ¿Siempre paseas tú al perro? Pensé que era de tu hermano.
    » Bueno, yo lo paseo por las mañanas porque mi hermano tiene que ir a clases, ¿verdad, Charlie?

PALABRA POR PALABRA Las tareas domésticas

1 🎧 **12** Listen to a series of conversations about household chores. Write the number of the conversation next to the appropriate image.

a. hacer la cama

b. tender la ropa

c. hacer la comida

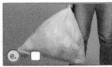
d. lavar los platos

e. tirar la basura

f. poner la mesa

g. poner la lavadora / el lavaplatos

h. planchar

i. barrer

j. pasear al perro

k. fregar el suelo

l. pasar la aspiradora

2 Fill in the blanks with the correct form of a verb from the list.

> fregar ○ tender ○ poner ○ limpiar ○ hacer ○ planchar ○ barrer ○ cambiar ○ pasar

a. Lo contrario de *quitar la mesa* es .... la mesa.
b. A veces cuando haces la cama también .... las sábanas.
c. Si limpio el suelo sin agua, lo ....; si lo limpio con agua y jabón, lo ....
d. Después de poner la lavadora, tengo que .... la ropa.
e. Lo hago con el polvo, los cristales y el baño y es lo contrario de *ensuciar*: ....
f. Antes de comer, ... la comida.
g. Antes de ponerte la ropa, la ....
h. Es más fácil .... la aspiradora que barrer.

3 Pilar has decided to assign one chore to each person in the family. Look at the images and indicate what Pilar tells each person to do and what they should be careful doing.

a. Abuelo, *plancha la ropa, pero ten cuidado de no quemarla...*

b. Antonio...

c. Nerea...

d. Javier...

4 Read the following article about organizing the household chores. Then decide whether the statements are true (T) or (F).

Responsabilidades del hogar

Organizar un hogar y una familia no es fácil. Por eso, es importante organizarse para distribuir las tareas y conseguir la colaboración de todos:

1. Haz un cuadro de tareas de tres columnas. En la primera, escribe todas las tareas del hogar. Pon, en primer lugar, las que se hacen todos los días, como pasear al perro por las mañanas, y, luego, las tareas semanales, como barrer, a continuación de las anteriores.
2. Piensa cuánto tiempo necesita cada tarea y escríbelo al lado, en la segunda columna.
3. Escribe en la tercera columna los nombres de las personas de la casa que crees que pueden hacer cada tarea. Asigna tareas de acuerdo con *(according to)* la edad, para que no sean demasiado difíciles para la persona que las realizará, o los horarios de cada uno.
4. Asigna a cada persona una o dos tareas diarias y una o dos semanales.
5. Planifica un horario rotativo y así nadie tendrá siempre los peores trabajos, como limpiar el baño o planchar.

Texto adaptado de: *http://www.ehowenespanol.com/distribuir-tareas-del-hogar-semana-como_206328/*

	T	F
a. La organización de las tareas en un hogar es una labor complicada.	☐	☐
b. Es necesario organizarse por horas.	☐	☐
c. Hay que separar las tareas diarias de las semanales.	☐	☐
d. La distribución de las tareas se hace en función del tiempo que duran *(it takes)*.	☐	☐
e. Cada tarea se asigna a cada miembro por sorteo *(randomly)*.	☐	☐
f. La organización de las tareas debe ser siempre la misma.	☐	☐

5 Discuss the following with a partner. What chores do you do at home? Which one is your favorite and which one is your least favorite? Why?

¿Qué tareas domésticas hacen ustedes en casa? ¿Cuál de ellas les gusta menos? ¿Por qué?

69

← **Previous Page**

Activity 2

- Have the students read the sentences and choose the correct verb for each.
- When they have finished, have them share with a partner. Ask individual students to read the complete sentences.

ANSWERS

Activity 1

a. 9; **b.** 11; **c.** 5; **d.** 3; **e.** 4; **f.** 2; **g.** 10; **h.** 6; **i.** 1; **j.** 12; **k.** 7; **l.** 8.

Activity 2

a. poner; **b.** cambiar; **c.** barro, friego; **d.** tender; **e.** limpiar; **f.** hago; **g.** planchas; **h.** pasar.

INSTRUCTIONAL STRATEGIES

Activity 3

- Read the model with the students and ask them which of the following best describes the meaning: ***El abuelo plancha la ropa*** or ***El abuelo tiene que planchar la ropa***. Ask students how they know this (Pilar is talking directly to the grandfather and telling him what to do). Ask them if they remember what form of the verb is used for cases like this (command form).
- Have students identify possible verbs they can use for each situation. Review ***haz*** for ***hacer***. Ask student what ***tener cuidado*** means and ask them for the command form: ***ten cuidado***. Have the students write the remaining sentences.
- Ask different students to say their answers aloud, while other students write them on the board to check.

Activity 4

- Read the text in sections and invite volunteers to repeat each section.
- Look at the statements below and have the students check True or False for each one. Have them share with a partner, before asking random students to give the correct answers.

Activity 5

Students sit in pairs to discuss the chores they do at home.

Extension

For additional practice with this vocabulary, use EA 2.2, ***Memory de las tareas del hogar*** to play a matching and memory game. Distribute photo and word cards to each group of 3 students and have them place the cards face down on separate sides. The object of the game is to identify the image in Spanish and match it to the corresponding expression. The student with the most matches wins.

ANSWERS

Activity 3

b. Antonio, pon la lavadora/lava la ropa, pero ten cuidado de no poner la ropa banca con la ropa de color; **c.** Nerea, haz/prepara la comida, pero ten cuidado de no quemarla; **d.** Javier, haz la cama, pero acuérdate de poner la manta.

Activity 4

a. T; **b.** F; **c.** T; **d.** T; **e.** F; **f.** F.

OBJECTIVES FOR LOS DEPORTES

- Present vocabulary needed to practice communicative and grammatical functions for the unit: Sports
- Describe how to play certain sports and games

STANDARDS

1.4 Engage in conversation
1.5 Understand the language
1.6 Present information
3.2 Acquire information
4.1 Compare languages and cultures

INSTRUCTIONAL STRATEGIES

Activity 6

- Have students look at the images and name the sports shown. If they are not sure, they should look at the vocabulary in the box or at the end of unit vocabulary list. Focus students' attention on **chutar** and ask them what they think it means (*to shoot*) and where they think it comes from (latinizing of *to shoot*). Explain that many sports terms, like technology terms, come from English. Then ask students which of these sports they play.
- Have them write the names of the sports at the top of each column and in the box below they write the words associated with each sport.
- Remind them that some words may be repeated. When they finish, have them share with a partner.
- Ask for volunteers to say a sport and the words associated with it.

Grammar Note

Share the following information with students about sports terms: *Red* corresponde a *tenis*, pero también se utiliza como sinónimo de *portería*; por otro lado, *balón* y *pelota* pueden usarse también como sinónimos, aunque se utiliza *balón* si su tamaño es más grande y *pelota* si es más pequeña; *golpear* podría clasificarse en todos los deportes, pero se prefiere para el tenis y el squash, ya que con fútbol se usa *chutar* y con balonmano y waterpolo se usa *lanzar*. *Cancha*, en algunos países de Hispanoamérica, se usa como sinónimo de *campo de fútbol*, pero no en España, que se refiere a un recinto cerrado.

Activity 7

- Have the students read the first set of rules with a partner and try to guess which sport is being described. When they finish, they do the same with the second card.
- Circulate around the room as they play, answering questions, checking pronunciation and helping with any vocabulary required.

Activity 8

- Each student chooses another sport and writes a set of rules, using ideas from Activity 7. They should not write the name of the sport.

PALABRA POR PALABRA Los deportes

6 Complete the chart with the name of the correct sport and the words associated with it. *¡Atención!* Some of the words can go in more than one column. Use the glossary if you need to.

~~fútbol~~ ∘ golpear ∘ tenis ∘ balón ∘ waterpolo ∘ pelota ∘ falta ∘ portería ∘ pared ∘ red ∘ squash ∘ pase ∘ raqueta ∘ portero ∘ chutar ∘ marcar un gol ∘ set ∘ lanzar ∘ cancha ∘ campo ∘ flotar ∘ botar ∘ ventaja ∘ balonmano ∘ jugador ∘ rebotar

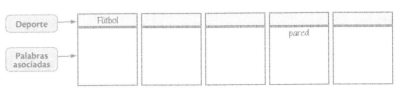

Deporte	Fútbol				
Palabras asociadas					pared

7 👥 Let's play. Read the rules with a partner to guess what sport is being described. The one who guesses the sport using the least number of rules is the winner! Play again with the second card.

A	B
• Consigue una raqueta y una pelota pequeña.	• Forma dos equipos. En cada uno tiene que haber un portero.
• Busca un adversario para jugar.	• Durante el partido, intenta marcar el mayor número de goles al equipo contrario.
• Si el jugador contrario te ha lanzado la pelota, no debes permitir que esta bote dos veces o más en el suelo o él conseguirá el punto.	• Para marcar un gol, lanza la pelota hacia la portería contraria. Si la metes dentro, habrás marcado.
• Para ganar puntos, intenta que el adversario no pueda responder a tus golpes.	• Intenta robar el balón al jugador del equipo contrario, pero no lo agarres porque cometerás falta. No cometas faltas porque podrás ser expulsado.
• Para poder jugar, encuentra un espacio cerrado rodeado de paredes.	• Para marcar gol, utiliza cualquier parte del cuerpo, pero si usas la mano, esta tiene que estar abierta.
• Golpea la pelota con la raqueta y haz que rebote en la pared frontal de la cancha.	• No pises el suelo de la piscina, está prohibido. Tienes que mantenerte flotando durante todo el partido.
Deporte:	Deporte: ....

8 👥 Think about another sport and write out the rules to explain how the sport is played. Use the words and expressions in Activity 6 as a guide. Then play again with a partner.

- Have the students exchange sets of rules and guess which sport is being described. They can continue exchanging with other students until you feel they have practiced enough.

ANSWERS

Activity 6

Fútbol: balón, falta, portería, red, portero, chutar, marcar un gol, campo, jugador, pase, botar; **Balonmano:** balón, falta, red, lanzar, cancha, jugador, pase, botar; **Tenis:** golpear, pelota, falta, red, raqueta, set, cancha, jugador, ventaja, botar; **Squash:** rebotar, golpear, pelota, falta, pared, raqueta, set, cancha, jugador, botar; **Waterpolo:** balón, falta, pase, portero, marcar un gol, lanzar, flotar, jugador.

Activity 7

A: squash; **B:** waterpolo.

9 Read about the basketball player, Vicky Alonso, in the following interview. Then organize the questions as they should appear in the interview.

Preguntas:

1. ¿En estos tiempos están todos los pabellones *(sports centers)* adaptados?
2. ¿Cómo es jugar en un equipo en donde los compañeros son hombres?
3. ¿Cómo llegó al mundo del deporte?
4. ¿Qué es lo mejor que le ha dado el deporte?
5. ¿Practicar un deporte adaptado supone un gran trabajo?

Vicky Alonso (Vigo, 1982) es una de las internacionales del deporte español. Lleva diez años en la élite del baloncesto en silla de ruedas, jugando en el Amfiv, un equipo con hombres, y está a punto *(ready)* de iniciar su quinto campeonato de Europa con la selección femenina. Dice que el deporte le ha hecho más fácil su minusvalía *(disability)*.

≫ (a) ....

≫ Llegué por casualidad. Cuando comencé a sacar el carné de conducir, mi profesor de la autoescuela, que era entrenador *(coach)*, me lo propuso, fui a probar y me gustó...

≫ (b) ....

≫ Yo creo que todo lo contrario, creo que el hecho de hacer deporte te ayuda muchísimo a superar la minusvalía, es todo lo contrario que en la vida cotidiana *(everyday)*.

≫ (c) ....

≫ En Vigo nunca hemos tenido dificultades, pero sí en alguna otra ciudad donde los pabellones no eran del todo accesibles...

≫ (d) ....

≫ Siempre he jugado sola entre hombres, pero la verdad es que es estupendo. Yo comencé a entrenar *(train)* con ellos y, la verdad, nunca he tenido ningún problema.

≫ (e) ....

≫ Lo mejor ha sido conocer a otras personas que están en la misma situación y que se han encontrado con las mismas dificultades que tú, gente que te hace pensar que no es tan trágico estar así y que tampoco es tan difícil salir adelante *(get ahead)*.

Adaptado de Castro Vigo: http://www.lavozdegalicia.es/coruna/2011/08/23/0003_201108H23P52991.htm

10 Think about Vicky Alonso. In a brief presentation, describe what she has accomplished and what she represents to you.

 Practice what you have learned with additional materials online.

INSTRUCTIONAL STRATEGIES

Activity 9

- Have the students look at the image and say which sport they think Vicky Alonso is playing.
- Have them read the questions and explain that they have to place them in the correct place in the interview.
- Explain that it is a good idea to look at the words after the blank to obtain an idea of which question will fit best.
- Have the students read the interview and write in the questions, ensuring that the answer fits the question.
- Circulate around the room offering assistance, and when they have finished, have them share with a partner.
- Ask for volunteers to give the correct answers.

Activity 10

- Have the students work in pairs to think and write about Vicky Alonso and her accomplishments and what they mean.
- Circulate around the class, offering assistance where required.
- Invite students to share their ideas with the class.

Extension

- Have the students choose a well-known sportsperson and research them on the Internet.
- Have them write a short text about that person's life and achievements and illustrate it with images from the Internet as a poster.
- The completed poster can be displayed on the classroom walls.

ANSWERS

Activity 9

a. 3; b. 5; c. 1; d. 2; e. 4.

OBJECTIVES FOR GRAMÁTICA 1

- Present grammatical structures needed to practice communicative functions of the unit:
  Affirmative commands of regular and irregular verbs
- Use affirmative command forms to tell different people what to do

CORE RESOURCES

- Extension activities EA 2.3
- Interactive Whiteboard Lesson: IWB 2.2
- Interactive Online Materials – ELEteca

STANDARDS

1.1 Engage in conversation
1.2 Understand the language
1.3 Present information
4.1 Compare languages

INSTRUCTIONAL STRATEGIES

1. Affirmative Commands

- Project the first chart of IWB 2.2, **El imperativo** to review affirmative commands. Have students fill in the empty spaces on the chart for the **tú** form of regular and irregular verbs. Then call on student volunteers to explain how they got the form (**tú** form of the present tense minus **s**). Call students up to fill in the blanks.
- To introduce the **usted** and **ustedes** forms, begin by filling in the forms of the present tense of regular verbs. As you do, ask students if they can explain the pattern (using the opposite endings). Continue practice with such verbs as: **lavar, limpiar, escribir, leer**, etc., for **usted** and **ustedes**. Then ask students to think of situation where these forms would be appropriate to use (formal and plural).
- Continue with the irregular forms and ask students to predict the forms. Then ask students to describe how the verbs went from **hacer** to **haga**, **tener** to **tenga** (begin with the **yo** form).

- Then have students open their books and review all the explanations.
- Go over the information in the box referring to the **vosotros** form. Explain that this is only used in Spain.
- Give extra practice by saying the beginning of a command and having the students complete it with their own ideas, for instance: **Ve al supermercado y...**, **Pon tu libro en la mesa y...**, etc., and then varying with **ustedes** form.
- Show students how pronouns are attached to the end of affirmative commands and explain that this often means an accent is required.

GRAMÁTICA

1. AFFIRMATIVE COMMANDS

- Affirmative commands are used to give an order, to invite, give advice, make recommendations, or give permission to someone.
  *Marcos, **limpia** tu habitación y después, **haz** la tarea.*

- For **tú** or informal commands, drop the **–s** from the present tense form of the verb. There are some irregular verbs for the **tú** form (**decir, hacer, poner, tener**...).

	REGULAR VERBS			IRREGULAR VERBS			
	COMPRAR	COMER	SUBIR	DECIR	HACER	PONER	TENER
tú	compra	come	sube	di	haz	pon	ten

- For **usted** or formal commands and **ustedes** or plural commands, start with the **yo** form of the present tense, drop the **–o** and switch to the opposite **–ar** or **–er/–ir** endings of the verb. For example, verbs ending in **–ar** will use the **–e/–en** endings in **usted** and **ustedes** commands. Verbs ending in **–er/–ir** will use the **–a/–an** endings in **usted** and **ustedes** commands.

- The informal affirmative command for **vosotros/as** has a different ending formed by substituting the **–r** in the infinitive with a **–d**:
  Compra**d** / come**d** / subi**d** / deci**d** / hace**d** / pone**d** / tene**d**...

- This form is used in Spain to tell a group of people you normally address as individually **tú** to do something.
  *Niños, **tened** cuidado al cruzar la calle. Children, be careful when crossing the street.*

REGULAR VERBS			
INFINITIVE	yo FORM	usted	ustedes
comprar	compro	compre	compren
comer	como	coma	coman
subir	subo	suba	suban

Compren fruta fresca y coman una al día.

IRREGULAR VERBS			
INFINITIVE	yo FORM	usted	ustedes
decir	digo	diga	digan
hacer	hago	haga	hagan
poner	pongo	ponga	pongan
tener	tengo	tenga	tengan

Ponga la lavadora y haga la cena.

72

■ With all affirmative commands, object pronouns are attached to the end of the verb.

Pon la mayonesa y la mostaza en el frigorífico.
Ponlas allí.
Put the mayonnaise and the mustard in the refrigerator.
Put them there.

Compra el pan. **Cómpralo.**
Buy the bread. Buy it.

1 Fill in the blanks with the affirmative commands of the verbs in parenthesis.

a. Por favor, (entrar, usted) ....
b. Muchachos, (guardar, ustedes) .... los libros.
c. (Mirar, ustedes) .... por la ventana.
d. (Escribir, ustedes) .... en el cuaderno.
e. Pedro, (leer, tú) .... este libro de poesía.
f. (Escuchar, usted) .... atentamente.
g. Por favor, (poner, tú) .... la mesa.
h. (Hacer, ustedes) .... las tareas para mañana.
i. (Decir, usted) .... lo que piensa.
j. (Tener, tú) .... cuidado al cruzar la calle.
k. (Hablar, tú) .... más alto, por favor, no te oigo bien.
l. (Estudiar, ustedes) .... mucho, mañana tienen un examen muy importante.
m. (Cerrar, usted) .... la ventana, por favor, hace mucho frío.
n. (Poner, ustedes) .... sus abrigos encima de la cama.

2 Daría's parents are going on a trip. Read the note that Daría's mom left for the grandfather and the children and write the affirmative command of the verbs in parenthesis.

Fernando, (a) .... (poner) el despertador para no quedarte dormido por la mañana y (b) .... (tener) cuidado de no dejarte el fuego de la estufa encendido. Marcos, puedes jugar un poco a los videojuegos si quieres, pero antes (c) .... (hacer) la tarea. Y Daría, tú (d) .... (sacar) al perro a pasear después de la escuela. Papá, (e) .... (tener) cuidado si sales a la calle y (f) .... (agarrar) las llaves, que siempre te las olvidas. Y, por favor, (g) .... (dejar) la casa ordenada.

73

INSTRUCTIONAL STRATEGIES

Activity 1

- Explain that they have to choose the correct command form of the verb (checking whether it is **tú**, **usted** or **ustedes**) and write it in the space provided.
- Do the first sentence with the class, asking for volunteers to say the correct form.
- Invite students to continue through the activity individually and then compare answers with a partner.
- Circulate while they work and answer any questions that may arise.
- When they have finished, ask for volunteers to call out the answers and write them on the board.
- If desired, ask them to change some of the commands to the **vosotros** form, for example b, c, d, h, l and n.

Activity 2

- Read the instructions and have the students read the text and write the correct form of the affirmative commands.
- Have them share their answers with a partner.
- Ask for volunteers to read each sentence with the correct command form.

Extension

Distribute copies of EA 2.3, **Mira la vida de Dani Martín**. Explain to students that Dani Martín is a well-known singer in Spain. Share with them the following Cultural Note.

Cultural Note

Daniel Martín García (Madrid, 1977) es un cantante, compositor y actor español de gran éxito. Anteriormente, fue líder del grupo de *El Canto del loco*, muy famoso entre los jóvenes. Actualmente prosigue su carrera en solitario.

- Then have students review the song lyrics and answer the questions in pairs.
- Play the song from the internet and have students just listen. Then call on students to review answers.
- Play the song again and have students follow along with the lyrics. Encourage students to sing along as well.

ANSWERS

Activity 1

a. entre; b. guarden; c. Miren; d. Escriban; e. lee; f. Escuche; g. pon; h. Hagan; i. Diga; j. Ten; k. Habla; l. Estudien; m. Cierre; n. Pongan.

Activity 2

a. pon; b. ten; c. haz; d. saca; e. ten; f. agarra; g. deja.

INSTRUCTIONAL STRATEGIES

Activity 3

- To review direct and indirect objects for students, write the model sentence on the board: **Pónganla en la estantería**. Ask students what **la** refers to (**la película**).
- Ask students what the correct order is when there are both a direct and an indirect object. Practice with **Dímelo**. Ask students what **lo** refers to (direct object pronoun taking the place of what is being said) and then **me** (person receiving the message).
- Tell them they have to use the correct affirmative command, checking which person is to be used, and then add the direct object pronoun to the end, which usually means adding an accent.
- Depending on the level of your students, you may want to have them underline the direct object in each sentence and prepare the corresponding pronoun as a middle step and ask individual students to say which pronouns they have chosen.
- Have the students work with a partner to choose the correct command form and then add the pronoun to the end, remembering to add an accent if necessary.
- Circulate as they work, answering questions and providing assistance where required.
- Ask for volunteers to read the answers and other volunteers to write them on the board. Ask the class where the accent should go if it is required.

OBJECTIVES FOR GRAMÁTICA 2

- Present grammatical structures needed to practice communicative functions of the unit:
- Negative commands of regular and irregular verbs
- Use negative command forms to tell different people what not to do

CORE RESOURCES

- Interactive Whiteboard Lesson: IWB 2.2

STANDARDS

1.1   Engage in conversation
1.2   Understand the language
1.3   Present information
4.1   Compare languages

INSTRUCTIONAL STRATEGIES

2. Negative Commands

- Project the second chart of IWB 2.2, **El imperativo** to introduce negative command forms. Begin by filling in the forms of regular verbs. As you do, ask students if they can explain the pattern (using the opposite endings). Then continue to complete the chart together. Next ask students to explain the forms for irregular verbs (originate with **yo** form).

GRAMÁTICA

3 **Change the following sentences into commands, replacing the nouns with their pronouns when possible.**

a. Poner la película en la estantería. (ustedes) .... *Pónganla en la estantería.*
b. Comprar la comida al perro. (tú) ....
c. Dejar las cosas en su sitio. (ustedes) ....
d. Meter los tamales en la nevera. (usted) ....
e. Poner el despertador a tu hermano. (tú) ....
f. Estudiar la lección para mañana. (ustedes) ....
g. Decir los verbos en imperativo. (tú) ....

2. NEGATIVE COMMANDS

- Negative commands are used to tell someone what not to do.

- To form the negative commands:
  - For **usted/ustedes**, use the same form as the affirmative command.

    (usted) compre ➞ **no compre**

    (ustedes) compren ➞ **no compren**

  - For **tú**, add **–s** to the negative command of **usted**.

    (usted) no compre ➞ (tú) **no compres**

REGULAR VERBS			
	COMPRAR	COMER	SUBIR
tú	no compres	no comas	no subas
usted	no compre	no coma	no suba
ustedes	no compren	no coman	no suban

IRREGULAR VERBS				
	DECIR	HACER	PONER	TENER
tú	no digas	no hagas	no pongas	no tengas
usted	no diga	no haga	no ponga	no tenga
ustedes	no digan	no hagan	no pongan	no tengan

- For **vosotros/as** (Spain) drop the **–ar**, **–er**, **–ir** ending of the infinitive and switch to **–éis** (for **–ar** verbs) or **–áis** (for **–er/–ir** verbs):

  no **compréis** / no **comáis** / no **subáis** / no **digáis** / no **hagáis**...

- Then walk the students through the explanation in the book and say a command in the affirmative for them to say in the negative, for instance: **Compra pan – No compres pan; Haz la tarea – No hagas la tarea; Ponga las cosas en la mesa – No ponga las cosas en la mesa**. etc. For this last sentence, point out that with negative commands, the pronouns come before the conjugated verb, and ask students to substitute a pronoun (**No las ponga en la mesa**).
- Point out the note that explains the **vosotros** form.

ANSWERS

Activity 3

b. Cómprasela; **c.** Déjenlas; **d.** Métalos; **e.** Pónselo; **f.** Estúdienla; **g.** Dilos.

■ With negative commands, pronouns always go before the conjugated verb.
*No **lo** bebas / no **me lo** digas / no **las** comas / no **lo** pienses / no **te** olvides...*
Don't drink it / don't tell it to me / don't eat them / don't think about it / don't forget....

4 **Fill in the blanks with the negative commands of the verbs in parenthesis.**

a. Necesito silencio para estudiar. (Poner, tú) .... música.
b. No nos gustan los productos de ese supermercado. (Comprar, ustedes) .... aquí.
c. En la planta de arriba hace mucho calor. (Subir, ustedes) ....
d. Es un secreto. (Decirlo, usted) ....
e. El pastel está malo. (Probarlo, tú) ....

5 **Daría's dad has also written a note to the children in the family. Fill in the blanks using the negative commands of the verbs in the box.**

> pelearse ○ comer ○ ensuciar ○ poner ○ olvidarse ○ quedarse ○ llegar

Marcos, no (a) .... solo pizzas, tienes que comer lo que cocine tu hermana.
Daría, tú eres la encargada de Hueso. No (b) .... de ponerle la comida y el agua todos los días, y ¡no (c) .... la cocina!
Fernando, no (d) .... tarde, ni (e) .... dormido viendo la tele en el sofá.
Abuelo, no (f) .... la radio muy alta, que después se quejan los vecinos.
Y a todos, por favor, no (g) ....

6 **Change the following sentences to negative commands and use pronouns when possible.**

a. Poner la película en la estantería. (ustedes) ....No la pongan en la estantería.
b. Comprar la comida al perro. (tú) ....
c. Dejar las cosas en su sitio. (ustedes) ....
d. Meter los tamales en la nevera. (usted) ....
e. Poner el despertador a tu padre. (tú) ....
f. Hacer la tarea a tu hermano. (tú) ....

7 **Put the words in order.**

a. le / nada / mi / hermano. / a / No / digas ....
b. Dale / perro. / comida / la / al ....
c. pongas / te / No / ese / jersey. ....
d. Ponte / gafas / las / sol. / de ....
e. se / No / peleen / primos. / sus / con ....
f. compres. / lo / No / me ....

 Practice what you have learned with additional materials online.

INSTRUCTIONAL STRATEGIES

Activity 4

• Have students write the correct form of the negative command and then share with a partner. Remind them that any direct object pronouns are placed before the command in the negative.
• Invite students to read their sentences to the class in order to correct.

Activity 5

• Run through the list of verbs ensuring students understand them all.
• Students work in pairs to write the negative command form in the blank provided.
• When they have finished, ask for volunteers to read a sentence and write the negative commands on the board.
• Point out the need for the letter **u** in this form of ***llegar***, and have the students think about which form will be used for the last command.

Activity 6

• Have the students look at the verbs and say the affirmative command form of each, according to the person in parenthesis.
• Read the model for the students and have half the class say the affirmative command form and the other half the negative.
• Have the students write the negative command for each sentence and change the direct object into a pronoun where possible.
• Have them compare answers with a partner.
• Invite students to say their answers aloud and write them on the board.

Activity 7

• Have the students work individually to put the words in the correct order.
• Ask them to share their answers with a partner.
• Have volunteers read their answers aloud.

ANSWERS

Activity 4

a. No pongas; **b.** No compren; **c.** No suban; **d.** No lo diga; **e.** No lo pruebes.

Activity 5

a. comas; **b.** te olvides; **c.** ensucies; **d.** llegues; **e.** te quedes; **f.** pongas; **g.** se peleen.

Activity 6

a. No la pongan en la estantería; **b.** No la compres; **c.** No las dejen desordenadas; **d.** No los meta en la nevera; **e.** No se lo pongas; **f.** No se la hagas.

Activity 7

a. No le digas nada a mi hermano; **b.** Dale la comida al perro; **c.** No te pongas ese jersey; **d.** Ponte las gafas de sol; **e.** No se peleen con sus primos; **f.** No me lo compres.

OBJECTIVES FOR DESTREZAS

- Learn to skim a brochure for information
- Asking the right questions

STANDARDS

- 1.1 Interpersonal communication
- 1.2 Understand the language
- 1.3 Present information

INSTRUCTIONAL STRATEGIES

Comprensión de lectura

Activity 1

- Have the students look at the image and ask if they can guess what the activity is going to be about.
- Talk the students through the strategy, and have them skim through the brochure.

Activity 2

- The students choose the correct ending for each statement.
- Have them compare answers with a partner.
- Ask for volunteers to give the correct answers.
- Ask questions about the information in the brochure, for instance: **¿Cuándo empieza el curso? ¿Cuánto cuesta el curso?**, etc.

ANSWERS

Activity 2

1. c; 2. c; 3. b; 4. a; 5. c; 6. c.

DESTREZAS

COMPRENSIÓN DE LECTURA

1 Before you complete the reading, review the strategy in Destrezas and follow the suggestion.

> **Destrezas**
>
> **Asking yourself questions**
> It is helpful to ask yourself questions as you read. Skim through the brochure and ask yourself if you have read similar brochures to sign up for an activity you liked.

Si te gusta la interpretación o simplemente quieres conocer gente nueva y pasarlo bien, apúntate ya a nuestro taller de teatro. Puedes hacerlo de 8:00 a 20:30h en el teléfono (33) 3563-9184; en la recepción de la **Casa Teatro El Caminante**, C/ Marcos Castellanos, 26, Guadalajara; o a cualquier hora a través de nuestra web: *www.casateatroelcaminante.mx*.

El plazo de inscripción finaliza el 30 de septiembre.
- Inicio de curso: viernes 5 de octubre.
- Horario: todos los viernes de 18:00 a 20:00h.
- Lugar: Casa de la Cultura.
- Edad: sin límite de edad.
- Precio: 450 pesos al mes. (350 pesos para menores de 21 años y mayores de 55).
- Final de curso: 24 de junio. Ese día harán una representación para mostrar a sus amigos y familiares todo lo que aprendieron.

2 Read the brochure again and circle the correct answer.

1. El taller de teatro va dirigido a...
   a. personas que quieren ser actores profesionales.
   b. personas que tienen experiencia en el teatro.
   c. personas a las que les gusta el teatro.

2. El curso...
   a. es de una hora a la semana.
   b. dura un año.
   c. es un día a la semana.

3. El curso es para...
   a. mayores de 55 años.
   b. todas las edades.
   c. personas de entre 21 y 55 años.

4. La inscripción...
   a. puede hacerse a cualquier hora.
   b. puede hacerse solo los viernes de 18:00 a 20:00h.
   c. empieza el 30 de septiembre.

5. El precio del curso...
   a. es de 450 pesos.
   b. es gratis.
   c. depende de la edad.

6. El último día de curso...
   a. hay una clase gratis para los amigos y familiares de los alumnos.
   b. los alumnos van a ver una obra de teatro.
   c. los alumnos hacen una obra de teatro.

EXPRESIÓN E INTERACCIÓN ORALES

UNIDAD 2

3 **Look at the image and choose one of the following options to talk about for 2 or 3 minutes.**

a. Describe el lugar, las personas, los objetos y las acciones.

b. Habla sobre las características físicas de las personas y sobre su ropa o las cosas que llevan.

PRONUNCIACIÓN La entonación

■ Intonation refers to the pitch or the rising and falling of one's voice. Intonation is important because it can change the meaning of a sentence. In Spanish, statements end in a falling pitch.

- **Entonación enunciativa.** *Estudio español. Está duchándose.*

- **Entonación exclamativa.** *¡Qué interesante! ¡Ya he terminado!*

- **Entonación interrogativa.**   Abierta: *¿Dónde vives?*

   Cerrada: *¿Tienes un diccionario?*

- **Entonación suspendida.** *Pues si no lo sabe él... ¡Es tan lindo...!*

1 🎧 ¹³ **Listen to the examples and repeat.**

2 🎧 ¹⁴ **Listen to the intonation and mark the statement you hear.**

a. ☐ Ya ha venido.   b. ☐ No lo quiere.   c. ☐ Habla español.   d. ☐ Es que no puede.
☐ ¡Ya ha venido!   ☐ ¡No lo quiere!   ☐ ¡Habla español!   ☐ ¡Es que no puede!
☐ ¿Ya ha venido?   ☐ ¿No lo quiere?   ☐ ¿Habla español?   ☐ ¿Es que no puede?
☐ Ya ha venido...   ☐ No lo quiere...   ☐ Habla español...   ☐ Es que no puede...

3 🎧 ¹⁵ **Listen to following dialogue and add the missing punctuation based on the intonation you hear.**

≫ Cuándo vendrá Marcos   ≫ Acaso te viene mal   ≫ Déjame que te explique
≫ Supongo que el domingo   ≫ Cómo dices eso   ≫ Pues habla ya
≫ Pues si viene el domingo   ≫ Quieres hablar claro

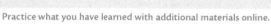
Practice what you have learned with additional materials online.   77

INSTRUCTIONAL STRATEGIES

Expresión e interacción orales

Activity 3

- Have the students look at the image.
- Tell them to choose either option *a* or *b* and take a few minutes to think about what they will say.
- Divide them into pairs (one having prepared *a* and the other *b*), and have them take turns to talk for about 3 minutes each.
- Circulate as they prepare and talk, answering questions and providing assistance where required.

OBJECTIVES FOR PRONUNCIACIÓN

- Practice correct intonation
- Listen and identify meaning through pronunciation

CORE RESOURCES

- Audio Program: Tracks 13, 14 and 15
- Interactive Online Materials – ELEteca

STANDARDS

   1.2   Understand the language
   3.2   Acquire information
   4.1   Compare languages

INSTRUCTIONAL STRATEGIES

- Walk the students through the explanation and go over the different intonations with them. Have them repeat each one.

🎧 **13 Activity 1**

Play the audio and have the students listen and repeat.

🎧 **14 Activity 2**

- Have students look briefly at the short sentences. Play the audio and have them check the statement that best matches the intonation they hear.
- Play the audio again while they confirm their answers. Ask for volunteers to give the correct answers.

Audioscript

a. ¡Ya ha venido!; **b.** ¿No lo quiere?; **c.** Habla español.; **d.** Es que no puede.

🎧 **15 Activity 3**

- Have the students read the exchanges silently. Then play the audio pausing for them to add the missing punctuation.
- Invite different students to write a sentence on the board with the correct punctuation. Play the audio one more time while they listen and look at the corrected activity.

Audioscript

≫ ¿Cuándo vendrá Marcos?   ≫ ¡Cómo dices eso!
≫ Supongo que el domingo.   ≫ ¿Quieres hablar claro?
≫ Pues si viene el domingo…   ≫ Déjame que te explique...
≫ ¿Acaso te viene mal?   ≫ ¡Pues habla ya!

OBJECTIVES FOR SABOR HISPANO

- Learn about manners in Spanish society
- Learn how other cultures have different norms

CORE RESOURCES

- Audio Program: Track 16

STANDARDS

2.1 Culture: practices and perspectives

2.2 Products and perspectives

3.2 Acquire information

5.2 Using language for personal enjoyment and enrichment

INSTRUCTIONAL STRATEGIES

 16

- Introduce the topic by asking what the students know about what is considered polite or rude in Spanish society and in U.S. society.
- Talk about the images and elicit what they already know and can share.
- Ask if any of them have noticed examples of good/bad manners.
- Have them look at the questions in **Antes de leer**.
- Tell the students to look at the **Glosario** on the next page to help them with any vocabulary they may not know.
- Read the first section of the text and invite a volunteer to read after you. After each section, ask questions such as: **¿Es importante llegar en punto en Alemania? ¿De dónde es Sebastian Rohde?**, etc. Continue with the other sections.
- Ask what the students have understood and invite those who understood more to help those who understood less.

SABOR HISPANO

¿SON MALEDUCADOS LOS ESPAÑOLES?

¿Hablas muy alto por teléfono?

Antes de leer

¿Qué son los buenos modales (*manners*), según tú?

¿Crees que la gente de tu país suele tener buenos modales?

¿Es importante ser educado? ¿Por qué?

 16 **Hablar alto, tocarse la nariz, empezar a comer antes que otros, llegar tarde... Mucha gente piensa que estos son malos modales pero, ¿son típicos de una persona maleducada o de una cultura?**

«Cuando me mudé a España me invitaron a una fiesta. La fiesta era a las 8 de la tarde. En Alemania la puntualidad es importante así que llegué a las 8 en punto. Pero mis amigos españoles no llegaron hasta las 8 y media... ¡Qué vergüenza!», dice Sebastian Rohde, una chico de 21 años de Berlín.

La experiencia de Sebastian no es única. En España no se considera de mala educación llegar tarde a una fiesta. «Si quedo con amigos a una hora determinada, se sobreentiende[1] que llegar algo más tarde es lo normal», dice Marisa López, una chica de Valencia.

«Pero en el ambiente laboral la actitud es muy distinta: con cosas relacionadas con el trabajo, la gente es muy profesional», dice Marisa.

«La primera vez que visité el Reino Unido, me chocó[1] mucho que la gente empezara a cenar antes que el resto de comensales[1]. En España eso se considera de mala educación», dice Samantha Borrás, una estudiante de Madrid que vive en el Reino Unido. «Preferimos comer la comida cuando está caliente», dice su novio inglés.

«¿Que si los españoles son maleducados? A veces sí lo parecen», dice Soraya Conti, una chica argentina que vive en España, «En mi país la gente que trabaja de cara al público utiliza muchas palabras de cortesía. En España se habla de forma más directa. Por eso, a algunos extranjeros les puede parecer que los españoles son maleducados».

«Creo que los españoles hablan muy alto. En Finlandia hablamos mucho más bajo. Allí se considera de mala educación hablar alto. Por eso algunas personas pueden pensar que los españoles son groseros[1]», dice Karen Laatvala, una estudiante que vive en Salamanca.

Una chica llega tarde a una cita.

¿Qué suelen pensar los extranjeros del comportamiento social de los españoles?

- Que no son puntuales.
- Que hablan alto.
- Que no tienen muy buena atención al cliente.
- Que interrumpen mucho.

5 comportamientos de buena educación en España

- Utilizar expresiones de cortesía.
- No comer hasta que todos los comensales hayan recibido su comida.
- Taparse la boca al toser* o estornudar*.
- No abrir la boca al comer.
- Comer con cubiertos*.

Un chico bosteza en público.

¿COMPRENDISTE?

Decide if the following statements are true (T) or false (F).

1. Sebastian y Karen hablan de los modales de los españoles. T ○ F ○
2. Soroya piensa que los españoles siempre hablan de forma cortés. T ○ F ○
3. Sebastian llegó tarde a la fiesta. T ○ F ○
4. Samantha prefiere esperar al resto de comensales. T ○ F ○
5. Comer con las manos es señal de buena educación en España. T ○ F ○

AHORA TÚ

What do you think? Answer the following questions and discuss your ideas with other students.

1. ¿Qué comportamientos se consideran correctos en tu país?
2. ¿Qué expresiones corteses usarías en español para pedir información?
3. ¿Has tenido alguna experiencia con otras culturas en las cuales has observado alguna señal de mala educación?
4. ¿Qué comportamientos son de mala educación, según tú?
5. ¿Te has comportado de forma grosera alguna vez? ¿Cuándo?

Un muchacho come muy rápido.

Glosario

chocar – to be in shock
el comensal – dinner guest
el cubierto – cutlery
estornudar – to sneeze
grosero/a – rude
sobreentender – understand perfectly
toser – to cough

Fuentes: Entrevistas personales a estudiantes de Erasmus, Guía de Protocolo, Protocolo.org.

79

INSTRUCTIONAL STRATEGIES

- Look at the pie graph and have the students interpret the information they see and make statements about it. Prompt with: *¿Qué piensa la mayoría de los extranjeros sobre los españoles? ¿Qué aspecto les molesta menos?* Ask students to share their own perspectives about Spanish-speakers and people in their own culture and communities. What behaviors do they have in common?
- Have students do the same with the bar graph. Then in pairs, ask students to categorize five behaviors they consider important. Call on volunteers to present. Then together as a class choose which five from the ones suggested best reflect American culture.

¿Comprendiste?

- Have the students read the statements in the box and then check through the text to see if they are true or false.
- Have them compare their answers with a partner.
- Invite individual students to share their answers with the class.

Ahora tú

- Read the questions with the students and have them think about the answers.
- Have the students answer the questions in pairs and then ask for volunteers to present to the class.

ANSWERS

1. T; 2. F; 3. F; 4. T; 5. F.

RELATO COMPREHENSIVE PRACTICE

OBJECTIVES FOR RELATO

- Revisit unit themes, grammar, vocabulary and culture in a new context
- Improve reading comprehension skills

STANDARDS

1.1 Engage in conversation
1.2 Understand the language
1.3 Present information
2.1 Practices and perspectives
5.3 Using language for personal enjoyment and enrichment

INSTRUCTIONAL STRATEGIES

Activity 1

- To introduce the activity, write the following quote on the board: **"En la vida hay que poner [el corazón] en lo que se hace. Si no, no sirve para nada"** leaving a blank for **corazón**. Ask students what word they think would complete the idea. Then have them read the quotation in the book.
- With a partner, have students answer and discuss the questions.
- Ask for volunteers to share their ideas with the class.

🎧 17 Activity 2

- Have the students read the title and look at the images to predict what they think the text will be about.
- Read the text in sections and ask individual students to repeat or play the audio.
- Ask questions about the text, such as: **¿Cómo se llama el libro encontrado? ¿Qué cuenta ese libro? ¿Por qué le gusta este libro?**, etc.

Cultural Note

Tell students: *La novela* Como agua para chocolate *es de la escritora mexicana Laura Esquivel.* Encourage students to learn more about her at *http://www.epdlp.com/escritor. php?id=2484*

ANSWERS

Activity 1

a. Se refiere a poner mucho esfuerzo y hacerlo todo lo mejor posible. **b., c.:** Answers will vary.

RELATO Mi abuela Eva

1 👥 **Read the following sentence and answer the questions with a partner.**

En la vida hay que poner el corazón en lo que haces. Si no, no sirve para nada.

a. ¿A qué crees que se refiere con "poner el corazón"?
b. ¿Estás de acuerdo con la frase?
c. Señala las cosas en las que pones el corazón: aficiones, deportes, estudios...

2 🎧 **17 Read the text.**

Mi abuela Eva

No sé si creer en las casualidades. Pero resulta que hoy, en el autobús, mientras iba a la escuela, alguien se había dejado olvidado un libro. Ya su portada me atraía a leerlo y a devorarlo *(devour it)*. Fíjate si estaba entusiasmada *(excited)* con la historia, que me pasé la parada de la escuela. El libro se llamaba *Como agua para chocolate* y cuenta la vida de Tita y su historia de amor con Pedro. La madre de Tita tuvo a su hija en la cocina, entre los olores *(smells)* de lo que estaba cocinando. Por eso, ya desde el principio, Tita sentía un gran amor por la cocina. Cuando cocinaba, su estado de ánimo *(mood)* influía en los platos que preparaba. Así, si hacía un plato estando alegre, cuando la gente lo comía, también se ponía contenta.

Ahora estoy en mi habitación y sigo leyéndolo sin parar. Quizás también me gusta esta historia porque me recuerda a mi abuela. Ella pasaba mucho tiempo en la cocina y le encantaba cocinar. Además, al igual que Tita, creía que era muy importante cómo te sentías cuando cocinabas. Siempre que podíamos, mi hermano y yo, a la vuelta de la escuela, pasábamos toda la tarde con ella. Cuando nos veía asomar *(peeking out)* la cabeza por la puerta siempre nos decía:

– Entren, entren. Miren qué estoy preparando.

Nosotros entrábamos hipnotizados. Dejábamos las mochilas en el suelo y nos poníamos manos a la obra *(get down to business)*.

– Manuela, ayúdame a cortar esta cebolla, y Tomás, lava las papas para cocerlas.

A mi hermano y a mí nos encantaba ser sus ayudantes en la cocina e imaginar que estábamos en uno de los mejores restaurantes de París.

– No, mira, si quieres que esté dulce, recítale un poema. Sí, así... Muy bien... En la vida hay que poner el corazón en lo que haces. Si no, no sirve para nada... Eso es, ponle alegría, que es para la familia...

UNIDAD 2

Daba igual si no lo hacíamos perfecto, ella siempre nos sonreía. Claro, que eso no era muy difícil, porque todo le parecía bien y casi siempre estaba de buen humor. Creo que solamente se enfadaba y se quejaba *(complain)* cuando cortaba la cebolla y le lloraban los ojos.

– Seguro que esto no es bueno. Si lloro ahora cocinando, ¿qué pasará cuando lo coman los invitados? Yo no quiero llorar cocinando. ¿Y si se me caen las lágrimas *(tears)* encima de la comida?

Un día, por su cumpleaños, se nos ocurrió regalarle unas gafas de buceo *(swimming mask)* para cortar cebollas y así perder el miedo a cocinar algo triste. Todavía recuerdo su sonrisa cuando se las puso. Nos dijo que era el mejor regalo del mundo.

3 **Fill in the blanks with the information from the text.**

a. Empezó a leer ....

b. Si estás triste y cocinas, ...

c. Estando con ella pensábamos ....

d. Las gafas de buceo le sirven para ....

e. La abuela siempre nos decía ....

f. El libro me recuerda a ella porque ....

4 **The book *Como agua para chocolate* (*Like Water for Chocolate*) belongs to a Latin-American literary movement called Magical Realism. Read the definition of this movement and answer the question.**

Este estilo se caracteriza por introducir elementos mágicos como algo normal de la vida cotidiana; forman parte de ella y son aceptados. La realidad y la fantasía se mezclan en la narración.

¿Qué idea del realismo mágico hay en el relato sobre la abuela Eva?

_____

_____

_____

_____

_____

_____

5 **Write about an important person in your life. Can you use Magical Realism in your writing?**

INSTRUCTIONAL STRATEGIES

Activity 3

- Ask the students to complete the sentences with information from the text.
- Have them compare their answers with a partner.
- Ask different students to say the correct answers aloud.

Activity 4

- Ask students to read the definition of magical realism and look for examples of it in the story with a partner.
- Ask for students to report to the class and discuss any ideas that emerge.

Activity 5

- Have the students choose an important person in their life and think about how they could use magical realism to write about that person.
- Have them write some sentences about the person and share them with a partner.

Extension

To help students understand magical realism and how it might be represented, share the following description from the movie version. Explain that Tita, as the youngest of the sisters and according to tradition, must remain unmarried to care for her mother. Yet she and Pedro have fallen in love. To stay a part of her life, Pedro decides to marry Tita's sister. Describe the following wedding scene for students to imagine.

Para la boda de su hermana, Tita, la protagonista de la historia, hace la torta de la boda para Pedro y su hermana Rosaura y después asiste a su boda. Tita no puede expresar las emociones por perder al amor de su vida que se casa con su hermana, pero sus lágrimas derramadas en la masa de la tarta de boda transmitirán sus emociones a todo aquel que la pruebe. El efecto del realismo mágico se ve en que toda la gente que come la tarta se pone enferma; sienten el dolor y la tristeza igual que si acabasen de perder a su amante.

ANSWERS

Activity 3

a. Empezó a leer un libro que alguien se había dejado olvidado en el autobús; **b.** Si estás triste y cocinas, transmitirás tu tristeza a las personas que coman lo que has cocinado; **c.** Estando con ella pensábamos que estábamos en uno de los mejores restaurantes de París; **d.** Las gafas de buceo le sirven para no tener que llorar mientras corta las cebollas y así evitar cocinar algo triste; **e.** La abuela siempre nos decía que en la vida hay que poner el corazón en lo que se hace porque si no, no sirve para nada; **f.** El libro me recuerda a ella porque también pasaba mucho tiempo en la cocina y le encantaba cocinar, además también creía que era muy importante cómo se sentía uno cuando cocinaba.

Activity 4

Answers will vary. Possible answer: Que el estado de ánimo que tenemos mientras cocinamos influye en los platos que preparamos y que estos lo transmiten a quien los come. Por ejemplo, en el texto aparece la idea de endulzar los platos recitando un poema o transmitir tristeza si se llora al cortar las cebollas.

OBJECTIVES FOR EVALUACIÓN

- Review grammar, vocabulary and culture from the unit
- Complete self-assessment

CORE RESOURCES

- Audio Program: Track 18
- Interactive Online Materials – ELEteca

STANDARDS

1.2   Understand the language
2.1   Practices and perspectives
4.1   Compare cultures

INSTRUCTIONAL STRATEGIES

- Activities can be completed individually and then reviewed with the class. Vary by asking students if they agree with the answer given and then writing it on the board. Provide explanations as needed.
- You may wish to assign point value to each activity as a way for students to monitor their progress.
- Direct students to the indicated pages in **En resumen** if they make more than one or two mistakes in any one section.

ANSWERS

Activity 1

1. e; **2.** c; **3.** b; **4.** d; **5.** a; **6.** f.

Activity 2

1. d, f; **2.** g, b; **3.** c, h; **4.** e, a.

Activity 3

a. pongan; **b.** Repártanlas; **c.** Tengan; **d.** hagan; **e.** Sean; **f.** pasen; **g.** limpien; **h.** Laven; **i.** lávenlos; **j.** Saquen; **k.** Sáquenla; **l.** se obsesionen.

EVALUACIÓN

ASKING, GIVING AND REFUSING PERMISSION. EXTENDING OR OFFERING INVITATIONS

1 **Match the items on the right with the items on the left.**

1. ¿Le importa si abro la ventana? Hace mucho calor. ......•
2. ¿Te importa si uso tu celular? ....•
3. ¿Puedo pasar? ....•
4. ¿Quieres un poco más de sopa? ....•
5. Tome, siéntese aquí. ....•
6. Mamá, si hago toda mi tarea y limpio mi habitación, ¿podría ir esta noche al cine? ....•

- a. Gracias, joven.
- b. ¡Claro! Pasa, pasa.
- c. Llama, llama.
- d. No, gracias, ya estoy lleno.
- e. No, por favor, ábrala.
- f. ¡Ni hablar!

INSTRUCTIONS, ADVICE, AND COMMANDS

2 **Match each sentence to the person that is saying it.**

a. Pues llámala.
b. Vale, pero si me voy es para siempre, así que no me llames más.
c. Perdone, ¿para ir al museo Picasso?
d. No llegues tarde, que van a venir tus abuelos a cenar.
e. Ayer me lo pasé genial con Aurora, ¿qué puedo hacer?
f. ¡Que síííííí…! ¡Ya me lo has dicho un montón de veces!
g. Agarra tus cosas y vete. No quiero verte más.
h. Sigue todo derecho, y al final de la calle gira a la izquierda.

COMMANDS AND PRONOUNS

3 **Fill in the blanks with the command form of the verb in parenthesis. Substitute pronouns for the nouns as indicated.**

Si van a compartir su apartamento con alguien (a) .... (poner, ustedes) unas normas para las tareas. (b) .... (Repartir, ustedes, las tareas) de forma justa y equitativa. (c) .... (Tener, ustedes) en cuenta los gustos y preferencias de la otra persona. No (d) .... (hacer, ustedes) solo las tareas que más les gustan a ustedes. (e) .... (Ser, ustedes) comprensivos el uno con el otro. Si quieren una casa limpia y ordenada, (f) .... (pasar, ustedes) la aspiradora y (g) .... (limpiar, ustedes) el baño, como mínimo, una vez a la semana. (h) .... (Lavar, ustedes) los platos cada día y (i) .... (lavar, ustedes, los platos) bien, también por debajo. (j) .... (Sacar, ustedes) la basura todos los días. (k) .... (Sacar, ustedes, la basura), si no, la casa olerá fatal. No (l) .... (obsesionarse, ustedes) con la limpieza. Si un día no hacen la cama, no pasa nada.

82

LAS TAREAS DOMÉSTICAS Y LOS DEPORTES

4 Fill in the blanks with the vocabulary words you have learned in this lesson.

a. No tengo ropa limpia, hay que ....

b. Mi madre es alérgica al polvo, así que tenemos que .... y pasar .... todos los días.

c. En mi casa se cambian las .... los domingos.

d. Bernardo es muy malo jugando al fútbol. El otro día, ... el balón y metió gol en su propia ....

e. Me han regalado una .... para jugar al tenis igual que la que usa Rafa Nadal.

INTONATION

5 **18** Listen to the conversation and choose Paco's answer.

Antonio: ¡Qué temprano vienes!

Paco: a. ☐ ¡Tú sí que has venido temprano!

b. ☐ ¿Tú sí que has venido temprano?

Antonio: Es que hoy no he perdido el bus. Por cierto, ¿qué hora es?

Paco: a. ☐ ¿Es que no tienes reloj?

b. ☐ Es que no tienes reloj…

Antonio: Lo he olvidado en casa. ¿A qué hora viene el jefe?

Paco: a. ☐ No lo sé.

b. ☐ ¡No lo sé!

Antonio: ¿Y si vamos a tomar un café?

Paco: a. ☐ ¡Otro café!

b. ☐ ¿Otro café?

Antonio: Es que no he desayunado.

Paco: a. ☐ Bueno, ¿te acompaño?

b. ☐ Bueno, te acompaño.

CULTURA

6 Answer the following questions with the information you learned in *¿Son maleducados los españoles?*

a. Si llegas tarde a una fiesta, ¿es de mala educación en España? ¿Y en tu país o región?

b. Si estás en España, ¿puedes empezar a cenar si no están todos los comensales? ¿Y en tu país o región?

c. Cuando un español habla en voz alta, ¿está enfadado? ¿Y en tu país o región?

d. ¿Qué hay que hacer en España si toses o estornudas? ¿Y en tu país o región?

e. En España, ¿se puede interrumpir a una persona que está hablando? ¿Y en tu país o región?

 Practice what you have learned with additional materials online.

---

 18 Activity 5

Audioscript

» ¡Qué temprano vienes!

» ¡Tú sí que has venido temprano!

» Es que hoy no he perdido el bus. Por cierto, ¿qué hora es?

» ¿Es que no tienes reloj?

» Lo he olvidado en casa. ¿A qué hora viene el jefe?

» No lo sé.

» ¿Y si vamos a tomar un café?

» ¿Otro café?

» Es que no he desayunado.

» Bueno, te acompaño.

ANSWERS

Activity 4

Answers may vary. Possible answers include: **a.** lavarla, poner la lavadora; **b.** barrer, la aspiradora; **c.** sábanas; **d.** chutó, portería; **e.** raqueta.

Activity 5

a. ¡Tú sí que has venido temprano!

b. ¿Es que no tienes reloj?

c. No lo sé.

d. ¿Otro café?

e. Bueno, te acompaño.

Activity 6

Answers will vary. **a.** En España no es de mala educación; **b.** En España tienes que esperar a todos los comensales; **c.** Cuando un español habla en voz alta no está necesariamente enfadado; **d.** En España, si toses o estornudas, tienes que taparte la boca con la mano; **e.** En España se puede interrumpir a una persona cuando está hablando.

OBJECTIVES FOR EN RESUMEN: VOCABULARIO

- Review unit vocabulary and expressions
- Practice communicative skills

STANDARDS

1.2 Understand the language
1.3 Present information
4.1 Evaluate similarities and differences in language

INSTRUCTIONAL STRATEGIES

- Encourage students to use self-adhesive notes to place on correct objects in their house.
- Index cards can be used as flashcards with the Spanish term on one side and the English term on the other, or a picture or drawing.
- Students work in pairs or groups, using vocabulary flashcards as they would the cards of a board game to help each other practice unit vocabulary.
- Encourage students to write labels or captions for the photos on this page. Remind them to use the vocabulary and expressions they have learned in this unit.

EN RESUMEN: Vocabulario

Verbos

aceptar *to accept*
agradecer *to thank*
botar *to throw away, to bounce*
chutar *to kick*

conceder *to grant*
dar permiso *to give permission*
decepcionar *to disappoint*
denegar *to refuse*
flotar *to float*
golpear *to hit*
lanzar *to throw*
limpiar *to clean*

marcar un gol *to score*
quejarse *to complain*
rechazar *to reject*
sonreír *to smile*

Los deportes

el balón *ball*
el campo *field*
la cancha *court*
la falta *fault*
el pase *pass*
la portería *goal*
el portero *goal keeper*

la raqueta *racket*

rebotar *to bounce*
la red *net*

Las tareas del hogar

la aspiradora *vacuum cleaner*
barrer *to sweep*
la basura *trash*
hacer la cama *make the bed*
hacer la comida *to cook lunch*

lavar los platos *wash the dishes*
planchar *to iron*
el polvo *dust*
poner la lavadora *to do the laundry*
poner la mesa *set the table*
las sábanas *bed sheets*

tender la ropa *hang out clothes*
tirar la basura *take out the trash*

Otras palabras útiles

apúntate *sign up*
decepcionado/a *disappointed*
equitativo/a *equitable, fair*
el esfuerzo *effort*
el estilo *style*

estricto/a *strict*
fatal *awful*
la inscripción *inscription*
la interpretación *interpretation*

la obra de teatro *theater play*

Pedir permiso, concederlo y denegarlo

¡De ninguna manera! *No way!*
¡Ni hablar! *Don't even mention it!*

No, (lo siento) es que... *No, (I'm sorry)*
¿Puedo / Podría...? *Can / Could I...?*
¿Quieres...? *Do you want...?*
¿Te / Le importa si...? *Do you mind if...*

Expresiones para pedir y dar instrucciones, órdenes y consejos

Perdone / Perdona, ¿para...? *Excuse me, how do I...?*
¿Por qué no...? *Why don't you...?*
¿Puedes / Podrías decirme cómo...? *Can / Could you tell me how...?*
¿Sabes cómo...? *Do you know how to...?*
Tendrías que / Deberías... *You should...*

84

EN RESUMEN: Gramática

AFFIRMATIVE COMMANDS
(See page 72)

- Affirmative commands are used to give an order, to invite, give advice, make recommendations, or give permission to someone.

- Verbs ending in **–ar** will use the **–e/–en** endings in **usted** and **ustedes** commands. Verbs ending in **–er/–ir** will use the **–a/–an** endings in **usted** and **ustedes** commands.

- With all affirmative commands, the object pronouns are attached to the end of the verb.

REGULAR VERBS			
	COMPRAR	**COMER**	**SUBIR**
tú	compra	come	sube
usted	compre	coma	suba
ustedes	compren	coman	suban

IRREGULAR VERBS				
	DECIR	**HACER**	**PONER**	**TENER**
tú	**di**	**haz**	**pon**	**ten**
usted	**diga**	**haga**	**ponga**	**tenga**
ustedes	**digan**	**hagan**	**pongan**	**tengan**

NEGATIVE COMMANDS
(See page 74)

- Negative commands are used to tell someone what not to do.

- To form the negative commands:

  - For **usted/ustedes**, use the same form as the affirmative command.
    (usted) compre ➡ *no compre*
    (ustedes) compren ➡ *no compren*

  - For **tú**, add **–s** to the negative command of **usted**.
    (usted) no compre ➡ *(tú)* **no compres**

- With negative commands, pronouns always go right before the conjugated verb.

REGULAR VERBS			
	COMPRAR	**COMER**	**SUBIR**
tú	no compre**s**	no coma**s**	no sub**as**
usted	no compre	no coma	no suba
ustedes	no compren	no coman	no suban

IRREGULAR VERBS				
	DECIR	**HACER**	**PONER**	**TENER**
tú	no **digas**	no **hagas**	no **pongas**	no **tengas**
usted	no **diga**	no **haga**	no **ponga**	no **tenga**
ustedes	no **digan**	no **hagan**	no **pongan**	no **tengan**

85

OBJECTIVES FOR EN RESUMEN: GRAMÁTICA
- Review unit grammar
- Practice communication skills

STANDARDS
1.2 Understand the language
1.3 Present information

INSTRUCTIONAL STRATEGIES
- Model how to review grammar.
- Have the students review the Learning Outcomes in the unit opener to assess whether they feel they have mastered the main ideas and skills.
- Ask them if they can remember additional examples for each grammar topic.
- Model how to find and go back to the appropriate page in the unit to review any grammar topic they may need help with.
- Invite students to review the grammar activities they completed in this unit.
- Ask them what grammar activities they found easy and which they found challenging. Encourage them to rework any activities they found particularly challenging.

Objectives for Ahora comprueba

- Review and recycle grammar, vocabulary and culture from the last two units
- Complete self-assessment

Core Resources

- Audio Program: Tracks 19 and 20

Standards

1.2   Understand the language
1.3   Present information
2.1   Practices and perspectives
4.1   Compare languages and cultures

Instructional Strategies

- Activities can be completed individually or in pairs and then reviewed with the class.
- When reviewing answers in class, expand by asking students if they agree with the answers given and then writing the correct answer on the board.
- You may wish to assign point value to each activity as a way for students to monitor their progress. If students achieve less than 80% on each activity, direct them to **En resumen** in the previous two units for page numbers to review.

Activity 1

- Introduce the theme or topic for the activities in this section, studying aboard through an exchange program.

🎧 19 Activity 2

- Before playing the audio, have students read the column heads to know what to focus on as they listen. Explain that they will be listening to six, short conversations and that more than one function can be selected.
- Play the audio and repeat as needed to help students check off the correct function or to confirm answers.

Audioscript

a. » ¿Puedo bajar después de comer a la piscina?
  » No, lo siento, es que después de comer vamos a ir a comprar.

b. » ¿Qué te pasa, Andrés?
  » Es que esta noche hay una fiesta y me gustaría ir. ¿Puedo ir, mamá?

c. » ¿Quieres más papas?
  » No gracias, ¡estoy lleno!

d. » ¿Qué transporte es el mejor para moverme por la ciudad, papá?
  » Lo mejor es comprar el abono transporte. Cómpralo el primer día del mes, cuesta 40 euros. Puedes tomar el metro, el autobús y el tren todas las veces que quieras.

e. » ¡Andrés! ¡Sal ya de la piscina y ven a comer!
  » ¡Ya voy!

1 Leo, an American student, is participating in an international student exchange. He is going to spend a few months in Madrid at Andrés's house. Read the following letter that Andrés wrote to Leo giving him some advice about living with his family. Write the verbs in parenthesis in the future tense.

¡Hola, Leo! Hoy he recibido tu carta y la verdad es que me alegra mucho saber que finalmente (a) .... (venir, tú) a Madrid en agosto. En esas fechas (b) .... (hacer) mucho calor, pero no te preocupes porque entre semana (c) .... (poder, tú) estar todo el día en la piscina de mi casa. No es muy grande pero (d) .... (pasártelo, tú) muy bien. Los fines de semana mi familia y tú seguramente (e) .... (ir) a la sierra, a casa de mi tía. Allí ya (f) .... (ver, tú) cómo no (g) .... (pasar, tú) tanto calor; incluso por la noche probablemente (h) .... (necesitar, tú) ponerte una chaqueta. Mi hermana seguro que (i) .... (querer) hacer alguna excursión y, si van a La Pedriza, (j) .... (bañarse, ustedes) en el río. Yo creo que (k) .... (llevarse, tú) muy bien con mi hermana porque, aunque es un poco pesada, la verdad es que es muy divertida. Mi padre es muy hablador, así que te (l) .... (contar) muchas historias de cuando él era joven. Mi madre también habla mucho y, además, te (m) .... (preguntar) mil veces si quieres algo más de comer y le (n) .... (dar) igual si quieres más o no, porque ella siempre te (ñ) .... (poner) tanta comida ¡que te (o) .... (salir) por las orejas!

2 🎧 19 Listen to the different conversations that Andrés's family is having and choose the category in which they belong.

	Pedir permiso	Conceder permiso	Denegar o rechazar permiso	Dar órdenes	Dar consejos	Dar instrucciones	Invitar u ofrecer
a.	☐	☐	☐	☐	☐	☐	☐
b.	☐	☐	☐	☐	☐	☐	☐
c.	☐	☐	☐	☐	☐	☐	☐
d.	☐	☐	☐	☐	☐	☐	☐
e.	☐	☐	☐	☐	☐	☐	☐
f.	☐	☐	☐	☐	☐	☐	☐
g.	☐	☐	☐	☐	☐	☐	☐
h.	☐	☐	☐	☐	☐	☐	☐

3 🎧 20 Listen to the chores that need to be done at Andres's home and write them in the correct column.

HACER	PONER	LIMPIAR	LAVAR	RECOGER

f. » Perdone, ¿para ir a la estación de Atocha?
  » Siga todo recto, al final de la calle gire a la derecha y después tome la primera a la izquierda.
  » Gracias.

g. » ¿Te importa si uso tu computadora? Es que quiero escribirles un email a mis amigos.
  » No, claro, hazlo.

h. » Andrés, ¿por qué no vamos a patinar esta tarde?
  » ¡Vale! ¡Buena idea!

4 Take a look at Andrés's room! Help him write an email to Leo telling him what to do before his parents arrive. Fill in the blanks with commands and the necessary pronouns.

Asunto: Ordenar la habitación

Para: leo@yamail.es

Leo, ¡ayúdame! ¡Con las prisas no me ha dado tiempo de ordenar la habitación! Esto es lo que hay que hacer:

a. Me dejé un vaso de agua al lado de la cama. Por favor, ...llévalo...... a la cocina.

b. No terminé de guardar la ropa en el armario. Por favor, ... tú.

c. Se me olvidó sacar la ropa de entrenar de la bolsa de deporte. .... de la bolsa y .... en la lavadora.

d. No me dio tiempo a hacer la cama. ....

e. No limpié el polvo de la estantería. ....

f. Dejé el escritorio muy desordenado. ....

g. Creo que, además, me dejé la computadora encendida. ....

¡Te prometo que te lo agradeceré toda la vida! :)

5 Look at the images and write what Andrés and his family will do over the weekend.

El fin de semana que viene ....

....

6 Imagine that an exchange student is coming to spend a month with you. Explain to him/her what your family is like, what you normally do, and how you share chores. Give him/her some advice about your family and what you have plan to do over his/her stay.

🎧 20 Activity 3

Point out to students that more than one possibility exists for arranging these chores.

Audioscript

Las ventanas, la compra, la mesa, los platos, el suelo, la cama, la habitación, la lavadora, el polvo de los muebles.

ANSWERS

Activity 1

a. vendrás; b. hará; c. podrás; d. te lo pasarás; e. irán; f. verás; g. pasarás; h. necesitarás; i. querrá; j. se bañarán; k. te llevarás; l. contará; m. preguntará; n. dará; ñ. pondrá; o. saldrá.

Activity 2

a. Pedir permiso y denegar o rechazar un permiso; b. Pedir permiso; c. Invitar u ofrecer; d. Dar consejos; e. Dar órdenes; f. Dar instrucciones; g. Pedir permiso y conceder un permiso; h. Invitar u ofrecer.

Activity 3

Answers may vary. Possible answers include: **Hacer:** la compra, la cama; **Poner:** la lavadora, la mesa; **Limpiar:** el polvo de los muebles, las ventanas; **Lavar:** los platos, el suelo; **Recoger:** la habitación.

INSTRUCTIONAL STRATEGIES

Activity 4

• Have the students read the text and choose the correct verb for each.

• When they have finished, have them share with a partner. Ask individual students to read the complete sentences.

Activity 5

Remind students to use the future tense in their description.

Activity 6

Remind students to use commands with and without pronouns, expressions for giving advice and instructions that they have learned in these two units.

ANSWERS

Activity 4

a. llévalo; b. guárdala; c. Sácala, ponla; d. Hazla; e. Límpialo; f. Arréglalo / Recógelo; g. Apágala.

Activity 5

Answers will vary. Possible answers include: El viernes estarán en Madrid y lloverá, por lo que irán al cine a la sesión de las ocho; El sábado irán de excursión a la Pedriza y hará buen tiempo. Allí pescarán y estarán al aire libre; El domingo estarán en Madrid y, como hará buen tiempo, irán por la mañana a la piscina y por la tarde al Museo del Prado.

OBJECTIVES FOR UNIT OPENER

- Introduce unit theme: *De cine*, about movies and theater
- Introduce culture for the unit: Learn about movies and theater

STANDARDS

- 1.1 Interpersonal communication
- 1.2 Understand the language
- 2.1 Practices and perspectives
- 4.2 Compare cultures

INSTRUCTIONAL STRATEGIES

- Introduce unit theme and objectives. Talk about the photo and have students state who they think the people are: **Son fans del cine**, **Están esperando la llegada de gente famosa**, **Están muy contentos**, etc.
- Have the students talk about themselves in the same context. Then have students work individually to write answers to the three questions on the page.
- Put students into pairs to share and discuss their answers.
- Call on volunteers to report back on their responses and discussions.
- Use the photograph to preview unit vocabulary: **¿Cuántos años crees que tienen? ¿Qué crees que van a hacer?**, etc.
- Ask related questions: **¿Tienes una cámara de video? ¿Te gusta hacer fotos? ¿Te gusta ir al cine? ¿Qué tipo de película te gusta más?**, etc.
- Help students formulate their ideas using **Tengo una cámara / un celular / una videocámara**, **Puedo hacer videos con mi celular**, **Mando fotos a mis amigos**, **Me gustan las películas de terror**, etc.

UNIDAD

3 DE CINE

¡Sonríe, que te están filmando!

》》 ¿Has filmado algún video con tus amigos o compañeros de clase?

》》 ¿Alquilas películas en un videoclub o las miras en tu computadora?

》》 Cuando eras pequeño, ¿cuál era tu película favorita?

88

ADDITIONAL UNIT RESOURCES

Extension Activities (EA) (Photocopiable)	Interactive Whiteboard Lessons (IWB)	Audio	Video	Online ELEteca
EA: 3.1, 3.2, 3.3	IWB: 3.1, 3.2	🎧 21 to 26	Diálogo 3	EXTENSIÓN DIGITAL

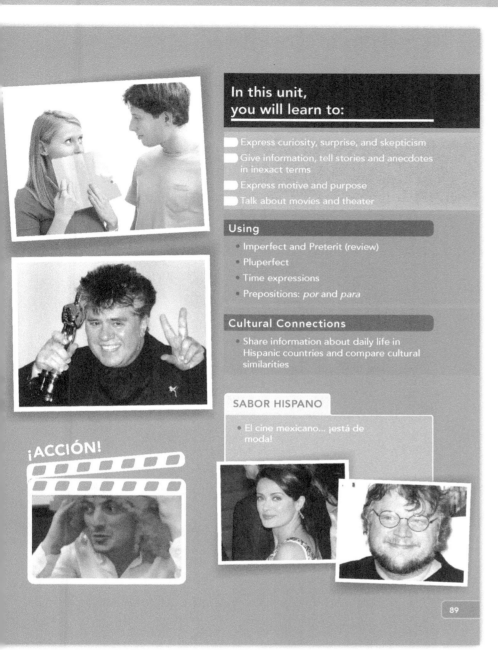

In this unit,
you will learn to:

- Express curiosity, surprise, and skepticism
- Give information, tell stories and anecdotes in inexact terms
- Express motive and purpose
- Talk about movies and theater

Using

- Imperfect and Preterit (review)
- Pluperfect
- Time expressions
- Prepositions: *por* and *para*

Cultural Connections

- Share information about daily life in Hispanic countries and compare cultural similarities

SABOR HISPANO

- El cine mexicano... ¡está de moda!

¡ACCIÓN!

89

LEARNING OUTCOMES

- Express curiosity, surprise and skepticism
- Give information and tell stories
- Express motive and purpose
- Talk about movies and theater
- Learn about daily life in Hispanic countries

INSTRUCTIONAL STRATEGIES

- Use unit opener to preview vocabulary and cultural topics for this unit.
- Have students look at the images on this page and relate them to the objectives listed. Ask questions such as: **¿Quiénes son estas personas? ¿Son famosos? ¿Por qué? ¿Qué tiene en la mano? ¿Cómo se siente?**, etc.
- Invite students to read the topic for **Sabor hispano** and preview that section in the unit. Ask questions such as: **¿Has visto alguna película mexicana? ¿Qué tipo de película era? ¿De acción, de miedo, romántica? ¿Qué actores o directores mexicanos conocen?**, etc.
- Ask students to anticipate what they think the episode for **¡Acción!** will be about. Ask: **¿Qué hace esta persona? ¿Qué tiene en la cabeza?**, etc.
- Have students work in pairs to talk about the images using the questions you have modeled. Then ask for volunteers to present to the class what they understand this unit to be about.

THREE MODES OF COMMUNICATION: UNIT 3			
	INTERPERSONAL	**INTERPRETIVE**	**PRESENTATIONAL**
HABLAMOS DE...		1, 2, 3, 4, 5, 6	1
COMUNICA	2, 4, 7	1, 5, 6	1, 3, 4, 7
¡ACCIÓN!	4	1, 2	3, 4
PALABRA POR PALABRA	1	2, 3, 4, 5, 6, 7	2, 4
GRAMÁTICA	4	1, 2, 3	4
DESTREZAS		1, 2, 3	
CULTURA		SABOR HISPANO	
RELATO		1, 2, 3	

OBJECTIVES FOR HABLAMOS DE...

- Understand language in context
- Preview vocabulary: Words and colloquial expressions relating to movies and theater
- Preview grammatical structures: Imperfect and preterit; Pluperfect; Time expressions; Prepositions **por** and **para**
- Read and listen to a conversation between two young people talking about a new theater workshop

CORE RESOURCES

- Audio Program: Track 21
- Interactive Whiteboard Lesson: IWB 3.1

STANDARDS

1.1 Engage in conversation
1.2 Understand the language
4.2 Compare cultures.

INSTRUCTIONAL STRATEGIES

Activity 1

- Ask students to talk about the people in the photos and describe what they see and what they think each represents. **¿Qué tipo de edificio creen que es? ¿Qué puede representar la estatua en número 3? ¿Qué están haciendo en número 4?**
- Have students work in pairs to answer and discuss the questions. Then ask: **¿Qué tienen todas las imágenes en común?** (**en todas hay un elemento relacionado con el cine o el teatro**). Guide students with questions to help them arrive at the same conclusion.

Activity 2

Have the students work individually to match the images to the correct description. Students will have an opportunity to confirm their answers in Activity 3.

Activity 3

- Explain to students that the headlines all appeared in the press and they should first try to match each headline to the appropriate image and then to a statement in Activity 2.
- Have students compare answers with a partner.
- Project IWB 3.1, **De cine y teatro** to review answers. Discuss each image and focus attention on the terms (**cine**, **teatro**, **director de cine**, **premio**, **taller de cine y teatro**). Make sure students understand the concept of **taller**. Explain as necessary in Spanish.

HABLAMOS DE... Cines y teatros

1 👥 **Look at the images below and talk with a partner about the following:**

- ¿Qué ves?
- ¿Reconoces a alguien?
- ¿Qué crees que pueden tener todas las imágenes en común?

2 Choose the best description for each of the images above.

- **a.** ☐ Es la entrega de un Oscar a un famoso director de cine español.
- **b.** ☐ Es un teatro en la capital uruguaya, Montevideo, que lleva el nombre del descubridor del Río de la Plata.
- **c.** ☐ Es un taller de teatro.
- **d.** ☐ Es un Goya, el premio de cine más prestigioso del cine español.

3 Match the letters of the statements in Activity 2 to the appropriate headline.

- **1.** ☐ Comienza el ciclo de teatro de vanguardia en el Solís.
- **2.** ☐ Este año las actividades extraescolares con más participación han sido los talleres de cine y teatro.
- **3.** ☐ La noche del cine español se viste de gala.
- **4.** ☐ Nunca antes un director español había pisado tantas veces la alfombra de Hollywood.

90

ANSWERS

Activity 2

a. 2; **b.** 1; **c.** 4; **d.** 3.

Activity 3

1. b; **2.** c; **3.** d; **4.** a.

4 🎧 21 **Listen to the conversation between Daniela and Ricardo as they discuss a new workshop at school. Fill in the blanks with the expressions you hear.**

Ricardo: ¿Te has enterado de los talleres de este curso? (a) .... van a ser totalmente diferentes.

Daniela: ¿(b) ....?

R.: Pues (c) .... han contratado a dos famosos para organizar un taller con el Departamento de Literatura.

D.: ¡(d) ....! Dos famosos trabajando en un instituto…

R.: Ya, pero, (e) ...., a estos los han elegido por su relación con la cultura y por su carrera profesional. He oído que son amigos de Paco, el de Literatura, parece que se conocieron cuando trabajaban juntos en una escuela de idiomas, creo que enseñaban español.

D.: ¡(f) ....! Dos profesores famosos, ¡(g) ....! Pero, (h) ...., que (i) .... ¿De qué es el taller? ¿Quién lo va a impartir (*teach*)?

R.: (j) ...., es un taller de cine y teatro…

D.: ¡(k) .... !

R.: La parte de cine la va a impartir la directora y guionista Anamar Orson y la parte de teatro el actor Cristian Pascual.

D.: ¿(l) ....? Pero si los dos son conocidísimos… ¡Cristian Pascual en el instituto! ¡(m) ....! ¿(n) ....?

R.: Sí, Daniela, sí, hablo en serio, aunque si quieres, llamamos para preguntar al Departamento de Literatura, porque no estoy demasiado seguro.

5 🎧 21 **Decide whether the statements are true (T) or false (F). Then listen to the conversation again and check your answers.**

	T	F
a. Daniela y Ricardo están hablando del nuevo profesor de Literatura.	☐	☐
b. Ricardo ha oído que este curso van a tener un taller de cine y teatro.	☐	☐
c. El taller lo va a impartir un importante director de cine.	☐	☐
d. El taller lo va a organizar el profesor de Literatura con dos amigos que son muy famosos.	☐	☐

6 **Select the expressions from the conversation (Activity 4) that communicate the meanings listed below. ¡*Atención!* Some meanings will have more than one example and some will not have any examples.**

1. Expresa sorpresa positiva o negativa. ➡ ....
2. Expresa seguridad. ➡ ....
3. No le interesa lo que le cuenta la otra persona. ➡ ....
4. Le parece difícil creer lo que le cuenta la otra persona. ➡ ....
5. Nunca dice quién le ha contado esa información. ➡ ..a... ....
6. Pide más información para continuar la conversación y expresa curiosidad. ➡ ..b... ....

91

INSTRUCTIONAL STRATEGIES

🎧 **21** **Activity 4**

- Inform the students that they are going to listen to a conversation between Daniela and Ricardo in which they talk about a new workshop.
- Tell students to close their books. Play the audio while the students listen.
- Ask how much they understood and have those who understood more explain what they heard.
- Play the audio again while the students follow in their books and fill in the missing words.
- Ask for volunteers to say the missing words and write them on the board.
- Explain vocabulary using examples in Spanish, for example: *impartir* (*dar clase*), *carrera* (*profesión*), *guionista* (*la persona que escribe la historia para la película*), etc.

🎧 **21** **Activity 5**

- Have the students read the sentences and decide whether they are true or false.
- Remind them to refer to the conversation in Activity 4 for help.
- Play the audio again for students to check their answers and tell them to correct the statements that are false.
- Review together as a class. Call on student volunteers to summarize the conversation.

Activity 6

- Help students understand the use of the expressions in the conversation. Explain that these expressions, in general terms, are either reactions to what was said or report information from unidentified sources. Ask students to identify examples for both types.
- Then review the descriptions in the activity and have students sort the expressions.
- Review answers by categories and write the examples on the board.

ANSWERS

Activity 4

a. He oído que; **b.** ¿Y eso?; **c.** parece que; **d.** ¡No me lo puedo creer!; **e.** según dicen; **f.** ¡Anda ya!; **g.** ¡imposible!; **h.** dime, dime; **i.** estoy intrigadísima; **j.** Al parecer; **k.** ¡Qué chévere!; **l.** ¿En serio?; **m.** ¡Qué fuerte!; **n.** ¿Hablas en serio?

Activity 5

a. falso (Están hablando sobre un nuevo taller de cine y teatro que se va a impartir en la escuela); **b.** verdadero; **c.** falso (La parte de cine la va a impartir la directora y guionista Anamar Orson y la parte de teatro el actor Cristian Pascual); **d.** verdadero.

Activity 6

1. d, k, l, m, n; **4.** d, f, g, l, n; **5.** a, c, e, j; **6.** b, h, i. (statements 2 and 3 do not have any examples).

OBJECTIVES FOR COMUNICA

- Present communicative functions of the unit:
  - Express surprise, skepticism, curiosity and give information
  - React to information you hear

CORE RESOURCES

- Extension Activities: EA 3.1
- Interactive Online Materials – ELEteca

STANDARDS

1.1 Engage in conversation
1.2 Understand the language
4.2 Compare cultures

INSTRUCTIONAL STRATEGIES FOR EXPRESSING SURPRISE, SKEPTICISM, CURIOSITY, AND GIVING INFORMATION

- Walk students through the explanations and ask them to comment on how the expressions were used in the conversation between Ricardo and Daniela.
- Say all the expressions using appropriate intonation for exclamations and interrogative expressions. Have the students repeat as necessary.

Activity 1

- Focus attention on the images and have the students look at the accompanying statements said by one of the people in the images.
- Guide students through a description of each scene and have them focus on what is being communicated in each.
- In pairs, the students take turns reacting to the situations with an expression from the section above.
- Circulate around the room as they speak, listening in and correcting pronunciation and intonation, or offering assistance where required.
- Invite different pairs to role-play a situation for the class.

Activity 2

- Have students divide into groups of three to create two more situations similar to those in Activity 1.
- The students take turns to role-play their situations.
- Invite some groups to perform for the class.
- You may choose to point out and ask students about the different verb tenses without getting into too much detail as these will be addressed more thoroughly in **Gramática**.

COMUNICA

EXPRESSING SURPRISE, SKEPTICISM, CURIOSITY, AND GIVING INFORMATION

- Para **dar una información** sin hablar de la fuente (*source*):
  - Pues parece que...
  - Según dicen...
  - ¿Te has enterado de...?
  - Al parecer...
  - He oído que...

- Para expresar **sorpresa**:
  - ¡Qué guay! (*sorpresa positiva*)
  - ¡Qué fuerte!
  - ¡No me digas!

- Para mostrar **interés** o **curiosidad** y pedir más información:
  - Cuenta, cuenta... / Dime, dime...
  - Estoy intrigadísimo/a.
  - ¿Y eso?

- Para expresar **incredulidad** y extrañeza:
  - ¡Anda ya!
  - ¡Imposible!
  - ¡No me lo puedo creer!
  - ¡Qué raro / extraño!
  - ¿(Hablas) En serio?

1 Look at the images below and take turns with a partner reacting to each situation. Choose from the expressions above and be prepared to justify your response as more than one expression could be right.

Esta semana ha llegado tarde cuatro veces.

Tengo que contarles algo muy fuerte que me pasó ayer.

Cuando mi abuela era joven ya usaba Internet.

El año pasado nadie suspendió Matemáticas.

¿Te has enterado de que este año no hay excursión de fin de curso?

El sábado conocí a una muchacha superinteresante.

2 Create two similar situations to present to a classmate for his/her reaction. Work in groups of three and take turns reacting to the situations presented.

3 📖 Write two experiences or situations on two pieces of paper about what you think other classmates did last week. Your partner will read the comment and react to it using one of the expressions already practiced. Then switch roles.

Modelo: E1 *(writes)*: Juan finalmente le ganó a Rosario en la competencia de Ciencias.
E2 *(reads and reacts)*: ¡No me lo puedo creer!

4 📖 Choose one of the following situations and present to your classmates. Then take turns listening and reacting to theirs.

Modelo: E1: Al parecer...
E2: Cuenta, cuenta...

Situación 1
• Ayer alguien tomó tus apuntes, hizo fotocopias y ahora los está vendiendo en Internet.

Situación 2
• Esta mañana te han llamado de tu compañía telefónica para informarte de que has ganado una computadora.

Situación 3
• Anoche cuando estabas en la cama escuchaste ruidos extraños en una casa vecina en la que no vive nadie.

Situación 4
• Ayer te pasó algo muy fuerte y todavía no se lo has dicho a nadie...

Situación 5
• Hoy el director de la escuela ha comunicado que este año no van a poder usar las computadoras en ninguna clase.

Situación 6
• Mañana tienen que empezar la primera clase de la mañana dos horas antes.

Situación 7
• Las navidades pasadas todos los compañeros de tu madre se hicieron millonarios, pero ella no, porque olvidó comprar la lotería de su empresa.

Situación 8
• ¡Las entradas que has comprado para el concierto son falsas!

Situación 9
• El viernes, en la clase de español, nos van a poner una película.

Situación 10
• Alguien dice que te vio en un centro comercial en horario de clase.

93

INSTRUCTIONAL STRATEGIES

Activity 3

- Read the model with the students and explain what they are to do.
- On separate pieces of paper, students write two experiences or situations about other classmates.
- Their partner reacts to the situation with an expression from the list.
- Then they change roles and the partner reads a situation.
- Ask for volunteers to perform for the class.

Activity 4

- Have the students read the situations in pairs or read them together as a class to ensure that students understand. See Cultural Note for more information about Situación 7. Explain that in Spain, the Christmas lottery is the largest one of the year and that people often buy tickets in large groups.
- Then have student pairs choose one each to perform for the class.
- Tell students to practice their conversation and to make sure each situation includes four exchanges. So in addition to reacting to the situation selected, students must add more information or details to elicit another reaction from their partner.
- When they are ready, invite them to perform for the rest of the class.

Cultural Note

- Explain to students that in Spain, the Christmas lottery also known as **el Gordo**, is the largest one of the year. Lottery tickets are printed with 5-digit numbers. Many organizations buy tickets and divide them up and sell them as participations to their customers or employees. In this way, the winnings from the number drawn are often shared among many participants, increasing everyone's chances for winning.
- Encourage students to research more about this historical national lottery that has been in place since 1812 and is the second oldest lottery in the world.

Extension

- Cut up situation cards from EA 3.1, **Situaciones** and put them face down for student pairs to select at random. Give students about 2 minutes to prepare and then have them perform the situation for the class.
- Set up categories for students to vote for the best, such as: Most believable, Most unbelievable, Best acting and reacting, Most exchanges, etc. Present the winning pairs with photocopy cutouts of **Premios Goya** as prizes.

OBJECTIVES FOR COMUNICA

- Present communicative functions of the unit:
Expressing purpose or motive of an action

STANDARDS

- 1.3 Engage in conversation
- 1.4 Understand the language
- 4.2 Compare cultures

INSTRUCTIONAL STRATEGIES FOR
EXPRESSING PURPOSE OR MOTIVE OF AN ACTION

- Introduce the topic by writing the following sentences on the board, leaving blanks as indicated: _____ **aprender español hay que viajar por países hispanos**, **Anoche cancelaron el concierto _____ la tormenta**. Ask students to fill in the blanks with **por** or **para**. Call on several students to give their answers without confirming which ones are correct. Ask students to try to explain why they chose **por** or **para**. In this way you introduce the general uses of **por** and **para**, motive for **por** and purpose, end goal for **para**.
- Point to **por** in the first sentence and explain that while the general rules are as stated, each preposition also can also have its own particular uses.
- Walk the students through the uses of **por** and **para** in the book.
- Ask a student to read the example in Spanish and another student to read the meaning in English.
- Focus attention on the extra information in the boxes.

Activity 5

- Students read the sentences and refer to the explanations above in order to fill in each blank with **por** or **para**.
- Ask for volunteers to say the correct answers and discuss any problems they may have encountered.
- Ask the students to point out which use of **por** or **para** from the explanation above was required in each case.

ANSWERS

Activity 5

a. para; **b.** por; **c.** Para; **d.** para; **e.** por.

COMUNICA

EXPRESSING PURPOSE OR MOTIVE OF AN ACTION

- Use **por** to express:
  - The **motive** behind an action
  *Los han elegido **por** su relación con la cultura y **por** su carrera profesional.* They were selected because of their association with culture and because of their professional careers.

- Other uses:
  - **Duration** of an event
  *Los Beatles triunfaron **por** los años sesenta.* The Beatles were successful in the seventies.
  - **Means** (teléfono, correo electrónico…)
  *Me enteré del premio de Ana **por** la tele.* I found out about Ana's prize on (by means of) television.
  - **Movement through**
  *Cuando miré **por** la ventana estaba lloviendo.* When I looked out (through) the window, it was raining.
  *Ana y Matilde han viajado **por** muchos países.* Ana and Matilde have traveled through many countries.
  - **Frequency**
  *Vamos al cine dos veces **por** semana (dos veces a la semana).* We go to the movies two times a week.

- Use **para** to express:
  - The **purpose**, **end goal** or **objective** behind an action
  *Han contratado a dos famosos **para** organizar un taller.* They have contracted two famous people to organize a workshop.

- Other uses:
  - **Deadline**
  *La tarea es **para** el próximo lunes.* The homework is due by next Monday.
  - **Recipient** of an action
  *Estos talleres son **para** estudiantes.* These workshops are for students.
  - **Opinion**
  Para mí, las películas románticas son muy aburridas. For me, romantic movies are very boring.

- Use an infinitive after **por**:
*Llegó tarde **por** estar en un atasco.* She arrived late due to being stuck in traffic.
- Use a conjugated verb after **porque** and **como** (since):
*Llegó tarde **porque** estuvo en un atasco.* She arrived late because she was stuck in traffic.
***Como** estuvo en un atasco, llegó tarde.* Since she was stuck in traffic, she arrived late.

- Use an infinitive after **para**:
*Estudió **para** ser directora de cine.* She studied in order to be a director.
- Other expressions that express **purpose**:
*Estudió **con el objetivo / el fin / la finalidad de** ser directora de cine.* She studied for the purpose of being / in order to be a movie director.

5 Fill in the blanks with *por* or *para*.
a. Esta carta no es .... mí, creo que ha habido un error.
b. Ayer el profesor de Matemáticas me riñó .... ser impuntual.
c. .... mi padre el cine comercial es de mala calidad.
d. Estudio español .... viajar por países hispanos.
e. Los documentos los enviaron .... correo electrónico.

6 Choose between *por* and *para* according to the context of the sentence. Then select the image most closely related to the sentence. ¡Atención! Not all of the sentences will have an image. Put an X for the sentence without an image.

1. ☐ Creo que el hotel está **por** / **para** el centro.
2. ☐ En vacaciones nos comunicamos **por** / **para** correo electrónico.
3. ☐ **Por** / **Para** los hispanos reunirse **por** / **para** comer es muy importante.
4. ☐ Tenemos que estar listos **por** / **para** las ocho.
5. ☐ Gracias **por** / **para** todo, estas flores son **por** / **para** ti.
6. ☐ Llamo **por** / **para** teléfono a mi abuela una vez **por** / **para** semana.
7. ☐ No me sonó el celular, es que estábamos pasando **por** / **para** un túnel.

7 Choose a role and complete the questions with *por* or *para*. Then use the questions to interview your partner.

Estudiante 1

a. ¿Qué haces .... mejorar tu español?
b. .... ti, ¿qué es mejor, ver una película en tu casa o en el cine?
c. ¿Has viajado mucho .... tu país?
d. ¿Cómo te comunicas más con tus amigos: .... Internet o .... teléfono?
e. ¿ .... quién piensas que deberían ser los descuentos en los teatros y los cines?

Estudiante 2

a. ¿Cuál es la mejor película .... ti?
b. ¿Cómo sueles entregar los trabajos de clase: .... correo electrónico o .... escrito?
c. ¿ .... quién piensas que se estrenan más obras de teatro?
d. ¿ .... qué países te gustaría viajar?
e. ¿Cuáles son los mejores consejos .... sacar buenas notas?

 Practice what you have learned with additional materials online.

INSTRUCTIONAL STRATEGIES

Activity 6

• Have students look at the images and read the sentences below.
• They choose **por** or **para** for each sentence.
• Then they decide which image is being referred to and write the number of the image in the box provided.
• The sentence that does not correspond with any image must be marked with an X.
• Have the students compare answers with a partner.
• Ask for volunteers to say the correct answers and identify the use for each.

Activity 7

• Have the students work in pairs and choose sentences in either *Estudiante 1* or *Estudiante 2*.
• Each student writes in **por** or **para** according to the meaning of the questions. Note that although each role has different questions, both sets contain the same uses so students can correct each other and discuss as needed.
• They interview each other using the completed questions.
• Circulate around the room as they talk, checking on correct usage of **por** and **para** and providing any assistance that may be required.
• Ask for volunteers to perform their interviews for the class.

ANSWERS

Activity 6

1. por, *movement through* (e); **2.** por, *means* (d); **3.** para, *opinion*, para, *purpose* (a); **4.** para, *deadline* (X); **5.** por, *motive*, para, *recipient* (c); **6.** por, *means*, por, *frequency* (f); **7.** por, *movement through* (b).

Activity 7

Estudiante 1: a. para; **b.** Para; **c.** por; **d.** por, por; **e.** Para.
Estudiante 2: a. para; **b.** por, por; **c.** Por; **d.** Por; **e.** para.

OBJECTIVES FOR ¡ACCIÓN!

- Provide students with a structured approach to viewing the video
- Contextualize the content of the unit in a familiar scenario

CORE RESOURCES

- Unit Video 3
- Interactive Online Materials – ELEteca

STANDARDS

1.5 Understand the language
2.1 Practices and perspectives
3.2 Acquire information
4.2 Compare cultures

INSTRUCTIONAL STRATEGIES

Previewing: Antes del video

Activity 1

Have students look at the frames and say what they think the video will be about. Ask the questions for each frame and have volunteers suggest answers.

Viewing: Durante el video

Activity 2

- Have students read the statements and listen for the information as they watch the video.
- Play the video without pauses.
- Answer any questions students may have about the vocabulary.
- Have the students write the letter of the statements in the appropriate category.
- Play the entire video again without pauses for them to confirm their answers.
- Ask for volunteers to give their answers.

Activity 3

- Ask students what they understood about the video.
- Have the students look at the questions and discuss their ideas with a partner.
- Play the video again and allow students to ask you to pause, as needed.

After viewing: Después del video

Activity 4

- In pairs, the students discuss who among their classmates would be best for each of the tasks listed.
- They write the names of the people for each task and provide a reason / reasons.
- Circulate while they work, providing assistance as required.
- Ask for volunteers to report their answers to the class.

¡ACCIÓN!

ANTES DEL VIDEO

1 Look at the scenes below from the video segment and answer the questions.

a. Estos dos estudiantes conocen en su escuela a dos personas famosas. ¿Qué crees que hacen dos famosos en una escuela?

b. Mira estas dos imágenes. Intenta descubrir a qué se dedican estos dos famosos.

c. ¿Alguna vez has recibido en tu escuela una clase especial o diferente? Habla con tu compañero.

DURANTE EL VIDEO

2 Decide which of the workshop coordinators is being described in the sentences below and write the letter in the appropriate category.

Anamar	Cristian	Los dos

a. Es actor.
b. Es directora de cine.
c. Vivió en Londres.
d. Trabajó en una escuela de español.
e. Conoce al profesor de Literatura.
f. Va a explicar cómo se hace una obra de teatro.
g. Está acostumbrado a hablar en público.
h. Hace mucho que no da una clase.

3 Answer the following questions.

a. ¿Por qué es diferente rodar una serie o una película a dar un curso a un grupo de jóvenes?
b. ¿Qué funciones tendrán los estudiantes en la obra de teatro?

DESPUÉS DEL VIDEO

4 Now stage your own play with a partner. Decide which classmates will be assigned to each task and explain why.

- Los directores serán .... porque ....
- Los guionistas serán .... porque ....
- Los decoradores serán .... porque ....
- Los actores serán .... porque ....

Practice what you have learned with additional materials online.

96

ANSWERS

Activity 2

Anamar: b, h; Cristian: a; Los dos: c, d, e, f, g.

Activity 3

a. Porque para dar un curso tienen que pensar en los estudiantes y no en el público y en los críticos como cuando filman una serie o una película;
b. Tendrán que hacer de actores, directores, guionistas, decoradores, etc.

PALABRA POR PALABRA El cine y el teatro   UNIDAD 3

1 👥 **With a partner, take turns talking about your preferences and experiences relating to movies and plays.**

- ¿Qué prefieres: el cine o el teatro?
- ¿Cuándo fuiste por última vez?
- ¿Qué obra de teatro o película viste?
- ¿Sobre qué trataba? ¿Te gustó?

2 **Review the words in the list below relating to movie and theater productions and list them under the appropriate category. Use each word only once.**

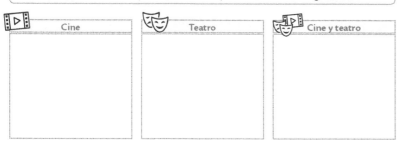

escenario ○ cámara ○ actor ○ director/a ○ guion ○ aplausos ○ interpretación
actriz ○ decorado ○ espectador/a ○ premio ○ escritor/a ○ obra ○
taquilla ○ telón ○ película ○ efectos especiales ○ festival ○ argumento

🎬 Cine	🎭 Teatro	🎬🎭 Cine y teatro

3 **Practice with the following word families to build vocabulary.**

a. Los protagonistas *protagonizan* una obra o película.
b. Los guionistas escriben el .... de una obra o película.
c. El telonero abre el .... en el teatro.
d. Los decoradores ganaron un premio por el .... de la obra.
e. Javier Bardem, uno de los intérpretes de la película, *No es país para viejos*, ganó un Oscar por su .... como Anton Chigurh.
f. Los espectadores aplaudieron a todos los actores de la obra, pero la actriz principal recibió los .... más fuertes.

97

OBJECTIVES FOR EL CINE Y EL TEATRO

- Present vocabulary needed to practice communicative and grammatical functions for the unit: Expressions relating to movies and theater
- Talk about the movie and theater industry and what people do

CORE RESOURCES

- Extension Activities: EA 3.2
- Interactive Online Materials – ELEteca

STANDARDS

1.1 Engage in conversation
1.2 Understand the language
1.3 Present information
3.2 Acquire information
4.1 Compare languages and cultures

INSTRUCTIONAL STRATEGIES

Activity 1

- Have students look at the images and express their preferences and routines regarding movies and plays. Ask the questions and have different students answer the question. It's important at this time to let students talk freely without correcting errors.
- Then have the students ask each other the questions in pairs.

Activity 2

- With books closed, write the following words on the board: **Cine**, **Teatro**, **Cine y teatro**.
- Have the students say words connected with these topics and classify them.
- Now have the students open their books and look at the vocabulary in the word bank. Tell them to add the new words to the headings on the board and discuss the meaning of any new words.
- The students copy the lists on the board into the columns in their books, using all the vocabulary in the box as well as any new words that may have been suggested.

Activity 3

- Have the students look at the activity and explain to them how words often come in 'families'.
- Read the model for them and show how ***protagonizar*** is connected with ***protagonista***.
- Ask for a volunteer to do the second sentence and ask the class if they agree.
- Now have them continue to work individually.
- When they have finished, ask them to share with a partner.

ANSWERS

Activity 2

Cine: cámara, guion, película, efectos especiales; **Teatro:** escenario, decorado, obra, telón; **Cine y teatro:** actor, director/a, aplausos, interpretación, actriz, espectador/a, premio, escritor/a, taquilla, festival, argumento.

Activity 3

a. protagonizan; **b.** guion; **c.** telón; **d.** decorado; **e.** interpretación; **f.** aplausos.

INSTRUCTIONAL STRATEGIES

Activity 4

- Look at the images and ask the students if they know or have seen any of these movies.
- Divide the class into groups of three and have each member of each group choose one of the movies.
- Focus attention on the chart at the foot of the page and tell the students that they are going to read about one of the movies and fill in the chart with the appropriate information for that movie.
- Check understanding of the terms in the chart and review the model with them.
- Now have them read the texts and begin to fill in the missing information, leaving the last point blank (***género***).
- If you like, distribute individual cards at random to each student in the group using EA 3.2, **De película**. Students can write the information on the back of their card.
- Circulate around the room as they work, providing assistance where required.
- When they have finished, they take turns asking and answering questions about 'their' movie, using the chart they have already completed.
- Invite volunteers to come to the front to tell the class about one of the movies.

ANSWERS

Activity 4

El laberinto del fauno

Nacionalidad: hispano-mexicana; **Año de estreno:** 2006; **Dirección:** Guillermo del Toro; **Protagonistas:** Ivana Baquero, Ariadna Gil, Maribel Verdú, Sergi López y Álex Angulo; **Lugares donde se rodó:** diferentes localizaciones rurales de España; **Género:** ciencia ficción / drama / histórica.

Los otros

Nacionalidad: española; **Año de estreno:** 2001; **Dirección:** Alejandro Amenábar; **Protagonistas:** Nicole Kidman; **Lugares donde se rodó:** en un pueblo de Cantabria; **Género:** terror.

El hijo de la novia

Nacionalidad: argentina; **Año de estreno:** 2001; **Dirección:** Juan José Campanela; **Protagonistas:** Ricardo Darín, Héctor Alterio y Norma Leandro; **Lugares donde se rodó:** Argentina; **Género:** drama / romántica.

PALABRA POR PALABRA

4 In groups of three, choose one of the following movies so that each of you has a different one. Read about the movie and complete the chart with the appropriate information. Then, take turns asking and sharing what you learned about the movie.

 En octubre de 2006 esta coproducción hispano-mexicana se presentó al público español en el Festival de Cine Fantástico de Sitges (Barcelona), pero meses antes ya había competido en Cannes. La película, escrita y dirigida por el mexicano Guillermo del Toro, fue filmada en diferentes localizaciones rurales de España. Protagonizada, entre otros, por Ivana Baquero, Ariadna Gil, Maribel Verdú, Sergi López y Álex Angulo, narra la historia de una niña que se traslada a un pueblo aragonés a vivir con su madre, recién casada con un militar franquista en plena represión de posguerra. La película sorprendió por la combinación de elementos propios del cine fantástico con uno de los episodios más dolorosos de la historia española.

 *Los otros* es considerada la película más taquillera del cine español. Obtuvo ocho premios Goya en su edición del año 2002, entre ellos el goya a la mejor dirección a Alejandro Amenábar. Un año antes ya había triunfado en las salas de EE. UU. En esta película, la famosa Nicole Kidman interpreta el papel de una madre obsesionada con proteger a sus hijos que viven en una enorme y oscura mansión. Un terrible secreto del pasado mantiene al espectador en un estado constante de suspense. Otro de los aspectos más valorados fue la atmósfera conseguida en el rodaje, una impresionante mansión ubicada en un pueblo de Cantabria, en el norte de España.

 Rafael dedica 24 horas al día a su restaurante, está divorciado, ve muy poco a su hija, no tiene amigos y no quiere comprometerse con su novia. Además, desde hace mucho tiempo no visita a su madre, internada en un geriátrico porque sufre el mal de Alzheimer. Una serie de acontecimientos inesperados le obligan a replantearse su vida. Entre ellos, la intención que tiene su padre de cumplir el viejo sueño de su madre: casarse por la Iglesia. Dirigida por Juan José Campanela en 2001 y protagonizada, entre otros, por Ricardo Darín, Héctor Alterio y Norma Leandro, esta producción argentina fue nominada al Oscar a la mejor película de habla no inglesa.

Modelo: E1: ¿De qué nacionalidad es la película...?
E2: Es...
E3: ¿Cuándo se estrenó?
E2: En el año...

> Nacionalidad: ....
> Año de estreno: ....
> Dirección: ....
> Protagonistas: ....
> Lugares donde se filmó: ....
> Género: ....

PALABRA POR PALABRA Géneros de cine   UNIDAD **3**

5 📖 Look at the following movie titles in Spanish. With a partner, classify the movies according to their genre or type. ¡Atención! They may fall into more than one category. Can you think of other examples?

- Rápido y furioso
- 12 años de esclavitud
- El señor de los anillos
- Star Trek: en la oscuridad
- El gran Gatsby
- Los juegos de hambre
- Carrie
- Mud
- Argo
- El reportero: la leyenda de Ron Burgundy

   comedia   drama   terror   romántica   ciencia ficción

    denuncia social   histórica   independiente   aventuras   acción

6 Fill in the blanks with the appropriate movie type that is being described.

a. No me gusta ir al cine para ver historias de amor tontas. Odio *(I hate)* esas películas .... tan típicas del cine comercial como *Querido John*. Prefiero sufrir un poco con las historias tristes y realistas de los .... como *Lee Daniels, el mayordomo*. Bueno, y también me gustan las películas ...., como *Argo*, donde puedes aprender sobre lo que sucedió en la historia reciente.

b. A mí me encanta pasar miedo viendo una peli de ...., como *Destino final*, o imaginar mundos de fantasía con una película de ...., como *El hobbit*. Otra opción para un viernes por la noche es reírse con una buena ...., como *Ladrona de identidades*. La risa es muy buena para la salud, por eso no me gustan las películas tristes.

c. Cuando voy al cine prefiero no pensar demasiado y divertirme, por eso no entiendo a la gente que odia el cine comercial. Dicen que el cine .... es muy artístico, pero muchas personas creemos que es demasiado serio y aburrido. En general, me gusta mucho el cine comercial, excepto las películas de ...., como *The Avengers: los Vengadores*, creo que son demasiado violentas.

7 Choose the best definition of the expressions in bold according to the context provided.

1. ≫ ¿Qué tal los exámenes?
   ≫ **Me ha ido de cine.**
   a. ☐ Me ha ido muy bien y lo he aprobado todo.
   b. ☐ Los resultados han sido normales.

2. ≫ ¿Vas a invitar a Matilde a tu fiesta?
   ≫ Es muy **cómica**.
   a. ☐ Es muy famosa.
   b. ☐ Es muy graciosa y divertida.

3. **¡No montes un drama!** Solo era un dólar.
   a. ☐ No exageres.
   b. ☐ No te preocupes.

4. Carlos es un **peliculero**.
   a. ☐ Filma películas.
   b. ☐ Es un poco mentiroso y exagerado.

  Practice what you have learned with additional materials online.

- Present vocabulary needed to practice communicative and grammatical functions for the unit: Movie types
- Talk about the types of movies you prefer

STANDARDS

- 1.1 Engage in conversation
- 1.2 Understand the language
- 1.3 Present information
- 3.2 Acquire information

INSTRUCTIONAL STRATEGIES

Activity 5

- Write the word ***género*** on the board and explain that this refers to types of movie.
- Ask the students to suggest movie types and write any correct ones on the board.
- Ask them to say the titles of movies of each type.
- When students have exhausted their ideas, add any remaining words from the types under the movie images and explain them if necessary.
- Have the students look at the list of movie titles and say which type they are, using the images and the list on the board to help them.
- Have them discuss the types of movies in pairs and add more examples in Spanish if they can.
- Ask students to report back to the class. List their responses on the board under the appropriate categories.
- Have students go back to the cards from Activity 4 and fill in the missing piece of information. Call on student volunteers to share and ask the class if they agree.

Activity 6

- Have students read the three short texts and fill in the missing words.
- Ask for volunteers to read the completed texts.

Activity 7

- Explain that many expressions have come into the language from movies.
- Have the students look at the examples in bold in this activity and select the best definition according to the context.

ANSWERS

Activity 5

Answers may vary. Possible answers include: **Comedia:** *El reportero: la leyenda de Ron Burgundy*; **Drama:** *Argo, 12 años de esclavitud*; **Terror:** *Carrie*; **Romántica:** *El gran Gatsby*; **Ciencia ficción:** *Star Trek: en la oscuridad*; **Denuncia social:** *12 años de esclavitud*; **Histórica:** *Argo, 12 años de esclavitud*; **Independiente:** *Mud*; **Aventuras:** *Los juegos de hambre, El señor de los anillos, Mud*; **Acción:** *Los juegos de hambre, Rápido y furioso*.

Activity 6

a. románticas, dramas, históricas; b. terror, aventuras, comedia; c. independiente, acción.

Activity 7

1. a; 2. b; 3. a; 4. b.

OBJECTIVES FOR GRAMÁTICA 1

- Present grammatical structures needed to practice communicative functions of the unit:
- Review of past tenses (preterit, imperfect and present perfect)
- Distinguish between the tenses and their uses

CORE RESOURCES

- Audio Program: Track 22
- Interactive Online Materials – ELEteca

STANDARDS

1.1   Engage in conversation
1.2   Understand the language
1.3   Present information
4.1   Compare languages

INSTRUCTIONAL STRATEGIES

1. Review of Past Tenses

- Have students go back to the conversation between Ricardo and Daniela on page 91 (Activity 4) and ask them to pick out all the verbs that refer to the past (**te has enterado, han contratado, han elegido, he oído, se conocieron, trabajaban, enseñaban**).
- Then have students say which tense is used for each verb and why. Provide cues to prompt their responses: does it refer to an action completed in the past, an ongoing or habitual action, or an action completed in the recent past?
- Walk students through the grammatical explanation in the book and review the sample sentences. Ask students what words or expressions help determine what tense to use (**anoche, cuando, este año**).

Activity 1

- Explain to students that most actions in stories are accompanied by time expressions so that we can understand when the action took place.
- Have the students read through the time expressions in the box and then the text. Ask them to explain what the message is about (**Cristian quiere hablar con Anamar sobre la posibilidad de colaborar en un taller de teatro con Paco**).
- Have them read through the text and fill in a correct time expression.
- Ask students to share their answers with a partner. Do not review answers with students yet.

🎧 22 Activity 2

- Play the audio for the students to correct their answers.
- Repeat the audio if necessary, pausing at each time expression.

ANSWERS

Activity 1

a. el otro día; **b.** entonces; **c.** En ese momento; **d.** luego; **e** .otra cosa.

GRAMÁTICA

1. REVIEW OF PAST TENSES

Preterit	Imperfect	Present Perfect
■ Use the preterit tense to talk about actions that were **completed** at a fixed point in the past. *Anamar **volvió** de Venecia anoche. Anamar returned from Venice last night.*	■ Use the imperfect to describe people, things or situations in the past, and to talk about ongoing or habitual actions in the past. *Cuando **vivian** en Madrid **estudiaban** juntos. When they lived in Madrid, they used to study together.*	■ Use the present perfect to say what a person **has done**. It describes actions completed in the recent past or in an unfinished period of time. *Este año Anamar **ha ganado** dos premios. This year Anamar has won two awards.*

1 Yesterday Cristian called Anamar, and left a message on her answering machine. Read what he said, and fill in the blanks with a time expression from the list.

> en ese momento ○ otra cosa ○ entonces ○ luego ○ el otro día

¡Anamar! Te he llamado mil veces esta semana. ¿Todavía no has vuelto de Berlín? Mira, te llamo para contarte que (a) .... quedé con Paco para tomar un café y me propuso colaborar en un taller de cine y teatro en su escuela. Yo acepté y (b) .... me sugirió organizarlo contigo. (c) .... dije que estabas muy ocupada, pero (d) .... pensé: "Solo van a ser cuatro semanas y siempre te ha encantado trabajar con jóvenes…" Ah, (e) ...., la respuesta tiene que ser urgente. Paco necesita confirmar nuestra colaboración para empezar a organizarlo.

2 🎧 22 Listen to the message and check your answers.

2. NARRATING IN THE PAST

3 Fill in the blanks with an expression from Activity 1 that fits the category.

■ To indicate when an action **approximately** takes place, use:	■ To indicate **continuity** or to **advance the story**, use:	■ To **add detail or specify additional information**, use:
• una vez • hace unos días / meses / minutos / años… • un día • .... •	• al principio • después • a continuación • más tarde • unos momentos después • .... •	• por cierto • ....

OBJECTIVES FOR GRAMÁTICA 2

- Present grammatical structures needed to practice communicative functions of the unit:
  Time expressions associated with past tenses
- Sequence actions in the past

STANDARDS

1.1   Engage in conversation
1.2   Understand the language
1.3   Present information

4 With a partner, prepare a conversation between Anamar and Cristian according to the information provided below. Then take turns role-playing the conversation with your partner.

Anamar
a. Llama a Cristian para responder a su mensaje de voz.
b. Acepta la propuesta del taller y pide disculpas por no responder antes. Cuéntale que anoche perdieron tus maletas en el aeropuerto, y que tuviste que esperar tres horas hasta que las encontraron. Llegaste al hotel muy tarde y no escuchaste el mensaje hasta hoy por la mañana.
c. Después pregunta a Cristian por Paco y reacciona ante la información que Cristian te da sobre él.

Cristian
a. Contesta a la llamada de Anamar y muestra alegría por hablar con ella.
b. Acepta las disculpas y reacciona ante la información de Anamar.
c. Coméntale a Anamar que este año Paco tiene un nuevo trabajo en una escuela y que está muy contento porque este curso el departamento lo ha elegido a él para organizar los talleres. Preséntale tu idea de organizar un taller de teatro y cine en esta escuela.

3. THE PLUPERFECT

■ We use the **pluperfect** or **past perfect** to talk about an action that took place before another action in the past. It is often referred to as the past within the past and corresponds to **had done** in English.

1.º Anamar llegó a Madrid a las 7:00h.

2.º Cristian dejó un mensaje a las 7:30h.

*Cuando Cristian dejó el mensaje, Anamar ya **había llegado** a Madrid.*
When Cristian left the message, Anamar had already arrived in Madrid.

■ The **pluperfect** is formed with the imperfect tense of **haber** and the past participle of the main verb.

		-AR	-ER	-IR
yo	había			
tú	habías			
usted/él/ella	había			
nosotros/as	habíamos	viaj**ado**	com**ido**	dorm**ido**
vosotros/as	habíais			
ustedes/ellos/ellas	habían			

101

◄ Previous Page

INSTRUCTIONAL STRATEGIES

2. Narrating in the Past

Activity 3

Read the information with the students and have them complete the chart with the time expressions from Activity 1 according to the context described in each heading.

ANSWERS

Activity 3

el otro día, en ese momento; entonces, luego; otra cosa.

INSTRUCTIONAL STRATEGIES

Activity 4

- Have the students prepare a conversation between Anamar and Cristian, using the guidelines provided.
- Have the students work in pairs and explain that Anamar is responding to Cristian's message. Anamar starts the conversation using the information in **a**. Cristian responds with the information on his card for **a** and so on.
- Circulate around the room as they work, listening in and providing assistance or correction where required. When they have practiced, invite pairs to perform the conversation for the class.

OBJECTIVES FOR GRAMÁTICA 3

- Present grammatical structures needed to practice communicative functions of the unit:
- The pluperfect tense
- Describe actions that took place before other actions in the past

CORE RESOURCES

- Extension Activities: EA 3.3
- Interactive Whiteboard Lesson: IWB 3.2

STANDARDS

- 1.2 Understand the language
- 1.3 Present information

INSTRUCTIONAL STRATEGIES

3. The pluperfect

- Walk the students through the explanation of the pluperfect. Focus attention on the images and the time line between Anamar's arrival at the airport and Cristian leaving her a message. Ask students when both actions took place (in the past) and which one happened first (Anamar's arrival).
- Emphasize the fact that the pluperfect is used to represent an action before another action in the past, and is often introduced by the word *ya*.

INSTRUCTIONAL STRATEGIES

- Draw attention to the fact that the past participles are those the students used in the present perfect, including all the irregulars.
- Ask the students to remember the irregular past participles: say **romper** and have them respond **roto**, etc.
- Have them look at the irregular past participles in the recycle box to check and confirm their ideas.

Activity 5

- Have the students focus on the information about the career of Anamar Orson.
- Read the introduction and have different students read each of the subsequent points. Pause to explain any unfamiliar words or expressions.
- Have the students read the sentences below the information and fill in the blanks with the correct form of the verb given, in the preterit or pluperfect as required.
- Remind them that the pluperfect is always the first action in time, or the oldest action, and that is not necessarily the first action in the sentence.
- Write the following examples on the board: *When Annie had finished her work, she left the office. Mark opened the letter after the mailman had disappeared down the road.* Ask the students to underline the actions in both sentences and number them according which action came first and which came second.
- Now have them fill in the blanks in the sentences.
- Have them share their answers with a partner.
- Ask for volunteers to read the correct answers.
- If necessary, write the sentences on the board and underline and number the actions as above.

Extension

- Distribute cut up copies of EA 3.3, **El pluscuamperfecto** to student pairs and tell students to arrange the fragments into complete sentences. Help students get started by telling them the order of the cards: pink, green, blue.
- Project IWB 3.2, **El pluscuamperfecto** to review answers. Ask students to identify which action occurred first (in blue). Ask students to explain the expressions in red (time frame).

ANSWERS

Activity 5

a. escribió, había comenzado; b. había escrito; c. terminó, había dejado; d. se hizo, se había cambiado.

GRAMÁTICA

- To form the past participle of a verb, drop the ending of the infinitive and add **–ado** for **–ar** verbs and **–ido** for **–er** / **–ir** verbs.

- Some verbs have irregular past participles.

  - abrir ➡ **abierto**
  - decir ➡ **dicho**
  - descubrir ➡ **descubierto**
  - escribir ➡ **escrito**
  - hacer ➡ **hecho**

  - morir ➡ **muerto**
  - poner ➡ **puesto**
  - romper ➡ **roto**
  - ver ➡ **visto**
  - volver ➡ **vuelto**

5 **Anamar is speaking at a performing arts workshop. First read the information about her career, and then fill in the blanks, using the preterit or the pluperfect. *¡Atención!* Think about what action happened before another one according to her timeline.**

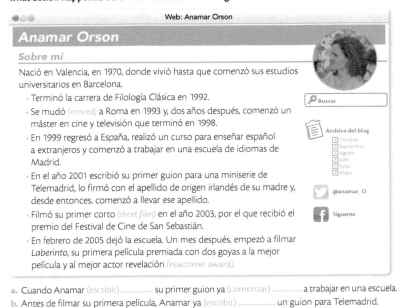

Web: Anamar Orson

Anamar Orson

Sobre mí

Nació en Valencia, en 1970, donde vivió hasta que comenzó sus estudios universitarios en Barcelona.

- Terminó la carrera de Filología Clásica en 1992.
- Se mudó *(moved)* a Roma en 1993 y, dos años después, comenzó un máster en cine y televisión que terminó en 1998.
- En 1999 regresó a España, realizó un curso para enseñar español a extranjeros y comenzó a trabajar en una escuela de idiomas de Madrid.
- En el año 2001 escribió su primer guion para una miniserie de Telemadrid, lo firmó con el apellido de origen irlandés de su madre y, desde entonces, comenzó a llevar ese apellido.
- Filmó su primer corto *(short film)* en el año 2003, por el que recibió el premio del Festival de Cine de San Sebastián.
- En febrero de 2005 dejó la escuela. Un mes después, empezó a filmar *Laberinto*, su primera película premiada con dos goyas a la mejor película y al mejor actor revelación *(newcomer award)*.

Buscar

Archivo del blog

@anamar_O

Sígueme

a. Cuando Anamar (escribir) .... su primer guion ya (comenzar) .... a trabajar en una escuela.
b. Antes de filmar su primera película, Anamar ya (escribir) .... un guion para Telemadrid.
c. Cuando (terminar) .... de filmar *Laberinto*, Anamar ya (dejar) .... la escuela de idiomas.
d. Cuando Ana se (hacerse) .... famosa por su primera película ya (cambiarse) .... el apellido.

 Practice what you have learned with additional materials online.

DESTREZAS

COMPRENSIÓN DE LECTURA

1 Before you read the text, review the strategy in Destrezas and follow the suggestions.

Destrezas

Focusing on relevant information

When reading about a topic that may be unfamiliar to you, use the following steps and include any notes.

1. Read the entire text to get a general idea of the topic.
2. Read each paragraph and highlight or list the main topic *(theme)* or subject *(person who performs the action)* as there could be more than one.
3. Look at each question. Is it asking about a topic or a person performing an action? Do you need a subject, a complement, a motive, a temporal expression, etc., to complete the sentence?
4. Go back to the highlighted text of the list you made for 2, look for information, and answer the question.
5. Remember that the question order follows the sequence of the information as it is presented in the text.

2 Read the text, and then choose the best answer to the questions.

XII EDICIÓN DE JÓVENES TALENTOS CINEMATOGRÁFICOS
Una apuesta por el cine más actual

El pasado 4 de marzo se celebró el duodécimo certamen de jóvenes talentos cinematográficos. Al evento asistieron no solo directores y actores noveles, sino que contó con la presencia de un buen número de veteranos que acudieron a interesarse por el trabajo de las nuevas generaciones.

Este año la Academia de las Artes y las Ciencias Cinematográficas de España, organismo dependiente del Ministerio de Cultura, ha contado con un presupuesto mucho más bajo que en años anteriores, por lo que, después de unos meses de muchas dudas, ha conseguido celebrar su duodécima edición con la ayuda de la publicidad de empresas privadas.

En la apertura del acto, la presentadora, Amelia Guillén, agradeció la colaboración de estas empresas patrocinadoras y pidió al público un fuerte aplauso para los más de 300 candidatos a los diferentes premios.

Antes de entregar el primer premio, Amelia Guillén dedicó unas palabras a todos los profesionales anónimos del séptimo arte, técnicos de sonido, cámaras, maquilladores, decoradores… "todos ellos absolutamente imprescindibles, pero invisibles para la gran mayoría del público", señaló la presentadora.

1. Al certamen acudieron…
   a. actores y directores jóvenes únicamente.
   b. actores y directores de diferentes generaciones.
   c. actores y directores de diferentes partes del mundo.

2. Este año el certamen ha estado en peligro…
   a. por las pocas ayudas recibidas del Estado.
   b. porque había pocas empresas patrocinadoras.
   c. por la falta de candidatos.

103

- Focus on relevant information

STANDARDS

1.1 Interpersonal communication
1.2 Understand the language
1.3 Present information

INSTRUCTIONAL STRATEGIES

Comprensión de lectura

Activity 1

- Talk the students through the strategy for focusing on relevant information.
- Answer any questions they may have at this stage.
- Have the students follow the instructions in the order they are set out. They should make notes.

Activity 2

- Ask the students to read the text and choose the best way to complete each statement.
- Have them use their notes and the instructions above to help them.
- When they have finished, have them compare answers with a partner.
- Ask for volunteers to say the correct answers.

ANSWERS

Activity 2

1. b (Al evento asistieron no solo directores y actores noveles, sino que contó con la presencia de un buen número de veteranos); **2.** a (Este año la Academia de las Artes y las Ciencias Cinematográficas de España, organismo dependiente del Ministerio de Cultura, ha contado con un presupuesto mucho más bajo que en años anteriores, por lo que, después de unos meses de muchas dudas, ha conseguido celebrar su duodécima edición con la ayuda de la publicidad de empresas privadas); **3.** c (En la apertura del acto, la presentadora, Amelia Guillén, agradeció la colaboración de estas empresas patrocinadoras); **4.** c (Antes de entregar el primer premio, Amelia Guillén dedicó unas palabras a todos los profesionales anónimos del séptimo arte, técnicos de sonido, cámaras, maquilladores, decoradores…).

INSTRUCTIONAL STRATEGIES

Activity 3

- Have the students read the information in the **Destrezas** box again and have them make notes for the text in this activity.
- Ask for volunteers to read the text aloud and pause to explain any unfamiliar words or expressions.
- Have the students answer the questions below the text.
- When they have finished, have them share their answers with a partner.
- Ask for volunteers to say the answers aloud for the class to correct.

ANSWERS

Activity 3

1. b (El 11 de octubre de 1896, Eduardo Jimeno Correas filmó *Salida de la misa de doce de la iglesia* con la primera cámara Lumière que un año antes había comprado en Lyon, Francia); **2.** a (El siglo XX comenzó con una producción de cine experimental, representado por directores como Luis Buñuel que, con impactantes películas como *Un perro andaluz*, consiguió el prestigio internacional y cierto escándalo en España); **3.** c (Las películas contrarias a la dictadura se censuraban, o simplemente se prohibían); **4.** b (A partir de los años ochenta comienza un gran periodo para el cine español. Directores como Pedro Almodóvar, José Luis Garci y Montxo Armendáriz, entre otros, iniciaron en estos años sus carreras y las desarrollaron con éxito nacional e internacional).

DESTREZAS

3. Amelia Guillén dio las gracias…
   a. a todos los participantes al certamen.
   b. al público que asistió a la ceremonia del certamen.
   c. a las empresas que colaboraron económicamente en el certamen.

4. La presentadora del certamen…
   a. pidió un gran aplauso a los profesionales anónimos.
   b. se emocionó al entregar el primer premio.
   c. reconoció el trabajo de profesionales del cine no conocidos por el público.

3 Read the following text and apply the same strategy as in Activity 1 before answering the questions that follow.

BREVE HISTORIA DEL CINE ESPAÑOL

El 11 de octubre de 1896, Eduardo Jimeno Correas filmó *Salida de la misa de doce de la iglesia* con la primera cámara Lumière que un año antes había comprado en Lyon, Francia. Un año después, el barcelonés Fructuós Gelabert filmó *Riña en un café*, la primera película española con argumento. El siglo XX comenzó con una producción de cine experimental, representado por directores como Luis Buñuel que, con impactantes películas como *Un perro andaluz*, consiguió el prestigio internacional y cierto escándalo en España.

Cuando en 1928 llegó el cine sonoro a España, pocas productoras habían desarrollado medios técnicos para realizar películas, esto provocó una crisis en la producción de trabajos cinematográficos.

Posteriormente, el cine producido durante la dictadura del General Francisco Franco fue, en general, un medio de propaganda de las ideas políticas, morales y religiosas oficiales. Las películas contrarias a la dictadura se censuraban, o simplemente se prohibían.

A partir de los años ochenta comienza un gran periodo para el cine español. Directores como Pedro Almodóvar, José Luis Garci y Montxo Armendáriz, entre otros, iniciaron en estos años sus carreras y las desarrollaron con éxito nacional e internacional. Además, en 1986 se fundó la Academia de las Artes y las Ciencias Cinematográficas, organismo encargado de la organización de los famosos premios Goya y que ha promocionado y difundido los méritos del cine producido en este país. En la actualidad son muchos los directores españoles con éxito y reconocimiento internacional.

1. La primera película española…
   a. fue de ficción.
   b. se filmó a la salida de una iglesia.
   c. se filmó con una cámara fabricada en España.

2. Las películas de Luis Buñuel tuvieron proyección internacional…
   a. pero no se entendieron muy bien en España.
   b. provocaron una crisis cinematográfica.
   c. fueron censuradas durante la dictadura de Franco.

3. El gobierno del dictador Francisco Franco…
   a. promocionó películas de cine experimental.
   b. estableció la Academia de las Artes y las Ciencias Cinematigráficas.
   c. prohibió películas contrarias a la dictadura.

4. El director Montxo Armendáriz inició su carrera profesional…
   a. durante la dictadura de Franco.
   b. en los años ochenta.
   c. en 1986 cuando fundó la Academia de las Artes y las Ciencias Cinematigráficas.

104

PRONUNCIACIÓN La letra *h*

1 As you know, in Spanish, the letter *h* is not pronounced (*hola, hoy, hablar*). Read the following information about when to use *h* when spelling in Spanish.

Se escriben con *h*:

Grupo 1
Las palabras que empiezan por **hue–, hie–, hui–**: *huevo, hierba, huida.*

Grupo 2
Las palabras que empiezan por los prefijos **hidro–, hiper–, hipo–, homo–, hetero–, heli–**: *hidrógeno, hipermercado, hipopótamo, homogéneo, heterogéneo.*

Grupo 3
La mayoría de las palabras que empiezan por **hosp–, horm–, horn–, herm–, hern–**: *hospital, hormiga, horno, hermético, hernia...* Hay excepciones como: *Ernesto, ermita.*

Grupo 4
Otras palabras se escriben con ***h*** por derivación de palabras de la misma familia: *habitante, habitar, habitación...*

2 🎧 **23** Listen to a series of words and write the number under the appropriate category in which they fall.

Grupo 1	Grupo 2	Grupo 3	Grupo 4

■ In Spanish there is a group of words or expressions that sound the same, but have different meanings. Here are some examples of homophones.

a (preposition)	**ha** (verb **haber**)	
ay (exclamation)	**hay** (verb **haber**)	**ahí** (adverb)
haber (verb)	**a ver** (preposition + verb)	
hecho (verb **hacer**)	**echo** (verb **echar**)	
hola *(greeting)*	**ola** *(wave, noun)*	

3 🎧 **24** Fill in the blanks with the homophones listed above. Then listen to the conversation and check.

a. Mónica .... vuelto .... Madrid.

b. ¿Ves estos libros de cine tan bonitos? Creo que los van .... vender todos y no va ....
   haber más hasta el próximo mes.

c. ¡ ...., Isaac! Quita la computadora de ...., ¿no ves que no .... espacio suficiente?

d. ¡ ...., Sergio! ¿Has visto qué .... tan buenas .... para hacer surf?

e. Otra vez he .... una tortilla horrible, siempre le .... demasiada sal.

Practice what you have learned with additional materials online.

105

OBJECTIVES FOR PRONUNCIACIÓN

• Practice pronouncing and spelling words containing the letter *h*

CORE RESOURCES

• Audio Program: Tracks 23 and 24
• Interactive Online Materials – ELEteca

STANDARDS

1.2 Understand the language
3.2 Acquire information
4.1 Compare languages

INSTRUCTIONAL STRATEGIES

Activity 1

Walk the students through the explanation and ask them to think of more examples for each group. Write the words on the board in their groups and make a special note to one side of any more exceptions.

🎧 **23** **Activity 2**

• Tell the students they are going to hear a series of words and they are to write them in the appropriate column according to which group they are in.
• Play the audio and have the students listen and repeat, and then write the word in the correct column.
• Repeat the audio and have the students confirm their answers.
• Repeat the audio if required.
• Ask random students to say which group each word is in.
• Read the note about homophones and have the students say the words so they can hear that they are pronounced the same in spite of being spelled differently.

Audioscript

1. habitual; **2.** helicóptero; **3.** había; **4.** hidroeléctrico; **5.** hiedra; **6.** hielo; **7.** hipersensible; **8.** homologar; **9.** honrado; **10.** hormonas; **11.** huele; **12.** huésped.

🎧 **24** **Activity 3**

• Introduce homophones by writing the following sentence on the board: ***El tren que llega _a las cuatro todavía no _a llegado***. Ask: ***¿Cuál de las dos "a" lleva hache?*** Review the examples in the box and clarify new vocabulary.
• Have the students read the sentences and fill in the missing homophones.
• Students work individually and then share their answers with a partner.
• Play the audio for students to confirm answers. Then ask for volunteers to read the completed sentences as you record them on the board.

ANSWERS

Activity 2

Grupo 1: 5, 6, 11, 12; Grupo 2: 2, 4, 7, 8; Grupo 3: 10, 9; Grupo 4: 1, 3.

Activity 3

a. ha, a; **b.** a, a; **c.** Ay, ahí, hay; **d.** Hola, olas, hay; **e.** hecho, echo.

OBJECTIVES FOR SABOR HISPANO

- Learn about the Mexican movie world
- Activate vocabulary connected with movies

CORE RESOURCES

- Audio program: Track 25

STANDARDS

2.1   Culture: practices and perspectives
2.2   Products and perspectives
3.2   Acquire information
5.2   Using language for personal enjoyment and enrichment

INSTRUCTIONAL STRATEGIES

🎧 25

- Introduce the topic by asking if the students know any Mexican actors / actresses / directors / movies.
- Look at the images with them and elicit what they already know and can share.
- Put students into pairs. Have them discuss the questions in the **Antes de leer** box. Encourage them to take notes about their partners' responses. Monitor their conversations and assist as needed.
- Have students switch partners and tell their new partners about their previous partners' responses. Monitor their conversations and assist as needed.
- Tell the students to look at the **Glosario** on the next page to help them with any vocabulary they may not know.
- Read the first section of the text and invite volunteers to read the questions.
- After each section, ask questions such as: **¿Qué tipo de películas le gustaban de niño? ¿Dónde estudió? ¿Cuándo filmó su primera película?**, etc.
- Ask what the students have understood and invite those who understood more to help those who understood less.
- Call on student volunteers to role-play the parts of interviewer and Guillermo del Toro.

SABOR HISPANO

EL CINE MEXICANO...
¡ESTÁ DE MODA!

El actor mexicano Diego Luna atiende las entrevistas de los periodistas.

Antes de leer
¿Qué tipo de películas te gustan?
¿Has visto alguna película en español? ¿Cuál?

🎧 25   **El cine en español, y en especial el mexicano, tiene cada vez más presencia en los festivales y cines internacionales. Lee estos extractos de entrevistas al director Guillermo del Toro.**

¿Cuándo supo que se quería dedicar al cine?
De niño crecí viendo películas de animación japonesas. Todas eran de monstruos japoneses y robots pilotados por humanos. Desde entonces quise contar historias a través de imágenes.

¿Cuándo comenzó?
Cuando estudiaba en el Instituto de Ciencias de Guadalajara comencé a filmar y a los 21 años filmé mi primera película. En esa época también fundé el Festival de Cine de Guadalajara.

¿Cuál es su especialidad?
La verdad es que no tengo ninguna. He filmado películas basadas en cómics, películas de terror, películas históricas, de fantasía, de ciencia ficción...

¿Cuáles son sus películas más importantes?
Sin duda, *El laberinto del fauno* y *El espinazo del diablo*.

¿Por qué?
Porque me dieron a conocer* en muchos países. A partir de ese momento comencé a trabajar en proyectos más ambiciosos e interesantes. Esas dos películas son muy queridas por mí... Tienen una temática que me interesa: en ellas hablo de la niñez* y de la política, y utilizo elementos fantásticos.

¿A qué otros directores mexicanos admira?
Admiro mucho a Luis Mandoqui porque tiene personalidad.

¿Dónde vive?
Ahora vivo en Los Ángeles, Estados Unidos. México es mi hogar pero Los Ángeles es la cuna* del cine.

¿Qué proyectos futuros tiene?
Estoy estudiando una propuesta para desarrollar *El increíble Hulk*, una historia basada en los cómics de Marvel.

Guillermo del Toro, en la presentación de la película *Don't be Afraid of the Dark*.

106

Estas son las películas más taquilleras del cine moderno mexicano

- No se aceptan devoluciones
- Nosotros los nobles
- El crimen del padre Amaro
- El laberinto del fauno
- Como agua para chocolate

Estos son los 5 actores mexicanos más famosos

- Salma Hayek
- Gael García Bernal
- Diego Luna
- Paulina Rubio
- Camila Sodi

La actriz mexicana Salma Hayek, en la alfombra roja del Festival de Cannes.

¿COMPRENDISTE?

Decide if the following statements are true (T) or false (F).

1. Diego Luna y Luis Mandoqui trabajan en el cine. T ◯ F ◯
2. Guillermo del Toro está orgulloso de *El espinazo del diablo.* T ◯ F ◯
3. Los Ángeles es el centro de la industria cinematográfica. T ◯ F ◯
4. Salma Hayek es una directora de cine importante. T ◯ F ◯
5. La película mexicana que ha conseguido más dinero es *No se aceptan devoluciones.* T ◯ F ◯

El director mexicano Luis Mandoqui, en una entrevista.

AHORA TÚ

What do you think? Answer the following questions and discuss your ideas with other students.

1. ¿Has visto alguna película de Guillermo del Toro? ¿Qué te ha parecido?

2. ¿Qué cualidades piensas que son importantes para contar historias a través del cine?

3. ¿Qué otros medios son buenos para contar historias?

4. ¿Qué se necesita para ser un buen actor?

5. ¿Qué películas te han marcado"? ¿Por qué?

Glosario

la cuna – cradle
dar a conocer – to become known
marcar – to influence
la niñez – childhood
taquillera – box office hit

Fuentes: *El País, La Vanguardia*, Prezi.com, Cineactual, *Fotogramas*, YouTube, *El Mundo*, Canal100.mx

107

INSTRUCTIONAL STRATEGIES

Las películas más taquilleras

- Call on a volunteer to read the title and description of the graph. Ask students to explain what *taquillera* means and to give examples of American movies that fit the description.
- Ask one or two questions to check students' understanding of the chart information, such as: **¿Conocen alguna de las películas de la lista? ¿Han visto alguna de ellas?**
- Ask students if they recognize any of the titles and can provide them in English. (*Instructions Not Included, We Are the Nobles, The Crime of Father Amaro, Pan's Labyrinth, Like Water for Chocolate*).

Los 5 actores mexicanos más famosos

- Call on a volunteer to read the title and description of the chart.
- Go online to project images of these actors. Ask students if they recognize any of them and if they can name any movies in which they appeared.

¿Comprendiste?

- Have the students read the statements in the box and check true or false. Then have them check through the text to see if they are correct.
- Have them compare their answers with a partner.
- Invite individual students to share their answers with the class.

Ahora tú

- Read the questions with the students and have them think about the answers.
- Have the students answer the questions in pairs or small groups and then ask for volunteers to present to the class.

ANSWERS

1. T; 2. T; 3. T; 4. F; 5. T.

OBJECTIVES FOR RELATO

- Revisit unit themes, grammar, vocabulary and culture in a new context
- Improve reading comprehension skills

CORE RESOURCES

- Audio Program: Track 26

STANDARDS

1.1. Engage in conversation
1.2 Understand the language
1.3 Present information
2.1 Culture: Practices and perspectives
5.3 Using language for personal enjoyment and enrichment

INSTRUCTIONAL STRATEGIES

Activity 1

- Have the students look at the image and title and guess what they think the text will be about. Ask them if they can name any other Hispanic poets or playwrights (or American ones).
- Introduce the poet and playwright, Federico García Lorca, and tell students that they are going to learn more about his life and works. Say to students: **Federico García Lorca nació en 1898 y murió en 1936. ¿Cuántos años tenía cuando murió?** (**38 años**), **¿Por qué creen que murió tan joven? ¿Estaba enfermo?** Then tell students they will find possible answers in the text, but to save their ideas for the end of the section when they will know more about Lorca.
- Before students begin to read, explain that the text is incomplete and that for now they should just read it for general understanding. Have students read through the text and write a summary statement and heading for each paragraph.
- Have them share their ideas with a partner.
- Discuss the themes and symbols in Lorca's works and share the following note with students.

Cultural Note

La simbología de Lorca es muy compleja y no tiene una sola interpretación, ya que depende del tema concreto de la obra. Dicho esto, se aceptan las siguientes interpretaciones: los elementos de la naturaleza y atmosféricos (el viento y el agua en movimiento, por ejemplo) como símbolo de libertad; el color verde: la muerte o la rebeldía; el negro: la represión, la falta de libertad y el fanatismo religioso; el caballo puede simbolizar la muerte, pero también la energía e incluso lo masculino; el rojo: la sangre, el dolor o la pasión; la luna representa la muerte, pero también la esterilidad; las flores: la felicidad; la sangre: los instintos; las palomas: la masculinidad…

Activity 2

- Have the students look through the text to find the numbers.
- Have them read the sentences and decide where each sentence should appear in the text. They write the number in the space provided.
- Have the students discuss their answers with a partner.

ANSWERS

Activity 2

a. 4; b. 1; c. 5; d. 3; e. 2.

RELATO Lorca y la Generación del 27

1 **Read about the famous Spanish poet and playwright, Federico García Lorca.**

Lorca y la Generación del 27

Federico García Lorca fue un escritor andaluz perteneciente a la Generación del 27, (1). La mayoría de los miembros del grupo estudió la obra de los clásicos españoles, publicó en las mismas revistas, vivió en la Residencia de Estudiantes y cultivó una literatura basada en la mezcla (*mixture*) de lo popular (*common*) y de lo culto (*cultured*), de lo tradicional y de lo moderno y miraba a su entorno (*surroundings*) español y al ámbito universal.

Lorca, como casi todos sus compañeros, apoyó (*supported*) públicamente las reformas democráticas de la Segunda República, en especial las dedicadas a la cultura y la educación, (2).

Cuando en 1939 Franco ganó la guerra civil muchos de estos escritores tuvieron que huir (*flee*) al extranjero por miedo a la represión del nuevo gobierno fascista. (3). Algún tiempo antes Lorca había recorrido España con *La Barraca* y había viajado a Nueva York y a Argentina, país en el que continuó con sus obras de teatro.

Sus poemas más conocidos son *Romancero Gitano* (1928), *Poeta en Nueva York* (1930) y *Poema del cante jondo* (1931). (4) (en todas se producen conflictos entre las normas establecidas y la libertad). Sus temas son el amor, la muerte, el destino, la soledad, la frustración, la tradición, el campo… Sus personajes favoritos, la mujer, los gitanos (*gypsies*), los niños y los marginados. Escribió con un cuidado estilo, tradicional y vanguardista al mismo tiempo, (5)…

2 **Read the following sentences extracted from the text and match them to the number in the text where they should appear.**

a. ☐ Sus obras de teatro más famosas son *Bodas de sangre* (1933), *Yerma* (1934) y *La casa de Bernarda Alba* (1936)

b. ☐ un grupo de escritores que compartieron experiencias y características literarias comunes.

c. ☐ y su lenguaje sigue siendo muy investigado por sus enigmáticos símbolos: la luna, el caballo, el agua, los gitanos

d. ☐ Federico García Lorca no tuvo tanta suerte (*luck*) y murió asesinado en 1936, el mismo año en el que estalló (*broke out*) la guerra civil

e. ☐ y fundó (*founded*) la compañía teatral *La Barraca* con la que estuvo dirigiendo e interpretando diversas obras de teatro por toda la geografía española

*108

3 🎧 **26** Read the following passages from two of Lorca's most well-known plays and identify the title of the play according to the descriptions that follow.

a	b
Bernarda: Niña, dame un abanico. **Amelia:** Tome usted. (*Le da un abanico redondo con flores rojas y verdes*). **Bernarda:** (*Tirando el abanico al suelo*). ¿Es este el abanico que se da a una viuda? Dame uno negro y aprende a respetar el luto de tu padre. **Martirio:** Tome usted el mío. **Bernarda:** ¿Y tú? **Martirio:** Yo no tengo calor. **Bernarda:** Pues busca otro, que te hará falta. En ocho años que dure el luto no ha de entrar en esta casa el viento de la calle. Haceros cuenta que hemos tapiado con ladrillos puertas y ventanas. Así pasó en casa de mi padre y en casa de mi abuelo.	(*Mira hacia la puerta*). **Yerma:** ¡María! ¿Por qué pasas tan deprisa por mi puerta? **María:** (*Entra con un niño en brazos*). Cuando voy con el niño, lo hago… ¡Como siempre lloras…! **Yerma:** Tienes razón. (*Toma al niño y se sienta*). **María:** Me da tristeza que tengas envidia (*envy*). (*Se sienta*). **Yerma:** No es envidia lo que tengo; es pobreza. **María:** No te quejes. **Yerma:** ¡Cómo no me voy a quejar cuando te veo a ti y a las otras mujeres llenas por dentro de flores, y viéndome yo inútil en medio de tanta hermosura!

Yerma

Obra teatral de Federico García Lorca que narra la historia de Yerma, una joven campesina que sufre porque desea tener un hijo. La directora Pilar Távora adaptó la obra y en 1999 se estrenó en el cine.

La casa de Bernarda Alba

Fue la última obra de teatro de Lorca. En ella Bernarda, mujer tradicional y autoritaria, encierra a sus hijas jóvenes en casa tras la muerte de su marido. La obra se llevó al cine en 1987 en una película del director Mario Camus.

4 Answer the following questions about Lorca's style according to the passages you read.

a. ¿Qué características de la obra de Lorca observas en los textos?
b. ¿Qué tienen en común ambas obras?

INSTRUCTIONAL STRATEGIES

🎧 **26** Activity 3

• Write the word **yerma** on the board and explain what it means: **inhabitado**, **incultivado**, **que no tiene cultivo ni labor** (*barren* in English). Project the image for the movie posters and point to the first one. Ask students, **¿A cuál de las dos creen que se refiere el título?**
• Next ask about the women in **La casa de Bernarda Alba** and ask: **¿Cuál es la relación entre esas mujeres? ¿Qué personalidades pueden tener?**
• Have the students read the brief information about the two plays, **Yerma** and **La casa de Bernarda Alba** below the excerpts to learn more about them.
• Tell students to read the passages from the two plays and decide which is which.
• Have them compare their answers with a partner.
• Play the audio while the students listen with books closed.
• Play the audio again as students follow in their books.
• Ask different students to say the correct answers aloud.

Activity 4

• Ask students to read the questions and discuss the answers in pairs.
• Ask for volunteers to express their ideas to the class.
• As a follow-up, ask students: **¿Cómo creen que se llaman los personajes presentados como "Señora" y "Chica joven y guapa"?** (**Bernarda Alba es la señora y Yerma es la chica joven y guapa**).

Extension

Go back to the question posed at the beginning of the lesson and ask students for their ideas regarding his death. Entertain different versions without confirming any just yet. Instead, encourage students to research online to learn what happened.

ANSWERS

Activity 3

　　a. *La casa de Bernarda Alba*; **b.** *Yerma*.

Activity 4

　　a. Personajes femeninos, la frustración, las tradiciones (como el luto), la falta de libertad…; **b.** Las dos son obras de teatro de Lorca, tienen personajes femeninos y han sido adaptadas al cine. También tienen argumentos de historias duras de falta de libertad y represión y ambas muestran un lenguaje lleno de símbolos.

OBJECTIVES FOR EVALUACIÓN

- Review grammar, vocabulary and culture from the unit
- Complete self-assessment

CORE RESOURCES

- Interactive Online Materials – ELEteca

STANDARDS

1.2 Understand the language
2.1 Practices and perspectives
4.1 Compare cultures

INSTRUCTIONAL STRATEGIES

- Activities can be completed individually and then reviewed with the class. Vary by asking students if they agree with the answer given and then writing it on the board. Provide explanations as needed.
- You may wish to assign point value to each activity as a way for students to monitor their progress.
- Direct students to the indicated pages in **En resumen** if they make more than one or two mistakes in any one section.

ANSWERS

Activity 1

1. c; **2.** a; **3.** d; **4.** b.

Activity 2

a. Como no sonó el despertador, llegué a clase tarde; **b.** El partido se canceló porque llovía; **c.** La película tuvo muy mala crítica por su violencia; **d.** Para mejorar las instalaciones, la biblioteca estará cerrada una semana.

Activity 3

a. por; **b.** por; **c.** por; **d.** por; **e.** para.

Activity 4

Answers will vary. Possible answer:
El otro día Daniela me llamó por teléfono para ir al cine. Pero media hora antes había hablado con Ricardo para ver una película en mi casa y entonces le comenté el plan y al final quedamos en mi casa.

EVALUACIÓN

EXPRESSING SURPRISE, SKEPTICISM, CURIOSITY, AND GIVING INFORMATION

1 **Match each sentence to its appropriate response.**

1. Los materiales del taller son gratis. .... •
2. ¡Han robado las cámaras del taller! .... •
3. Han publicado las notas del examen de español. .... •
4. Te aseguro que te envié el correo. ¿De verdad que no lo has recibido? •

- **a.** ¡Qué fuerte! Las compraron ayer.
- **b.** No, ¡qué raro!
- **c.** ¡Qué guay!
- **d.** ¡Anda ya!, si lo hicimos ayer.

EXPRESSING PURPOSE OR MOTIVE OF AN ACTION

2 **Rewrite the following sentences using the words in parenthesis. Make changes as needed.**

a. Llegué tarde a clase porque no sonó el despertador. (como) ....

b. El partido se canceló por la lluvia. (porque) ....

c. La película tuvo muy mala crítica debido a su violencia. (por) ....

d. Con el objetivo de mejorar las instalaciones, la biblioteca estará cerrada una semana. (para) ....

USING POR AND PARA

3 **Fill in the blanks with por or para as needed.**

a. El estreno de su primera película fue .... mayo.
b. Mis padres van al cine una vez .... semana.
c. Mi sueño es poder viajar .... el mundo.
d. Gracias .... todo.
e. Es una película muy fuerte, no es adecuada .... todas las edades.

NARRATING IN THE PAST

4 **Look at the following timeline of events and write a short story about what happened. Use the time expressions and the information below to help you develop your story. ¡Atención!** Today is Monday.

| media hora antes ○ y entonces ○ al final ○ El otro día |

- Había hablado con Ricardo para ver una película en mi casa (viernes, 5:00h)
- Le comenté el plan (viernes, 5:35h)
- Quedamos en mi casa (viernes, 8:00h)
- Daniela me llamó para ir al cine (viernes, 5:30h)

Modelo: El otro día Daniela me llamó...

REVIEW OF PAST TENSES

5 **Write the correct form of the verb in parenthesis in the past. Use the preterit, imperfect, present perfect, and past perfect (pluperfect) as needed.**

Cristian (a) .... (nacer) en 1971 en Bilbao, ciudad en la que (b) .... (realizar) sus estudios de Bellas Artes *(Fine Arts)*. Tres meses antes de terminar la carrera *(degree)*, (c) .... (decidir) que quería ser actor y (d) .... (mudarse) a Londres para perfeccionar su inglés y estudiar interpretación. Durante el tiempo en que (e) .... (vivir) en Londres, por las mañanas (f) .... (estudiar) Arte Dramático y por las tardes (g) .... (enseñar) español. Encontró ese trabajo con la ayuda de Paco, un profesor de español que (h) .... (conocer) antes de subir al avión en Madrid. En 1999 (i) .... (trasladarse) a Madrid, donde (j) .... (continuar) trabajando como profesor de español, de nuevo con Paco, que ya (k) .... (regresar) a España un año antes. En la escuela (l) .... (conocer) a Anamar y en el año 2002 (m) .... (actuar) por primera vez en una serie de televisión que (n) .... (escribir) su compañera Anamar el verano anterior. Por esta serie se hizo muy famoso y desde entonces no (ñ) .... (parar) de trabajar en cine, televisión y teatro. De hecho, se rumorea que últimamente (o) .... (recibir) varias ofertas de algunos de los directores más prestigiosos del mundo del cine.

EL CINE Y EL TEATRO

6 **Complete the sentences with a word or expression relating to the movies or the theater.**

a. Un tipo de cine más relacionado con el arte que con la taquilla es el cine ....
b. Cuando he tenido un gran día o todo me ha salido bien digo que me ha ido ....
c. Cuando vamos al cine para ver una .... podemos escuchar muchas carcajadas de risa.
d. Para comprar los boletos de una peli o una obra tienes que pasar por la ....

THE LETTER *H*

7 **Choose the correct option.**

a. Quita el bolso de **hay** / **ahí** / **ay**, no es un lugar seguro.
b. Esta semana hemos **hecho** / **echo** muchos exámenes.
c. Hoy es un poco peligroso bañarse en el mar con estas **holas** / **olas**.
d. Corren porque creen que no va a **ver** / **haber** entradas.

CULTURA

8 **Answer the following questions with the information you learned in *El cine mexicano*.**

a. ¿Quién es Guillermo del Toro y cuál ha sido su trayectoria?
b. ¿Qué tipo de películas captó su imaginación como niño? ¿Tiene alguna especialidad?
c. ¿Qué actores mexicanos ya conocías de la lista que se presentó? Y de las películas, ¿conocías alguna?
e. ¿Crees que los directores mexicanos están de moda? Explica.

 Practice what you have learned with additional materials online.

ANSWERS

Activity 5

a. nació; **b.** realizó; **c.** decidió; **d.** se mudó; **e.** vivió; **f.** estudiaba; **g.** enseñaba; **h.** había conocido; **i.** se trasladó; **j.** continuó; **k.** había regresado; **l.** conoció; **m.** actuó; **n.** había escrito; **ñ.** ha parado; **o.** ha recibido.

Activity 6

a. independiente; **b.** de cine; **c.** comedia; **d.** taquilla.

Activity 7

a. ahí; **b.** hecho; **c.** olas; **d.** haber.

Activity 8

Answers may vary. **a.** Guillermo del Toro es director de cine. Nació en México y filmó su primera película a los 21 años. Sus películas más taquilleras son *No se aceptan devoluciones* y *Nosotros los nobles*; **b.** De niño le gustaban mucho las películas japonesas de animación.

OBJECTIVES FOR EN RESUMEN: VOCABULARIO

- Review unit vocabulary and expressions
- Practice communicative skills

STANDARDS

1.2 Understand the language
1.3 Present information
4.1 Evaluate similarities and differences in language

INSTRUCTIONAL STRATEGIES

- Encourage students to use self-adhesive notes to place on correct objects in their house.
- Index cards can be used as flashcards with the Spanish term on one side and the English term on the other, or a picture or drawing.
- Students work in pairs or groups, using vocabulary flashcards as they would the cards of a board game to help each other practice unit vocabulary.
- Encourage students to write labels or captions for the photos on this page. Remind them to use the vocabulary and expressions they have learned in this unit.

EN RESUMEN: Vocabulario

Cine y teatro

la alfombra de Hollywood *the red carpet*
el aplauso *applause*
el argumento *plot, story line*
la cámara *camera*
el cámara *cameraman*
el cineasta *filmmaker*
la comedia *comedy*
el corto *short film*
el decorado *set*
el decorador *set designer*
el director de cine *film director*
el drama *drama*
los efectos especiales *special effects*
la escena *scene*
el escenario *stage*
el escritor *writer*
el espectador *spectator*
el estreno *premiere*
el guionista *scriptwriter*
la obra *work*
la obra de teatro *play*
la película de aventuras *adventure*
la película de ciencia ficción *science fiction*
la película de denuncia social *social protest*
la película de terror *horror movie*
la película histórica *historical film*
la película independiente *indie*
el premio *award*
el protagonista *leading actor*

el rodaje *film shoot*
el taller de teatro *performing arts workshop*
la taquilla *box office*
el telón *curtain*
la trayectoria *career*

Verbos

abrir *to open*
escribir *to write*
estrenar *to release*
filmar *to shoot*
interpretar *to perform*
protagonizar *to have the leading role*
rodar *to shoot*
vestirse de gala *to dress for a special event*

Marcadores temporales

a continuación *next*
al principio *in the beginning*
después *after*
el otro día *(the) other day / another day*
en ese momento *at that time*
entonces *then*
hace unos días / meses / años... *days / months / years ago...*
luego *then*
más tarde *later*
por cierto *by the way*
un día *one day*
una vez *once*
unos momentos después *moments later*

Para dar una información

Pues parece que... *Well, it seems that...*
Al parecer... *Apparently...*
Según dicen... *According to what they are saying...*
He oído que... *I have heard that...*

¿Te has enterado de...? *Have you noticed / realized that...*

Para mostrar interés o curiosidad

Dime, dime... *Tell me, tell me...*
Estoy intrigadísimo/a. *I'm so intrigued.*
¿Y eso? *What's that about?*

Para expresar sorpresa

¡Qué guay! *cool*
¡Qué fuerte! *pretty rough*
¡No me digas! *You must be kidding!*

Para expresar incredulidad

¡Anda ya! *Go on now!*
¡No me lo puedo creer! *I can't believe it!*
¡Qué raro / extraño! *How weird / strange!*
¿(Hablas) En serio? *Are you serious?*

Coloquialismos

de cine *Awesome, amazing*
montar un drama *to make a fuss*
ser peliculero/a *to be a show off*
ser muy protagonista *to be self centered*
ser cómica *to be funny*

112

EN RESUMEN: Gramática

PAST TENSES (REVIEW)

(See page 100)

INTERPRETAR			
	PRETERIT	IMPERFECT	PRESENT PERFECT
yo	interpreté	interpretaba	he interpretado
tú	interpretaste	interpretabas	has interpretado
usted/él/ella	interpretó	interpretaba	ha interpretado
nosotros/as	interpretamos	interpretábamos	hemos interpretado
vosotros/as	interpretasteis	interpretabais	habéis interpretado
ustedes/ellos/ellas	interpretaron	interpretaban	han interpretado

Preterit

- Use the preterit tense to talk about actions that were **completed** at a fixed point in the past.
  *Anamar **volvió** de Venecia anoche. Anamar returned from Venice last night.*

Imperfect

- Use the imperfect to describe people, things or situations in the past, and to talk about ongoing or habitual actions in the past.
  *Cuando **vivían** en Madrid **estudiaban** juntos. When they lived in Madrid, they used to study together.*

Present Perfect

- Use the present perfect to say what a person **has done**. It describes actions completed in a recent past or in an unfinished period of time.
  *Este año Anamar **ha ganado** dos premios. This year Anamar has won two awards.*

PLUPERFECT OR PAST PERFECT TENSE

(See page 101)

- Use the pluperfect to talk about an action that took place before another past action.
- To form the pluperfect tense:

	IMPERFECT TENSE OF *HABER*	PAST PARTICIPLE	IRREGULAR PAST PARTICIPLES	
yo	había			
tú	habías		abierto	muerto
usted/él/ella	había	viajado	dicho	puesto
nosotros/as	habíamos	comido	descubierto	roto
vosotros/as	habíais	dormido	escrito	visto
ustedes/ellos/ellas	habían		hecho	vuelto

OBJECTIVES FOR EN RESUMEN: GRAMÁTICA

- Review unit grammar
- Practice communication skills

STANDARDS

- 1.2 Understand the language
- 1.3 Present information

INSTRUCTIONAL STRATEGIES

- Model how to review grammar.
- Have the students review the Learning Outcomes in the unit opener to assess whether they feel they have mastered the main ideas and skills.
- Ask them if they can remember additional examples for each grammar topic.
- Model how to find and go back to the appropriate page in the unit to review any grammar topic they may need help with.
- Invite students to review the grammar activities they completed in this unit.
- Ask them what grammar activities they found easy and which they found challenging. Encourage them to rework any activities they found particularly challenging.

Objectives for Unit Opener

- Introduce unit theme: ***¡Superespacio!***, about healthy lifestyles and giving advice
- Introduce culture for the unit: Learn about pop culture and teen magazines in the Hispanic world

Standards

1.1 Interpersonal communication
1.2 Understand the language
2.1 Practices and perspectives
4.2 Compare cultures

Instructional Strategies

- Introduce unit theme and objectives. Talk about the photo and have students state who they think the people are: ***Son compañeras de clase***, ***Una de ellas tiene una revista***, ***Están mirando la revista***, etc.
- Have the students discuss the questions and talk about themselves in the same context.
- Use the image to preview unit vocabulary: ***¿Cuántos años crees que tienen? ¿Qué crees que van a hacer?***, etc.
- Ask related questions: ***¿Compran alguna revista regularmente? ¿Les gustan las revistas? ¿Qué tipo de artículos hay en las revistas que leen?***, etc.
- Help students formulate their ideas using ***A veces / todas las semanas / cada dos semanas compro una revista***, ***Me gustan los artículos sobre la moda joven***, etc.

UNIDAD 4

¡SUPERESPACIO!

Tres amigas comparten la lectura de una revista.

⟫ ¿Qué tipo de revista crees que están leyendo?
⟫ ¿Sueles leer revistas? ¿Cuáles te interesan más?
⟫ ¿Prefieres leerlas en formato impreso o digital?

114

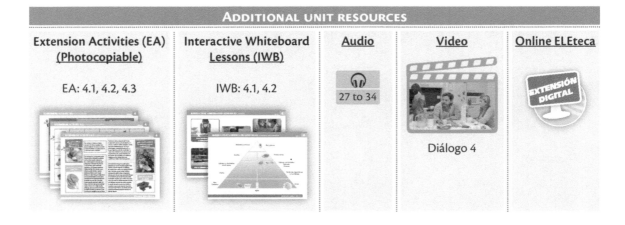

ADDITIONAL UNIT RESOURCES				
Extension Activities (EA) (Photocopiable)	**Interactive Whiteboard Lessons (IWB)**	**Audio**	**Video**	**Online ELEteca**
EA: 4.1, 4.2, 4.3	IWB: 4.1, 4.2	🎧 27 to 34		EXTENSIÓN DIGITAL
			Diálogo 4	

**In this unit,
you will learn to:**

☐ Ask and give advice and recommendations
☐ Ask for permission and favors
☐ Express probability or hypothesis in the past
☐ Talk about food and health

Using

• The Conditional

Cultural Connections

• Share information about pop culture and teen magazines in Hispanic countries and compare cultural similarities

SABOR HISPANO

• La dieta mediterránea... ¿mito o realidad?

¡ACCIÓN!

LEARNING OUTCOMES

• Ask and give advice and recommendations
• Ask for permission and favors
• Express probability or hypothesis in the past
• Talk about food and health
• Share information about pop culture and teen magazines in Hispanic countries

INSTRUCTIONAL STRATEGIES

• Use unit opener to preview vocabulary and cultural topics for this unit.
• Have students look at the images on this page and relate them to the objectives listed. Ask questions such as: *¿Qué tipo de revista es esta? ¿Ven a alguna persona famosa? ¿Qué hace este muchacho en la segunda imagen? ¿Dónde está?*, etc.
• Invite students to read the topic for **Sabor hispano** and preview that section in the unit. Ask questions such as: *¿Qué tipo de comida les gusta más? ¿Qué ingredientes ven aquí? ¿Cómo se llama este plato? ¿Qué ven en la botella?*, etc.
• Ask students to anticipate what they think the episode for **¡Acción!** will be about. Ask: *¿Quiénes son? ¿Dónde están? ¿Creen que van a comer o que ya han comido?*, etc.
• Have students work in pairs to talk about the images using the questions you have modeled. Then ask for volunteers to present to the class what they understand this unit to be about.

115

THREE MODES OF COMMUNICATION: UNIT 4			
	INTERPERSONAL	**INTERPRETIVE**	**PRESENTATIONAL**
HABLAMOS DE...		1, 2, 3, 4, 5	6
COMUNICA	4	1, 2, 3, 5, 6, 7	4, 6, 8
¡ACCIÓN!	1, 4	2, 3	3
PALABRA POR PALABRA	4, 7	1, 2, 3, 5, 6	4, 7
GRAMÁTICA	8	1, 3, 4, 5, 6	2, 7, 8
DESTREZAS		1, 2	
CULTURA		SABOR HISPANO	
RELATO		1, 2, 3, 4	2, 5

OBJECTIVES FOR HABLAMOS DE...

- Understand language in context
- Preview vocabulary: Talking about pop culture, food and health
- Preview grammatical structures: The conditional
- Read and listen to a conversation between two girls talking about the latest issue of a teen magazine

CORE RESOURCES

- Audio Program: Track 27

STANDARDS

1.1 Engage in conversation
1.2 Understand the language
4.2 Compare cultures

INSTRUCTIONAL STRATEGIES

Activity 1

- Tell students to talk about the people in the photos on the magazine cover and say what they are doing and where they are or who they are. Ask students for the name of these types of magazines in Spanish (**revistas del corazón**, **la prensa rosa**, **los cotilleos**). Ask if they are famous and what kind of TV program or movie they think each one appears in.
- Then ask: **¿Leen este tipo de revistas? ¿Quiénes suelen aparecer en ellas? ¿Qué temas suelen tratar?**, etc.
- Have students complete the activity individually.

Activity 2

- Have the students look at the images from the magazine cover and match each one to a description.
- Ask random students to read a sentence and other students to give the corresponding answer.

Extension

Go online and project other teen magazine covers in Spanish. Discuss the topics on the cover. You may choose to use some of these magazines to motivate students to read more about topics that interest them.

Cultural Note

En gran cantidad de revistas, tanto de adultos como de jóvenes, se especula bastante sobre las relaciones amorosas de la gente famosa. Ejemplos de revistas españolas para adolescentes son la revista *SuperPop* y la revista *Bravo*. *People en español*, en Estados Unidos.

ANSWERS

Activity 1

1. c; **2.** b; **3.** a; **4.** a.

Activity 2

b; c; a; d.

HABLAMOS DE... Revistas juveniles

1 Look at the images and articles included, and choose the correct option.

1. La imagen representa...
   a. ☐ una revista de moda.
   b. ☐ una revista de cocina.
   c. ☐ una revista para jóvenes.

2. Maruchi es...
   a. ☐ actriz.
   b. ☐ cocinera.
   c. ☐ bailarina.

3. ¿Qué tipo de programa crees que es *Amor en directo*? Un programa...
   a. ☐ para encontrar pareja *(partner)*.
   b. ☐ de canciones de amor.
   c. ☐ de cotilleos *(gossip)* de amor.

4. Mónica Pérez es...
   a. ☐ una famosa actriz.
   b. ☐ una cocinera.
   c. ☐ la participante de un concurso para encontrar pareja.

2 Select the letter of the image from the cover that corresponds to the following headlines.

☐ **Parece ser que el amor está en el aire. Varios rumores circularon días atrás sobre la famosa pareja, aunque esta foto parece confirmar que se aman.**

☐ **Una receta infalible: descúbrela con nuestra cocinera favorita.**

☐ **"De pequeño ya sabía que quería ser actor", confiesa.**

☐ **Josefa y Benjamín se conocen en el plató, ¿habrá flechazo?**

3 🎧 ²⁷ **Listen to the conversation between Lucía and Carla about the latest issue of** *SuperEspacio* **and choose between the two girls to respond to the questions below.**

	Carla	Lucía
a. ¿Quién está muy "enamorada" de Maxi Castro?......................	☐	☐
b. ¿Quién sabe más sobre la vida de Mónica Pérez?......................	☐	☐
c. ¿A quién no le gusta la comida sana?......................	☐	☐
d. ¿Quién pide ayuda para contestar un test?......................	☐	☐
e. ¿Quién cree que la entrevista tiene mucha información sobre la vida de Maxi?....	☐	☐

4 **Now read the conversation and answer true (T) or false (F). If a statement is false, give the correct information, according to the conversation.**

Lucía: Mira, Carla, las fotos que trae esta semana *SuperEspacio*. Hay una entrevista a Maxi Castro.

Carla: ¿Maxi Castro? ¡Ay!, Lucía, déjame ver... Yo estoy enamoradísima de ese actor... Es tan guapo y tan simpático.

Lucía: Mira... también viene un test para saber si conoces bien la vida de Maxi... Y si aciertas *(answer correctly)* todas las preguntas, participas en el sorteo *(sweepstake)* de un viaje a París, la ciudad del amor. ¿Podrías ayudarme?

Carla: Claro, yo conozco todos los secretos de la vida de Maxi. De todos modos, yo que tú primero leería la entrevista y después contestaría el test. Seguro que esa entrevista contiene mucha información.

Lucía: ¿Has visto que parece que Mario Medina y Mónica Pérez están juntos?

Carla: ¿Mónica Pérez es la actriz de la película *La soga*?

Lucía: Carla, deberías estar más informada... Es la actriz de la serie *Sombras*. Es la que hace el papel *(role)* de mala.

Carla: Bueno, vale. También sale la cocinera esa de *Salud al día*, el programa de televisión... A mi madre le encanta y en casa nos lo pone todos los días.

Lucía: A mí no me saques de las hamburguesas y las papas fritas. Odio las verduras.

Carla: ¿En serio? No me lo puedo creer. Pues deberías comer más verdura. Es muy buena para la salud.

	T	F
a. Maxi Castro es un cantante muy famoso.	☐	☐
b. *Salud al día* es un programa de cocina sana.	☐	☐
c. La actriz Mónica Pérez es protagonista en una serie de televisión.	☐	☐
d. La cocinera y el actor tienen un romance.	☐	☐

INSTRUCTIONAL STRATEGIES

🎧 **27** Activity 3

- Tell the students they are going to listen to a conversation between Lucía and Carla about the latest issue of *SuperEspacio*.
- Have the students read the questions and tell them they have to decide which of the two girls is speaking for each question.
- Play the audio with books closed.
- Have the students open their books and play the audio again while they check the boxes.
- Ask for volunteers to give the correct answers.

Activity 4

- Now have the students look at the true or false statements in their books.
- Have them read the dialogue and check the boxes.
- Ask them to compare their answers with a partner.
- Play the audio again as they follow in their books, pausing at the answers to the questions for them to confirm.

ANSWERS

Activity 3

a. Carla; **b.** Lucía; **c.** Lucía; **d.** Lucía; **e.** Carla.

Activity 4

a. falso (Maxi Castro no es cantante, es actor); **b.** verdadero; **c.** verdadero; **d.** falso (El actor Mario Medina tiene un romance con la actriz Mónica Pérez, y no con la cocinera Maruchi).

INSTRUCTIONAL STRATEGIES

Activity 5

- Have the students focus on the sentences marked in bold in the conversation.
- Tell them that they contain a new tense: the conditional.
- Have them connect the expressions with the uses of the conditional on the right.
- Remind them to refer to the conversation in Activity 4 for help.
- Ask for volunteers to say the correct answers.

Activity 6

- Provide context for students before they discuss the questions with a partner. Engage students in a conversation about these magazines and ask: **¿Qué piensan de las personas que salen en estas revistas? ¿Por qué creen que reciben tanta atención? ¿Es por su talento, su comportamiento, su apariencia física? ¿Es fácil hacerse famoso? ¿Les gustaría ser famosos? ¿Qué ventajas o desventajas creen que tiene la fama?** Note answers on the board as necessary to guide students in their discussion later.
- Have the students look at the magazine covers illustrated.
- Ask questions such as: **¿Reconocen a esta persona? ¿Cómo se llama?**
- Now have them ask and answer the questions in pairs.
- Circulate around the room to check that students are on task, provide support, and correct students as needed.

Extension

Have students go online and research some of the people on the covers and report back to the class on what they discovered. Who is the person, what does he/she do, why is he/she famous, why is he/she appearing in this issue.

ANSWERS

Activity 5

1. b; 2. a; 3. a; 4. a.

HABLAMOS DE...

5 Read the conversation again and focus on the expressions in bold. Can you recognize the verbs? These verbs are conjugated in a new tense. Connect the sentences with the explanations for using the conditional tense.

1. ¿Podrías ayudarme? .... •
2. Yo que tú leería la entrevista y después contestaría el test. .... •
3. Deberías estar más informada... .... •
4. Deberías comer más verdura. .... •

- a. Para dar una recomendación o un consejo.
- b. Para pedir un favor.

6 Look at the following magazine covers. Then with a partner, take turns answering the following questions about them.

a. ¿Qué tipo de revistas son?
b. ¿A qué tipo de público piensas que va dirigida cada una?
c. ¿Sueles leer algunas de estas revistas? ¿Qué contenidos te gustan más?
d. ¿Te interesan las revistas del corazón?
e. ¿Qué tipos de famosos suelen aparecer en ellas?
f. ¿Te parece que han ganado la fama de una manera justa?
g. ¿Piensas que es fácil hacerse famoso?
h. ¿Te gustaría llegar a ser famoso?
i. ¿Qué ventajas o desventajas crees que tiene la fama?

COMUNICA

ASKING FOR AND GIVING ADVICE

■ Para **pedir consejos**:

¿Qué puedo hacer? *What can I do?*

¿Tú qué harías? *What would you do?*

¿Podrías aconsejarme? *Could you advise me?*

■ Para **dar consejos** o recomendaciones:

Yo / Yo que tú / Yo en tu lugar, comería de una manera más saludable. *If I were you, I would eat healthier.*

Deberías / podrías acostarte. Es tarde. *You should / could go to sleep. It's late.*

■ Otras formas:

¿Por qué no vas al médico? *Why don't you go to the doctor?*

Toma un taxi, llegarás más rápido. *Take a taxi, you'll get there faster.*

¿Y si comes menos fritos? *And if you eat less fried food?*

Juan y tú **tienen que** ir a ver esa película. *Juan and you have to go see that movie.*

No fumes. Te hace daño. *Don't smoke. It's harmful.*

1 Maxi Castro is shooting a new movie, and the producers have organized a special cast call. They need to find a new actress to play opposite him. Carla has signed up for the auditions, but now she is nervous and thinks she won't do well. Help her out and complete the sentences with some useful advice.

a. .... me aprendería muy bien el papel.

b. ¿Y si ....? Van a ser muchos en el casting.

c. .... me tomaría un té de hierbas relajante antes de la prueba.

d. Deberías ....

e. ¿Por qué no ....? Tú lo haces muy bien y eso es un punto extra a tu favor.

2 Maruchi, the chef, gives her viewers some advice for how to follow a healthy and delicious diet. Complete the conversations with a verb from the list below.

Carlos: Maruchi, te veo todos los días en la tele y me encanta tu programa. Mi problema es que últimamente estoy engordando mucho, ¿tú qué (a) .... para adelgazar?

Maruchi: Yo que tú (b) .... con moderación y (c) .... las comidas con aceite de oliva, preferentemente crudo. También (d) .... el consumo de azúcar y de sal.

Carlos: ¡Uf!... todo eso ya lo hago, pero engordo...

Maruchi: A lo mejor consumes más calorías de las que necesitas. En ese caso, yo en tu lugar, (e) .... ejercicio diariamente.

Alicia: Hola, Maruchi, me encanta tu programa. Mira, mi problema es que últimamente me encuentro muy cansada y, a veces, me duele la cabeza. El médico dice que estoy sanísima, pero yo me siento sin energías, ¿(f) .... darme algunos consejos?

Maruchi: Alicia, querida, ¿seguro que te alimentas bien? En primer lugar, (g) .... incluir legumbres y frutos secos en tu dieta. Para el dolor de cabeza, yo que tú (h) .... abundante cantidad de agua durante todo el día.

3 🎧 **28** Listen to the audio and check your answers.

119

OBJECTIVES FOR COMUNICA

• Present communicative functions of the unit:
  Ask for and give advice

CORE RESOURCES

• Audio Program: Track 28
• Extension Activities: EA 4.1
• Interactive Online Materials – ELEteca

STANDARDS

1   Engage in conversation
2   Understand the language
4.2   Compare cultures

INSTRUCTIONAL STRATEGIES FOR
ASKING FOR AND GIVING ADVICE

• Tell the class you have a problem and would like some advice from them, for instance: **Mis hijos no ayudan en las tareas de la casa. ¿Qué puedo hacer?**

• Have the students make recommendations and give advice. They may need help at first with structures, so suggest: **¿Por qué no...?** or **Podrías...**, etc.

• Once they have made some recommendations, walk them through the explanations on this page to learn how to ask for and give advice.

Activity 1

• Explain to students that many of the activities in **Comunica** expand on the topics presented in *SuperEspacio*. Ask students to describe the fictitious Maxi Castro to provide context for the activity.

• Explain that there are several possible answers. Have the students complete the sentences and then share their answers with a partner.

• Ask for volunteers to say the correct sentences and have the rest of the class say any alternative answers.

Activity 2

• Review the words from this list: **podría**, **practicaría**, **tomaría**, **deberías**, **comería**, **harías**, **disminuiría**, **prepararía** to make sure students recognize the infinitive. For now, have students repeat after you to become familiar with the form and sound of these verbs.

• Have students read the first conversation and fill each blank with the correct verb. Have them share their answers with a partner.

• Ask them to continue on to the second conversation and do the same.

• Invite pairs to read the completed conversations for the class.

🎧 **28** Activity 3

• Play the audio and have the students follow in order to correct the completed conversations from Activity 2.

ANSWERS

Activity 1

Answers will vary. **a.** Yo / Yo que tú / Yo en tu lugar; **b.** inventas algo original; **c.** Yo / Yo que tú / Yo en tu lugar; **d.** ser tú misma; **e.** cantas una canción.

Activity 2

a. harías; **b.** comería; **c.** prepararía; **d.** disminuiría; **e.** practicaría; **f.** podrías; **g.** deberías; **h.** tomaría.

COMUNICA COMMUNICATIVE FUNCTIONS

INSTRUCTIONAL STRATEGIES

Activity 4

- Have the students work in pairs, with each of them looking at a different card (one holds the book upside down).
- Each student reads through the information and asks the other for advice, taking turns. Their partner reacts to the situation with an expression of advice.
- Circulate around the room as they work, providing assistance and answering questions as required.
- Ask for volunteers to perform for the class.

Alternative Activity

Distribute two sets of cards from EA 4.1, **Tengo un problema** to student pairs. Explain to students that their partner is going to choose a card and give them advice about a problem they have. They in turns have to guess what that problem is based on the advice they receive. Partners must continue giving advice until the student guesses the problem. Then they switch roles.

OBJECTIVES FOR COMUNICA

- Present communicative functions of the unit:
  Ask for favors and permission

STANDARDS

- 1.1 Engage in conversation
- 1.2 Understand the language
- 4.2 Compare cultures

INSTRUCTIONAL STRATEGIES FOR
ASKING FOR FAVORS AND PERMISSION

- Pretend to feel cold and ask a student: **¿Podrías dejarme tu chaqueta? Es que tengo frío**. Use mime and exaggeration to help convey the meaning.
- Ask similar questions, such as: **¿Podrías acercarme una silla? Es que quiero sentarme, ¿Podrías prestarme tu lápiz? Es que necesito apuntar algo**, etc.
- Walk the students through the expressions presented in the book for asking for favors and permission. Point out that in this context **dejar** and **prestar** have similar meanings.

Activity 5

- Remind students that **Amor en directo** is the program presented in the magazine, *SuperEspacio*.
- Have them combine the two halves of the sentences. When they have finished, ask them to share with a partner.
- Ask for volunteers to say the completed sentences.

ANSWERS

Activity 5

1. b; **2.** e; **3.** c; **4.** d; **5.** f; **6.** a.

COMUNICA

4 👥 **Working with a partner, ask each other for advice based on the following situations.**

> **Estudiante 1**
>
> a. ¡No soy popular en Facebook!
> b. Siempre que tengo un examen me pongo muy nervioso y no me puedo concentrar.
> c. Tengo muchos granos (*pimples*) pero no puedo dejar de comer chocolate.
> d. Lloro viendo todas las películas.
> e. Mis padres quieren que salga con el hijo / la hija de sus amigos, pero a mí no me gusta.

> **Estudiante 2**
>
> a. Necesito ver mi celular constantemente.
> b. Creo que en mi casa hay un fantasma.
> c. El muchacho / La muchacha que me gusta me ha invitado a una fiesta pero pero nadie me cree.
> d. No puedo dormir por las noches.
> e. Me encanta la ropa de mi hermano/a mayor pero no me la deja.

ASKING FOR FAVORS AND PERMISSION

- Para **pedir permiso** decimos:
  ¿Te importa si me llevo estos libros? *Do you mind if I take these books?*
  ¿Puedo cerrar la puerta? *Can I close the door?*
  ¿Podría salir un poco antes de clase? *Could I leave class a little early?*
  ¿Me dejas usar tu teléfono? *Will you allow me to use your phone?*

- Para **pedir favores** decimos:
  ¿Me prestas un boli? *Will you lend me a pen?*
  ¿Te importaría llevar estos libros a la biblioteca? (formal) *Would you mind taking these books to the library?*
  ¿Podrías prestarme tu diccionario de español? (formal) *Could you lend me your Spanish dictionary?*
  ¿Sería tan amable de decirme la hora? (muy formal) *Would you be so kind as to tell me the time?*

- Para **explicar** o **justificar** el porqué de la petición se utiliza **es que**…:
  Es que he perdido mi boli. *It's just that I lost my pen.*

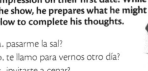

5 The program *Amor en directo* is a popular program featuring people looking for romance. Benjamin, the next participant, is looking for a girlfriend. He wants to make a good impression on their first date. While waiting in the dressing room before the show, he prepares what he might say to her. Combine the sentences below to complete his thoughts.

1. ¿Te importa si ⋯⋯ •
2. ¿Podría ⋯⋯⋯ •
3. ¿Puedo ⋯⋯⋯ •
4. ¿Me dejas ⋯⋯ •
5. ¿Le importaría ⋯⋯ •
6. ¿Podrías ⋯⋯⋯ •

- a. pasarme la sal?
- b. te llamo para vernos otro día?
- c. invitarte a cenar?
- d. acompañarte a casa?
- e. aconsejarnos en la comida?
- f. tomarnos una foto juntos?

120

6 Write the number of the sentences from Activity 5 next to the situations in which Benjamin could use them.

a. ☐ Están cenando y la comida está sosa *(bland)*.

b. ☐ Acaban de salir del restaurante.

c. ☐ Se acaban de sentar en la mesa del restaurante y piden ayuda al camarero.

d. ☐ Se están despidiendo después de la cita.

e. ☐ Han salido del plató *(set)* de *Amor en directo* y están pensando qué hacer.

f. ☐ Están pasando una buena noche y le pide al camarero un recuerdo de ella.

EXPRESSING PROBABILITY IN THE PAST

■ Si queremos **expresar probabilidad** en el pasado, decimos:

Anoche **cenaría** *sobre las 7.* (Serían aproximadamente las siete, pero no estoy seguro).
Last night I must have had dinner around seven.

Tendría *unos 15 años cuando conocí a Sara.* (No recuerdo con exactitud la edad que tenía).
I must have been about 15 when I met Sara.

7 Guess what must have happened to the following people based on the images. Choose from the expressions in the list below.

estar nervioso/a por el examen de Historia ○ perder la cartera ○ quedarse dormido/a ○
perder el metro o el autobús ○ quedarse chateando por Internet hasta tarde

a. Ayer Pepe llegó tarde a clase... *Perdería el autobús.*

b. Hoy Carlos se ha dormido en clase...

c. Ayer María tenía la luz de la habitación encendida a las 4 de la mañana...

d. Ayer llamé a Laura por teléfono y estaba muy rara...

e. Ayer estaba en la cafetería y un cliente muy bien vestido se fue sin pagar...

8  The girl that Benjamin was supposed to meet on the program did not show up. With your partner, come up with some possible scenarios for what must have happened.

Sería...   Se quedaría...
Tendría...   Estaría...

 Practice what you have learned with additional materials online.

INSTRUCTIONAL STRATEGIES

Activity 6

- Have students connect the expressions in Activity 5 with the situations given here.
- They write the number of the favor requested in the box.
- Have them share their answers with a partner.
- Ask for volunteer pairs to read the requests and situations for the class.

OBJECTIVES FOR COMUNICA

- Present communicative functions of the unit: Express probability in the past

CORE RESOURCES

- Interactive Whiteboard Lesson: IWB 4.1

STANDARDS

1.1   Engage in conversation

1.2   Understand the language

4.2   Compare cultures

INSTRUCTIONAL STRATEGIES FOR
EXPRESSING PROBABILITY IN THE PAST

- Read the explanation with the class and focus on the form of the verb for expressing probable cause in the past (what must have happened).

Activity 7

- Project IWB 4.1, **¡Qué raro!** and say to students, **Ayer Pepe llegó tarde a clase**. **¿Por qué creen que llegó tarde?** Tell students to look at the images and read the captions. Ask them to come up with possible explanations for the situation. Help students with the forms as necessary.

- Have the students complete the activity individually.
- Circulate around the room as they work and provide assistance where required.
- Ask for volunteers to read the completed sentences to the class.

Activity 8

- Have the students work in pairs to conjecture about why the girl did not show up to meet Benjamin on the program.
- Ask for volunteers to read out their suggestions while you record them on the board. Vote on the best and worst excuse for what must have happened to her.

ANSWERS

Activity 6

a. 6a; b. 4d; c. 2e; d. 1b; e. 3c; f. 5f.

Activity 7

a. Perdería el autobús; b. Se quedaría chateando por Internet hasta tarde; c. Se quedaría dormida; d. Estaría nerviosa por el examen de Historia; e. Perdería la cartera.

OBJECTIVES FOR ¡ACCIÓN!

- Provide students with a structured approach to viewing the video
- Contextualize the content of the unit in a familiar scenario

CORE RESOURCES

- Unit Video 4
- Interactive Online Materials – ELEteca

STANDARDS

1.3 Understand the language

2.1 Practices and perspectives

3.2 Acquire information

4.2 Compare cultures

INSTRUCTIONAL STRATEGIES

Previewing: Antes del video

Activity 1

- Have the students work in pairs asking and answering the questions about their study habits.
- Circulate as they work, correcting pronunciation and any grammatical errors.
- Have students report back to class about their partner's preferences.

Activity 2

- Have students look at the frames and say what they think the video segment will be about.
- Ask the questions for each frame and have volunteers suggest answers.
- Ask for any alternative answers.
- Follow up by having students talk about what else they see happening in each frame.

¡ACCIÓN!

ANTES DEL VIDEO

1 👥 **With a partner, take turns asking and answering the following questions.**

  a. ¿Dónde estudias normalmente?
  b. ¿Crees que es importante el lugar y las condiciones del lugar para estudiar mejor?
  c. ¿Cuáles crees que deben ser esas condiciones?
  d. ¿Cómo son las condiciones del lugar en el que tú estudias?

2 **Look at the scenes from the video segment and answer the questions.**

  a. ¿Dónde están estas personas?
  b. ¿Qué relación crees que hay entre ellas?
  c. ¿Qué hora piensas que es? ¿Por qué?
  d. ¿Qué está haciendo cada uno?
  e. ¿Qué crees que están mirando?
  f. ¿Cómo crees que se llevan (get along) entre ellos?
  g. ¿De qué crees que van a hablar en unos minutos más?

  h. ¿Cómo te imaginas que es Carla?   i. ¿Qué crees que está haciendo?

DURANTE EL VIDEO

3 Number the following sentences in the order in which they occurred in the video.

a. ☐ La televisión me ayuda a concentrarme.

b. ☐ Lo mejor es que dejes el móvil aquí.

c. ☐ Deberías estudiar en un lugar más tranquilo, ¿es que no te molesta la televisión o cuando hablamos?

d. ☐ No deberías tener la tele encendida mientras estudias.

e. ☐ El profesor me tiene manía.

f. ☐ ¿Por qué no le pides al profesor que te explique las cosas un poco mejor?

g. ☐ Yo en tu lugar prestaría más atención en clase y me dejaría de tonterías.

h. ☐ Podrías haber estudiado ayer o la semana anterior, pero no ahora.

i. ☐ ¡En esta casa nadie me comprende!

j. ☐ Yo lo entiendo todo perfectamente, ¿vale?

DESPUÉS DEL VIDEO

4 With your partner, talk and answer the following questions.

a. ¿Qué consejos le da el padre a Carla?

b. ¿Qué consejos le da la madre a Carla?

c. ¿Cómo reacciona Carla?

d. ¿Cómo se sienten los padres de Carla?

e. ¿Cuál es tu opinión acerca de esta situación? ¿Qué crees que debería hacer Carla?

f. ¿Has estado alguna vez en esta situación?

g. ¿Qué consejos te dan tus padres?

 Practice what you have learned with additional materials online. 123

INSTRUCTIONAL STRATEGIES

Viewing: Durante el video

Activity 3

- Have the students read the statements and pencil in the information as they watch the video.
- Play the video without pauses.
- Answer any questions students may have about the vocabulary.
- Play the entire video again without pauses for them to confirm their answers.
- Ask for volunteers to give their answers.

After viewing: Después del video

Activity 4

- Ask students what they understood about the video.
- Have the students look at the questions and discuss their ideas with a partner.
- Play the video again and allow students to ask you to pause, as needed.
- Replay sections students found hard to understand.
- Have volunteers who understand help those students who understood less.
- Show the entire video again without pauses. Ask students to share how their understanding has improved.

ANSWERS

Activity 3

a. 4; b. 9; c. 2; d. 3; e. 5; f. 6; g. 8; h. 1; i. 10; j. 7.

OBJECTIVES FOR LA COMIDA

- Present vocabulary needed to practice communicative and grammatical functions for the unit: Foods and healthy eating
- Talk about foods and following a healthy diet

CORE RESOURCES

- Audio Program: Track 29
- Interactive Whiteboard Lessons: IWB 4.2
- Extension Activities: EA 4.2
- Interactive Online Materials – ELEteca

STANDARDS

1.1 Engage in conversation
1.2 Understand the language
3.1 Knowledge of other disciplines
3.2 Acquire information

INSTRUCTIONAL STRATEGIES

🎧 29 Activity 1

- Invite the students to look at the images and name any items they already know.
- Have the students look at the categories and discuss what they mean.
- Now have them categorize the foodstuffs and write the letter of the image next to the correct word. Have them share the results with a partner.
- Play the audio for the students to check their answers. Check that students understand **entera** and **desnatada**. Ask students if they recognize a cognate in **entera** (entire) and think what kind of milk it can refer to. Tell students that **nata** means cream and what they think **desnatada** refers to.
- Ask questions to practice the new vocabulary, such as: **¿Comes sano? ¿Qué tipo de comida te gusta más? ¿Con qué frecuencia comes carne / pescado / dulces...? ¿Cuántas veces a la semana comes carne / pescado / dulces...?**, etc.

PALABRA POR PALABRA La comida

1 🎧 29 Match the types of food to the appropriate images. Make your best guesses at unfamiliar words. Then listen to the audio to check your answers.

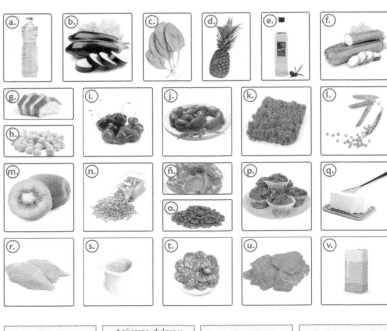

Aceites	Azúcares, dulces y pastelerías	Verduras y vegetales	Frutas
1. aceite de oliva ☐	3. bizcocho ☐	5. berenjena ☐	8. cereza ☐
2. aceite de girasol ☐	4. magdalena ☐	6. calabacín ☐	9. piña ☐
		7. espinacas ☐	10. kiwi ☐

Legumbres	Carnes y derivados	Lácteos y derivados de la leche
11. guisantes ☐	15. carne picada ☐	21. leche entera / desnatada ☐
12. lentejas ☐	16. chuleta de cerdo ☐	22. mantequilla ☐
13. frijoles ☐	17. pechuga de pollo ☐	23. yogur natural /
14. garbanzos ☐	18. bistec ☐	desnatado / con futas ☐
	Embutidos *(cold cuts)*	
	19. salchichón ☐	
	20. chorizo ☐	

Audioscript

a. aceite de girasol
b. berenjena
c. espinacas
d. piña
e. aceite de oliva
f. calabacín
g. bizcocho
h. garbanzos
i. cereza
j. chorizo
k. carne picada
l. guisantes
m. kiwi
n. lentejas
ñ. chuleta de cerdo
o. frijoles
p. magdalena
q. mantequilla
r. pechuga de pollo
s. yogur natural / desnatado / con futas
t. salchichón
u. bistec
v. leche entera / desnatada

ANSWERS

Activity 1

1. e; **2.** a; **3.** g; **4.** p; **5.** b; **6.** f; **7.** c; **8.** i; **9.** d; **10.** m; **11.** l; **12.** n; **13.** o; **14.** h; **15.** k; **16.** ñ; **17.** r; **18.** u; **19.** t; **20.** j; **21.** v; **22.** q; **23.** s.

2 Combine words from both columns to forms common food pairs.

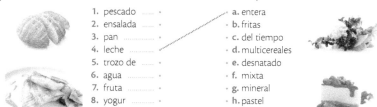

1. pescado ...... •
2. ensalada ...... •
3. pan .... •
4. leche .... •
5. trozo de ...... •
6. agua .... •
7. fruta .... •
8. yogur .... •
9. papas .... •

• a. entera
• b. fritas
• c. del tiempo
• d. multicereales
• e. desnatado
• f. mixta
• g. mineral
• h. pastel
• i. a la plancha

3 Mónica Pérez, the actress, and Maruchi, the famous chef, are talking about how to improve Mónica's eating habits. Read their conversation and fill in the blanks with word pairs from Activity 2.

Maruchi: Primero, vamos a analizar qué es lo que comes habitualmente. A ver, ¿qué sueles desayunar?
Mónica: Tomo un vaso de (a) ....
Maruchi: ¿Y qué más?
Mónica: Pues, nada más.
Maruchi: ¿Solo eso? Bueno, ¿y luego? ¿A la hora de la comida?
Mónica: Como una hamburguesa con (b) .... y una Coca-Cola.
Maruchi: ¿Tomas postre?
Mónica: Sí, un (c) .... de chocolate.
Maruchi: ¿Y para cenar?
Mónica: Para cenar tomo (d) .... como salmón o sardinas con una (e) .... y de postre, un (f) ....

Maruchi: Bien. En realidad, creo que tenemos que hacer algunos cambios, sobre todo en el desayuno y la comida. Para desayunar, yo tomaría café o té, con leche desnatada, pero lo acompañaría con (g) .... y mermelada. Lo que yo cambiaría bastante es la comida. Para empezar, la haría más variada, incorporando verduras y legumbres de todo tipo. Por otro lado, yo en tu lugar abandonaría completamente los dulces y tomaría una (h) .... de postre. ¡Ah! y olvídate también de las bebidas con gas, mucho mejor beber (i) ....

4 Take turns asking each other the following set of questions about your own eating habits. Comment on what your partner says and offer advice as needed.

Estudiante 1

a. ¿En qué consiste tu dieta?
b. ¿Te gusta la comida rápida?
c. ¿Te interesa comer de forma saludable?
d. ¿Has cambiado algo de tu alimentación en los últimos años?

Estudiante 2

a. ¿Con qué frecuencia comes verdura?
b. ¿Vas mucho a restaurantes de comida rápida?
c. ¿Dónde crees que tienes una alimentación más sana: en casa o en la escuela?
d. ¿Crees que comes bien?

125

 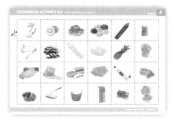

OBJECTIVES FOR ¡A COCINAR!

- Present vocabulary needed to practice communicative and grammatical functions for the unit: Cooking
- Talk about food preparation and recipes

CORE RESOURCES

- Extension Activities: EA 4.3

STANDARDS

1.1 Engage in conversation
1.2 Understand the language
1.3 Present information
3.2 Acquire information

INSTRUCTIONAL STRATEGIES

- Begin by asking students: **¿Les gusta cocinar? ¿Saben preparar algún plato o alguna receta? ¿Qué saben preparar?** Then tell students they are going to learn some tricks of the trade in cooking.

Activity 5

- Introduce the verbs on the left and act them out as in charades to provide context for students before they begin the activity. Then have the students match the verbs with their definitions on the right.
- When they have finished, have them share with a partner.
- Ask for volunteers to say the correct answers and provide assistance if necessary.

Activity 6

- Have the students look at the images and say what they can see.
- Ask them to use the verbs from the previous activity to fill in the blanks in the cooking tips while they look at the images which illustrate the actions.
- When students finish, have them share their answers with a partner.
- Ask for volunteers to say the correct answers.

Extension

Distribute cut up questions and texts of EA 4.3, *Curiosidades culinarias* so that some students have questions and others have answers. Have students search out their match among the other students. Then call on student pairs to read and answer the question. Encourage students to share their own *curiosidades* about food and health.

PALABRA POR PALABRA ¡A cocinar!

5 The following words are generally associated with cooking. Match the words with their definitions. Work with a partner and use context clues in the definitions to help you.

1. añadir .... •
2. escurrir .... •
3. aliñar .... •
4. poner en remojo ... •
5. lavar .... •
6. cocer .... •
7. congelar .... •
8. triturar .... •

- **a.** Poner un alimento en agua durante un tiempo para poder cocinarlo bien el día siguiente.
- **b.** Quitar el agua de un alimento después de cocinar.
- **c.** Limpiar con agua un alimento.
- **d.** Cortar un alimento en trozos más pequeños. Hay máquinas que lo hacen muy bien y muy rápido.
- **e.** Poner alimentos a temperaturas muy frías para conservarlos frescos.
- **f.** Poner un alimento, como la verdura, en agua caliente durante un tiempo determinado.
- **g.** Poner sal, aceite y vinagre a la ensalada.
- **h.** Poner ingredientes adicionales poco a poco o al final.

6 Maruchi also prepares different recipes for the magazine *SuperEspacio* where she shares some cooking tricks. Fill in the blanks with verbs from the previous exercise and use the images as a guide.

1. Para conseguir unos garbanzos tiernos *(tender)*, los tienes que (a) .... la noche anterior. Para las lentejas no es necesario, pero las tendrás que (b) .... lentamente.
2. Si has comprado mucha carne y no la vas a comer en el mismo día, la puedes (c) ...., así conservará todas sus propiedades.
3. Después de cocer la pasta, la tendrás que (d) .... antes de (e) .... la salsa de tomate.
4. Para cambiar la consistencia de la sopa de verduras, la puedes (f) .... y hacer un puré de verduras.
5. Antes de comer fruta, la deberás (g) ....
6. Para darle más sabor a la ensalada, la puedes (h) .... con aceite de oliva.

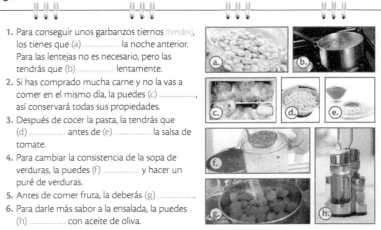

7 Do you like to cook? In small groups, take turns describing what you know how to make. Use the expressions you learned to explain how you prepare it. Then decide who is the most knowledgeable cook in the group.

Practice what you have learned with additional materials online.

Activity 7

- Divide the class into small groups and have them discuss how to prepare a simple dish.
- Student groups can present their recipe to the class orally or in writing.

ANSWERS

Activity 5

1. h; **2.** b; **3.** g; **4.** a; **5.** c; **6.** f; **7.** e; **8.** d.

Activity 6

a. poner en remojo; **b.** cocer; **c.** congelar; **d.** escurrir; **e.** añadir; **f.** triturar; **g.** lavar; **h.** aliñar.

GRAMÁTICA

UNIDAD **4**

1. THE CONDITIONAL TENSE: REGULAR VERBS

	CANTAR	COMER	ESCRIBIR
yo	cantaría	comería	escribiría
tú	cantarías	comerías	escribirías
usted/él/ella	cantaría	comería	escribiría
nosotros/a	cantaríamos	comeríamos	escribiríamos
vosotros/as	cantaríais	comeríais	escribiríais
ustedes/ellos/ellas	cantarían	comerían	escribirían

Note that all endings have a written accent on the **í**.

The simple conditional is used to:

■ Give **advice** and make recommendations:
Yo / Yo que tú / Yo en tu lugar, comería más fruta y verdura. *If I were you, I would eat more fruit and vegetables.*
Deberías / Podrías dejarle un mensaje. Creo que está preocupado. *You should / could leave him a message. I think he's worried.*

■ Ask for **favors** and **permission**:
¿Te importaría hacerme un favor? Es que mañana tengo un examen…
Would you mind doing me a favor? It's just that tomorrow I have a test…

■ Express **probability** or **hypothesis** in the past:
En aquella época yo **ganaría** unos 1.000 euros al mes. *Back then I was probably earning some 1.000 euros a month.*

1 Josefa, the girl Benjamin was supposed to meet on *Amor en directo*, has finally agreed to appear, thanks to her friend Diana who convinced her. But now Josefa is a nervous wreck. Read the conversation as Diana tries to calm down her friend. Fill in the blanks with the verbs in parenthesis.

Josefa: ¡Qué vergüenza! ¿Y qué hago si me hace una pregunta indiscreta?
Diana: Yo le (a) .... (responder) con otra pregunta.
Josefa: ¿Y si lo veo y no me gusta?
Diana: Pues yo que tú le (b) .... (dar) una oportunidad y (c) .... (cenar, yo) con él. Si después de la cena no te gusta, no (d) .... (participar, yo) más en el programa.
Josefa: ¿Y si me gusta?
Diana: Pues entonces (e) .... (seguir) conociéndolo y sobre todo (f) .... (quedar) con él fuera de las cámaras, ya sabes que la televisión engaña *(misleads)* mucho… Si no que te lo digan a ti, que no querías ni ir…
Josefa: Tienes razón, (g) .... (deber, yo) conocerlo mejor. Pero, igual me enamoro de él y él no de mí, ¿te imaginas?
Diana: ¡Ay, Josefa! Yo no lo (h) .... (pensar) más, ¡solo es un concurso! (i) .... (Ir), (j) .... (divertirse) un rato, (k) .... (conocer) a gente nueva y quién sabe…, igual es el hombre de tu vida…
Josefa: ¿Y si lo es?
Diana: Pues entonces yo (l) .... (casarse) con él, y (m) .... (ser, yo) muy feliz.
Josefa: Y entonces… ¿me (n) .... (ayudar, tú) a elegir vestido de novia?
Diana: ¡¡Grrrrrr!! Que sí, ¡¡pesada!!

127

OBJECTIVES FOR GRAMÁTICA 1

- Present grammatical structures needed to practice communicative functions of the unit:
  The conditional tense of regular verbs
- Use the conditional to give advice

CORE RESOURCES

- Interactive Online Materials – ELEteca

STANDARDS

1.1   Engage in conversation
1.2   Understand the language
1.3   Present information
4.1   Compare languages

INSTRUCTIONAL STRATEGIES

1. The Conditional Tense: Regular Verbs

- Explain to students that the form of the verb they have been using is called the conditional tense. Explain that the tense is formed by adding **-ía, -ías, -ía, -íamos, -íais, -ían** endings to the infinitive. Ask students what other tense is formed by adding endings to the infinitive (future).
- Have students turn back to the conversation between Mónica and Maruchi in Activity 3 (page 125) and underline the verbs in the conditional in the section on the left (Maruchi's recommendations). Then ask students to explain one of the uses of the conditional (give advice and recommendations).
- Walk students through the grammatical explanation of this tense and the uses that follow.
- Provide practice by saying a verb and asking students to say the form of the conditional for the person given. For instance, say **hablar – él**. Students should respond: **hablaría**, etc.

Activity 1

- Have the students focus on the images and identify the two girls. Remind students again of who the characters in the conversation are and ask them to provide background information on the show: **Amor en directo**.
- Have students read through the text and fill in the blanks with a form of the conditional of the verb in parenthesis.
- Ask students to share their answers with a partner. Ask questions to check comprehension: **¿Qué siente Josefa? ¿Qué consejos le da su amiga para el primer encuentro? ¿Qué haría Diana por Josefa?**
- Ask for two volunteers to read the completed conversation.

ANSWERS

Activity 1

a. respondería; **b.** daría; **c.** cenaría; **d.** participaría; **e.** seguiría; **f.** quedaría; **g.** debería; **h.** pensaría; **i.** Iría; **j.** me divertiría; **k.** conocería; **l.** me casaría; **m.** sería; **n.** ayudarías.

INSTRUCTIONAL STRATEGIES

Activity 2

- Have the students look at the image of Benjamin and read the information.
- Remind students to use the previous activity as a model and the expressions in **Comunica** to give Benjamin advice.
- Circulate around the room as they work, ensuring they are using the conditional correctly. Invite volunteers to read their advice aloud.

OBJECTIVES FOR GRAMÁTICA 2

- Present grammatical structures needed to practice communicative functions of the unit:
  The conditional tense of irregular verbs
- Use the conditional to ask for favors and express probability

CORE RESOURCES

- Audio Program: Track 30

STANDARDS

- 1.1 Engage in conversation
- 1.2 Understand the language
- 1.3 Present information
- 4.1 Compare languages

INSTRUCTIONAL STRATEGIES

2. The Conditional Tense: Irregular Verbs

- Ask students to recall the irregular stems used in the future tense and write them on the board, prompting students as necessary. Explain to students that these verbs are also irregular in the conditional and use the same stem.
- Read through the explanation in the book and point out that the endings for irregular verbs are the same as those for regular verbs.
- Practice the irregular verbs in the conditional by saying a person an irregular verb and having the students say the correct form of that verb.

Activity 3

- Have the students read the sentences and fill in the blanks with the conditional of one of the verbs in the box.
- Remind them to check which verbs are irregular and underline them before they begin to answer. When they have finished, have them share with a partner.
- Ask for volunteers to report back to the class.

Activity 4

- Have the students look at the images taken from the *SuperEspacio* magazine and identify the characters and give as much background information as they remember. Have them match them with the sentences in the previous activity.
- Ask for volunteers to say the answers for the class.

GRAMÁTICA

2 Benjamin is also very nervous to finally meet Josefa. Since you already know what Josefa thinks, what kind of advice would you give Benjamin? Write him a short note.

Modelo: *Querido Benjamin, yo en tu lugar...*

2. THE CONDITIONAL TENSE: IRREGULAR VERBS

■ For all irregular verbs in the conditional, the endings remain the same as with regular verbs, only the stem changes as follows:

IRREGULAR VERBS			
poder → podr-			ía
salir → saldr-	tener → tendr-		ías
caber → cabr-	poner → pondr-	hacer → har-	ía
haber → habr-	venir → vendr-	decir → dir-	íamos
saber → sabr-	valer → valdr-		íais
querer → querr-			ían

What other tense uses these same stems?

3 Fill in the blanks with the appropriate verb from the list, using the conditional tense.

poner ○ saber ○ decir ○ tener ○ animar

a. .... unos cuatro años cuando empecé a dar mis primeros pasos como actor.
b. No tengo nada que decir respecto a mi relación con Mario Medina. Yo que tú .... en la revista que solo somos buenos amigos.
c. Yo no .... qué hacer sin los consejos de mi amiga Diana.
d. Yo .... a todos los jóvenes que una alimentación con muchas verduras es una garantía de salud para el futuro.
e. Yo .... a los jóvenes tímidos a buscar pareja a través de *Amor en directo*.

4 Think back to the stories from *SuperEspacio* magazine. Who said what? Match the sentences in Activity 3 with the appropriate person.

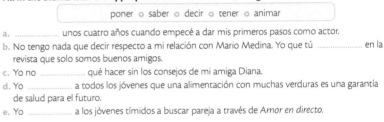

| Mónica Pérez | Josefa | Maxi Castro | Maruchi | Benjamin |

ANSWERS

Activity 3

a. Tendría; **b.** pondría; **c.** sabría; **d.** diría; **e.** animaría.

Activity 4

1. b; **2.** c; **3.** a; **4.** d; **5.** e.

5 🎧 30 **Listen to interviews from *SuperEspacio* and identify the person being interviewed.**

Benjamin ○ Maruchi ○ Maxi ○ Mónica

a. .... b. .... c. .... d. ....

6 🎧 30 **Listen again to the interviews and fill in the blanks with the appropriate verb in the conditional.**

	Uso
≫ ¿Qué .... si a tu hijo no le gusta el sabor de casi ninguna?	c
≫ .... usar tu imaginación.	☐
≫ .... la primera vez que venía a la tele.	☐
≫ ¿Y tú qué .... entonces, Luz?	☐
≫ Mira, yo	☐
≫ Sí, ... decir que sí.	☐
≫ Creo que no .... hacer otra cosa.	☐
≫ ¿Te .... firmarme un autógrafo para mi hija?	☐
≫ ¿ .... decirnos cuándo nació esa bonita amistad?	☐
≫ Reconoces que Mario Medina .... parte de tu vida privada.	☐
≫ .... limitarte a escribir lo que digo.	☐
≫ Yo que tú lo .... claro de una vez.	☐

7 👥 **Check your answers to Activity 6 with a partner. Then, together, identify the use of the conditional in each sentence above using the following list. The first one has been done for you.**

a. dar consejo
b. expresar probabilidad o hipótesis en el pasado
c. pedir consejo
d. pedir un favor

8 👥 **How would you react in the following situations? Prepare two responses for each. Then in small groups, take turns sharing your reaction. Who had the best responses?**

a. Vas al programa de Maruchi, *Salud al día*, y como siempre, invita a algunos espectadores a probar el plato que acaba de preparar. Te escoge a ti, pero cuando lo pruebas *(taste)*, ¡sabe fatal! ¿Qué harías?

b. Ahora vas a la grabación del programa *Amor en directo*. Presentan al primer concursante y ves que sale tu novio/a al escenario. ¿Qué harías?

c. Ya no puedes más, y necesitas tomar un café. Estás esperando en cola en uno de esos cafés de moda y ves a la actriz Mónica Pérez con Maxi Castro sentados en una mesa. Parece que están enamorados. Se levantan y salen por una puerta de atrás, tomados por la mano. ¿Qué harías?

 Practice what you have learned with additional materials online.

129

INSTRUCTIONAL STRATEGIES

🎧 30 **Activity 5**
- Tell the students they are going to hear some interviews and need to identify the person being interviewed.
- Play the audio.
- Repeat the audio for the students to confirm their answers.
- Have the students write the names in the spaces provided.
- Ask for volunteers to say the correct answers.

See audioscript on page APP1

Activity 6
- Have the students read over the interviews and play the audio again while they fill in the blanks with an appropriate verb in the conditional.
- Tell them not to do anything as yet with the last column.

Activity 7
- Have the students check their answers to the previous activity with a partner.
- Now have them identify the uses of the conditional from the list provided.
- They write the letter of the use in the box in the previous activity using the list provided.
- Ask for volunteers to say the correct uses.

Activity 8
- Have the students read quickly through the situations and identify which image matches which situation.
- Read the first situation and ask for reactions from the class.
- Now have the students divide into small groups and read the other situations and react to them in at least two ways.
- Ask for volunteers to read a situation and react to it.

ANSWERS

Activity 5

a. Maruchi; **b.** Benjamin; **c.** Maxi; **d.** Mónica.

Activities 6 and 7

harías (c); deberías (a); Sería (b); harías (c); esperaría (a); podríamos (b); sabría (b); importaría (d); Podrías (d); formaría (b); Deberías (a); dejaría (a).

OBJECTIVES FOR DESTREZAS

• Identify the format of a text

STANDARDS

1.1 Interpersonal communication
1.2 Understand the language
1.3 Present information

INSTRUCTIONAL STRATEGIES

Comprensión de lectura

Activity 1

• Talk the students through the strategy for identifying the format of a text.
• Answer any questions they may have at this stage.
• Have the students follow the instructions in the order they are set out, filling in the boxes for each of the texts in Activity 2.

Activity 2

• Ask the students to read each short text and the corresponding question on the next page.
• Have them use their notes and the instructions above to help them.
• When they have finished, have them compare answers with a partner.
• Ask for volunteers to say the correct answers.

Cultural Note

Share the following information about Madrid.

La Puerta del Sol es el centro neurálgico de Madrid. A pesar de su nombre, en el lugar donde se encuentra no hay ninguna puerta, pero en sus orígenes fue uno de los accesos de la cerca que rodeaba Madrid en el siglo XV. Esta cerca recogía en su perímetro los arrabales medievales que habían ido creciendo extramuros, en torno a la muralla cristiana del siglo XII. El nombre de la puerta proviene de un sol que adornaba la entrada, colocado ahí por estar orientada la puerta hacia el este.

El Oso y el Madroño es una estatua que se encuentra en la Puerta del Sol y que es el símbolo de Madrid.

El Madroño es un árbol típico de la Comunidad de Madrid y con sus frutos se hace el licor de madroño.

La chocolatería San Ginés es un lugar típico de Madrid para ir a tomar chocolate con churros. Es tradición tomar esta bebida en la madrugada de Año Nuevo.

ANSWERS

Activity 2

1. b; **2.** b; **3.** b.

DESTREZAS

COMPRENSIÓN DE LECTURA

1 Before you begin reading, review the strategy in Destrezas and follow the suggestion.

Destrezas

Identifying the format of a text

Look at the images, headings, and layout to help you understand the purpose of the text. Then follow these steps:

	Texto 1	Texto 2	Texto 3
1. Read the text and the question connected to this text for a general sense of the content.			
2. Highlight the most important word or phrase in the question or write it in the column to the right.			
3. Go back to the main text and look for related nouns or verbs.			
4. Read the supporting details. Do they answer what is asked?			

2 Read the texts and answer the questions in the next page.

La revista para jóvenes a partir de 15 años.

Suscripción a la revista

Ahora podrás disfrutar de las más interesantes noticias sobre actualidad, videojuegos, música, cine, deportes, literatura; propuestas de escapadas de fin de semana, salir por tu ciudad, talleres, concursos; entrevistas a tus ídolos, los consejos de Maruchi... ¡Todo esto y mucho más en la puerta de tu casa!

No te lo pienses más y aprovecha la oferta: si te suscribes este mes, ¡recibirás gratis la revista durante 6 meses!

Participa en el sorteo y ¡gana un viaje a París, la ciudad del amor!

¿Cómo puedes participar?

Es muy fácil, tan solo tienes que leer la entrevista a Maxi Castro y responder al cuestionario sobre su vida que encontrarás en el interior de la revista. Después envíanos tus respuestas, bien por correo ordinario o por Internet a través de nuestra revista digital. Entre los participantes que acierten todas las preguntas se realizará un sorteo ante notario. El nombre del ganador se dará a conocer en la publicación del mes de febrero. No lo dudes, participa y ¡gana!

¿Qué ver en Madrid?

El paseo comienza en la Puerta del Sol, centro de Madrid. No olvides fotografiarte junto al Oso y el Madroño, uno de los símbolos de la ciudad. Después, dirige tus pasos a la calle Arenal y busca la chocolatería San Ginés, donde puedes desayunar un chocolate con churros.

130

1. Si quieres suscribirte a la revista *SuperEspacio*...
   a. Debes tener más de 15 años.
   b. No necesitarás bajar al quiosco a comprarla.
   c. No tendrás que abonar ningún importe.

2. Podrás participar en el sorteo...
   a. tan solo con contestar el cuestionario y enviar tus respuestas a la revista.
   b. si has contestado correctamente al cuestionario.
   c. si acudes a la celebración del sorteo que se realizará ante notario.

3. El texto sobre Madrid recomienda...
   a. recorrer la calle Arenal.
   b. encontrar la chocolatería en la calle Arenal.
   c. evitar ir a la calle Arenal.

PRONUNCIACIÓN Las letras y y x

■ To form the plural of a word ending in **y**, add **-es: rey / reyes**. Notice that the **y** is now pronounced as a consonant.

■ Verbs like **oír, caer, creer** and those ending in **-uir** like **construir, destruir**, and **huir** (to flee) will have a **y** in the **usted/él/ella** and **ustedes/ellos/ellas** form in the preterit.

oír ➡ o**y**ó   caer ➡ ca**y**eron   creer ➡ cre**y**ó
construir ➡ constru**y**ó   destruir ➡ destru**y**eron   huir ➡ hu**y**eron

1 Fill in the blanks with the correct form of the verbs in parenthesis.

a. Ayer Juan (oír) .... un ruido extraño y (creer) .... que era un ladrón. Salió corriendo para atraparlo, (caerse) .... y el ladrón (huir) .... con todo el dinero.
b. Isabel la Católica fue una gran reina, ya que (construir) .... un gran imperio.
c. El huracán (destruir) .... la casa de mis tíos en Santo Domingo.

■ The letter **x** is used in place of s before the consonant pairs **pl-** and **pr-: explorar, exprimir**.

2 Fill in the blanks with *x* or *s*, according to the rule you have just learned.

a. e ☐ plotar   c. e ☐ timado   e. e ☐ tupidez   g. e ☐ presar
b. e ☐ plicar   d. e ☐ presión   f. e ☐ tatuto   h. e ☐ tirar

  Practice what you have learned with additional materials online.

131

OBJECTIVES FOR PRONUNCIACIÓN
• Practice pronouncing and spelling words containing the letters **y** and **x**

CORE RESOURCES
• Interactive Online Materials – ELEteca

STANDARDS
  1.2   Understand the language
  3.2   Acquire information
  4.1   Compare languages

INSTRUCTIONAL STRATEGIES
• Walk the students through the explanation and ask them to think of more examples for each group. Write the words on the board in their groups.

Activity 1
• Have the students fill the blanks with the correct form of the verbs in parenthesis. Remind them to check the list above to verify spellings.
• Have the students share their answers with a partner.
• Invite students to come to the front and write the correct sentences on the board.
• Ask for volunteers to read the sentences to the class.

Activity 2
• Have the students read the note about the use of **x** or **s**.
• Students work individually to fill in the missing letter according to the information above and then share their answers with a partner.
• Ask for volunteers to read the completed words.
• Have the students comment on any difficulties and discuss these with the class.
• The first group to complete their dictation correctly is declared the winner.

ANSWERS
Activity 1
  a. oyó, creyó, se cayó, huyó; **b.** construyó; **c.** destruyó.

Activity 2
  a. explotar; **b.** explicar; **c.** estimado; **d.** expresión; **e.** estupidez; **f.** estatuto; **g.** expresar; **h.** estirar.

OBJECTIVES FOR SABOR HISPANO

- Learn about the Mediterranean diet and healthy eating
- Activate vocabulary connected with food and cooking

CORE RESOURCES

- Audio Program: Track 31

STANDARDS

2.1 Culture: practices and perspectives
2.2 Products and perspectives
3.2 Acquire information
5.2 Using language for personal enjoyment and enrichment

INSTRUCTIONAL STRATEGIES

🎧 31

- Introduce the topic by asking the students to look at the images and say any words they already know.
- Put students in pairs to discuss the questions in the **Antes de leer** box.
- Before playing the audio, tell students to listen for the question posed at the beginning of the audio and be prepared to answer it. Either have students close their books while they listen or follow along with the text in the book.
- Elicit responses to the target question. Ask for different opinions and explanations.
- Play the audio of the text in sections as students follow along. After each section, ask questions such as: **¿De dónde es típica la dieta mediterránea? ¿Cuál es el factor más importante? ¿Qué ingredientes tienen en común muchos de los platos típicos?**, etc.
- Ask what the students have understood and invite those who understood more to help those who understood less.
- To help build vocabulary, have students locate and underline any words from the glossary on the next page in the text. Then have them make and share new sentences with the words. You may choose to have them work individually or in pairs.

SABOR HISPANO

LA DIETA MEDITERRÁNEA...

Vegetales, queso, aceitunas, sal, pimienta y aceite de oliva, ingredientes típicos de la dieta mediterránea.

¿MITO O REALIDAD?

Antes de leer

¿Qué tipo de comida sueles comer?
¿Te gusta la comida rápida? ¿Por qué?
¿Qué ingredientes son sanos?

🎧 31 **La comida mediterránea es típica de los países que rodean[*] el mar Mediterráneo. España es uno de ellos. Pero, ¿esta dieta existe o es un mito?**

«El clima es el factor más importante de la dieta mediterránea, ya que produce una serie de ingredientes típicos de esta gastronomía», dice el Doctor José Ordovas.

Hay muchos platos típicos de los países mediterráneos que tienen ingredientes en común, como los vegetales, las aceitunas[*], el pescado, el marisco, las frutas, el aceite de oliva y algunos condimentos.

«Culturalmente, los países del Mediterráneo pueden ser muy distintos. Y, claro, su gastronomía también puede diferir, pero los ingredientes son los mismos», dice el doctor.

España es uno de estos países. Sin embargo, solo una parte del país está en el Mediterráneo y disfruta de[*] este clima cálido. El norte de España, por ejemplo, tiene un clima más frío y lluvioso.

«En España, al hablar de los hábitos alimentarios, no se puede generalizar. El clima y la dieta varían mucho de norte a sur, o de este a oeste. En el norte se come marisco, pero también mucha carne y patatas. En el centro son típicos los guisos[*]», asegura Mariona Coslada, nutricionista.

Además, la dieta está cambiando. Las familias ya no tienen tanto tiempo para cocinar y suelen preparar platos rápidos, a menudo no muy saludables.

Una encuesta[*] reciente reveló que muchos jóvenes ahora prefieren la comida rápida, o comida basura, a la dieta mediterránea. «A mí me encanta la comida rápida, la verdad. Hamburguesas, papas fritas, aros de cebolla… », dice Mario Velázquez, un estudiante de 20 años.

La hamburguesa se considera un ejemplo de comida rápida en España.

132

Estos fueron los alimentos más consumidos en España en 2013

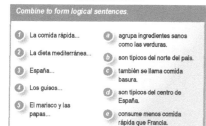

16%
2%
3%
4%
6%
13%
14%
22%
20%

Carne
Pescado
Verduras
Leche y lácteos
Pan
Café o té
Refrescos
Bollería
Otros

Gasto en comida rápida en el mundo (euros por habitante)

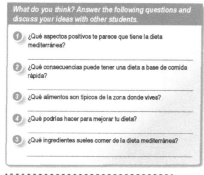

169 166
116.5
94 83.5 76.4
54.6 45.5
30.1 27.4

Japón
Estados Unidos
Canadá
Reino Unido
Australia
Francia
Alemania
México
Italia
Brasil

España está en el puesto número 14 (21.8).

La carne fue el alimento más consumido en España en 2013.

¿COMPRENDISTE?

Combine to form logical sentences.

1. La comida rápida...
2. La dieta mediterránea...
3. España...
4. Los guisos...
5. El marisco y las papas...

a. agrupa ingredientes sanos como las verduras.
b. son típicos del norte del país.
c. también se llama comida basura.
d. son típicos del centro de España.
e. consume menos comida rápida que Francia.

La paella, un plato típico de la dieta mediterránea.

AHORA TÚ

What do you think? Answer the following questions and discuss your ideas with other students.

1. ¿Qué aspectos positivos te parece que tiene la dieta mediterránea?

2. ¿Qué consecuencias puede tener una dieta a base de comida rápida?

3. ¿Qué alimentos son típicos de la zona donde vives?

4. ¿Qué podrías hacer para mejorar tu dieta?

5. ¿Qué ingredientes sueles comer de la dieta mediterránea?

Glosario

aceitunas – olives
disfrutar de – to enjoy
encuesta – poll
el guiso – stew
rodear – surround

Fuentes: *El País*, Ministerio de Agricultura, Pesca y Alimentación de España, EAE Business School, Unitedexplanations.org, *ABC*, Friedman School of Nutrition.

133

INSTRUCTIONAL STRATEGIES

Alimentos más consumidos

- Call on a volunteer to read the caption and chart data aloud.
- Elicit examples of food items that belong to some of the categories to recycle unit vocabulary.
- Review any common errors with the class, eliciting the corrections.
- Put students into pairs to discuss whether or not they consume similar percentages of food as the people in Spain. Have them come up with their own percentages for each category and add any new categories of their own.
- Call on volunteers to report back on their similarities or differences with the data from Spain.

Gasto en comida rápida

- Call on a volunteer to read the title. Then call on others to describe the information that follows.
- Check students' understanding of the information by asking questions, such as: **¿En qué puesto está Estados Unidos? ¿Hay algún dato que les sorprende? ¿Qué tipo de comida consideran comida rápida en Estados Unidos?**
- Help students calculate the equivalent spent in dollars by providing the current exchange rate. Ask students for their impressions of the dollar amounts spent.
- Have students write three questions about the data.
- Put them into pairs to take turns asking and answering the questions.
- Monitor their conversations and assist as needed. Take note of any common errors that you hear in their discussions.

¿Comprendiste?

- Have the students combine the phrases in the box. Then have them check through the text to see if they are correct.
- Have them compare their answers with a partner.
- Invite individual students to share their answers with the class.

Ahora tú

- Read the questions with the students and have them think about the answers.
- Have the students answer the questions in pairs or small groups and then ask for volunteers to present to the class.

ANSWERS

1. c; **2.** a; **3.** e; **4.** d; **5.** b.

OBJECTIVES FOR RELATO

- Revisit unit themes, grammar, vocabulary and culture in a new context
- Improve reading comprehension skills

CORE RESOURCES

- Audio Program: Track 32

STANDARDS

1.1 Engage in conversation
1.2 Understand the language
1.3 Present information
2.1 Practices and perspectives
5.3 Using language for personal enjoyment and enrichment

INSTRUCTIONAL STRATEGIES

Activity 1

- Have the students look at the photo and introduce José Lezama Lima as an internationally recognized Hispanic author and poet of the twentieth century.
- Ask them if they can name any other Cuban poets or writers (or American poets).
- Explain to students that Lezama's works exemplify a baroque style of writing. Ask students if they have ever heard of this term and can explain what it means. Share the Cultural Note below with students to set the tone for the fragment they will be reading.
- Read the questions with the students and remind them that reading the questions often provides useful information about the text.
- Have them read through the biography and answer the questions together with a partner. Invite volunteers to share their answers with the class.

Cultural Note

Los escritores barrocos hispanoamericanos usaban un lenguaje muy decorado, abundante, complicado, cargado de adornos literarios como la metáfora y el hipérbaton en el cual el autor juega con el orden lógico de las palabras para producir otro efecto. Su objetivo era el de complicar el significado del texto.

Extension

Project images of different styles of baroque architecture from Spain and Latin America. Include images of pre-Columbian art, which also factored into the baroque expression of Latin-American writers.

Activity 2

- Have the students look at the words taken from the next text and guess their meaning.
- Now have them read quickly through the text in Activity 3 and locate and underline the words in the text.

RELATO *Paradiso*

1 Read about José Lezama Lima, a poet, essayist and novelist from Cuba. Then answer the questions that follow.

José Lezama Lima nació en Cuba en 1910 y murió en 1976.

Aunque se dedicó principalmente a la poesía y al ensayo, se le recuerda sobre todo por su faceta de novelista, en concreto por su obra *Paradiso*, publicada en 1966 y de gran repercusión internacional.

De estilo barroco, y considerado uno de los autores más importantes de la literatura hispanoamericana, ha influido en una gran cantidad de escritores de su época y posteriores *(later)*.

El argumento de su principal novela se centra en la infancia y juventud de José Cemí, el protagonista, a través del cual *(through which)* el autor construye todo un mundo poético en el que se mezclan la realidad, el mito y la fantasía, escritos con un excelente dominio de la lengua española.

Tras su publicación, en 1971, el hecho de abordar *(tackle)* temas controvertidos hizo que su novela no fuera bien vista por las autoridades cubanas, que acusaron al autor de participar en actividades contrarrevolucionarias, algo que actualmente han rectificado.

Para muchos, Lezama fue el reinventor del lenguaje cuando parecía que todo estaba ya dicho, describiendo una nueva realidad a través de la metáfora y la imagen.

a. ¿Por qué obra se reconoce internacionalmente a Lezama Lima? ¿Tuvo éxito?
b. ¿Fue entendida en su época la obra por parte de las autoridades cubanas? ¿Por qué?
c. ¿Esa misma situación continúa actualmente?
d. ¿Qué tipo de estilo desarrolló Lezama Lima en *Paradiso*?
e. ¿En qué personaje se centra la novela?
f. ¿Qué etapas de la vida del protagonista desarrolla?
g. ¿Qué tipo de mundo construye Lezama Lima en *Paradiso*?

2 The following list of words were taken from a chapter in Lezama Lima's novel, *Paradiso*. Working with a partner, choose the correct definition of these words, using the dictionary if necessary.

a. lascas del pavo: patas / trozos / plumas
b. garzones: adultos / niñas / jóvenes
c. refinamiento: elegancia, buen gusto / calidad de estrecho / mal sabor
d. pachorra: nombre de persona / tranquilidad excesiva / de broma
e. acatar: ordenar / saborear la comida / obedecer
f. paladar: parte interior de la boca, fundamental para el sentido del gusto / parte interior de la boca que sirve para morder y triturar los alimentos / parte interior de la boca, fundamental para el sentido del olfato

---

- Have the students discuss their answers with a partner.
- Have those students who understood more help those who understood less.
- Offer a dictionary for students to check any words still unknown.
- Ask for volunteers to give the correct answers.

ANSWERS

Activity 1

a. Se le reconoce internacionalmente por su obra *Paradiso* que tuvo mucho éxito; **b.** La obra no fue bien vista por las autoridades cubanas porque abordaba temas controvertidos; **c.** No, actualmente las autoridades cubanas han rectificado su postura; **d.** Un estilo barroco, con el que describe una nueva realidad a través de la metáfora y la imagen; **e.** Se centra en el personaje de José Cemí; **f.** Se centra en su infancia y juventud; **g.** Lezama Lima construye un mundo poético donde se mezclan realidad, mito y fantasía.

3 🎧 **32** **Read the text.**

(1) Los mayores solo probaron algunas lascas del pavo, (2) pero no perdonaron el relleno que estaba elaborado con unas almendras que se deshacían y con unas ciruelas que parecían crecer de nuevo con la provocada segregación del paladar.

(3) Los garzones, un poco huidizos aún al refinamiento del soufflé, crecieron su gula habladora en torno al almohadón de la pechuga, donde comenzaron a lanzarse tan pronto el pavón (*peacock*) dio un corto vuelo de la mesa de los mayores a la mesita de los niños, que cuanto más comían, más rápidamente querían ver al pavón todo plumado, con su pachorra (*sluggishness*) en el corralón.

Al final de la comida, doña Augusta quiso mostrar una travesura (*prank*) en el postre. Presentó en las copas de champagne la más deliciosa crema helada. Después que la familia mostró su más rendido acatamiento (*acceptance*) al postre sorpresivo, doña Augusta regaló la receta: "(4) Son las cosas sencillas, que podemos hacer en la cocina cubana, (5) la repostería más fácil, y que enseguida el paladar declara incomparables. Un coco rallado en conserva, más otra conserva de piña rallada, unidas a la mitad de otra lata de leche condensada, y llega entonces el hada, es decir, la viejita Marie Brizard, para rociar con su anisete la crema olorosa. Al refrigerador, se sirve cuando está bien fría".

Luego la vamos saboreando, recibiendo los elogios de los otros comensales que piden con insistencia el bis (*encore*), como cuando oímos alguna pavana de Lully.

Al mismo tiempo que se servía el postre, doña Augusta le indicó a Baldovina que trajese el frutero, (6) donde mezclaban sus colores las manzanas, peras, mandarinas y uvas.

4 **Find the numbered sentences in the text above that correspond to the descriptions below.**

a. ⃞ El relleno del pavo estaba compuesto por almendras muy tiernas y buenas y con ciruelas muy ricas.
b. ⃞ En el frutero había frutas de diferentes colores.
c. ⃞ Los postres cubanos son de fácil preparación pero exquisitos.
d. ⃞ Los jóvenes no estaban acostumbrados a esa comida tan refinada y se dedicaron a comer pollo.
e. ⃞ Los adultos probaron un poco de pavo.
f. ⃞ La señora habla de la sencillez de la comida cubana.

5 📖 **Look for more information on Lezama Lima and his work, *Paradiso*. Prepare your answers to the following questions. Then discuss your findings with a partner.**

a. ¿En qué lugar pasó José Cemí, el protagonista de *Paradiso*, su primera infancia?
b. ¿Qué tipo de niño era José Cemí?
c. ¿Qué importante papel juega Oppiano Licario en la vida de José Cemí?
d. ¿Quién lo inicia en el mundo de la poesía?
e. ¿A qué corriente o periodo literario pertenece la obra de Lezama Lima?
f. Además de Lezama Lima, ¿qué otros autores pertenecen a este movimiento?

↰ **Previous Page**

Activity 2

a. trozos; **b.** jóvenes; **c.** elegancia, buen gusto; **d.** tranquilidad excesiva; **e.** obedecer; **f.** parte interior de la boca, fundamental para el sentido del gusto.

INSTRUCTIONAL STRATEGIES

🎧 **32** **Activity 3**

• To introduce the reading have the students talk about Thanksgiving and the types of food which are prepared especially for that festivity. Then play the audio while the students listen with books closed.
• Play the audio again as students follow in their books.
• Discuss any vocabulary or expressions that may still give difficulty.

Activity 4

Ask students to read the sentences and look for the corresponding numbered sentences in the text. Have them share their answers with a partner.

Activity 5

• Read the questions with the students and have them research the answers on the Internet.
• Once they have some information, they report to the class and compile more complete answers to the questions.

ANSWERS

Activity 4

a. 2; **b.** 6; **c.** 5; **d.** 3; **e.** 1; **f.** 4.

Activity 5

Answers will vary. Possible answers include:
a. José Cemí pasó su primera infancia en un campamento militar adonde su padre, coronel de artillería, se había trasladado con toda la familia; **b.** José Cemí era un niño asmático, mimado por las mujeres de la familia y la servidumbre; **c.** Oppiano Licario es una extraña figura que aparece como maestro, precursor y protector espiritual de José Cemí; **d.** De niño, su tío Alberto Olaya lo inicia en los misterios de la poesía y a través de él conoce a Oppiano Licario, personaje fundamental en su historia futura; **e.** La obra de Lezama Lima pertenece al movimiento de la novela hispanoamericana del siglo XX y se la suele clasificar dentro de la narrativa metafísica. Para conocer las características de esta literatura y sus diferentes etapas se puede consultar el siguiente enlace: *http://curro2m.awardspace.com/Selectividad/novelahispanoamericana.pdf* cuyo contenido hemos resumido en el apartado de notas culturales; **f.** Borges, Alejo Carpentier, Miguel Ángel Asturias…

OBJECTIVES FOR EVALUACIÓN

- Review grammar, vocabulary and culture from the unit
- Complete self-assessment

CORE RESOURCES

- Interactive Online Materials – ELEteca

STANDARDS

1.2 Understand the language
2.1 Practices and perspectives
4.1 Compare cultures

INSTRUCTIONAL STRATEGIES

- Activities can be completed individually and then reviewed with the class. Vary by asking students if they agree with the answer given and then writing it on the board. Provide explanations as needed.
- You may wish to assign point value to each activity as a way for students to monitor their progress.
- Direct students to the indicated pages in **En resumen** if they make more than one or two mistakes in any one section.

ANSWERS

Activity 1

Answers will vary. **a.** Podrías guardar un poco para después; **b.** Yo que tú ordenaría un poco la ropa; **c.** Yo en tu lugar haría la cama nada más levantarme; **d.** Deberías conducir más despacio; **e.** Yo que tú me olvidaría de ese muchacho; **f.** Deberíais comprar menos cosas.

Activity 2

1. d; **2.** a; **3.** e; **4.** b; **5.** c.

Activity 3

a. saldría; **b.** pondría; **c.** Tendrían; **d.** vendría; **e.** sabría; **f.** diría; **g.** Podríamos.

Activity 4

Carnes: solomillo de ternera, pechuga de pollo, salchichón; **Frutas:** piña, manzana, cerezas; **Legumbres:** frijoles, lentejas, garbanzos; **Verduras:** calabacín, guisantes, espinacas, berenjena.

EVALUACIÓN

GIVING ADVICE OR RECOMMENDATIONS

1 Give advice to the people in the following images.

THE CONDITIONAL TENSE

2 Match the sentences with the appropriate use of the conditional.

1. Estoy hecho un lío, ¿tú qué harías? .... •
2. Yo que tú, cortaría la relación con ese muchacho. .... •
3. ¿Podría hacer una llamada? .... •
4. Ayer Nacho llegó muy tarde. Regresaría sobre las cuatro de la mañana. .... •
5. ¿Podrías dejarme tu boli azul? .... •

- a. Dar consejos o recomendaciones.
- b. Expresar probabilidad o hipótesis en el pasado.
- c. Pedir un favor.
- d. Pedir consejo.
- e. Pedir permiso.

3 Complete the sentences with the verbs in the conditional tense.

a. Yo que tú, no (salir) .... a la calle sin abrigo, hace mucho frío.
b. Yo, no (poner) .... tanto peso en la estantería, creo que no lo va a resistir.
c. (Tener, ustedes) .... que tener más cuidado con el mando de la tele, ¡siempre se les cae al suelo!
d. Yo creo que ayer (venir, él) .... sobre las dos. Yo estaba ya en la cama.
e. No (saber, yo) .... qué decirte. Por un lado, te entiendo, pero por otro creo que él también tiene razón.
f. Yo en tu lugar, le (decir, yo) .... realmente lo que pienso.
g. ¿(Poder, nosotros) .... entregar el trabajo la semana que viene?

LA COMIDA

4 Sort out the following words in the appropriate category in the chart.

piña ○ frijoles ○ calabacín ○ solomillo de ternera ○ lentejas ○ pechuga de pollo salchichón ○ guisantes ○ manzana ○ espinacas ○ cerezas ○ berenjena ○ garbanzos

CARNES Y DERIVADOS	FRUTAS	LEGUMBRES	VERDURAS Y HORTALIZAS

5 Fill in the blanks with the words from the list below to get the recipe for a delicious dish.

> lavar ○ añadir ○ poner en remojo ○ guisar ○ cocer ○ escurrir (2)

Necesitas medio kilo de garbanzos. Para ablandarlos, los tendrás que (a) .... el día anterior. Pasado ese tiempo, los deberás (b) .... bien, quitándoles el agua sobrante. Las espinacas, si son frescas, se deben (c) .... muy bien para eliminar la tierra que pueden traer; también se pueden usar las espinacas congeladas.

En primer lugar, debemos (d) .... las espinacas cubriéndolas de agua, a fuego lento durante unos diez minutos. Después de retirarlas del fuego, para quitarles el agua, las tenemos que (e) .... y dejar a un lado.

A continuación, por separado, tenemos que (f) .... los garbanzos con agua, aceite, ajo, cebolla y pimienta. Una vez tiernos los garbanzos, ya podemos (g) .... las espinacas. Lo dejamos todo en el fuego durante unos dos minutos y ya tendremos listo ¡un delicioso guiso de garbanzos con espinacas!

THE LETTERS Y AND X

6 Fill in the missing letters in the following words. Then use the words to complete the sentences below.

> ca☐ó ○ e☐plotar ○ re☐es ○ hu☐ó ○ e☐presionista ○ le☐es

a. Las .... de mi país son muy estrictas.
b. El periódico *El País* publicó una noticia sobre los .... de España.
c. Si sigues comiendo así, vas a ....
d. La semana pasada mi hermano se .... en la ducha y se golpeó la cabeza.
e. El ladrón .... por los edificios con la famosa obra de arte *La Gioconda*.
f. El estilo .... pertenece al siglo XX.

CULTURE

7 Answer the following questions with the information you learned in *La dieta mediterránea... ¿mito o realidad?*

a. ¿Cuáles son algunos de los ingredientes típicos de la gastronomía mediterránea?
b. ¿Cómo es el clima de estos países? ¿Qué parte de España no está incluida en este clima? ¿Por qué?
c. ¿De qué manera está cambiando la dieta y cuál es el resultado?
d. Últimamente, ¿qué prefieren comer los jóvenes? ¿Y tú?
e. ¿Qué alimento consumen más los españoles? ¿Crees que es igual en Estados Unidos?
f. ¿Qué alimento se consume menos en España? ¿Crees que es igual en Estado Unidos?

Practice what you have learned with additional materials online.

Activity 5

a. poner en remojo; **b.** escurrir; **c.** lavar; **d.** cocer; **e.** escurrir; **f.** guisar; **g.** añadir.

Activity 6

a. leyes; **b.** reyes; **c.** explotar; **d.** cayó; **e.** huyó; **f.** expresionista.

Activity 7

Answers may vary.

a. Los ingredientes típicos son los vegetales, el queso, las aceitunas, la sal, la pimienta y el aceite de oliva; **b.** El clima de estos países es cálido, pero el norte de España es diferente porque tiene un clima más frío y lluvioso; **c.** Las familias ya no tienen tanto tiempo para cocinar y suelen preparar platos rápidos, a menudo no muy saludables; **d.** Últimamente los jóvenes prefieren comer comida rápida; **e.** El alimento que más se consume en España es la carne; **f.** El alimento que menos se consume en España es la bollería.

OBJECTIVES FOR EN RESUMEN: VOCABULARIO

- Review unit vocabulary and expressions
- Practice communicative skills

STANDARDS

1.2 Understand the language
1.3 Present information
4.1 Evaluate similarities and differences in language

INSTRUCTIONAL STRATEGIES

- Encourage students to use self-adhesive notes to place on correct objects in their house.
- Index cards can be used as flashcards with the Spanish term on one side and the English term on the other, or a picture or drawing.
- Students work in pairs or groups, using vocabulary flashcards as they would the cards of a board game to help each other practice unit vocabulary.
- Encourage students to write labels or captions for the photos on this page. Remind them to use the vocabulary and expressions they have learned in this unit.

EN RESUMEN: Vocabulario

Verbos

adelgazar *to lose weight*
aliñar *to dress (salad)*
añadir *to add*
cocer *to boil, cook*
congelar *to freeze*
consumir *to consume*
engordar *to gain weight*
escurrir *to drain*
estar enamorado/a de *to be in love with*
lavar *to rinse*

poner en remojo *to soak*
triturar *to grind*

Descripciones

a la plancha *grilled*
crudo *raw*
desnatado/a *skimmed*
entero/a *whole*
saludable *healthy*
sano/a *healthy*
soso/a *bland*

Pedir y dar consejos

Deberías... *You should...*
Es que... *It's just that...*
¿Me dejas...? *Will you allow me to...?*
Para pedir permiso. *Asking for permission.*
¿Podría...? *Could I...?*
¿Podrías...? *Could you...?*
¿Puedo...? *Can I...?*
¿Qué puedo hacer? *What can I do?*

¿Sería tan amable de...? *Would you be so kind as to...?*
¿Te importaría...? *Would you mind...?*
¿Te importa si...? *Do you mind if...?*
¿Tú qué harías? *What would you do?*
Yo que tú / Yo en tu lugar... *If I were you...*

Los alimentos

el aceite de girasol *sunflower oil*
el aceite de oliva *olive oil*

la berenjena *eggplant*

el bistec *steak*
el bizcocho *cake*

el calabacín *zucchini*
la carne picada *ground beef*

las cerezas *cherries*
el chorizo *sausage*

la chuleta de cerdo *pork chop*
los dulces *sweets*
los embutidos *cold cuts*
las espinacas *spinach*
los frijoles *beans*
los garbanzos *chick peas*

los guisantes *peas*
las lentejas *lentils*
la magdalena *muffin*

la mantequilla *butter*

la pechuga de pollo *chicken breast*
la piña *pineapple*
el sabor *taste, flavor*
la sal *salt*
el salchichón *salami*
la salsa *sauce*
el trozo de *piece of*
el vinagre *vinegar*

EN RESUMEN: Gramática

ASKING FOR AND GIVING ADVICE

(See page 119)

■ Para **pedir consejos**:

¿Qué puedo hacer?　　　*¿Tú qué harías?*　　　*¿Podrías aconsejarme?*

■ Para **dar consejos** o recomendaciones:

Yo / Yo que tú / Yo en tu lugar, comería de una manera más saludable.

Deberías / podrías acostarte. Es tarde.

■ Otras formas:

¿Por qué no vas al médico?　　　*Juan y tú tienen que ir a ver esa película.*

Toma un taxi, llegarás más rápido.　　　*No fumes. Te hace daño.*

¿Y si comes menos fritos?

THE CONDITIONAL TENSE

(See pages 127 and 128)

■ Regular verbs.

REGULAR VERBS			
	CONGELAR	COCER	ESCURRIR
yo	congelaría	cocería	escurriría
tú	congelarías	cocerías	escurrirías
usted/él/ella	congelaría	cocería	escurriría
nosotros/as	congelaríamos	coceríamos	escurriríamos
vosotros/as	congelaríais	coceríais	escurriríais
ustedes/ellos/ellas	congelarían	cocerían	escurrirían

■ Irregular verbs.

IRREGULAR VERBS			
poder ➡ **podr-**			ía
salir ➡ **saldr-**	tener ➡ **tendr-**		ías
caber ➡ **cabr-**	poner ➡ **pondr-**	hacer ➡ **har-**	ía
haber ➡ **habr-**	venir ➡ **vendr-**	decir ➡ **dir-**	íamos
saber ➡ **sabr-**	valer ➡ **valdr-**		íais
querer ➡ **querr-**			ían

■ The conditional is used to:

• Give **advice** or **recommendations**:

Yo / yo que tú / yo en tu lugar, comería más fruta y verdura. Comes fatal.

Deberías escribirle un mensaje. Creo que está preocupado.

Podrías dedicarte al deporte a nivel profesional. Eres muy bueno.

• Ask for **favors** or **permission**:

¿Te importaría hacerme un favor? Es que mañana tengo un examen…

• Express **probability** or **hypothesis** in the past:

En aquella época yo ganaría unos 1.000 euros al mes.

139

AHORA COMPRUEBA

OBJECTIVES FOR AHORA COMPRUEBA

- Review and recycle grammar, vocabulary and culture from the last two units
- Complete self-assessment

CORE RESOURCES

- Audio Program: Tracks 33 and 34

STANDARDS

1.2   Understand the language
4.1   Compare languages

INSTRUCTIONAL STRATEGIES

To introduce the theme, ask students what sections they would include in a monthly magazine at their school. Encourage students to think back to the content presented in the previous units.

Activity 1

- As a warm-up, tell students to react to the following: **Un famoso director de cine ha aceptado ser entrevistado para la revista de la escuela pero todavía no les puedo decir quién es.** Prompt as needed to elicit reactions of surprise, incredulity, and curiosity. Record student responses on the board.
- Have students match the responses in the activity.

Activity 2

- Have students select the appropriate response.
- As a follow-up, ask students to provide additional reactions and turn back to the section in the unit where these were presented.

Activity 3

In this activity students practice with **por** and **para** plus the uses of all past tenses including the pluperfect.

ANSWERS

Activity 1

1. b; **2.** c; **3.** a.

Activity 2

a. 3; **b.** 1; **c.** 2.

Activity 3

había regresado; para; para; conocí; conoció; han ganado; filmé; recibí; por; había ganado.

AHORA COMPRUEBA

LA REVISTA DE LA ESCUELA

Some high school students have decided to create their own magazine. They will include interviews, a section to give advice, another on movies, theatre and literature, and they will also report on workshops or activities organized at the school.

1 Connect the students' comments, on the left, with what they express, on the right.

1. Cuenta, cuenta, ¿de quién ha sido la idea de crear la revista? .... •
2. ¡Qué fuerte! ¿Has visto? ¡Entrevistan a la directora de cine Anamar Orson! ...... •
3. ¡Imposible! ¡Anamar Orson entrevistada por estudiantes de la escuela! .... •

- **a.** Incredulidad.
- **b.** Interés y curiosidad.
- **c.** Sorpresa.

2 Complete the students' comments with a comment from the previous exercise.

a. Cuando me dijeron que los creadores de la revista habían hablado personalmente con ella, me sorprendí muchísimo. Lo primero que dije al escucharlo fue:

b. Cuando estaba desayunando en la cafetería con Lucía, escuchamos a Dani contar que unos alumnos le habían propuesto a Paco, el profe de Literatura, crear una revista para la escuela, y en ese momento yo le interrumpí:

c. Ayer en la puerta de la escuela estaban repartiendo ejemplares del primer número de la revista. Agarré uno y solo ver la portada ¡me quedé alucinada!, ¡no me lo podía creer! ¿Cómo lo habían conseguido? Así que fui corriendo a buscar a Carla y le dije:

3 Some students have talked to Anamar Orson. Read an excerpt from the interview and choose the correct verb forms and preposition: *por* or *para*.

Entrevistador: Pero, entonces, Anamar, ¿usted y el actor Cristian Pascual se conocen desde hace mucho tiempo?

Anamar Orson: Sí, somos viejos amigos. Nos conocemos desde el 99, yo **regresé** / **había regresado** a España **por** / **para** hacer un curso **por** / **para** enseñar español y fue entonces cuando **conocí** / **había conocido** a Cristian.

E.: Y fue en esa misma época cuando **conoció** / **había conocido** también a Paco, nuestro profesor de Literatura, ¿no?

A.O.: Efectivamente.

E.: Por lo que sabemos, sus trabajos **han ganado** / **habían ganado** un total de tres premios cinematográficos.

A.O.: Sí, así es. En el año 2005 **filmé** / **he filmado** mi primera película y **recibí** / **había recibido** dos premios Goya. Pero este no fue mi primer premio **para** / **por** mi trabajo en el cine. Dos años antes **había ganado** / **ha ganado** la Concha de Oro del Festival de San Sebastián al mejor corto español.

4 🎧 **33** **Listen to the comments on the new high school magazine. Write the number next to the piece of advice or appropriate recommendation.**

a. ⬜ ¿Por qué no hablas sinceramente con ellos? Seguro que te entenderán.

b. ⬜ ¿Y si le pedimos una suya? Es tan maja que seguro que nos da alguna.

c. ⬜ Deberías organizarte, estudiar un poco todos los días y hacerte resúmenes y esquemas, porque si lo dejas todo para antes del examen, te agobiarás más.

d. ⬜ ¿Por qué no echas un vistazo a las sugerencias para el finde de la revista? Proponen un montón de planes alternativos: desde rutas turísticas por la ciudad, hasta intercambios de idiomas, excursiones a la sierra… Seguro que encuentras algo interesante.

e. ⬜ No te preocupes, tu problema tiene solución. Es evidente que te esfuerzas, pero creo que no estás dando los pasos acertados. Yo en tu lugar buscaría un profesor particular.

f. ⬜ Eso se llama pánico escénico. Yo que tú intentaría aprender algunas técnicas de relajación y centraría mis esfuerzos en prepararme bien el guion.

5 🎧 **34** **Listen to the complete dialogues and check your preceding answers.**

6 **Read the following pieces of advice or recommendations, taken from the magazine. Then link to the correct text.**

1. ¿Por qué no haces el siguiente test de compatibilidad?
2. Yo que tú esperaría un poco más y aclararía antes mis ideas.
3. Deberías contactar con la gente del lugar a pesar del miedo.
4. Trata de alcanzar una velocidad de cuatro a nueve kilómetros por hora.

a. ⬜ Imaginemos que viajas para hacer un curso de español a España. Aterrizas y te das cuenta de que todos tus miedos son reales. Te cuesta entender a la gente, entras en pánico y tomas el camino fácil: te juntas con personas de tu país de origen y hablas todo el tiempo tu lengua materna. ¡¡¡Error!!!

b. ⬜ ¡Sorpresa! Maxi Castro, nuestro actor favorito, se está dejando de nuevo el pelo largo, eso ya lo veíamos venir, ¿verdad? Pero lo que no sabíamos es que se volvería a dejar el pelo como en sus inicios. Si quieres saber si eres compatible con Maxi,…

c. ⬜ Caminata rápida. Este ejercicio es uno de los más recomendables. El único equipo necesario es calzado cómodo y un camino. Alarga el paso y ve a un ritmo bastante rápido.

d. ⬜ Querida Alicia: Sé que estás pasando por un mal momento y que tal vez piensas que ese muchacho es el apoyo que necesitas, pero ahora mismo no te conviene empezar una relación.

7 **The new magazine is still being tested. The editors are looking for a good title and some content suggestions among the students. Write them a letter, considering:**

a. Propón un título para esta.

b. Da algunas sugerencias y recomendaciones sobre sus contenidos.

c. Pide algún consejo.

d. Envía una receta de cocina para su próximo concurso de recetas.

141

🎧 **33** **Activity 4**

• To introduce the listening activity and in keeping with the theme about creating a school magazine, tell students that they are going to listen to excerpts of students talking about their school magazine either as part of the editorial team that put the publication together, the students in charge of the advice section, or students reading the magazine.

• Have students read through the statements and ask them to think about which might be the logical context for each.

• Play the audio. Students will have the opportunity to confirm their answers in the next activity.

Audioscript

1. He suspendido otra vez Matemáticas…, no sé cómo voy a aprobar esta asignatura, estudio un montón pero es que soy muy malo para los números.

2. ¡Qué horror! ¡¡¡Esta fotografía queda fatal!!! Se la ve desde muy lejos y borrosa, casi no se reconoce que es ella.

3. No sé qué hacer… Por un lado, quiero seguir con la tradición familiar de ser médico y no quitarles la ilusión a mis padres, pero por otro pienso que es mi futuro lo que está en juego y que a mí lo que me apasiona es el periodismo.

4. Estoy aburrida de hacer siempre lo mismo el fin de semana: o película o discoteca. ¿Es que a nadie se le ocurre algún plan más interesante?

5. Nunca conseguiré que me seleccionen para el papel, cuando estoy en el escenario se me olvida todo y no me salen ni las palabras.

6. No sé qué hacer para aprobar Historia: es demasiada información y no retengo nada.

🎧 **34** **Activity 5**

• Here students will have the opportunity listen to the entire conversations for each of the statements in Activity 4.

• Play the audio and have students confirm their answers.

See audioscript on page APP1

Activity 6

Students may work in pairs or individually.

Activity 7

• Remind students that the letter they are composing is directed to the students on the editorial team of the magazine so they should choose their approach accordingly. Students can refer to appropriate structures presented in the units.

• Tell students that they must address all four points.

ANSWERS

Activity 4

a. 3; b. 2; c. 6; d. 4; e. 1; f. 5.

Activity 6

a. 3; b. 1; c. 4; d. 2.

OBJECTIVES FOR UNIT OPENER

- Introduce unit theme: **¡Ojalá!** about expressing wishes and emotional reactions to events
- Introduce culture for unit: Learn about opportunities for volunteering in Hispanic countries

STANDARDS

- 1.1 Engage in conversation
- 2.1 Practices and culture

INSTRUCTIONAL STRATEGIES

- Before students open their books, write **tareas solidarias** on the board. Elicit a definition and examples. If students struggle to understand or contribute, consider giving them examples of two different actions, one that exemplifies volunteer work and one that doesn't. Have them guess which one is an example of a **tarea solidaria**. Then ask them for more examples of their own.
- Have students open their books. Focus their attention on the photo. Invite them to share things they see or notice. You can prompt them to provide simple and obvious statements as well, such as: **Hay cuatro personas**, **Son amigos**, **Están sonriendo**, **Llevan guantes y tienen bolsas de plástico**, etc.
- Have students work individually to write answers to the three questions on the page.
- Put students into pairs to share and discuss their answers.
- Call on volunteers to report back on their responses and discussions.
- Help students formulate their ideas using **Van a recoger basura**, **Creo que están en su comunidad o cerca de su escuela**, **Sí, he participado en una campaña solidaria, he cocinado para personas sin hogar**.

UNIDAD 5 ¡OJALÁ!

Cuatro amigos comparten su tiempo realizando tareas solidarias.

⟫ ¿Qué van a hacer los muchachos?

⟫ ¿Dónde crees que están desarrollando su tarea?

⟫ ¿Has participado alguna vez en campañas solidarias? ¿Qué has hecho?

142

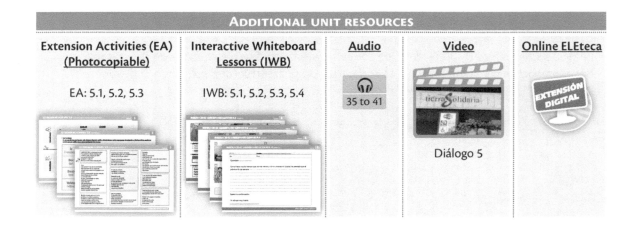

ADDITIONAL UNIT RESOURCES

Extension Activities (EA) (Photocopiable)	Interactive Whiteboard Lessons (IWB)	Audio	Video	Online ELEteca
EA: 5.1, 5.2, 5.3	IWB: 5.1, 5.2, 5.3, 5.4	35 to 41	Diálogo 5	EXTENSIÓN DIGITAL

**In this unit,
you will learn to:**

- Discuss emotional reactions to events
- Situate events in time
- Express purpose
- Use appropriate responses in social situations
- Talk about volunteering and NGOs

Using

- Present Subjunctive
- The subjunctive with adverbial conjunctions
- Common expressions

Cultural Connections

- Share information about volunteering in Hispanic countries and compare cultural similarities

SABOR HISPANO

- «Me encanta ser voluntario»

¡ACCIÓN!

tierra Solidaria

143

LEARNING OUTCOMES

- Discuss emotional reactions to events
- Situate events in time
- Express purpose
- Use appropriate responses in social situations
- Talk about volunteering and NGOs

INSTRUCTIONAL STRATEGIES

- Use the unit opener to preview vocabulary and cultural topics for this unit.
- Have students look at the images on this page and try to relate them to the objectives listed.
- Exploit the two main photos a bit further: ***Miren la foto del edificio: ¿En qué país creen que está? ¿Por qué? ¿Qué tipo de edificio creen que es?*** (It's a church in the Plaza de la Constitución in Guatemala City). ***Miren la foto de las dos manos: ¿Quiénes son? ¿Cuál es su historia? ¿Cómo se sienten cuando ven esta foto?***
- Invite students to read the topic for **Sabor hispano** and preview that section in the unit. Ask questions, such as: ***¿Te gusta ser voluntario? ¿Por qué?***
- Ask students to anticipate what they think the episode for **¡Acción!** will be about.

THREE MODES OF COMMUNICATION: UNIT 5		
	INTERPERSONAL	**INTERPRETIVE**	**PRESENTATIONAL**

	INTERPERSONAL	INTERPRETIVE	PRESENTATIONAL
HABLAMOS DE...	6	1, 2, 3, 4, 5	6
COMUNICA	4, 7	1, 2, 3, 5, 6	3
¡ACCIÓN!		1, 2, 3, 4	
PALABRA POR PALABRA	1, 9	1, 2, 3, 4, 5, 6, 7, 8	
GRAMÁTICA	3, 6, 8	1, 2, 4, 5, 7	6, 8
DESTREZAS		1, 3	2, 4
CULTURA		SABOR HISPANO	
RELATO		1, 2, 3, 4	5

OBJECTIVES FOR HABLAMOS DE...

- Understand language in context
- Preview vocabulary: Expressing wishes
- Preview grammatical structures: The present subjunctive
- Read and listen to a conversation between Paula and Irene about their summer plans

CORE RESOURCES

- Audio Program: Track 35

STANDARDS

1.2 Understand the language

1.3 Present the language

INSTRUCTIONAL STRATEGIES

Activity 1

- Have students look at the illustrations. Ask: **¿Qué tipo de relación creen que tienen los personajes de las imágenes?** Discuss their ideas until they reach agreement. Guide them to the conclusion that the first scene is between a mother and her son, and the second scene is between a doorman or super and a resident of the building.
- Put students into pairs to ask and answer the questions.
- Call on volunteers to report back. You might to challenge student responses to encourage discussion.

Activity 2

- Working in the same pairs as Activity 1, have students match the speech bubbles to the correct scene.
- Go over the answers as a class and ask for student volunteers to present.
- Once the answers are reviewed, ask students: **¿En qué situación se utiliza la expresión "¡Que aproveche!"?** (**se dice antes de empezar a comer o cuando ves a alguien que está comiendo**). You can also point out to students that these are phrases and expressions that people use frequently to express wishes and social courtesies. Tell students to note that these expressions use a new form of the verb that they are going to learn in this unit: the present subjunctive.

🎧 35 Activity 3

- Have students close their books. Tell the students that they are going to listen to a phone call between two friends, Paula and Irene. Write two question on the board to focus their attention on the first listening: **¿Por qué llamó Irene a Paula? ¿Qué va a hacer Paula este verano?**
- Play the audio. Call on volunteers to offer answers to the target questions.
- Have students open their books. Tell them they are going to listen again to determine whether the sentences are true or false.

ANSWERS

Activity 1

Escena 1: Lo está acostando; **Escena 2:** Estar un poco enfermo.

Activity 2

Escena 1: ¡Que duermas bien! **Escena 2:** ¡Que se mejore!

Activity 3

a. F; **b.** F; **c.** T; **d.** T; **e.** T; **f.** F; **g.** F.

HABLAMOS DE... Expresar deseos

1 👥 Look at the images in the two scenes above. Answer the questions and explain why. Work with your partners.

Escena 1: ¿La madre está acostando o despertando al niño?

Escena 2: ¿Pachucho es un tipo de enfermedad o significa "estar un poco enfermo"?

2 👥 Read the expressions below. Then with a partner, match the expression to the appropriate speech bubble in each of the scenes above. **¡Atención!** Only two of the expressions will work.

a. ¡Que se mejore!   **b.** ¡Que tengas suerte!   **c.** ¡Que aproveche!   **d.** ¡Que duermas bien!

3 🎧 35 Listen to the conversation. Choose with true (T) or false (F).

	T	F
a. Paula va a Guatemala a un colegio que han construido allí.	☐	☐
b. Va a estar en Guatemala dos semanas en julio.	☐	☐
c. Va a hacer un curso para aprender a convivir y trabajar en equipo.	☐	☐
d. Quiere dormir durante el viaje en avión.	☐	☐
e. Irene le desea buena suerte en su viaje.	☐	☐
f. El viaje de Paula es unos días después de terminar las clases.	☐	☐
g. Paula le contará muchas cosas a Irene desde Guatemala.	☐	☐

144

4 **Read the conversation and check your answers.**

Irene: ¡Hola, Paula! Oye, ¿has hablado ya con Ana? Es que esta mañana me ha dicho que (a) quiere que vayamos este verano a la casa que tienen sus tíos en la Costa Brava, y que si queremos podemos pasar todo el mes de julio allí. Ellos ya no van nunca y la casa está vacía.

Paula: Sí, precisamente te llamo por eso. Es que me han ofrecido la posibilidad de ir a Guatemala para ayudar a construir un colegio. Así que yo no podré ir con ustedes.

I.: ¡Qué me dices! Eso es estupendo, Paula. ¿Y vas tú sola?

P.: Bueno, voy a través de una ONG que se llama *Ayuda en Acción*. La verdad es que no conozco mucho a la gente pero, (b) antes de irnos, nos van a dar un curso durante dos semanas para saber lo que tenemos que hacer allí, conocer la situación, su cultura… y también para que nos conozcamos entre nosotros. ¡Vamos a estar un mes conviviendo y trabajando! (c) Espero llevarme bien con todos.

I.: Ya verás como sí. ¿Y cuándo te vas?

P.: (d) En cuanto terminemos las clases. De hecho, el avión sale el mismo día por la noche. ¡Ay, Irene! Son doce horas de avión y ¡odio

volar *(to fly)*! ¡(e) Ojalá me quede dormida pronto en el avión!

I.: ¡Uf! ¡Doce horas! Bueno, tú llévate el libro que nos ha recomendado el profesor de Filosofía y seguro que te duermes enseguida. Yo lo intenté empezar el otro día pero, (f) en cuanto lo abrí, me quedé dormida *(fell asleep)*. Oye, ahora en serio, me parece genial tu idea de ir a Guatemala, creo que va a ser toda una experiencia y (g) te deseo de todo corazón que te vaya muy bien y (h) ojalá tu esfuerzo sirva para que esos niños puedan vivir mejor.

P.: Muchas gracias. Ya te contaré (i) cuando vuelva. ¡Ah! y yo también (j) espero que se lo pasen muy bien en la Costa Brava. Dense un bañito en la playa por mí.

I.: ¡Eso seguro! Pero, bueno, nos veremos (k) antes de que te vayas para despedirnos, ¿no?

P.: ¡Claro! ¡Faltaría más!

5 **Arrange the highlighted expressions from the conversation in the appropriate category below.**

Alguien expresa un deseo para otra persona	Alguien desea algo para sí mismo	Se habla del futuro	Se habla del pasado
a.			

6  You and two other classmates have decided to volunteer for a project in Latin America. Choose a country and the type of project it will be: social, educational or environmental. Use the following expressions to present your plan to the rest of the class.

- antes de irnos…
- mientras estemos…
- después de estar…
- esperamos…
- deseamos…
- ojalá…

145

INSTRUCTIONAL STRATEGIES

Activity 4

- Have students read the conversation individually. Monitor their progress and assist with vocabulary as needed.
- Then put students into pairs and have them check their answers to Activity 3 with a partner. Encourage them to use the transcript to correct any mistakes.
- Go over the answers as a class. Once again, point out the new form of the verb and ask students if they recognize the form (same as **usted** command) and if they can begin to figure out when it is used.

Activity 5

- Working individually or in pairs, have the students sort the highlighted expressions from the transcript into the correct categories. The first one has been done for them.
- After reviewing the answers, ask students what sentences a, g, h, j have in common with d, i, k (they all use the subjunctive form of the verb). Explain that these are some of the functions that they're going to be focusing on in this unit.

Activity 6

- Put students into small groups. Write categories on the board: **País** and **Proyecto**. Elicit examples of different countries in Latin America and possible volunteer projects. Write a few examples on the board under the appropriate categories.
- Give students 2 minutes to decide in their groups on the country and project they want to focus on. Monitor their progress and assist as needed.
- Focus students' attention back on the board. Add the categories: **antes de irnos**, **mientras estemos**, **después de estar**. Ask students to think of things that they would need or want to do before, during, and after the project. Take note of their ideas on the board under the appropriate categories and ask if these actions refer to the present, past, or future (future).
- Then, write the category **deseamos**, **esperamos**, **ojalá** on the board. Continue eliciting examples of wishes or aspirations related to the volunteer project. Take notes on the board using infinitive expressions. For example, **Deseamos ayudar a los niños**, etc. For now, tell students to try to use the new verb form after **ojalá**. Provide some examples, **Ojalá que ayude a mucha gente**, **Ojalá que tenga una experiencia inolvidable**, etc.
- Give students 5 minutes to use their notes and the expressions in the book to write their own sentences for their presentation. Suggest that they divide up responsibilities so each person in the group writes a few sentences and prepares to share them. Monitor their progress and assist as needed, especially with the writing of sentences that might require the subjunctive.
- Finally, have each group present their volunteer project to the rest of the class.

ANSWERS

Activity 5

Alguien expresa un deseo para otra persona: **a**, **g**, **h**, **j**; Alguien desea algo para sí mismo: **c**, **e**; Se habla del futuro: **b**, **d**, **i**, **k**; Se habla del pasado: **f**.

OBJECTIVES FOR COMUNICA

- Present communicative functions of the unit:
  Expressing the moment when an action takes place
- Identify whether a sentence is referring to a habit, a past
  action, or a future action

CORE RESOURCES

- Interactive Whiteboard Lesson: IWB 5.1
- Audio Program: Track 36
- Interactive Online Materials – ELEteca

STANDARDS

1.2   Understand the language
4.1   Compare languages

INSTRUCTIONAL STRATEGIES FOR EXPRESSING THE MOMENT WHEN AN ACTION TAKES PLACE

- To introduce the topic, project IWB 5.1, **Cuando...** and go
  over it as a class.
- Have students look at the images. Call on volunteers to
  read the sentences in number 1, and match them with the
  appropriate images. Ask students to think about when the
  actions take place as you review answers.
- Then tell students to match each of the sentences in number
  1 with the correct time periods in number 2.
- Use the answers from number 2 to elicit the correct formulas
  in number 3. Encourage them to write the formulas in the
  chart in their notebooks for future reference. Then have
  students open their books, and walk them through the
  examples.
- Note that the examples **Antes de que** and **Después de que**
  are not modeled in the category for **pasado** because they
  require the past/imperfect subjunctive (**Salí antes de que /
  después de que cenaras**), which students haven't studied yet.

🎧 36 Activity 1

- Have students work on their own to complete the
  conversation with the phrases in the box.
- Monitor their progress and assist as needed.
- Play the audio to allow them to go over their answers. Ask
  if they need any clarification; offer to play the audio again, if
  necessary.
- Put the students in pairs, and have them practice the
  conversations. Have them practice both roles.

COMUNICA

EXPRESSING THE MOMENT WHEN AN ACTION TAKES PLACE

- Para relacionar dos acciones en el **futuro**:
  Al *llegar a casa, cenaré.* Upon arriving home, I will have dinner.
  Cuando / En cuanto *llegue a casa, cenaré.* When / As soon as I get home, I will have dinner.
  Saldré **antes de / después de** *cenar.* I'll leave before / after having dinner.
  Saldré **antes de que / después de que** *vengan mis padres.* I'll leave before / after my parents come.
  Veré la tele **hasta que** *cene.* I'll watch TV until I have dinner.

- Para relacionar dos acciones en el **pasado**:
  Al *terminar la clase, salí con mis amigos.* When class ended, I left with my friends.
  Cuando / En cuanto *terminó la clase, salí con mis amigos.* When / As soon as class ended, I left with my friends.
  Salí **antes de / después de** *terminar la clase.* I left before / after class ended.
  Hablé por teléfono con Marta **hasta que** *llegaron mis padres.* I spoke to Marta on the phone until my parents arrived.

- Para hablar de verdades universales o **hábitos**:
  Al *llegar a casa, hago la tarea.*
  Upon arriving home, I do my homework.
  Cuando / En cuanto *llego a casa, hago la tarea.*
  When / As soon as I get home, I do my homework.
  Siempre **hago la tarea antes de / después de** *salir de clase.*
  I always do my homework before / after getting home.
  A veces escucho música **hasta que** *llego a casa.*
  Sometimes I listen to music until I get home.

En cuanto llego a casa, hago la tarea.

1 🎧 **36** Complete the conversations with an expression from the list. Use the chart above for
reference. Then listen to the audio and check your work.

> al ○ cuando ○ antes de ○ después de ○ en cuanto ○ hasta que

» ¡Oh! ¡Qué colgante *(pendant)* tan bonito!
» Gracias, me lo ha regalado Marina. Dice que si me lo pongo
  (a) .... haga el examen de Química, me dará suerte.
» Uf... yo no creo en esas supersticiones. Lo que tienes que hacer es
  estudiar (b) .... hacer el examen.

» ¡Que tengas buen viaje, cariño! ¡No te olvides de llamarme (c) .... llegar al hotel!
» Descuida. Te llamaré (d) .... llegue.
» Eso espero, porque la última vez no me llamaste.
» ¡Cómo que no! Sí te llamé.
» Sí, me llamaste, pero tres días (e) .... llegar.
» No, también te llamé antes, pero no contestaste. De todas formas, no te
  preocupes, esta vez no dejaré de llamarte (f) .... me contestes.

146

ANSWERS

IWB 5.1

Futuro: *Cuando* + verbo en subjuntivo: Cuando llegue a la portería, no
lo dudaré, chutaré y meteré un gol (Imagen 3); **Pasado:** *Cuando* + verbo
en indicativo: Cuando llegué a la portería, no lo dudé, chuté y metí el gol
(Imagen 1); **Acción habitual:** *Cuando* + verbo en indicativo: Qué suerte, yo
cuando llego a la portería, me pongo tan nervioso que no consigo ni chutar
(Imagen 2).

Activity 1

a. cuando; **b.** antes de; **c.** al; **d.** en cuanto; **e.** después de; **f.** hasta que.

EXPRESSING PURPOSE OR OBJECTIVE

2 Read the uses of *para* and *para que*. Then find other examples from the conversation on page 145 for each case.

■ Para expresar la finalidad *(purpose)* o el motivo por el que se hace algo se usa **para** o **para que**.

• **Para** + infinitivo ➡ Si los dos sujetos *(subjects)* de la oración son los mismos, o uno de los dos no está especificado.

(Yo) *he hecho muchas fotos* **para (yo) colgarlas** *en Facebook.*

(a) ....

• **Para que** + subjuntivo ➡ Si hay sujetos diferentes.

(Yo) he traído *las fotos de las vacaciones* **para que (tú)** *las* **veas**.

(b) ....

3 Look at the images and, with your partner, decide what these people are doing. Use *para* and *para que* in your descriptions to express purpose.

Sofía y Ramiro

Borja y su madre

las amigas

Tomás

Emilia y sus amigos

los novios

el padre, Alicia y su madre

la profesora y Alberto

147

OBJECTIVES FOR COMUNICA

• Present communicative functions of the unit: Expressing purpose or objective
• Recognize and practice expressions of purpose, objective, and wishes

CORE RESOURCES

• Interactive Whiteboard Lesson: IWB 5.2

STANDARDS

1.1   Engage in conversation
3.2   Acquire information

INSTRUCTIONAL STRATEGIES

FOR EXPRESSING PURPOSE OR OBJECTIVE

Activity 2

• Walk students through the explanations and examples on the page.
• Have students find examples of **para** and **para que** from the conversation on page 145 to complete the chart. Focus their attention on the subjects of each sentence and the use of the subjunctive.
• In preparation for the next activity, elicit the subjunctive conjugations of the forms of **ver**. Do the same with an **–ar** verb, such as **hablar**. Ask what they notice about the endings for the **–er** verb versus the **–ar** verb. Again, you may wish to remind students that they have already seen these forms in Unidad 2 with the command forms.

Activity 3

• Note that these images are also available for projection: IWB 5.2, **¿Para qué...?**

• Then brainstorm other ideas with students for the first situation listing them under the headings **para** and **para que**, and modeling correct forms.
• Put students into pairs to discuss their ideas for each scene. Have them write down their descriptions so they are prepared to share them with the class.
• Call on volunteers to offer their descriptions for each picture. Ask questions such as **¿Para qué ha llamado por teléfono?** (**Para preguntarle qué tal está**) to encourage students to offer different examples with **para** and **para que**. Help students self-correct, if necessary.

ANSWERS

Activity 3

Possible answers might include the following: **a.** La chica le llama por teléfono para preguntarle cómo está; **b.** Anima a su amigo para que sople las velas; **c.** Han quedado para comer juntas; **d.** Mira al cielo para ver si llueve; **e.** Va a la estación para despedirse y para que tengan buen viaje; **f.** Se acercan a los novios para desearles que sean muy felices; **g.** Van al centro para pasear un rato; **h.** Le ha comprado una colección de libros de su autora favorita para que los lea este verano.

INSTRUCTIONAL STRATEGIES

Activity 4

- Read the first sentence and focus students' attention on **ojalá** and the language note. Call on students to read the remaining sentences to discuss any vocabulary.
- Then individually, have students select the ones that are true for them.
- Take a class poll for each wish on the list. Have students give a thumbs up for each wish they selected. Discuss which ones are the most popular.

Activity 5

- Put students into pairs to complete the chart. Remind students to use the examples in Activity 4 to get them started and then, to focus on what happens to the rest of the sentence after these verbs.
- Have student pairs compare their answers with another pair.
- Confirm the answers as a class making sure students understand who the subject is in each sentence. Review a few more examples from the wish list.

OBJECTIVES FOR COMUNICA

- Present communicative functions of the unit: Other expressions of wishes and social responses
- Practice using appropriate social responses in a variety of situations

CORE RESOURCES

- Audio program: Track 37

STANDARDS

- 1.1 Engage in conversation
- 1.2 Understand the language
- 4.1 Compare languages

INSTRUCTIONAL STRATEGIES FOR
OTHER EXPRESSIONS AND SOCIAL RESPONSES

🎧 37 Activity 6

- Explain to the students that they are going to listen to a series of conversations. Each conversation contains an expression appropriate to the social context presented. Give them a few minutes to skim the different contexts presented.
- Play the audio and repeat as necessary. Have students compare their answer with a partner. Confirm the correct responses as a class.

See audioscript on page APP2

Activity 7

- Tell student pairs to first choose a role and then read the sentence on the card to elicit an appropriate response from their partner.

COMUNICA

4 👥 The following is a wish list expressed by the students in the class. With a partner, talk about the wishes and the ones that are also true for you.

- **Ojalá** que algún día dejen de existir los exámenes.
- Este año **espero** no recibir menos de C en ninguna asignatura.
- El año que viene **quiero** ir a España a estudiar español.
- **Deseo** que mis amigos me hagan una fiesta sorpresa para mi cumpleaños.
- **Espero** que este curso no sea tan difícil como nos han contado.
- **Deseo** hacer un safari por África.

 The expression **ojalá** comes from an Arabic expression meaning "God (Allah)" and is used as the equivalent of "I hope that, let's hope that" It may be used with or without **que**.

5 👥 Look again at the expressions in bold in Activity 4 and complete the chart accordingly with *desear, esperar, infinitivo, querer* and *subjuntivo*.

| (a) .... | verbo en (d) .... (si el sujeto de las dos acciones es el mismo).
(Yo) Quiero (yo) ir mañana a la playa. |
| (b) .... + | |
| (c) .... | **que** + verbo en (e) .... (si el sujeto de las dos acciones es diferente).
(Yo) Quiero que (tú) me compres un helado. |

OTHER EXPRESSIONS AND SOCIAL RESPONSES

6 🎧 37 Listen to the dialogues and complete the chart.

- A alguien que se va a dormir.
  Que duermas bien. (a) ....
- A alguien que va a empezar a comer o está comiendo. (b) ....
- A alguien que tiene un examen o una entrevista de trabajo.
  Que tengas suerte. (c) ....
- A alguien que está enfermo.
  Que te mejores.

- A alguien que va a hacer algo divertido.
  Que disfrutes. (d) ....
  Que (te) lo pases bien.
- A alguien que ha tenido una mala noticia.
  (e) ....
- A alguien que ha tenido una buena noticia.
  Enhorabuena. (f) ....
- A alguien que se va por mucho tiempo.
  (g) ....

7 👥 Taking turns with a partner, respond accordingly to the social situation presented by your partner.

Estudiante 1

Dices:
1. ¡Ana / Juan y yo nos casamos!
2. Me voy a dormir.
3. Esta noche voy a un concierto.

Estudiante 2

Dices:
1. El partido va a comenzar.
2. ¡Van a quitar los exámenes!
3. Me voy a estudiar al extranjero seis meses.

 Practice what you have learned with additional materials online.

- To correct the activity together assign half the class to **Estudiante 1** and the other to **Estudiante 2**. One student from the first group says one of the sentences to one of the students in the other group, who responds appropriately and continues in the same way choosing to whom he/she directs the comments until all responses are reviewed.

ANSWERS

Activity 5

a. Querer; **b.** Esperar; **c.** Desear; **d.** infinitivo; **e.** subjuntivo.

Activity 6

a. Que descanses; **b.** Que aproveche; **c.** Que te vaya bien; **d.** Que te diviertas; **e.** Lo siento mucho; **f.** Felicidades; **g.** Cuídate.

¡ACCIÓN!

UNIDAD 5

ANTES DEL VIDEO

1 Look at the scenes from the video segment and answer the questions. Then compare your answers with a partner. Do you agree?

¿Qué crees que representa el cartel?

¿Dónde crees que están?

¿Quién crees que es?

¿Qué crees que está haciendo en este momento?

DURANTE EL VIDEO

2 Check your answers to the previous activity against the information provided in the video.

DESPUÉS DEL VIDEO

3 Choose the correct option.

1. El responsable de la ONG ha reunido a los estudiantes…
   a. para organizar una visita a una ONG.
   b. para informar a los estudiantes de una nueva ONG.
   c. para informar a los estudiantes del proyecto de una ONG y para que estos se hagan voluntarios.

2. Los estudiantes quieren…
   a. que el responsable les ayude a completar el formulario de inscripción *(registration)* de voluntario.
   b. saber en qué consiste su trabajo en el proyecto y que el responsable les diga la fecha.
   c. dar dinero para ayudar a la ONG.

3. El proyecto presentado consiste en…
   a. enviar profesores a Guatemala.
   b. visitar colegios necesitados en Guatemala.
   c. viajar a Guatemala y construir una escuela.

149

OBJECTIVES FOR ¡ACCIÓN!
- Provide students with a structured approach to viewing the video
- Contextualize the content of the unit in a familiar scenario

CORE RESOURCES
- Unit Video 5
- Interactive Online Materials – ELEteca

STANDARDS
1.3 Understand the language
2.1 Practices and perspectives

INSTRUCTIONAL STRATEGIES

Previewing: Antes del video

Activity 1
- Put students into pairs. Go over the instructions. Explain that they are going to make predictions before watching the video.
- Monitor their discussions and assist as needed. Encourage them to give reasons for their predictions.
- Call on volunteers to report back on their discussions and share their predictions.

Viewing: Durante el video

Activity 2
- Tell students to watch and listen for the correct answers to the questions in Activity 1.
- Play the video. Discuss the answers to the questions from Activity 1.

ANSWERS

Activity 1
Answers will vary. Possible answers might include the following:
Imagen 1: El cartel representa una organización que hace tareas solidarias; **Imagen 2:** Creo que están en una aula; **Imagen 3:** Creo que es un responsable de la ONG; **Imagen 4:** Creo que les está explicando a un grupo de alumnos lo que significa la palabra ONG y algún proyecto relacionado con esta organización.

INSTRUCTIONAL STRATEGIES

After viewing: Después del video

Activity 3

- Give students some time to read and attempt the activity based on what they remember from the first viewing.
- Play the video again, allowing the students to select or confirm their answers.
- Put students in pairs to review their answers.
- Go over the answers as a class, clarifying any disagreement in responses between partners.

Activity 4

- Have students work individually –or in the same pairs as Activity 3– to read the statements about each character and answer whether they are true or false.
- Monitor students' progress. Play the video again, if necessary.
- Go over the answers as a class.

ANSWERS

Activity 3

1. c; 2. b; 3. c; 4. a; 5. c.

Activity 4

Person 1: **a.** F; **b.** T; **c.** F.

Person 2: **a.** F; **b.** T; **c.** T.

Person 3: **a.** F; **b.** F; **c.** T.

Person 4: **a.** T; **b.** T; **c.** F.

Person 5: **a.** T; **b.** T; **c.** F.

Persons 6: **a.** F; **b.** T; **c.** T.

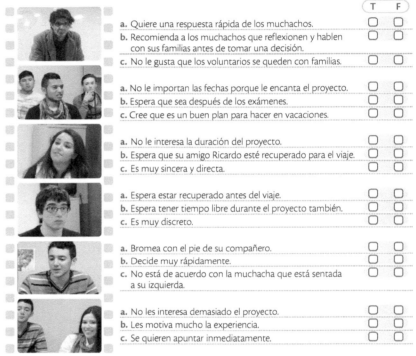

¡ACCIÓN!

4. Los muchachos conocerán la fecha exacta del proyecto...
   a. cuando se sepa el número exacto de voluntarios.
   b. cuando les den las notas de junio.
   c. cuando lo consulten con sus familias.

5. La ONG...
   a. pagará el viaje y el hotel de los voluntarios.
   b. no pagará el viaje y no es responsable del alojamiento.
   c. pagará parte del viaje y organizará el alojamiento de los voluntarios en casas habitadas por familias del lugar.

4 Decide whether the statements are true (T) or false (F) for the people in each of the images.

	T	F
a. Quiere una respuesta rápida de los muchachos.	☐	☐
b. Recomienda a los muchachos que reflexionen y hablen con sus familias antes de tomar una decisión.	☐	☐
c. No le gusta que los voluntarios se queden con familias.	☐	☐
a. No le importan las fechas porque le encanta el proyecto.	☐	☐
b. Espera que sea después de los exámenes.	☐	☐
c. Cree que es un buen plan para hacer en vacaciones.	☐	☐
a. No le interesa la duración del proyecto.	☐	☐
b. Espera que su amigo Ricardo esté recuperado para el viaje.	☐	☐
c. Es muy sincera y directa.	☐	☐
a. Espera estar recuperado antes del viaje.	☐	☐
b. Espera tener tiempo libre durante el proyecto también.	☐	☐
c. Es muy discreto.	☐	☐
a. Bromea con el pie de su compañero.	☐	☐
b. Decide muy rápidamente.	☐	☐
c. No está de acuerdo con la muchacha que está sentada a su izquierda.	☐	☐
a. No les interesa demasiado el proyecto.	☐	☐
b. Les motiva mucho la experiencia.	☐	☐
c. Se quieren apuntar inmediatamente.	☐	☐

Practice what you have learned with additional materials online.

PALABRA POR PALABRA Las ONG
UNIDAD **5**

1 👥 Look at the following images and describe what the people are doing. What do they all have in common?

2 👥 With a partner, match the images in Activity 1 to the expressions below. ¡Atención! Each expression will have more than one letter or image. Then list other expressions you know in Spanish relating to NGOs (Non-Governmental Organizations).

1. catástrofes naturales ➡ ...a....
2. conflictos bélicos *(armed)* ➡ ....
3. labores humanitarias ➡ ....
4. protección del medioambiente ➡ ....

5. comercio justo ➡ ....
6. donativo ➡ ....
7. voluntario ➡ ....
8. labor social ➡ ....

3 Look at these logos. Do you recognize them?

4 👥 Decide whether the following statements about Cruz Roja are true (T) or false (F). Then compare your answers with a partner.

	T	F
a. La Cruz Roja nació después de un viaje de su fundador por los países del tercer mundo.	☐	☐
b. La Cruz Roja es una organización que atiende a personas de todo el planeta.	☐	☐
c. La mayoría de los países dan parte de su Producto Interior Bruto o PIB *(Gross Domestic Producto or GDP)* a las ONG para ayudarlas a financiarse.	☐	☐
d. Las personas que trabajan en las ONG son todas voluntarias.	☐	☐

151

OBJECTIVES FOR LAS ONG

- Present vocabulary needed to practice communicative and grammatical functions for the unit: Non-governmental organizations or NGOs
- Identify and discuss different causes for which people often volunteer

CORE RESOURCES

- Interactive Whiteboard Lesson: IWB 5.3
- Interactive Online Materials – ELEteca

STANDARDS

1.2 Understand the language

3.1 Knowledge of other disciplines

INSTRUCTIONAL STRATEGIES

Activity 1

- Before students open their books, project IWB 5.3, **Las ONG**. Hide the phrases beneath the images. Look at the images one at a time.
- Ask students to describe what they see. Ask questions, such as: **¿Dónde están? ¿Qué están haciendo? ¿Cuál es el problema? ¿Qué tienen todos en común?**

Activity 2

- Review the first item with the class. Put students into pairs and have them work together on the remaining items.
- Project IWB 5.3, **Las ONG** again to review answers as a class. Check their understanding of the phrases by asking for definitions or additional examples.

Activity 3

- Take a class poll to find out how many students recognize each organization.
- Elicit basic explanations of what each organization does.
- Give examples of different scenarios and see if they can correctly identify which of the three organizations helps in each situation.

Activity 4

Put students into pairs. Tell them to read statements about the Red Cross. Have them work together to decide if the statements are true or false based on what they may already know about this organization. Tell them to guess if they are unsure of the answers. Do not review answers until you review Activity 5.

Previous Page

ANSWERS

Activity 1

Todos son voluntarios de distintas ONG.

Activity 2

1. a, d; **2.** b; **3.** b, c; **4.** a, d; **5.** b; **6.** b; **7.** a, b, c, d; **8.** b, c.

Activity 3

a. Unicef (Fondo de Naciones Unidas para la Infancia, encargado de ayudar a los niños y proteger sus derechos); **b.** Cruz Roja (movimiento humanitario mundial, que realiza campañas de ayuda humanitaria, de intervención en casos de desastres, prevención de enfermedades, etc.); **c.** WWF (organización independiente para la conservación de la naturaleza, cuya misión es detener la degradación del ambiente natural del planeta).

INSTRUCTIONAL STRATEGIES

Activity 5

- The goal of this activity is for students to learn vocabulary associated with NGOs in an appropriate context so that they will be able to discuss NGOs and what they do.
- Explain to students that the abbreviation of NGOs in Spanish is **las ONG** (**o-ene-ge**) and that unlike English, acronyms in Spanish are never pluralized. Only the article will indicate number.
- Call on a volunteer to read the first paragraph. Go over the answer to the first question from Activity 4. Have a student correct the false statement.
- Have another volunteer read the second paragraph, and check students' answers to the second questions from Activity 4.
- Continue with another volunteer and the third paragraph. Encourage students to explain their answers and find the related lines in the text.
- Finally, have a volunteer read the fourth paragraph and answer the last question from Activity 4. Have him/her correct the false statement.

Activity 6

- The purpose of this activity is to help students recognize the prepositions that are used with these verbs. You may want to review them first with students. For example: **luchar por** (on behalf of), **luchar en** (in), **luchar a favor** (followed by preposition **de**), **luchar contra** (against), **trabajar por** (on behalf of).
- Have students work individually to match the phrases.
- Monitor their progress and assist as needed.
- Go over the answer as a class.

ANSWERS

Activities 4 and 5

a. F (Surgió después de un viaje a Italia); **b.** T; **c.** T; **d.** F (Aunque la mayoría son voluntarios, las ONG también cuentan con trabajadores asalariados).

Activity 6

1. f, g; **2.** a, e; **3.** d; **4.** c; **5.** g; **6.** d; **7.** a, e; **8.** f; **9.** a, b, c; **10.** d.

PALABRA POR PALABRA Las ONG

5 Read the following text and check your answers to Activity 4.

Las siglas ONG significan **Organización No Gubernamental**. La primera ONG que se conoce como tal es la Cruz Roja, que fue fundada en 1864 por el suizo (Swiss) Henry Dunant. El 8 de mayo de 1859, Dunant, que era un hombre de negocios, se encontraba en el norte de Italia. Allí fue testigo de una cruel batalla y de cómo las víctimas quedaban desatendidas en medio de las calles. Fueron las mujeres de los pueblos cercanos quienes se hacían cargo de aquellos pobres hombres.

Le impactó tanto aquella experiencia que pensó en la necesidad de crear organizaciones, **sin ánimo de lucro** e independientes de poderes (power) políticos e ideologías, para atender a las víctimas en los **conflictos bélicos** o en caso de **catástrofes naturales**. Así nació la Cruz Roja Internacional que hoy en día está presente en los cinco continentes.

Desde entonces el número de ONG ha aumentado en todo el mundo y también han ampliado su campo de trabajo. Algunas están enfocadas más a las **labores humanitarias** y otras a la **protección del medioambiente**. La mayoría de países aportan parte de su **PIB** a la **financiación** de las ONG. Otra forma de **recaudar fondos** son las **campañas de sensibilización** para captar socios (partners) o la venta de artículos de **comercio justo**, aunque hay algunas que prefieren, para mantener su libertad, financiarse solo con **donativos**.

La mayoría de personas que trabajan en las ONG son **voluntarios**, es decir, personas que combinan sus responsabilidades diarias, estudios o trabajos con ofrecer una **ayuda desinteresada** a otras personas. Sin embargo, también cuentan con trabajadores asalariados (salaried), ya que, sobre todo (especially) las grandes ONG, requieren de personal cualificado y dedicado a tiempo completo (full time) para su buen funcionamiento.

6 Combine elements from both columns to form complete sentences about what NGOs do on a daily basis around the world. ¡Atención! You should be able to create a total of 10 sentences.

a. Luchar por	**1.** ◯ campañas de sensibilización.
b. Luchar en	**2.** ◯ la protección del medioambiente.
c. Luchar a favor	**3.** ◯ la explotación infantil.
d. Luchar contra	**4.** ◯ de los derechos humanos.
e. Trabajar por	**5.** ◯ actos benéficos para recaudar fondos.
f. Ofrecer	**6.** ◯ la pobreza.
g. Organizar	**7.** ◯ el comercio justo.
	8. ◯ orientación laboral.
	9. ◯ la defensa de los animales.
	10. ◯ el calentamiento global.

7 Here is a list of just a few of the organizations NGOs support. Link the sentences you created in Activity 6 to an appropriate organization below. Think of other actions or tasks that benefit these organizations.

Medioambiente	Países subdesarrollados	Discapacitados
ECOL★GISTAS Trabajar por la protección del medioambiente...		♪ONCE

Personas sin hogar	Inmigrantes	Mujeres y niños
sintecho	acoge	mujeres

8 📖 Read about the following volunteers and their experiences. Then choose the appropriate description from the list below that conveys the same meaning as the sentences in bold.

Inés, 35 años, Malawi
Cuando terminé Arquitectura intenté encontrar trabajo en España, pero no lo conseguí, así que decidí empezar mi carrera profesional como voluntaria en África. Hace 10 años llegué a Malawi para colaborar en la construcción de un hospital y sigo aquí. Lo mejor es que **(a) trabajamos codo con codo con la** población de aquí. Así, todos aprendemos de todos y esperamos que en el futuro no nos necesiten, porque eso significará que ellos tendrán los medios para **(b) salir adelante.** Es una manera de tener un **(c) trabajo** satisfactorio y **(d) ser solidario** al mismo tiempo.

Walter, 15 años, Buenos Aires
Yo soy voluntario porque quiero que el mundo sea mejor cada día. Todos podemos hacer algo por los demás, no tienen que ser grandes gestos, porque si cada uno **(e) pone su granito de arena,** al final se pueden hacer cosas muy importantes.

Rocío, 22 años, Sevilla
Cada año organizamos un mercadillo benéfico. La gente trae las cosas que ya no necesita pero que están en buen estado.
Nosotros no ponemos precio, sino que la gente **(f) da la voluntad.** La verdad es que se recoge bastante dinero.

1. ◯ Realizar un trabajo que te hace feliz.
2. ◯ Realizar un trabajo en colaboración con otra persona.
3. ◯ Superar una situación difícil.
4. ◯ Dar el dinero que tú quieres.
5. ◯ Ser generoso.
6. ◯ Colaborar.

9 👥 With a partner, discuss the following topics.
- ¿Qué ONG de tu país conoces?
- ¿Colaboras con alguna ONG o conoces a alguien que lo haga?
- Habla sobre el tipo de trabajo que haces o que hace esa persona.

Practice what you have learned with additional materials online.

153

INSTRUCTIONAL STRATEGIES

Activity 7
- Go over the instructions and sample answer. Then have students continue working individually to sort their sentences from Activity 6 under the correct NGO.
- Monitor their progress and assist as needed. Encourage students to add at least one more action or task in each NGO.

Extension
- Divide the class into groups and assign each group one of the NGOs.
- Have the groups research their NGO on the Internet to determine its main functions, actions, and tasks. Websites: www.ecologistasenaccion.org; www.redacoge.es; www.globalhumanitaria.org; www.once.es; www.sin-techo.es; www.fundacionmujeres.es.
- Then put the students into new groups, each person from a different NGO, to share their findings and add to their lists.

Activity 8
- Have three volunteers read each of the volunteer experiences aloud. Ask a comprehension question or two after each description to check students' understanding, for example: **¿Por qué decidió Inés ir a Malawi? ¿A qué edad se fue allí? ¿Dónde vive Walter? ¿Él piensa que es necesario dedicar un montón de tiempo a las tareas solidarias? ¿De dónde es Rocío? ¿Cada cuánto tiempo organiza el mercadillo?**
- Put the students into pairs to match the definitions with the correct phrases from the text. Go over the answers as a class.

Activity 9
- Call on a volunteer. Model a conversation based on the questions provided.
- Put students into pairs, and have them take turns asking and answering the questions on the page. Monitor their conversations and assist as needed.
- Call on students to report back on interesting details from their conversations.

ANSWERS

Activity 7
Medioambiente: trabajar por la protección del medioambiente, luchar en defensa de los animales, trabajar por el comercio justo; **Países subdesarrollados:** luchar contra la pobreza, trabajar por el comercio justo, luchar contra la explotación infantil, luchar a favor de los derechos humanos, organizar actos benéficos para recaudar fondos; **Discapacitados:** Organizar campañas de sensibilización, organizar actos benéficos para recaudar fondos, ofrecer orientación laboral; **Personas sin hogar:** luchar a favor de los derechos humanos, organizar campañas de sensibilización de la población, ofrecer orientación laboral, organizar actos benéficos para recaudar fondos; **Inmigrantes:** ofrecer orientación laboral, organizar campañas de sensibilización de la población, luchar contra la pobreza. **Mujeres y niños:** luchar contra la explotación infantil, ofrecer orientación laboral, luchar a favor de los derechos humanos, organizar campañas de sensibilización de la población.

Activity 8
1. c; 2. a; 3. b; 4. f; 5. d; 6. e.

GRAMÁTICA GRAMMAR IN CONTEXT

OBJECTIVES FOR GRAMÁTICA 1

- Present grammatical structures needed to practice communicative functions of the unit:
- The present subjunctive: regular verbs
- Learn to conjugate regular verbs in the present subjunctive

CORE RESOURCES

- Extension Activities: EA 5.1
- Interactive Online Materials – ELEteca

STANDARDS

- 1.1 Engage in conversation
- 1.1 Understand the language
- 4.1 Compare languages

INSTRUCTIONAL STRATEGIES

1. The Present Subjunctive: Regular Verbs

- Before presenting the grammar, distribute copies of EA 5.1, **Presente de subjuntivo: verbos regulares**, giving half the class the chart for **Estudiante A** and the other half the chart for **Estudiante B**. The purpose is to have students work out the forms of the subjunctive based on examples they have already seen and patterns they recognize.
- Have students work individually to try to complete their charts.
- Then put students into A/B pairs. Explain that **Estudiante A** has the answers to **Estudiante B**'s chart, and vice versa. Have the students ask each other and answer questions of each other to check their answers.
- Then have students open their books to check their answers. Go over the uses of the present subjunctive and the sample sentences on the page.

Activity 1

- Have students work individually to complete the sentences.
- Go over the answers as a class. Ask students to reflect on the use of the subjunctive in each case (wishes, hopes, and future actions) and why the infinitive is needed in the other cases (no change of subject).

Activity 2

- Have students work individually to match the sentences from Activity 2 to the images. Put the students in small groups to compare and explain their answers.

GRAMÁTICA

1. THE PRESENT SUBJUNCTIVE: REGULAR VERBS

- In this unit you have learned to express wishes, hopes, and desires as well as goals for the future using a new form of the verb. This form is called the subjunctive mood. Unlike the indicative, which states facts, the subjunctive describes reality from the point of view of the speaker.

  Quiero un helado. vs. *Quiero que me compres un helado.*

  Este curso es muy difícil. vs. *Espero que este curso no sea muy difícil.*

  Cuando llegué a casa, cené. vs. *Cuando llegue a casa, cenaré.*

- Here are the forms of the present subjunctive.

	–AR HABLAR	–ER COMER	–IR VIVIR
yo	hable	coma	viva
tú	hables	comas	vivas
usted/él/ella	hable	coma	viva
nosotros/as	hablemos	comamos	vivamos
vosotros/as	habléis	comáis	viváis
ustedes/ellos/ellas	hablen	coman	vivan

1 Complete these sentences using the subjunctive or an infinitive.

- a. ¡Ojalá me (llamar) .... Juanjo!
- b. Cuando (hablar, tú) .... en español, intenta abrir más la boca.
- c. ¡Te quedas sentada a la mesa hasta que te (terminar) .... todo el pescado!
- d. Mario y Sara han venido para (presentar) .... su nuevo disco.
- e. Susana nos va a explicar una receta muy sencilla para que (aprender, nosotros) .... a hacer paella.
- f. Cuando (independizarse, yo) ...., espero que mis amigos (vivir) .... cerca de mí.
- g. ¡Que la fuerza te (acompañar) .... !
- h. Quiero (cambiar, yo) .... mi número de teléfono.

2 Match the sentences in Activity 1 to the appropriate image below. Explain your choices.

Extension

Have each student write a sentence on a piece of paper using the present subjunctive expressing a wish or hope that students in class can associate with him/her. Collect all the sentences. Read a few of them aloud, and have the class guess which student wrote each one.

ANSWERS

Activity 1

a. llame; **b.** hables; **c.** termines; **d.** presentar; **e.** aprendamos; **f.** me independice, vivan; **g.** acompañe; **h.** cambiar.

Activity 2

1. g; **2.** e; **3.** d; **4.** b; **5.** c; **6.** a; **7.** f; **8.** h.

3 🔲 **Respond to your partner's statements.**

Estudiante 1

Dices:

a. "Soy el genio de la lámpara maravillosa: pide tres deseos y te serán concedidos".

b. Te vas de vacaciones dentro de una semana, ¿qué quieres hacer?

c. Imagina que es fin de año. ¿Qué deseos pides para el año que empieza?

d. ¿Qué le pides al muchacho/a ideal?

e. Piensa en ti dentro de quince años. ¿Qué le pides a la vida?

Estudiante 2

Dices:

a. Estás en una isla desierta y al parecer el resto del mundo se ha olvidado de ti. ¿Qué desearías?

b. Se acerca tu cumpleaños, ¿cuáles son tus deseos?

c. Imagina que vas a conocer al presidente de tu país, ¿qué le pides?

d. Mañana empieza el curso y tenéis nuevo profesor de español. ¿Cómo quieres que sea?

e. ¿Qué le pides a la ciudad ideal?

2. THE PRESENT SUBJUNCTIVE: IRREGULAR VERBS

■ Almost all **irregular verbs** in the present indicative are also irregular in the present subjunctive.

Stem-changing verbs

	QUERER	**VOLVER**	**JUGAR**	**PEDIR**
	e → ie	o → ue	u → ue	e → i (en todas las personas)
yo	quiera	vuelva	juegue	pida
tú	quieras	vuelvas	juegues	pidas
usted/él/ella	quiera	vuelva	juegue	pida
nosotros/as	queramos	volvamos	juguemos	pidamos
vosotros/as	queráis	volváis	juguéis	pidáis
ustedes/ellos/ellas	quieran	vuelvan	jueguen	pidan

4 **Complete the chart with the correct forms of the subjunctive for the following stem-changing verbs.**

ENTENDER	ENCONTRAR	REPETIR

155

INSTRUCTIONAL STRATEGIES

Activity 3

Put students into pairs. Have them choose who is **Estudiante 1** and who is **Estudiante 2**. Explain that they are going to take turns reading the statements on their cards, and their partners are going to respond appropriately using the present subjunctive. Model a conversation with a volunteer.

Extension

• Have students write down three wishes for themselves, e.g. *Deseo aprobar esta asignatura*.

• Then have them pass those wishes to another classmate. That classmate must respond to each wish, e.g. *Espero que apruebes esta asignatura*.

• Have the students return their papers to the original writers and check or correct the usage of the present subjunctive.

OBJECTIVES FOR GRAMÁTICA 2

• Present grammatical structures needed to practice communicative functions of the unit:
The present subjunctive: irregular verbs

• Learn to conjugate irregular verbs in the present subjunctive.

CORE RESOURCES

• Extension Activities: EA 5.2

STANDARDS

1.1   Engage in conversation

1.1   Understand the language

4.1   Compare languages

INSTRUCTIONAL STRATEGIES

2. The Present Subjunctive: Irregular Verbs

• Explain that there are three different kinds of irregularities in the present subjunctive:

1. **Stem-changing verbs.** Almost all verbs that stem change in the **yo** form of the present indicative also stem-change in the present subjunctive in all forms except in −**ar**/−**er nosotros**/**vosotros** forms. Note other exceptions such as **dormir** and **morir**.

2. **Irregular yo form verbs.** Verbs with irregular **yo** forms in the indicative are also irregular in the present subjunctive in all forms.

3. **Completely irregular.** Some verbs have unique irregular forms in the present subjunctive.

• Go over the charts one at a time, doing Activity 4 after presenting the chart of stem-changing verbs and Activity 5 after presenting the chart of irregular **yo** form verbs.

Stem-changing verbs

Remind students again of the rule: Stem-changing verbs ending in −**ar** and −**er** will stem-change in the present subjunctive in all forms except **nosotros**/**vosotros**.

Previous Page

Activity 4

- Put students in pairs to complete the chart.
- Monitor their progress and assist as needed.
- Go over the answers as a class, eliciting corrections from other students as needed.

ANSWERS

Activity 4

Entender: entienda, entiendas, entienda, entendamos, entendáis, entiendan; **Encontrar:** encuentre, encuentres, encuentre, encontremos, encontréis, encuentren; **Repetir:** repita, repitas, repita, repitamos, repitáis, repitan.

INSTRUCTIONAL STRATEGIES

Stem-changing –ir verbs and dormir / morir

- For stem-changing verbs ending in **–ir**, it may be simpler to have students remember the forms of **dormir** and **morir** then to explain the type of stem-change that occurs as there are very few **–ir** verbs students are likely to use in the present subjunctive form that stem-change **e ➡ ie** (and that would therefore change to only **i** in the **nosotros/vosotros** forms.) For example: **preferir ➡ prefiera, prefiramos.**

Irregular yo form verbs

- Remind students again of the general rule for forming the present subjunctive form: Begin with the **yo** form of the present indicative, drop the **o** and switch to the opposite endings. In this way, verbs with irregular **yo** forms will also have irregular forms in the present subjunctive.

Activity 5

- Put students in pairs to complete the chart.
- Monitor their progress and assist as needed.
- Go over the answers as a class, eliciting corrections from other students as needed.

Completely irregular verbs

Tell students that these are the last category of irregular verbs in the present subjunctive. Point out that as in most other forms, these verbs are irregular here too.

Extension

After reviewing the charts, put students in groups of three and distribute a copy of EA 5.2, **Tres en raya** to each group. Explain that they will take turns choosing a square and correctly conjugating the verb in the present subjunctive form. If the conjugation is correct, they write their name in the square. The first person to get three squares in a row correct, wins.

ANSWERS

Activity 5

Poner: ponga, pongas, ponga, pongamos, pongáis, pongan; **Decir:** diga, digas, diga, digamos, digáis, digan; **Construir:** construya, construyas, construya, construyamos, construyáis, construyan.

GRAMÁTICA

- The verbs **dormir** and **morir** have two stem changes in the present subjunctive: **o ➡ ue** and **o ➡ u** as follows:

	DORMIR	MORIR
yo	duerma	muera
tú	duermas	mueras
usted/él/ella	duerma	muera
nosotros/as	durmamos	muramos
vosotros/as	durmáis	muráis
ustedes/ellos/ellas	duerman	mueran

Irregular yo form verbs

- The present subjunctive of verbs with irregular **yo** forms is as follows:

TENER	SALIR	TRAER
tenga	salga	traiga
tengas	salgas	traigas
tenga	salga	traiga
tengamos	salgamos	traigamos
tengáis	salgáis	traigáis
tengan	salgan	traigan

5 Complete the chart with the correct forms of the subjunctive for the following verbs with irregular **yo** forms.

PONER	DECIR	CONSTRUIR

- The following verbs have irregular subjunctive forms:

HABER	IR	SABER	ESTAR	SER	VER	DAR
haya	vaya	sepa	esté	sea	vea	dé
hayas	vayas	sepas	estés	seas	veas	des
haya	vaya	sepa	esté	sea	vea	dé
hayamos	vayamos	sepamos	estemos	seamos	veamos	demos
hayáis	vayáis	sepáis	estéis	seáis	veáis	deis
hayan	vayan	sepan	estén	sean	vean	den

156

6 Complete these sentences with your own ideas. Then, in small groups, take turns sharing your ideas. Did you all have similar responses?

a. Cuando tenga 20 años,...

b. Quiero que mis padres me compren...

c. Ojalá que mañana...

d. Mi profesor espera que yo...

e. Cuando mis amigos se van de vacaciones les digo que...

f. Pienso vivir en casa hasta que...

g. Cuando seamos mayores,...

7 Fill in the blanks with the verbs in parenthesis to learn more about *Antoñito el fantasioso* and his hopes for the future.

Antoñito era un niño que se pasaba el día soñando.

– Cuando (a) ....(ser) mayor, me iré a vivir a Australia –decía siempre.

– Sí, te irás a Australia, pero tendrás que saber inglés –le respondía su madre.

– Bueno, estudiaré y cuando (b) ....(saber, yo) hablarlo bien, me iré. Por cierto, mamá, quiero que me (c) .... (comprar, tú) un buen diccionario, que me hará falta. Ojalá me (d) ....(dar) una beca *(scholarship)* para ir a estudiar a Australia... –pensaba siempre Antoñito–. Eso sí, espero que no me (e) ....(poner, los profesores) tantas tareas como aquí y que no (f) ....(llamar) a mi madre y le (g) .... (decir) que no estoy estudiando mucho. ¡Ay! –suspiraba Antoñito–. ¡Ojalá me (h) .... (hacer) mayor pronto...!

Los padres de Antoñito, que ya sabían que a su hijo le encantaba construir castillos en el aire, le decían:

– Sí, Antoñito, pero tú, hasta que no (i) ....(crecer, tú), estudia, hijo, estudia...

Antes de dormir, Antoñito le preguntaba a su madre:

– Mamá, cuando (j) ....(vivir, yo) en Australia, vendrás a verme, ¿no?

– Sí, hijo, sí, buenas noches, que (k) ....(dormir) bien y que (l) ....(soñar) con los angelitos, perdón, con los canguritos –se corregía su madre.

Lo curioso es que hoy Antoñito es uno de los principales importadores de jamón en Australia, porque, aunque no siempre es bueno construir castillos en el aire, también es verdad que quien quiere, puede.

8 Think about your own goals for the future. Then share your goals with your partner and ask about his/her goals.

Modelo: *Cuando termine los estudios en la secundaria, iré a estudiar a una universidad fuera de mi ciudad. Cuando esté en la universidad, estudiaré Periodismo. Cuando termine Periodismo, me haré corresponsal y cuando...*

Practice what you have learned with additional materials online.

157

INSTRUCTIONAL STRATEGIES

Activity 6

• Have students work individually to complete the sentences with their own ideas.

• Put students into small groups to share and compare their ideas.

• Have groups report back on any interesting aspects of their discussions.

Activity 7

• Have students work individually to complete the sentences.

• Monitor their progress and assist as needed.

• Put the students in pairs to share their sentences.

• Go over the answers as a class.

Activity 8

• Review the instructions and read the model aloud. Give students some time to jot down notes about their own goals for the future.

• Then put students into pairs. Tell them to listen closely to what their partners say, because they will be asked to report back (orally or in writing) about their partner's goals to the rest of the class. Encourage students to take notes.

• Monitor their conversations and assist as needed.

• Either call on students to orally relay their partner's goals or have them submit them to you in writing. If the students write their summaries, read them to the class, and have students guess whose goals they are.

ANSWERS

Activity 6

Answers will vary but should all include correct present subjunctive forms.

Activity 7

a. sea; b. sepa; c. compres; d. den; e. pongan; f. llamen; g. digan; h. haga; i. crezcas; j. viva; k. duermas; l. sueñes.

OBJECTIVES FOR DESTREZAS

- Develop writing skills by learning how to use a chart to organize information
- Learn strategies for writing an email

CORE RESOURCES

- Interactive Whiteboard Lesson: IWB 5.4

STANDARDS

1.3   Present information
5.1   Spanish in the community

INSTRUCTIONAL STRATEGIES

Expresión e interacción escritas (1)

Activity 1

- Review the instructions and **Destrezas** box aloud.
- Point out that the categories in the chart were generated from the survey below. Have students find the corresponding questions or sections in the survey. Explain that **motivos** refers to reasons why they are traveling to Ecuador and why they like to travel in general.
- Give students time to complete the chart with a few of their own details related to each category. Encourage them to use notes, not sentences, at this stage.
- Monitor their progress and assist as needed.

Activity 2

- Read (or have a student read) the instructions and the situation. Explain that students are going to use their notes to complete the survey.
- Have students work individually to complete the survey.
- Put students into pairs to interview each other so they can share and compare their responses.

Extension

- For additional practice with the survey or just for fun, have students answer the questions imagining that they are a famous person.
- Then put students into pairs to interview each other once again, but this time they should not reveal their fictitious names. The partners need to guess who they are based on their responses to the questions.

Next Page

INSTRUCTIONAL STRATEGIES

Expresión e interacción escritas (2)

Activity 3

- Have students think about how they organize their email messages. Elicit the parts of an email from students. Project IWB 5.4, **Querido/a** to give them a visual example of the form of an email message. Elicit alternative phrases or sentences they might use in each of the parts on display.
- Call on a student to read the instructions and the strategies in the book. Elicit an example of a sentence with the conditional tense to confirm their understanding. Quickly review the form, if necessary.

DESTREZAS

EXPRESIÓN E INTERACCIÓN ESCRITAS (1)

1 In this activity you will be filling out a survey form. Before you begin, review the strategy in Destrezas and follow the suggestion.

Destrezas

Using a personal chart

Create a chart to organize your personal information. Review the form and identify major categories of information you will need to provide. Decide which categories require more thought and preparation. Select those to include in your chart.

Categoría	Detalles
trabajo	
estudios	
tiempo libre (aficiones, deporte, viajes)	
motivos	

2 Read the following situation and complete the task requested.

Acabas de llegar a Guayaquil, Ecuador, y has ido a la oficina de turismo de la ciudad para solicitar información. Antes de marcharte, la dirección te pide que rellenes este formulario para un estudio que están haciendo sobre las características de los jóvenes turistas de la ciudad.

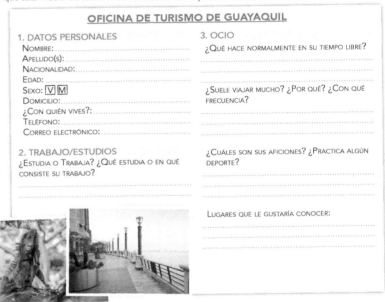

OFICINA DE TURISMO DE GUAYAQUIL

1. DATOS PERSONALES
NOMBRE: ....
APELLIDO(S): ....
NACIONALIDAD: ....
EDAD: ....
SEXO: [V] [M]
DOMICILIO: ....
¿CON QUIÉN VIVES?: ....
TELÉFONO: ....
CORREO ELECTRÓNICO: ....

2. TRABAJO/ESTUDIOS
¿ESTUDIA O TRABAJA? ¿QUÉ ESTUDIA O EN QUÉ CONSISTE SU TRABAJO?
....
....

3. OCIO
¿QUÉ HACE NORMALMENTE EN SU TIEMPO LIBRE?
....
....

¿SUELE VIAJAR MUCHO? ¿POR QUÉ? ¿CON QUÉ FRECUENCIA?
....
....

¿CUÁLES SON SUS AFICIONES? ¿PRACTICA ALGÚN DEPORTE?
....
....

LUGARES QUE LE GUSTARÍA CONOCER:
....
....

EXPRESIÓN E INTERACCIÓN ESCRITAS (2)

3 Before you begin to write, review the strategy in Destrezas and follow the suggestion.

Destrezas

Strategies for writing an email

a. Keep in mind that 10 words are generally 1 sentence. Do not count the opening or the greeting as a sentence.

b. Divide the sentences by the number of topics you are required to write about -in this case, 5. Now you know how to organize your writing.

c. Choose the opening: formal (*Estimado/a...*) or informal (*Querido/a..., Hola, Juan...*).

d. The conditional tense also expresses courtesy. Use it!

e. Choose the greeting: formal (*Reciba un cordial saludo, Me despido de usted*), or informal (*Cuídate mucho, Un abrazo, Hasta pronto*).

4 Write an email between 80-100 words according to the situation below.

Escribe a un amigo ecuatoriano para invitarle a pasar un fin de semana en tu ciudad. Explícale qué cosas van a hacer, qué van a visitar, cómo es la ciudad y qué tiempo hace. Dile también cómo esperas que sea el fin de semana.

PRONUNCIACIÓN Los diptongos e hiatos: acentuación

- In addition to representing their own vowel sounds, the letters **i** and **u** may also represent glides, which are brief, weak sounds that combine with a vowel to form a single syllable (**diptongo**):
  - *nue-vo, sie-te, vein-te, gua-po, eu-ro.*
  In these cases, remember to follow the rules for written accents in general:
  - *ha-céis, can-ción, pen-sáis, des-pués, cuí-da-lo.*

- However, the letters **i** and **u** are not always glides when next to other vowels. Whey they are vowels and not glides, a written accent mark is used (**hiato**):
  - *dí-a, rí-o, pa-ís, Ra-úl.*

1 **38** Listen to the audio and write the words you hear.

_____

2 **38** Listen again to the words you wrote in Activity 1. Then divide them into syllables.

3 Arrange the list of words in the appropriate category. Remember to include accents as needed.

Diptongos: _____
Hiatos: _____

Practice what you have learned with additional materials online.

Activity 4

- Encourage students to use the organizational chart in Activity 1 with the pertinent categories to organize their email. Have them number their notes and the chart categories so they can determine the best order and necessary number of paragraphs for their email.
- After they've written their first drafts, have students exchange papers and correct each other's work.

OBJECTIVES FOR PRONUNCIACIÓN

- Practice the correct pronunciation of diphthongs and hiatuses

CORE RESOURCES

- Audio Program: Track 38
- Interactive Online Materials – ELEteca

STANDARDS

1.2 Understand the language
4.1 Compare languages

INSTRUCTIONAL STRATEGIES

- Walk students through the notes and examples on the page. Focus their attention on the use of accent marks when *i* and *u* do not combine with other vowel sounds.
- Elicit one or two more examples of Spanish words with two consecutive vowels. Determine as a class whether there is a glide or not between them and whether or not they need an accent.

 38 Activity 1

- Tell the students that they are going to listen to a list of words and that they should write the words they hear. Tell them not worry about accent marks at this stage.
- Play the audio and repeat if necessary. Don't write the words on the board just yet. Have students focus their listening.

Audioscript

guion, bonsái, autor, filosofía, huésped, océano, crucial, habláis, veintiún, acuático, raíz, dehesa.

---

 38 Activity 2

Tell the students that this time when they listen they should listen closely to the syllables in each word. Model a few words, clapping to the syllables, so they can understand how to identify them.

Activity 3

- Have students work individually or in pairs to correctly sort and write the words.
- Go over the answers as a class.

ANSWERS

Activity 2

guion, bon-sái, au-tor, fi-lo-so-fí-a, hués-ped, o-cé-a-no, cru-cial, ha-bláis, vein-tiún, a-cuá-ti-co, ra-íz, de-he-sa.

Activity 3

Diptongos: guion, bonsái, autor, huésped, crucial, habláis, veintiún, acuático; **Hiatos:** filosofía, océano, raíz, dehesa.

OBJECTIVES FOR SABOR HISPANO

- Learn about a student's gap year experience as a volunteer in Guatemala
- Compare rates of volunteerism in different countries

CORE RESOURCES

- Audio Program: Track 39

STANDARDS

2.1 Practices and perspectives

3.2 Acquire information

4.2 Compare cultures

INSTRUCTIONAL STRATEGIES

🎧 39

- Focus students' attention on the image at the top of the page. Ask where it was taken. Have them guess what they think is happening.
- Then have students look at the picture of Ryan and read the caption and the title of the text. Have them predict what the text is going to be about.
- Put students into pairs. Have them discuss the questions in the **Antes de leer** box. Encourage them to take notes about their partner's responses. Monitor their conversations and assist as needed.
- Have students switch partners and tell their new partners about their previous partner's responses. Monitor their conversations and assist as needed.
- Have students close their books. Tell them you are going to play the audio about Ryan's experience. To focus their listening, ask them to write down three activities that Ryan talks about.
- Play the audio. Then call on volunteers to give examples of Ryan's activities.
- Have students open their books. Play the audio again, this time allowing students to follow along.
- Ask again about the context of the main photo at the top of the page: **¿Qué estaban celebrando?** Have them find the relevant section of the text that reveals the answer.
- Point out the glossary of terms at the bottom of the next page. Have students find and underline those terms in the text.

SABOR HISPANO

«ME ENCANTA SER VOLUNTARIO»

Una alfombra de flores en Antigua, Guatemala.

Ryan piensa que ser voluntario es genial.

Antes de leer

¿Adónde te gustaría viajar para hacer un voluntariado internacional? ¿Por qué?

¿Qué tipo de tareas te gustaría hacer?

🎧 39 Cada vez hay más gente joven que prefiere hacer un voluntariado en el extranjero[°] a ir directamente a la universidad. Ryan, un chico norteamericano, habla de su experiencia.

«Ser voluntario es genial. Mi vida cambió completamente después de pasar un mes en Guatemala», dice Ryan, un muchacho norteamericano de 16 años que viajó al país centroamericano en 2013. «Cuando llegué a Antigua, hablaba muy poco español. Pero una familia me recibió en su casa y hablando con ellos mi español mejoró[°] rápidamente», cuenta. «Después de estar un mes con ellos, me siento parte de la familia. Ojalá pueda verlos pronto otra vez».

«Mis tareas en Antigua eran ayudar a construir casas en un barrio nuevo», explica Ryan. «Allí había también otros voluntarios internacionales. Hice amistad con una muchacha española, Ainhoa, que ya está de vuelta en Madrid. Espero que sigamos en contacto por correo electrónico y Skype».

«Como tenía las tardes libres, me invitaron a dar clases de inglés a la escuela del barrio», dice. «Me tocó[°] una clase de muchachos de ocho años y hablamos muchísimo. Me hicieron preguntas sobre la vida en Illinois, donde yo vivo. También me enseñaron trabalenguas[°] en español, ¡aunque son dificilísimos!», cuenta Ryan. «Me gustaría que vinieran a visitarme».

Además de pasar tiempo con los niños, Ryan recorrió[°] las antiguas ciudades mayas y los parques naturales. «También participé en las fiestas de la Semana Santa, haciendo alfombras enormes de aserrín[°] y flores», dice.

160

Países con más voluntarios

Estos son los países con más voluntarios que vienen de otros países, en millones de personas.

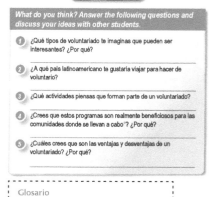

- 157
- 115
- 52
- 45
- 34
- 27
- 21

- ■ India
- ■ EE. UU.
- ■ Indonesia
- ■ China
- ■ Nigeria
- ■ Filipinas
- ■ México

Países solidarios

Existe un *ranking* que mide la cantidad de gente en un país que ayudó a un desconocido durante los últimos 30 días. Estos son los países con la gente más solidaria, en porcentaje de la población.

- 77%
- 73%
- 72%
- 70%
- 68%
- 67%
- 67%

- ■ EE. UU.
- ■ Qatar
- ■ Libia
- ■ Colombia
- ■ Senegal
- ■ Camerún
- ■ Nueva Zelanda

Los mexicanos son los latinoamericanos que más voluntariados hacen.

¿COMPRENDISTE?

Decide if the following statements are true (T) or false (F).

1. Se pueden hacer voluntariados en todo el mundo. T ○ F ○
2. El país latino con más voluntarios es México. T ○ F ○
3. Ryan es un chico de EE. UU. que habla de las cooperativas. T ○ F ○
4. Ryan visitó Nicaragua y México. T ○ F ○
5. Según estadísticas recientes, Colombia es un país solidario. T ○ F ○

En Colombia, la mayoría de las personas ayudaría a un desconocido.

AHORA TÚ

What do you think? Answer the following questions and discuss your ideas with other students.

1. ¿Qué tipos de voluntariado te imaginas que pueden ser interesantes? ¿Por qué?
2. ¿A qué país latinoamericano te gustaría viajar para hacer de voluntario?
3. ¿Qué actividades piensas que forman parte de un voluntariado?
4. ¿Crees que estos programas son realmente beneficiosos para las comunidades donde se llevan a cabo? ¿Por qué?
5. ¿Cuáles crees que son las ventajas y desventajas de un voluntariado? ¿Por qué?

Glosario

el aserrín – sawdust
el extranjero – abroad
llevarse a cabo – to take place
mejorar – to improve
recorrer – to tour
tocar – to be given
el trabalenguas – tongue-twister

161

Fuentes: Cooperatour, *Lonely Planet*, World Giving Index.

Países con más voluntarios

- Call on a volunteer to read the title and description of the chart.
- Ask a question or two to check students' understanding of the chart information, such as: *¿Cuál es el país de Latinoamérica con más voluntarios?*
- Have students write down two questions of their own about the chart and pass them forward. Hold on to them for a moment.

Países solidarios

- Call on a volunteer to read the title and description of the chart.
- Ask a question or two to check students' understanding of the chart information, such as: *¿Qué porcentaje de la población de Camerún ha ayudado a un desconocido durante los últimos 30 días?*
- Have students write down two questions of their own about the chart and pass them forward. Hold on to them for a moment.
- Put students into small groups. Mix up the questions and pass them out the different groups. Have students work together to answer the questions on their papers.

¿Comprendiste?

- Have students work individually to answer the questions.
- Monitor their progress and assist as needed.
- Go over the answers as a class. Have them explain the false answers.

Ahora tú

- Have students work individually to answer the questions.
- Monitor their progress and assist as needed.
- Put students into pairs. Have them take turns asking each other the questions and responding with their written answer. Encourage students to ask follow-up questions for more information.
- Ask each pair to report back to the class on something interesting from their conversation.

ANSWERS

¿Comprendiste?

1. T; 2. T; 3. F; 4. F; 5. T.

OBJECTIVES FOR RELATO

- Revisit unit themes, grammar, vocabulary and culture in a new context
- Improve reading comprehension skills

CORE RESOURCES

- Audio program: Tracks 40 and 41
- Extension Activities: EA 5.3

STANDARDS

1.2 Understand the language
1.3 Present the language
5.2 Using the language for personal enjoyment and enrichment

INSTRUCTIONAL STRATEGIES

Activity 1

- Before reading the text, write **Pablo Neruda** on the board. Find out what students may already know about him. (You may choose to consult *http://www.neruda.uchile.cl* to find out more information for yourself). Tell them you are going to read about him. Perhaps go over the meaning of some new vocabulary in the text, such as **cónsul**, **natal**, and **oda**. Finally, pose a simple question or two for students to keep in mind while they read.
- Read the text as a class. Then call on volunteers to answer the simple questions you posed before reading.
- Put students into pairs to answer the four questions at the bottom of the reading. Encourage them to refer back to the text.

🎧 40 Activity 2

- Tell students that they are going to listen to an excerpt of one of Neruda's poems. Before playing the audio, give students a chance to read the statements. Perhaps encourage them to underline key words to listen for to help them determine which statement is correct.
- Play the audio. Then take a class poll as to whether they think the correct statement is **a**, **b**, or **c**.
- Play the audio again. After the second listening, take a class poll again. Have students explain the reasons for their answers.
- Confirm the correct answer, clarifying it, if necessary.

Cultural Note

The first part of the poem evokes the Madrid that Neruda experienced when he arrived in 1935, a Madrid with an intense cultural life favored by the liberal and progressive government of the Second Republic (1931–1936). The second part of the poem (verse 36) talks about how that ideal Madrid disappeared with the outbreak of the war, provoked by the uprising of the National Party (verse 43), led by General Franco, who would use the power to install a dictatorship (1936–1975). The poem makes reference (verse 18) to the Spanish poets Rafael Alberti and Federico García Lorca (already assassinated), both part of the Generation of 27 For more information, you can consult the document *http://www.cdechamps-lycee-delacroix.fr/IMG/pdf/Aide_a_l_explication_de_Explico_algunas_cosas.pdf*, where there's an analysis of the poem.

RELATO Pablo Neruda, Soneto LXXXIX

1 **Read about the poet Pablo Neruda and answer the questions.**

Ricardo Eliecer Neftalí Reyes Basoalto (Chile, 1904-1973), más conocido como Pablo Neruda, ha sido uno de los poetas más influyentes en la literatura del siglo XX y así se le reconoció cuando en 1971 ganó el Premio Nobel de Literatura. Su obra es muy variada y extensa. En sus primeros años se caracteriza por el romanticismo y la melancolía, influenciado por el modernismo hispanoamericano de Rubén Darío y de su gran amiga, la poetisa Gabriela Mistral. De esta época es quizá *(possibly)* una de sus obras más famosas: *Veinte poemas de amor y una canción desesperada* (1924).

En 1927 empieza a trabajar como cónsul *(diplomat)*. Gracias a esto, viaja por todo el mundo y conoce a los políticos y artistas más importantes de la época, convirtiéndose en un hombre culto y comprometido *(committed)* socialmente. Entre otros, conoce a Federico García Lorca en Buenos Aires, a Picasso en Barcelona y a los autores de la Generación del 27 en Madrid. Al estallar la guerra civil española en 1936, Neruda tiene que regresar a su país natal. Allí, impresionado por la guerra y el asesinato de Federico García Lorca, del que se había hecho muy amigo, escribió su obra *España en el corazón* (1937), un libro de poemas sobre el horror de la guerra y el dolor de las víctimas.

Pero Neruda siguió escribiendo bellos poemas de amor como los recogidos en *Cien sonetos de amor* (1959). Y no solo escribió sobre temas profundos, también los objetos más cotidianos *(everyday)* fueron fuentes *(sources)* de su inspiración. Ejemplo de ello son su famosas *Odas elementales*: "Oda a la cebolla", "Oda al tomate", "Oda a los calcetines"… Neruda decía que él escribía para gente sencilla, incluso para los que no sabían leer.

a. ¿A qué época de la obra del autor pertenece *Veinte poemas de amor y una canción desesperada*?

b ¿Por qué se caracteriza dicha época?

c. ¿Qué hechos mueven al autor a escribir *España en el corazón*?

d. ¿En qué se inspiran las *Odas elementales*?

2 **🎧 40** **Read excerpts from one of Neruda's poems on the next page and indicate which statement is correct.**

a. El poema se llama "Oda a Madrid". Neruda primero hace una descripción de Madrid antes y después de la guerra y, más tarde, lo compara con su país natal.

b. El poema se llama "Explico algunas cosas", pertenece a su obra *España en el corazón* y habla de cómo vivió Neruda el estallido de la guerra civil española y por qué cambió su estilo.

c. El poema se llama "Yo vivía en un barrio", pertenece a la primera época de Neruda y trata sobre la nostalgia que Neruda siente por Madrid.

[...]
Yo vivía en un barrio
de Madrid, con campanas,
con relojes, con árboles.

Desde allí se veía
5 el rostro seco de Castilla
como un océano de cuero.
Mi casa era llamada
la casa de las flores, porque por todas partes
estallaban geranios: era
10 una bella casa
con perros y chiquillos.

[...]
Y una mañana todo estaba ardiendo
y una mañana las hogueras
salían de la tierra
devorando seres,
15 y desde entonces fuego,
pólvora desde entonces,
y desde entonces sangre.

[...]
Preguntaréis por qué su poesía
no nos habla del sueño, de las hojas,
20 de los grandes volcanes de su país natal.

3 The next poem is part of *Cien sonetos de amor*, which Neruda dedicated to his third wife, Matilde Urrutia, his great love, his muse and his companion until his death. With a partner, choose from the words in the list below to complete the poem.

amé ○ arena ○ luz ○ manos ○ mar ○ muera ○ oídos ○ pelo ○ viento ○ vivas

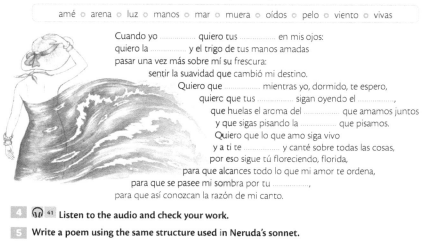

Cuando yo .... quiero tus .... en mis ojos:
quiero la .... y el trigo de tus manos amadas
pasar una vez más sobre mí su frescura:
        sentir la suavidad que cambió mi destino.
                Quiero que .... mientras yo, dormido, te espero,
        quiero que tus .... sigan oyendo el ....,
            que huelas el aroma del .... que amamos juntos
                y que sigas pisando la .... que pisamos.
            Quiero que lo que amo siga vivo
            y a ti te .... y canté sobre todas las cosas,
        por eso sigue tú floreciendo, florida,
    para que alcances todo lo que mi amor te ordena,
    para que se pasee mi sombra por tu ....,
    para que así conozcan la razón de mi canto.

4 🎧 41 Listen to the audio and check your work.

5 Write a poem using the same structure used in Neruda's sonnet.

Cuando yo ....
quiero ....

Quiero que ....
quiero que ....
que ....

y que ....
Quiero que ....

por eso ....
para que ....
para que ....
para que ....

ANSWERS

Activity 1

a. Pertenece a sus primeros años; **b.** Por el romanticismo, la melancolía y la influencia del modernismo hispanoamericano de autores como Rubén Darío y Gabriela Mistral; **c.** La Guerra Civil española y el asesinato de Federico García Lorca; **d.** En los objetos más cotidianos y aparentemente insignificantes.

Activity 2

b.

Extension

Copy and cut out the sections of the poem in EA 5.3, *Explico algunas cosas*. Have the students work in groups to put the poem in the correct order. To check that their answers are correct, have them listen to a recording of the poem, spoken by Pablo Neruda himself, available online by searching "Pablo Neruda, Explico algunas cosas". You may choose to further analyze the poem together as a class, which will serve to teach students more about the history of Spain.

INSTRUCTIONAL STRATEGIES

Activity 3

Read the instructions aloud. Have students work in pairs to complete the poem.

🎧 41 **Activity 4**

• Play the audio so that students can check their answers to Activity 3.

• Confirm any responses that students may have missed in the audio.

• Encourage students to share their opinions about the poem and pick out their favorite verses.

Activity 5

• Go over the instructions. Allow students to spend a few minutes thinking about a moment in their future that they want to write about. Encourage them to jot down ideas first before completing the template.

• Direct students' attention back to the template. Ask them to identify where they need to use the subjunctive. Then give them time to write their poems.

• Monitor their progress and assist as needed.

• Have students take turns presenting their poems to the class or in small groups. If you have students present the poems to the entire class, consider having them vote and choose a winner for the following categories: the most original, the most fun, and the best presentation.

ANSWERS

Activity 3

muera, manos, luz, vivas, oídos, viento, mar, arena, amé, pelo.

OBJECTIVES FOR EVALUACIÓN

- Review grammar, vocabulary and culture from the unit
- Complete self-assessment

CORE RESOURCES

- Interactive Online Materials – ELEteca

STANDARDS

1.2 Understand the language

4.1 Compare languages

INSTRUCTIONAL STRATEGIES

- Have students complete the activities individually.
- Go over the answers as a class. Encourage students to learn from each other by asking if they agree with the answers given. Provide explanations as needed.
- You may wish to assign point value to each activity as a way for students to monitor their progress.
- Direct students to the indicated pages in **En resumen** if they make more than one or two mistakes in any one section.

ANSWERS

Activity 1

Answers will vary. Possible answers might include the following:

a. Yo lo llevo fatal, la Física nunca ha sido lo mío, espero que no sea muy difícil; **b.** ¡Hala, qué suerte! Pues espero que te diviertas; **c.** Bueno, de aquí al fin de semana quedan unos días, espero que te haga buen tiempo; **d.** ¡Vaya, qué mala suerte! Pues dile a tu hermano de mi parte que se mejore; **e.** Pues, ¡que aproveche!

Activity 2

Answers will vary. Possible answers might include the following:

a. me guste el instituto y mis profesores y compañeros; **b.** aprenda a hablar perfectamente en español; **c.** conocer la ciudad y a la gente de allí; **d.** ir a ver un partido del América en el estadio Azteca; **e.** mis amigos vengan a verme muy pronto.

Activity 3

a. En cuanto; **b.** Al; **c.** hasta que; **d.** Después de; **e.** Después de que; **f.** hasta que; **j.** Cuando.

Activity 4

a. para que sepan; **b.** para hacer; **c.** para que veamos; **d.** para que pienses; **e.** para hacer.

EVALUACIÓN

EXPRESSING WISHES

1 You are chatting with a friend. Complete the conversation using some of the expressions that you have learned.

» ¡Hola! ¿Cómo llevas el examen de Física? ¿Tú crees que será muy difícil?

» ....

» Uf, yo no puedo concentrarme, porque estoy pensando en el fin de semana. ¡Me voy a Ibiza!

» ....

» Lo malo es que he visto en la tele que está lloviendo mucho.

» ....

» Mi hermano también iba a venir, pero se ha roto el brazo, así que no va a poder ser.

» ....

» Gracias, bueno, te dejo que me voy cenar.

» ....

2 Next year you are moving to México D.F. Complete the sentences.

a. Espero que ....

b. Ojalá ....

c. Quiero ....

d. Deseo ....

e. Quiero que ....

EXPRESSING THE TIME WHEN AN EVENT OCCURS

3 Choose the correct option.

a. **En cuanto / Hasta que** llegues al aeropuerto, lo primero que debes hacer es facturar la maleta.

b. **Al / Después** llegar la primavera los campos se llenan de flores.

c. Me quedaré en casa **hasta que / antes de** pare de llover.

d. **Después de / Después** irnos, llegó Pedro.

e. **Antes de / Después de** que salgamos del cine, iremos a tomar algo.

f. Si quieres, puedes ver la tele **después / hasta que** sea la hora de cenar.

g. **Cuando / Después de** cumpla los dieciocho, podré votar.

EXPRESSING A PURPOSE

4 Fill in the blanks with *para* o *para que* and the verbs in parenthesis in the appropriate form.

a. El profesor les ha mandado hacer un trabajo sobre las ONG (saber, ustedes) .... más cosas acerca de ellas.

b. He comprado pan (hacer, yo) .... unos bocadillos.

c. He venido (ver, nosotros) .... una película.

d. Te he hecho esta bufanda (pensar, tú) .... en mí en Irlanda.

e. Este aparato sirve (hacer, el aparato) .... helados.

164

INDICATIVE, SUBJUNCTIVE, INFINITIVE

5 Complete the sentences using the correct form of the verb.

a. ¿Cuándo (venir, tú) .... a visitarnos? Tenemos muchas ganas de verte.

b. Quiero (beber, yo) .... algo fresco.

c. Hasta que no (irse) .... Juan no voy a decir nada.

d. Cuando mis abuelos (jubilarse) ...., se fueron a vivir a Málaga.

e. Mi hermana me ha dado un libro para que no (aburrirse, yo) .... durante el viaje.

f. Espero que hoy (salir, nosotros) .... puntuales de la clase de español.

g. Me voy antes de que (llover) ....

h. Cuando (terminar, yo) .... la universidad, espero (trabajar, yo) .... en una buena empresa.

i. Espero que no (dormirse, nosotros) .... con la película. Dicen que es un rollo.

j. ¡Ojalá (aprobar, yo) .... todos los exámenes!

k. He venido para que me (contar, tú) .... lo que pasó ayer.

l. Deseo que Pablo y tú (ser) .... muy felices y (tener) .... muchos hijos.

m. ¿Quieres que (empezar, nosotros) .... ya a cenar o prefieres esperar?

n. Su padre no quiere que (ver, ustedes) .... el regalo que les ha comprado.

ñ. Este bolígrafo no sirve para (corregir) ...., necesitas otro de diferente color.

o. No te levantes hasta que yo te lo (decir) ....

p. En cuanto (traer, ellos) .... mi equipaje, me iré de este hotel.

DIPHTHONGS, HIATUS

6 Look at the underlined stressed vowel and mark an accent when needed. Then look for diphthongs or hiatus.

> boina ○ Eugenio ○ estadounidense ○ anciano ○ buho ○ aullar ○ copia ○ acentua ○ orquidea ○ coreografo ○ barbacoa ○ actuo ○ adios ○ violencia ○ buitre ○ diurno ○ buey

CULTURA

7 Answer the following questions with the information you learned in *Me encanta ser voluntario*.

a. ¿Qué beneficios experimentaron algunos jóvenes después de hacer un voluntariado internacional?

b. ¿En qué tipo de actividades participaban los voluntarios?

c. ¿Fue todo trabajo o pudieron hacer otras cosas? Da ejemplos.

d. ¿Te sorprende que EE. UU. sea el primer país con el mayor número de gente que ayuda a los demás? ¿Por qué (no)?

 Practice what you have learned with additional materials online.

ANSWERS

Activity 5

a. vendrás; b. beber; c. se vaya; d. se jubilaron; e. me aburra; f. salgamos; g. llueva; h. termine, trabajar; i. nos durmamos; j. apruebe; k. cuentes; l. sean, tengan; m. empecemos; n. vean; o. corregir; p. diga; q. traigan.

Activity 6

Diptongos: boina, Eugenio, estadounidense, anciano, aullar, copia, actuó, adiós, violencia, buitre, diurno, buey.

Hiatos: búho, acentúa, orquídea, coreógrafo, barbacoa, actúo.

Activity 7

Answers will vary. Possible answers might include the following:

a. Los jóvenes mejoraron su español y aprendieron costumbres nuevas; b. Construir casas, dar clases de inglés; c. Pudieron participar en fiestas, viajar por el país y hacer amistades con otros jóvenes; d. Answers will vary.

OBJECTIVES FOR EN RESUMEN: VOCABULARIO

- Review unit vocabulary and expressions
- Practice communicative skills

STANDARDS

1.2 Understand the language
1.3 Present the language

INSTRUCTIONAL STRATEGIES

- Have students role-play scenarios similar to what they see in the images and practice using the correct *Expresiones de deseo*.
- Have students write sentences with the words and phrases in the other vocabulary sections. Call on students to write their sentences on the board – but leaving a blank line where the vocabulary word or phrase should be. Then have the rest of the class write down the answers. Go over the answers as a class.
- Index cards can be used as flashcards with the Spanish term on one side and the English term, a picture, or a drawing on the other.
- Working in pairs or groups, students can use the flashcards to help each other practice unit vocabulary.

EN RESUMEN: Vocabulario

Expresiones de deseo
Cuídate. *Take care.*
Enhorabuena. *Congratulations.*

Felicidades. *Congratulations.*

Lo siento mucho. *I'm so sorry.*

ojalá *I hope, let's hope (that)*
Que aproveche. *Enjoy your meal, Bon appétite.*

Que disfrutes. *Have fun.*

Que duermas bien. *Sleep well.*

Que lo pases bien. *Have a good time.*

Que te mejores. *Get well.*

Que tengas buen viaje. *Have a good trip.*

Que tengas suerte. *Good luck.*

Expresiones temporales
dentro de un rato *in a moment*
dentro de... (periodo de tiempo) *within a (period of time)*
el mes que viene *next month*
pasado mañana *day after tomorrow*

Hacer conjeturas y promesas
al *upon*
cuando *when*

en cuanto *as soon as*
hasta (que) *until*
mientras (que) *while*

Las ONG
la ayuda desinteresada *selfless aid*
la campaña de sensibilización *awareness campaign*
la catástrofe natural *natural disaster*
el comercio justo *fair trade*
el conflicto bélico *armed conflict*
los derechos humanos *human rights*
los discapacitados *handicapped people*

el donativo *donation*
la labor social *social work*
las labores humanitarias *humanitarian relief*
la orientación laboral *workforce readiness*
la protección del medioambiente *environmental protection*
sin ánimo de lucro *non-profit*

Verbos
defender (e>ie) *to defend*
desatender *to neglect*
desear *to wish, desire*
esperar *to hope, to wait for*
luchar (por, en, a favor de, contra) *to fight (for, in, in favor of, against)*
ofrecer *to offer*
recaudar fondos *to raise money*

166

EN RESUMEN: Gramática

PRESENT SUBJUNCTIVE: REGULAR VERBS

(See page 154)

	−AR HABLAR	−ER COMER	−IR VIVIR
yo	hable	coma	viva
tú	hables	comas	vivas
usted/él/ella	hable	coma	viva
nosotros/as	hablemos	comamos	vivamos
vosotros/as	habléis	comáis	viváis
ustedes/ellos/ellas	hablen	coman	vivan

PRESENT SUBJUNCTIVE: IRREGULAR VERBS

(See page 155 and 156)

Stem-changing verbs

QUERER	VOLVER	JUGAR	PEDIR
e → ie	o → ue	u → ue	e → i (en todas las personas)
quiera	vuelva	juegue	pida
quieras	vuelvas	juegues	pidas
quiera	vuelva	juegue	pida
queramos	volvamos	juguemos	pidamos
queráis	volváis	juguéis	pidáis
quieran	vuelvan	jueguen	pidan

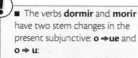

■ The verbs **dormir** and **morir** have two stem changes in the present subjunctive: **o → ue** and **o → u**:

- **duerma, duermas, duerma, durmamos, durmáis, duerman.**
- **muera, mueras, muera, muramos, muráis, mueran.**

Verbs with irregular *yo* forms

poner → **pong**-	traer → **traig**-	-a
tener → **teng**-	hacer → **hag**-	-as
salir → **salg**-	caer → **caig**-	-a
venir → **veng**-	construir → **construy**-	-amos
decir → **dig**-	conocer → **conozc**-	-áis
		-an

Verbs that are completely irregular

HABER	IR	SABER	ESTAR	SER	VER	DAR
haya	vaya	sepa	esté	sea	vea	dé
hayas	vayas	sepas	estés	seas	veas	des
haya	vaya	sepa	esté	sea	vea	dé
hayamos	vayamos	sepamos	estemos	seamos	veamos	demos
hayáis	vayáis	sepáis	estéis	seáis	veáis	deis
hayan	vayan	sepan	estén	sean	vean	den

167

OBJECTIVES FOR UNIT OPENER

- Introduce unit theme: *¡Hoy me siento bien!* about feelings and emotions
- Introduce culture for the unit: Share information about the arts in Hispanic countries

STANDARDS

- 1.1 Interpersonal communication
- 1.2 Understand the language
- 2.1 Practices and perspectives

INSTRUCTIONAL STRATEGIES

- Introduce unit theme and objectives. Talk about the photo and have students state who they think the people are and what they are going: *¿Dónde están estos muchachos? ¿Qué están haciendo? ¿Cuál es la relación entre ellos? ¿Cómo están vestidos? ¿Para ir a una fiesta, para ir al campo...?*, etc.
- Help students formulate their ideas: *Están contentos porque ganaron un concurso de baile*, etc. Encourage students to use their imagination to create various scenarios.
- Have students work individually to write answers to the three questions on the page.
- Put students into pairs or small groups to share and discuss their answers.
- Call on volunteers to report back on their responses and discussions. See if you can get the class to reach agreement.

ANSWERS

Answers will vary. Possible answers are:
- Están felices porque han ganado un concurso de baile. Es la gran final.

UNIDAD 6

¡HOY ME SIENTO BIEN!

¡Ojalá que lo consigamos!

▶▶ ¿Cómo se sienten estos muchachos? ¿Por qué están así? ¿Es una fecha especial o ha pasado algo extraordinario?

▶▶ Y tú, ¿cómo te sientes hoy?

168

ADDITIONAL UNIT RESOURCES

Extension Activities (EA) (Photocopiable)	Interactive Whiteboard Lessons (IWB)	Audio	Video	Online ELEteca
EA: 6.1, 6.2, 6.3, 6.4, 6.5, 6.6, 6.7, 6.8	IWB: 6.1	42 to 53	Diálogo 6	EXTENSIÓN DIGITAL

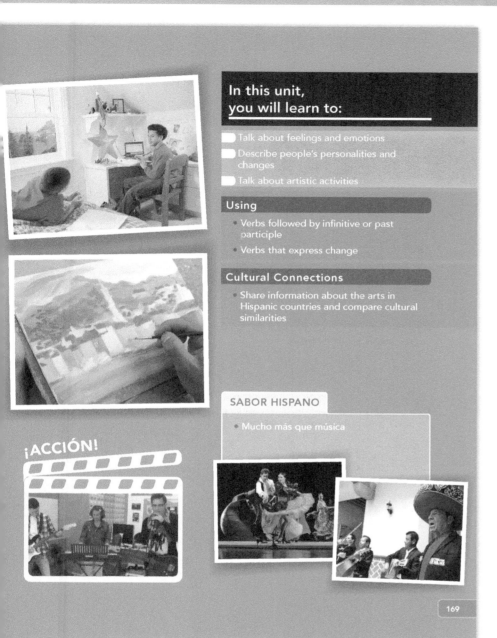

**In this unit,
you will learn to:**

Talk about feelings and emotions

Describe people's personalities and changes

Talk about artistic activities

Using

• Verbs followed by infinitive or past participle

• Verbs that express change

Cultural Connections

• Share information about the arts in Hispanic countries and compare cultural similarities

SABOR HISPANO

• Mucho más que música

¡ACCIÓN!

169

LEARNING OUTCOMES

• Talk about feelings and emotions
• Describe people's personalities and changes
• Talk about artistic activities

INSTRUCTIONAL STRATEGIES

• Use unit opener to preview vocabulary and cultural topics for this unit.
• Have students look at the images on this page and relate them to the objectives listed. Ask questions such as: **¿Quiénes son estas personas? ¿Dónde están? ¿Cómo crees que son? ¿Te gusta la pintura? ¿Quién es tu artista favorito? ¿Qué estilo tiene? ¿Qué otras actividades artísticas pueden nombrar?**
• Invite students to read the topic for **Sabor hispano** and preview that section in the unit. Ask questions such as: **¿Reconocen el tipo de baile y el estilo de música que se presentan en las imágenes?** (el flamenco y la música de los mariachis) **¿Te gusta bailar? ¿Qué tipos de bailes hispanos conoces?**
• Ask students to anticipate what they think the episode for **¡Acción!** will be about.
• Have students work in pairs to talk about the images using the questions you have modeled. Then have volunteers present to the class what they understand this unit to be about.

THREE MODES OF COMMUNICATION: UNIT 6			
	INTERPERSONAL	**INTERPRETIVE**	**PRESENTATIONAL**
HABLAMOS DE...	2, 6, 7	1, 3, 4, 5	
COMUNICA	1, 4, 8	2, 3, 5, 6, 7	8
¡ACCIÓN!	1	2, 3, 4, 5	2
PALABRA POR PALABRA	4, 8, 10	1, 2, 3, 5, 6, 9, 11	1, 7, 9, 12, 13
GRAMÁTICA	2, 7	1, 4, 5, 6	3, 6
DESTREZAS		2, 4	
CULTURA		SABOR HISPANO	
RELATO	6, 7	1, 2, 4	3, 5

OBJECTIVES FOR HABLAMOS DE...

- Talk about feelings and emotions
- Preview vocabulary: Feelings, personality, and emotions
- Preview grammatical structures: Verbs followed by infinitive or past participle and verbs that express change

CORE RESOURCES

- Audio Program: Track 42

STANDARDS

1.1 Engage in conversation
1.2 Understand the language
1.3 Present information
4.2 Compare cultures

INSTRUCTIONAL STRATEGIES

Activity 1

- Ask students to talk about the people in the photo and in pairs, ask: **¿Quiénes creen que son las personas que ven? ¿Qué relación puede haber entre ellas? ¿Dónde están? ¿Qué llevan? ¿Qué están haciendo? ¿Qué les llama la atención a ustedes?**
- Have students complete the activity individually and compare their answers with another student. Remind students that they may not have the same answers and more than one answer can be correct.

Activity 2

- Tell students to compare their answers with the words listed in the word bank. Ask students how well they were able to predict the text completions. Ask students to share other options and confirm whether they are correct.
- Then have students complete the activity again using the words provided.
- Correct the activity with the whole class and be sure they understand the text.

Activity 3

- Introduce the activity by asking students to come up with some ideas about what each person in the image is probably thinking. Record responses on the board.
- In this activity students will review the present subjunctive. Ask students to read the first bubbles and identify the form of the verb. Then have them read the remaining thought bubbles and ask whether they all need the subjunctive. Review the forms as necessary.
- Have students to do the activity individually completing the sentences and writing the name of the person who is probably thinking it.

ANSWERS

Activity 1

a. escuela; **b.** clase; **c.** trabajo; **d.** profesor; **e.** compañero; **f.** gusta; **g.** vergüenza; **h.** nerviosa; **i.** contenta.

Activity 3

a. pase, intentaré: Adrián; **b.** salude, se pondrá: Antonia; **c.** llegue, tenemos: Raquel; **d.** entre, diré: el profesor.

HABLAMOS DE... Los sentimientos

1 Look at the image and fill in the blanks in the paragraph.

Antonia y Raquel son dos compañeras de la (a) .... que están en la puerta de (b) .... hablando sobre un (c) .... que tienen que presentar en clase. Esperan a que llegue el (d) .... de Historia para entrar en clase y, mientras hablan, ven a Adrián, que es un (e) .... de clase que le (f) .... a Antonia. Esta, al ver que él para a saludarla, se pone roja como un tomate de la (g) .... Raquel le sonríe a Antonia para animarla a hablar con él. Sabe que Antonia está (h) ...., pero también (i) .... porque Adrián se ha fijado en ella.

2 Check your answers with a partner. Do you have similar answers? Then check them against the words from the list below.

compañero ○ vergüenza ○ nerviosa ○ escuela ○ gusta ○ profesor
encantada ○ trabajo ○ clase

3 Complete the sentences with the correct form of the verb in parenthesis. Then write the name of the person who is probably thinking it.

a. Cuando (pasar) ....pase.... por aquí, (intentar) .... hablar con ella.

b. Seguro que cuando lo (saludar) ...., (ponerse) .... rojo.

c. Antes de que (llegar) .... el profesor, (tener) .... que estar sentados.

d. En cuanto (entrar) .... en clase, les (decir) .... que hay examen la semana que viene.

170

4 Read the conversation between Antonia and Raquel and fill in the blanks with a word from the list below.

atenta ○ musa ○ vergüenza ○ tonta ○ abierta ○ amor ○ enamorada ○ loca

Raquel: ¡Antonia! ¡Antoooonia!
Antonia: ¡Ay! Hola, Raquel, no te había visto.
R.: ¿Cómo me vas a ver con lo distraída que vas?
A.: Es que estaba pensando en una canción que me encanta y…
R.: ¿Qué canción?
A.: La nueva de *Nerea*, ¿la has escuchado?
R.: Sí, está bien, ella tiene una voz espectacular, pero… es demasiado romántica, ¿no? Bueno, para ti es perfecta porque con lo (a) .... que estás últimamente…
A.: Para nada, ¿pero qué dices?
R.: ¿Que no? Pero si se te nota de lejos que estás (b) .... por Adrián. Cada vez que lo ves, pones una cara de (c) ....…
A.: Ok, ok, lo que tú digas. Por cierto, compuse un tema nuevo para el concierto.
R.: ¡Súper! Oye, mira quién viene por ahí, tu (d) ....
A.: ¡Ay, caray, qué (e) ....! Tú ahora no te vayas y no me dejes sola. Es que cuando estoy con él no sé qué me pasa que nunca sé qué decirle y me da rabia que piense que soy una tonta…

R.: Pues dile, por ejemplo, que le has escrito una canción y que quieres que vaya a nuestro concierto. Seguro que cuando te oiga dedicándole "su" canción subida a un escenario, se queda con la boca (f) ....
A.: ¿Qué dices? No me atrevo *(dare)*… ¿Por qué no se lo dices tú?
R.: ¿Yooo? ¡Pero si a mí no me gusta!
A.: ¡Ay! ¡Qué nervios! Ya viene y me está mirando…
R.: Sí, y acaba de tocar el timbre para entrar en clase. Así que mejor dejas tu declaración de (g) .... para otro momento, que cuando nos vea el profe hablando en la puerta…
A.: Sí, mejor entramos. Por cierto, ¿tienes los apuntes del otro día? Es que no estuve muy (h) ....
R.: Sí, vamos, y a ver si hoy escuchas más al profe y compones menos.
A.: Bueno, es que la inspiración llega cuando menos te lo esperas.

5 🎧 42 Listen to the conversation and check your answers.

6 👥 What about you? Talk to a partner about your own experiences. Use the following questions as a guide.
• ¿Cómo reaccionas cuando sientes vergüenza? ¿Te pones rojo/a?
• ¿En qué clases estás menos atento/a? ¿Por qué?
• ¿Te has quedado con la boca abierta en alguna situación? ¿Qué pasó?

7 👥 Look at the highligthed sentences in the conversation. Which ones use the subjunctive? Then with a partner, take turns completing the sentences with your own examples related to the conversation.
a. Cuando el profe vea a los estudiantes hablando en la puerta…
b. Antonia no quiere que Raquel…
c. Raquel cree que Adrián se va a quedar con la boca abierta cuando…
d. En mi opinión,… llega cuando menos te lo esperas.

171

Activity 4
• Review the words in the list and have students identify the ones that describe people. You may want to preteach **descargar**, **descargado**, **componer** and **ensayar** asking students to look and see if they recognize the cognates.
• Ask students to read the conversation and fill in the blanks with the appropriate words. Then, work in pairs to compare their answers.

🎧 42 Alternative activity
Play the audio first and tell students they are going to listen to a conversation between Antonia and Raquel with their books closed. Afterwards, ask questions to see how much they have understood. For example: *¿Por qué Antonia no había visto a Raquel? ¿Qué le pasa a Antonia últimamente? ¿Qué le pasa a Antonia cuando está cerca de Adrián?* After the discussion, they can do Activity 4.

🎧 42 Activity 5
Play the audio so students can check their answers to Activity 4.

Activity 6
• The purpose of the activity is to help students identify with the topic and provide opportunities for them to talk about their own experiences and similar feelings. If they don't feel comfortable talking about their own situations they should feel free to invent their own.
• Have students to work in pairs taking turns to complete the activity.

Activity 7
• Ask students to review the highlighted expressions. Call on volunteers to read one aloud and explain the use for the subjunctive or indicative: **No te vayas** / **No me dejes sola** (negative commands), **Quieres que vaya** (subjunctive: expressing wishes), **Cuando te oiga** / **Cuando nos vea** (subjunctive: after **cuando** when the action takes place in the future), **Cuando menos te lo esperas** (indicative: everyday occurrence).
• Then have students complete the sentences with their own examples. Record student responses on the board to ensure correct use of subjunctive or indicative.

Extension
Preview the use of the subjunctive with expressions of emotion. Tell students to look for the following expressions in the conversation: **Me da rabia** and **les encanta que**. Then have students look at the form of the verb after **que** and ask students why they think the subjunctive is used and what type of expression introduces the subjunctive.

ANSWERS
Activity 4
a. enamorada; **b.** loca; **c.** tonta; **d.** inspiración; **e.** vergüenza; **f.** abierta; **g.** amor; **h.** atenta.

Activity 7
Answers will vary but should include the following forms of the verb: **a.** future / *ir a* + infinitive; **b.** subjunctive; **c.** subjunctive; **d.** present indicative.

OBJECTIVES FOR COMUNICA

- Present communicative functions of the unit:
- Talk about feelings and emotions

STANDARDS

1.1 Engage in conversation
1.2 Understand the language
1.3 Present information
4.1 Compare languages

CORE RESOURCES

- Audio Program: Tracks 43 and 44
- Extension Activities: EA 6.1, 6.2, 6.3, 6.4
- Interactive Online Materials – ELEteca

INSTRUCTIONAL STRATEGIES FOR
EXPRESSING FEELINGS AND EMOTIONS (1)

- Use EA 6.1 and 6.2, *Estados de ánimo* to activate vocabulary to describe moods and to introduce the section. Distribute cut up cards to student pairs and have them match the images to the descriptions.
- Review with students the expressions for feelings and emotions in the chart and create a sample sentence for each of the endings to emphasize the different uses with nouns, infinitives, indicative and subjunctive forms. Write the samples sentence on the board.
- Share with students one situation explaining your feelings and emotions. Ask a couple of students to do the same. If you or your students do not feel comfortable sharing real situations, invent one.

COMUNICA

EXPRESSING FEELINGS AND EMOTIONS (1)

Estoy (estar)	contento	con *la nueva profesora.*	→ noun
	encantado	cuando / si *juega mi equipo.*	→ indicative
	nervioso	de *estar aquí.*	→ infinitive: same subject
	aburrido	de que *te vayas.*	→ subjunctive: different subject
	triste...		

Me pongo (ponerse) *I get / I become*	alegre	
	furioso	cuando *escucho mi música favorita.*
	nervioso	
Me siento (sentirse) *I feel*	contento	si me *cuentan el final de una película.*
	de buen / mal humor...	
	bien / mal / fatal...	

Adoro *I love*		
No soporto / aguanto *I can't stand*	los paisajes del Caribe.	→ noun
	madrugar *(to get up early).*	→ infinitive: same subject
Odio *I hate*	que me empujen *(shove)* en el metro.	→ subjunctive: different subject

> (!) **Estoy preocupado por** *Álex. Hace dos días que no viene a clase.*
> *I'm worried about Álex. He hasn't been to class for two days.*

1 👥 **Describe to your partner how you typically feel in the following situations.**

a. un día de lluvia
b. antes de un examen
c. en un concierto
d. si ves una pelea *(fight)*
e. en el dentista
f. de vacaciones

2 Complete the following conversations by filling in the numbered blanks with an appropriate verb to express feelings and emotions. Select an adjective from the list below for the lettered blanks.

> nervioso ○ histérica ○ tranquilo ○ preocupado ○ serio

a. » Pero, ¿qué te pasa? Desde que llegaste, (1) .... muy (a) ....
» Es que (2) .... (b) .... por el examen de mañana. He estudiado mucho, pero ahora creo que estoy hecho un lío y no entiendo nada.
» Bueno, eso es normal, yo también (3) .... (c) .... antes de un examen. Mira, hazte un té y acuéstate temprano, ya verás como mañana, después de descansar, (4) .... más (d) .... y te acuerdas de todo.

172

Activity 1

- Model some examples to help students get started: **Estoy aburrido/a cuando llueve, Me pongo triste cuando llueve, No soporto los días de lluvia.**
- In pairs, have students to express how they are feeling in each situation and have the other student react.

Activity 2

- Ask students to look at the images and describe the following: **¿Quiénes creen que son las personas que aparecen? ¿Qué relación hay entre ellas? ¿De qué creen que están hablando? ¿Cuál es su estado de ánimo o cómo creen que se sienten?**
- Have students work individually and then compare their answers with a partner. Students will have an opportunity to confirm their answers after listening to the audio.

ANSWERS

Activity 2

a. **1.** estás; **a.** serio; **2.** estoy; **b.** preocupado; **3.** me pongo; **c.** nervioso; **4.** estás; **d.** tranquilo.
b. **5.** soporto; **6.** odio; **7.** te pongas; **e.** histérica.

b. » Sergio, ¿fuiste tú el que ha usado mi computadora?
» ¡Ay, sí! Es que le he dejado mi portátil a Santi.
» ¿Y por qué no me lo pides? ¡Te he dicho mil veces que no (5) .... que me agarren las cosas sin pedírmelas!
» Bueno, no te pongas así, fue un momento…
» Que no, Sergio, que no, además sabes que (6) .... que me toquen mi computadora, pero nada, tú siempre igual…
» ¡Ok, ok, mujer! No (7) .... (e) ...

3 🎧 ⁴³ **Now listen to the conversations and check your answers.**

4 📖 **Using the new expressions you have learned, tell your partner again how you feel in the situations in Activity 1.**

EXPRESS FEELINGS AND EMOTIONS (2)

	da/n	rabia *(infuriates me, you...)* vergüenza *(embarrasses me)* igual *(makes no difference to me)* lástima / pena *(it makes me feel pity)*	***ver una película empezada.*** ❗ Use the infinitive when the person who feels the emotion and the one who performs the activity is the same person.
(A mí) **me** (A ti) **te** (A usted/él/ella) **le** (A nosotros/as) **nos** (A ustedes/ellos/ellas) **les**	**pone/n**	triste *(makes me sad)* histérico/a *(makes me hysterical)* de los nervios *(makes me crazy)*	***que la gente hable en el cine.*** ❗ Use the subjunctive when the person who feels the emotion and the one who performs the activity are different.
		molesta/n *(bothers me)* indigna/n *(makes me indignant)* impresiona/n *(strikes / affects me)*	***las películas de amor.*** ❗ Also followed by singular and plural nouns.

❗ ■ These verbs have the same construction as **gustar / encantar** and must agree with the subject that follows.
Me ponen triste **las personas** que no tienen casa.
Me pone triste **la música** romántica.
(A nosotros) **Nos pone** nerviosos **(nosotros) tener** que esperar antes de entrar al cine.
(A mí) **Me da** rabia que en el cine **(otras personas) hablen** durante la película.

173

INSTRUCTIONAL STRATEGIES

🎧 **43 Activity 3**
- Play the audio and have students check their answers.
- Have students practice the conversations with a partner.
- Circulate around the room to check that students are on task and actively participating.

Activity 4
- Have students go back to Activity 1 and work again on these situations. This time students need to express feelings and emotions using the expressions they have learned in this section.
- Provide a model to help students get started: **No aguanto que llueva todo el día. Me pongo de mal humor cuando cancelan los partidos por la lluvia.**
- Call on student volunteers to share examples with the class.

INSTRUCTIONAL STRATEGIES FOR
EXPRESSING FEELINGS AND EMOTIONS (2)
- Ask students to describe everything they know about the verb **gustar**. Record responses on the board and provide cues as needed to ensure students cover all aspects of the structure. Then ask students for other verbs like **gustar** (**encantar**, **molestar**, **doler**, etc.).
- Explain to students that the expressions in the chart follow the same pattern as **gustar**. List these on the board separately to help students access meaning. For example, start with **me da rabia**, **me da vergüenza**, and then have students continue calling out the combinations. Move on to **me pone triste**, etc., pausing as needed to clarify meaning, and so on until all expressions have been covered and recorded on the board.

Extension
- For additional practice with meaning, shuffle the cards from EA 6.3, **¿Qué sientes cuando…?** Ask a student to pick a card and formulate a question using **¿Qué sientes cuando…?** and the action pictured in the image. The student then calls on a classmate to match it with one of the expressions listed on the board. You may choose to project the complete set of images to prepare the situations first.

- Next, go over the different ways to express feelings and emotions about something else. Call on students to combine elements to create sample sentences. Make sure they are logical before recording on the board. Go over the uses with infinitives, subjunctive, and nouns.
- Share with students another situation about things that bother you, make you sad, etc., using some of these verbs and a variety of endings. Have students prepare some of their own.

INSTRUCTIONAL STRATEGIES

🎧 44 Activity 5

- You have different options to do this activity. Play the audio first so students can fill in the blanks and then correct their answers, or ask students to fill in the blanks first and then play the audio to check their answers.
- Either way, have students compare answers with a partner before going over the answers.

Activity 6

Have students do these activities individually and compare answers with a partner. Correct the activity together.

Activity 7

- Remind students that *me*, *te*, *le*, *nos*, and *les* must be used with these expressions and that the adjectives must show agreement.
- Have students complete the activity and compare answers with a partner.

Activity 8

- Have students work in pairs and express feelings and emotions using the expressions they have learned.
- Observe, provide support, and correct students as needed.
- Call on students to report what their partners said. To liven up the review, ask for volunteers to report back on the strangest, funniest, most surprising things their partners said as well as situations they had in common to practice with *nos*.

Extension

For additional practice with these expressions, distribute copies of EA 6.4, *Expresar sentimientos y estados de ánimo*. Review the instructions with students and have them work individually. Project the answers to self-correct.

ANSWERS

Activity 5

a. aburren; b. pena; c. miedo, pánico; d. lo mismo; e. nerviosa; f. enferma; g. contenta.

Activity 6

1. d; 2. c; 3. b; 4. e; 5. a.

Activity 7

a. Me ponen enfermo/a; b. Me da pena; c. Me pone de buen humor; d. le dan miedo; f. Me molesta.

COMUNICA

5 🎧 44 Listen to the conversation between María and Ana as they talk about the movie they have just seen and where they are going to go next. As you listen, fill in the blanks with one of the words from the list. ¡*Atención!* Not all the words will be used.

> aburren ○ contenta ○ enferma ○ lo mismo ○ maleducada
> miedo ○ nerviosa ○ pánico ○ pena ○ triste

a. Ya sabes que me .... los dramas y las películas de amor.
b. Es verdad que te da mucha .... el final.
c. A mí las películas de vampiros me dan .... Bueno, me dan ....
d. Sabes que a mí me da .... ir a un sitio que a otro.
e. Me pone muy .... que tarden tres horas en atenderte.
f. Es que me pone .... que la gente sea tan maleducada.
g. Verás qué ....te ponen unas buenas tapas.

6 Match each expression with its logical completion.

1. Me da vergüenza... .... •   • a. que llegue a casa de noche, nunca voy solo.
2. Me pone de mal humor... .... •   • b. que salga de casa sin hacer mi cama.
3. A mi madre le da mucha rabia... .... •   • c. que la gente hable por teléfono en el autobús.
4. Me aburren... .... •   • d. actuar delante de tanta gente.
5. Mamá, no sé por qué te da miedo... . •   • e. las películas históricas.

7 Fill in the blanks with an appropriate verb from the list below.

> le dan miedo ○ me da pena ○ me molesta ○ me pone de buen humor ○ me ponen enfermo/a

a. .... las personas que se cuelan en la cola (*cut the line*) del cine.
b. .... que el guitarrista de *La sonrisa de Eva* quiera dejar el grupo.
c. .... escuchar música alegre.
d. A mi hermana .... las películas de terror, pero a mí no.
e. .... que no sea gratis entrar a los museos.

8 Antonia likes Adrián, but talking to him makes her nervous. Take turns with a partner describing situations that make you feel in the following ways.

- Me molesta que...   - Me aburren...   - Me da rabia...
- Me pone nervioso/a que...   - Me da lástima que...   - Me ponen de buen humor...
- Me da pena...   - Me dan miedo...   - Me pone de mal humor...

Modelo: *Me molesta que pongan anuncios cuando estoy viendo una película en la televisión.*

 Practice what you have learned with additional materials online.

EA 6.4

1. a. de; 1. regresar; b. de que; 2. estemos; c. que; 3. se termine; d. cuando; 4. abrí; e. con; f. cuando; 5. tengo; g. si; 6. hay; 7. volar; h. que; 8. llames; 9. hacer; 10. hagas.

2. 1. se pone; 2. está, me da; 3. les pone, le dan; 4. se pone; 5. Me ponen; 6. le pone; 7. se siente; 8. me pone, le da; 9. se ponen; 10. me pongo; 11. le dan, se pone; 12. me siento.

¡ACCIÓN!

UNIDAD 6

ANTES DEL VIDEO

1 With a partner, take turns asking and responding to the following questions.

a. ¿Te gustan los conciertos? ¿Tocas algún instrumento?

c. ¿Cuándo fue la última vez que escuchaste música en vivo (live)?

d. ¿Te gustaría formar parte de un grupo musical?

2 Look at the following scene segment and answer the questions.

Estos tres amigos están ensayando (rehearsing).

¿Qué instrumentos musicales están tocando?

¿Qué tipo de música crees que tocan?

DURANTE EL VIDEO

3 Select which of the people below did the following things according to the video segment.

a. ¿Quién llegó anoche más tarde a casa? ○ ○ ○
b. ¿Quién llega más tarde al ensayo? ○ ○ ○
c. ¿Quién es el primero que empieza a tocar en el ensayo (rehearsal)? ○ ○ ○
d. ¿Quién le dedicó ayer un tema a una chica? ○ ○ ○
e. Según Sandra, ¿quién es un conquistador? ○ ○ ○

4 During the segment, Antonio receives a text message from Adriana. What did it say?

DESPUÉS DEL VIDEO

5 List each instrument from the list under the appropriate category.

De viento	De cuerda	De percusión

tambor o arpa
violín o flauta
platillos o saxofón
guitarra

Practice what you have learned with additional materials online.

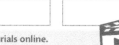

175

OBJECTIVES FOR ¡ACCIÓN!

- Provide students with a structured approach to viewing the video
- Contextualize the content of the unit in a familiar scenario

CORE RESOURCES

- Unit Video 6
- Interactive Online Materials – ELEteca

STANDARDS

1.2. Understand the language
2.1 Practices and perspectives
3.2 Acquire information
4.2 Compare cultures

INSTRUCTIONAL STRATEGIES

Previewing: Antes del video
Activity 1
Have students work in pairs and share the answers to the questions.

Activity 2
Ask students to look at the image and discuss the questions with a partner. When they finish, invite different students to offer their answers to the class. Allow time for discussion of different answers.

Viewing: Durante el video
Activity 3
- Play the entire video without pauses and ask students what they understood.
- Play again and allow students to ask you to pause, as needed.
- Replay sections students found hard to understand.
- Have volunteers who understand help those students who do not.
- Show the entire video again without pauses.

Activity 4
Give the students a few minutes to think about the text message, then have them compare answers in pairs.

After viewing: Después del video
Activity 5
Ask students to do this activity individually and then share the answers with a partner.

ANSWERS

Activity 3
a. Antonio; b. Sandra; c. Roberto; d. Antonio; e. Roberto.

Activity 4
De viento: flauta, saxofón; De cuerda: arpa, violín, guitarra; De percusión: tambor, platillos.

OBJECTIVES FOR ADJETIVOS CALIFICATIVOS

- Present vocabulary needed to discuss attributes and characteristics
- Describe the qualities of people and things

CORE RESOURCES

- Interactive Online Materials – ELEteca

STANDARDS

1.1   Engage in conversation
1.2   Understand the language
1.3   Present information
4.1   Compare languages and cultures

INSTRUCTIONAL STRATEGIES

- Tell students that in this section they will build vocabulary using adjectives they already know.
- Use the following examples to present the shortened form of adjectives: **Es una buena muchacha / Es un buen muchacho**. Ask students to describe the difference. Then explain that this happens with **bueno** and **malo**.
- Write the following sentence pairs on the board to explain the change in meaning that occur when certain adjectives are placed before the noun: **Es un amigo viejo / Es un viejo amigo**. Ask students to guess at the meanings.
- Finally, write **paciente ≠ impaciente** to show opposites. Then ask students to provide the opposites of **simpático** and **tranquilo** by adding a prefix.
- Walk students through the explanations in the chart to reinforce the information just presented.

Activity 1

- Review the model with students to make sure students understand what they have to do. Ask students to provide other explanations for the model to help them get started. Then work in pairs.
- Call on volunteers to share their answers. Follow up their responses with examples from the sample answers provided below.

Activity 2

- Ask students to work individually and then compare answers with a partner.
- Review as a class.

ANSWERS

Activity 1

Answers will vary. Possible answers include: **a.** Es una empresa grande, en ella trabajan más de 1000 empleados. / Es una gran empresa, su prestigio es conocido a nivel internacional; **b.** Es un alumno viejo, después de jubilarse decidió matricularse en la universidad y volver a estudiar. / Es un viejo alumno y, aunque ya habla español muy bien, sigue viniendo a la escuela para perfeccionarlo; **c.** Es una única obra, al principio pensaron en hacer más, pero el presupuesto no lo permitió. / Es una obra única, según los expertos, ninguna hasta el momento la ha podido igualar.

Activity 2

a. sincero, falso; **b.** tranquilo; **c.** generoso, egoísta; **d.** sociable; **e.** flexible; **f.** tolerante; **g.** preocupado.

PALABRA POR PALABRA Adjetivos calificativos

- Descriptive adjectives describe a trait or quality of the noun they modify.

- In Spanish, descriptive adjectives generally follow the noun, with some exceptions.

- The adjectives **bueno** and **malo** drop the final -o when placed before the noun.
  *Es un **buen** hijo.*
  *No es un **mal** ejemplo.*

- The adjective **grande** becomes **gran** before singular nouns.
  *Es una **gran** película.*

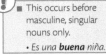

- This occurs before masculine, singular nouns only.
  - *Es una **buena** niña.*

- Placing certain adjectives before the noun changes the meaning of the adjective.

*Es un **gran** libro.*	➡	quality
*Es un libro **grande**.*	➡	size
*Es un **viejo** amigo.*	➡	time
*Es un amigo **viejo**.*	➡	age
*Es un **único** ejemplar.*	➡	quantity
*Es un ejemplar **único**.*	➡	without parallel

impaciente.

- Add a prefix, such as **im-**, **in-** or **des-**, to form the opposite of an adjective describing a trait or characteristic: **paciente / impaciente**, **útil / inútil**, **agradable / desagradable**.

1 Together with a partner, add information to the following sentences to clarify their meaning.

Modelo: Es un hombre **grande**. *Es el más alto y fuerte de la clase.*
Es un **gran** hombre. *Es generoso y todo el mundo lo respeta.*

a. Es una empresa **grande**. / Es una **gran** empresa. ➡ ....
b. Es un alumno **viejo**. / Es un **viejo** alumno. ➡ ....
c. Es una **única** obra. / Es una obra **única**. ➡ ....

2 Fill in the blanks with the correct form of the adjectives from the list.

tranquilo ○ preocupado ○ sociable ○ generoso ○ tolerante
sincero ○ flexible ○ falso ○ egoísta

a. Si siempre digo la verdad, soy ...., pero si no digo lo que pienso, soy ....
b. Cuando no estoy nervioso, estoy ....
c. Si me gusta compartir lo mío con los demás, soy ....: pero si lo quiero todo para mí y no pienso en los demás, soy ....
d. Si me gusta relacionarme con las personas, soy ....
e. Cuando me adapto fácilmente a las situaciones y acepto los cambios, soy ....
f. Si acepto otras opiniones y a las personas diferentes a mí, soy ....
g. Cuando tengo un problema, estoy ....

3 Write the opposite of the following adjectives. ¡Atención! Not all are formed with prefixes.

a. flexible ➡ .... f. tolerante ➡ .... k. optimista ➡ ....
b. ordenado ➡ .... g. fuerte ➡ .... l. introvertido ➡ ....
c. educada ➡ .... h. tranquilo ➡ .... m. trabajadora ➡ ....
d. preocupada ➡ .... i. puntual ➡ .... n. seguro ➡ ....
e. responsable ➡ .... j. sociable ➡ .... ñ. paciente ➡ ....

4 👥 Prepare a description of yourself and one of your partner. Then exchange information. Were your descriptions of each other accurate?

5 🎧 45 Match the words from the list to the appropriate image below. ¡Atención! Some images will have more than one possibility. Then listen to the audio to check your answers.

1. ⬜ acueducto   5. ⬜ galería de   8. ⬜ museo   12. ⬜ poema
2. ⬜ violín   arte   9. ⬜ músico   13. ⬜ poeta
3. ⬜ escultura   6. ⬜ guitarra   10. ⬜ orquesta   14. ⬜ retrato
4. ⬜ estatua   7. ⬜ guitarrista   11. ⬜ pintura   15. ⬜ actuar

177

INSTRUCTIONAL STRATEGIES

Activity 3

- Tell students that the prefix **in-** has some variations depending on the first letter of the adjective. Use **irr-** with adjectives starting with **r-** (**regular/irregular**), **im-** with adjectives starting with **p-** (**paciente** / **impaciente**).
- Students write individually the opposite of the adjectives from the list. Remind them that not all these adjectives are formed with prefixes.
- Correct the activity with the entire class.

Extension

Play charades. Have students write adjectives on separate pieces of paper. Then in groups of 3 or 4, students pick from the cards and act out the adjective for the others to guess. The group with the most correct answers wins.

Activity 4

- Have students prepare a description of themselves and then of their partner. Tell them to include adjectives from the section.
- Have them share the descriptions to check if they were accurate. Discuss together as a class.

OBJECTIVES FOR ¡QUÉ ARTE!

- Present vocabulary needed to talk about the arts
- Talk about artistic activities

CORE RESOURCES

- Audio Program: Track 46
- Extension Activities: EA 6.5

STANDARDS

1.1   Engage in conversation
1.2   Understand the language
3.2   Acquire information

INSTRUCTIONAL STRATEGIES

🎧 45 Activity 5

After the presentation, have students work individually to match the words and images. Then play the audio for students to check their answers.

Audioscript

a. acueducto; **b.** estatua; **c.** museo; **d.** escultura; **e.** galería de arte; **f.** retrato; **g.** pintura; **h.** guitarrista; **i.** guitarra; **j.** músico; **k.** violín; **l.** actuar; **m.** poeta; **n.** poema; **ñ.** orquesta.

ANSWERS

Activity 3

a. inflexible; **b.** desordenado; **c.** maleducada; **d.** despreocupada / tranquila; **e.** irresponsable; **f.** intolerante; **g.** débil; **h.** intranquilo / nervioso; **i.** impuntual; **j.** insociable; **k.** pesimista; **l.** abierto / extrovertido; **m.** vaga; **n.** inseguro; **ñ.** impaciente.

Activity 5

1. a; **2.** k; **3.** d; **4.** b; **5.** e; **6.** i; **7.** h; **8.** c; **9.** j; **10.** ñ; **11.** g; **12.** n; **13.** m; **14.** f; **15.** l.

INSTRUCTIONAL STRATEGIES

Activity 6

- Ask students if they know who the figure in the center is. Explain that Athena (Roman name Minerva) was the goddess of the arts and wisdom. She was the patron goddess of Athens. Her symbol was the owl.
- Have students complete the charts individually and then compare their answers with a partner.
- Review together and clarify meaning as needed.

Activity 7

- In pairs, have students practice with word families to build vocabulary and expand on what they already know.
- Tell students to create two more definitions using the new vocabulary for their partner to guess.
- Call on student volunteers to quiz the class.

Activity 8

- To introduce the activity, present the expression: **Yo creo que soy bueno/a en... porque...** and ask students to talk about themselves. Model some examples to get them started. For example: **Yo creo que soy bueno en fotografía porque dedico mucho tiempo a sacar fotos**.
- Have students ask each other about their talents and interests in the arts.
- Call on students to report back on what they learned about their partners.

Extension

Distribute cards from of EA 6.5, **Pictionary de las artes** to play Pictionary or charades in groups of four. Divide the groups into two teams with each group receiving a set of cards.

ANSWERS

Activity 6

Música: melodía, compositor, violinista, canción, orquesta, guitarrista, ensayar; **Arquitectura:** acueducto, diseñar; **Danza:** baile, ballet, bailarín, ensayar; **Escultura:** estatua, galería de arte, escultor; **Literatura:** obra, novelista, aventuras, poema, poeta, histórica, contar, cuento, tema, novela; **Pintura:** obra, cuadro, retrato, galería de arte, pintar.

Activity 7

a. pintor; **b.** compositor; **c.** arquitecto; **d.** músicos; **e.** escultor; **f.** escritores.

PALABRA POR PALABRA ¡Qué arte!

6 Arrange the following words according to the category in which they belong. *¡Atención!* Some words may appear in more than one category. Who does the figure in the middle represent?

> melodía ○ compositor ○ obra ○ cuadro ○ acueducto ○ violinista ○ novelista ○ ensayar ○ aventuras ○ estatua ○ retrato ○ canción ○ poema ○ galería de arte ○ pintar ○ escultor ○ baile ○ orquesta ○ ballet ○ diseñar ○ poeta ○ bailarín ○ histórica ○ contar ○ cuento ○ tema ○ guitarrista ○ novela

MÚSICA

ARQUITECTURA

DANZA

ESCULTURA

LITERATURA

novela

PINTURA

7  Practice with word families and fill in the blanks with an appropriate profession. Then create two of your own using the vocabulary from Activities 5 and 6 for your partner to guess.

- **a.** Un .... pinta cuadros y retratos de personas famosas.
- **b.** Un .... compone música y melodías.
- **c.** Un .... diseña edificios y otras estructuras como, por ejemplo, puentes.
- **d.** Hay unos cien .... en las orquestas sinfónicas.
- **e.** Un .... crea esculturas de hierro, mármol y otros materiales.
- **f.** Muchos de los .... escriben novelas, poemas y obras de teatro.

8 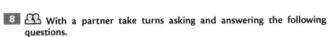 With a partner take turns asking and answering the following questions.

- **a.** ¿Has practicado alguna de estas actividades artísticas? ¿Cuál?
- **b.** ¿Hay alguna que te gustaría practicar y aún no lo has hecho?
- **c.** ¿Crees que tienes alguna aptitud artística? ¿Eres bueno haciendo algo?
- **d.** ¿Cuál es tu obra favorita de cada actividad artística? ¿Por qué?

PALABRA POR PALABRA La música

9 👥 With a partner, discuss whether you think the following statements are true or false. Then read the text that follows regarding the relationship between music and emotions. Were your assumptions correct?

	T	F
a. La cultura es un sentimiento universal y está por encima de la cultura en la que hemos crecido o que conocemos.	☐	☐
b. La música influye en nuestro estado de ánimo, incluso en nuestro comportamiento.	☐	☐
c. Todas las sociedades poseen escritura, pero algunas no poseen música.	☐	☐
d. La música nos ayuda a comunicarnos y a entender mejor a los demás.	☐	☐

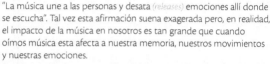

La música de las emociones

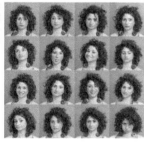

"La música une a las personas y desata *(releases)* emociones allí donde se escucha". Tal vez esta afirmación suena exagerada pero, en realidad, el impacto de la música en nosotros es tan grande que cuando oímos música esta afecta a nuestra memoria, nuestros movimientos y nuestras emociones.

Estudios realizados por científicos, demostraron que, tanto un aborigen como un moderno ingeniero, cuando escuchaban la misma música, reaccionaban de la misma forma. Otra investigación, realizada en Camerún entre personas que no habían oído nunca música occidental antes, demostró que estas eran capaces *(able)* de reconocer en ella la alegría, la tristeza o el terror... Todos son sentimientos comunes que provoca una misma melodía a personas de diferentes culturas. Por eso, hay canciones universales que consiguen ponernos tremendamente tristes y otras que, en cambio, nos contagian *(transmit)* alegría y buen humor, seamos de donde seamos.

Otra de las grandes cualidades de la música es su inmenso poder de unión social. Hay sociedades sin escritura, pero ninguna sin música. Las melodías nos unen, nos hacen compartir estados de ánimo.

A lo largo de la historia los seres humanos nos hemos unido para bailar, cantar y celebrar rituales. De hecho, no hay celebración que no vaya acompañada de música.

10 👥 **Based on the reading and what you know about music, what type of music do you listen to in the following situations? Talk about your music preferences with a partner and include the name of artists, composers and other relevant information to describe your emotions.**

Modelo: *Cuando estoy enamorado/a, me gusta escuchar... porque...*

- estás enamorado/a
- te apetece mucho *(feel like)* bailar
- quieres relajarte
- quieres cantar y bailar al mismo tiempo
- estás de mal humor

179

OBJECTIVES FOR LA MÚSICA

- Present vocabulary needed to talk about styles of music
- Talk about musical preferences

STANDARDS

1.1 Engage in conversation
1.2 Understand the language
1.3 Present information
3.2 Acquire information
4.1 Compare languages and cultures

INSTRUCTIONAL STRATEGIES

Activity 9

- Have students read the statements and decide if they are true or false based on what they think they know about the relationship between music and emotions.
- Then have students read the text and check whether their opinions were supported by the reading.
- Find out how many students had the correct answers with a show of thumbs up or down. Encourage students to talk about the ones they got wrong and where the correct information was presented in the text.

Activity 10

- Brainstorm with students different genres of music and list them on the board. Include all types from classical music to show tunes (***melodías de espectáculos musicales***) to give students a broad range from which to choose.
- Have students work in pairs or groups of three. Tell them to use the vocabulary and the expressions they have learned in this section.
- Circulate around the room to check that students are on task and responding with more than just a type of music. Provide support as needed to help students expand on their answers.

ANSWERS

Activity 9

a. T; b. T; c. F; d. T.

INSTRUCTIONAL STRATEGIES

Activity 11

- Before students begin the activity, go over the meaning of the following words to facilitate comprehension of the text: **seguidor, puntero, encabezar, listas de éxitos, ejercer, imitar, compases, decantarse** (*opt for*) and **arriesgadas fusiones**. For the words that are already glossed in text, ask students to locate them and explain in their own words using context clues. For the others, explain in Spanish or have students look for familiar words.

- Have students read the text, ignoring the blanks for now. Ask some comprehension questions such as: **¿Qué tipo de música tiene el mayor número de seguidores? ¿Cuándo empezó la música pop a sonar en España? ¿Qué estilo de música ha influido en la música pop?**

- Then in pairs, have students match the missing sentences to their correct spot in the text. After reviewing the answers, call on student volunteers to read a paragraph inserting the new sentences.

Activity 12

- Have students select one of the musical groups mentioned in the reading and research more information about them on Internet or project some of their videos in class.

- Have students discuss their opinions in pairs. Then ask students to share with the class.

- Review the note on **la movida madrileña** and encourage students to seek more information about this transformative period in music.

Extension

As a follow up to Activity 12 and an introduction to Activity 13, have students choose from the following topics: **la Escuela Popular de Música**, **flamenco-chill**, **flamenco errante**, **ska**, **Alaska y Dinarama**... to do additional research online about what interests them. Encourage students to bring in pictures from the Internet to present and discuss in class.

Activity 13

With a different partner, ask students to discuss these questions.

ANSWERS

Activity 11

a. 2; **b.** 4; **c.** 1; **d.** 5; **e.** 3.

PALABRA POR PALABRA La música

11 Read the following text about the evolution of pop music in Spain. Then match the letters in the text to the sentences that would logically follow in the sequence.

Sin duda, el género que más seguidores (*followers*) tiene hoy en España es el pop, (a) .... En los 60 y 70, (b) ...., fueron famosos grupos como los Brincos, los Bravos o Fórmula V.

En los 80, influidos por la conocida movida madrileña, surgen grupos como Alaska y Dinarama, los Secretos o Radio Futura. (c) ....

Actualmente, grupos pop que destacan (*stand out*) en el panorama musical español (d) .... son: Maldita Nerea, el Canto del Loco, Amaral o Pereza, entre otros.

Es importante señalar también que el flamenco ha ejercido una gran influencia en muchos de los grupos y cantantes de la actualidad: así, (3) ...., como es el caso de Chambao y su *flamenco-chill*, o el Bicho y su *flamenco errante*.

1. .... ➡ Después les seguirán Hombres G, Mecano o Duncan Dhu, líderes indiscutibles de aquella década

2. .... ➡ música que se puede cantar y bailar, y que se desarrolla con la llegada del rock a España en los años 50

3. .... ➡ mientras grupos como Ojos de Brujo imitan sus compases, otros se decantan por nuevas y arriesgadas fusiones

4. .... ➡ décadas conocidas como la *era dorada de los grupos españoles*

5. .... ➡ y que suelen encabezar (*top*) las listas de éxitos (*hits*)

■ La movida madrileña fue un movimiento contracultural que surgió (*emerged*) durante los primeros años de la transición de la España después de la muerte de Franco (1975), y se prolongó hasta mediados de los años ochenta. Fue parte del cambio y liberalización cultural e ideológica que experimentó la gran mayoría de la sociedad española. *Flamenco-chill* es un subgénero musical derivado de la fusión del flamenco y música electrónica ambiental (*background*). Se desarrolló con la colaboración de Henrik Takkenberg y el grupo Chambao. El Bicho es un grupo que se conoció en la Escuela Popular de Música de Madrid y en pocas semanas comenzaron a tocar en pequeñas salas (*lounges*) y por la calle, atrapando a la gente que pasaba con sus canciones de una belleza y sencillez deslumbrante (*stunning*).

12 Search online for more information about these groups and watch some of their music videos. Which ones did you like? Discuss your thoughts with a partner.

13 Take turns with a partner asking and responding to the following questions.

a. ¿Conoces alguno de los estilos musicales que se mencionan en el texto?
b. ¿Y los grupos musicales o cantantes?
c. ¿Conoces otros grupos musicales o cantantes hispanos? ¿Qué tipo de música hacen?

Practice what you have learned with additional materials online.

GRAMÁTICA

UNIDAD **6**

1. VERBS FOLLOWED BY AN INFINITIVE OR PRESENT PARTICIPLE

■ To express the beginning point of an activity use **empezar / ponerse a** + infinitive.
*He **empezado a leer** un libro muy interesante. I have started reading an interesting book.*
*Luis, ¡**ponte a hacer** las tareas ahora mismo! Luis, start doing your homework right now!*

■ To express the repetition of an activity use **volver a** + infinitive.
*El año pasado fui a Sevilla y este año **volveré a ir**.*
Last year I went to Sevilla and this year I'm going to go again.

Plaza de España, Sevilla.

■ To express an activity that is ongoing use **seguir / continuar** + present participle.
Sigo estudiando en la misma escuela que el año pasado.
I'm still studying in the same school as last year.
*El año pasado iba a clases de teatro y este **continuaré yendo**.*
Last year I was going to acting classes and this year I will continue going.

■ To express an activity that has just finished use **acabar de** + infinitive.
*¡**Acabo de ver** al muchacho que conocimos ayer en el concierto!*
I just saw the guy we met yesterday at the concert!

■ To express the interruption of an activity use **dejar de** + infinitive.
*He **dejado de ir** a clases de guitarra porque no tengo tiempo.*
I stopped going to guitar classes because I don't have time.

1 Fill the blanks with the appropriate verb construction. **¡Atención!** Be sure to use the correct past tense of the verbs.

> ●●● Asunto: Cosas que pasan
> De: Roberto   Para: NachoVela@hotmail.com
>
> Nacho, ¡no te lo vas a creer lo que pasó esta mañana!
> (Nosotros) (a) .... de entrar en clase cuando el
> profesor (b) .... a escribir en el pizarrón los acordes
> *(chords)* de una canción. Todos la reconocimos rápidamente y
> (c) .... a cantarla en voz baja. Pero, de pronto, Antonia
> (d) .... a cantar en voz alta, mirando hacia Adrián.
> Entonces el profesor le mandó callar *(to be quiet)*, pero Antonia
> (e) .... cantando, mientras Adrián y el resto de la
> clase la mirábamos alucinados *(amazed)*. Cuando el profesor la
> (f) .... a mandar a callar, amenazando con castigarla,
> Antonia (g) .... de cantar, pero antes le dijo a Adrián
> que quería decirle las palabras de esa canción desde hacía
> mucho tiempo.

181

OBJECTIVES FOR GRAMÁTICA 1

• Present grammatical structures needed to practice communicative functions of the unit:
Verbs that are followed by an infinitive or the present participle
• Talk about the beginning, end, continuity, and repetition of an action

CORE RESOURCES

• Interactive Online Materials – ELEteca

STANDARDS

1.1   Engage in conversation
1.2   Understand the language
1.3   Present information
4.1   Compare languages

INSTRUCTIONAL STRATEGIES

1. Verbs Followed by an Infinitive or Present Participle

• To introduce the topic write the following expressions on the board: ***empezar a, dejar de, volver a, seguir, acabar de***. Explain to students that you are going to talk about yourself and things that you have started to do or have done again, things you have stopped doing, etc., using the expressions on the board. Ask them to listen for what comes after these expressions in your story and to jot them down. Tell students (pointing to the expressions as you say them): ***Empecé a andar cuando tenía 10 meses. Dejé de montar en bicicleta a los 17 años porque empecé a conducir. He vuelto a montar en bicicleta para hacer ejercicio pero todavía sigo conduciendo. Acabo de comprar un coche híbrido que ahorra mucho en gasolina***. Ask students what forms they heard and for which expressions.

• Walk students through the grammatical explanation in the book. Read the examples, review the explanations, and answer any questions they may have.

• Ask personalized questions with each verb so students can give you real examples. Allow students time to write their sentences. Ask: **¿Cuándo empezaste a hablar español / jugar a los videojuegos...? ¿Qué hacías cuando tenías 10 años y que sigues haciendo ahora? ¿Qué has dejado de hacer?**

Activity 1

• Ask students if they remember the characters Adrián and Antonia from earlier in the unit, and what they know of them.
• Have students complete this activity individually. Then have students compare their answers with a partner.
• Project the activity with the answers inserted. Review with students the expressions: ***cantar en voz alta / baja, callar, castigar***.
• Then ask students to describe what happened in class between Adrián and Antonia.

ANSWERS

Activity 1

a. Acabábamos; **b.** empezó; **c.** empezamos; **d.** se puso; **e.** siguió; **f.** volvió; **g.** dejó.

INSTRUCTIONAL STRATEGIES

Activity 2

- Have students walk around the class to find a classmate who has done some of these things. Students will need to write the names next to the appropriate sentence and ask for more information.
- Have three or four students share their findings with the class.

Alternative Activity

Tell students that they need to go around the class and find someone who answers 'yes' to all the questions. The student who completes all the sentences first, wins. Be aware that it is necessary to answer 'yes' to the first question in order to move to the next question.

Activity 3

- Have students write out their sentences on a separate piece of paper, reminding them to include some activities that are not true for them.
- Then in small groups, have students exchange lists with others in the group. Tell them to read their classmate's experiences and try to pick out the facts from fiction, writing **sí** or **no** next to the activities and then return the list to its owner. Take turns responding to false statements using thumbs up or down. Who made the best guesses?

OBJECTIVES FOR GRAMÁTICA 2

- Present grammatical structures needed to practice communicative functions for the unit:
  Verbs that express change
- Describe changes that can occur in professions, lifestyles, and emotions.

CORE RESOURCES

- Audio Program: Track 46
- Interactive Whiteboard Lesson: IWB 6.1

STANDARDS

1.4 Engage in conversation
1.5 Understand the language
1.6 Present information
4.1 Compare languages

INSTRUCTIONAL STRATEGIES

2. Verbs that Express Change

- Project IWB 6.1, **¡Vaya cambio!** to introduce the concept of change. Review each set of images and ask students to think about the type of change depicted: a. a change in profession; b. a change in lifestyle; c. a physical change; d. an emotional change. Then guide students to explain using **antes era**... / **ahora es**... and **antes** (+ imperfect) / **ahora** (+ present) to describe actions.
- Walk the students through the explanation in the book and invite volunteers to read the examples for the class.

GRAMÁTICA

2 Read the following list of activities your classmates may or may not have done. Walk around the class and find a classmate who has done any of the following things. Write his/her name in the appropriate box and ask for more information. Share your findings with the class.

	¿Quién?	Más información
Ha empezado a practicar algún deporte nuevo.		¿Cuál?
Alguna vez se ha puesto a llorar viendo una película en el cine.		¿Qué película?
Sigue viviendo en la misma casa en la que nació.		¿En qué lugar?
Acaba de comprar una computadora nueva.		¿Cómo es?
Continúa teniendo un juguete de cuando era pequeño.		¿Qué juguete?
Ha dejado de practicar algún *hobby* que antes practicaba.		¿Qué *hobby*?
Ha empezado a leer un libro recientemente.		¿Cómo se titula?
Ha dejado de colgar *(post)* fotos en su Facebook.		¿Por qué?

3 Make a list of five activities you have started to do, have done and are planning to do again, stopped doing, or have just done. Include real life experiences as well as some that are not true for you.

Modelo: El año pasado fui de vacaciones a China y este año volveré a ir. Acaba de comprar mi boleto de avión.

---

2. VERBS THAT EXPRESS CHANGE

■ To express temporary changes in a person or changes that happen spontaneously use **ponerse** + adjective.
Se pone muy nervioso al hablar en público. *He becomes / gets very nervous when speaking in public.*
Se puso rojo cuando le preguntaron. *He turned / became red when they asked him a question.*

■ **Quedarse** shows the result, the final condition.
Se quedó muy sorprendido por la noticia. *He was very surprised by the news (and remained so).*

> **!** ■ **Quedarse** can sometimes express permanent changes.
> • Mi abuelo **se quedó calvo** a los 50 años.
>   *My grandfather went bald at age 50.*

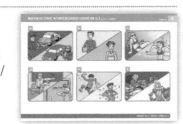

UNIDAD 6

- To express permanent changes use **volverse** *(not voluntary)* or **hacerse** *(voluntary or gradual change)* + adjective.
  Se ha vuelto un antipático. Antes no era así. He has become unlikable. He wasn't like that before.
  Jugó a la lotería y se volvió millonario. He played the lottery and became a millionaire.
  Con esa situación se hizo fuerte. He became strong.

- **Hacerse** can be used with adjectives and nouns that describe profession, religion, and ideology.
  Antes era abogado y ahora se ha hecho juez. Before he was a lawyer and now he became a judge.
  Viajó al Tíbet y se hizo budista. He traveled to Tibet and became a Buddhist.

4 Fill in the blanks with the correct verb of change. ¡Atención! Keep in mind the type of change being expressed. There may be more than one possibility.

a. .... un antipático
b. .... blanco
c. .... guapo
d. .... más delgado
e. .... contento
f. .... más sociable
g. .... vegetariano
h. .... un irresponsable
i. .... empresario

5 Complete the sentences with an appropriate expression from the previous activity.

a. Desde que es famoso siempre contesta mal a todo el mundo,...................................
b. Los invitaron a la inauguración de una galería de arte,...................................
c. Estudió un máster de negocios muy prestigioso y ....
d. Desde que es bailarina ....
e. Cuando le dieron la nota del examen de Literatura ....
f. Desde que trabaja en una ONG en defensa de los animales ....

6 46 Blanca and Esther have been friends since high school. Listen as Blanca talks about a class reunion Esther was not able to attend. Complete the chart with what has changed.

	Martín	Carolina	Gustavo	Antonio	Elena	Dani
Aspecto físico						
Carácter						
Profesión						
Ideología						
Vida personal						

7 You are all at your 10th year class reunion. Walk around the room and tell each other what has changed in your life.

 Practice what you have learned with additional materials online.

INSTRUCTIONAL STRATEGIES

Activity 4
Have students complete the activity individually and review as a class.

Activity 5
- Have students do this activity individually and then correct the answers with a partner.
- Ask for a couple of volunteers to ask and respond to each other taking turns: **¿Cuándo fue la última vez que te pusiste nervioso / muy contento / enfermo / rojo...?**

Extension
As a follow-up, project IWB: 6.1, ¡Vaya cambio! and ask students to describe the changes once again, but this time using the new expressions.

46 Activity 6
- Explain to students that they will be listening to a conversation between two friends, one of whom attended their high-school reunion.
- Have students review the names and the categories they will need to complete to document changes observed by Blanca at the reunion.
- Play the audio and ask students to complete the chart while listening. Tell them there will be a brief pause between each one. Repeat the audio another time so students can check their answers. Review as a class.

See audioscript on page APP2

Activity 7
- Allow students time to prepare 2 or 3 predictions about how their lives have changed since the last time they were in class. Then tell students to form a circle within a circle to ensure everyone gets a turn.
- Then call on volunteers to share the most drastic changes they heard about their classmates.

ANSWERS

Activity 4
a. Volverse; **b.** Quedarse; **c.** Volverse; **d.** Quedarse; **e.** Ponerse; **f.** Volverse; **g.** Volverse; **h.** Volverse; **i.** Hacerse.

Activity 5
a. se ha vuelto un antipático; **b.** se pusieron contentos; **c.** se hizo empresario; **d.** se ha quedado más delgada; **e.** se puso blanco; **f.** se ha vuelto más sociable.

Activity 6
Martín: Se ha puesto guapísimo; Se ha vuelto mucho más sociable y hablador; No ha dejado de hacer deporte, tiene novia; **Carolina:** Sigue siendo igual de guapa que antes; Se hizo modelo, ahora trabaja para una organización humanitaria; Se hizo budista; Dejó de ser una esclava de la imagen; **Gustavo:** Se puso muy gordo, se está quedando calvo; Sigue siendo tan simpático como siempre; Dejó de hacer deporte, se ha casado y acaba de tener un niño; **Antonio:** Se puso a trabajar en un restaurante, después volvió a estudiar y se hizo profesor de español; Ya no vive en España, dejó de estudiar y se fue a Toronto; **Elena:** Ahora se ha puesto muy guapa, se quedó mucho más delgada; Empezó a llevar un estilo de vida más saludable, se hizo vegetariana; Ya no sale con Dani; **Dani:** Empezó a trabajar por las noches en una discoteca, se ha hecho empresario; Se volvió más irresponsable y despreocupado; Ya no sale con Elena.

OBJECTIVES FOR DESTREZAS

• Anticipate content before listening

CORE RESOURCES

• Audio Program: Tracks 47 and 48

STANDARDS

• Understand the language

INSTRUCTIONAL STRATEGIES

Comprensión auditiva (1)

Activity 1

• Review the strategy with students and give them time to prepare.
• Ask them to look at the images to anticipate the answers to the questions.
• Ask students to discuss it in pairs. They will discover if they were correct after listening the audio (Activity 2).

🎧 47 Activity 2

• Tell students that each conversation will be played twice with a pause in between.
• Ask students to give the correct answer.

Audioscript

Conversación 1

» Has estado hoy en clase con Juan, ¿no? ¿Le has dicho que hemos quedado en el café de la esquina?
» No, no ha venido, ha vuelto a faltar. Se lo diré después en la biblioteca.

Conversación 2

» Perdona, me quiero probar estos jeans en la talla 30, esta camiseta y este jersey, pero en verde.
» A ver… Es que camisetas solo nos quedan en la talla grande y los jeans no nos quedan en ninguna talla, acaban de llevarse los últimos. El jersey aquí lo tienes y resulta que es el último que hay en la tienda.

INSTRUCTIONAL STRATEGIES

Comprensión auditiva (2)

Activity 3

• Review the strategy with students and give them time to prepare.
• Tell students they will listen to an announcement. In this case, students will hear a longer selection.

ANSWERS

Activity 2

Conversación 1: a; Conversación 2: a.

DESTREZAS

COMPRENSIÓN AUDITIVA (1)

1 Before you listen, read the strategy in Destrezas and follow the suggestion.

Destrezas

Anticipating content

Read the question carefully before listening to the audio. Look at the interrogative word to determine what type of response is needed. Is it asking for a person, a place, a thing, etc.? Then look at the choice of images and prepare ahead the vocabulary you might expect to hear.

Conversación 1: ¿Dónde creía el muchacho que ella había hablado con Juan?

Conversación 2: ¿Qué prenda está agotada en la tienda?

2 🎧 47 You will now listen to two very short conversations that will be played twice. After the second time, choose the correct option from the choices given.

Conversación 1: ¿Dónde creía el muchacho que ella había hablado con Juan?

Conversación 2: ¿Qué prenda está agotada en la tienda?

 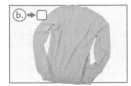 

COMPRENSIÓN AUDITIVA (2)

3 Next, you will listen to an announcement. Before you listen, read the strategy in Destrezas and follow the suggestions.

Destrezas

Listening to longer selections

To prepare for longer listening selections, first read the questions you will be asked to answer. Underline or highlight key words you will need to listen for. Say them softly aloud to yourself so you can hear how they are pronounced. Focus on these words and do not be distracted by unfamiliar words.

184

4 🎧 **48** In this activity you will be listening to an announcement over the public address system in a school. It will be played twice. After the second listening, decide whether the statements are true (T) or false (F).

	T	F
a. Las bases del concurso se pueden consultar en Internet y en los tablones informativos del centro.	☐	☐
b. El sobre en el que tienen que enviar el escrito se puede recoger en el Departamento de Lengua y Literatura del centro.	☐	☐
c. La modalidad del trabajo es libre.	☐	☐

PRONUNCIACIÓN Los extranjerismos *(foreign words)*

■ En español usamos algunas palabras que proceden de otras lenguas. Se dividen en:

• **Voces adaptadas**
Se adaptan a la ortografía y pronunciación del español: *estrés, eslogan, cabaré…*

• **Voces no adaptadas**
Se escriben igual que en la lengua original y su pronunciación es más o menos aproximada a ella: *pizza, rock and roll, jazz, pendrive…*

1 🎧 **49** Listen to some foreign words that are commonly used among Spanish speakers and write them below.

....

....

....

2 👥 Compare the words you have written with a partner. Then, decide which of the words have been adapted to Spanish and which have not.

3 Fill in the blanks with the appropriate word or expression you have learned in this section.

a. Necesito ir a la .... para comprarme un vestido.
b. A mi hermana le encantan los .... con tomate.
c. Marta y Juan han quedado para jugar al .... esta tarde.
d. Mis padres desayunan un .... y un café con leche.
e. El .... es el equipamiento lógico de un sistema informático.

 Practice what you have learned with additional materials online.

185

INSTRUCTIONAL STRATEGIES

🎧 **48** Activity 4

• Tell students that the audio will be played twice with a pause between each one. Correct the activity with the whole class.

See audioscript on page APP3

ANSWERS

Activity 4

a. verdadero; **b.** falso (Los trabajos deberán introducirse en un sobre grande que facilita la Consejería del centro y se entregarán al Departamento de Lengua y Literatura); **c.** falso (Solo se admitirán trabajos en la modalidad de cuento, el tema será libre).

OBJECTIVES FOR PRONUNCIACIÓN

• Learn about foreign words adapted to Spanish and those that stay in the original

CORE RESOURCES

• Audio Program: Track 49
• Interactive Online Materials – ELEteca

STANDARDS

1.2 Understand the language
3.2 Acquire information
4.1 Compare languages

INSTRUCTIONAL STRATEGIES

• Write on the board the following words: ***estrés, eslogan, email, iphone, pizza, espaguetis, tenis, fútbol***, etc.
• Ask students to tell you which of these words have been adapted to Spanish and which ones remain in their original language.

🎧 **49** Activities 1 and 2

• Play the audio and have students write each word.
• Ask students to tell you which words have been adapted to Spanish and which ones have not.
• In pairs, ask students to expand the list. Write the words on the board.

Audioscript

escáner, boutique, máster, stock, marketing, ranking, espaguetis, estatus, yogur, playback, espray, software, ballet, pádel, blus, cruasán.

Activity 3

Ask students to do this activity individually. Correct together as a class.

ANSWERS

Activity 1

See audioscript.

Activity 2

Adapted to Spanish: escáner, máster, espaguetis, estatus, yogur, espray, pádel, blus, cruasán.
Stay in the original: boutique, stock, marketing, ranking, playback, software, ballet.

Activity 3

a. boutique; **b.** espaguetis; **c.** tenis; **d.** cruasán; **e.** software.

OBJECTIVES FOR SABOR HISPANO

- Learn about Hispanic music
- Learn about different type of Hispanic music and dance

CORE RESOURCES

- Audio Program: Track 50

STANDARDS

2.1. Practices and perspectives

2.2 Products and perspectives

3.2 Acquire information

5.2 Using language for personal enjoyment and enrichment

INSTRUCTIONAL STRATEGIES

🎧 50

- Introduce the topic by asking what the students know about Hispanic music and dance.
- Talk about the images and elicit what they already know and can share.
- Put students in pairs to discuss the questions in the **Antes de leer** box.
- Monitor their conversations and assist as needed.
- Call on volunteers to report back on their discussions.
- Before playing the audio, tell students to listen for the type of stories are told by **los corridos mexicanos**. Either have students close their books while they listen or follow along with the text in the book.
- Elicit responses to the target question. For more detail, ask: **¿Cuándo empezaron los corridos mexicanos? ¿Qué papel tenían en cuanto a la revolución? Y ahora, ¿qué tipo de historias cuentan?**
- To help build vocabulary, have students locate and underline any words from the glossary on the next page in the text. Then have them make and share new sentences with the words. You may choose to have them work individually or in pairs.

SABOR HISPANO

MUCHO MÁS QUE MÚSICA

Una banda de mariachis de Puebla, Mexico.

Antes de leer

¿Qué música o artistas mexicanos conoces?

¿Piensas que los mariachis son divertidos o están pasados de moda? ¿Por qué?

🎧 50 **En el mundo hispano hay muchísimos tipos de música y baile. No solamente son expresiones artísticas: a veces, como los corridos mexicanos, son una forma de contar historias de actualidad.**

Los corridos son canciones populares mexicanas que cuentan una historia. La melodía suele ser muy sencilla, y la letra° es fácil de recordar. Eran habituales ya en 1910, en la época de la Revolución mexicana, y cumplían la importante función de diseminar° las noticias en todo el territorio. Los temas de los corridos son variados: a veces hablan sobre un héroe popular, a veces son divertidos, y otras tienen contenido político. Muchas veces, las bandas de mariachis cantan corridos. Desde 1930, el contenido de los corridos incorpora noticias relacionadas con el narcotráfico. En los últimos años, este género se ha hecho más popular, especialmente en los estados del norte del país como Chihuahua, Nuevo León, Baja California y Sinaloa, donde se concentra la violencia del narcotráfico. En muchos estados, está prohibido reproducir narcocorridos en conciertos, discotecas y bares. «Este tipo de canciones presenta a los narcotraficantes con glamur», dicen las autoridades.

En la actualidad, los Tigres del Norte son una banda muy famosa de música norteña, que incluye los corridos. Son conocidos internacionalmente y han ganado cinco premios Grammy. Sin embargo, varios pueblos les han puesto multas° por cantar narcocorridos en sus conciertos. «La prohibición no es justa°, estas canciones son parte de la cultura actual», dicen.

Un edificio público en Culiacán, Sinaloa, tierra del narcocorrido.

186

El tango

Todos los años se celebra un festival internacional de tango en la ciudad de Buenos Aires. Más de 70.000 turistas y bailarines de todo el mundo llegan para participar en el evento. Estos son los principales países representados en el festival, además de Argentina.

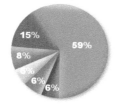

- 59%
- 15%
- 8%
- 6%
- 6%
- 6%

- ■ Colombia
- ■ Estados Unidos
- ■ Japón
- ■ Brasil
- ■ Francia
- ■ Argentina

Los top 5 del flamenco

Para muchos turistas, el flamenco es sinónimo de cultura española, aunque proviene* del sur del país. Te contamos cinco cosas que debes saber sobre esta apasionada* danza.

1. Combina la cultura **andaluza**, **sefardí**, **gitana** y **árabe**.
2. Una de sus formas se llama «**cante jondo**».
3. El bailarín se llama «**bailaor**» y la bailarina, «**bailaora**».
4. Gran parte del baile es **improvisación**.
5. Los lugares donde se baila flamenco se llaman «**tablaos**».

El tango nació en Buenos Aires, y siempre se baila en pareja.

¿COMPRENDISTE?

Decide if the following statements are true (T) or false (F).

1. No todos los corridos hablan sobre el narcotráfico.   T ○ F ○
2. Los Tigres del Norte piensan que los narcocorridos son parte de la cultura.   T ○ F ○
3. Colombia es el país extranjero mejor representado en el festival de tango.   T ○ F ○
4. Los pasos del baile flamenco están todos planeados con anticipación.   T ○ F ○
5. El tango se puede bailar de forma individual.   T ○ F ○

El flamenco es la música y baile típicos del sur de España.

AHORA TÚ

What do you think? Answer the following questions and discuss your ideas with other students.

1. ¿Qué tipo de música te gusta? ¿Cuál es su atractivo, en tu opinión?
2. ¿Qué tipo de música no escuchas nunca, y por qué?
3. ¿Qué forma musical norteamericana presenta estilos de vida polémicos con glamur?
4. ¿Te gusta bailar? ¿Cuándo fue la última vez que bailaste y qué tipo de música había?
5. ¿Prefieres bailar de forma individual o en pareja? ¿Por qué?
6. Entre el tango y el flamenco, ¿qué estilo musical te parece más interesante? ¿Por qué?

Glosario

apasionado/a – passionate
diseminar – to spread
justo/a – fair
la letra – lyrics
la multa – fine
la pareja – couple
pasado de moda – out of date
provenir – to originate

Fuentes: BBC Mundo, Tango BA, Buzzle.

INSTRUCTIONAL STRATEGIES

El tango

- Call on a volunteer to read the caption and chart data aloud.
- Have students write three questions about the data.
- Put them into pairs to take turns asking and answering the questions.
- Monitor their conversations and assist as needed. Take note of any common errors that you hear in their discussions.
- Review any common errors with the class, eliciting the corrections.

Los top 5 del flamenco

- Call on a volunteer to read the title and information that follows.
- Check students' understanding of the information by asking questions, such as: *¿Qué culturas están representadas en el flamenco? ¿Qué tipo de baile es? ¿Qué quiere decir?*

¿Comprendiste?

- Have the students say if the statements are true or false.
- Ask for volunteers to point out where in the text they can find the information.
- Discuss any vocabulary that may be unknown, and ask those that have understood to help those that have not.

Ahora tú

- Read the questions with the students and have them think about the answers.
- Have the students answer the questions in pairs and then present to the class. Each student may take a turn at speaking.

ANSWERS

¿Comprendiste?

1. T; 2. T; 3. F; 4. F; 5. F.

OBJECTIVES FOR RELATO

- Revisit unit themes, grammar, vocabulary and culture in a new context
- Improve reading comprehension skills

CORE RESOURCES

- Audio Program: Track 51

STANDARDS

1.1 Engage in conversation
1.2 Understand the language
1.3 Present information
2.1 Practices and perspectives
5.3 Using language for personal enjoyment and enrichment

INSTRUCTIONAL STRATEGIES

Activity 1

- Before doing the activity, ask students to provide the names of famous Hispanic poets or writers they have studied so far, ask them to name different genres, and say which one was their favorite and why.
- The purpose of the activity is to preview the vocabulary that will appear in the text and to facilitate comprehension.
- Ask students to look at the images and match the words with their definitions.
- Help students to access meaning since some of these words are used more in literary texts than in everyday conversations.

🎧 51 Activity 2

- Ask students if they know what animal is pictured. Ask them to talk about its color and why they think its name is **Platero**.
- Before students read the text, review glossed words such as: **peludo**, **blando**, **algodón**, **huesos**, **prado**, **tibiamente**, **celeste**, **naranjas**, **mandarinas**, **uvas moscateles**, **morado**, **cristalino**, **gota** y **miel**.
- Tell students that the sentence **"Tien' asero..."** refers to the way they speak in Andalucía.

Activity 3

- Have the students read the questions and skim the text to look for the correct answer.
- Explain what a **comparación** is (a literary device in which a writer compares or contrasts two people, places, things, or ideas) and a **metáfora** (a type of analogy that achieves its effects via association, comparison or resemblance).

ANSWERS

Activity 1

1. d; **2.** a; **3.** i; **4.** b; **5.** f; **6.** c; **7.** g; **8.** e; **9.** h.

Activity 3

a. Un burro; **b.** Físicamente es pequeño, peludo, suave, con los ojos muy negros. De carácter es tierno, y mimoso, alegre, pero también es fuerte; **c.** *Tan blando que se diría todo de algodón; los espejos de azabache de sus ojos son duros como dos escarabajos de cristal negro; Camina con un trotecillo alegre que parece que se ríe; es tierno y mimoso igual que un niño, que una niña; es fuerte y seco como una piedra; tiene acero y plata de luna.*

RELATO Platero y yo

1 **Match the following words to their definitions.**

1. azabache ......
2. escarabajo ....
3. hocico ....
4. gualdo/a ....
5. trote ....
6. cascabeleo ...
7. higo ....
8. ámbar ....
9. despacioso ..

- a. Insecto que busca excremento de otros animales para alimentarse.
- b. Amarillo. Se dice así porque hay una flor de ese color con el mismo nombre.
- c. Sonido que producen los cascabeles.
- d. Tipo de carbón, de color negro, que se usa como adorno en collares, pulseras...
- e. Resina fósil de color amarillo, que se emplea en collares, etc.
- f. Modo de caminar acelerado de algunos animales, que avanzan saltando.
- g. Fruto de la higuera, dulce, de color verde por fuera y blanco o rojo por dentro.
- h. Lento, pausado.
- i. Parte de la cabeza de algunos animales, en la que están la boca y la nariz.

2 🎧 **51** **Read the following excerpt from Juan Ramón Jiménez's novel, *Platero y yo*.**

Platero y yo

Platero es pequeño, peludo (*hairy*), suave; tan blando (*soft*) por fuera, que se diría todo de algodón, que no lleva huesos (*bones*). Solo los espejos de azabache de sus ojos son duros cual (*like*) dos escarabajos de cristal negro.

Lo dejo suelto y se va al prado, y acaricia (*caresses*) tibiamente con su hocico, rozándolas apenas, las florecillas rosas, celestes y gualdas... Lo llamo dulcemente: "¿Platero?", y viene a mí con un trotecillo alegre que parece que se ríe, en no sé qué cascabeleo ideal...

Come cuanto le doy. Le gustan las naranjas mandarinas, las uvas moscateles, todas de ámbar; los higos morados, con su cristalina gotita de miel...

Es tierno y mimoso (*affectionate*) igual que un niño, que una niña...; pero fuerte y seco por dentro, como una piedra... Cuando paso sobre él, los domingos, por las últimas callejas del pueblo, los hombres del campo, vestidos de limpio y despaciosos, se quedan mirándolo:

- "Tien' asero...".

Tiene acero (*steel*). Acero y plata de luna, al mismo tiempo.

3 👥 **Work with a partner and answer the following questions.**

- a. Según el texto y la imagen, ¿qué animal es Platero?
- b. ¿Cómo es físicamente? ¿Y su carácter o personalidad?
- c. El autor utiliza metáforas y comparaciones para describir a Platero. ¿Podrías localizarlas en el texto? ¿Sabes qué significan todas?

4 Number the following paragraphs in the appropriate order to learn about the author, Juan Ramón Jiménez. The first one has been done for you.

☐ De carácter hipersensible, la melancolía lo acompañó a lo largo de su vida. En 1913 conoce en Madrid al gran amor de su vida, Zenobia Camprubí, con la que se casó durante su viaje a Estados Unidos en 1916.

☐ En 1936, al estallar la Guerra Civil, abandonan España para no regresar nunca. Estados Unidos, Cuba y Puerto Rico fueron sus lugares de residencia a partir de entonces.

☐ La primera se caracteriza por ser íntima, emotiva y sentimental, abundan las descripciones del paisaje como reflejo del alma del poeta, y también la melancolía, la música, los recuerdos y los ensueños. El modernismo de Rubén Darío y el simbolismo francés influirán en esta etapa de juventud. Es el tiempo en el que escribió la obra que lo inmortalizó, *Platero y yo*,

☐ Juan Ramón Jiménez nació en Huelva (España) en 1881, fue un niño solitario y su infancia transcurrió en el pueblo de Moguer, en contacto con la naturaleza.

☐ el libro español traducido a más lenguas del mundo, junto con *El Quijote*. Escrito en prosa poética, está inspirado en la amistad del autor con un burro pequeño y peludo que lo acompañó en sus paseos por su pueblo natal.

☐ Ya en el colegio se sintió atraído primero por la pintura, después por la música y finalmente por la poesía.

☐ Otra de sus obras más conocidas, *Diario de un poeta recién casado* (1917), escrito a partir de su viaje por mar a Estados Unidos, representa una ruptura con la poesía sensitiva, iniciándose así una poesía más intelectual que lo situará en el camino hacia otra más metafísica y depurada en su última etapa.

☐ En 1956, tres días antes de la muerte de su esposa, recibió el Premio Nobel de Literatura, él morirá tan solo dos años después. Su obra es muy extensa y su poesía pasa por distintas etapas.

5 In the first stage of his literary career, the author focuses on creating descriptions to provoke certain feelings. What feelings do you get from Platero's description?

6 Do you have or have you ever had a pet? Write a description of your pet using metaphors and comparisons as Jiménez did in his. If you do not have a pet, you can describe a person you cared deeply about.

7 🗪 Discuss the following with a partner.

· ¿Piensas que el tener animales es bueno para desarrollar algunos sentimientos positivos?

· ¿Crees que puede ayudar a superar otros negativos? ¿Cuáles?

Draw here the described pet or person

INSTRUCTIONAL STRATEGIES

Activity 4

- Tell students to go online and find out more information about Juan Ramón Jiménez and his poetry.
- Ask students to read the text and order the paragraphs to learn more about the author.
- Choose to do this activity individually or in pairs.

Activity 5

- Drawing from the structures and expressions students have learned in this unit, have them discuss their feelings in pairs.
- Ask a couple of volunteers to share their feelings after the reading.

Activity 6

- Have students write a description of their favorite pet using adjectives, comparisons and metaphors as modeled in ***Platero y yo***.
- Provide students with the following examples for comparisons: ***Tus ojos se parecen al mar***, ***Tus ojos son como el mar*** and metaphors that connect two nouns in apposition using ***ser***: ***Tus ojos son el mar***.
- Ask them to draw their pet to complete the description.
- Ask a couple of students to read their descriptions and draw their pets on the board.
- Have the rest of the students vote for the most interesting / funny / crazy… pet.

Activity 7

- Have students work in pairs to discuss their feelings about pets and what they bring to people's lives.
- You can bring to class articles, texts or some news about animals. You can create a debate with two big groups: one group should be in favor and the other against controversial topics like: bullfights, cockfights, fur coats, etc.

ANSWERS

Activity 4

3, 4, 6, 1, 7, 2, 8, 5.

OBJECTIVES FOR EVALUACIÓN

- Review grammar, vocabulary and culture from the unit
- Complete self-assessment

CORE RESOURCES

- Interactive Online Materials – ELEteca

STANDARDS

1.2 Understand the language

2.1 Practices and perspectives

4.1 Compare cultures

INSTRUCTIONAL STRATEGIES

- Activities can be completed individually and then reviewed with the class. Vary by asking students if they agree with the answer given and then writing it on the board. Provide explanations as needed.
- You may wish to assign point value to each activity as a way for students to monitor their progress.
- Direct students to the indicated pages in **En resumen** if they make more than one or two mistakes in any one section.

ANSWERS

Activity 1

a. lleguen; **b.** me despido; **c.** se pone; **d.** tire; **e.** entregar; **f.** hacer; **g.** espero.

Activity 2

Poner: de mal humor; triste; de los nervios; **Dar:** pena; rabia; lástima; igual; miedo

Activity 3

a. Juan ha vuelto a reprobar el examen de Música; **b.** Ana y Luis dejaron de hablarse; **c.** María sigue estudiando solfeo; **d.** He empezado a ir a clase de guitarra; **e.** Acabo de ver al profesor de Música; **f.** A Carlos le continúa gustando ver caricaturas.

EVALUACIÓN

EXPRESSING FEELINGS AND EMOTIONS

1 **Fill in the blanks with the correct form of the verb in parenthesis.**

a. Estoy contenta de que (llegar) .... las vacaciones.

b. Estoy triste cuando (despedirse, yo) .... de un amigo por mucho tiempo.

c. Me enfado si mi hermana (ponerse) .... mi ropa sin pedírmela.

d. Me molesta que la gente (tirar) .... papeles al suelo.

e. Nos preocupa no (entregar, nosotros) .... el trabajo a tiempo.

f. Odio (hacer, yo) .... mi cama por las mañanas.

g. Me pongo nervioso cuando (esperar, yo) .... el autobús y tarda mucho en llegar.

2 **Place the following words in the proper column.**

de mal humor ○ pena ○ rabia ○ triste ○ lástima ○ igual ○ de los nervios ○ miedo

PONER	DAR

Now write a sentence using the following verbs.

a. Poner ....

b. Dar ....

VERBAL CONSTRUCTIONS WITH INFINITIVE OR PRESENT PARTICIPLE

3 **Rewrite the following sentences using a verb followed by infinitive or present participle as in the example.**

a. Juan ha reprobado el examen de Música de nuevo.

(volver a) ....

b. Ana y Luis eran muy amigos, pero hace un mes se enfadaron y ahora no se hablan.

(dejar de) ....

c. María empezó a estudiar solfeo a los 8 años y ahora con 16 años todavía lo estudia.

(seguir) ....

d. Me he apuntado a clases de guitarra y voy desde hace una semana.

(empezar a) ....

e. Vi al profesor de Música hace cinco minutos.

(acabar de) ....

f. A Carlos le gustaba ver caricaturas de pequeño y ahora también le gusta.

(continuar) ....

190

VERBS THAT EXPRESS CHANGE

4 **Choose the correct option in each sentence.**

a. Como dejó el deporte, **se puso** / **se volvió** / **se quedó** muy gorda.
b. Desde que le robaron **se ha puesto** / **se ha vuelto** / **se ha quedado** más desconfiada.
c. Como ya sabe que aprobó, **se ha puesto** / **se ha vuelto** / **se ha quedado** tranquila.
d. Como la invitaron a un concierto, **se puso** / **se volvió** / **se quedó** muy contenta.
e. Desde que vive sola **se ha puesto** / **se ha vuelto** / **se ha quedado** más independiente.

5 **Describe what a person with each of the following characteristics is like. Then write the opposite adjective.**

a. egoísta ➡ .... ➡ ....
b. sincera ➡ .... ➡ ....
c. vaga ➡ .... ➡ ....
d. tolerante ➡ .... ➡ ....

LAS ARTES

6 **Fill in the blanks with a word from the list below.**

aventuras o paisaje o pintor o retrato o pirámides o novela

 Las (a) .... de Chichen Itzá son de origen maya.

 Estuvimos en Costa Rica y el (b) .... era tan bonito que tomé un montón de fotografías.

Estoy leyendo una (c) .... de (d) .... que trata de tesoros y piratas.

Los cuadros de ese (e) .... me encantaron, sobre todo el (f) .... ce su mujer.

FOREIGN WORDS

7 **Mark the words that have adopted Spanish spelling and pronunciation.**

☐ estrés ☐ pizza ☐ cruasán ☐ cabaré ☐ software
☐ estatus ☐ yogur ☐ pendrive ☐ blus ☐ piercing

CULTURA

8 **Answer the following questions with the information you learned in *Mucho más que música*.**

a. ¿De qué trataban los primeros corridos mexicanos? ¿Qué función tenían?
b. Y ahora, ¿de qué tratan muchos de los corridos modernos?
c. ¿Por qué han recibido multas los Tigres del Norte? ¿Crees que es justo?
d. ¿Qué se celebra cada año en Buenos Aires y qué países participan?
e. Cuenta tres cosas que aprendiste sobre el flamenco.

 Practice what you have learned with additional materials online.

Activity 4

a. se puso; b. se ha vuelto; c. se ha quedado; d. se puso; e. se ha vuelto.

Activity 5

a. Persona que piensa en sí misma y no en los demás; solidaria, generosa.
b. Persona que dice lo que piensa; falsa, hipócrita.
c. Persona perezosa, a la que no le gusta trabajar; trabajadora.
d. Persona que respeta las ideas de los demás; intolerante.

Activity 6

a. pirámides; b. paisaje; c. novela; d. aventuras; e. pintor; f. retrato.

Activity 7

estrés, estatus, yogur, cruasán, cabaré, blus.

Activity 8

a. Los primeros corridos mexicanos trataban de la Revolución mexicana. Su función era diseminar las noticias en todo el territorio; b. Muchos corridos modernos tratan del narcotráfico; c. Los Tigres del Norte han recibido multas por cantar narcocorridos en sus conciertos; d. Se celebra un festival internacional de tango. Participan países del todo el mundo pero especialmente de Colombia, Estados Unidos, Japón, Brasil, Francia y Argentina.

OBJECTIVES FOR EN RESUMEN: VOCABULARIO

• Review unit vocabulary and expressions
• Practice communicative skills

STANDARDS

1.2 Understand the language
1.3 Present information
4.1 Evaluate similarities and differences in language

INSTRUCTIONAL STRATEGIES

• Encourage students to use index cards used as flashcards with the Spanish term on one side and the English term on the other, or a picture or drawing.
• Students work in pairs or groups, using vocabulary flashcards as they would the cards of a board game to help each other practice unit vocabulary.
• Encourage students to write labels or captions for the photos on this page. Remind them to use the vocabulary and expressions they have learned in this unit.

EN RESUMEN: Vocabulario

Verbos

adorar *to adore*
apetecer *to feel like*
atreverse *to dare*
colarse (o>ue) *to cut in, to sneak in*
colgar (o>ue) *to hang, to post online*
dar igual *to care less*

dar lástima / pena *to feel pity*

dar lo mismo *to be ambivalent*
dar rabia *to infuriate*

dar vergüenza *to feel embarrassed*

diseñar *to design*

ensayar *to rehearse*
hacer cola *to stand in line*
indignar *to anger*
molestar *to bother*
odiar *to hate*

ponerse *to become*
relajarse *to relax*
sentirse (e>ie) *to feel*

Descripciones

agotado/a *sold out, exhausted*
atento/a *attentive*
egoísta *selfish*
falso/a *fake*
gran *great*
histórico/a *historic*
leal *loyal*
preocupado/a *worried*
seguro/a *assured*
sociable *sociable*
tierno/a *tender*
tolerante *tolerant*
tranquilo/a *calm*

Las artes

el acueducto *aqueduct*
las aventuras *adventures*
el bailarín / la bailarina *ballet dancer*
el compositor *composer*
el cuadro *painting*
la escultura *sculpture*

la estatua *statue*

el género *genre, style*
la galería de arte *art gallery*
el guitarrista *guitarist*
la melodía *melody*
el músico *musician*
el novelista *novelist*
la obra *work*
la orquesta *orchestra*
la pintura *painting*
el poema *poem*
el poeta *poet*
el retrato *portrait*
el violinista *violinist*

Los instrumentos musicales

el arpa *harp*
la flauta *flute*
la guitarra *guitar*
los platillos *cymbals*
el saxofón *saxophone*
el tambor *drum*
el violín *violin*

192

EN RESUMEN: Gramática

EXPRESSING FEELINGS AND EMOTIONS
(See page 174)

■ To express feelings and emotions use:

• **estar** + adjective + **con** + noun	• **No soportar** *(can't stand)*	
• **estar** + adjective + **de (que)**	• **No aguantar** *(can't take)*	+ noun
	• **Odiar** *(to hate)*	+ infinitive
	• **Adorar** *(to love)*	+ **que** + subjunctive

• **ponerse / sentirse / estar** + adjective + **cuando / si** + present tense

• **me / te / le / nos**... + **da rabia / pone alegre / molesta** + **que** + subjunctive

• **me / te / le / nos**... + **da rabia / pone alegre / molesta** + infinitive

*Mi hermana **está muy contenta con** su profesora de música.*
*Yo **me pongo furioso cuando** dejo un libro y no me lo devuelven.*
***Odio que** me digan lo que tengo que hacer.*
*A mí **me da vergüenza** hablar en público.*

VERBS FOLLOWED BY INFINITIVE OR PRESENT PARTICIPLE
(See page 183)

■ Some of these constructions are made up of a conjugated verb followed by a preposition and an infinitive. Others are followed by the present participle.

■ Use **empezar / ponerse a** + infinitive to express the start point of an activity.
***Empecé a leer** una novela muy interesante.*
*En cuanto llegué a casa **me puse a estudiar** para el examen del día siguiente.*

■ Use **volver a** + infinitive to express the repetition of an activity.
*El año pasado me apunté a clases de teatro y este año me **volveré a apuntar** de nuevo.*

■ Use **seguir / continuar** + present participle to express that an activity is ongoing.
*Nos conocimos en la guardería y hoy todavía **seguimos siendo** amigos.*
*Este verano **continuaré yendo** a clases de inglés, no quiero olvidar lo que he aprendido.*

■ Use **acabar de** + infinitive to express that an activity has just finished.
*Si quieres pastel, espera a que se enfríe un poco, que **acabo de sacarlo** del horno.*

■ Use **dejar de** + infinitive to express the interruption of an activity.
***He dejado de ir** a clases de guitarra porque este año no tengo tanto tiempo.*

VERBS THAT EXPRESS CHANGE
(See page 184)

■ To express spontaneous or temporary changes in a person we use **ponerse** + adjective; **quedarse** shows the result, the final situation.
***Se pone muy nervioso** al hablar en público.*
***Se puso rojo** cuando le preguntaron.*
***Se quedó muy sorprendido** por la noticia.*

■ To express permanent changes use **volverse** (non voluntary) or **hacerse** (voluntary or gradual change).
***Se ha vuelto** un antipático.*
*Antes era abogado y ahora **se ha hecho** juez.*
*Con esa situación **se hizo** fuerte.*

193

OBJECTIVES FOR EN RESUMEN: GRAMÁTICA

• Review unit grammar
• Practice communication skills

STANDARDS

1.2   Understand the language
1.3   Present information

INSTRUCTIONAL STRATEGIES

• Model how to review grammar.
• Have the students review the Learning Outcomes in the unit opener to assess whether they feel they have mastered the main ideas and skills.
• Ask them if they can remember additional examples for each grammar topic.
• Model how to find and go back to the appropriate page in the unit to review any grammar topic they may need help with.
• Invite students to review the grammar activities they completed in this unit.
• Ask them what grammar activities they found easy and which they found challenging. Encourage them to rework any activities they found particularly challenging.

AHORA COMPRUEBA

OBJECTIVES FOR AHORA COMPRUEBA

- Review and recycle grammar, vocabulary and culture from the last two units
- Complete self-assessment

CORE RESOURCES

- Audio Program: Tracks 52 and 53
- Extension Activities: EA 6.6, 6.7, 6.8

STANDARDS

1.2 Understand the language
1.3 Present information
2.1 Practices and perspectives
4.1 Compare languages and cultures

INSTRUCTIONAL STRATEGIES

Activity 1

- To introduce the theme for the section, ask students to think about the title **Dame vida** and say what they think it means. Go online and search on YouTube for *Dame vida Huecco* so students can check to see if they were on track with their predictions.
- Ask students to look at the images and discuss with a partner what they have in common.

Cultural Note

Huecco es un joven cantante español. Su música es una fusión de estilos muy diversos: rock, hip-hop, rumba y ritmos latinos. Ha saltado a la fama gracias a poner letra y voz a varios proyectos solidarios en los que él mismo ha colaborado. Aunque principalmente se le conoce en España e Hispanoamérica, ha publicado sus discos en varios países de Europa. Para más información consultar su página web: *www.huecco.es*

🎧 52 Activity 2

- Present the expression **hacer ilusión** and tell students it has the same structure as **gustar**.
- Have students review the questions first before listening to the audio. Then play the audio for students to write the answers.

See audioscript on page APP3

Activity 3

Ask students to complete the activity individually. After correcting the activity, review the tenses.

ANSWERS

Activity 1

1. El cantante Huecco; **2.** El futbolista del F.C. Barcelona, David Villa; **3.** El jugador de baloncesto de Los Ángeles Lakers (NBA), Pau Gasol; **4.** Unos niños de un poblado pobre del Sahara; **5.** Un balón que se carga de energía y puede dar luz; **6.** El corredor de motociclismo G.P., Jorge Lorenzo.

AHORA COMPRUEBA

1 👥 **Look at the images of the following people. What do you think they have in common? Discuss your ideas with a partner.**

DAME VIDA

2 🎧 52 **In addition to a song title, *Dame vida* is a foundation dedicated to helping others. Listen to the conversation between Carlos and Abel, and answer the questions.**

a. ¿Por qué no le gustan los conciertos a Carlos?
b. ¿Qué le molesta a Abel de los conciertos?
c. ¿Por qué le hace ilusión ir al concierto de Raquel?
d. ¿Para qué es el concierto?
e. ¿Cómo funciona el balón?
f. ¿Dónde se puede comprar?
g. ¿Quién lo inventó?
h. ¿Por qué Abel cree que es tan bueno el proyecto del balón?
i. ¿Qué desea Carlos en relación al proyecto y al cantante?
j. ¿Al final irá Carlos al concierto? ¿Por qué?

3 **Fill in the blanks with the correct form of the verb in parenthesis.**

a. *Dame vida* es una fundación que desea (recaudar) .... fondos para (ayudar) .... a los necesitados.
b. Jessica Mathews y Julia Silverman son las creadoras del *soccket*, un balón con un acumulador de energía dentro que (recargarse) .... con las patadas que se le dan.
c. Cuando la pelota (cargarse) .... de energía, esta se convertirá en horas de luz para las familias pobres.
d. *Dame vida* quiere que cada hogar sin electricidad (tener) .... un balón con luz.
e. Huecco contactó con varios de los mejores deportistas del mundo para que (colaborar, ellos) .... en la grabación del videoclip de la canción.
f. Vicente del Bosque, seleccionador español de fútbol, ha declarado que le encanta (poder) .... colaborar en el video y que cuando el cantante lo (llamar) .... para (participar) .... no lo dudó un momento.
g. Huecco declaró que quiere (dar) .... las gracias de corazón a todos los que participaron en el videoclip.
h. *Dame vida* quiere que la música (servir) .... para que los más jóvenes (practicar) .... deporte.
i. La fundación también espera que a través de la práctica del deporte (generar) .... energía eléctrica limpia.
j. Huecco declaró que el deporte y la música son las energías más limpias y que este proyecto servirá para (llenar) .... de luz limpia el mundo.

Activity 2

a. Porque el público canta y no puede escuchar la música; **b.** Que la gente le pise y le empuje; **c.** Porque lo organiza una ONG; **d.** Para recaudar fondos para fabricar una pelota que se carga de energía; **e.** El balón funciona con el movimiento, se va cargando de energía y después esta se aprovecha en forma de luz eléctrica; **f.** El balón todavía no se puede comprar, antes necesitan recaudar dinero para fabricarlo; **g.** Dos estudiantes americanas; **h.** Porque servirá para dar electricidad a la gente pobre y es bueno para el medioambiente; **i.** Carlos desea que el proyecto tenga éxito y que se puedan fabricar muchos balones; **j.** Sí, porque quiere colaborar en esta causa solidaria.

Activity 3

a. recaudar, ayudar; **b.** se recarga; **c.** se carga; **d.** tenga; **e.** colaboren; **f.** poder, llamó, participar; **g.** dar; **h.** sirva, practiquen; **i.** se genere; **j.** llenar.

4 This foundation also participates in two other projects. Read the excerpts that your teacher is going to distribute and match the description to the appropriate project image below. Then create a title for each project.

Título: _____

Título: _____

5 🎧 53 You are going to listen a radio program in which the presenter talks about the three projects that Huecco is involved with. Match the experiences he recounts to the appropriate person below.

Jessica Matthews
Proyecto:

Aganju
Proyecto:

Pau Gasol
Proyecto:

Yveline
Proyecto:

Juan
Proyecto:

6 Fill in the blanks with the correct form of the verbs below and learn more about volunteer experiences.

acabar de ○ ponerse ○ seguir ○ llevar ○ ponerse a ○ dejar de ○ quedarse ○ volver a ○ empezar a

Todo empezó cuando recibí un correo electrónico en el que buscaban colaboradores para construir escuelas para niños pobres en Guatemala. Al llegar allí (a) _____ muy impresionada de ver cómo aquella gente vivía con tan poco. Al principio fue muy duro, yo no estaba acostumbrada a ver tanta pobreza y cuando (b) _____ trabajar fue todavía peor, (c) _____ muy nerviosa porque había muchas cosas que no sabía hacer y me sentí inútil. (d) _____ llegar y ya quería hacer las maletas y regresar a España... Pero después, un compañero me tranquilizó diciéndome que era normal sentirse así al principio y que ellos también habían tenido que aprender, pero que mi trabajo era importante y que tenía que seguir adelante. Lo pensé mejor y (e) _____ trabajar sin preocuparme de si lo hacía bien o mal.
Desde que trabajé codo con codo con ellos me he vuelto más responsable y menos egoísta y (f) _____ preocuparme por cosas que en realidad no son importantes. Ya (g) _____ tres años colaborando con la organización y estoy deseando que llegue el verano para (h) _____ ir a Guatemala y (i) _____ ayudando a los niños de allí.

7 Have you ever done a good deed? Think about that experience and write what it was like and how you felt.

INSTRUCTIONAL STRATEGIES

Activity 4

- Ask students to look at the images and tell them to guess what other two social projects this foundation also participates in.
- Distribute copies of EA 6.6, **Proyectos solidarios**. In pairs, ask students to classify the paragraph according to the project they belong and write a title for each project.
- Explain the following vocabulary words: **granja**, **orfanato**, **potable**, **violencia de género**.

🎧 53 **Activity5**

- Have student guess who these people are.
- Write on the board: **soccket**, **Haití** and **mujeres**, and have students match the images with these words.
- Play the audio and allow students time to complete this activity individually.

See audioscript on page APP3

Activity 6

Ask students to do this activity individually.

Activity 7

Ask students to write about their experiences and provide as many details as possible.

Extension

- Go to YouTube and play **Se acabaron las lágrimas**. Then distribute copies of EA 6.7 and 6.8, **Se acabaron las lágrimas** de **Huecco**. In pairs, students take turns and one of them gives a definition from his/her card and the other student will guess it.
- While they are guessing these words, they write the missing words to complete the song.

ANSWERS

Activity 5

Jessica Mathews: soccket; **Aganju:** Haití; **Pau Gasol:** soccket; **Yveline:** Haití; **Juan:** mujeres.

Activity 6

a. me quedé; b. empecé a; c. me ponía; d. Acababa de; e. me puse a; f. he dejado de; g. llevo; h. volver a; i. seguir.

OBJECTIVES FOR UNIT OPENER

- Introduce unit theme: *¡Que no te engañen!* about advertising and Internet
- Introduce culture for the unit: Learn about the role of advertisements and the Internet in Hispanic countries, and compare cultural similarities

STANDARDS

1.1   Engage in conversation
2.2   Products and culture

INSTRUCTIONAL STRATEGIES

- Before students open their books, write the unit title on the board: *¡Que no te engañen!* Give examples of what **engañar** means. For example, **Compras un carro usado y dentro de unos días ya no funciona. Te engañaron**, **Vas a la tienda y le das al cajero veinte dólares en efectivo y te da el cambio para diez dólares. Te engañaron**. Elicit other ideas from the students and then ask what they think the title means (don't let them fool / trick you) and what content they think they'll encounter in the unit.
- Have students open their books, look at the image, and read the caption. Ask: **¿Dónde están las personas? ¿Qué hacen? ¿Por qué crees que hay tantos jóvenes?**
- Have students work individually to write answers to the questions on the page.
- Monitor their progress and assist as needed.
- Put students into pairs or small groups to share and discuss their answers.
- Call on volunteers to report back on their responses and discussions.
- Help students formulate their ideas using **Están en una tienda de ropa / en unos grandes almacenes**, **Están comprando ropa**, **Hay jóvenes porque hay rebajas y la ropa cuesta menos**, **Creo que las rebajas son un buen momento para comprar las cosas que necesitas / gustan a buen precio**, etc.

UNIDAD 7

¡QUE NO TE ENGAÑEN!

De rebajas.

40% DESCUENTO

- ¿Qué están haciendo las personas de la imagen?
- ¿Qué opinas sobre las rebajas?
- ¿Qué piensas de los eventos especiales como el Cyber Monday o las rebajas de enero?
- ¿Sueles aprovechar las rebajas para comprar?

196

ADDITIONAL UNIT RESOURCES

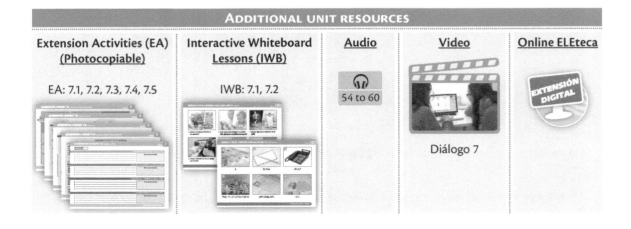

Extension Activities (EA) (Photocopiable)	Interactive Whiteboard Lessons (IWB)	Audio	Video	Online ELEteca
EA: 7.1, 7.2, 7.3, 7.4, 7.5	IWB: 7.1, 7.2	54 to 60	Diálogo 7	EXTENSIÓN DIGITAL

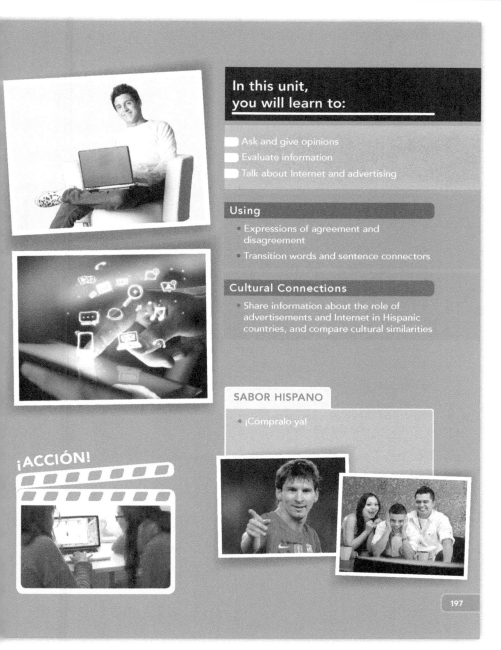

**In this unit,
you will learn to:**

- Ask and give opinions
- Evaluate information
- Talk about Internet and advertising

Using

- Expressions of agreement and disagreement
- Transition words and sentence connectors

Cultural Connections

- Share information about the role of advertisements and Internet in Hispanic countries, and compare cultural similarities

SABOR HISPANO

- ¡Cómpralo ya!

¡ACCIÓN!

197

LEARNING OUTCOMES

- Ask and give opinions
- Evaluate information
- Talk about Internet and advertising

INSTRUCTIONAL STRATEGIES

- Use the unit opener to preview vocabulary and cultural topics for this unit.
- Have students look at the images on this page and try to relate them to the objectives listed.
- Exploit the first main photo a bit further by asking questions, such as: *¿Cuánto tiempo pasan navegando por Internet cada día? ¿Para qué utilizan el Internet? ¿Te crees todo lo que lees en Internet? ¿Qué sitios son los más fiables? ¿Y los menos?*
- Exploit the second photo a bit further by asking questions, such as: *¿Qué iconos ven? ¿Qué significan?*
- Invite students to read the topic for **Sabor hispano** and preview that section in the unit. Ask questions, such as: *¿Reconocen al futbolista? ¿Cómo se llama?* (*Lionel Messi*) *¿En qué equipo juega?* (*Barcelona o el Barça*).
- Ask students to anticipate what they think the episode for **¡Acción!** will be about.

THREE MODES OF COMMUNICATION: UNIT 7			
	INTERPERSONAL	**INTERPRETIVE**	**PRESENTATIONAL**
HABLAMOS DE...	1, 5	2, 3, 4, 5	
COMUNICA	2, 4, 6, 7	1, 3, 5	6, 7
¡ACCIÓN!	1, 4	2, 3, 4	
PALABRA POR PALABRA	3, 4, 6, 9	1, 2, 4, 5, 7	3, 8
GRAMÁTICA	4	1, 3	2, 4
DESTREZAS		1, 2, 3, 4	
CULTURA		SABOR HISPANO	
RELATO	2, 7	3, 4	1, 5, 6

OBJECTIVES FOR HABLAMOS DE...

- Understand language in context
- Preview vocabulary: Internet and advertising
- Preview grammatical structures: Transition words and phrases and other connectors
- Read and listen to a conversation between four friends about an anticonsumerist advertising campaign

CORE RESOURCES

- Audio Program: Track 54

STANDARDS

1.1 Engage in conversation
2.2 Products and culture
3.2 Acquire information

INSTRUCTIONAL STRATEGIES

Activity 1

- Write the word **publicidad** on the board. Elicit related words from students, such as: **cartel, marca, anuncio, eslogan, consumidores, vender, convencer**...
- To generate interest, ask questions such as: **¿Les gusta la publicidad? ¿Creen que es necesaria? ¿Cuál es su objetivo? ¿Es actual? ¿Es honesta?**
- Have students open their books and look at the image at the top of the page. Tell them to focus on the sign and ask: **¿Qué es? ¿Qué representa? ¿Qué significa el texto y la imagen? ¿Les parece raro ver un anuncio así en una tienda o centro comercial? ¿Por qué creen que está? ¿Te parece buena idea tener un día destinado a no comprar?**
- Put students into pairs to ask and answer the questions and discuss their ideas.
- Call on volunteers to report back on their ideas.

Activity 2

- Go over the instructions and review the list of verbs. Ask what kind of verbs they are (like **gustar**) and what that means to the structure (use indirect object pronouns). Model –or elicit– a sample sentence for the class.
- Have students work in pairs to make sentences based on the characters in the photo.
- Monitor their progress and assist as needed. Remind them that they can make negative sentences as well.
- Call on volunteers to share their sentences with a class. Encourage students to explain their ideas.

Cultural Note

Share the following information about Adbusters with students. Then ask if they are familiar with the magazine.

Adbusters es una organización anticonsumista que critica y ataca a los medios de comunicación y la filosofía consumista que estos promocionan. Su objetivo es utilizar la publicidad como un medio de comunicación para hacer burla de los productos y compensar así la manipulación que tiene la publicidad sobre la sociedad. La organización aparece en 1989 y en 1994 publican la revista del mismo nombre.

HABLAMOS DE... Las opiniones

Andrés Nélida Germán Silvia

1 Look at the image above and discuss the following with a partner.

a. ¿Qué crees que están mirando?
b. ¿Qué sensación crees que les provoca ver el cartel de la campaña?
c. ¿Puedes estar un día sin comprar?

2 Combine elements from the columns to form sentences about how Andrés and his friends feel about this upcoming ad campaign.

A mí		encantan	la imagen.
A Nélida y a mí		pone nerviosas	que la gente deje de comprar.
A Germán	le	da miedo	que exista tanta publicidad.
A los cuatro	les	indigna	las novedades.
A Nélida	(no) me	impresiona	ver cosas diferentes.
A Nélida y a Silvia	nos	preocupa	que la gente gaste demasiado.
A Silvia		gusta	que no se entienda el mensaje.

198

3 🎧 54 **Read the conversation among the four friends and fill in the blanks with words from the choices below. Then listen and check your answers.**

> manipulación o feminidad o iconos o anticonsumista o virilidad o
> ventanas emergentes o machista

Andrés: ¿Qué les parece el cartel de la campaña? ¡Es una obra de arte!

Nélida: Yo creo que es increíble que esté en un centro comercial, ¿no les parece?

Germán: Pues yo no pienso que sea para tanto. Solo es más publicidad, ¿no?

Silvia: Es terrible que intenten confundirnos. ¿El cartel significa que no compremos? ¡Puf!... No lo entiendo y no me gusta. Por cierto, ¡qué es Adbusters?

A.: ¡¿No los conoces!? Es una organización (a) .... que ataca a los medios de comunicación. Su objetivo es utilizar la publicidad para criticar la (b) .... que esta hace sobre la sociedad. También tienen una revista.

S.: Bueno, en mi opinión, la publicidad trata de informar a un público objetivo sobre lo que hay.

N.: Sí, estoy de acuerdo con que trata de informar, pero para cambiar nuestras opiniones y deseos, ¡claro!

A.: Por supuesto, la publicidad lleva muchos años vendiéndonos el mensaje de la juventud, de la salud, de la (c) ...., de la (d) .... La imagen siempre es la misma: jóvenes, ricos y guapos.

G.: Lo que quiere, desde luego, es provocar. Y tienes razón, a veces incorrectamente, y es racista, sexista, e incluso (e) ....

N.: ¡Ya lo creo! ¿Y qué pasa con la protección de los jóvenes, con el derecho a la intimidad, y con el respeto?

S.: ¡Claro, claro! ¿Y con la libertad de expresión? Pero, de acuerdo, está claro que debe haber límites. En cualquier caso, creo que la gente no le hace tanto caso a la publicidad, hay demasiada: en la calle, en la tele, en los periódicos, en las revistas, en Internet...

A.: ¡Uf! Sí, es ridículo que las redes sociales estén tan llenas de anuncios, no es lo que vas a ver allí. Me preocupa que utilicen nuestra información personal para vender. Y en muchas páginas te atacan las (f) .... que se te abren todo el tiempo.

S.: Pues, a mi modo de ver, no pienso que toda la publicidad sea mala y, como dijiste antes, es arte, creación... Son (g) .... de nuestra cultura, por ejemplo, mira algunas obras de Andy Warhol.

G.: En esto todos estamos de acuerdo, siempre hay cosas bien hechas.

4 **Search in the text for a synonym of the following words.**

a. *Pop-up.* ....
b. Masculinidad, valor, fortaleza. ....
c. Imagen, modelo. ....
d. Femineidad, delicadeza, ternura. ....
e. Cambio que se hace para conseguir algo. ....
f. Prepotencia de hombres sobre mujeres. ....
g. En contra de la compra innecesaria. ....

5 👥 **Answer the following questions. Then compare answers with a partner. Do you agree?**

a. ¿Qué es Adbusters? ....
b. ¿Qué piensa Silvia de la publicidad? ....
c. ¿Están de acuerdo sus amigos con ella? ....

199

INSTRUCTIONAL STRATEGIES

🎧 **54 Activity 3**

- Tell the students that they are going to listen to a conversation between the four friends in the photo on the previous page. Go over the instructions.
- Give students a moment to read the words in the box before playing the audio. Elicit students' initial ideas about the meanings of the words. Explain that the conversation will provide context to help them determine the meanings.
- Have students read the conversation and try to complete it with the words from the box. Monitor their progress and assist as needed.
- Play the audio and go over the answers as a class.

Activity 4

- Go over the instructions. Have students work individually to find the synonymns in the conversation.
- Then go over the answers as a class.

Activity 5

- Go over the instructions. Have students answer the questions individually.
- Monitor their progress and assist as needed.
- Put students into pairs to compare answers. Encourage them to explain their answers to each other.
- Call on volunteers to share their answers with a class.
- Follow up by asking students for their own opinions on the topic. For example: **¿Qué piensas de la publicidad? ¿Es algo necesario? ¿Por qué? ¿En qué medios de comunicación te molesta más la publicidad?**

ANSWERS

Activity 3

a. anticonsumista; **b.** manipulación; **c.** virilidad; **d.** feminidad; **e.** machista; **f.** ventanas emergentes; **g.** iconos.

Activity 4

a. ventanas emergentes; **b.** virilidad; **c.** icono; **d.** feminidad; **e.** manipulación; **f.** machista; **g.** anticonsumista.

Activity 5

Answers will vary. Possible answers may include the following:
a. Una organización anticonsumista que ataca a los medios de comunicación. Su objetivo es utilizar la publicidad para criticar la manipulación que esta ejerce sobre la sociedad;
b. Piensa que informa pero que debe haber límites, también cree que hay publicidad que se ha convertido en arte y que es un icono de nuestra cultura; **c.** En parte sí y en parte no. Están de acuerdo en que la publicidad bien hecha es arte, pero Andrés y Nélida, por ejemplo, no piensan que solo trate de informar, sino que creen que esta intenta manipularnos.

OBJECTIVES FOR COMUNICA

- Present communicative functions of the unit: Expressing opinion
- Practice using different phrases to ask about and share opinions

CORE RESOURCES

- Interactive Online Materials – ELEteca

STANDARDS

3.1 Knowledge of other disciplines

4.1 Compare languages

INSTRUCTIONAL STRATEGIES FOR EXPRESSING OPINION

- Before opening their books, ask students for examples of ways to express opinions (**Creo que**, **Para mí**, etc.). Ask them how to ask for someone's opinion. Write their ideas on the board.
- Have students open their books and read the examples. Ask students which expressions use the indicative and which use the subjunctive. Make sure students understand that **No creo que**, **No pienso que**, **No me parece que** all take subjunctive when used with **no**.
- Model a few questions and answers with volunteers so students can see the language in use. You might ask students for their opinions about celebrities, TV shows, or sports.

Activity 1

- Have students read the text on their own or read it together as a class.
- Put students into pairs to determine the main idea of the text and share their opinions about it. To focus their discussion, consider asking them to come up with an example that demonstrates the use of each of the three main strategies.
- Go over the main idea as a class. Call on volunteers to share the examples of the different strategies they have identified.

Activity 2

- Project the images of the ads and ask students to give their opinion about them. Make sure students understand what is being promoted.
- Put students into pairs to express their opinions about the advertising campaigns.
- Remind them to use the phrases for asking and expressing opinions at the top of the page. Encourage them to give reasons for their opinions.
- Call on volunteers to share their answers with the class.

Extension Activity

Pass out different advertisements, or have students find ads of their own. Have students write about the ways in which their ads do or don't adhere to the blueprint described in the text. Have them present their analyses to the class or share them in small groups.

COMUNICA

EXPRESSING OPINION

- Para **pedir opinión** usamos:

  ¿Qué piensas / crees / opinas de / sobre las compras por Internet?

  ¿(A ti) qué te parece el blog del que nos habló Carlos?

  En tu opinión / Desde tu punto de vista / Según tú, ¿cuál es el anuncio más inteligente?

- Para **dar opinión** usamos:

  En mi opinión / Desde mi punto de vista el blog (no) es muy interesante.

  Creo / Pienso / Opino / Me parece que el logo de una marca (no) es muy importante.

  No creo / pienso / me parece que el logo sea tan importante como la calidad de sus productos.

1 Read the following text describing elements of successful advertising campaigns. Then, with a partner, pick out the main ideas and discuss your opinions.

La publicidad, ¿cómo actúa sobre el público?

El mensaje publicitario obedece a un esquema de interpretación del comportamiento del público al que se dirige:

- el anuncio debe llamar la atención, despertar el interés, provocar el deseo y mover a la acción (...);
- se busca llevar una señal al inconsciente del individuo;
- el producto o la marca se identifica con un grupo social o una serie de valores admitidos o admirados por una parte de la sociedad. Al comprarlo, se dispone de un símbolo de promoción, social.

http://recursos.cnice.mec.es/media/publicidad/bloque7/pag8.htm

2 The three images below are part of different advertising campaigns. With a partner, exchange opinions about the following:

a. Desde tu punto de vista, ¿cuál es la campaña más original? ¿Y la menos?

b. ¿Estás de acuerdo con tu compañero/a?

c. ¿Crees que los anuncios cumplen *(meet)* con los requisitos que se mencionan en el texto que acabas de leer?

Modelo: E1: Creo que el mejor anuncio es...

E2: No creo que sea el mejor porque...

TO EXPRESS AGREEMENT AND DISAGREEMENT WITH AN OPINION

■ Para **expresar acuerdo o desacuerdo** con una opinión usamos:

(No) estoy	a favor de	todo **tipo** de anuncios. (noun)
	estoy en contra de	**ser manipulado** por la publicidad. (same subject)
	(del todo) de acuerdo con	**que** nos **hagan** encuestas. (different subjects)

3 👥 With a partner, read the expressions and list them in the appropriate columns below.

a. Sí, claro.
b. Yo pienso lo mismo que tú.
c. ¡Qué va!
d. ¡Desde luego!
e. Por supuesto.
f. ¡(Pero) qué dices!

g. A mi modo de ver, ese no es el problema / el tema...
h. Bueno, lo que pasa es que...
i. ¡A poco!
j. Yo no diría eso...
k. ¡No, no!

l. ¡No, de ninguna manera!
m. ¡Y que lo digas!
n. Tienes razón, pero...
ñ. ¡Anda ya!
o. Sí, es una idea interesante, pero por otra parte...

Expresar acuerdo	Expresar desacuerdo	Suavizar (soften) el desacuerdo

4 👥 Discuss the following topics with a partner using the expressions above. Do you agree or disagree?

a. Facebook a cambio (in exchange for) de nuestra privacidad.
b. Las descargas (downloads) gratuitas y la piratería contra los derechos de autor (copyright).
c. El poder adictivo de las computadoras, Internet o los videojuegos.
d. El peligro de chatear con extraños o colgar nuestras fotos en Internet.
e. Las amistades virtuales y las amistades reales.
f. Las identidades falsas en Facebook y las redes sociales.
g. Las modas y las marcas, ¿estilo o falta de personalidad?

201

UNIDAD 7

OBJECTIVES FOR COMUNICA

- Present communicative functions of the unit: Expressing agreement and disagreement with an opinion
- Practice using different expressions for agreeing and disagreeing

CORE RESOURCES

- Extension Activity: EA 7.1

STANDARDS

1.1 Engage in conversation
4.1 Compare languages

INSTRUCTIONAL STRATEGIES FOR EXPRESSING AGREEMENT AND DISAGREEMENT WITH AN OPINION

- To introduce the idea of agreement and disagreement, elicit a student's opinion about something, for example, sushi or some other food. Elicit more students' opinions until one person expresses the same opinion and one expresses a different opinion. After each new opinion, ask: **¿Tienen la misma opinion? (Sí/No). Entonces, (no) están de acuerdo**. Write **acuerdo** and **desacuerdo** on the board. Go through the examples in the chart.
- Write the following expressions on the board: **Estoy totalmente de acuerdo contigo, con él/ella, No estoy del todo de acuerdo, No estoy nada de acuerdo.** Ask students what they think the purpose of the underlined expressions is (emphasis).
- Distribute copies of EA 7.1, **Expresar acuerdo y desacuerdo** to student pairs and have students sort the expressions under the appropriate categories. Review by having students tape the words to the board. Then ask, **¿Están de acuerdo?** as a way to prompt students to use one of the expressions on the board.

Activity 3

- Put students into pairs to sort the expressions into the appropriate categories.
- Monitor their progress and assist as needed. Go over the answers as a class.

Activity 4

- Put students into pairs to discuss the topics and take turns sharing opinions. To ensure they use a variety of expressions, have them use the cards from EA 7.1, and hold them up to respond to their partner.
- Since there is a long list of topics, you may want to have students switch partners after each topic or after every two topics. This will help add some variety and keep them focused on each new topic.

ANSWERS

Activity 3

Expresar acuerdo: a, b, d, e, m; Expresar desacuerdo: c, f, i, k, l, ñ; Suavizar el desacuerdo: g, h, j, n, o.

- Present communicative functions of the unit:
  Making value judgements
- Practice using different expressions to make value judgements

CORE RESOURCES

- Audio Program: Track 55
- Extension Activity: EA 7.2
- Interactive Whiteboard Lesson: IWB 7.1

STANDARDS

1.1 Engage in conversation
1.2 Understand the language
4.1 Compare languages

INSTRUCTIONAL STRATEGIES
FOR MAKING VALUE JUDGEMENTS

- Explain that making value judgements is another way of expressing opinions.
- Review the chart in the book and read aloud different options for explaining how you feel about the topics presented in the sample sentences. Call on students to provide other combinations. Then write these formulas on the board:

Está claro / Es obvio / Es verdad + indicativo

Ser / parecer + adjetivo + que + subjuntivo

No está claro / No es obvio / No es verdad + subjuntivo

- Put students into pairs to discuss their opinions about the topics presented. Start by calling on students individually and then have them work in pairs. Circulate around the class and take note of common errors to address later as a class.

🎧 55 Activity 5

- Have students work individually first to complete the conversations.
- Monitor their progress and assist as needed. Refer them back to the chart for help.
- Play the audio, and have students listen and check their answers.
- Put students into pairs to practice the conversations. Then have them switch roles and practice the conversations again.

Extension Activity

Have students do the information gap activity EA 7.2, **Opinar y valorar**. Put students into pairs, giving one the card for **Estudiante A** and the other the card for **Estudiante B**. Have them work individually first to correctly conjugate the verbs in their version of the text. Then have them practice the conversation together, checking each other's answers.

ANSWERS

Activity 5

a) **a.** diga; **b.** haces; **c.** tengas; **b) a.** se muestre; **b.** reduzcan; **c.** haga.

EA 7.2

Estudiante A: reúna, has estado pensando, podrías, sería, perdería, conozcas.
Estudiante B: sea, pruebes, toques, aparezcan, cambie, preocupe, pruebe.

COMUNICA

MAKING VALUE JUDGEMENTS

- Para **pedir valoración** usamos:
  ¿**Te parece bien** poder usar buscadores para hacer trabajos de clase?
  ¿**Te parece mal** el sueldo de un publicista?
  ¿**Te parece una tontería** (foolish) **que** los publicistas ganen mucho dinero?
- Para **valorar** usamos:

Me parece **Es**	(parecer) bien / mal (ser) bueno / malo triste / increíble / cómico / justo ridículo / exagerado / preocupante... una tontería / una vergüenza	**que** haya tanta publicidad en Internet.
Está claro **Es obvio / verdad**	**que** la publicidad es creación.	
¡Qué bien / interesante	este anuncio! poder compartir tanta información a través de Facebook! que nuestra escuela tenga una página web!	

- To form the **present subjunctive**: yo (present) ➞ drop o ➞ add **opposite endings**:
  -ar ➞ -e, -es, -e, -emos, -éis, -en   -er/-ir ➞ -a, -as, -a, -amos, -áis, -an.

5 🎧 55 **Complete the conversations with the correct form of the verbs in parenthesis. Use the table above for reference. Then listen and check your answers.**

a. » Me encanta el anuncio del perfume FreeMan.
» Es increíble que tú (a) .... (decir) eso. Hace unos días le decías a Elena que odiabas las marcas y mencionaste precisamente FreeMan.
» Bueno, lo que pasa es que Elena me gusta un montón...
» No, si está claro que tú por Elena (b) .... (hacer) lo que sea, pero me parece un poco triste que (c) .... (tener) que mentir para impresionarla.

b. » Me parece fatal que en la publicidad (a) .... (mostrarse) una imagen tan poco real de los jóvenes: todos frívolos y de fiesta continua.
» Tienes razón, y... ¡¿qué me dices de las muchachas? !Es ridículo que nos (b) .... (reducir) a una cara o a un cuerpo. Y casi siempre anoréxico. ¡Qué triste!
» ¡Ya lo creo! ¿A quién le gusta eso?
» Pues no sé, la verdad, pero es preocupante que nadie (c) .... (hacer) nada por cambiarlo, es una mala influencia para los más jóvenes.

6 Discuss the following questions with a partner. Do you agree?

a. ¿Qué aspectos positivos y negativos piensas que tiene la publicidad?

b. ¿Te parece que la imagen que da de los jóvenes es real?

c. Según tu opinión, ¿cuándo es necesaria la publicidad?

d. ¿Cuál es el último ejemplo de buena publicidad que recuerdas? ¿Y de mala publicidad? ¿Por qué crees que son buenos o malos ejemplos?

e. ¿Qué opinas de la publicidad y el consumismo?

7 Take turns asking and describing to your partner what you think about the following topics. Use the expressions you learned in this section.

a. ¿Comer productos frescos o congelados?

b. ¿Las nuevas tecnologías se asocian solo a jóvenes o también a mayores?

c. En el tiempo libre, ¿hacer deporte o relajarse en el sofá?

d. ¿Tener animales en casa o verlos por la tele?

e. ¿Vivir en una ciudad grande o en un pueblo?

f. ¿Hacer turismo cultural o turismo de sol y playa?

 Practice what you have learned with additional materials online.

203

INSTRUCTIONAL STRATEGIES

Activity 6

- Have students work individually first to jot down notes with their ideas.
- Put students into pairs to share and discuss their answers.
- Monitor their progress and assist as needed. Encourage them to explain their opinions and ask each other questions for more information. Remind them to use the expressions they have learned for opinions, agreement, disagreement, and value judgements.
- Invite volunteers to share interesting aspects of their conversations with the class.

Alternative Activity

Put students into groups of five, and arrange them in a circle. Assign each student a different question from the list and have him or her write a complete response to the question. Then have them pass their questions and responses to the person on their right. Have them write a statement agreeing or disagreeing with the original. Have them continue passing the questions and responses to the write until they have all responded to each question.

Activity 7

- Focus students' attention on the images. To activate schema and remind them of relevant vocabulary, invite them to comment on what they see or notice about each image.
- Go over the instructions. Then put students into pairs to ask and answer the questions posed under the images and discuss their opinions.
- Monitor their conversations and assist as needed. Take note of any common errors you hear in their conversations.
- Review any common errors, eliciting corrections from the class.
- Call on volunteers to share any of their partners' opinions that they found interesting.

Alternative Activity

These images are also available for projection in IWB 7.1, *Valorar*. Before going over the activity in the book, you may want to project the images, masking the questions. Have students analyze the images and try to generate the questions themselves.

OBJECTIVES FOR ¡ACCIÓN!

- Provide students with a structured approach to viewing the video
- Contextualize the content of the unit in a familiar scenario

CORE RESOURCES

- Unit Video 7
- Interactive Online Materials – ELEteca

STANDARDS

1.1 Engage in conversation

1.2 Understand the language

INSTRUCTIONAL STRATEGIES

Previewing: Antes del video

Activity 1

- Go over the instructions. Put students in pairs to ask and answer the questions. You may choose to have them write down their partner's responses to keep them focused on the task.
- Monitor their progress and assist as needed.
- Call on volunteers to report back on their discussions, or have students hand in their written responses.

Activity 2

- Have students work individually to speculate about what they see in the images and will see in the video. Have them write down their answers.
- Monitor their progress and assist as needed.
- Put students into pairs to share and compare their hypotheses.

Viewing: Durante el video

Activity 3

- Before doing this activity, you may want to play the video through once so that students can find out if their responses in Activity 2 were accurate.
- Play the video. Go over the answers to Activity 2 as a class.
- Then focus students' attention on Activity 3. Give them time to read the phrases before you play the video again.
- Play the video again. Go over the answers to Activity 3 as a class.

After viewing: Después del video

Activity 4

- Go over the instructions. Before putting students into pairs, give them some time to answer the questions on their own.
- Put students into pairs to compare answers. Monitor their conversations and assist as needed.
- Call on volunteers to report back on their discussions.

ANSWERS

Activity 3

1. c; 2. f; 3. a; 4. e; 5. b; 6. d.

¡ACCIÓN!

ANTES DEL VIDEO

1 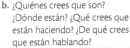 **Take turns with a partner asking and answering the following questions.**

  a. ¿Tienes computadora en casa? ¿Una personal o de la familia? ¿Tienes Internet?

  b. ¿Para qué usas la computadora: para consultas de las asignaturas de clase, para ver películas, para escuchar música…?

  c. ¿Qué crees que se puede comprar por Internet?

  d. ¿Compras por Internet? Si lo haces, ¿qué compras? ¿Conoces a alguien que compre por Internet?

2 **Look at the scenes from the video segment and answer the questions.**

  a. ¿A qué lugar crees que pertenecen estas imágenes? Describe qué ves en ellas.

  b. ¿Quiénes crees que son? ¿Dónde están? ¿Qué crees que están haciendo? ¿De qué crees que están hablando?

DURANTE EL VIDEO

3 **Combine elements from both columns to form logical sentences.**

  1. Me parece que .... •

  2. Yo creo que todas .... •

  3. No me parece que .... •

  4. Estoy pensando que pronto .... •

  5. ¿Creen que .... •

  6. Es increíble que Internet .... •

  • **a.** sea difícil.

  • **b.** podríamos encontrar una cena regalo?

  • **c.** han reunido las marcas que más gustan a unos precios superbajos.

  • **d.** te permita hacer estas cosas.

  • **e.** es el cumpleaños de tu padre.

  • **f.** sabemos qué nos gusta y cuál es nuestra talla.

DESPUÉS DEL VIDEO

4 **Answer the following questions. Then compare your answers with a partner.**

  a. ¿Cómo funcionan las páginas de compra de ropa por Internet?

  b. ¿Qué otras cosas puedes comprar además de ropa?

  c. ¿Qué quiere hacer la madre?

  d. ¿Cuál es tu opinión sobre estas páginas?

 Practice what you have learned with additional materials online.

PALABRA POR PALABRA Internet
UNIDAD **7**

1 Read the following Internet terms and their definitions. Then match the terms to their corresponding image.

a. Usuario: persona que utiliza una computadora o cualquier sistema informático.

b. Banner o banderola: formato publicitario en Internet que consiste en incluir una pieza publicitaria dentro de una página web.

c. Logo: representación de una empresa u organización. Puede tener letras e imagen.

d. Buscador: sitio especializado para facilitar la búsqueda de información entre los millones de páginas web existentes.

e. Portal o web portal: sitio que sirve para ofrecer acceso a una serie de recursos y de servicios relacionados con un mismo tema. Puede incluir: enlaces, buscadores, foros, documentos, aplicaciones, compra electrónica...

f. Botón: permite al usuario comenzar una acción, como buscar, aceptar una tarea, interactuar...

g. Enlace: conexión de una página web con otra mediante una palabra que representa una dirección de Internet. Generalmente está subrayado y es azul. También sirve para la descarga de ficheros, abrir ventanas, etc.

205

OBJECTIVES FOR INTERNET

• Present vocabulary needed to practice communicative and grammatical functions for the unit: Online environments and the Internet

• Understand and use terms related to the Internet

CORE RESOURCES

• Extension Activities: EA 7.3

• Interactive Online Materials – ELEteca

STANDARDS

1.2   Understand the language

1.3   Present information

INSTRUCTIONAL STRATEGIES

Activity 1

• Before students open their books, activate students' schema about online environments and Internet. You may choose to write Internet on the board and invite students to suggest related terms, which they or you can add to the board.

• These might include: ***computadora***, ***portátil***, ***correo electrónico***, ***Google***, ***contraseña***, ***página web***, ***YouTube***, ***Facebook***...

• Explain to students that they are going to learn the expressions in Spanish for common Internet terms. Have students open their books. Go over the instructions. You may choose to read the definitions aloud as a class. Have students work individually to match the definitions with the images.

• Monitor their progress and assist as needed.

• Go over the answers as a class. Call on students to read the definitions aloud.

ANSWERS

Activity 1

1. a; 2. g; 3. c; 4. e; 5. d; 6. f; 7. b.

INSTRUCTIONAL STRATEGIES

Activity 2

- Go over the instructions. Have students work individually to complete the sentences with the words from Activity 1.
- Monitor their progress and assist as needed.
- Go over the answers as a class.

Activity 3

- Before beginning the activity, invite students to give examples of their favorite websites and explain what they like about them in terms of both their content and their design.
- Read through the sections and indicate the parts that need to be filled in (indicated by brackets). Distribute copies of EA 7.3, **Crea tu web** and put students into groups of three to create a web page. Tell them to use the model on the page as a guide but to write their information, once the content has been decided, directly on the sheet. Encourage students to be creative and draw their own logo.
- Monitor their progress and assist as needed. Encourage them to think about what makes their website unique or special. Remind them that each member of the group should speak during the presentation and to decide on their parts.
- Have the groups present their webpages to the class.

Activity 4

- Go over the instructions. Have students work individually to answer the questions.
- Put students into pairs to compare answers.
- Monitor their conversations and assist as needed. Remind them to use the expressions they learned for expressing opinions, agreeing, and disagreeing.
- Call on volunteers to report back on their opinions. Encourage them to give reasons for their answers. Then explain that they will have an opportunity to confirm their answers after reading the article in Activity 5.

ANSWERS

Activity 2

a. usuario; b. buscador; c. enlaces; d. botón; e. logos; f. banners; g. web portal.

Activity 4

Answers will vary. After doing Activity 5, they may reassess their answers as follows:
a. T; b. F (Pasan más tiempo conectados a Internet); c. F (Tuenti); d. T; e. T; f. F.

PALABRA POR PALABRA Internet

2 Complete the following sentences with words from Activity 1.

a. Mi nombre de .... en Facebook no es mi nombre real. Es necesario proteger la intimidad.

b. Cuando hago un trabajo de investigación, voy a un .... para encontrar lo que necesito.

c. Los .... que encuentro en un artículo del periódico en Internet me dan más información relacionada con la noticia.

d. En la web de mi marca favorita de pantalones el .... de compra es siempre una tentación para mí.

e. Me encantan los diseños de los .... de algunas compañías, dan muy buena imagen.

f. La sofisticación de algunos .... me impresiona, pero también me molesta que aparezcan cuando solo quiero escribir un correo electrónico.

g. La .... de mi centro tiene mucha información útil para los alumnos y es muy fácil de usar.

3 In groups of three, create your own web page using the model below. Choose the name of your web and a description of what it can do. Then present your web page to the class.

Crea tu web

[BANNER]

SU WEB [NOMBRE]
Pongan aquí una descripción principal de su web.

[Aquí una frase motivadora]

Aquí su Logo

Bienvenido a su Web [NOMBRE]

:: Inicio
:: Sobre nosotros
:: Contáctenos
:: Sección 1

[Aquí botones para las secciones]

Descargar ▼

[Aquí podrán incorporar texto de bienvenida para sus usuarios. Podrán adjuntar tanto texto como deseen, pero recuerden que no es bueno abusar de contenidos para no agobiar al lector]

Sección Destacada

[imagen]

[Esta sección de inicio puede dedicarse a llamar la atención de algo importante]

4 Read the following statements and decide whether you think they are true (T) or false (F). Then compare your answers with a partner. Do you agree?

	T	F
a. Los jóvenes españoles hablan más con sus amigos a través de Internet que en la realidad.	☐	☐
b. Los adolescentes españoles pasan más tiempo viendo la tele que conectados a Internet.	☐	☐
c. La red social preferida de los adolescentes españoles es Facebook.	☐	☐
d. Muchos adolescentes tienen personas que no conocen dentro de sus redes sociales.	☐	☐
e. La mayoría de españoles tiene su primer celular a los 16 años.	☐	☐
f. Las redes sociales son muy seguras.	☐	☐

5 Fill in the blanks with words from the list below. Then check your answers from Activity 4 based on the information from the reading. Did you guess correctly?

> desconocidos ○ Internet ○ personal ○ fotos ○ virtuales ○ tuitear
> perfil ○ cuenta ○ usarios ○ quedar

Las redes sociales y los jóvenes españoles

Una de las actividades preferidas por los jóvenes españoles es quedar con los amigos. Sin embargo, los encuentros con sus amigos, en los últimos años, son más (a) .... que reales. Es decir, hablan más a través de las redes sociales o servicios de mensajería instantánea como What'sApp o Line, que en persona. Prueba *(Proof)* de esto es que palabras como *chatear* (del inglés *chat*), *wasapear* (de la aplicacción What'sApp) o (b) .... (de Twitter), se  han convertido en palabras cotidianas que demuestran esta realidad.

El 80% de los jóvenes españoles tiene (c) .... en alguna red social. La mayoría (casi el 80%) prefiere Tuenti, la versión española de Facebook, aunque aproximadamente la mitad tiene abierta una (d) .... en dos o tres redes sociales a la vez. Las más frecuentes son Tuenti, Facebook y Twitter.

Según estudios realizados, los adolescentes españoles tienen 177 "amigos" de media, pero curiosamente, el 30% de estos amigos no son conocidos directos, es decir, que son amigos de los amigos o incluso completos (e) ....

Desde las sedes de las principales redes sociales como Facebook o Twitter aconsejan a los jóvenes que solo acepten a aquellos (f) .... cue son realmente amigos, y que no publiquen mucha información (g) .... , ya que esta puede ser manipulada y causarles problemas.

 Los jóvenes españoles utilizan las redes sociales para pasar el tiempo, hablar con sus amigos, compartir (h) .... u organizar "quedadas" (encuentros) de amigos. También las usan para abrir grupos de deporte, donde cuelgan las fotos de los partidos y se anuncian los horarios de las competiciones.

Es la primera generación de españoles que dedica más tiempo a (i) .... que a la televisión. La mayoría se conecta diariamente una media de dos horas y los fines de semana más. También es la primera generación que ya no llama para (j) .... con sus amigos, sino que "wasapea".

6 👥 In small groups, discuss with your classmates the following questions.

a. ¿Qué tienen en común con los jóvenes españoles?
b. ¿En qué aspectos son diferentes?

INSTRUCTIONAL STRATEGIES

Activity 5

- Go over the instructions. Have students work individually to complete the text.
- Monitor their progress and assist as needed.
- Go over the answers as a class. Go back to Activity 4 and reassess those answers. Encourage students to explain their false answers.

Cultural Note

Tuenti is Spanish social networking website with over 5 million users. Although it may sound like the English word *twenty*, Tuenti actually comes from **tu entidad** (your core, essence) which is then shortened to *tuenti*. Like other social networking site, Tuenti users create profiles, upload photos, link videos and connect with others. Unlike most sites such as Facebook, Tuenti does not allow banner advertisements or other forms of obstructive advertising.

Activity 6

- Go over the instructions. Put students in small groups to discuss the questions.
- Monitor their progress and assist as needed. Take notes of any errors that you might hear.
- Call on volunteers to share interesting aspects of their discussions.
- Go over any common errors that you heard, eliciting corrections from the class.

ANSWERS

Activity 5

a. virtuales; **b.** tuitear; **c.** perfil; **d.** cuenta; **e.** desconocidos; **f.** usuarios; **g.** personal; **h.** fotos; **i.** Internet; **j.** quedar.

OBJECTIVES FOR LA PUBLICIDAD EN INTERNET

- Present vocabulary needed to practice communicative and grammatical functions for the unit: Online advertising
- Write about and discuss issues related to online advertising

CORE RESOURCES

- Audio Program: Track 56

STANDARDS

1.2 Understand the language

5.1 Spanish in the community

INSTRUCTIONAL STRATEGIES

 56 Activity 7

- Give students time to read items and multiple-choice options before they listen. Encourage them to underline key words to help focus their listening.
- Play the audio. Have students choose the correct options on their own.
- Put them in pairs to compare answers. Encourage them to explain their answers to each other. You may choose to play the audio again for students to resolve any discrepancies in their responses. Go over the answers as a class.

See audioscript on page APP4

Activity 8

- Go over the instructions. Focus students' attention on the prompts in the online forum.
- Before students write, engage them in a prewriting task. For the first prompt, encourage them to make a list of main ideas from the audio. Offer to play the audio from Activity 7 again. To help them along, you may choose to elicit responses to some comprehension questions about the audio, such as: **¿Por qué es gratis el uso de Google y Yahoo? ¿Hay publicidad en las bitácoras? ¿Cómo reciben tus datos las compañías que generan la publicidad?**
- For the second prompt, suggest that they make a T-chart to list advantages and disadvantages of online advertising. Encourage them to brainstorm different ideas.
- Have students work individually to write their responses to the forum prompts.
- Put students into pairs and have them exchange their papers. Encourage them to respond to each other orally: asking additional questions, expressing new opinions, agreeing, or disagreeing with each other.

Activity 9

- Put students into pairs to discuss the two questions. Tell students to be prepared to report back on their discussions with the class.
- Have pairs report back with a brief summary or a few interesting ideas from their discussions.
- Go over any common errors you heard, eliciting corrections from the class.

ANSWERS

Activity 7

1. a; **2.** b; **3.** a.

PALABRA POR PALABRA La publicidad en Internet

7 **56** Listen to an article about advertising on the Internet and choose the correct option that explains the meaning of these and other terms used online.

1. **Entrar y hacer** clic en los enlaces de las páginas web significa...
   a. dinero y publicidad.
   b. que aceptas pagar tú el uso de la página.
   c. ver la información sin ninguna consecuencia económica para los propietarios de la web.

2. Un segundo sistema de publicidad son los **anuncios de texto** que consisten en...
   a. un botón para comprar el producto.
   b. un pequeño recuadro, un título del producto o empresa, un texto corto de descripción, y la **dirección web** con enlace a la página.
   c. un amplio catálogo de productos o servicios disponibles para comprar.

3. Un **blog** (bitácora) en Internet es...
   a. un sitio en el que un autor o autores publican artículos de su interés. Es posible hablar de temas muy variados. Se incluye publicidad en ellos.
   b. una **página web** exclusivamente publicitaria.
   c. algo parecido a un **chat** para presentar temas de interés.

8 This month's theme at your high school's website is "Internet advertising". For this reason a forum has been created to find out what students think about it. Log into the forum and give us your opinion.

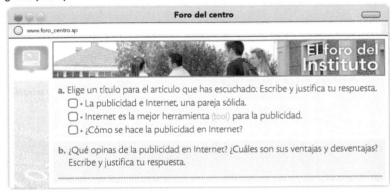

a. Elige un título para el artículo que has escuchado. Escribe y justifica tu respuesta.
- La publicidad e Internet, una pareja sólida.
- Internet es la mejor herramienta *(tool)* para la publicidad.
- ¿Cómo se hace la publicidad en Internet?

b. ¿Qué opinas de la publicidad en Internet? ¿Cuáles son sus ventajas y desventajas? Escribe y justifica tu respuesta.

9 Talk with a classmate about the following topics.
a. ¿Cómo crees que será en el futuro la publicidad?
b. ¿Cuáles serán sus canales *(channels)* para llegar a los posibles consumidores?

Practice what you have learned with additional materials online.

GRAMÁTICA

1. TRANSITION WORDS AND PHRASES

1 **Read the following text and complete the chart that follows with the appropriate transition words and phrases.**

En los medios de comunicación, por la calle, en gigantescos espectaculares *(billboards)* o de formas novedosas, muchos rostros *(faces)* conocidos se asoman a la publicidad para aumentar sus beneficios. Por un lado están los deportistas, con un espacio muy importante. Y, sin duda, son los que más dinero generan para las marcas, que se pelean por contar con ellos. Por ejemplo: Cristiano Ronaldo, Messi, Pau Gasol o Rafa Nadal.

Por otro (lado), actrices y modelos. Y es que nadie escapa de la tentación de conseguir dinero extra si su ocupación profesional no pasa por su mejor momento. Sobre eso tendría mucho que contarnos Andie McDowell, que lleva un tiempo alejada de las carteleras y ya es un clásico de los anuncios de cosméticos y productos de belleza. Algo parecido ocurre con Claudia Schiffer. También prestaron su imagen para anunciar todo tipo de productos desde cantantes hasta humoristas, presentadores, antiguas celebridades o hijos de famosos, como es el caso en España de Enrique Iglesias.

Asimismo, podemos recordar grandes personajes que también sucumbieron a la publicidad. Como Mijaíl Gorbachov, que llegó a hacer una campaña para una conocida marca de comida rápida norteamericana, o Sarah Ferguson, que también tuvo sus momentos publicitarios hace ya unos años.

Y es que el dinero que mueve la publicidad es muy goloso *(appetizing)*.

Adaptado de www.noticiasterra.es

■ Para distinguir dos argumentos:
  · **En primer lugar / En segundo lugar**…
    La juventud es muy crítica. **En primer lugar** *no acepta cualquier cosa y,* **en segundo lugar,** *busca lo que quiere.*

■ Para **oponer** dos argumentos:
  · .... / ....
    Comer es importante. .... *es necesario,* .... *un placer.*

■ Para **añadir** argumentos:
  · .... / **además** / .... / ....
    La creatividad está presente en la publicidad, **además** *de la originalidad, por supuesto.*

■ Para **ejemplificar** y **explicar**:
  · .... / **es decir / o sea**
    El alto nivel de competencia hace necesario invertir en publicidad, **es decir,** *hay muchos productos buenos y similares en el mercado, pero algo te hace elegir uno.*

■ Para **aludir a un tema** ya planteado *(mentioned)*:
  · **(Con) respecto a (eso de / eso)** / ....
    Con respecto a eso *que dijiste antes, siento no estar totalmente de acuerdo contigo.*

209

OBJECTIVES FOR GRAMÁTICA 1

- Present grammatical structures needed to practice communicative functions of the unit: Transition words and phrases
- Learn and practice using transitional words and phrases in writing

CORE RESOURCES

- Extension Activity: EA 7.4
- Interactive Online Materials – ELEteca

STANDARDS

1.2 Understand the language
4.1 Compare languages

INSTRUCTIONAL STRATEGIES

1. Transition Words and Phrases

Activity 1

- To introduce the lesson, elicit examples from the class of famous people who have marketed different products in commercials and other forms of advertising. Ask if they can recall the product that the person was promoting, if they liked the advertisement or not, and if they thought the famous person helped to sell the product or not. You may choose to put students into pairs to discuss their favorite advertisements with famous people and explain their preferences. (This will also help them prepare for Activity 2).
- Have students open their books, and go over the instructions. You may choose to read the text as a class or have students read it silently to themselves.
- Have students work invidually to complete the chart with the phrases form the text. Monitor their progress and assist as needed.
- Put students into pairs to compare their answers.
- Go over the answers as a class.

ANSWERS

Activity 1

Para oponer dos argumentos: **Por un lado… por otro (lado)**; Para añadir argumentos: **Y, también, asimismo**; Para ejemplificar y explicar: **Por ejemplo**; Para aludir a un tema ya planteado: **Sobre eso.**

INSTRUCTIONAL STRATEGIES

Activity 2

- You may choose to have students work individually or in pairs on the essays.
- Remind them of the three main parts of the essay: the introduction, the body, and the conclusion. Discuss the basic components of each section. Model a possible outline on the board, eliciting examples from the class to complete it together.
- Have students create their own outlines.
- Have students discuss their outlines with a partner or another pair to see to ensure that they have a good plan for their essays.
- Have students write their first drafts.
- Focus students' attention on the first draft questions. Have students exchange papers and markup their first drafts based on the questions provided.
- Have students return the marked up essays and write their second drafts.
- Focus students' attention on the second draft questions. Have students exchange papers and markup their second drafts based on the questions provided.
- Have students write their final drafts, checking their own work based on the final reflection questions in the book.
- If you like, you can distribute copies of EA 7.4, **Guía para escribir y mejorar un texto** to use as a checklist.

OBJECTIVES FOR GRAMÁTICA 2

- Present grammatical structures needed to practice communicative functions of the unit:
  Other sentence connectors
- Learn new sentence connectors and apply them to appropriate contexts

CORE RESOURCES

- Audio Program: Track 57

STANDARDS

1.2   Understand the language
4.1   Compare languages

GRAMÁTICA

2 Write an essay about a well-known person or celebrity that often appears in advertisements or commercials. Use transition words and phrases to organize your ideas. Follow the suggested guidelines:

Haz un esquema (outline)

- Escribe las ideas principales que le den progreso al tema elegido.
- Marca en cada una de ellas las ideas secundarias, evita las repeticiones.
- Busca y utiliza sinónimos que den coherencia y variedad léxica.
- Organiza y relaciona las partes del texto con los conectores adecuados.
- Finaliza con un resumen o una conclusión.

Primera lectura (first draft)

Comprueba que la información del texto tiene sentido:

- ¿El tipo de texto y el esquema están bien desarrollados?
- ¿Has incluido la información que es más importante para el lector?
- ¿Presentas la información de una forma clara y lógica?
- ¿Has excluido la información no necesaria?

Segunda lectura

Comprueba que las palabras y frases son correctas:

- ¿Puedes cambiar palabras de contenido general por otras más precisas?
- ¿Describes bien y con precisión lo que quieres decir?
- ¿La ortografía, la puntuación y la gramática son correctas?

Reflexión final

- ¿Añadirías o eliminarías algo?
- Como lector, ¿qué crítica le harías al texto?

2. OTHER SENTENCE CONNECTORS

■ Para **añadir razones** en un orden de fuerza creciente (increasing):
- **incluso**
María trabaja todos los días, **incluso** los domingos.

■ Para **contraponer** (counter) razones:
- **bueno**   - **no obstante**   - **pero**   - **en cambio**   - **sin embargo**

El rojo es mi color preferido, **sin embargo** nunca llevo ropa de ese color.

■ Para expresar **consecuencia**:
- **así que**   - **de ahí que**   - **así pues**   - **de modo que**   - **de manera que**   - **pues**

Me encantan las películas, **así que** voy al cine siempre que puedo.

■ Para sacar **conclusiones**:
- **entonces**   - **en resumen**   - **total que**
- **por lo tanto**   - **para terminar**   - **en conclusión**

Fuimos a la montaña sin botas ni ropa adecuada, **total que** pasamos muchísimo frío.

3 🎧 **57** **A group of teenagers from Mexico D.F. participated in an advertising campaign for a famous sports shoes brand. Listen to their experiences and arrange the following statements in the correct order. Then, fill in the blanks with an appropriate connector.**

Foro

www.foro_opinion.sp

a. ☐ La clave del éxito de esta campaña fue, ... , el volverse parte de la vida del consumidor y Nike llegó hasta sus propias casas.

b. ☐ Se consiguieron más de 4.000 jóvenes, ... había que implicarlos en el proyecto, ... se crearon las mascotas que representaban a los diferentes barrios de la ciudad. .... aparecieron como grafiti y estaban dibujadas sobre los bancos y en las estaciones de autobuses de todo México.

c. ☐ La campaña de las famosas zapatillas utilizó mercadotecnia *(marketing)* de calle .... de una campaña en redes sociales para conseguir el éxito.

d. ☐ Se empezó con un video que se subió a Youtube donde muchachos de la ciudad jugaban al fútbol en la calle, ... un muchacho hablaba y decía: "El fútbol es diversión, juegues donde juegues".

e. ☐ La idea era organizar un torneo de fútbol con jóvenes de México D.F., ... hubo una convocatoria *(announcement)* en la página Facebook de Nike que tiene 811.000 seguidores allí.

---

4 👥 **Work with a partner and complete the following sentences with an appropriate ending.**

a. Las redes sociales llegan a muchísimas personas en cualquier país, **así que** ....
b. Toda la información es muy accesible con Internet. **Total que** ....
c. En los anuncios la música atrae la atención, **pero** ....
d. El tiempo que dura un anuncio cuesta caro, **de modo que** ....
e. Los protagonistas de los anuncios son modelos perfectos, **en cambio** ....
f. Me gustaría participar en un anuncio, **incluso** ....

 Practice what you have learned with additional materials online.

211

Previous Page

INSTRUCTIONAL STRATEGIES

2. Other Sentence Connectors

• Before students open their books, put the four categories of other sentence connectors on the board. Have them brainstorm examples of each. Discuss their ideas before checking them against the chart in the book.
• Go over the examples of sentence connectors. After each bullet point, elicit new examples of the phrases in context from the class.
• Consider reciting a few new examples of your own. Elicit what the connector is doing in the sentence, e.g. adding a reason, expressing a consequence, etc.

🎧 **57** **Activity 3**

• Go over the instructions. Give students time to read the sentences before they listen and anticipate their correct order.
• Play the audio. Have them number the sentences.
• Put students in pairs to compare their answers.
• Then, individually, students complete each sentence with an appropriate connector. Remind them to refer back to the charts on the previous pages to find the appropriate connectors.
• Go over the answers as a class.

See audioscript on page APP4

Activity 4

• Go over the instructions. Model the first example for the class. Ask what the connector **así que** indicates about the type of information that will follow. Elicit a possible ending.
• Put students into pairs to complete the sentences with their own ideas.
• Monitor their progress and assist as needed.
• Have two pairs join each other to share their ideas.
• Call on volunteers to share their examples with the class.

ANSWERS

Activity 3

Answers will vary. Possible answers: **a.** (4) por lo tanto; **b.** (3) sin embargo, así que, Incluso; **c.** (5) además; **d.** (2) entonces; **e.** (1) de modo que.

Activity 4

Answers will vary. Possible answers may include the following: **a.** son muy utilizadas por las marcas; **b.** todos podemos conocer qué pasa en cualquier rincón del mundo; **c.** suben demasiado el volumen; **d.** son muy cortos; **e.** la gente real no es así; **f.** hacer cine.

OBJECTIVES FOR DESTREZAS

- Develop grammar and vocabulary comprehension skills
- Learn strategies for preparing for assessments

STANDARDS

1.2 Understand the language

INSTRUCTIONAL STRATEGIES

Comprensión de gramática y vocabulario (1)

Activity 1

- Before beginning the lesson, have a quick discussion about standardized tests and test-taking strategies. Ask questions, such as: *¿En general, cómo se preparan para los exámenes? ¿Tienen rituales que siguen antes de los exámenes? ¿Cómo se sienten antes, durante y después de los exámenes? ¿Qué hacen cuando no saben la respuesta a una pregunta en un examen?*
- Have students open their books. Go over the strategy.

Activity 2

- Go over the instructions. Have students work individually to select the correct options.
- Put students into pairs to compare their answers. Encourage them to explain their answers by referring back to the questions posed in the **Preparing for assessments (1)** box.
- Go over the answers as a class.

Activity 3

Go over the instructions and strategy as a class.

ANSWERS

Activity 2

1. a; **2.** b; **3.** a; **4.** b; **5.** c; **6.** c.

Next Page →

INSTRUCTIONAL STRATEGIES

Comprensión de gramática y vocabulario (2)

Activity 4

- Go over the instructions as a class. Do the first example together. Elicit the part of speech of all the possible answers (verbs). Have students identify all of the verbs in the target sentence. Write the sentence on the board and underline the verbs. Have a volunteer explain which verb is incorrect, what the replacement should be, and why.
- Have students work individually to correct the remaining sentences.
- Monitor their progress and assist as needed. Remind them to underline key words and identify the structure that needs to be replaced.
- Put students in pairs to compare their answers.
- Go over the answers as a class.

DESTREZAS

COMPRENSIÓN DE GRAMÁTICA Y VOCABULARIO (1)

1 At some point you may need to take a standardized test is Spanish. Read the strategy in Destrezas and follow the suggestion.

Destrezas

Preparing for assessments (1)

In some testing formats, you may be asked to demonstrate your overall knowledge of the language. In these cases, you will need to identify expressions or sentences that convey the same message. Focus on the message. Is it about something happening now, has it happened in the past or will it happen in the future? Is it a fact, an opinion, a hope, a command, etc.?

2 Select the option that corresponds to the context presented.

1. Alberto, no es bueno que pierdas tanto tiempo viendo la televisión.
   a. No te parece bien que Alberto vea mucho tiempo la televisión.
   b. No te importa que Alberto vea mucho tiempo la televisión.
   c. Crees que Alberto ve poco la televisión.

2. De segundo, me gustaría tomar pollo rostizado con ensalada.
   a. En un supermercado.
   b. En un restaurante.
   c. En el cine.

3. Es obvio que el atleta ganará este maratón.
   a. Estás convencido de la victoria del atleta.
   b. Crees que el atleta no llegará a la final.
   c. Estás seguro que el atleta participará en el maratón.

4. Encontré mi licencia, de modo que puedo ir a la discoteca esta noche.
   a. Tienes licencia pero no puedes entrar en la discoteca.
   b. No podías ir a la discoteca pero ahora ya sí.
   c. No tienes edad para ir a la discoteca aún.

5. Dime si estás de acuerdo o no.
   a. Pides un deseo.
   b. Pides una acción física.
   c. Pides una opinión.

6. Compré un billete de lotería, sin embargo, creo que he perdido el dinero.
   a. Sé que voy a ganar el primer premio.
   b. Perdí el dinero cuando iba a comprar el billete.
   c. No creo que vaya a ganar ningún premio.

3 Another testing format includes replacing words in a sentence with a better choice based on the meaning and tone of the context. Read the following strategy in Destrezas and follow the suggestion.

Destrezas

Preparing for assessments (2)

In the following group of sentences, a word or expression in boldface does not fit the sentence. You will need to choose from the list of options the word or expression that is not only correct but appropriate in the context provided. To do so, read the item carefully and underline key words. Be sure to identify the structure that needs to be replaced. Is it a verb, a noun, an adjective, an expression?

ANSWERS

Activity 4

1. b; **2.** c; **3.** c; **4.** d; **5.** c; **6.** c.

COMPRENSIÓN DE GRAMÁTICA Y VOCABULARIO (2)

4 There is a wrong word or phrase in the following sentences. Change that word with one from the list below each sentence.

1. Creo que beber en botella de plástico no es bien.

   a. funciona   b. está   c. sea   d. bebe   e. sepa

2. ¡A poco! Yo también creo que el domingo es el mejor día de la semana.

   a. ¿Seguro?   b. Me parece   c. Desde luego   d. No estoy seguro   e. ¿Pero cómo dices?

3. En el cartel de perfumes se escucha mi música preferida.

   a. el foro   b. el enlace   c. el anuncio   d. la web   e. el blog

4. No me parece que estudiar es lo más aburrido que puedes hacer.

   a. fue   b. era   c. eres   d. sea   e. sería

5. He trabajado duro mucho tiempo, si ahora tengo un buen trabajo.

   a. porque   b. sí   c. por lo tanto   d. desde   e. como

6. » La clase de Lengua de hoy ha sido muy divertida.

   » ¡Qué va! Nunca me había reído tanto.

   a. ¡También!   b. No   c. ¡Y que lo digas!   d. ¡En absoluto!   e. ¡Claro que sí!

PRONUNCIACIÓN Siglas, acrónimos y abreviaciones

SIGLA	ACRÓNIMO	ABREVIACIÓN
• Palabra formada por el conjunto de letras iniciales de una expresión: **GPS** [ge-pe-ese], **PC** [pe-ce], **FM** [efe-eme]. Su plural es invariable (does not change): las ONG.	• Siglas que pueden leerse como palabras. **ONU** (Organización de Naciones Unidas o **UNO** en inglés), **UNESCO** (United Nations Educational, Scientific and Cultural Organization).	• Representación reducida de una palabra o grupo de palabras. Al leerlas, leemos la palabra entera: **etc.** (etcétera); **Dña.** (doña); **dcha.** (derecha); **Ud.** (usted); **C.P.** (código postal).

1 🎧 58 Listen to the following acronyms and abbreviations as they are read to you. Do you know what they represent?

PIB ○ Adena ○ ADN ○ TIC ○ VV. AA. ○ UNAM ○ CD ○ FMI ○ FIFA ○ pyme ○ n.º
VIP ○ Sr. ○ Banxico ○ Láser ○ JJ. OO. ○ NBA ○ GPS ○ DVD

2 Identify the letters in the first column as *abreviaciones* (AB), *acrónimos* (AC), or *siglas* (S). Then match them with their meaning.

		AB	AC	S
1. VV. AA. •	• a. Unión Europea.	☐	☐	☐
2. JJ. OO. •	• b. Varios Autores.	☐	☐	☐
3. TIC •	• c. Pequeña y Mediana Empresa.	☐	☐	☐
4. pyme •	• d. Juegos Olímpicos.	☐	☐	☐
5. UE •	• e. Tecnologías de Información y Comunicación.	☐	☐	☐

Practice what you have learned with additional materials online.

213

OBJECTIVES FOR PRONUNCIACIÓN

• Listening for and pronouncing initials, acronyms, and abbreviations

CORE RESOURCES

• Audio Program: Track 58
• Interactive Whiteboard Lesson: IWB 7.2
• Interactive Online Materials – ELEteca

STANDARDS

1.2   Understand the language
4.1   Compare languages

INSTRUCTIONAL STRATEGIES

🎧 58 **Activity 1**

• To introduce the topic, write **USA** and **EE.UU.** on the board. Elicit what they stand for (*United States, Estados Unidos*).
• Then project IWB 7.2, **Abreviaturas**. Show the photos one at a time, keeping the abbreviations covered. Elicit the abbreviations for each. Ask questions to guide students along as needed.
• Have students open their books. Go over the explanations and examples of **siglas**, **acrónimos**, and **abreviaciones** together.
• Go over the instructions. Play the audio.
• Discuss what the acronyms and abbreviations represent. Practice pronunciations.

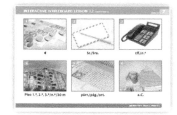

Activity 2

• Go over the instructions. Have students work individually or in pairs to select the correct columns and match the meanings.
• Monitor their progress and assist as needed.
• Go over the answers as a class.

ANSWERS

Activity 1

PIB (Producto Interior Bruto, *GDP: Gross Domestice Product*); Adena (Asociación para la Defensa de la Naturaleza); ADN (Ácido Desoxirribonucleico, *DNA*); TIC (Tecnologías de Información y Comunicación); VV.AA. (Varios Autores); UNAM (Universidad Nacional Autónoma de México); CD (Disco Compacto); FMI (Fondo Monetario Internacional, *IMF: International Monetary Fund*); FIFA (Fédération Internationale de Football Association); pyme (Pequeña y Mediana Empresa, *SME: Small and Medium Size Enterprises*); n° (número); VIP (del inglés *Very Important People*, Persona muy importante); Sr. (señor); Banxico (Banco de México); Láser (de la sigla inglesa *Light Amplification by Stimulated Emission of Radiation*); JJ.OO. (Juegos Olímpicos); NBA (Asociación Nacional de Baloncesto); GPS (Sistema de Posicionamiento Global); DVD (del inglés *Digital Video Disc*).

Activity 2

1. b (AB); **2.** d (AB); **3.** e (AC); **4.** C (AC) c; **5.** a (S).

SABOR HISPANO

OBJECTIVES FOR SABOR HISPANO

- Learn about the role of advertisements and Internet in Hispanic countries
- Compare cultural similarities about the role of advertisements and Internet around the world

CORE RESOURCES

- Audio Program: Track 59

STANDARDS

2.2 Products and perspectives
4.2 Compare cultures

INSTRUCTIONAL STRATEGIES

🎧 59

- Put students in pairs to discuss the questions in the **Antes de leer** box.
- Monitor their conversations and assist as needed.
- Call on volunteers to report back on their discussions.
- Focus students' attention on the images and their captions. Ask who they are, where they are from, and why they are famous.
- Before playing the audio, tell students to listen for the question posed at the beginning of the audio and be prepared to answer it. Either have students close their books while they listen or follow along with the text in the book.
- Elicit responses to the target question. For more detail, ask: **¿Quiénes tienen más influencia y poder para convencer al consumidor en España: los actores y los cantantes, o los deportistas? ¿Cómo lo saben?**
- To help build vocabulary, have students locate and underline any words from the glossary on the next page in the text. Then have them make and share new sentences with the words. You may choose to have them work individually or in pairs.

SABOR HISPANO

¡CÓMPRALO YA!

Lionel Messi.

Antes de leer

¿Comprarías un producto porque una persona famosa hace la publicidad?? ¿Por qué (no)?

🎧 59 **Muchos famosos usan su imagen y su éxito para vender productos. Pero... ¿funciona esta estrategia en España? ¡Lee para saberlo!**

Lionel Messi es uno de los futbolistas más famosos del mundo. Su fortuna asciende a´ 172 millones de dólares. Pero hoy, Lionel está concentrado en convencerte: quiere que compres la tableta de una famosa marca´. Para eso, participa en un video usando el producto. La idea es que, cuando lo veas, te imagines viviendo la glamurosa vida de una estrella de fútbol internacional.

Shakira también quiere que compres algo, y no es solamente la entrada a su último concierto. La cantante colombiana pone su sonrisa´ para vender pasta de dientes en videos y publicidades en revistas y periódicos.

Ellos no son los únicos que usan su imagen para comercializar productos: Jennifer López vende celulares, Salma Hayek vende champú y Antonio Banderas vende vino en publicidades y eventos.

Aunque parezca una receta infalible, en la mayoría de los casos la cara de un famoso deportista o artista no es suficiente para convencer al consumidor. En España, solamente el 5% de la gente compraría un producto porque un actor o cantante hace la publicidad. Los deportistas son, al parecer, más efectivos: el 8% de las personas consultadas en una encuesta´ de la empresa Nielsen compraría un producto porque lo recomienda un atleta.

Shakira.

214

Anuncios que más destacan

De acuerdo con su tono o contenido, algunos anuncios quedan en la memoria colectiva. Estas son las estrategias que mejor funcionan.

- con humor
- escenas cotidianas
- valores
- con familias
- con deportistas
- con artistas

¿Quién te convence?

Estas son las razones que llevan a los españoles a consumir un producto o servicio.

87% 59% 56% 45%

- mi familia y amigos
- críticas en Internet
- un artículo periodístico
- un anuncio en prensa

Las críticas en Internet son útiles para el consumidor.

¿COMPRENDISTE?

Decide if the following statements are true (T) or false (F).

1. Lionel Messi pone su imagen para vender tecnología. T ◯ F ◯
2. Las publicidades con famosos son muy efectivas. T ◯ F ◯
3. El humor es la estrategia menos efectiva en los anuncios publicitarios. T ◯ F ◯
4. La mayoría de los españoles confía en las recomendaciones de su familia y amigos. T ◯ F ◯
5. Para mucha gente, los artículos en prensa escrita son útiles para decidir la compra de un producto. T ◯ F ◯

Las anuncios con humor son los más recordados.

AHORA TÚ

What do you think? Answer the following questions and discuss your ideas with other students.

1. ¿Qué cosas son importantes para convencerte de comprar un producto? Nombra dos.
2. ¿Por qué crees que los deportistas tienen más éxito en las publicidades que los artistas?
3. Si fueras famoso/a, ¿qué producto no publicitarías nunca? ¿Por qué?
4. ¿Qué famoso norteamericano tiene credibilidad, en tu opinión? ¿Por qué?
5. ¿Cuál es tu publicidad favorita? Descríbela brevemente y explica por qué te parece efectiva.

Glosario

ascender a – to amount to
confiar – to trust
destacar – to stand out
la encuesta – survey
hacer la publicidad – to promote
la marca – brand
la publicidad – advertising
la sonrisa – smile
valores – value

Fuentes: Nielsen, Msn Latino, *El País*.

215

OBJECTIVES FOR RELATO

- Revisit unit themes, grammar, vocabulary and culture in a new context
- Improve reading comprehension skills

CORE RESOURCES

- Audio Program: Track 60

STANDARDS

1.3 Present information
2.2 Products and perspectives
3.1 Knowledge of other disciplines

INSTRUCTIONAL STRATEGIES

Activity 1

- To activate schema, elicit words related to feelings and emotions in Spanish and write them on the board, for example: **alegría**, **pérdida**, **amistad**, **comunicación**, **imaginación**, **fantasía**, **dependencia**, **independencia**, **soledad**, **organización**…
- Go over the instructions. Focus students' attention on the images. Model a possible response based on one of the images using your own experiences and feelings.
- Have students work individually to write their own ideas.
- Monitor their progress and assist as needed. Encourage them to be creative.
- Call on volunteers to share their ideas.

Activity 2

- Go over the instructions. Tell students to be prepared to report back on their partners' responses.
- Put students into pairs to ask and answer the questions.
- Monitor their progress and assist as needed. Encourage them to take notes to focus on what their partner is saying. Listen to any common errors in their discussions.
- Have students' switch partners and report back on their previous partners' responses.
- Go over any common errors you heard, eliciting corrections from the class.

🎧 60 Activity 3

- Read the instructions as a class. Focus students' attention on the title. Ask students what they think the text will include. Elicit ideas and check their understanding of the vocabulary in the title.
- Play the audio, and have students read along.
- Call on volunteers to share their impressions of the text. Ask questions, such as: **Según el texto, ¿creen que el autor piensa que es bueno recibir un reloj de regalo? ¿Por qué sí o por qué no?**
- Put students into pairs to discuss how they can use the ideas in the text in an advertisement.
- Monitor their progress and assist as needed.
- Have volunteers report back on their ideas.

---

1 Look at the following objects and write about what they represent for you and what emotions, feelings or memories you associate with them.

2 👥 Take turns asking and answering the following questions with your partner.

a. ¿Cuál usas con más frecuencia?
b. ¿Cuál es el más indispensable para ti?
c. ¿Imaginas tu vida sin él? ¿Cómo cambiaría tu vida?

3 🎧 60 At the advertising agency where you work, you come across the following literary text. Read it and then discuss with your partner how you could use it in an advertisement.

Preámbulo a las instrucciones para dar cuerda a un reloj

Piensa en esto: cuando te regalan un reloj te regalan un pequeño infierno florido, una cadena (*chain*) de rosas, un calabozo (*jail cell*) de aire. No te dan solamente el reloj, que los cumplas muy felices y esperamos que te dure porque es de buena marca, suizo con áncora (*anchor*) de rubíes; no te lo regalan solamente ese menudo picapedrero que te atarás a la muñeca (*wrist*) y pasearás contigo. Te regalan –no lo saben, lo terrible es que no lo saben–, te regalan un nuevo pedazo frágil y precario de ti mismo, algo que es tuyo pero no es tu cuerpo, que hay que atar (*tie*) a tu cuerpo con su correa como un bracito desesperado colgándose de tu muñeca. Te regalan la necesidad de darle cuerda (*wind*) todos los días, la obligación de darle cuerda para que siga siendo un reloj; te regalan la obsesión de atender a la hora exacta en las vitrinas de las joyerías, en el anuncio por la radio, en el servicio telefónico. Te regalan el miedo a perderlo, de que te lo roben, de que se te caiga al suelo y se rompa. Te regalan su marca, y la seguridad de que es una marca mejor que las otras, te regalan la tendencia de comparar tu reloj con los demás relojes. No te regalan un reloj, tú eres el regalado, a ti te ofrecen para el cumpleaños del reloj.

4 The previous text is an excerpt from *Historias de cronopios y de famas* (1962) by Julio Cortázar. Read about this writer and his work. Then, find the word in the text with the same meaning as the expression below.

a. Obra que narra la vivencias personales del autor. ➡ ....
b. Los hechos que se narran no siguen un orden cronológico. ➡ ....
c. La obra del autor que más se ha vendido. ➡ ....
d. Composición de carácter poético no escrita en verso. ➡ ....

Julio Cortázar nació en Bélgica, el 26 de agosto de 1914 y murió en Francia el 12 de febrero de 1984. Fue un escritor, traductor e intelectual argentino nacionalizado francés. Se le considera uno de los autores más innovadores y originales de su tiempo. Maestro del relato corto, la prosa poética y la narración breve en general, destaca, por ejemplo, su obra autobiográfica *Bestiario*. Fue creador de importantes novelas que inauguraron una nueva forma de hacer literatura en el mundo hispano, rompiendo los moldes clásicos: no existe la linealidad temporal y los personajes tienen autonomía y una profundidad psicológica. Debido a que los contenidos de su obra están en la frontera entre lo real y lo fantástico, se le suele relacionar con el surrealismo. Su mayor éxito editorial, *Rayuela*, la cual le valió el reconocimiento de ser parte del *boom* latinoamericano, se convirtió en un clásico de la literatura argentina. También escribió teatro y poesía. Vivió buena parte de su vida en París, pero también en Argentina, España y Suiza.

5 **Think about an object that is special to you and write a text similar to Cortazar's about this object.**

Piensa en esto:

- Cuando te regalan ....
- Te regalan un ....
- No te dan solamente ....
- No te regalan solamente ....
- Te regalan la necesidad de ....
- Te regalan la obsesión de ....
- Te regalan el miedo de ....
- Te regalan su marca y la seguridad de que ....
- Te regalan la tendencia de ....
- No te regalan un ....
- Tú eres el regalado. A ti te regalan para el cumpleaños del ....

6 **With this information, you have now created the copy for your ad. Decide on a slogan along with the images and music you would use. Then present your ad to the class.**

7 **Talk to your partner about some of your favorite ads. Use the following questions as a guide.**

a. ¿Cuál es el anuncio publicitario que más te ha llamado la atención?

b. ¿Dónde lo has visto?

c. ¿Por qué te ha impresionado?

INSTRUCTIONAL STRATEGIES

Activity 4 (From previous page)

- Go over the instructions. Read the text as a class.
- Have students work individually to find the words in the text with the same meaning.
- Go over the answers as a class.
- Consider asking a few questions to check their comprehension of the text, such as: **¿De dónde es Julio Cortázar? ¿Dónde vivió? ¿Por qué es famoso?**

Activity 5

- Go over the instructions. Have students work individually or in pairs to brainstorm ideas and complete the sentences.
- Monitor their progress and assist as needed. Encourage them to be creative.

Activity 6

- Go over the instructions. Elicit examples of slogans from current ad campaigns. Discuss the qualities of good slogans; they are often concise, clever, and catchy.
- Have students review their sentences from Activity 5 and come up with a catchy slogan to help sell their object. In addition to the images and music, you may even choose to have students mock up a logo, a rough design of a print ad, or a storyboard for a commercial.
- Have students present their ads to the class.

Activity 7

- Put students into pairs or small groups to discuss the questions.
- Monitor their conversations and assist as needed.
- Call on volunteers to report back on interesting aspects of their conversations.

ANSWERS

Activity 4

a. Autobiográfica; **b.** No existe la linealidad; **c.** Su mayor éxito editorial; **d.** Prosa poética.

OBJECTIVES FOR EVALUACIÓN

- Review grammar, vocabulary and culture from the unit
- Complete self-assessment

CORE RESOURCES

- Extension Activities: EA 7.5
- Interactive Online Materials – ELEteca

STANDARDS

1.2 Understand the language

4.1 Compare languages

INSTRUCTIONAL STRATEGIES

- Have students complete the activities individually.
- Go over the answers as a class. Encourage students to learn from each other by asking if they agree with the answers given. Provide explanations as needed.
- You may wish to assign point value to each activity as a way for students to monitor their progress.
- Direct students to the indicated pages in **En resumen** if they make more than one or two mistakes in any one section.

Extension

Give students a copy of EA 7.5, *Autoevalación*. Have them complete the charts with the information they have learned and the mistakes they have made so they may better understand where they need the most improvement.

ANSWERS

Activity 1

a. deben; **b.** se dejen; **c.** pidan; **d.** desarrollan; **e.** hacen; **f.** vayamos / vayan.

Activity 2

a. No es ridículo que; **b.** No es verdad que; **c.** Es una tontería que; **d.** Es increíble que; **e.** Está claro que.

Activity 3

Answers will vary. Possible answers may include the following:

a. Yo no creo que eso sea verdad, pienso que en verano cada uno elige según sus posibilidades; **b.** En mi opinión sucede todo lo contrario, los medios nos bombardean continuamente con ella; **c.** A mí me parece que es totalmente cierto porque es un sector de la población muy influenciable; **d.** Yo no estoy nada de acuerdo porque el arte puede expresarse a través de cualquier medio.

Activity 4

a. ¡Y que lo digas!; **b.** ¡Qué va!; **c.** ¡Desde luego!; **d.** ¡Anda ya!

EVALUACIÓN

EXPRESSING WISHES

1 Write the correct form of the verb in parenthesis.

a. Me parece que las escenas en los anuncios (deber) .... ser variadas y dinámicas.

b. No pienso que los jóvenes (dejarse) .... influir tanto por la publicidad.

c. No creo que los niños (pedir) .... los productos que ven en la televisión.

d. Opino que los consumidores (desarrollar) .... un espíritu crítico ante tanta información.

e. Desde mi punto de vista, las asociaciones anticonsumo (hacer) .... un buen trabajo en la sociedad.

f. No me parece bien que todos (ir) .... con la misma ropa y los mismos tenis.

MAKING VALUE JUDGEMENTS

2 Complete the sentences with an appropriate expression from the list.

Está claro que ○ Es increíble que ○ Es una tontería que ○ No es verdad que ○ No es ridículo que

a. .... los padres vigilen cuántas horas de televisión ven sus hijos pequeños.

b. .... los anuncios sean sinceros.

c. .... las personas crean que un perfume las hará perfectas.

d. .... no sepamos elegir por nosotros mismos.

e. .... los medios de comunicación tienen un gran poder sobre la sociedad.

SHOWING AGREEMENT AND DISAGREEMENT

3 Indicate whether you agree or disagree with the following opinions.

a. En verano somos más influenciables por la publicidad porque queremos tener unas buenas vacaciones.

b. En la actualidad, hay poca publicidad y por eso todos la siguen con mucha atención.

c. En las redes sociales hay mucha publicidad porque los jóvenes las visitan con mucha frecuencia.

d. La fotografía y el diseño gráfico no son arte.

4 Complete the following conversations with a response showing support for or against the statement.

a. » Es ridículo que el cine sea tan caro, me gustaría ir más.

» ¡...................... ! A mí también me gustaría.

b. » Creo que hay fiestas solo comerciales, como San Valentín.

» ¡......................! Es la fiesta del amor y el romanticismo.

c. » Es impresionante que compres tantos libros digitales. A mí me gustan en papel.

» ¡......................! Es mucho mejor en papel, pero pesan y ocupan más.

d. » Me he comprado el último libro de Vargas Llosa. ¡Estoy muy contento!

» ¡......................! Eres un antiguo. Yo lo llevo en mi ebook.

TRANSITION WORDS AND SENTENCE CONNECTORS

5 **Match elements from both columns.**

1. El fútbol es un gran deporte. Sin embargo .... •
2. La fotografía en el cine es fundamental. Por ejemplo, ... •
3. Los jóvenes no ven la publicidad, incluso .... •
4. Pienso que seré seleccionado para el comercial de Axo; en la última entrevista que hice les gusté mucho. Además, ... •
5. El gasto de las compañías en publicidad es muy alto. Total que .... •
6. Por un lado, los anuncios me divierten por su fantasía, pero por otro lado, ... •

- a. yo diría que no les interesa.
- b. sus procuctos son muy caros.
- c. no es el único.
- d. me aburre que haya tantos.
- e. había muy poca gente.
- f. en *Memorias de África* es impresionante, ¿la recuerdas?

INTERNET Y LA PUBLICIDAD EN INTERNET

6 **Fill in the blanks with the words and phrases from the list below.**

> botón ○ enlaces ○ texto publicitario ○ usuario ○ web portal ○ logo

Mi centro ha creado una (a) .... que es un sitio en Internet que sirve para que podamos acceder a recursos y servicios relacionados con la vida estudiantil. Puede incluir: enlaces, buscadores, libros, documentos, aplicaciones, compra electrónica. Así, el (b) ...., es decir, la persona que utiliza la web portal, podrá acceder a ella y buscar información solo pinchando un (c) .... Además, podemos conectar con otras páginas web, descargar ficheros o abrir ventanas a través de (d) .... Por suerte, no sufriremos los continuos anuncios, porque no está permitido incluir ningún (e) .... Lo que no me gusta de la página es el (f) ...., vamos, la combinación de letras e imagen que representa el centro escolar.

INITIALS, ACRONYMS AND ABBREVIATIONS

7 **Write the initials, acronym or abbreviation for the following.**

a. Unión Europea. ⇒ ....
b. Pequeña y Mediana Empresa. ⇒ ....
c. Organización de Naciones Unidas. ⇒ ....
d. Estados Unidos. ⇒ ....
e. Tercero izquierda. ⇒ ....
f. Juegos Olímpicos. ⇒ ....

CULTURA

8 **Answer the following questions with the information you learned in ¡Cómpralo ya!**

a. ¿Cuál es la estrategia de poner a un futbolista como Lionel Messi a vender productos?
b. ¿Qué producto promociona Shakira? ¿Crees que han acertado? ¿Por qué?
c. Según los datos presentados, ¿es suficiente tener a un personaje famoso para convencer al consumidor?
d. ¿Qué tipo de anuncio tiene el mayor éxito a la hora de vender?
e. En el caso de los españoles, ¿cómo se les convence mejor para que compren algo?

Practice what you have learned with additional materials online.

Answers

Activity 5

1. c; 2. f; 3. a; 4. e; 5. b; 6. d.

Activity 6

1. web portal; 2. usuario; 3. botón; 4. enlaces; 5. texto publicitario; 6. logo.

Activity 7

a. UE; b. pyme; c. ONU; d. EE. UU.; e. 3.º izq.; f. JJ. OO.

Activity 8

Answers will vary. Possible answers might include the following:

a. La idea es que, cuando lo veas, te imagines viviendo la glamurosa vida de una estrella de fútbol internacional; b. Shakira promociona pasta de dientes; c. No, no es suficiente; d. Tienen más éxito los anuncios con humor; e. A los españoles les convencen más las recomendaciones de familia y amigos.

OBJECTIVES FOR EN RESUMEN: VOCABULARIO

- Review unit vocabulary and expressions
- Practice communicative skills

STANDARDS

- 1.2 Understand the language
- 1.3 Present information

INSTRUCTIONAL STRATEGIES

- Have students write sentences with the words and phrases in the other vocabulary sections.
- Call on students to write their sentences on the board –but leave a blank line (or give multiple choices, in some cases) where the vocabulary word or phrase should be. Then have the rest of the class write down the answers to complete the sentences
- Go over the answers as a class. You may choose to create a competition and keep score by individual or group.

Alternative Activity

Index cards can be used as flashcards with the Spanish term on one side and the English term, a picture, or a drawing on the other. Working in pairs or groups, students can use the flashcards to help each other practice unit vocabulary.

EN RESUMEN: Vocabulario

La publicidad
la campaña *campaign*
el cartel *sign, poster*
el consumidor *consumer*
el derecho a la intimidad *right to privacy*
la encuesta *survey*
el espectacular *billboard*

la libertad de expresión *freedom of expression*
la manipulación *manipulation*
la marca *brand*
la mercadotecnia / el mercadeo *marketing*
la novedad *fad, novelty*
el público *public*

el punto de vista *point of view*
las rebajas *sales*

las redes sociales *social networks*

el respeto *respect*
el valor *value*

Descripciones
anticonsumista *one who opposes consumerism*
machista *chauvinist*
preocupante *worrisome, alarming*

Verbos
abrir ventanas *to open a new window*
atacar *to attack*
consumir *to consume*

cumplir *to accomplish*
descargar *to download*
hacer caso *to pay attention to*
provocar *to provoke*
tratar de *to try to (do something)*
tuitear *to tweet*

utilizar *to use*

Internet
la amistad virtual *virtual friend*
la banderola *banner*

el botón *button*
el buscador *search engine*

la dirección web *web address*
el enlace *link*
el fichero / el archivo *computer file*
el foro *forum*
el icono *icon*
el logo *logo, branding*
la página web *web page*
el perfil *profile*

la piratería *piracy*

el portal *web portal*
el sitio (web) *(web) site*
el usuario *user*
las ventanas emergentes *pop-up windows*

220

EN RESUMEN: Gramática

EXPRESSING OPINION
(See page 200 and 201)

- To **ask opinion**:
  ¿Qué piensas / crees / opinas de / sobre...?
  ¿(A ti) qué te parece...?
  ¿En tu opinión / Desde tu punto de vista / Según tú + question sentence?

- To **express agreement** and **disagreement** with an opinion:

(No) estoy	a favor de	+ noun
	estoy en contra de	+ infinitive *(same subject)*
	(del todo) de acuerdo con	+ **que** + present subjunctive *(different subjects)*

- To **express opinion**:
  En mi opinión / Desde mi punto de vista... + opinion
  Me parece que / Creo que / Pienso que + indicative
  No me parece que / No creo que + subjunctive

MAKING VALUE JUDGEMENTS
(See page 202)

- To **ask for evaluation or value judgementes** we use:
  ¿Te parece bien / mal + noun / infinitive / que + present subjunctive?

- To **value judgements**:

Me parece Es	(parecer) bien / mal (ser) bueno / malo triste / increíble / cómico / justo ridículo / exagerado / preocupante... una tontería / una vergüenza	**que** + present subjunctive
Está claro Es obvio / verdad		**que** + indicative
¡Qué bien / interesante		noun / infinitive / **que** + subjunctive!

TRANSITION WORDS AND PHRASES TO ORGANIZE THE IDEAS OF A TEXT
(See page 209)

- To **distinguish** two arguments: En primer lugar... / En segundo lugar...
- To **set out** two arguments: Por un lado / una parte... por otro (lado) / por otra (parte)...
- To **add** arguments: Y / además / también / asimismo...
- To **explain and give examples**: Por ejemplo / es decir / o sea...
- To **mention a previously-raised theme**: (Con) respecto a (eso de / eso) / sobre (eso)...

OTHER SENTENCE CONNECTORS
(See page 210)

- To **add reasons** in strength-raising order: Incluso.
- To **oppose reasons**: Bueno / pero / sin embargo / no obstante / en cambio.
- To **express consequence**: Así que / de modo que / de manera que / de ahí que / así pues / pues.
- To draw **conclusions**: Entonces / total que / por lo tanto / en resumen / en conclusión / para terminar.

221

OBJECTIVES FOR EN RESUMEN: GRAMÁTICA
- Review unit grammar
- Practice communication skills

STANDARDS
1.2 Understand the language
4.1 Compare languages

INSTRUCTIONAL STRATEGIES
- Focus students' attention on the key grammar topics of the unit.
- Have students review the Learning Outcomes in the unit opener to assess whether they feel they have mastered the main ideas and skills.
- Ask them if they can remember additional examples for each grammar topic.
- Model how to find and go back to the appropriate page in the unit to review any grammar topic they may need help with.
- Invite students to review the grammar activities they completed in this unit.
- Ask them what grammar activities they found easy and which they found challenging. Encourage them to rework any activities they found particularly challenging.

OBJECTIVES FOR UNIT OPENER

- Introduce unit theme: **¿Sueño o realidad?** about expressing real and hypothetical situations and stories
- Introduce culture for the unit: Learn about letter writing and formal correspondence in Hispanic countries

STANDARDS

1.1 Engage in conversation

2.2 Products and culture

INSTRUCTIONAL STRATEGIES

- Before students open their books, write the unit title on the board: **¿Sueño o realidad?** Elicit ideas from the students about the material they think they will encounter in the unit.
- Have students open their books, look at the image, and read the caption. Ask: **¿Dónde se puede encontrar esta imagen? ¿Cómo se llama el autor? ¿Cómo se titula el libro? ¿Qué significa el título?** Ask students to recall another title by the same author (**La sombra del viento**).
- Have students work individually to write answers to the three questions on the page. Remind them to use the image of the cover to answer the questions.
- Monitor their progress and assist as needed.
- Put students into pairs or small groups to share and discuss their answers.
- Call on volunteers to report back on their responses and discussions. See if you can get the class to reach agreement.

Cultural Note

Carlos Ruiz Zafón is a Spanish author. He wrote the fiction novel *El Juego del Ángel* in 2008 as a prequel to his 2001 novel entitled *La Sombra del Viento*. *El Juego del Ángel* is about David Martín, a young writer in Barcelona in the 1920s and 1930s, and his encounters with a mysterious man who wants him to write a book. The novel retains two specific settings from *La Sombra del Viento*: The Cemetery of Forgotten Books and Sempere & Sons bookshop.

UNIDAD
8

¿SUEÑO O REALIDAD?

La portada del libro, *El juego del ángel*, de Carlos Ruiz Zafón.

>> ¿Será este libro un ensayo, una novela, un libro de poesía o de cuentos?

>> ¿Qué historia te imaginas que cuenta el autor?

>> ¿Qué tipo de personaje crees que representa la imagen?

222

ADDITIONAL UNIT RESOURCES

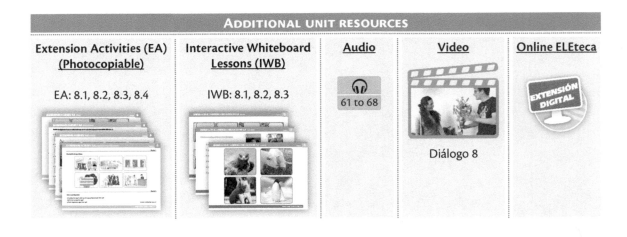

Extension Activities (EA) (Photocopiable)	Interactive Whiteboard Lessons (IWB)	Audio	Video	Online ELEteca
EA: 8.1, 8.2, 8.3, 8.4	IWB: 8.1, 8.2, 8.3	61 to 68	Diálogo 8	EXTENSIÓN DIGITAL

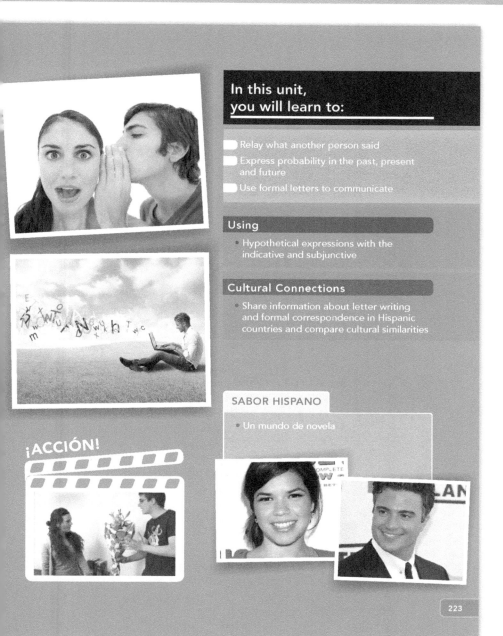

In this unit,
you will learn to:

- Relay what another person said
- Express probability in the past, present and future
- Use formal letters to communicate

Using

- Hypothetical expressions with the indicative and subjunctive

Cultural Connections

- Share information about letter writing and formal correspondence in Hispanic countries and compare cultural similarities

SABOR HISPANO

- Un mundo de novela

¡ACCIÓN!

223

LEARNING OUTCOMES

- Relay what another person said
- Express probability in the past, present, and future
- Use formal letters to communicate

INSTRUCTIONAL STRATEGIES

- Use the unit opener to preview vocabulary and cultural topics for this unit.
- Have students look at the images on this page and try to relate them to the objectives listed.
- Exploit the first main photo a bit further by asking questions, such as: *¿Qué le está diciendo el muchacho a la muchacha? ¿Cuál es la reacción de ella? ¿Por qué creen que se siente así?*
- Move on to the second photo and ask questions, such as: *¿Todavía escriben cartas formales? ¿Cuándo? ¿A quiénes escriben cartas formales? ¿Cuáles son las diferencias entre las cartas formales y las cartas informales?*
- Invite students to read the topic for **Sabor hispano** and preview that section in the unit. Ask questions, such as: *¿Reconocen a estas personas? ¿Cómo se llaman?* (*América Ferrera*, *Jaime Camil*) *¿Por qué son famosos?*
- Ask students to anticipate what they think the episode for **¡Acción!** will be about.

THREE MODES OF COMMUNICATION: UNIT 8		
	INTERPERSONAL	**INTERPRETIVE**	**PRESENTATIONAL**
HABLAMOS DE...	1	1, 2, 3, 4, 5	
COMUNICA	4, 7, 9, 10	1, 2, 3, 5, 6, 8	4, 10
¡ACCIÓN!	5	1, 2, 3, 4	
PALABRA POR PALABRA	5	1, 2, 3, 4, 6, 7, 8, 10	6, 9, 10
GRAMÁTICA	2, 8, 9	1, 2, 3, 4, 5, 7	6, 8, 9
DESTREZAS	3	1, 2, 3	2, 3
CULTURA		SABOR HISPANO	
RELATO	1, 2, 6, 8	3, 4, 5, 7	

OBJECTIVES FOR HABLAMOS DE...

- Understand language in context
- Preview vocabulary: reading fiction
- Preview grammatical structures: hypothetical expressions with the indicative and the subjunctive
- Read and listen to a conversation between Daniela and José about selecting a birthday gift for a friend

CORE RESOURCES

- Audio Program: Track 61
- Extension Activities: EA 8.1
- Interactive Whiteboard Lesson: IWB 8.1

STANDARDS

1.1 Engage in conversation
2.2 Products and culture
3.2 Acquire information

INSTRUCTIONAL STRATEGIES

Activity 1

- Before students open their books, activate their schema by asking questions, such as: **¿Les gusta leer? ¿Qué cosas leen? ¿Prefieren leer para aprender algo o por diversión? ¿Qué libros pueden recomendar?**
- Have students open their books and look at the images at the top of the page. Put students into pairs to ask and answer the questions and discuss their ideas.
- Monitor their conversations and assist as needed.
- Call on volunteers to report back on their ideas.

Activity 2

- Refer students back to the book covers and have them work individually to answer the questions. Encourage students to make educated guesses if they don't know the answers.
- Go over the answers as a class. Then share the following note with students.

HABLAMOS DE... Libros y cómics

1 Look at the image and talk to your partner about the following.

a. ¿Dónde están los muchachos?
b. ¿Cuál de los dos libros piensas que es más adecuado para un muchacho de tu edad?
c. ¿Cuál comprarías tú?
d. ¿Cuál es el último libro que compraste o leíste?

2 Decide which of the two books would contain the following information based on the covers you see.

	El Quijote	Mafalda
a. Es del año 1964.	☐	☐
b. Es del año 1605.	☐	☐
c. Su autor es Cervantes.	☐	☐
d. Su autor es Quino.	☐	☐
e. Otros personajes que aparecen son Felipe, Miguelito y Susanita.	☐	☐
f. Otros personajes que aparecen son Dulcinea, Sancho y Rocinante.	☐	☐
g. Es de origen español.	☐	☐
h. Es de origen argentino.	☐	☐

224

Cultural Note

- **Mafalda** es un personaje argentino, creado por el dibujante Quino, que aparecía en tiras cómicas y que es muy popular en Hispanoamérica y en varios países europeos. Mafalda es una niña que desea que el mundo sea mejor, pero también refleja el pesimismo de la sociedad de los años 60.
- **Don Quijote de la Mancha** es quizás el personaje literario español más popular internacionalmente. Creado en 1605 por Cervantes, es un personaje que ha perdido la razón después de leer muchos libros de caballería. Sale de su pueblo acompañado de Sancho Panza para vivir el tipo de aventuras que ha leído en esos libros.

ANSWERS

Activity 2

El Quijote: b, c, f, g; **Mafalda:** a, d, e, h.

3 🎧 61 **Listen to the conversation between Daniela and José. Then answer true (T) or false (F).**

	T	F
a. Daniela quiere comprar dos libros.	☐	☐
b. Felipe lee solo novelas modernas.	☐	☐
c. Daniela disfrutaba mucho con los cómics de Mafalda cuando era pequeña.	☐	☐
d. A José el cómic no le parece un buen regalo.	☐	☐
e. José ya tiene regalo para Felipe.	☐	☐

4 **Read the conversation and check your answers to Activity 3.**

Daniela: No sé qué libro comprarle a Felipe para su cumpleaños, ¡estoy hecha bolas!

José: La verdad es que es bastante complicado, tienes razón.

D.: Creo que finalmente voy a regalarle uno de estos dos, pero no sé por cuál decidirme. Son muy diferentes.

J.: Me parece que a Felipe le gusta leer novelas. Pero quizás no le guste *El Quijote*, es un poco antiguo para él.

D.: Es verdad que es un poco antiguo, pero Felipe lee toda clase de libros. En su casa tiene una colección enorme de novelas de todas las épocas. Es increíble que a un muchacho de 17 años le guste tanto leer.

J.: ¿Y sabes si también lee cómics? A lo mejor

el libro de Mafalda es un poquito infantil.

D.: ¿Infantil? Todo lo contrario. En mi opinión deberían leerlo los adultos, es un poco filosófico. En estas historietas aparece una niña preocupada por la paz del mundo y por la humanidad. Yo, cuando era pequeña, tenía un montón de libros de Mafalda, pero no los entendí del todo hasta que no fui adulta.

J.: Pues quizás sea esa una buena opción. Me parece que es más atractivo y más original como regalo.

D.: Pues ya está decidido. ¡Me lo llevo! Le voy a decir al dependiente que me lo envuelva. Oye, ¿y tú qué le vas a comprar?

J.: Ni idea, voy a darme una vuelta por aquí a ver si encuentro algo.

5 **Here are some popular Spanish comic books. Identify the characters for each comic book series using the options listed below.**

detectives o superhéroe o niños traviesos o trabajador de una editorial

a.

b.

c.

d.

225

INSTRUCTIONAL STRATEGIES

🎧 61 **Activity 3**

- Have students close their books. Tell the students that they are going to listen to a conversation between two friends, Daniela and José. Write two questions on the board to focus their attention on the first listening: **¿Dónde creen que están Daniela y José? ¿Por qué?**
- Play the audio. Call on volunteers to offer answers to the target questions.
- Have students open their books. Tell them they are going to listen again to determine whether the sentences are true or false. Give them a little time to read over the sentences and play the audio again.

Activity 4

- Put students into pairs. Have them check their answers with a partner. Encourage them to use the transcript to correct any mistakes.
- Monitor their progress and assist as needed.
- Go over the answers as a class. Have students explain the false answers.
- As a follow-up, ask students to suggest gifts José might buy for Felipe based on what you have learned about him.

Activity 5

- Review the instructions and the names of the comic books. Point out that in Spain they are called **tebeos**. The word comes from the name of a magazine published in Barcelona in 1917, TBO.
- Have students match the character descriptions with the covers of the comic books.
- Monitor their progress and assist as needed. Go over the answers as a class.

Alternative Activity

Have students research the comics online to be able to match the characters and covers with more confidence.

Extension

Project the comic strip with the empty speech bubbles from IWB 8.1, **Tebeos** and distribute copies of EA, 8.1, **Tebeos** to each student. Ask some basic questions about the images to activate vocabulary. Then give the students some time to fill in their own speech bubbles for each scene. Put them into small groups to share their comics. Have each group collaborate to produce the best comic strip from the samples provided to be presented to the class. Finally, reveal the speech bubbles in the original comic strip. Compare it to those produced by the students. Discuss its meaning by asking questions, such as: **¿Qué creen que ha querido transmitirnos su autor?**

ANSWERS

Activity 3

a. F; **b.** F; **c.** T; **d.** F; **e.** F.

Activity 5

a. niños traviesos; **b.** detectives; **c.** trabajador de una editorial; **d.** superhéroe.

COMUNICA COMMUNICATIVE FUNCTIONS

OBJECTIVES FOR COMUNICA

- Present communicative functions of the unit:
  Relaying information from others
- Talk about what others said and asked

CORE RESOURCES

- Audio Program: Track 62
- Interactive Online Materials – ELEteca

STANDARDS

1.1 Engage in conversation
1.2 Understand the language
4.1 Compare languages

INSTRUCTIONAL STRATEGIES FOR
RELAYING WHAT ANOTHER PERSON SAID AND ASKED

- Before opening their books, introduce students to the concept of indirect speech. You might ask students if they talked to anyone before class and what that person said. Tell them that relaying what someone else said is called indirect (or reported) speech.
- Have students open their books and walk them through the chart of examples of direct speech converted to indirect speech. Point out that it's important not only to make changes in the verbs but also in the possessives, demonstratives, etc.
- Write an example of direct speech on the board. Elicit how they might convert that to indirect speech. Help them along as needed.
- Next go over the examples of direct speech questions converted into indirect speech statements. Point out the use of **si** in *yes/no* questions and the repetition of the interrogative in information questions.
- Write another example of a *yes/no* question and an information question on the board. Elicit the transformations from the class.

Activity 1

- Have students work on their own to convert direct speech into indirect speech.
- Go over the answers as a class. Point out the expressions that introduce questions in reported speech: ***pregunta que...***, ***me/te/le/nos/les pregunta que...***

Activity 2

- Put students into pairs to complete the conversation. Encourage them to guess if they are not sure. Students will be able to confirm their answers in Activity 3.

🎧 62 Activity 3

- Play the audio to allow them to check their answers. Ask if they need any clarification; offer to play the audio again, if necessary.
- Put the students in pairs, and have them practice the conversations.

COMUNICA

RELAYING WHAT ANOTHER PERSON SAID

DIRECT SPEECH	INDIRECT SPEECH
"**Eres** lo mejor de **mi** vida".	➡ *Dice que soy* lo mejor de **su** vida.
"**Estuve aquí** comiendo con Ana".	➡ *Dice que estuvo allí* comiendo con Ana.
"**Creo** que **tenemos este** libro".	➡ *Dice que cree* que **tienen ese** libro.
"**Compra pan**".	➡ *Me ordena* que **compre** pan.

- To report what was said, use verbs like: **decir**, **comentar** or **confesar** (e ➡ ie).
- To repeat an order or request, use verbs like **ordenar**, **aconsejar**, **sugerir** or **recomendar** plus the present subjunctive.

> ❗ ■ The present perfect can also be used in indirect speech:
> **Ha dicho que / Me ha ordenado que...**

RELAYING WHAT ANOTHER PERSON ASKED

"¿Hicieron la tarea?".	➡ El profesor *pregunta* si hicimos la tarea.
"¿Cuándo harán la tarea?".	➡ El profesor nos *pregunta* **cuándo** haremos la tarea.

1 Report what the following people said using the expressions provided.
a. "Me acosté porque tenía sueño". ➡ Dice que ....
b. "Visita Madrid si quieres divertirte". ➡ Me recomienda ....
c. "Este libro lo escribimos entre mi mejor amigo y yo". ➡ Me confiesa ....
d. "¿Fuiste a la fiesta de Juan?". ➡ Me pregunta ....
e. "¿Dónde vive tu hermano?". ➡ Te pregunta ....

2 👥 **Marta is talking to her friend Pedro about the day she spent with their other friend Elena. Work with a partner and complete the phone conversation below.**

Marta: Elena me (a) .... que se va a cambiar de casa. Que está muy contenta porque (b) .... encontró trabajo.
Pedro: Vaya, qué suerte.
M.: Me (c) .... que realmente no está enamorada de su novio y (d) .... quiere dejarlo.
P.: La verdad es que no hacen buena pareja.
M.: Tienes razón. Por lo visto el otro día discutieron en el cine... Por cierto, me (e) .... la película que vio, (f) .... que es muy buena.
P.: Pues si quieres, vamos a verla este viernes.
M.: Bueno... ¡Ah! y también me (g) .... que cree que el mes que viene va a Ámsterdam a visitar a su hermano y a su cuñada, y me preguntó (h) .... quiero ir con ella.

3 🎧 62 **Now listen to the complete conversation and check your answers.**

226

ANSWERS

Activity 1

a. Dice que se acostó porque tenía sueño; **b.** Me recomienda que visite Madrid si quiero divertirme; **c.** Me confiesa que ese libro lo escribieron entre su mejor amigo y él/ella; **d.** Me pregunta si fui a la fiesta de Juan; **e.** Te pregunta dónde vive tu hermano.

Activity 2

a. ha dicho; **b.** ayer; **c.** ha confesado; **d.** que; **e.** ha recomendado; **f.** dice; **g.** ha dicho; **h.** si.

4 👥 **In groups of three, take turns asking each other a question. Then report back to the group what you learned.**

Modelo: E1: ¿Cuál es tu libro favorito?
　　　　E2: El señor de los anillos.
　　　　E1: Luis dice que El señor de los anillos es su libro favorito.

REPORTING INFORMATION IN THE PAST

■ The preterit can also be used to introduce reported speech, but will require additional changes in the sentence.

Direct speech information	Verb in indirect speech does not change tense	Verb in indirect speech changes tense as follows
	Dice / Ha dicho que...	*Dijo que...*
• Present	• Present ➡	• Imperfect
"Estudio español".	*...estudio español.*	*...estudiaba español.*
• Preterit	• Preterit ➡	• Preterit or Pluperfect
"Estudié español".	*...estudié español.*	*...estudió / había estudiado español.*
• Future	• Future ➡	• Conditional
"Estudiaré español".	*...estudiaré español.*	*...estudiaría español.*
• Conditional	• Conditional ➡	• Conditional
"Estudiaría español".	*...estudiaría español.*	*...estudiaría español.*
• Imperfect	• Imperfect ➡	• Imperfect
"Estudiaba español".	*...estudiaba español.*	*...estudiaba español.*
• Pluperfect	• Pluperfect ➡	• Pluperfect
"Había estudiado español".	*...había estudiado español.*	*...había estudiado español.*

Pedro dijo que le gustabas tú y no Raquel.

5 **Select the correct option.**

a. "Tienes que estudiar más".
Todos los días mi madre me dice que **tengo** / **tenía** que estudiar más.

b. "Fui al cine con mi familia".
Ayer me dijo que **iría** / **había ido** al cine con su familia.

c. "En los últimos años he ido pocas veces a la playa".
Me dijo que **va** / **había ido** pocas veces a la playa en los últimos años.

d. "Me encantaría tener otro perro".
Hoy me dice que le **encantaría** / **encantará** tener otro perro.

e. "Mañana, antes de cenar, prepararé la maleta'.
Me dijo que antes de cenar **prepararía** / **preparó** la maleta.

227

INSTRUCTIONAL STRATEGIES

Activity 4

• Put students into groups of three. Have each member of the group ask the others a question and note the responses.

• Then put students into new groups. Have each student report his/her previous group members' responses to the new group.

Alternative Activity

Play a game of "telephone." Have students sit in a circle. Each student whispers a question into the ear of the person on their right and writes down that person's response; each student also answers the question from the person to the left and writes down that person's question. Then, out loud, each student reports back on the answer from the person to their right and the question from the person to their left.

OBJECTIVES FOR COMUNICA

• Present communicative functions of the unit: Reporting information in the past

• Learn how to introduce reported speech with the preterit

CORE RESOURCES

• Extension Activities: EA 8.2

STANDARDS

　1.1　Engage in conversation
　4.1　Compare languages

INSTRUCTIONAL STRATEGIES FOR REPORTING INFORMATION IN THE PAST

• Ask students what they think happens when you introduce reported speech with a phrase in the past tense. Ask what happens in English.

• Have students open their books. Walk students through the chart contrasting sentences introduced by ***Dice que*** and ***Dijo que***.

• Point out that while no changes in tense occur to the second part of the sentence after ***Dice que***, some changes in verb tenses occur when the reported speech is introduced by ***Dijo que***. Explain that these changes occur in sentences that were originally in the future and in the preterit only. The future changes to the conditional after ***dijo que*** and the preterit changes to pluperfect.

• Depending on the level of the group and whether you think it might help them to remember, you may choose to explain that *would* (conditional) is actually the past tense of *will* (future). Also that the pluperfect (*had done*) describes the past within the past making it a logical choice to indicate that the direct speech took place place before it was reported.

Activity 5

• Have students work individually to complete the sentences. Encourage them to answer without referring to the chart.

• Monitor their progress and assist as needed.

• Go over the answers as a class.

ANSWERS

Activity 5

　a. tengo; b. había ido; c. había ido; d. encantaría; e. prepararía.

INSTRUCTIONAL STRATEGIES

Activity 6

- Distribute copies of EA 8.2, **Estilo indirecto** and have students first underline the verbs in each sentence and other words that may need to be changed such as possessive adjectives, etc. Ask students to think about the person the questions are posed to and what change needs to be made (change from **tú** to **yo** form).
- Have students work individually to convert the direct speech to indirect speech.
- Put students into pairs to compare answers (or exchange papers for peer correction). Go over the answers as a class.

Activity 7

- Give students some time to read through the questions and jot down notes for the own answers.
- Put students into pairs. Have them take turns asking and answering the questions. Monitor their conversations and assist as needed.
- Call on students to report back on interesting parts of their conversation.

OBJECTIVES FOR COMUNICA

- Present communicative functions of the unit:
  Expressing probability in the past, the present, and the future
- Practice expressing probability by speculating and making assumptions

CORE RESOURCES

- Extension Activities: EA 8.3

STANDARDS

1.1 Engage in conversation
1.2 Understand the language
4.1 Compare languages

INSTRUCTIONAL STRATEGIES FOR EXPRESSING PROBABILITY IN THE PAST, THE PRESENT AND THE FUTURE

- To introduce the theme of the section, focus students' attention on the image. Have them imagine what happened to Luis and elicit some responses. Explain that since we don't know for sure, we have to base our answers on assumptions. Write **Está enfermo** and **Estará enfermo** on the board and compare the difference between them. Explain: **En el primer caso conozco esta información y estoy 100% seguro de ella y en el segundo, desconozco la información, pero**

COMUNICA

6 Report what the following people said using indirect speech. Begin each sentence with *Dijo que* and make any necessary changes.

a. "En agosto fui a mi pueblo a ver a mis abuelos".
b. "Ayer habíamos salido de fiesta cuando nos llamaron ustedes por teléfono".
c. "Esta mañana hemos ido a tu casa pero no estabas allí".
d. "¿Quieres entrar en esta cafetería?".
e. "Creo que mañana iré al teatro con ustedes".
f. "¿Sabes que ayer estrenaron la nueva película de Brad Pitt?".
g. "Tengo que llamar a su padre antes de las cinco".
h. "Cuando tu padre era pequeño solía echarse la siesta después de comer".
i. "Todavía no he visitado el museo del Prado y llevo diez años viviendo en Madrid".

7  Prepare your answers to the following. Then take turns sharing the information with a partner.

a. ¿Quién te ha dicho algo muy bonito? ¿Qué te dijo?
b. ¿Quién te ha dicho algo que no te gustó? ¿Qué te dijo?
c. ¿Quién te ha dado el mejor consejo? ¿Qué te dijo?
d. ¿Quién te pide muchos favores? ¿Qué te pide?
e. ¿Qué te ha mandado el profesor?
f. ¿Quién te ha confesado una mentirita (*little white lie*)? ¿Qué te confesó?

> Sara me dijo que iba a ir al cine con Carlos.

EXPRESSING PROBABILITY IN THE PAST, THE PRESENT AND THE FUTURE

¿QUÉ LE PASA A LUIS?

Conozco la información	Imagino la información
Está enfermo. (Present)	➡ **Estará** enfermo. (Future)
El profesor no **ha llegado**. (Present Perfect)	➡ El profesor no **habrá llegado**. (future of **haber** + Past Participle)
No durmió anoche porque **estaba** nervioso. (Imperfect)	➡ No durmió porque **estaría** nervioso. (Conditional)
Ayer **fue** a una fiesta. (Preterit)	➡ Ayer **iría** a una fiesta. (Conditional)

■ Para hacer preguntas:

Sabemos que la persona que escucha la pregunta sabe la respuesta:	Sabemos que nadie conoce la respuesta o estamos solos
¿Qué hora **es**? (alguien tiene reloj)	➡ ¿Qué hora **será**? (nadie tiene reloj)
¿Todavía no **ha salido** el autobús?	➡ ¿Ya **habrá salido** el autobús?
¿Quién **rompió** el cristal ayer?	➡ ¿Quién **rompería** el cristal ayer?
¿Cuánta gente **había** ayer en la fiesta?	➡ ¿Cuánta gente **habría** ayer en la fiesta?

imagino que puede ocurrir esto.

- Explain that we have to use a different form of the verb when we speculate about something versus when we know something is true. Direct their attention to the first chart, and walk them through the examples. (After this explanation, you may choose to proceed with Activity 8).
- Explain that the same verb changes apply to questions when you are not sure of the answer. Again ask students to explain the difference between **¿Qué hora es?** and **¿Qué hora será?** Then walk students through the examples in the second chart. (After this explanation, you may choose to proceed with Activity 9).

8 This dog is very sad. Change the statements to make assumptions as to why he is sad.

a. Le **duele** el estómago. ➡ ....

b. **Está buscando** a su dueño. ➡ ....

c. Ayer lo **llevaron** al veterinario porque no **se encontraba** bien. ➡ ....

d. Se **perdió**. ➡ ....

9 🗣 Take turns asking and answering the following questions about the dog in Activity 8. What can you guess about his situation?

a. ¿Cómo (llamarse)? ➡ ....

b. ¿(Comer, hoy)? ➡ ....

c. ¿(Tener) dueño? ➡ ....

d. ¿(Escaparse, ayer) de la perrera (dog pound)? ➡ ....

e. ¿(Estar, ayer) con sus dueños (owners) y los (perder) de vista? ➡ ....

f. ¿Sus dueños le (abandonar, hoy) para irse de vacaciones? ➡ ....

10 🗣 With a partner, come up with some possible explanations for the following images. Describe what you think is happening now and what must have happened before.

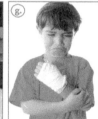

Practice what you have learned with additional materials online.

229

Previous Page

ANSWERS

Activity 6

a. Dijo que en agosto fue a su pueblo a ver a sus abuelos; b. Dijo que ayer habían salido de fiesta cuando los llamaron por teléfono; c. Dijo que esa mañana habían ido a tu casa pero que no estabas allí; d. Me preguntó si quería entrar en esa cafetería; e. Dijo que creía que mañana iría al teatro con nosotros; f. Me preguntó si sabía que ayer habían estrenado la nueva película de Brad Pitt; g. Dijo que tenía que llamar a su padre antes de las cinco; h. Me dijo que cuando mi padre era pequeño solía echarse la siesta después de comer; i. Dijo que todavía no había visitado el Museo del Prado y que llevaba 10 años viviendo en Madrid.

INSTRUCTIONAL STRATEGIES

Activity 8

• Have students work individually to transform the sentences. Encourage them to refer back to the charts for help.

• Go over the answers as a class.

Activity 9

• To prepare for this activity, you may choose to have students work individually to write the correct forms of questions first, which they can compare with a partner or you can go over as a class.

• Put students into pairs to ask and answer the questions. Have them take notes on their responses.

• Call on volunteers to share the ideas they discussed with their partners.

Activity 10

• Focus students' attention on the images. To activate schema and remind them of relevant vocabulary, ask them what they see or notice about each picture. Encourage them to first share what they *know* about each image, not what they speculate.

• Then put students into pairs to discuss their hypotheses regarding the circumstances behind each image. Have them talk about what they think is happening now and what they think must have happened before.

• Monitor their conversations and assist as needed.

• Have each pair share their favorite hypotheses with the class.

Alternative Activity

These images are also available in EA 8.3, **Hipótesis**. You can divide the class into groups and give each group a different image. Have them write about what is happening using the future, future perfect, and conditional tenses. Then exchange the pictures and descriptions between the groups and have them correct each other's work and add new ideas.

ANSWERS

Activity 8

a. dolerá; b. Estará buscando; c. llevaría, se encontraría; d. perdería.

Activity 9

a. ¿Cómo se llamará?; b. ¿Habrá comido?; c. ¿Tendrá dueño?; d. ¿Se escaparía de la perrera?; e. ¿Estaría con sus dueños y los perdería de vista?; f. ¿Sus dueños le habrán abandonado para irse de vacaciones?

OBJECTIVES FOR ¡ACCIÓN!

- Provide students with a structured approach to viewing the video
- Contextualize the content of the unit in a familiar scenario

CORE RESOURCES

- Unit Video 8
- Interactive Online Materials – ELEteca

STANDARDS

1.2 Understand the language
1.3 Present information

INSTRUCTIONAL STRATEGIES

Previewing: Antes del video

Activity 1

- Have students work individually to match the descriptions with the image.
- Go over the answers as a class. Have students explain their answers.
- Then in pairs, have students follow the correct sequence of images and create a brief conversation for each. For example, ask students to think about what Paloma could say to remind Jorge that it's her birthday tomorrow and what Jorge might say in response.
- Allow student time to practice. Then call on different pairs to present their complete versions to the class. Or assign a scene to different pairs to present in order.

Activity 2

- Have students work individually to speculate about what will happen after each scene. Have them write down their answers.
- Monitor their progress and assist as needed.
- Put students into pairs to share and compare their hypotheses.
- Call on different students to share their ideas while you list them on the board by scenes. Tell students that they will have an opportunity to confirm their hypotheses after viewing the segment.

ANSWERS

Activity 1

1. d; **2.** a; **3.** c; **4.** b.

¡ACCIÓN!

1 Match the following sentences with the scenes from the video segment.

a. Cuando Jorge llega a casa, su hermana Paloma le recuerda que mañana es su cumpleaños.

b. Los hermanos se sientan a charlar y ella insiste en recordar que mañana es su cumpleaños, después intenta que su hermano le diga cuál será su regalo.

c. De repente, llega a casa un ramo de flores.

d. Más tarde reciben nuevos mensajes…

2 Make assumptions about what you think is going to happen next using the following images.

Quizás…   Es probable que el ramo de flores…

Tal vez la carta sea…

Es posible que su hermano…

DURANTE EL VIDEO

3 Watch the video and check to see if your hypothesis was correct.

DESPUÉS DEL VIDEO

4 Answer true (T) or false (F).

	T	F
a. Al inicio de la conversación la hermana quiere que su hermano la invite a cenar.	☐	☐
b. Paloma fue muy generosa y puntual con el regalo de cumpleaños de su hermano.	☐	☐
c. Jorge no le quiere decir cuál será su regalo pero le da algunas pistas para que ella lo averigüe.	☐	☐
d. Paloma decide buscar el regalo de su hermano mientras él no está.	☐	☐
e. El ramo de flores es un regalo de sus compañeros de clase.	☐	☐
f. La madre llega con una tarjeta de felicitación que Paloma no había tomado del buzón.	☐	☐
g. Paloma cree que sus compañeros y sus tíos son un desastre con las fechas.	☐	☐
h. El hermano de Paloma insiste en no decirle cuál será su regalo.	☐	☐
i. La madre ayuda a Paloma a decidir qué le va a regalar su hermano.	☐	☐

5 **Think of a present for your partner and ask questions to guess what he/she is going to give you.**

Modelo: E1: A ver... ¿Es algo para hacer deporte?
E2: Sí.
E1: Entonces... será una raqueta de tenis, que es mi deporte favorito.
E2: ...

Practice what you have learned with additional materials online.

231

INSTRUCTIONAL STRATEGIES

Viewing: Durante el video
Activity 3
- Tell students that they are going to watch and listen to the video to find out if their hypotheses in Activity 2 were correct.
- Play the video, stopping it after each scene in Activity 2. Ask questions to check their understanding of what indeed happened next in each case. Then take a tally of how many students had the correct hypotheses.

AFTER VIEWING: DESPUÉS DEL VIDEO
Activity 4
- Have students work individually –or in the same pairs as Activity 3– to read the statements about each character and answer whether they are true or false.
- Monitor students' progress. Play the video again, if necessary.
- Go over the answers as a class.

Activity 5
- Go over the instructions.
- Put students into pairs. Have students write down their ideas for a birthday gift for their partners, but tell them not to let their partners see their ideas. Then have students ask and answer questions to try to guess what birthday presents they're going to give to each other. Encourage them to ask at least six questions before revealing their gift ideas.
- Monitor their conversations and assist as needed.
- Have students report back on whether or not they correctly guessed their gifts and whether or not they liked them.

ANSWERS
Activity 4
a. F; b. F; c. T; d. F; e. F; f. T; g. T; h. T; i. F.

OBJECTIVES FOR Cartas formales y celulares

- Present vocabulary needed to practice communicative and grammatical functions for the unit: Letter-writing and cell phone issues
- Learn the parts of a formal letter to write a letter of complaint
- Use language associated with cell phones to talk about what can go wrong

CORE RESOURCES

- Audio Program: Track 63
- Interactive Online Materials – ELEteca

STANDARDS

1.2 Understand the language
3.1 Knowledge of other disciplines

INSTRUCTIONAL STRATEGIES

Activity 1

- Before students open their books, activate students' schema about formal letters. Ask questions, such as: **¿Han escrito alguna vez una carta? ¿Cuándo fue y para qué? ¿En qué situación o por qué escribirían una carta formal?**
- Have students open their books. Put them in pairs to work together to try to identify the different parts of a formal letter. Point out the language box as a reminder for where some parts go.
- Monitor their progress and assist as needed.
- Go over the answers as a class. Ask students to explain in Spanish such terms as: **el remitente (la persona que escribe la carta), el destinatario (la persona a quien va dirigida la carta / la persona que va a recibir la carta), despedida (decir adiós)**, and so on.

Activity 2

- Go over the instructions. Encourage students to begin by first writing down the name of the section (using the phrases from Activity 1) and then numbering them in the order in which they should appear. Have students work individually to put the letter in order.
- Monitor their progress and assist as needed.
- Go over the answers as a class, calling on students to read each section of the letter aloud.

ANSWERS

Activity 1

a. 5; **b.** 2; **c.** 7; **d.** 4; **e.** 1; **f.** 6; **g.** 3.

Activity 2

Fecha, 3; Dirección del destinatario, 2; Despedida, 6; Dirección del remitente, 1; Motivo, 5; Saludo, 4; Firma, 7.

1 Identify the parts of a formal letter according to the sample letter on the right. Use word families to guess at unfamiliar words.

a. ☐ motivo e. ☐ dirección del remitente
b. ☐ dirección del destinatario f. ☐ despedida
c. ☐ firma g. ☐ fecha
d. ☐ saludo

■ Remember, the sender's address always goes first in a formal letter, followed by the date.

2 Arrange the elements of this letter, sent by a customer to his cell phone carrier, in the correct order. Then identify what part of the letter each one belongs to. The first one has been done for you.

Bogotá, 13 de enero de 2014

Movilindo
Paseo de la Antena, 33
110988 Bogotá

Atentamente,

Juan Mora
C/ Cliente, 130
117592 Bogotá

Dirección del remitente

Les escribo esta carta porque llevo varios días teniendo problemas con mi teléfono celular. Hace cinco meses me regalaron un nuevo **aparato** por llevar como cliente en su empresa más de tres años. Pues bien, este **celular** no deja de darme problemas. A continuación les explico punto por punto cada uno de ellos. La **pantalla táctil** no funciona bien. Cada vez que intento marcar un número, el teléfono se apaga. En muchos lugares no **tiene cobertura**. Es decir, que cuando salgo de la ciudad tengo muy poca señal y no puedo ni **llamar** ni **recibir llamadas**. Cuando puedo llamar, **se corta** la **conversación** después de dos minutos. Además, cuando intento **cargar el teléfono**, la **batería** solo dura cinco horas y, después, tengo que cargarlo otra vez. Al principio pensé que era problema del **cargador**, pero he probado con otro y sigo teniendo el mismo problema. Debido a todos estos inconvenientes, espero que me cambien el **celular** o me regalen uno nuevo. En caso contrario cambiaré de compañía telefónica.

Estimados señores:

Next Page

INSTRUCTIONAL STRATEGIES

Activity 3

- Direct students' attention to the phrases highlighted in orange in the letter on the previous page. Confirm their understanding as to which one refers to the greeting and which to the closing parts of a letter. Have them write the words in the appropriate columns of the chart.
- Have students work individually to sort the other greetings and closings in the word box.
- Monitor their progress and assist as needed.
- Go over the answers as a class.

3 The highlighted words in the letter are examples of a formal greeting and closing for business letters or correspondence. List the following greetings and closings in the appropriate column.

> Distinguido señor/a o Se despide atentamente o Muy señor/a mío/a
> Reciba un cordial saludo o Señor/a o En espera de sus noticias o Cordialmente

Saludos	Despedidas

4 Match the expressions to their correct definition.

1. el aparato .... •
2. la pantalla táctil .... •
3. cobertura .... •
4. recibir llamadas .... •
5. se corta .... •
6. cargar .... •
7. el cargador .... •
8. la batería .... •

- • **a.** Acumula electricidad.
- • **b.** Intrumento que conecta la electricidad con la batería.
- • **c.** Instrumento o mecanismo que tiene una función determinada.
- • **d.** Acción de recuperar la batería.
- • **e.** Una de las funciones principales de un celular.
- • **f.** Extensión geográfica de los servicios de telecomunicaciones.
- • **g.** Cuando se pierde una llamada.
- • **h.** Parte de algunos aparatos electrónicos que funciona con el contacto.

5 🗨 Talk to your partner about the following situations.

a. ¿Has tenido problemas con tu teléfono celular? ¿Cuáles?
b. ¿Los solucionaste? ¿Cómo?
c. ¿Cuáles son algunas otras quejas *(complaints)* que tienes con tu celular o el servicio que recibes?
d. ¿Cómo sería tu celular ideal?

6 🎧 63 **Now listen to the conversation between Movilindo's director and his secretary, and explain the director's plan of action.**

....
....
....
....

233

Instructional Strategies

Activity 4

- To introduce the vocabulary relating to cell phones, have students search for terms in the letter that fit the following categories: **Sinónimos**, **Acciones**, **Partes**. Start with the first word in boldface (***aparato***) and ask students to select the correct category (**Sinónimos**) and continue to work through the list.
- Then have students work individually to match the phrases in Activity 4. Encourage them to go back to the letter to see the words in context and better deduce their meanings. Go over the answer as a class.

Activity 5

- Before starting the activity, have students turn back to the letter and ask students to explain the customer's reason for writing it.
- Tell students that they are going to have discussions in pairs and that they should be prepared to report back on their partners' responses using indirect speech. Encourage them to take notes.
- Put students into pairs to ask and answer the questions. Then have students change partner's and report on their previous partner's responses.

🎧 63 Activity 6

- Go over the instructions. Point out that Movilindo is the same company that Juan Mora was writing to about his cell phone on the previous page.
- Play the audio. Give students time to write their responses.
- Call on a volunteer to share the director's plan. Have the class confirm whether or not they heard and understood the same course of action. If it seems like many of them did not hear the director's plan, play the audio again.

See audioscript on page APP4

Answers

Activity 3

Saludos: Distinguido señor/a, Muy señor/a mío/a, Señor/a; **Despedidas:** Se despide atentamente, Reciba un cordial saludo, En espera de sus noticias, Cordialmente.

Activity 4

1. c; **2.** h; **3.** f; **4.** e; **5.** g; **6.** d; **7.** b; **8.** a.

Activity 6

Answers will vary. Possible answers might include the following:

El director le dice a la secretaria que no se preocupe, que él mismo se pondrá en contacto con el departamento comercial y que le escribirán un correo disculpándose. También que le ofrecerán un móvil más moderno que no dé problemas.

OBJECTIVES FOR LOS CORREOS ELECTRÓNICOS

- Present vocabulary needed to practice communicative and grammatical functions for the unit: email language and expressions
- Practice reading and responding to emails
- Learn how to say common electronic symbols

STANDARDS

1.2 Understand the language

1.3 Present information

INSTRUCTIONAL STRATEGIES

Activity 7

- Go over the instructions. Focus students' attention on the email. Ask questions to have them engage with its parts, such as: **¿Cuál es el saludo? ¿Cuál es la despedida? ¿A quién está escribiendo Movilindo? ¿De qué está escribiendo?**
- Before they read, consider posing a question to focus their reading, such as: **¿Qué le pide el director a Juan Mora?**
- Have students read the email quietly to themselves. Elicit a response to the question you posed.

Activity 8

- Have students work individually or in pairs to match the symbols with their meaning and then go over the answers as a class.
- Put students into pairs, if they are not already, to take turns reading the email from Activity 7 aloud to each other, using the correct words for the symbols.

Culture Note

Websites from Spain end in *.es*, which is read aloud as *punto es*.

Activity 9

- Go over the instructions. As a class, elicit ideas as to other possible responses that the director of Movilindo might give to Juan Mora.
- Give students some time to brainstorm additional ideas for their own responses. Remind them to refer back to Juan Mora's initial letter in Activity 2 and respond to his specific complaints.
- Have students work individually to write their own responses to Juan Mora.
- Have students exchange emails with a partner.

Activity 10

- Have students read their partner's emails from Activity 9. You may want to have them first correct any errors they notice.
- Put students into small groups to report back on their partner's email using indirect speech.

---

7 Read the response from Movilindo.

> Asunto: Nuevo celular
>
> De: movilindo@mundoreal.es   Para: juanmora@edimail.com
>
> Estimado cliente:
> Nos dirigimos a usted con la finalidad de expresarle nuestras disculpas por los problemas causados. Comprendemos perfectamente las molestias que puede haber tenido con el último celular que recibió y, por esa razón, ponemos a su disposición un nuevo modelo. Por favor, para recibir este nuevo aparato mándenos un correo electrónico con la dirección donde quiere recibirlo a *movilindo-aparatos@mundoreal.es*. Si desea ver el modelo que le ofrecemos, puede hacer clic en el siguiente enlace: *www.movilesmovilindo/nuevos*.
> Atentamente,
> Movilindo
> Paseo de la Antena, 33
> 110988 Bogotá

8 Match the following symbols to their meaning.

1. @ .... •
2. / .... •
3. : .... •
4. .. .. •
5. _ .... •
6. .com •
7. www •

- **a.** guion *(hyphen)*
- **b.** punto com
- **c.** arroba
- **d.** triple doble ve
- **e.** barra
- **f.** dos puntos
- **g.** guion bajo

9 As Movilindo's director, write a different response to your customer. Then exchange emails with a partner.

> Asunto: Nuevo celular
>
> De: movilindo@mundoreal.es   Para: juanmora@edimail.com
>
> Estimado señor Mora:

10 Read your partner's email and relay the message to the class.

Modelo: El director de Movilindo dice que...

Practice what you have learned with additional materials online.

- Finally, have students return the emails back to the original writers so that they can see any corrections that were made.
- As a class, discuss the most common responses and rank how effective they are from a customer service point of view.

ANSWERS

Activity 8

1. c; **2.** e; **3.** f; **4.** a; **5.** g; **6.** b; **7.** d.

GRAMÁTICA

UNIDAD **8**

1. HYPOTHETICAL EXPRESSIONS WITH THE INDICATIVE

■ Other ways to express hypothesis or probability using the indicative:

Creo / Me parece		ese modelo de celular no **es** uno de los mejores.
Me imagino / Supongo	**que**	si está en la sierra no **tendrá** cobertura, llámalo mañana.
Para mí / Yo diría		**llovió** anoche, las calles están mojadas.

A lo mejor / Lo mismo / Igual *(maybe)*	**es** un problema de tu compañía porque yo sí tengo cobertura.

> **!** ■ **Suponer** *(to suppose)* is conjugated like the verb **poner.**

1 **Edu has found a house he is interested in buying but would like more information about it. Fill in the blanks with the correct form of the verbs from the list.**

> vivir ○ poder ○ querer ○ tener ○ haber ○ costar ○ pertenecer

Me encantaría comprar esta casa, pero antes me gustaría tener información sobre ella. **Supongo que** (a) .... muchísimo dinero, pero **creo que** mis padres (b) .... ayudarme. Parece una casa grande, **me imagino que** .... más de tres habitaciones y al menos dos baños. **Lo mismo** en algún baño (d) .... un jacuzzi, sería genial. **Yo diría que** antes (e) .... una familia numerosa, **a lo mejor** la (f) .... vender para irse a vivir a otra ciudad. **Igual** la parte de atrás (g) .... también a la casa y hay una piscina y todo, quién sabe.

2  **Look at the following images and write three explanations for each situation using the expressions you have just learned. Then, in groups of three, take turns exchanging your impressions.**

¿Por qué no hay nadie?	¿Por qué está llorando?	¿Qué le pasa?
a.	a.	a. ....
b.	b.	b. ....
c.	c.	c. ....

235

OBJECTIVES FOR GRAMÁTICA 1

• Present grammatical structures needed to practice communicative functions of the unit:
Hypothetical expressions with the indicative

• Learn and practice using hypothetical expressions with the indicative

CORE RESOURCES

• Audio Program: Track 64
• Interactive Online Materials – ELEteca

STANDARDS

> 1.1 Understand the language
> 4.1 Compare languages

INSTRUCTIONAL STRATEGIES

1. Hypothetical Expressions with the Indicative

• Before presenting the grammar, elicit ways to express hypotheses, to speculate, or to imagine that students have already been using and that do not require use of the future or conditional tenses (**creo que**, **pienso que**, etc.).You may want to write some of their ideas on the board.

• Go over the examples of hypothetical expressions with the indicative in the book. Then have students write down a hypothesis using one of the expressions in the chart. Give students a topic such as the weather (**el tiempo**), an important game coming up (**el partido**, **el campeonato**), the next episode of a popular series (**el próximo capítulo de la serie**…). Then ask them to share their hypotheses with the class or with a partner. Guide any necessary corrections.

Activity 1

Have students work individually to complete the sentences with the correct forms of the verbs in the word box. Remind them to refer to the chart above for help. Go over the answers as a class.

Activity 2

• Focus students' attention on the images. Elicit descriptions of what they see to help activate relevant vocabulary.
• Put students into small groups. Encourage them to discuss their ideas before writing them.
• Have a member from each group present their ideas to the class. Guide any necessary corrections.

ANSWERS

Activity 1

> **a.** cuesta / costará; **b.** pueden / podrán; **c.** tiene; **d.** hay; **e.** vivía; **f.** quieren; **g.** pertenece.

Activity 2

> Answers will vary. Possible answers might include the following:
> **Imagen 1:** Supongo que es la hora del descanso; Igual se ha confundido y es fiesta; Me imagino que llegarán tarde; **Imagen 2:** Creo que el novio la ha dejado plantada; Igual se le ha roto el vestido; Para mí que es la emoción; **Imagen 3:** Creo que está enfermo; Para mí que tiene dolor de tripa; Lo mismo ha comido algo en malas condiciones.

INSTRUCTIONAL STRATEGIES

🎧 64 Activity 3

- Tell students that they are going to listen to the end of three arguments. To focus their listening, have them write down key words or phrases that they hear.
- Play the first part of the audio. Then put students into pairs. Have them share the key words or phrases that they heard with a partner and give them time to write their hypotheses as to the cause of each argument. Remind them to use the expressions they just learned.
- Have a member from each pair write their hypotheses on the board. Go over the hypotheses as a class.
- Play the complete conversations. As a class, discuss which, if any, of the hypotheses on the board were correct.

See audioscript on page APP4

OBJECTIVES FOR GRAMÁTICA 2

- Present grammatical structures needed to practice communicative functions of the unit:
- Hypothetical expressions with the indicative and the subjunctive
- Use the indicative or subjunctive to express how certain you feel

CORE RESOURCES

- Audio program: Track 65

STANDARDS

1.1   Engage in conversation
1.2   Understand the language
4.1   Compare languages

INSTRUCTIONAL STRATEGIES

2. Hypothetical Expressions with the Indicative and the Subjunctive

🎧 65 Activity 4

- Before playing the audio, explain that there are some expressions for hypothetical situations that can use the indicative or the subjunctive forms of the verbs, but they have different connotations. Tell students that for now just listen to the conversations and fill in the missing expressions in the first column of the chart. Point out that the expressions will be repeated in different conversations in case they miss them the first time.
- Play the audio and go over the answers as a class, listing them on the board.
- Write out the sample sentences with **Probablemente** and the indicative, then with the subjunctive. Ask students to identify which sentence expresses that the speaker is more confident or certain about the outcome than the other.
- Give other examples from the audio (recited aloud), and

GRAMÁTICA

3 🎧 64 👥 Listen to the end of three arguments. Then, with a partner, provide a hypothesis about the reason that started them. Afterwards, listen to the complete conversation and check your answers. Were you right?

a. ....
b. ....
c. ....

2. HYPOTHETICAL EXPRESSIONS WITH THE INDICATIVE AND THE SUBJUNCTIVE

4 🎧 65 👥 Listen to the following conversations and complete the chart with the missing expressions.

Probablemente / .... Seguramente / .... Tal vez		la compañía telefónica **se pone** / **se ponga** en contacto conmigo después de mi reclamación. (indicativo/subjuntivo)
.... / **Es probable** **Puede ser** /	que	mi celular **tenga** algún defecto de fábrica, me lo compré hace poco y no me dura nada la batería. (subjuntivo)

- With the first group of expressions, the use of the indicative or the subjunctive depends on how certain the speaker feels that the action will take place.
  - **Problablemente** la compañía telefónica **se pone** en contacto conmigo.
    (Speaker feels there's a strong likelihood the company will contact him / her = indicative)
  - **Problablemente** la compañía telefónica **se ponga** en contacto conmigo.
    (Speaker feels there is less likelihood that the company will contact him / her = subjunctive)

5 Choose the correct option in each sentence. In some cases, both options are correct.
a. Es probable que mañana **llueve** / **llueva**.
b. Seguramente **tiene** / **tenga** más de veinte años.
c. Tal vez **viene** / **venga** mi hermana conmigo.
d. Es posible que **consigue** / **consiga** el trabajo.
e. Quizás no **quiere** / **quiera** trabajar con nosotros.
f. Puede ser que **necesitan** / **necesiten** nuestra ayuda.
g. No le hagas caso, posiblemente lo **hace** / **haga** para molestarte.
h. Puede que mañana **vamos** / **vayamos** a la playa.

6 Write your own endings to the following sentences.
a. ¡Qué raro que no haya llegado Juan! Él es muy puntual. Es posible que...
b. La compañía telefónica me está cobrando un servicio que no utilizo. Seguramente...
c. Me dijo que me iba a llamar esta tarde pero no lo ha hecho todavía. Tal vez...
d. Le he escrito un correo electrónico y no le ha llegado aún. Puede que...
e. He salido de casa y cuando he entrado en el metro no llevaba el monedero. Probablemente...
f. No encuentro mis gafas por ningún sitio. Quizás...

have students identify whether you feel confident about the outcome based on how you express it.
- Continue going over the examples of hypothetical expressions that must use the subjunctive. Point out that both **quizás** and **quizá** are considered correct
- Play the conversations again and encourage students to listen for the form of the verb that follows the expressions.

See audioscript on page APP5

ANSWERS

Activity 4

Posiblemente, Quizás (con indicativo/subjuntivo); Es posible, Puede (con subjuntivo).

7 Complete the following sentences using what you learned about expressing hypothesis and probability. ¡Atención! Be sure to use the correct form of the verb.

a. Es probable que (ser) .... su cumpleaños porque invitó a cenar a todos sus amigos.

b. Igual (mudarse, él) .... Hace mucho tiempo que quería cambiar de casa.

c. Quizás (comprarse, yo) .... un teléfono celular nuevo. Este ya no funciona.

d. A lo mejor Juan (ser) .... alérgico a los gatos. No para de estornudar.

e. Posiblemente yo (organizar) .... la fiesta. Soy su mejor amigo.

f. Yo diría que Carmen y Sonia (estar) .... enfadadas. Ya nunca van juntas.

g. Seguramente (ganar) .... el premio. Está haciendo un buen trabajo.

h. Me parece que Carlos no (estar) .... contento con su nuevo trabajo.

i. Puede que (saber) .... hablar italiano. Vivió un tiempo en Roma.

j. » ¡Qué raro que Pepe no esté todavía aquí! Es muy puntual.
» Oye, lo mismo (pasarle) .... algo. ¿Lo llamamos al celular?

8 Talk to a classmate about what you are planning to do for the following events or situations. Indicate that your plans are not certain by using the appropriate expression.

Tu próximo cumpleaños	Tus próximas vacaciones	Tus próximos estudios

9 Prepare a brief description of what you think your classmate's life will be like when he/she is 50. Include information such as: profession, family, where he/she lives, what he/she looks like, etc. Then exchange impressions. Were you surprised? Do you think your partner's description of you is accurate?

Modelo: *Cuando tengas 50 años, es probable que / seguramente...*

Practice what you have learned with additional materials online.

Previous Page

Extension

To exploit the audio further, you may choose to develop questions that check students' general and specific comprehension of the conversations – with less emphasis on the target grammar structures and more on the content.

INSTRUCTIONAL STRATEGIES

Activity 5

• Have students work individually to select the correct answers. Remind them to think about what the expressions mean rather than having to memorize the chart.

• Go over the answers as a class. Guide any necessary corrections.

Activity 6

• Have students work individually to complete the sentences with their own ideas.

• Put students into small groups to share their ideas. Encourage them to explain the reasoning for their own hypotheses and respond to each other's ideas.

ANSWERS

Activity 5

a. llueva; **b.** tiene / tenga; **c.** viene / venga; **d.** consiga; **e.** quiere / quiera; **f.** necesiten; **g.** hace / haga; **h.** vayamos.

INSTRUCTIONAL STRATEGIES

Activity 7

• Have students work individually to complete the sentences and then compare their answers with a partner. Encourage students to peer correct.

• Go over the answers as a class.

Activity 8

• Before putting students into pairs, give them some time to brainstorm and jot down ideas in each category. Remind them to use appropriate expressions to indicate how certain they are or aren't about their plans.

• Have students report back on one of their partner's plans.

Activity 9

• Model a pre-writing technique on the board: create a mind map (or word web) using the categories in the instructions. Write the name of a famous young person in the center. Have students imagine what he or she will be like at age 50. Elicit their ideas, and write them in the mind map on the board.

• Give students time to create their own mind maps before they write. Monitor their progress and assist as needed.

• Focusing their attention back on the board, discuss how they can use their mind maps to create a paragraph. Call on a volunteer to convert one of the notes on the board into a sentence.

• Give students time to write their descriptions. Monitor their progress and assist as needed.

• Once completed, have students exchange their descriptions with their partners. Then have students report back on whether or not they think their partner's descriptions of them are accurate and explain why or why not.

ANSWERS

Activity 7

a. sea; **b.** se ha mudado / se mudó; **c.** me compre / me compro; **d.** es; **e.** organice / organizo; **f.** están; **g.** gana / gane; **h.** está; **i.** sepa; **j.** le pasa / ha pasado.

OBJECTIVES FOR DESTREZAS

- Simulate multiple choice testing formats in preparation for international testing certificates as the DELE (*Diploma de Español como Lengua Extranjera*) or in preparation for other state and/or national assessments
- Use strategies presented throughout the units

CORE RESOURCES

- Extension Activity: EA 8.4

STANDARDS

1.1 Engage in conversation

1.3 Present information

2.1 Practices and perspectives

INSTRUCTIONAL STRATEGIES

Comprensión de gramática y vocabulario

Activity 1

- Before reading the letter, activate students' schema about parties and party planning by asking questions, such as: *¿Les gustan las fiestas? ¿Les gusta preparar y organizar las fiestas? En su opinión, ¿qué cosas son necesarias para tener una buena fiesta?*
- Go over the instructions. Have students work individually to choose the correct answers.
- Monitor their progress and assist as needed.
- Put students into pairs to compare answers. Have them reach agreement in the cases where they selected different answers.
- Go over the answers as a class. Have students taking turns reading the paragraphs aloud. Guide any necessary corrections.

INSTRUCTIONAL STRATEGIES

Expresión e interacción orales

Activity 2

- Go over the instructions. Have students work individually to write their own responses to the questions.
- Put students into pairs to share their ideas. Encourage them to take notes on their partner's responses, as they will be asked to report back on them.
- As a model, call on a volunteer to report back on his or her partner's response to the first question. Encourage him or her to use reported speech.
- Then put students into new pairs and have them report on their previous partner's responses.

ANSWERS

Activity 1

a. en; **b.** para; **c.** asistan; **d.** vayas; **e.** Puede que; **f.** buena; **g.** están / estén; **h.** había; **i.** bailen; **j.** seguramente.

DESTREZAS

COMPRENSIÓN DE GRAMÁTICA Y VOCABULARIO

1 Read the response a reader received to his letter asking for advice. Then, choose the correct option from the choices provided.

Una fiesta inolvidable

Querido amigo Álex:

Si estás pensado (a) **de** / **en** / **para** preparar una fiesta para impresionar a tu familia y amigos, a continuación te daremos algunos consejos (b) **para** / **por** / **en** convertir esa celebración en algo inolvidable.

En primer lugar, deberás ponerte en contacto con las personas a las que quieres invitar para decidir el día. Un mensaje de texto o un correo electrónico masivo será la forma más rápida de hacerlo. Lo mejor será proponer un día del fin de semana, ya que es más probable que (c) **asisten** / **asistirán** / **asistan** más personas si no hay que madrugar al día siguiente.

Al menos un par de días antes del evento deberás ir al supermercado para comprar todo lo que necesitas cuando (d) **ve** / **irás** / **vayas** a preparar la comida.

Piensa en sorprender a tus invitados con originales bocadillos. Además, es importante que haya gran variedad de ellos para satisfacer los gustos y exigencias de todos. (e) **Tal vez** / **Quizás** / **Puede que** alguno sea vegetariano, que otro no coma ciertos productos o incluso que haya algún alérgico a cualquier alimento.

Otra cosa importante para causar (f) **buen** / **buena** / **grande** impresión es la decoración. Igual los globos y las guirnaldas de las tiendas (g) **están** / **estén** / **sean** ya muy vistos, así que te recomendamos que crees tú mismo tu propia decoración, no hay nada como un toque personal para impresionarlos.

Y la música, por supuesto; alguien dijo una vez que no (h) **hubo** / **había** / **habría** fiesta que mereciera tal nombre sin música. Para que todos (i) **bailan** / **bailen** / **bailarán** sin parar, te recomendamos que la música sea movida y sobre todo variada, por aquello de la diversidad de gustos que ya te comentábamos.

Las canciones lentas resérvalas para el final, (j) **igual** / **seguramente** / **imaginamos que** sean la excusa perfecta para aquellos que quieran sacar a bailar a alguna muchacha.

¡Ah! y sentimos decirte que, por muy cansado que estés, deberás ser el último en retirarte.

Si sigues todos estos pasos, te convertirás en el rey de las fiestas.

EXPRESIÓN E INTERACCIÓN ORALES

2 Answer the following questions about yourself.

a. ¿Te gustan las fiestas? ¿Qué tipo de fiestas son las que más te gustan?

b. ¿Prefieres las fiestas en casa, o en locales o discotecas? ¿Por qué?

c. ¿Te gusta invitar a tus amigos a una fiesta o prefieres que te inviten?

d. ¿Cuál es la última fiesta a la que fuiste? ¿Cómo fue?

3 👥 **With a partner, role-play the following situation.**

Te invitaron a una fiesta en un restaurante. Cuando llegas, el portero no te deja entrar porque dice que vas con zapatillas de deporte. En la invitación no se especifica cómo hay que ir vestido. Solicitas hablar con el encargado del restaurante. Cuando salga, exponle tu queja contándole lo que te dijo el portero y lo que no dice la invitación.

PRONUNCIACIÓN Palabras con diferente significado

1 **Read the conversation on the left and then fill in the blanks to complete the explanation on the right.**

1. » ¿**A dónde / adónde** podemos ir a almorzar?
   » **A donde / adonde** tú quieras.
   » ¿**Dónde** decías que hacían esas quesadillas tan buenas?
   » ¡Ah! Te refieres al sitio **donde** te conté que fui con Marcos.

(a) dónde / adónde o (a) donde / adonde
• Usamos el adverbio (a) .... para indicar lugar y (b) .... o (c) .... indistintamente cuando indicamos también dirección o destino mediante la preposición **a**.
• Usamos (d) ...., (e) .... o (f) .... cuando las formas anteriores son exclamativas o interrogativas.

2. » No entiendo el **porqué** de su reacción, no me lo explico.
   » Pues yo creo que actuó así **porque** no podía más y al final explotó.
   » Pero, ¿**por qué** no le dijo a nadie que necesitaba ayuda?
   » Es que es muy orgulloso y le da pena reconocerlo.
   » Yo voto **por que** hablemos con él y le ofrezcamos nuestra ayuda.

porque / porqué / por que / por qué
• Usamos (a) .... para expresar la causa o motivo de lo que se expresa a continuación y (b) .... para preguntar por esa causa o motivo.
• Usamos (c) .... cuando nos referimos al sustantivo que significa "la causa, el motivo o la razón".
• Usamos (d) .... para referirnos a la preposición **por** seguida del pronombre **que**.

3. » Su **sino** no es quedarse quieto viendo la vida pasar, **sino** llegar muy lejos.
   » Tienes razón, no solo es muy decidido, **sino** también muy trabajador.
   » **Si no** cambia será alguien muy importante en el futuro, tal vez un político.
   » Sí, además sabe escuchar, tiene carisma, es elegante y, **asimismo**, discreto.
   » Sí, pues **así mismo** se lo haremos saber cuando lo veamos.

sino / si no
• Usamos (a) .... como sustantivo que significa "destino"; para introducir una información que reemplaza o sustituye a la negada en la oración precedente.
• Usamos (b) .... para referirnos a la conjunción condicional **si** seguida del adverbio negativo **no**.

asimismo / así mismo
• Usamos (c) .... en el sentido de "también" y (d) .... en el sentido de "de la misma manera".

 Practice what you have learned with additional materials online.

INSTRUCTIONAL STRATEGIES

Activity 3

• Go over the situation with the class.
• Put students into pairs. Instead of role playing the situation right away, you may want to have students write a script together. Encourage them to write a conversation in which each of them speaks at least three times.
• Monitor their progress and assist as needed.
• Have each pair –or volunteers– perform their conversations in front of the class.

Extension

For additional writing practice, pass out copies of EA 8.4, **Expresión e interacción escritas**. Tell students to use the images in part 1 to write a narrative and to respond to the questions in part 2 with their own likes and preferences.

OBJECTIVES FOR PRONUNCIACIÓN

• Distinguish words with similar spellings or pronunciations but with different meanings

CORE RESOURCES

• Interactive Online Materials – ELEteca

STANDARDS

    1.2   Understand the language
    4.1   Compare languages

INSTRUCTIONAL STRATEGIES

Activity 1

• Explain that there are some words in Spanish that sound very similar –and are sometimes spelled exactly same, apart from a space or an accent mark– but have different meanings.
• Go over the instructions. Read the first group of sentences together. Elicit the answer to item **a**. Have the student explain his or her answer and identify which sample sentence from the group illustrates that usage.
• Have students work individually or in pairs to complete the other items related to the first group only. Monitor their progress and assist as needed. Go over the answers as a class. Guide any necessary corrections.
• Continue the same process of the second and third group of sample sentences.

ANSWERS

Activity 1

    1. a. donde; **b.** a donde; **c.** adonde; **d.** dónde; **e.** a dónde; **f.** adónde; **2. a.** porque; **b.** por qué; **c.** porqué; **d.** por que; **3. a.** sino; **b.** si no;
    4. a. asimismo; **b.** así mismo.

OBJECTIVES FOR SABOR HISPANO

- Learn about Hispanic soap operas
- Compare soap operas from the Spanish-speaking world to the United States

CORE RESOURCES

- Audio Program: Track 66

STANDARDS

2.2   Products and perspectives

4.2   Compare cultures

INSTRUCTIONAL STRATEGIES

🎧 66

- Write the word **telenovela** on the board. Elicit a definition and examples from the class.
- Put students in pairs to discuss the questions in the **Antes de leer** box.
- Monitor their conversations and assist as needed.
- Call on volunteers to report back on their discussions.
- Focus students' attention on the image at the top of the page and its captions. Ask who she is, where she is from, and why she is famous.
- Before playing the audio, pose a question or two to the class to focus their listening, such as: **¿Qué reflejan las telenovelas? ¿Cuál es una función importante de las telenovelas?** You can also give students a moment to locate and skim the glossary on the next page to prepare them for unfamiliar vocabulary in the text and throughout the lesson.
- Either have students close their books while they listen or follow along with the text in the book.
- Elicit responses to the target questions. Have them find the answers in the text.

Cultural Note

In addition to being dubbed the Queen of Latin Pop for her wildly successful singing and musical career, Thalía earned herself another title as the Queen of Telenovelas by accruing enormous sucess as an actress as well. Her first major role was in the telenovela **Quinceañera** in 1987, and her first lead role was in the telenovela **Luz y Sombra** in 1989. Her most popular role, however, was in the telenovela **María Mercedes** in 1992, the first of a trilogy of telenovelas which also included **Marimar** in 1994 and **María la del Barrio** in 1995. Her telenovelas have been aired in over 180 countries and seen by over 2 billion people.

SABOR HISPANO

UN MUNDO DE NOVELA

Thalia, cantante y actriz mexicana, conocida como ela reina de las telenovelas».

Antes de leer

¿Qué programas de televisión te gustan? ¿Por qué? ¿Sueles ver alguna telenovela de la televisión norteamericana? ¿Has visto alguna telenovela en español? ¿Qué sabes de estas telenovelas?

🎧 66   **La telenovela es una expresión cultural típica del mundo hispano. En estos programas de televisión no faltan dramas, villanos... ¡ni capítulos!**

Las telenovelas son programas de televisión dramáticos. Pero no son cualquier programa: están estrechamente° conectadas con la forma de ser de los países hispanos. Las historias de las telenovelas reflejan las tradiciones, las aspiraciones y, muchas veces, los temas de actualidad de la sociedad que las mira. «Las telenovelas son exitosas porque generan emoción y entretenimiento», explica Nora Mazziotti, investigadora argentina y autora de libros sobre telenovelas.

Aunque cada telenovela tiene una historia diferente, hay elementos comunes que están presentes en todas ellas. Suelen tener entre 100 y 200 capítulos. Hay un galán° (normalmente, rico) y una heroína (normalmente, pobre). Hay una villana que hace todo lo posible por separarlos. Y hay varios personajes secundarios que aportan° historias divertidas, para equilibrar° el melodrama de la historia central.

Cada país latinoamericano produce telenovelas con un estilo distinto. «Las telenovelas mexicanas son las más tradicionales: son muy conservadoras.

Las brasileñas tienen elementos modernos. Las colombianas tienen historias muy creativas. Las argentinas suelen tener toques de comedia», dice Mazziotti.

Además de entretener, una importante función de las telenovelas es educar. Muchas de las historias incorporan personajes que atraviesan° enfermedades graves, o viven situaciones serias como la decisión de adoptar un hijo o la pérdida° de un trabajo.

Las telenovelas son famosas por sus escenas dramáticas.

240

Los mejores finales de las villanas

1. **Catalina Creel** (*Cuna de Lobos*, 1987). Tomó veneno, se vistió elegantemente y declaró que, a pesar de usar un parche° en el ojo derecho, veía perfectamente con los dos.

2. **Soraya Montenegro** de la Vega (*María la del barrio*, 1996). Quiso encerrar a los protagonistas en una casa en llamas° y quedó atrapada en el incendio°.

3. **Valeria del Castillo** (*Rosalinda*, 1993). Después de muchos planes para separar a los protagonistas, esta villana acaba en la cárcel.

La más exitosa

Yo soy Betty, la fea es una telenovela colombiana. Trata sobre una joven lista y culta° que asciende profesionalmente gracias a su talento pero es despreciada° por su apariencia física. Es la telenovela latinoamericana más exitosa de la historia. Este es un perfil en números de su éxito:

7 millones de personas vieron el primer beso de Betty con Armando, el galán.

100 países emitieron esta telenovela.

15 son los idiomas a los que se tradujo.

338 es el número de capítulos.

2001 es el año en que terminó.

La actriz América Ferrera protagonizó la versión norteamericana de Yo soy Betty, la fea.

¿COMPRENDISTE?

Decide if the following statements are true (T) or false (F).

1. Las telenovelas son solamente dramáticas. T ○ F ○
2. Muchas telenovelas incorporan elementos de actualidad. T ○ F ○
3. Cada país latinoamericano produce telenovelas diferentes. T ○ F ○
4. Yo soy Betty, la fea fue un éxito solamente en Colombia. T ○ F ○
5. Yo soy Betty, la fea tiene más capítulos de lo habitual en las telenovelas. T ○ F ○

El actor Jaime Camil, protagonista de la telenovela Por ella soy Eva.

AHORA TÚ

What do you think? Answer the following questions and discuss your ideas with other students.

1. ¿Qué telenovela de las mencionadas te gustaría ver y por qué?
2. ¿Qué programas en la televisión norteamericana tienen la función de entretener y educar? Da dos ejemplos.
3. Piensa en tu género televisivo favorito y haz una lista de los elementos que lo componen, según el ejemplo del texto.
4. Las villanas de las telenovelas siempre tienen un final violento. ¿Por qué?
5. ¿Por qué crees que las antagonistas de las telenovelas suelen ser mujeres?

Glosario

ahorrar – to save
aportar – to add
atravesar – to go through
culto – educated
despreciado – despised
en llamas – burning
equilibrar – to balance
estrechamente – closely
el galán – leading man
el incendio – fire
el parche – patch
la pérdida – loss

Fuentes: Terra, Univisión, Página 12.

241

Los mejores finales de las villanas

- Call on a volunteer (or volunteers) to read the text aloud.
- Check students' understanding of the information by asking questions, such as: **¿Cuál de las tres villanas murió en un incendio? ¿La villana de qué telenovela tomó veneno? ¿Quién acabó en la cárcel?**
- Have students think about what happened to the villain in their favorite TV show or movie and share the information with a partner.
- Monitor their conversations and assist as needed.
- Call on volunteers to share their examples with the class.

La más exitosa

- Call on a volunteer to read the title and information that follows.
- Check students' understanding of the information by asking questions, such as: **¿De qué trata la telenovela Yo soy Betty, la fea? ¿De qué país es originaria? ¿Cuántos países emitieron la telenovela? ¿Quién protagonizó la version norteamericana de la telenovela?**

¿Comprendiste?

- Have students work individually to answer the questions.
- Monitor their progress and assist as needed.
- Go over the answers as a class. Have them explain the false answers.

Ahora tú

- Have students work individually to answer the questions.
- Monitor their progress and assist as needed.
- Put students into pairs or small groups to share their ideas. Have them take turns asking and answering the questions. Encourage them to ask each other follow-up questions for more information.
- Ask each pair or group to report back to the class on something interesting from their conversation.

ANSWERS

¿Comprendiste?

1. F; 2. T; 3. T; 4. F; 5. T.

RELATO COMPREHENSIVE PRACTICE

OBJECTIVES FOR RELATO

- Revisit unit themes, grammar, vocabulary and culture in a new context
- Improve reading comprehension skills

CORE RESOURCES

- Audio Program: Track 67
- Interactive Whiteboard Lesson: IWB 8.2

STANDARDS

2.2   Products and perspectives

3.1   Knowledge of other disciplines

INSTRUCTIONAL STRATEGIES

Activity 1

- Put students into pairs, assigning one to the role of **Estudiante 1** and the other to **Estudiante 2**. Monitor their progress and assist as needed. Possible questions for students to ask each other: **Estudiante 1: a. ¿Cómo se llamaba?; c. ¿En qué año nació?; e. ¿Cuál es el título de una de sus obras más importantes? Estudiante 2: b. ¿Dónde nació?; d. ¿Cuántas obras escribió?**
- Pose *yes/no* questions with incorrect information to the class and call on students to correct you, for example: **¿Calderón de la Barca es de México? ¿Es guionista de películas famosas? ¿Ha escrito solamente dos obras?**

Activity 2

- Have students jot down ideas on their own first. Encourage them to come up with five possibilities, one for each phrase in the box.
- Then put students into pairs to share their ideas. Have each group report back on their favorite hypothesis.

Activity 3

- Explain that the sentences represent the basic plot of the play **La vida es sueño** but that the sentences are out of order.
- Working individually or in pairs, have students put the plot in order.
- Go over the answers as a class to find out if any of the students' original hypotheses were correct.

Next Page

INSTRUCTIONAL STRATEGIES

🎧 67 Activity 4

- Before listening to the audio, consider giving students some time to read through the excerpt and footnoted definitions to familiarize themselves with the new vocabulary.
- Play the audio. Then have students read the three interpretations and select the correct one.
- Go over the answer as a class. Encourage students to explain their answers.

ANSWERS

Activity 4

Segismundo no puede entender qué ha hecho para ser encerrado por su padre.

RELATO *La vida es sueño*

1 Calderón de la Barca was one of the most important writers of the Golden Age of literature. Take turns asking and answering questions to learn more about this figure and complete his biographical data.

Estudiante 1

a. Nombre:

b. Lugar de nacimiento: Madrid.

c. Año de nacimiento:

d. N.º de obras escritas: más de 200.

e. Una de sus obras más importantes:

La vida es sueño.

e. Una de sus obras más importantes:

d. N.º de obras escritas:

c. Año de nacimiento: 1600.

b. Lugar de nacimiento:

a. Nombre: Pedro.

Estudiante 2

2 Segismundo, the main character in the play *La vida es sueño*, has been locked in a tower since he was born. Can you imagine what the reasons for this might be? Share your ideas with a partner.

- Creo que...
- Tal vez...
- Es posible que...
- A lo mejor...
- Puede que...

3 To confirm your hypothesis, put the following sentences in the right order to learn the plot of the play, *La vida es sueño*.

a. ◯ Para que nadie sepa que existe un príncipe sucesor, lo encierra en una torre.

b. ◯ Segismundo finalmente gana, pero muestra respeto por su padre, porque es el rey. Basilio en ese momento es consciente de que su hijo será un buen rey en el futuro y le deja el trono.

c. ◯ Una vez en libertad, actúa de forma violenta contra todo el mundo y lo encierran otra vez.

d. ◯ El rey Basilio cuando nace su hijo Segismundo cree en una superstición que dice que ese niño no será un buen sucesor del trono.

e. ◯ El pueblo descubre que existe un príncipe heredero y lo liberan. Segismundo lucha contra su padre.

f. ◯ En una ocasión decide darle una oportunidad para comprobar si podrá ser un buen rey y lo saca de la torre.

4 🎧 67 **Follow along as you listen to the following excerpt where Segismundo speaks from his locked cell in the tower. Then, select the correct interpretation.**

¡Ay, mísero[1] de mí, ay infelice!
Apurar[2], cielos[3], pretendo,
ya que me tratáis así
qué delito[4] cometí
contra vosotros naciendo;
aunque si nací, ya entiendo
qué delito[5] he cometido:
bastante causa ha tenido
vuestra justicia[6] y rigor[7],
pues el delito mayor
del hombre es haber nacido.

Solo quisiera saber
para apurar[8] mis desvelos[9]
dejando a una parte, cielos,
el delito de nacer,
qué más os puede ofender
para castigarme más.
¿No nacieron los demás?
Pues si los demás nacieron,
¿qué privilegios[10] tuvieron
que yo no gocé[11] jamás?

1. Wretched; 2. To find out, discover; 3. The Heavens, plea to God; 4. Offense, mistake; 5. Refers to Original Sin; 6. Refers to the Heaven justice; 7. Severity; 8. Finish, conclude; 9. Worry, suffering; 10. Advantage, better luck; 11. Enjoy.

a. Segismundo no puede entender qué hizo para ser encerrado por su padre.
b. Segismundo está preocupado por el medioambiente.
c. Segismundo piensa que nacen muchos niños en el mundo.

5 **Throughout the play, Segismundo thinks he is sleeping and that his life is a dream. What do the words *sueño* or *soñar* mean to you? List all the words that come to mind in Spanish when you think about these words.**

6 👥 **In groups of 3 or 4, discuss the following.**

a. ¿Sueñas con frecuencia?
b. ¿Sueles tener sueños agradables o pesadillas?
c. ¿Hay algún sueño que tengas a menudo?
d. ¿Recuerdas tu último sueño?

7 **Link the following words and expressions related to dreams with their meanings.**

1. No pegar ojo. ....
2. Dormir como un tronco. ....
3. Tener sueño. ....
4. Soñar con los angelitos. ....
5. Pasar la noche en blanco. ....
6. Cumplirse un sueño. ....
7. Tener un sueño. ....

- a. Estar cansado y con ganas de dormir.
- b. Hacerse realidad algo muy deseado.
- c. No poder dormir.
- d. Desear algo con mucha intensidad.
- e. En lenguaje infantil, dormir.
- f. Dormir muy profundamente.

8 👥 **What dream would you like to achieve in real life? Share your thoughts with a partner.**

INSTRUCTIONAL STRATEGIES

Activity 5

- Write the words **sueño** and **soñar** on the board. Elicit a few examples of other words that students relate to these, and write them on the board as well.
- Have students work individually to brainstorm and jot down more ideas.
- Monitor their progress and assist as needed.
- Call on volunteers to share some of their examples. Invite them explain their word associations if the connections are more tenuous.

Alternative Activity

Create a competition. Each student shares his or her list of associated words or phrases. If other students have the same word or phrase on their own lists, they must cross it off. Students only receive points for those words or phrases that no one else has.

Extension

Project IWB 8.2, **Los sueños**. Have the students match the phrases with the images to learn more vocabulary associated with dreaming.

Activity 6

- Put students into small groups to discuss the questions.
- Monitor their conversations and assist as needed.
- Call on volunteers to report back on interesting aspects of their conversations.

Activity 7

- Go over the instructions. Have students work individually to match the expressions with their meanings. Point out that one definition will be used twice.
- Go over the answers as a class.

Activity 8

- Give students some time to jot down their ideas first.
- Then put students into pairs to share their ideas. Encourage students to ask each other questions for more information.
- Have students change partners and report on their previous partner's dreams.
- Ask students if they were surprised by any of the dreams they heard and explain why or why not.

ANSWERS

Activity 7

1. c; **2.** f; **3.** a; **4.** e; **5.** c; **6.** b; **7.** d.

IWB 8.2

1. c; **2.** a; **3.** e; **4.** b; **5.** f; **6.** d.

OBJECTIVES FOR EVALUACIÓN

- Review grammar, vocabulary and culture from the unit
- Complete self-assessment

CORE RESOURCES

- Interactive Online Materials – ELEteca

STANDARDS

1.2 Understand the language

4.1 Compare languages

INSTRUCTIONAL STRATEGIES

- Have students complete the activities individually.
- Go over the answers as a class. Encourage students to learn from each other by asking if they agree with the answers given. Provide explanations as needed.
- You may wish to assign point value to each activity as a way for students to monitor their progress.
- Direct students to the indicated pages in **En resumen** if they make more than one or two mistakes in any one section.

ANSWERS

Activity 1

a. Me dice que tiene frío y que necesita un abrigo y que si no le sirve uno mío, va a comprarse uno; **b.** Me pregunta dónde tiene que ir, qué tiene que hacer y cuándo debe volver; **c.** Me confesó que no había hecho nada y que, cuando vuelva de su viaje, me lo demostrará; **d.** Me preguntó si estaba muy lejos la casa de mi primo porque estaba un poco cansado de caminar; **e.** Me pide que le diga la verdad.

Activity 2

1. b; **2.** e; **3.** d; **4.** a; **5.** c.

Activity 3

a. era; **b.** haremos; **c.** fueron; **d.** nació; **e.** está / estará; **f.** cocinan / cocinarán.

Activity 4

a. Lo mismo; **b.** Probablemente; **c.** Puede ser que; **d.** Quizás; **e.** Es posible que; **f.** Quizás.

EVALUACIÓN

RELATING INFORMATION SAID BY OTHERS

1 Change the following sentences into indirect speech.

a. Tengo frío y necesito un abrigo. Si no me sirve uno tuyo, voy a comprarme uno.
Me dice ....

b. ¿Dónde tengo que ir? ¿Qué tengo que hacer? ¿Cuándo debo volver?
Me pregunta ....

c. No hice nada y, cuando vuelva de mi viaje, te lo demostraré.
Me confesó ....

d. ¿Está muy lejos la casa de tu primo? Es que estoy un poco cansado de caminar.
Me preguntó ....

e. Dime la verdad.
Me pide ....

HYPOTHETICAL EXPRESSIONS WITH THE INDICATIVE AND THE SUBJUNCTIVE

2 Match the following columns to create logical conclusions.

1. ¡Muchas gracias por el regalo de cumpleaños! .... •
2. (¡Riiinnnggg!) Son las doce de la noche y no espero ninguna llamada. .... •
3. No encuentro las llaves de casa por ningún sitio. .... •
4. No sé por qué se escuchan tantas sirenas de policía. .... •
5. Sara me dice que el abrigo que se compró la semana pasada ahora está mucho más barato. .... •

- a. ¿Qué habrá pasado?
- b. ¿Qué será?
- c. ¿Cuánto costaría antes?
- d. ¿Dónde las habré puesto?
- e. ¿Quién será?

3 Write the correct form of the verb in parenthesis.

a. Me parece que ayer (ser) .... el cumpleaños de mi primo y se me olvidó llamarlo.

b. Creo que (hacer, nosotros) .... los ejercicios mañana. Ahora no tenemos tiempo.

c. A lo mejor (ir, ellos) .... a clase la semana pasada pero esta semana no vinieron.

d. Yo diría que (nacer, él) .... en el sur de España. Baila flamenco muy bien.

e. Me imagino que (estar, él) .... en casa. Desde aquí veo que hay luz dentro.

f. Suponemos que (cocinar, ustedes) .... bien, pero nunca nos han invitado a comer.

4 Choose the correct option in each sentence.

a. **Lo mismo / Es posible que** está en la recámara.

b. **Es probable que / Probablemente** sabe dónde trabaja.

c. **Me parece que / Puede ser que** diga la verdad.

d. **Quizás / A lo mejor** haga el pastel para tu cumpleaños.

e. **Igual / Es posible que** cambie de casa en los próximos días.

f. **Es probable que / Quizás** puede llevarte en su carro.

CARTAS FORMALES

5 Link to create formal greetings and closings.

1. se despide .... •
2. muy .... •
3. reciba .... •
4. en espera .... •
5. estimado .... •

• a. de sus noticias
• b. un cordial saludo
• c. atentamente
• d. señor
• e. señor mío

CORREOS ELECTRÓNICOS

6 Complete the following email with the symbols studied.

●○○   Mensaje nuevo

De: carol.sanz@gmail.com   Para: Laural.a@hotmail.com

Hola Laura (dos puntos) ....
Te envío la dirección de correo electrónico de Pepe para que le envíes las fotos.
Es (PepeguionbajoCruzarrobahotmailpuntocom) ....
Un besito, Carolina.

WORDS WITH DIFFERENT MEANINGS

7 Select the correct option.

a. **¿Dónde / A dónde** vas? No quiero que juegues **adonde / donde / dónde** no hay valla.
b. No fue Pedro quien me lo dijo, **sino / si no** Juan.
c. Déjalo **asimismo / a sí mismo**, ya está bien.
d. » **¿Porqué / Por qué / Porque** me pasarán estas cosas a mí?
   » **Porque / Porqué / Por qué** eres un despistado y no te fijas en lo que haces.

CULTURA

8 Answer the following questions with information you learned in *Un mundo de novela*.

a. ¿De qué manera están conectadas las telenovelas a los países hispanos?
b. ¿Cuáles son algunos de los elementos que tienen en común las telenovelas? ¿Qué elementos tienen en común con las telenovelas en Estados Unidos?
c. Además de entretener, ¿qué intentan hacer las telenovelas? Y las telenovelas en Estados Unidos, ¿qué temas sociales suelen tocar?
d. ¿Cuáles son las características del personaje Betty de la telenovela *Betty la fea*? ¿Piensas que es una exageración u ocurre así en la vida real?

 Practice what you have learned with additional materials online.

ANSWERS

Activity 5
1. c; 2. e; 3. b; 4. a; 5. d.

Activity 6
1. : (dos puntos); 2. Pepe_Cruz@hotmail.com

Activity 7
a. A dónde, donde; b. sino; c. así mismo; d. Por qué, Porque.

Activity 8
Answers will vary. Possible answers might include the following:
a. Cada país latinoamericano produce telenovelas con un estilo distinto. Las telenovelas reflejan las tradiciones, las aspiraciones, y los temas de actualidad de la sociedad que las mira; b. Suelen tener entre 100 y 200 capítulos. Generalmente, hay un galán rico, una heroína pobre, y una villana que hace todo lo posible por separarlos. Como las telenovelas en los Estados Unidos, son melodramáticas; c. Intentan educar. Suelen tocar temas sociales, por ejemplo, la pobreza, la homosexualidad, el abuso, la violencia, el cáncer, y mucho más; d. Betty es una joven inteligente y capaz que asciende profesionalmente pero es despreciada por su apariencia física.

OBJECTIVES FOR EN RESUMEN: VOCABULARIO

- Review unit vocabulary and expressions
- Practice communicative skills

STANDARDS

1.2   Understand the language
1.3   Present information

INSTRUCTIONAL STRATEGIES

- Have students write sentences with the words and phrases in the other vocabulary sections.
- Call on students to write their sentences on the board –but leave a blank line (or give multiple choices, in some cases) where the vocabulary word or phrase should be. Then have the rest of the class write down the answers to complete the sentences.
- Go over the answers as a class. You may choose to create a competition and keep score by individual or group.

Alternative Activity

Index cards can be used as flashcards with the Spanish term on one side and the English term, a picture, or a drawing on the other. Working in pairs or groups, students can use the flashcards to help each other practice unit vocabulary.

EN RESUMEN: Vocabulario

Cartas formales

a continuación *following*
la despedida *closing (of a letter)*
destinatario *addressee, recipient of letter*
las disculpas *apologies*
la fecha *date*
la finalidad *purpose*
la firma *signature*
la molestia *bother*
el motivo *motive, subject*
la queja *complaint*
el remitente *sender (of a letter)*
el saludo *greeting*

Telecomunicaciones

el aparato *mechanical device*
la arroba *at, @*

la barra *slash*
la batería *battery*

el cargador *charger*

cargar *to charge*
dos puntos *colon*
el guion *hyphen*
el guion bajo *underscore*
hacer clic *to click*

la pantalla táctil *touch screen*

punto com *dot com*
se corta *to be cut, dropped (as in a call)*
la señal *signal*
tener cobertura *to have coverage*
la triple doble ve *www*

Verbos

aconsejar *to advise*

comentar *to comment*
confesar (e > ie) *to confess*
durar *to last*
ordenar *to order*
recomendar (e > ie) *to recommend*
suponer *to suppose*

Expresiones para expresar hipótesis

a lo mejor *maybe*
es probable *it's possible*
igual *maybe*
lo mismo *maybe*
posiblemente *possibly*
probablemente *probably*
puede ser / puede que *it can be that*
seguramente *surely*
tal vez *maybe*

246

EN RESUMEN: Gramática

REPORTED SPEECH
(See pages 226 and 227)

- To relate some information we use the verbs **decir, comentar** or **confesar** in present tense.

  *"**Eres** lo mejor de **mi** vida".* ➜ **Dice que soy** lo mejor de **su** vida.

  *"**Estuve aquí** comiendo con Pedro".* ➜ **Dice que estuvo allí** comiendo con Pedro.

  *"**Creo** que **tenemos** este libro".* ➜ **Dice que** cree que tienen ese libro.

- In these cases there are no changes in the verb tenses, but there are changes in:
  - **Personal pronouns:** *"**Yo** quiero ir".* ➜ Dice que **él** / **ella** quiere ir.
  - **Demonstrative adjectives** and **pronouns:** *"Te daré **este** libro".* ➜ Dice que me dará **ese** libro.
  - **Possessive adjectives** and **pronouns:** *"Este es **mi** coche".* ➜ Dice que ese es **su** coche.
  - **Adverbs allí, ahí, aquí:** *"Este de **aquí** es mi hermano".* ➜ Dice que **aquel** de **ahí** / **allí** es su hermano.
  - Verbs *ir, venir, traer, llevar* also change: *"Voy a **ir** a tu casa".* ➜ Dice que va a **venir** a mi casa.
  - **Time adverbs:**

hoy ➜ aquel día	mañana ➜ al día siguiente	ayer ➜ el día anterior
ahora ➜ entonces	luego / después ➜ más tarde	

- When a command or request is related, the present subjunctive is used.

  "Compra pan". ➜ **Me ordena** que **compre** pan.

  In this case we relate the information using introductory verbs such as **ordenar, aconsejar, sugerir** or **recomendar**.

- When we relate questions:

  "¿Hicieron la tarea?". ➜ El profesor **pregunta** si hicimos la tarea.

  "¿Cuándo harán la tarea?". ➜ El profesor nos **pregunta cuándo** haremos la tarea.

  When repeating questions, use the interrogative word in the question (**cómo, dónde, qué, cuándo**…) or **preguntar** + **si** (for questions without interrogatives).

VERBS AND EXPRESSIONS
TO EXPRESS HYPOTHESIS OR PROBABILITIES
(See pages 235 and 236)

Creo / Me parece		ese modelo de celular no **es** uno de los mejores.
Me imagino / Supongo	**que**	si está en la sierra no **tiene** cobertura, llámalo mañana.
Para mí / Yo diría		**llovió** anoche, las calles están mojadas.
A lo mejor / Lo mismo / Igual *(maybe)*		**es** un problema de tu compañía porque yo sí tengo cobertura.
Probablemente / Posiblemente		la compañía telefónica **se pone** / **se ponga** en contacto conmigo
Seguramente / Quizás		después de mi reclamación. (indicativo/subjuntivo)
Tal vez		
Es posible / Es probable	**que**	mi celular **tenga** algún defecto de fábrica, me lo compré hace
Puede ser / Puede		poco y no me dura nada la batería. (subjuntivo)

- We can also express probability using some tenses:

Present ➜ Simple Future	*Javier no ha llegado, **estará** todavía en el metro.*
Present Perfect ➜ Future Perfect	*Javier no ha llegado, ¿le **habrá pasado** algo?*
Simple Past ➜ Conditional	*Si Javier no vino ayer, **tendría** algún motivo.*

247

- " Review unit grammar
- Practice communication skills

STANDARDS

1.2 Understand the language

4.1 Compare languages

INSTRUCTIONAL STRATEGIES

- Focus students' attention on the key grammar topics of the unit.
- Have students review the Learning Outcomes in the unit opener to assess whether they feel they have mastered the main ideas and skills.
- Ask them if they can remember additional examples for each grammar topic.
- Model how to find and go back to the appropriate page in the unit to review any grammar topic they may need help with.
- Invite students to review the grammar activities they completed in this unit.
- Ask them what grammar activities they found easy and which they found challenging. Encourage them to rework any activities they found particularly challenging.

AHORA COMPRUEBA

OBJECTIVES FOR AHORA COMPRUEBA

- Review and recycle grammar, vocabulary and culture from the last two units
- Complete self-assessment

CORE RESOURCES

- Audio Program: Track 68
- Interactive Whiteboard Lessons: IWB 8.3

STANDARDS

1.2 Understand the language

4.1 Compare languages

INSTRUCTIONAL STRATEGIES

🎧 68 Activity 1

- Focus students' attention on the image and ask: **¿Conocen la historia? ¿Han visto la película? ¿Recuerdan los nombres de los personajes?** Elicit what they know about the story and its characters.
- Give students time to read the questions before playing the audio. Encourage them to underline key words to listen for and to take notes while they listen.
- Play the audio. Have students compare their notes with a partner and answer the questions in pairs. Play the audio again so they can check their answers. Go over the answers as a class.

See audioscript on page APP5

Activity 2

- Have students work individually to complete the conversation.
- Put students into pairs to compare their answers. Then go over the answers.
- Have the pairs practice the conversation. Then have them switch roles.

Activity 3

Have students work individually to create sentences. Then go over the answers as a class and have students continue telling the rest of the story.

ANSWERS

Activity 1

a. En el teatro Lope de Vega en Madrid, c/ Gran Vía, 57; **b.** En metro: estaciones de Callao y Plaza de España o en coche con parking en la Plaza de España; **c.** A través de la página web: *www.elreyleon.es* o en el teléfono 902 888 788. También en la taquilla todos los días desde las 12 p.m. hasta el inicio de la última función; **d.** Una butaca que ofrece una visita guiada al *backstage* de *El rey León* y la posibilidad de conocer a los actores después de la función; **e.** *El rey León, el musical que conmueve a todo el mundo.*

Activity 2

1. Qué te parece; **2.** impresionante; **3.** ¡Pero qué dices!; **4.** es asombroso que; **5.** No creo que; **6.** Además; **7.** Desde luego; **8.** creo que.

Activity 3

a. 4, B; **b.** 1, D; **c.** 3, A; **d.** 2, C.

AHORA COMPRUEBA

1 🎧 **68** Listen to the following commercial about the musical *El Rey León (The Lion King)* and answer the questions.

a. ¿Dónde puedes ver El Rey León?
b. ¿Cómo puedes llegar?
c. ¿Dónde y cómo puedes comprar los boletos?
d. ¿Qué es la "butaca de oro"?
e. ¿Cuál es el eslogan?

2 Complete the conversation between Nélida and Silvia with the following expressions.

> creo que ○ además ○ desde luego ○ es asombroso que ○
> no creo que ○ impresionante ○ qué te parece ○ pero qué dices

Nélida: ¿(a) .... ir a ver el musical de *El Rey León*? Vi la película cuando era pequeña y me parece (b) .... poder ver ahora el musical en Madrid.

Silvia: ¡(c) .... ! No me gustan nada los musicales.

N.: ¿No has visto su anuncio en la tele? Creo que (d) .... estén tan bien caracterizados los actores para parecer animales. Ya solo eso me parece increíble... Y las canciones fueron escritas por Elton John y el letrista Tim Rice, que ganaron un Oscar y un Tony.

S.: (e) .... sea el tipo de espectáculo para mí, prefiero una película. (f) .... , el teatro es carísimo.

N.: ¡(g) .... que es caro! Pero lo vale la emoción del directo, los actores cantando y bailando delante de ti, los efectos de iluminación... Es tan espectacular que (h) .... es imposible verla y que no se te pongan los pelos de punta.

S.: ¡¡Imposible?! Hummm...

3 Combine elements from the three columns to create sentences describing the plot of *El Rey León*.

a. Simba es un cachorro y sucesor al trono, ...
b. Scar organiza la muerte de Mufasa, el padre de Simba, y le hace creer que es culpa suya, ...
c. Simba tiene dos nuevos amigos que le adoptan y, ...
d. Su tío Scar toma el trono, ...

- 1. por eso ....
- 2. incluso ....
- 3. además, ...
- 4. sin embargo ....

- A. le enseñan la filosofía de vivir sin preocupaciones: el *Hakuna Matata*.
- B. su tío Scar quiere ser el próximo rey y prepara un plan para ocupar el trono.
- C. llega a hacer pensar a todos los animales que Simba murió. ¿Volverá a recuperar su reino?
- D. se siente culpable y escapa a la selva.

4 Complete the following conversation between two friends as they talk about the play. Neither of them knows much about it. Read the answers and come up with the question that was posed. The first one has been done for you.

Sandra: ¿Cuánto costarán los boletos?
Mateo: Ni idea, pero imagino que serán caros.
S.: (a) ....
M.: Imagino que en la taquilla del teatro o por Internet, pero no estoy seguro.
S.: (b) ....
M.: Creo que está por el centro de Madrid. Lo podemos mirar en la página web del teatro.
S.: (c) ....
M.: Me imagino que sí ha ganado muchos premios.
S.: (d) ....
M.: Supongo que más de dos horas, como todos los musicales.
S.: (e) ....
M.: Tal vez. Si no, pues buscamos un estacionamiento.
S.: (f) ....
M.: Ya sabes que yo tampoco lo sé, pero normalmente las funciones son sobre las ocho de la tarde, ¿no?
S.: (g) ....
M.: Seguramente. La están representando en muchos países, entonces supongo que sí, que la vieron muchas personas.

5 Many animals appear in the story told in *El Rey León*. **Match the image to the appropriate word for each.**

1.
a. ☐ toro
b. ☐ rinoceronte
c. ☐ jabalí

2.
a. ☐ elefante
b. ☐ ciervo
c. ☐ cerdo

3.
a. ☐ pingüino
b. ☐ oso panda
c. ☐ cebra

4.
a. ☐ loro
b. ☐ águila
c. ☐ tucán

6 Now write your hypothesis using different transition words and expressions.

1.	2.	3.	4.

INSTRUCTIONAL STRATEGIES

Activity 4

- Go over the instructions and the model. Point out the key bit of information that neither person knows much about the play. Elicit from the students what that suggests about the grammar and kinds of expressions they should use.
- Put students into pairs. Have them work together to write an appropriate question for each response.
- Monitor their progress and assist as needed.
- Call on volunteers to role-play their conversations in front of the class.

Activity 5

- Go over the instructions. Have students work individually to match the pictures with the correct words.
- Monitor their progress and assist as needed. Encourage them to guess if they are not sure.
  Before going over the answers, have students continue with Activity 6.

Activity 6

- Have students write hypotheses that reflect how confident they are or are not in their guesses in Activity 5.
- Put students in pairs to compare their hypotheses.
- Project IWB 8.3, **Animales** to reveal the answers. To create more suspense, consider revealing the images one at a time, piece by piece. Confirm whether or not their hypotheses were correct.

ANSWERS

Activity 4

Answers will vary. Possible answers might include the following:
1. ¿Dónde podremos comprarlas?; **2.** ¿Dónde estará el teatro?; **3.** ¿Habrá ganado algún premio?; **4.** ¿Cuánto durará la obra?; **5.** ¿Podremos aparcar allí?; **6.** ¿A qué hora serán las funciones?; **7.** ¿La habrá visto mucha gente?

Activity 5

1. b; **2.** c; **3.** a; **4.** b.

APÉNDICES

- Resumen y expansión gramatical
- Tabla de verbos

RESUMEN GRAMATICAL

THE FUTURE TENSE

■ Regular verbs:

	−AR VIAJAR	−ER COMER	−IR VIVIR
yo	viajar**é**	comer**é**	vivir**é**
tú	viajar**ás**	comer**ás**	vivir**ás**
usted/él/ella	viajar**á**	comer**á**	vivir**á**
nosotros/as	viajar**emos**	comer**emos**	vivir**emos**
vosotros/as	viajar**éis**	comer**éis**	vivir**éis**
ustedes/ellos/ellas	viajar**án**	comer**án**	vivir**án**

■ Irregular verbs:

IRREGULAR VERBS			
poder ➡ **podr–**	tener ➡ **tendr–**	hacer ➡ **har–**	**é**
salir ➡ **saldr–**	poner ➡ **pondr–**	decir ➡ **dir–**	**ás**
caber ➡ **cabr–**	venir ➡ **vendr–**		**á**
haber ➡ **habr–**	valer ➡ **valdr–**		**emos**
saber ➡ **sabr–**			**éis**
querer ➡ **querr–**			**án**

The future is often used with the following temporal expressions:

El año / mes / la semana / primavera **que viene**

Dentro de dos años / un rato / unos días

El/la próximo/a semana / mes / año

Mañana / **Pasado mañana**

SI + PRESENT + FUTURE

■ To talk about future actions that will occur if a certain condition is met, use the following:

- **Si** + **present** + **future**

  Si   no llueve,   iremos a la playa.

AFFIRMATIVE COMMANDS

■ Affirmative commands are used to give an order, to invite, give advice, make recommendations, or give permission to someone.

■ Verbs ending in −**ar** will use the −**e**/−**en** endings in **usted** and **ustedes** commands. Verbs ending in −**er**/−**ir** will use the −**a**/−**an** endings in **usted** and **ustedes** commands.

REGULAR VERBS			
	COMPRAR	COMER	SUBIR
tú	compra	come	sube
usted	compre	coma	suba
ustedes	compren	coman	suban

IRREGULAR VERBS				
	DECIR	HACER	PONER	TENER
tú	di	haz	pon	ten
usted	diga	haga	ponga	tenga
ustedes	digan	hagan	pongan	tengan

AFFIRMATIVE COMMANDS + PRONOUNS

■ Direct, indirect, and reflexive pronouns are attached to affirmative commands to form one word.

Pon el queso en la nevera. ➡ **Ponlo**.   *Dime el secreto.* ➡ **Dímelo**.

EXPANSIÓN GRAMATICAL

Other irregular verbs:

	VENIR	IR	SER	SALIR
tú	ven	ve	sé	sal
usted	venga	vaya	sea	salga
ustedes	vengan	vayan	sean	salgan

Stem-changing verbs in the command form maintain their stem change:

	CERRAR	DORMIR	JUGAR	PEDIR	CONSTRUIR
	e ➡ ie	o ➡ ue	u ➡ ue	e ➡ i	i ➡ y
tú	cierra	duerme	juega	pide	construye
usted	cierre	duerma	juegue	pida	construya
ustedes	cierren	duerman	jueguen	pidan	construyan

NEGATIVE COMMANDS

■ Negative commands are used to tell someone what not to do.

■ To form the negative commands:

• For **usted/ustedes**, use the same form as the affirmative command.

(usted) compre ➡ **no compre**   (ustedes) compren ➡ **no compren**

• For **tú**, add –**s** to the negative command of **usted**.

(usted) no compre ➡ (tú) **no compres**

REGULAR VERBS			
	COMPRAR	COMER	SUBIR
tú	no compres	no comas	no subas
usted	no compre	no coma	no suba
ustedes	no compren	no coman	no suban

IRREGULAR VERBS				
	DECIR	**HACER**	**PONER**	**TENER**
tú	no **digas**	no **hagas**	no **pongas**	no **tengas**
usted	no **diga**	no **haga**	no **ponga**	no **tenga**
ustedes	no **digan**	no **hagan**	no **pongan**	no **tengan**

NEGATIVE COMMANDS AND PRONOUNS

■ Direct, indirect, and reflexive pronouns are placed before negative commands.

*No **lo** pongas en la estantería.*   *No **se lo** digas a nadie.*

EXPANSIÓN GRAMATICAL

Other irregular verbs:

	VENIR	**IR**	**SER**	**SALIR**
tú	no **vengas**	no **vayas**	no **seas**	no **salgas**
usted	no **venga**	no **vaya**	no **sea**	no **salga**
ustedes	no **vengan**	no **vayan**	no **sean**	no **salgan**

Stem-changing verbs in the command form maintain their stem change:

	CERRAR	**DORMIR**	**JUGAR**	**PEDIR**	**CONSTRUIR**
	e ➡ ie	o ➡ ue	u ➡ ue	e ➡ i	i ➡ y
tú	no **cie**rres	no **due**rmas	no **jue**gues	no **pi**das	no construy**as**
usted	no **cie**rre	no **due**rma	no **jue**ge	no **pi**da	no construy**a**
ustedes	no **cie**rren	no **due**rman	no **jue**guen	no **pi**dan	no construy**an**

UNIDAD 3

THE PLUPERFECT (PAST PERFECT)

The pluperfect is formed with the imperfect of **haber** + past participle of the verb.

yo	había			
tú	habías			
usted/él/ella	había	**–ado** (–ar verbs)	lleg**ado**	
nosotros/as	habíamos	**–ido** (–er / ir verbs)	com**ido**	
vosotros/as	habíais		viv**ido**	
ustedes/ellos/ellas	habían			

Irregular past participles	
abrir ➡ **abierto**	escribir ➡ **escrito**
hacer ➡ **hecho**	ver ➡ **visto**
decir ➡ **dicho**	poner ➡ **puesto**
romper ➡ **roto**	volver ➡ **vuelto**

EXPANSIÓN GRAMATICAL

■ Uses:

• To talk about an action that ended before another past action. Note the use of **todavía** and **ya**:
   *Cuando llegué al cine la película no **había comenzado** todavía / la película todavía no **había comenzado**.*
   (Llegué al cine a las 17:59, la película comenzó a las 18:00)
   *Cuando llegué al cine la película **había comenzado** ya / la película ya **había comenzado**.*
   (Llegué al cine a las 18:05 y la película comenzó a las 18:00)

• To talk about an action that took place before another past action, but with a sense of immediacy:
   *Le compré un juguete y al día siguiente ya lo **había roto**.*
   *Para mi cumpleaños me regalaron una novela y a la semana siguiente ya la **había leído**.*

• To talk about an action that we had never done before. Note the use of **nunca** and **nunca antes**:
   *Nunca / Nunca antes **había estado** aquí / No **había estado** aquí nunca / nunca antes.*
   *Nunca / Nunca antes **habíamos viajado** en globo / No **habíamos viajado** en globo nunca / nunca antes.*

• To ask if a person had ever done something before. Note the use of **antes** and **alguna vez**:
   *¿**Habías estado** en Madrid alguna vez / antes?*
   *¿**Habías estado** alguna vez / antes en Madrid?*

UNIDAD 4

THE CONDITIONAL TENSE

■ Regular verbs:

	HABLAR	COMER	ESCRIBIR
yo	hablar**ía**	comer**ía**	escribir**ía**
tú	hablar**ías**	comer**ías**	escribir**ías**
usted/él/ella	hablar**ía**	comer**ía**	escribir**ía**
nosotros/as	hablar**íamos**	comer**íamos**	escribir**íamos**
vosotros/as	hablar**íais**	comer**íais**	escribir**íais**
ustedes/ellos/ellas	hablar**ían**	comer**ían**	escribir**ían**

■ Irregular verbs:

caber ➡ **cabr**–	tener ➡ **tendr**–	hacer ➡ **har**–		**ía**
haber ➡ **habr**–	poder ➡ **podr**–	decir ➡ **dir**–		**ías**
saber ➡ **sabr**–	poner ➡ **pondr**–			**ía**
querer ➡ **querr**–	venir ➡ **vendr**–		+	**íamos**
	salir ➡ **saldr**–			**íais**
	valer ➡ **valdr**–			**ían**

■ Uses:

• To **give advice** or recommendations:
   *Yo / yo que tú / yo en tu lugar, **le diría** la verdad, seguro que lo entiende.*
   ***Deberías** comer menos dulces, no son muy saludables.*
   ***Podrías** presentarte al casting para el programa de baile, lo haces muy bien.*

• To **ask for permission** and favors:
   *¿**Te importaría** acercarme la chaqueta? Es que yo no alcanzo.*

• To express **probability** or **hypothesize** in the past:
   ***Tendría** 20 años cuando empezó a cantar.*

THE PRESENT SUBJUNCTIVE

- Regular verbs:

  To form the present subjunctive, start with the **yo** form of the present indicative, drop the **o** and switch to the opposite endings. For –**ar** verbs use: –**e**, –**es**, –**e**, –**emos**, –**éis**, –**en**. For –**er** / –**ir** verbs use: –**a**, –**as**, –**a**, –**amos**, –**áis**, –**an**.

	HABLAR	COMER	ESCRIBIR
yo	habl**e**	com**a**	escrib**a**
tú	habl**es**	com**as**	escrib**as**
usted/él/ella	habl**e**	com**a**	escrib**a**
nosotros/as	habl**emos**	com**amos**	escrib**amos**
vosotros/as	habl**éis**	com**áis**	escrib**áis**
ustedes/ellos/ellas	habl**en**	com**an**	escrib**an**

- Irregular verbs:

  Almost all verbs that are irregular in the present indicative will be irregular in the present subjunctive.

Stem-changing verbs

	QUERER **e → ie**	VOLVER **o → ue**	JUGAR **u → ue**	PEDIR **e → i** (en todas las personas)
yo	qu**ie**ra	v**ue**lva	j**ue**gue	p**i**da
tú	qu**ie**ras	v**ue**lvas	j**ue**gues	p**i**das
usted/él/ella	qu**ie**ra	v**ue**lva	j**ue**gue	p**i**da
nosotros/as	queramos	volvamos	juguemos	p**i**damos
vosotros/as	queráis	volváis	juguéis	p**i**dáis
ustedes/ellos/ellas	qu**ie**ran	v**ue**lvan	j**ue**guen	p**i**dan

- The verbs **dormir** and **morir** have two stem changes in the present subjunctive: **o → ue** and **o → u**:
  - d**ue**rma, d**ue**rmas, d**ue**rma, d**u**rmamos, d**u**rmáis, d**ue**rman.
  - m**ue**ra, m**ue**ras, m**ue**ra, m**u**ramos, m**u**ráis, m**ue**ran.

Verbs with irregular *yo* forms

poner ➡ **pong**–	traer ➡ **traig**–	**a**
tener ➡ **teng**–	hacer ➡ **hag**–	**as**
salir ➡ **salg**–	caer ➡ **caig**–	**a**
venir ➡ **veng**–	construir ➡ **construy**–	**amos**
decir ➡ **dig**–	conocer ➡ **conozc**–	**áis**
		an

Verbs that are completely irregular

HABER	IR	SABER	ESTAR	SER	VER	DAR
haya	vaya	sepa	esté	sea	vea	dé
hayas	vayas	sepas	estés	seas	veas	des
haya	vaya	sepa	esté	sea	vea	de
hayamos	vayamos	sepamos	estemos	seamos	veamos	demos
hayáis	vayáis	sepáis	estéis	seáis	veáis	deis
hayan	vayan	sepan	estén	sean	vean	den

■ Uses:

• To express **wishes** or **desires**. If there is only one subject in the sentence, use an infinitive. If there are different subjects, use the subjunctive:

*(Yo) Quiero (yo) **hablar** contigo. / (Yo) Quiero que (nosotros) **hablemos**.*

*(Yo) Espero (yo) **verte** pronto. / (Yo) Espero que (nosotros) nos **veamos** pronto.*

• To express **purpose** or **goals in the future**. If there is only one subject in the sentence or a subject that is not specified, use an infinitive. If there are different subjects, use the subjunctive:

*He hecho una tortilla para **cenar**. / He hecho una tortilla para que **cenéis** Carla y tú.*

• To express **future actions** after **adverbial conjunctions**:

》*¿Cuándo volverá Ana?*　　　　　　　　》*Cuando **salga** de trabajar.*

EXPANSIÓN GRAMATICAL

Other verbs with irregular forms in the subjunctive:

e ➜ ie (except in the nosotros and vosotros forms)		
cerrar ➜ c**ie**rra	encender ➜ enc**ie**nda	mentir ➜ m**ie**nta
comenzar ➜ com**ie**nce	encerrar ➜ enc**ie**rre	querer ➜ qu**ie**ra
despertarse ➜ se desp**ie**rte	entender ➜ ent**ie**nda	recomendar ➜ recom**ie**nde
divertirse ➜ se div**ie**rta	gobernar ➜ gob**ie**rne	sentarse ➜ se s**ie**nte
empezar ➜ emp**ie**ce	manifestar ➜ manif**ie**ste	sentir ➜ s**ie**nta

o ➜ ue (except in the nosotros and vosotros forms)		e ➜ i (en todas las personas)
acordarse ➜ se ac**ue**rde	rogar ➜ r**ue**gue	competir ➜ comp**i**ta
acostarse ➜ se ac**ue**ste	soler ➜ s**ue**la	despedir ➜ desp**i**da
contar ➜ c**ue**nte	sonar ➜ s**ue**ne	despedirse ➜ se desp**i**da
llover ➜ ll**ue**va	soñar ➜ s**ue**ñe	impedir ➜ imp**i**da
probar ➜ pr**ue**be	volar ➜ v**ue**le	medir ➜ m**i**da
resolver ➜ res**ue**lva	volver ➜ v**ue**lva	repetir ➜ rep**i**ta

EXPRESSING FEELINGS AND EMOTIONS

■ To express changing moods and feelings use the following structures:

• Verb **estar** + adjective + **con** + noun.
Mi hermana está muy contenta con su profesora de música.

• Verb **estar** + adjective + **de** + infinitive (if the subject of both verbs is the same).
Estamos encantadas de asistir al estreno de la nueva película de Mario Casas.

• Verb **estar** + adjective + **de que** + subjunctive (if the subject of both verbs is different).
Estoy encantada de que te quedes unos días más con nosotros.

• Verbs **ponerse**, **sentirse** o **estar** + adjective + **cuando** / **si** + indicative.
Yo me pongo furioso cuando dejo un libro y no me lo devuelven.

Yo me siento mal si veo una noticia triste.

■ Other verbs:

• **No soportar**	+ noun *Odio los lunes.*
• **No aguantar**	+ infinitive (same subject)
• **Odiar**	*No soporto madrugar.*
• **Adorar**	+ **que** + subjunctive (different subjects) *No aguanto que me empujen en el metro.*

■ Verbs like **gustar**:

• **Me**, **te**, **le**, **nos**… + **da rabia**, **pone alegre/s**, **molesta** + infinitive (if the person experiencing the emotion and carrying out the action is the same).
A mí me da vergüenza hablar en público.

• **Me**, **te**, **le**, **nos**… + **da rabia**, **pone alegre/s**, **molesta** + **que** + subjunctive (if the person experiencing the emotion and the person carrying out the action are different).
A mí me da rabia que la gente toque los cuadros en los museos.

• Remember that adjectives must agree with the subject in number and gender.
*A mi **madre** le pone **enferma** que no recoja mi habitación.*

VERBS FOLLOWED BY INFINITIVES OR PRESENT PARTICIPLES

■ In some of these constructions, the first verb, which is always conjugated, may be followed by a preposition.

• **Empezar** / **ponerse a** + infinitive expresses the beginning of an action.
He empezado a leer una novela muy interesante.
En cuanto llegué a casa me puse a estudiar para el examen del día siguiente.

• **Volver a** + **infinitive** expresses the repetition of an action.
El año pasado me apunté a clases de teatro y este año he vuelto a apuntarme.

• **Seguir** / **continuar** + **present participle** expresses an action that continues.
Nos conocimos en la guardería y hoy todavía seguimos siendo amigas.
Este verano continuaré yendo a clases de inglés, no quiero olvidar lo que he aprendido.

- **Acabar de** + **infinitive** expresses an action that just occurred.

  Si quieres pastel espera a que se enfríe un poco, que acabo de sacarlo del horno.

- **Dejar de** + **infinitive** expresses the interruption of an action (to stop doing something).

  He dejado de ir a clases de guitarra porque este año no tengo tanto tiempo.

VERBS THAT EXPRESS CHANGE

- To express **spontaneous** or **temporary changes** in a person, use:

  - **Ponerse** + adjective.

    Al hablar se ha puesto muy nervioso.   *Se ha puesto rojo cuando le han preguntado.*

  - **Quedarse** (describes the end result).

    Se ha quedado muy sorprendido por la noticia.   *¡Mi madre se ha quedado embarazada!*

    Quedarse *can sometimes express permanent changes: Mi abuelo* **se quedó calvo**.

- To express **permanent changes**, use:

  - **Volverse** + adjective / noun (not voluntary)

    Se ha vuelto un antipático. Antes no era así.   *Desde su divorcio, se ha vuelto más reservada.*
    Jugó a la lotería y se volvió millonario.

  - **Hacerse** (gradual or voluntary change).

    Antes era abogado y ahora se ha hecho juez.

    Hacerse *can be used with adjectives and nouns that express* **profession**, **religion** *and* **ideology**.

    Estudió Medicina y **se hizo médico**.   *Con esa situación* **se hizo fuerte**.
    Viajó al Tíbet y **se hizo budista**.

UNIDAD 7

EXPRESSING OPINIONS

- To **ask for an opinion**:

  - **¿Qué piensas / crees / opinas de / sobre…?**
    ¿Qué piensas de este periódico?

  - **¿(A ti)** qué **te parece…?**
    ¿A ti qué te parece lo que está pasando con la organización de la fiesta?

  - **En tu opinión / Desde tu punto de vista / Según tú** + question.
    Desde tu punto de vista, ¿cuál es el anuncio más inteligente?

- To **give an opinion**:

  - **En mi opinión / Desde mi punto de vista…**
    En mi opinión el blog no es muy interesante.

  - **Me parece que / Creo que / Pienso que** + indicative.
    Nos parece que la marca es muy importante.

  - **No me parece que / No creo que** + present subjunctive.
    No nos parece que la marca sea tan importante.

■ To show agreement and disagreement:

• **(No) estoy a favor de**	+ noun
• **(No) estoy en contra de**	+ infinitive (same subject)
• **(No) estoy (del todo) de acuerdo con**	+ que + present subjunctive (different subjects)

No estoy de acuerdo con todo tipo de anuncios.
Estoy en contra de ser manipulado por la publicidad.

Estoy a favor de que nos pidan opinión antes de vendernos sus productos.

■ Other ways to express:

AGREEMENT	SOFTEN A DISAGREEMENT	DISAGREEMENT
• Sí, claro.	• Yo no diría eso…	• ¡No, no!
• ¡Desde luego!	• Tienes razón, pero…	• ¡No, de ninguna manera!
• ¡Claro, claro!	• Sí, es una idea interesante, pero por otra parte…	• ¡Qué va!
• Yo pienso lo mismo que tú.	• A mi modo de ver, ese no es el problema / el tema…	• ¡(Pero) qué dices! (coloquial)
• Por supuesto.	• Lo que pasa es que…	• ¡Anda ya! (coloquial)
• ¡Y que lo digas! (coloquial)		

MAKING VALUE JUDGEMENTS

■ To **ask**:

• **¿Te parece bien / mal** /… + noun / infinitive / **que** + present subjunctive?
¿Te parece mal el sueldo de un publicista?
¿Te parece bien poder usar buscadores para hacer trabajos de clase?
¿Te parece una tontería que los publicistas ganen mucho dinero?

■ To **respond**:

• **Me parece bien / mal**	
• **Me parece / Es triste / increíble / cómico**…	+ **que** + present subjunctive
• **Me parece / Es una tontería / una vergüenza**…	
• **Es bueno / malo**	

Es increíble que se gasten tanto en anunciar sus productos.
Me parece bien que se entienda como una inversión y no como un gasto.
Creo que es una tontería que siempre veas los anuncios.

• **Está claro**	+ **que** + indicative
• **Es obvio / verdad**	

Está claro que la publicidad es creación.

• **¡Qué + bien / interesante**… + sentence!
¡Qué interesante este artículo!
¡Qué bien poder compartir tanta información a través de Facebook!
¡Qué guay que nuestro instituto tenga una página web!

TRANSITION WORDS AND SENTENCE CONNECTORS

- To present a **series** of reasons or points in an **argument**: **En primer lugar… en segundo lugar…**
  La juventud es muy crítica. En primer lugar no acepta cualquier cosa y en segundo lugar busca lo que quiere.

- To present **opposing views**: **Por un lado / una parte… por otro (lado) / por otra (parte)…**
  Comer bien es importante. Por un lado es necesario, por otro un placer.

- To **add points** or arguments: **Y / además / también / asimismo**
  La creatividad está presente en la publicidad, además de la originalidad por supuesto.

- To provide **examples** and **explanations**: **Por ejemplo / es decir / o sea**
  El alto nivel de competencia hace necesario invertir en publicidad, es decir, hay muchos productos buenos y similares en el mercado, pero algo te hace elegir uno.

- To refer to a topic **previously presented**: **(Con) respecto a (eso de / eso) / Sobre (eso)…**
  Con respecto a eso que has dicho antes, siento no estar totalmente de acuerdo contigo.

- To **add reasons** to an argument: **Incluso**
  María trabaja todos los días, incluso los domingos.

- To **contrast reasons**: **Bueno / pero / sin embargo / no obstante / en cambio**
  El rojo es mi color preferido, sin embargo nunca llevo ropa de ese color.

- To express **consequence**: **Así que / de modo que / de manera que / de ahí que / así pues / pues**
  Me encantan las películas, así que voy al cine siempre que puedo.

- To draw **conclusions**: **Entonces / total que / por lo tanto / en resumen / en conclusión / para terminar**
  Fuimos a la montaña sin botas ni ropa adecuada, total que pasamos muchísimo frío.

UNIDAD 8

INDIRECT SPEECH

- To repeat information use verbs like **decir**, **comentar** or **confesar** in the present or present perfect tenses:
  "Eres lo mejor de mi vida". ➡ *Dice / Ha dicho* **que soy** lo mejor de **su** vida.
  "Estuve aquí comiendo con Pedro". ➡ *Dice / Ha dicho* **que estuvo allí** comiendo con Pedro.
  "Cree que tenemos este libro". ➡ *Dice / Ha dicho* **que** cree que **tienen ese** libro.

- While the verb tenses in these cases do not change, other changes will take place in the following:
  - Subject Pronouns
    "**Yo** quiero ir". ➡ *Dice que* **él/ella** *quiere ir.*
    "**Tú** quieres hablar siempre". ➡ *Dice que* **yo** *quiero hablar siempre.*
  - Demonstrative Adjectives and Pronouns
    "**Te** daré **este** libro". ➡ *Dice que* **me** *dará* **ese** *libro.*
  - Possessive Adjectives and Pronouns
    "Este es **mi** coche". ➡ *Dice que ese es* **su** *coche.*
  - Adverbs **allí**, **ahí**, **allí**
    "Este de **aquí** es mi hermano". ➡ *Dice que aquel de* **ahí** / **allí** *es su hermano.*
  - Verbs **ir**, **venir**, **traer**, **llevar** also need to change.
    "Voy a **ir** a tu casa". ➡ *Dice que va a* **venir** *a mi casa.*

- Adverbs of time

hoy ➡ aquel día	ahora ➡ entonces
mañana ➡ al día siguiente	luego / después ➡ más tarde
ayer ➡ el día anterior	

■ When repeating a command, the command form changes to the present subjunctive. Note that the information is relayed using verbs like **ordenar**, **aconsejar**, **sugerir** or **recomendar**:

"Compra el pan". ➡ *Me ha ordenado que compre el pan.*

■ When repeating questions, use the interrogative word in the question (**cómo**, **dónde**, **qué**, **cuándo**…) or **preguntar** + **si** (for questions without interrogatives):

"¿Han hecho la tarea?". ➡ *El profesor nos ha preguntado si hemos hecho la tarea.*
"¿Cuándo van a hacer la tarea?". ➡ *El profesor nos ha preguntado cuándo vamos a hacer la tarea.*

■ The preterit can also be used to introduce reported speech, but will require additional changes in the sentence.

DIRECT SPEECH	INDIRECT SPEECH (dice / ha dicho)	INDIRECT SPEECH (dijo)
Present	No change	Imperfect
Preterit	No change	Preterit or Pluperfect (Past Perfect)
Present perfect	No change	Pluperfect (Past Perfect)
Imperfect	No change	Imperfect
Pluperfect (Past perfect)	No change	Pluperfect (Past Perfect)
Future	No change	Conditional
Conditional	No change	Conditional

HYPOTHETICAL EXPRESSIONS WITH THE INDICATIVE AND THE SUBJUNCTIVE

- **Creo / me parece que**
- **Me imagino / aupongo que**   + indicative   *Creo que ese modelo de móvil **es** uno de los mejores.*
- **Para mí / yo diría que**

- **A lo mejor / lo mismo / igual** + indicative
  *Igual **es** un problema de tu compañía.*
- **Probablemente / posiblemente / seguramente / quizás / tal vez** + indicative / subjunctive
  *Quizás la compañía se **pone / ponga** en contacto conmigo después de mi reclamación.*
- **Es posible / es probable / puede (ser) + que** + subjunctive
  *Puede que mi teléfono **tenga** algún defecto de fábrica, me lo compré hace poco y no me dura nada la batería.*

■ We can also express probability with the following verb tenses:

- Present ➡ Future
  ≫ *¿Sabes dónde está Javier?*
  ≫ *No sé, **estará** todavía en el metro.*

- Present Perfect ➡ Future perfect
  ≫ *¿Sabes cuándo ha llegado hoy?*
  ≫ *Pues no sé, **habrá llegado** a la misma hora de siempre.*

- Preterit ➡ Conditional
  ≫ *¿Sabes cómo vino ayer a clase?*
  ≫ *No lo sé. **Vendría** andando.*

TABLA DE VERBOS

Affirmative Commands

Regular verbs

CANTAR	COMER	VIVIR
canta	come	vive
cante	coma	viva
canten	coman	vivan

Irregular verbs

CAER	CONDUCIR	CONOCER	CONSTRUIR	CONTAR
cae	conduce	conoce	construye	cuenta
caiga	conduzca	conozca	construya	cuente
caigan	conduzcan	conozcan	construyan	cuenten

DECIR	DORMIR	ELEGIR	EMPEZAR	HACER
di	duerme	elige	empieza	**haz**
diga	duerma	elija	empiece	**haga**
digan	duerman	elijan	empiecen	**hagan**

HUIR	IR	JUGAR	LLEGAR	OÍR
huye	**ve**	juega	llega	**oye**
huya	**vaya**	juegue	llegue	**oiga**
huyan	**vayan**	jueguen	lleguen	**oigan**

PEDIR	PENSAR	PONER	SABER	SALIR
pide	piensa	**pon**	sabe	**sal**
pida	piense	**ponga**	**sepa**	**salga**
pidan	piensen	**pongan**	**sepan**	**salgan**

SER	TENER	VENIR	VESTIR	VOLVER
sé	**ten**	**ven**	viste	vuelve
sea	**tenga**	**venga**	vista	vuelva
sean	**tengan**	**vengan**	vistan	vuelvan

Future Tense

Regular verbs

CANTAR	COMER	VIVIR
cantar**é**	comer**é**	vivir**é**
cantar**ás**	comer**ás**	vivir**ás**
cantar**á**	comer**á**	vivir**á**
cantar**emos**	comer**emos**	vivir**emos**
cantar**éis**	comer**éis**	vivir**éis**
cantar**án**	comer**án**	vivir**án**

Irregular verbs

CABER	DECIR	HABER	HACER
cabré	diré	habré	haré
cabrás	dirás	habrás	harás
cabrá	dirá	habrá	hará
cabremos	diremos	habremos	haremos
cabréis	diréis	habréis	haréis
cabrán	dirán	habrán	harán

PODER	PONER	QUERER	SABER
podré	pondré	querré	sabré
podrás	pondrás	querrás	sabrás
podrá	pondrá	querrá	sabrá
podremos	pondremos	querremos	sabremos
podréis	pondréis	querréis	sabréis
podrán	pondrán	querrán	sabrán

SALIR	TENER	VALER	VENIR
saldré	tendré	valdré	vendré
saldrás	tendrás	valdrás	vendrás
saldrá	tendrá	valdrá	vendrá
saldremos	tendremos	valdremos	vendremos
saldréis	tendréis	valdréis	vendréis
saldrán	tendrán	valdrán	vendrán

The pluperfect (past perfect)

yo	había			
tú	habías			llegado
usted/él/ella	había	–ado (–ar verbs)		comido
nosotros/as	habíamos	–ido (–er / ir verbs)		vivido
vosotros/as	habíais			
ustedes/ellos/ellas	habían			

Irregular past participles

abrir ➡ **abierto**		escribir ➡ **escrito**	
hacer ➡ **hecho**		ver ➡ **visto**	
decir ➡ **dicho**		poner ➡ **puesto**	
romper ➡ **roto**		volver ➡ **vuelto**	

The conditional

Regular verbs

	HABLAR	COMER	ESCRIBIR
yo	hablar**ía**	comer**ía**	escribir**ía**
tú	hablar**ías**	comer**ías**	escribir**ías**
usted/él/ella	hablar**ía**	comer**ía**	escribir**ía**
nosotros/as	hablar**íamos**	comer**íamos**	escribir**íamos**
vosotros/as	hablar**íais**	comer**íais**	escribir**íais**
ustedes/ellos/ellas	hablar**ían**	comer**ían**	escribir**ían**

Irregular verbs

caber ➡ **cabr**–	tener ➡ **tendr**–	hacer ➡ **har**–	**ía**
haber ➡ **habr**–	poder ➡ **podr**–	decir ➡ **dir**–	**ías**
saber ➡ **sabr**–	poner ➡ **pondr**–		**ía**
querer ➡ **querr**–	venir ➡ **vendr**–	+	**íamos**
	salir ➡ **saldr**–		**íais**
	valer ➡ **valdr**–		**ían**

The present subjunctive

Regular verbs

	HABLAR	COMER	ESCRIBIR
yo	habl**e**	com**a**	escrib**a**
tú	habl**es**	com**as**	escrib**as**
usted/él/ella	habl**e**	com**a**	escrib**a**
nosotros/as	habl**emos**	com**amos**	escrib**amos**
vosotros/as	habl**éis**	com**áis**	escrib**áis**
ustedes/ellos/ellas	habl**en**	com**an**	escrib**an**

Irregular verbs

Stem-changing verbs

	QUERER	VOLVER	JUGAR	PEDIR
	e ➡ ie	**o ➡ ue**	**u ➡ ue**	**e ➡ i** (en todas las personas)
yo	qu**ie**ra	v**ue**lva	j**ue**gue	p**i**da
tú	qu**ie**ras	v**ue**lvas	j**ue**gues	p**i**das
usted/él/ella	qu**ie**ra	v**ue**lva	j**ue**gue	p**i**da
nosotros/as	queramos	volvamos	juguemos	p**i**damos
vosotros/as	queráis	volváis	juguéis	p**i**dáis
ustedes/ellos/ellas	qu**ie**ran	v**ue**lvan	j**ue**guen	p**i**dan

■ The verbs **dormir** and **morir** have two stem changes in the present subjunctive: **o ➡ ue** and **o ➡ u**:
 • d**ue**rma, d**ue**rmas, d**ue**rma, d**u**rmamos, d**u**rmáis, d**ue**rman.
 • m**ue**ra, m**ue**ras, m**ue**ra, m**u**ramos, m**u**ráis, m**ue**ran.

AUDIOSCRIPTS Student book

UNIT 0: VOLVEMOS A VERNOS

Track 2..page **25**

1. Al acabar la escuela secundaria, empecé a ir a la universidad; **2.** De pequeño, jugaba mucho al fútbol con mis amigos; **3.** Me casé con la mujer de mi vida; **4.** Ahora estoy jubilado; **5.** De joven tenía muchas novias; **6.** Trabajaba muchas horas para mantener a mi familia; **7.** Con 5 años aprendí a montar en bici; **8.** Esta mañana he ido al parque y ahí he leído el periódico tranquilo; **9.** A esa edad me afeité por primera vez.

UNIT 1: CONSTRUYENDO UN FUTURO

UNIT 2: COSAS DE CASA

UNIT 3: DE CINE

UNIT 4: ¡SUPERESPACIO!

Track 30.. page **129**

a. **Isabel:** Sí, si eso lo sabemos todas las madres, pero, ¿qué harías si a tu hijo no le gusta el sabor de casi ninguna?
Maruchi: Entonces, amiga mía, deberías usar tu imaginación, hay muchas salsas que disimulan el sabor de los alimentos. ¿Has probado con el kétchup, la mayonesa o la mostaza con miel? A ellos les encanta…

b. **Luz:** Bueno, sería la primera vez que venía a la tele y le daría muchísima vergüenza, pero eso no significa que no te quiera conocer.
Benjamin: ¿Y tú qué harías entonces, Luz?
Luz: Mira, yo esperaría. Hemos tenido muchos casos de invitados que no vienen al primer programa y que después se lo piensan mejor y cambian de opinión.

c. **Isabel:** Eso quiere decir que casi empezaste a actuar antes que a hablar.
Maxi: ¡Ja, ja! Sí, podríamos decir que sí.
Isabel: ¿Y no te cansa tener que ensayar y filmar durante tantas horas?
Maxi: Bueno, forma parte de mi trabajo, es verdad que es la parte menos divertida, pero creo que no sabría hacer otra cosa, provengo de una familia de actores y para mí la vida sin el cine es inimaginable.

Isabel: ¿Te importaría firmarme un autógrafo para mi hija?
Maxi: Sí, claro, cómo no.
Isabel: Es que si le digo que te he entrevistado y llego sin un autógrafo… ¡no entro en casa!
Maxi: ¡Ja, ja, ja!

d. **Luz:** Entonces… ¿podrías decirnos cuándo empezó esa bonita amistad?
Mónica: Mira, de verdad, es que no me gusta hablar de mi vida privada.
Luz: Pero entonces reconoces que Mario Medina formaría parte de tu vida privada…
Mónica: No, yo no he dicho eso, deberías limitarte a escribir lo que digo y no buscar dobles sentidos a mis palabras.
Luz: Bueno, no te enfades, pero piensa que los lectores quieren saber más de tu vida y, si realmente no hay nada serio entre ustedes, yo que tú lo dejaría claro de una vez.

Track 34.. page **141**

1. ≫ He suspendido otra vez Matemáticas…, no sé cómo voy a aprobar esta asignatura, estudio un montón pero es que soy muy malo para los números.
   ≫ No te preocupes, tu problema tiene solución. Es evidente que te esfuerzas, pero creo que no estás dando los pasos acertados. Yo en tu lugar buscaría un profesor particular.

2. ≫ ¡Qué horror! ¡Esta fotografía queda fatal! Se la ve desde muy lejos y borrosa, casi no se reconoce que es ella.
   ≫ ¿Y si le pedimos una suya? Es tan maja que seguro que nos da alguna.

3. ≫ No sé qué hacer… Por un lado, quiero seguir con la tradición familiar de ser médico y no quitarles la ilusión a mis padres, pero por otro pienso que es mi futuro lo que está en juego y que a mí lo que me apasiona es el periodismo.
   ≫ ¿Por qué no hablas sinceramente con ellos? Seguro que te entenderán.

4. ≫ Estoy aburrida de hacer siempre lo mismo el fin de semana: o película o discoteca. ¿Es que a nadie se le ocurre algún plan más interesante?
   ≫ ¿Por qué no echas un vistazo a las sugerencias para el finde de la revista? Proponen un montón de planes alternativos: desde rutas turísticas por la ciudad, hasta intercambios de idiomas, excursiones a la sierra… Seguro que encuentras algo interesante.

5. ≫ Nunca conseguiré que me seleccionen para el papel, cuando estoy en el escenario se me olvida todo y no me salen ni las palabras.
   ≫ Eso se llama pánico escénico. Yo que tú intentaría aprender algunas técnicas de relajación y centraría mis esfuerzos en prepararme bien el guion.

6. ≫ No sé qué hacer para aprobar Historia: es demasiada información y no retengo nada.
   ≫ Deberías organizarte, estudiar un poco todos los días y hacerte resúmenes y esquemas, porque si lo dejas todo para antes del examen, te agobiarás más.

UNIT 5: ¡OJALÁ!

≫ Pedro, vamos a pedir unas pizzas para cenar y a ver una película, ¿te unes?

≫ ¡Uf!, qué va, me voy a la cama, estoy supercansado y, además, mañana tengo un examen y me quiero levantar pronto para repasar.

≫ Bueno, pues que descanses.

Madre: ¡Hola, Daniel! ¿Qué tal las clases?

Daniel: Bien, bien, mamá. Ha venido Carlos para que le deje unos apuntes.

Madre: Vale, pero no tarden mucho que la comida está ya lista.

Carlos: Hola, señora Carmen. Ummm, ¡qué bien huele!

Madre: Hola, Carlos. ¿Te quieres quedar a comer?

Carlos: No, gracias, que mi madre también me estará esperando.

Daniel: Toma, Carlos, aquí están.

Carlos: Bueno, gracias, nos vemos luego. Adiós, señora Carmen, y que aproveche.

Hija: Adiós, mamá, me voy a clase.

Madre: Pero si todavía es muy pronto, ¿no?

Hija: Sí, pero es que hoy tenemos una presentación y hemos quedado un rato antes para organizarnos.

Madre: Bueno, pues que te vaya bien.

Hija: Gracias, mamá. Adiós.

≫ ¡Cómo me duele la cabeza!

≫ ¿Te has tomado algo?

≫ Sí, unas pastillas que me recomendó el médico, pero, por ahora, no me han hecho nada…

≫ ¡Vaya! Bueno… me tengo que ir, que te mejores.

≫ ¡Hola, Irene! Te llamo para despedirme.

≫ ¡Ay! Hola, Pedro.

≫ ¿Qué?, ¿ya tienes todo preparado?

≫ Sí, más o menos, solo me falta poner unas cosas en la maleta y ¡poder cerrarla!

≫ Las chicas, siempre igual. Seguro que te llevas media casa para solo dos semanas… Oye, ¿cuándo sale el avión?

≫ A las 7. Ahora cuando venga mi padre, me lleva al aeropuerto.

≫ Bueno, pues un beso y ¡que te diviertas!

María: Mira, por ahí viene Lucas, pobrecillo, está muy triste porque acaba de morir su perro.

Lucas: Hola, chicos.

Álex: Hola, Lucas, oye, que María me acaba de contar lo de Toby, lo siento mucho.

Lucas: Gracias, Álex.

≫ ¡Chicos! ¡Me han admitido en el conservatorio! ¡No me lo puedo creer!

≫ Bueno, ¡felicidades! ¡Esto hay que celebrarlo por todo lo alto!

≫ ¡Enhorabuena! ¿Lo ves? ¡Si es que eres la mejor!

≫ Bueno, aprende mucho inglés y aprovecha tu año en Michigan, pero no te olvides de nosotros. Cuelga muchas fotos y conéctate al Facebook, anda.

≫ Claro, eso seguro. Además, hasta que no empiece a conocer a gente me voy a sentir muy sola.

≫ Te voy a echar mucho de menos, sobre todo de camino la escuela.

≫ Yo también. Bueno, ya tengo que entrar. ¡Adiós!

≫ Adiós y ¡cuídate!

UNIT 6: ¡HOY ME SIENTO BIEN!

Esther: Bueno, cuenta, cuenta… ¿Qué tal la reunión?

Blanca: ¡Buah!, genial. Nos lo pasamos superbién. Qué pena que no pudiste venir.

Esther: Ya… Bueno, ¿y quién fue?

Blanca: Pues prácticamente todos. Bueno, menos tú, Antonio y alguno más.

Esther: Y Antonio, ¿por qué no fue?

Blanca: Pues es que ya no vive aquí. Parece que dejó de estudiar y se fue a Toronto. Al principio se puso a trabajar en un restaurante, pero después, volvió a estudiar y se hizo profesor de español allí.

Esther: ¿Profesor de español? Pero si él quería ser abogado, ¿no?

Blanca: Sí, pero todos dicen que está encantado con su nueva profesión.

Esther: ¡Qué bien! Oye, viste a Gustavo, ¿sigue siendo tan guapo como en el colegio?

Blanca: ¡Que va, hija! Si lo ves, no lo reconoces.

Esther: ¿Y eso?

Blanca: Pues nos contó que tuvo una lesión y dejó de hacer deporte, así que está más gordo y, además, está casi calvo.

Esther: ¡No me digas! Con lo guapo que era…

Blanca: Eso sí, sigue siendo tan simpático como siempre, fue la alegría de la fiesta. ¡Ah! y ¿sabes? Se ha casado y acaba de tener un niño.

Esther: ¡Qué bien! Me alegro por él.

Blanca: ¡Ah!, pero, ¿sabes quién sí se ha puesto guapísimo?

Esther: ¿Quién?

Blanca: Martín.

Esther: ¡¿Martín!?

Blanca: Sí, chica, Martín… Se ve que él no ha dejado de hacer deporte. Cuando lo vimos, ¡nos quedamos con la boca abierta! ¡Qué guapo!

Esther: Bueno, ¿y él está casado?

Blanca: Casado no, pero tiene novia. Nos contó muchas cosas. Se ha vuelto mucho más sociable y hablador que en la escuela.

Esther: Vaya… ¡Ah! ¿Y Carolina?

Blanca: Bueno, ella también ha cambiado mucho.

Esther: ¿Sí?

Blanca: A ver, está tan guapa como antes, lo que pasa es que se fue unos años al Tíbet y se hizo budista. Ahora trabaja para una organización humanitaria y, claro, dejó de ser una esclava de la moda como antes.

Esther: Pues si ella quería ser modelo…

Blanca: Sí, sí, se hizo modelo. Estuvo trabajando en Nueva York y todo, pero le cansó ese mundo y decidió cambiar de vida de forma radical.

Esther: ¡Qué interesante…! Oye, ¿y fue Elena?

Blanca: ¡Claro!

Esther: ¿Sigue saliendo con Dani?

Blanca: Qué va, rompieron hace un año. Elena me contó que Dani empezó a trabajar por las noches en una discoteca y que cambió mucho, que se volvió más irresponsable y despreocupado y que al final rompieron. Creo que él se ha hecho empresario y tiene varias discotecas.

Esther: ¿Sí? No me lo imagino, pero…, y Elena, ¿cómo está?

Blanca: Ella muy bien. Me contó que empezó a llevar un estilo de vida más saludable y se hizo vegetariana y que, a partir de entonces, se quedó más delgada y se ha puesto muy guapa.

Esther: Qué bien, oye y…

Track 47 .... **page 184**

Track 48 .... **page 185**

Atención a todos los alumnos. Recuerden que el 19 de abril nuestra escuela celebrará, en colaboración con la editorial Edinumen, su tradicional concurso para jóvenes escritores. Las bases del concurso, que estarán colgadas tanto en los tablones informativos del centro como en nuestro portal de Internet, son las siguientes: podrán participar todos los alumnos de la escuela, solo se admitirán trabajos en la modalidad de cuento, el tema será libre y las composiciones deberán ir firmadas con un pseudónimo.

Además, los trabajos deberán introducirse en un sobre grande que estará disponible en la oficina principal del centro y se entregará al Departamento de Lengua y Literatura. El plazo de presentación de los trabajos finalizará el día 19 de marzo, un mes antes de la votación del jurado, que dará a conocer el nombre del ganador y de los finalistas del concurso el mismo día de la celebración. Además de la entrega de premios, se realizarán actividades como la lectura de fragmentos de las obras participantes y diferentes talleres de creación literaria impartidos por miembros de la editorial.

Track 49 .... **page 185**   **Track 50** .... **page 186**

Track 51 .... **page 188**

Track 52 .... **page 194**

Abel: ¡Oye, Carlos! ¿Te apetece ir este sábado al concierto de Huecco con Raquel y conmigo?

Carlos: Uf, no sé, es que a mí los conciertos no me gustan mucho. Odio que la gente empiece a cantar, ahí, gritando… Prefiero oír el disco tranquilamente en mi casa.

Abel: ¡Hombre, pero no es lo mismo! A mí no me importa que la gente cante. Lo que sí me molesta es que la gente me pise y me empuje, pero los concierto son así. Además, es un concierto benéfico, y ya sabes que a Raquel le encanta todo lo relacionado con las ONG, así que le hace mucha ilusión que vayamos.

Carlos: ¿Y para qué ONG es?

Abel: No lo sé muy bien, solo sé que es para recaudar fondos para fabricar unos balones que producen electricidad y llevarlos después a los países pobres.

Carlos: ¡¿Qué?! ¿Un balón que produce electricidad?

Abel: Sí, es un balón que dentro tiene una batería. Al jugar con él, el movimiento del balón produce energía y esta energía se guarda dentro de la batería. Después puedes enchufar cualquier tipo de aparato y ¡ya funciona!

Carlos: ¿En serio? Entonces el balón funciona como una batería, ¿no?

Abel: Exactamente.

Carlos: Pero tendrás que jugar durante mucho rato para que produzca energía, ¿no?

Abel: No, con 15 minutos es suficiente para tener unas cuantas horas de luz.

Carlos: ¿Y este balón se puede comprar en las tiendas?

Abel: Todavía no, porque lo han inventado unas estudiantes americanas y necesitan dinero para poder fabricarlo. Yo, en cuanto esté en las tiendas, me compro uno; porque además de ayudar a la gente, la verdad es que es algo muy práctico.

Carlos: ¡Qué buena idea! Ojalá inventen más aparatos como estos. ¿Te imaginas? ¡Podríamos tener energía gratis!

Abel: Sí, esta idea es genial, porque no solo van a ayudar a personas sino que además es bueno para el medioambiente… y para que la gente **haga deporte.**

Carlos: Estoy completamente de acuerdo contigo. Espero que este proyecto tenga mucho éxito y ojalá Huecco venda muchos discos para que gane mucho dinero y se puedan fabricar muchos balones.

Abel: Bueno, entonces, ¿vienes al concierto?

Carlos: Pues mira, sí, ¡todo sea por una buena causa!

Track 53 .... **page 195**

Buenos días, queridos radioyentes. Hoy tenemos el placer de hablarles de un gran proyecto solidario que conseguirá que familias de todo el mundo puedan tener luz eléctrica en sus hogares.

El proyecto, *Dame vida*, cuenta con la colaboración de numerosos rostros famosos del mundo del deporte como nuestro querido bicampeón del baloncesto de la NBA con Los Ángeles Lakers, quien declaró que los deportistas, además de ganar partidos, tienen otra obligación más allá del deporte que es la de ayudar y colaborar con los que más lo necesitan. Por eso, los deportistas, admirados por tantos jóvenes, deben dar ejemplo con acciones solidarias como la de este fantástico balón. Por su parte, una de las inventoras del *soccket* nos confesó que, cuando recibió la llamada del cantante y le propuso colaborar con su invento, fue tal su sorpresa que tardó unos minutos en reaccionar, claro que después contestó que sí inmediatamente.

Pero *Dame vida* no es solo el nombre de este fantástico proyecto, es también una fundación que colabora en otros proyectos sociales como, por ejemplo, el de la *lucha contra la violencia de género*, donde llevan una activa labor en contra de los malos tratos y diversos programas de integración social. Un joven madrileño de 23 años nos contaba que, por desgracia, este es un tema del que se habla casi todos los días en las noticias y que tenemos que ayudar a estas personas para que recuperen su vida anterior lo antes posible.

Otro de los proyectos en los que trabaja es el de la *Ayuda a Haití*, donde tanto queda por hacer a pesar de haber pasado ya varios años desde aquel terrible terremoto que conmocionó al mundo.

Claro que no podíamos cerrar este programa sin acordarnos de los principales protagonistas de estos proyectos, aquellos para los que su vida sería todavía mucho más difícil sin la acción solidaria de personas como Huecco.

Nos referimos a personitas como esta niña de 11 años, que nos contaba que después del terremoto estaba muy triste, porque este destruyó su casa y también su escuela, pero que ahora, gracias a la ayuda de personas buenas, ha podido volver a estudiar.

O el testimonio de un chico de 13 años, quien nos contaba que todos están muy contentos en su pueblo porque haciendo deporte, lo que más les gusta, pueden ayudar en casa para tener luz por las noches.

UNIT 7: ¡QUE NO TE ENGAÑEN!

En la actualidad, *Yahoo* y *Google* tienen un sistema propio de publicidad en Internet. Los enlaces a las páginas web de las empresas se colocan en los buscadores y por cada clic del usuario la empresa paga un precio al buscador; por eso, el uso de estas páginas es gratis para los usuarios. El entrar y hacer *clic* en los enlaces supone publicidad para la empresa y dinero para el buscador.

Como segundo sistema tienen los anuncios de textos. Estos consisten en un pequeño recuadro, con un título del producto o empresa, un texto corto de descripción, y la dirección web con enlace a la página. Puede aparecer tanto en las barras a los lados, como en la superior e inferior de la web. Por lo tanto, la publicidad en Internet está en los clics que realiza el usuario y la información de imagen y texto que recibe.

Existen otros muchos fenómenos que se suelen aprovechar, por ejemplo, el blog o la bitácora, páginas en las que se publica desde un diario hasta artículos sobre cualquier tema de interés para su autor o autores. A veces permiten conversaciones a través de comentarios entre los lectores y el autor. Aquí aparecen a menudo anuncios Google, banners, botones y logos, que llevan a la página en promoción.

Por lo tanto, la publicidad en Internet puede existir en todo sitio. En los últimos años, las grandes protagonistas han sido las redes genéricas, tipo Facebook, en las que el usuario comparte todo tipo de información con sus contactos, y sin ser muy consciente, con las compañías que utilizan y acceden a estos datos para generar su publicidad en estas mismas páginas.

Internet es un gran mundo lleno de posibilidades para todos, y para la publicidad es barato, atractivo, fácil y con un alcance extraordinario. Si nos molesta, tenemos que recordar que nos permite acceder a muchos servicios e información gratis.

La campaña *City Cup* de Nike fue más que un anuncio publicitario; logró comunicarse con los jóvenes apasionados del fútbol de México D.F., poniéndolos a competir en un torneo para que defendieran la bandera de su barrio. Así, Nike alcanzó el 9% de conocimiento de marca y se convirtió en uno de los 13 monstruos de la mercadotecnia de la revista *Expansión* en 2011.

El vídeo que Nike subió a YouTube para promocionar su torneo *City Cup* mostraba, en un primer momento, a un par de adolescentes que jugaban en la calle y entonces uno de ellos decía: "El fútbol es diversión, juegues donde juegues".

A través de las redes sociales, convocaron a los chicos del D.F. a participar en el torneo y defender a su barrio. En tres días reclutaron a 4.000 jóvenes de entre 16 y 19 años. La razón de hacer una campaña con enfoque digital era obvia, pues Nike es la marca de productos de consumo en México con más seguidores en Facebook, casi 811.000. Como los adolescentes son leales a su barrio, se crearon 32 mascotas inspiradas en la cultura prehispánica que representaban las 32 casas en que fue dividido el México D.F. para esta competición. Además de los contenidos en redes sociales, el *branding* de calle, por medio de las mascotas oficiales del torneo, apareció en grafiti sobre 144 metros cuadrados de muros y en 32.000 plantillas plasmadas sobre bancos, bases de postes de luz y en estaciones de autobuses en todo México. "El joven encontró identidad inmediata con una marca global que le rinde tributo directamente a su cuadra", comenta Reynoso, publicista de la campaña. La mejor estrategia para destacar es volverse parte de la vida del consumidor, y Nike llegó hasta la puerta de su casa.

El *mix* de medios incluye mercadotecnia de calle y redes sociales. No solo fue digital, sino que hubo un torneo detrás. "Lo interesante es que lo *online* se fue a lo *offline*, es decir, al mundo real, para intensificar la experiencia de la marca", dice Reynoso.

UNIT 8: ¿SUEÑO O REALIDAD?

Secretaria: Con permiso, Señor Marín.
Director: Dígame.
Secretaria: Hemos recibido una carta de uno de nuestros mejores clientes, se llama Juan Mora y dice que el nuevo teléfono que le regalamos no para de darle problemas. Dice que la pantalla táctil no funciona bien, que en muchos lugares no tiene cobertura y no puede llamar, que cuando llama, la conversación siempre se corta en el minuto 2. También dice que la batería no dura más de cinco horas.
Director: Muy bien, no se preocupe. Yo mismo me pondré en contacto con el departamento comercial. Le escribiremos un correo electrónico para pedirle disculpas. Además le ofreceremos un nuevo teléfono celular mucho más moderno. Yo lo tengo y no creo que con él tenga problemas. Gracias por la información.

a. Marta: ¡Pero bueno! ¿Se puede saber dónde están la ensalada de papa y los bocadillos que había en la cocina?
   Nacho: Ejem… ¿La ensalada de papa y los bocadillos?
   Marta: Sí, los estuve preparando ayer por la noche porque hoy nos vamos de excursión al campo, ¿no te acuerdas que te lo comenté? A ver si alguien los ha metido en el refrigerador…
   Nacho: Ejem… No, en el refrigerador no busques que no están.
   Marta: ¿No? pero entonces, ¿dónde están?, ¿tú lo sabes?, ¿los has puesto en algún sitio?
   Nacho: No, es que…
   Marta: ¡Ay, Nacho! ¡Es que ¿qué?!
   Nacho: Pues… es que… yo no sabía que eran tuyos y ayer cuando llegamos del partido teníamos mucha hambre y…

Marta: ¡¡Qué!? ¿Que te has comido la ensalada entera y todos los bocadillos!?

Nacho: No, yo solo no, es que vine con Carlos y con Armando y…

Marta: ¡No me lo puedo creer, Nacho! ¡Eres lo peor y me parece terrible lo que has hecho! ¿Es que no sabías que lo había preparado todo para hoy?

b. Hija: Por favor, papá, vamos a comprar uno, si son un amor.

Padre: Que no, Carmen, que ya te he dicho que no quiero animales en casa.

Hija: Pero mira qué bonito es, además seguro que no da apenas trabajo, ¿no ves lo pequeñito que es? Si casi ni se ve…

Padre: Desde luego… si casi lo pisan al pobre.

Hija: Anda, papá, te prometo que lo cuido yo.

Padre: ¡Que no! ¡Ya te he dicho mil veces que no! No me importa si es grande o pequeño o si se ve o no, cuando tú seas mayor haces lo que quieras, pero mientras vivas en casa no.

c. Toni: Tengo que conseguir rescatar a la princesa del castillo antes de que se derrumbe.

Mónica: Sí, pero necesitamos la llave, si no, no podemos entrar en el castillo.

Toni: Pero es que cada vez que intento agarrar la llave sale el dragón y me lanza bolas de fuego, no sé cómo esquivarlas.

Mónica: Es que no tienes que saltar cuando lanza las bolas sino cuando las tienes más cerca.

Toni: A ver, lo intento.

Mónica: ¡No! ¡Todavía no saltes! ¡Te he dicho que saltes cuando la bola de fuego esté más cerca! Si saltas antes, caes justo encima de la bola. Déjame a mí y yo te lo paso.

Toni: No, lo tengo que conseguir yo.

Mónica: Bueno, pues hazlo justo cuando te digo, solo te queda una vida.

Toni: A ver…

Mónica: ¡No! ¡Aún no! Se acabó. Te dije que si volvías a hacerlo no tendrías más oportunidades.

Track 65 ....page **236**

a. ≫ ¿Has visto mis gafas? Es que las estoy buscando por todas partes y no las encuentro.

≫ Pero, ¿estás seguro de que has vuelto a casa con ellas? Posiblemente te las dejaste en la oficina.

≫ Pues me parece que sí, ahora que lo dices creo que me las quité para lavarme la cara y seguramente estén en el baño de la oficina.

b. ≫ No me funciona Internet en el celular.

≫ A ver…, pues a mí sí me funciona, quizás sea un problema de conexión de tu compañía.

≫ No, yo creo que es mi celular, me da problemas desde que me lo compré.

≫ Pero es bastante nuevo, está en garantía aún, ¿no?

≫ Sí.

≫ Pues llévalo a la tienda, posiblemente sea una tontería y si no, seguramente te lo cambien por otro celular.

c. ≫ Qué raro, Juan no está en la biblioteca.

≫ Bueno, quizás se ha quedado estudiando en casa.

≫ No creo, me dijo que vendría a estudiar aquí si yo venía también,

que tenía algunas dudas y que así las comentábamos juntos.

≫ No sé, puede que llegue más tarde, todavía es pronto.

≫ Voy a llamarlo.

≫ ¿Qué?

≫ Salta el contestador, dice que no tiene cobertura, probablemente esté en el metro y viene de camino.

d. ≫ ¿Oíste lo de Santi?

≫ No…

≫ Pues me contó que es posible que a su padre lo manden a trabajar a Hong Kong.

≫ ¿Es verdad? Y si lo mandan ahí, ¿él que haría?

≫ Pues me dijo que lo están pensando en casa y que tal vez se vaya toda la familia con él.

≫ ¡Pero si él no sabe chino!

≫ Bueno, irse allí es una buena forma de aprenderlo, ¿no? Además en Hong Kong todo el mundo habla inglés.

≫ Sí, seguramente, pero ¿y en la escuela? Las clases serán en chino, digo yo…

≫ Pues es verdad…, no sé, puede que se tenga que matricular en un curso intensivo antes de irse.

≫ Pero el chino es muy difícil…

Track 66 .... page **240**   **Track 67** .... page **243**

Track 68 ....page **248**

El rey León, el musical que conmueve a todo el mundo.

El rey León transporta al espectador al exotismo africano, con evocadoras músicas y un diseño artístico extraordinario. Representa un nuevo hito en el mundo del espectáculo y es, sin duda alguna, un musical que a nadie deja indiferente.

El rey León es un espectáculo único, cargado de valores familiares, que demuestra la conexión de cada uno de nosotros con nuestras raíces. Nos hace pensar sobre la importancia de todas nuestras acciones y el efecto que causan en nuestro entorno. Además, es un canto al respeto y al amor por la naturaleza.

¿Dónde? En el Teatro Lope de Vega, calle Gran Vía, 57.

Con una duración de 2h y 30 minutos, incluido el descanso.

¿Cómo puedes llegar? Recomendamos el transporte público, porque la zona es de mucho tráfico. Si vas en metro, las estaciones son Callao y Plaza de España. Encontraréis parking público en Plaza de España.

El horario de la función es: martes, miércoles y jueves a las ocho y media de la tarde, viernes y sábados a las seis y a las ocho, y los domingos a las siete.

El precio de la entrada va desde los 20 a los 80 euros, dependiendo de la zona del teatro y del día de la semana. Puedes comprarla en la siguiente página web: *www.elreyleon.es* o en el teléfono 902 888 788. También en la taquilla todos los días desde las 12 del mediodía hasta el inicio de la última función.

Descubre con la Butaca de Oro los secretos que esconde este extraordinario musical detrás del escenario. Disfrutarás de una asombrosa visita guiada al *backstage* de *El rey León* y del encuentro con los actores después de la función.

¡No esperes más! Ya están disponibles las entradas para los meses de marzo, abril y mayo.

VIDEOSCRIPTS Student book

UNIT 1: CONSTRUYENDO UN FUTURO

Pitonisa: Pasá, pasá, linda. A ver, ¿qué te trae por aquí?

Paula: Hola, verá, es que yo quería saber algo sobre mi futuro, en qué universidad estudiaré, qué estudiaré... Es que no sé si quiero ser arquitecta o médica.

Pitonisa: Veremos, sentate. Cortá la baraja con la mano izquierda, que es la del corazón (...) Veamos. Cerrá los ojos y concentrate. (...) ¡Cerrá los ojos!

Paula: ¡Lo siento!

Pitonisa: Muy bien, ya podés abrir los ojos. Uhhh.

Paula: ¿Qué está viendo?

Pitonisa: ¡Chsss! Te irás a vivir a otra ciudad porque...

Paula: ¿Por qué?, ¿por qué?

Pitonisa: Porque estudiarás allá. En una universidad de una ciudad muy grande.

Paula: Y, ¿de qué es? ¿Qué estudiaré?

Pitonisa: A ver. Vivirás cerca de la universidad, junto con otros estudiantes. Tendrás un coche rojo, no muy grande, más bien pequeño y un poco viejo. Pero tendrás suerte en el amor. Conocerás a un chico muy especial en esa ciudad. Mmm, esperá, ahora te veo andando junto con una chica que irá a la universidad con vos. Es una chica rubia de pelo rizado, con gafas, alta...

Paula: Esa es Celia. ¡Qué bien! Estudiaremos juntas. Pues, entonces, creo que estudiaré Arquitectura, porque es lo que quiere hacer ella.

Pitonisa: Esperá, no, la chica rubia entra en otro edificio y vos seguís andando. Es por la tarde y hace frío.

Paula: El tiempo no me interesa.

Pitonisa: ¡Chsss! Callate, que me desconcentrás. Te acercás a otro edificio, es una biblioteca, sí. Es una biblioteca. Te sentás y abrís un libro de...

Paula: ¿De qué? ¿De Medicina?

Pitonisa: Lo siento, amor, ya no veo más nada.

Paula: Pero...

Pitonisa: Pero si venís mañana, a lo mejor veo más. Y ahora, si me disculpás, tengo que irme. El presidente me está esperando, quiere saber si podrá cumplir con algunas de las promesas que hizo en las pasadas elecciones.

UNIT 2: COSAS DE CASA

Santi: ¡Ey! Marcos, ¿qué tal?

Paula: Hola.

Eva: Hola.

Marcos: Bien.

Paula: ¿Bien? Pues, no lo parece. ¿Qué te pasa?

Marcos: Nada, es que quería ir al concierto de U2, pero la entrada es muy cara y no tengo dinero. Llevaba todo el año esperando este concierto. No sé qué hacer.

Santi: Pues, pídeles el dinero a tus padres.

Marcos: Ya lo he hecho, pero me han dicho que ya me pagaron el viaje a esquiar.

Eva: Bueno, yo te puedo dejar algo de dinero.

Marcos: No, no, gracias.

Paula: Ya sé, puedes buscar algo para ganar un dinero extra.

Santi: Eso. Como un trabajo después de clase.

Marcos: Pero, ¿el qué?

Eva: ¡Ya lo tengo! Mi prima mayor está buscando a alguien que cuide de su hijo unas horas después del colegio. Podrías ser tú.

Marcos: Es que los niños no se me dan nada bien.

Paula: Pero, ¡qué dices! Si tú eres muy divertido.

Eva: Venga, inténtalo.

Marcos: No sé.

Santi: Yo creo que es una buena idea, y así podrás ir al concierto.

Eva: Claro, mira, yo te doy su número. Y tú la llamas y le dices que eres mi amigo.

Marcos: Bueno, dame el teléfono.

Eva: 657

Marcos: 657

Eva: 67

Marcos: 67

Eva: 66

Marcos: 66

Eva: 890

Marcos: 890

Eva: Se llama María.

Marcos: Bueno, a ver qué me dice.

[...]

Paula: ¿Qué te ha dicho?

Marcos: Pues que sería ir a buscarle al colegio y llevarle un rato al parque, solo una hora, hasta que ella vuelva de trabajar. Parece fácil.

Santi: ¿Sí? Problema solucionado, ¿no?

Marcos: Pues sí. Gracias, chicos.

Eva: De nada. Para eso están los amigos.

Paula: Oye, ¿qué os parece si vamos esta tarde a mi casa a jugar a la Play?

Santi: ¡Genial!

Eva: Yo me apunto.

Marcos: Yo, también.

UNIT 3: DE CINE

Daniela: Hola, ¿podemos pasar?

Anamar: Sí, sí, claro. Aunque llegáis un poco temprano, ¿no?

Ricardo: Es que estamos intrigadísimos. Pero, ¡veo que es verdad!

Cristian: Que es verdad, ¿qué? No te entiendo.

Daniela: ¡Dos famosos en nuestro instituto! Es que no nos lo podíamos creer.

Anamar: Ah, eso. Bueno, no es la primera vez que damos algún taller en institutos.

Cristian: Y tampoco es la primera vez que enseñamos juntos, ¿verdad? ¿Sabíais que nos conocimos hace algunos años dando clases de español en una escuela?

Ricardo: Sí, sí, eso había oído.

Daniela: Disculpa si soy indiscreta, pero ¿es verdad que sois amigos de Paco, el de Literatura?

Cristian: Sí, claro. Él nos propuso hacer el taller y como estos meses vamos a estar algo más tranquilos y, además, estamos rodando en Madrid, pues pensamos que estaría bien volver a trabajar con Paco. Bueno, ¡y con vosotros!

Ricardo: ¡Ah!, ¡qué guay! Entonces, ¿os conocisteis los tres en aquella escuela de español?, ¿no?

Cristian: No exactamente. Yo a Paco lo conocí antes, cuando fui a vivir a Londres. Luego coincidimos los tres en aquella escuela de español y hasta hoy.

Daniela: Oye, una pregunta. Y después de tanto tiempo sin dar una clase, ¿estáis nerviosos?

Ricardo: ¡Daniela! Que estás hablando con un actor y una directora de cine que además han sido profesores. ¿Cómo van a estar nerviosos?

Cristian: Bueno, bueno. Es cierto que estamos acostumbrados a hablar en público y delante de las cámaras, pero dar una clase a un grupo de estudiantes es diferente.

Ricardo y Daniela: ¿Diferente?

Anamar: Sí, claro. Cristian tiene razón. No es lo mismo rodar una serie o una película que dar un curso para veinte jóvenes como vosotros. Además, hace mucho que no doy una clase.

Cristian: Eso es. Un taller de teatro no es como una película. No es lo mismo pensar en el público y en los críticos que en un grupo de estudiantes.

Ricardo: Ya, no es lo mismo, pero solo tenéis que explicarnos cómo se hace una obra de teatro, ¿no?

Anamar: Sí, y, además, queremos hacer un taller interesante y práctico. Y necesitamos vuestra colaboración. No es tan fácil, ¿eh?

Daniela: Seguro que nos encanta. Además, Paco nos conoce muy bien. Seguro que os ayuda mucho. Una cosa: ¿tendremos que actuar?

Cristian: Tendréis que hacer muchas cosas. Algunos haréis de directores, otros de guionistas, otros de decoradores… Y algunos tendréis que hacer de actores. Vais a crear vosotros mismos vuestra propia obra de teatro.

Ricardo: Y, ¿Paco va a actuar también?

Cristian: Claro. Paco es un gran actor, seguro que os sorprende mucho.

Daniela: Bueno, Paco nos sorprende todos los días. Y una última pregunta.

Anamar: No más preguntas, por favor, que parecéis dos periodistas. Venga, chicos, que tenemos que preparar el aula y esto parece un taller de periodismo. ¿Nos ayudáis con el escenario?

Daniela y Ricardo: ¡Claro!

UNIT 4: ¡SUPERESPACIO!

Padre: Carla, deja ya el libro y termina el desayuno.

Carla: Pero, si estoy estudiando.

Padre: De eso se trata. Yo en tu lugar estudiaría por la tarde, cuando llegas de clase, o en cualquier otro momento del día, pero no a primera hora de la mañana.

Carla: Pero, es que el examen de Historia lo tengo hoy.

Padre: Pues, por eso mismo, Carla. Podrías haber estudiado ayer, o la semana anterior. Pero no ahora. Además, mira, has tirado todos los cereales encima del libro.

Madre: Tiene razón tu padre, Carla. De esta manera no te lo vas a saber mejor. Además, ya que te lo dejas para el mismo día del examen, por lo menos estudia en un lugar tranquilo. ¿O es que no te molesta la televisión, ni tu padre y yo cuando hablamos?

Padre: Eso. Eso es exactamente lo que haces normalmente y no deberías: tener la tele encendida mientras estudias.

Carla: Lo hago porque me ayuda a concentrarme.

Padre: Eso no es verdad. Sabes perfectamente que la televisión te desconcentra.

Madre: A ver, Carla, tenemos que hablar seriamente de tus estudios. Últimamente, no estás sacando muy buenas notas, especialmente en Historia.

Carla: Mamá, es que el profesor me tiene manía.

Madre: Pues si te tiene manía, no sé, habla con él.

Padre: Que no, Pepa, que el profesor no le tiene manía, que es ella que no estudia.

Carla: Jo, papá, si estoy todo el día estudiando.

Padre: No estás estudiando todo el día, y lo sabes. Más bien no estudias nada.

Madre: Estoy de acuerdo. ¿Por qué no le pides al profesor que te explique las cosas un poquito mejor?

Carla: Mamá, que yo lo entiendo todo perfectamente, ¿vale?

Padre: Yo, en tu lugar, prestaría más atención en clase y me dejaría de tonterías. ¿No estarás así con el móvil en clase, verdad?

Madre: Mira, lo mejor es que te dejes el móvil aquí. Sabes que en el instituto no lo necesitas para nada…

Carla: ¡Uf! ¡En esta casa nadie me comprende!

UNIT 5: ¡OJALÁ!

Responsable: Chicos, chicos, perdonad. Os he reunido hoy aquí para informaros de que desde la ONG estamos organizando un viaje a Guatemala para construir un colegio y necesitamos voluntarios. Como la mayoría de vosotros tendréis pronto las vacaciones, os queríamos proponer la posibilidad de viajar con nosotros a Guatemala y ayudarnos en la ONG.

Muchacho 1: ¡Yo me apunto!

Muchacha 1: ¡Yo, también!

Muchacha 2: Pero, ¿qué día saldríamos?

Responsable: Saldríamos a finales de junio. Cuando sepamos cuántos vais a venir, os diremos el precio de los billetes y la fecha exacta.

Muchacho 3: Pues espero que sea a partir del día 25, ¿no?, que es cuando estamos todos ya de vacaciones.

Responsable: Sí, eso ya lo tenemos en cuenta.

Muchacha 1: Y, exactamente, ¿en qué consistirá nuestro trabajo?

Muchacho 2: Sí, ¿qué tendremos que hacer? Espero que no solo sea poner ladrillos, porque yo con mi esguince no creo que pueda ayudar.

Muchacho 1: ¡Pero, hombre! ¡Tú cómo vas a ir a Guatemala con un esguince en el pie...!

Muchacho 2: Bueno, supongo que para finales de junio ya estaré bien.

Muchacho 1: Bueno, pues entonces, ya podrás poner ladrillos, ¿no? A mí lo que me parece es que tú no quieres trabajar.

Responsable: A ver, chicos, no solo hay que poner ladrillos, ¿eh? El trabajo allí será muy duro. Y, además, vosotros no estáis acostumbrados al clima de allí, ni al esfuerzo físico. No va a ser fácil, ¿eh?

Muchacho 2: Pero también tendremos tiempo para descansar, ¿no?

Responsable: Por supuesto, que también tendréis momentos para hacer otras cosas, incluso para que hagáis algo de turismo, pero no estáis de vacaciones, ¿eh? Esto es una ONG y tenéis que ser conscientes de que vais allí a ayudar y a trabajar.

Muchacha 1: ¿Y cuánto tiempo vamos a estar?

Responsable: Más o menos un mes. La ONG os pagará parte del billete y allí nos alojaremos en la casa de la gente del pueblo al que vamos. Es gente muy humilde, pero muy hospitalaria. Quiero que os comportéis muy bien con ellos, porque, por experiencia de proyectos anteriores, es gente muy generosa, ¿eh? Que lo poco que tiene, lo da.

Muchacha 2: Pues a mí me parece muy interesante porque, además de ir ayudar, podremos conocer otra cultura y hacer nuevos amigos.

Muchacho 1: Sí, yo lo tengo muy claro. A mí, apúntame.

Responsable: Bueno, bueno, todavía falta tiempo, ¿eh? Así que quiero que os lo penséis bien y que también habléis con vuestras familias. Y cuando estéis completamente seguros, me lo decís. Entonces, tendremos otra reunión para explicaros mejor el proyecto y también para que os conozcáis entre vosotros.

Muchacho 2: Eso, si vamos a pasar muchos días juntos, deberíamos conocernos mejor.

Muchacha 1: De verdad, Ricardo, que no te moleste lo que voy a decir, pero espero, quiero y deseo con todas mis fuerzas... ¡que no puedas venir!

UNIT 6: ¡HOY ME SIENTO BIEN!

Roberto: ¡Eh! ¡Qué cara de felicidad traes!, ¿eh? Al final, ¿a qué hora llegaste a casa?

Antonio: Ummm, la verdad es que bastante tarde.

Roberto: No, no, eso seguro. Ya era supertarde cuando yo me fui y vosotros aún seguíais hablando.

Antonio: Ya ves, mi madre me ha echado una bronca... Buf, imagínate. Me ha dicho que como vuelva a llegar tarde, esto de los ensayos del grupo se acaba.

Roberto: Oye, oye, pues ten cuidado. A ver si ahora que empezamos a tocar en sitios, nos vamos a quedar sin cantante en el grupo.

Antonio: Sí, me tendré que portar bien durante una temporadita. Oye, ¿y Sandra?

Roberto: ¡Ah! Mira, por ahí viene. ¡Venga, Sandra!, que no tenemos todo el día para ensayar. Parece que a ti también te ha costado levantarte, ¿eh?

Sandra: Ay, no me grites, Roberto, que ayer viernes me acosté a las tantas y me duele un montón la cabeza.

Roberto: ¡Claro! ¡Si es que no se puede trasnochar tanto! ¿A qué hora te fuiste tú?

Sandra: Puf, pues no sé, pero vamos, que cuando yo me fui, este tortolito seguía de charla con su enamorada. Bueno, ¿y qué te dijo? Cuenta, cuenta...

Antonio: Puf. Lo que me faltaba, ahora tú también. ¿Empezamos a ensayar o qué?

Roberto: ¡Eso!, que estamos perdiendo el tiempo. ¿Empezamos por *Eres*?

Antonio: Venga.

Roberto: Por cierto, ¡vaya temazo! Sabía que era bueno, pero es que en directo, ¡es una pasada!

Sandra: Es verdad, Antonio. Para mí, tu mejor tema.

Antonio: Mola, ¿verdad?

Roberto: Ya ves... Es ahora y ¡se me ponen los pelos de punta! ¡Fue increíble! Toda la gente del bar se emocionó cuando la tocamos. Creo que va a ser nuestro mejor tema.

Antonio: Tenemos muchos temas muy buenos.

Sandra: Sí, sí, pero es que este fue especial. No sé, yo creo que fue por lo que transmitías mientras lo cantabas. Además, solo tenías ojos para Adriana, ¿eh?

Antonio: Bueno…, ya empieza.

Sandra: Pero, ¡es que es verdad! Todo el mundo lo notó. Eso sí, ayer ya no te pusiste tan nervioso. Anda…, cuéntanos qué pasó cuando os quedasteis hablando los dos. ¿Qué te dijo?

Roberto: Eso, cuéntanoslo ya de una vez. A ver si ensayamos ya.

Antonio: Jo, ¡qué pesados!

Sandra y Roberto: Anda…

Antonio: Pues a ver… Me dijo que le hizo mucha ilusión que le dedicara una canción y ¡que yo también le gustaba!

Roberto: ¿Lo ves? Si es que lo sabía. Si es que a la que les dedicas una canción, se vuelven locas por ti.

Sandra: Mira quién fue a hablar, el conquistador.

Antonio: ¡Que no! Que no es solo por eso.

Roberto: Ah, ¿no?

Antonio: Pues no. Me dijo que ella también se había fijado ya en mí, que le gusta mi forma de ser, que sea independiente, bohemio… Pero como ella es muy tímida le daba corte hablar conmigo.

Roberto: Uy, ¿quién será? Seguro que por la cara que pones tiene que ser… Adriana.

Sandra: Uy, uy, uy… Esto suena a romance. Bueno, di. ¿Qué te pone en el mensaje?

Antonio: Gracias por la canción, fue algo inolvidable.

Roberto y Sandra: ¡Oh!

Antonio: Pero, bueno. ¿Es que nunca se va a poder ensayar o qué? Vamos. Un, dos, tres…

UNIT 7: ¡QUE NO TE ENGAÑEN!

María: Hola, chicas.

Rebeca y Lucía: Hola.

María: ¿Qué hacéis? ¿Estudiando?

Rebeca: No, estamos buscando un pantalón de Lavise en estas páginas de compra por Internet, porque Lucía es socia. Y, la verdad, es que me parece que han reunido las marcas que más molan a unos precios superbajos. ¡Qué alucinante!

María: ¡A ver! Está bien, ¿eh? No conocía esto. Nunca había buscado ropa por Internet. Lo único que no me gusta es que no te la puedes probar. ¿Cómo te vas a comprar unos vaqueros sin saber cómo te quedan?

Lucía: Bueno, si quieres, luego vas a la tienda, los puedes ver, probártelos, comparar precios y después ¡tú decides!

Rebeca: Pues sí, ¡totalmente de acuerdo! Además, yo creo que todas sabemos qué nos gusta, y cuál es nuestra talla. No me parece que sea difícil.

María: Vale, vamos a ver… ¿Cómo funciona? ¿Y cómo te haces socia? ¿Hay que pagar algo para ello?

Lucía: ¡Claro que no! Solo necesitas conocer a alguien que ya sea socio, por ejemplo, a mí. Yo te invito y tengo un vale de 5€ en mi próxima compra. Julián fue quien me hizo socia a mí. ¡Y está superbién para los dos!

Rebeca: ¿Julián también compra por Internet? Ya decía yo que siempre iba a la última y con las marcas más caras.

Lucía: ¡Pues claro! Estas páginas de ofertas se lo permiten. Hay descuentos del 50%, y hasta del 70%, y no solo en ropa. También hay páginas de viajes, hoteles, restaurantes, masajes, teatro… ¡Absolutamente de todo!

María: ¡Mmmm! Estoy pensando que pronto es el cumple de tu padre y que le encanta la comida alemana desde que estuvimos en Berlín el verano pasado. ¿Creéis que podríamos encontrar alguna oferta en estas páginas para una cena regalo?

Lucía: Ah, ¡pues qué gran idea! Será superfácil. ¡Vamos a buscarlo!

María: Desde luego, es increíble que Internet te permita hacer estas cosas.

UNIT 8: ¿SUEÑO O REALIDAD?

Paloma: Bueno, hermanito, recuerdas que mañana es mi cumpleaños, ¿verdad?

Jorge: Sí, claro. Imagino que me invitarás a algo, no sé, a cenar por lo menos. Te recuerdo que en mi cumple te invité a ti, a papá y a mamá a tu restaurante favorito. Así que ya sabes.

Paloma: Es cierto que nos invitaste, pero imagino que te acordarás del maravilloso reloj que te regalé, ¿no?

Jorge: Sí, claro. Recuerdo perfectamente que te olvidaste que era mi cumpleaños y que me diste el reloj una semana después.

Paloma: Bueno, vale. Ya sabes que soy un desastre con las fechas. Pero como tú no eres como yo, imagino que ya me habrás comprado algún regalito.

Jorge: Algo he comprado.

Paloma: ¡Qué bien! Por favor, dame una pista. Por favor. ¿Cómo es?

Jorge: No, no pienso decirte ni una palabra hasta mañana.

Paloma: Por favor.

Jorge: ¡Que no!

Paloma: Bueno, al menos, déjame que te haga algunas preguntas. ¿Es pequeño?

Jorge: Tal vez.

Paloma: ¿Es caro?

Jorge: Posiblemente.

Paloma: Me extraña que sea caro. Tú nunca gastas mucho en los regalos.

Jorge: Pues quizá te lleves una sorpresa y sea mejor de lo que imaginas.

Paloma: ¿Es algo para hacer deporte?

Jorge: Frío, frío.

Paloma: ¿Es algo para la casa?

Jorge: Caliente, caliente.

Paloma: ¡Guay! A ver, es algo pequeño, caro, sirve para casa... Ay, ¿qué será?

Jorge: Hombre, yo no he dicho que sea pequeño. Solo te diré que es más grande que un teléfono móvil y más pequeño que no sé, nuestra televisión.

Paloma: Ay, ¿qué será?

Jorge: Mira, han traído este ramo de flores para ti. ¿Quién te lo habrá enviado?

Paloma: ¡Guau! ¡Qué bonito!

Jorge: Mira, ahí hay una tarjeta, ábrela y saldremos de dudas.

Paloma: Pues, será de los tíos de Málaga, que no sé lo que les pasa que siempre se equivocan y me dan los regalos un día antes de mi cumple. ¡Efectivamente! Son ellos. ¡Son preciosas!

Madre: Mira, Paloma, esto estaba en el buzón. Una carta para ti.

Paloma: ¡Es una tarjeta de cumpleaños! ¡De mis compañeros de clase! ¡Qué desastres! Mira que les dije que era mañana. Ay, bueno, ¡ya tengo dos regalos! Hermanito, dentro de poco son las diez de la noche, ¿por qué no me das tu regalo? ¡Anda!

Jorge: Pero, ¡qué hermana más impaciente tengo! Mira, mañana por la mañana te lo daré.

Paloma: Mamá, ¿tú sabes lo que me ha comprado?

Madre: Posiblemente.

Paloma: Ah, ¿que tú también lo sabes?

Madre: Pues sí, pero tu hermano me ha dicho que no puedo decirte nada.